CARRIAGE OF
GOODS BY SEA

FIFTH EDITION

John F Wilson

Emeritus Professor of Law
at the Institute of Maritime Law
University of Southampton

PEARSON
Longman

Harlow, England • London • New York • Boston • San Francisco • Toronto
Sydney • Tokyo • Singapore • Hong Kong • Seoul • Taipei • New Delhi
Cape Town • Madrid • Mexico City • Amsterdam • Munich • Paris • Milan

Pearson Education Limited

Edinburgh Gate
Harlow
Essex CM20 2JE
England

and Associated Companies throughout the world

Visit us on the World Wide Web at:
www.pearsoned.co.uk

First published under the Pitman Publishing imprint in Great Britain 1988
Second edition published in 1993
Third edition published in 1998
Fourth edition published in 2001
Fifth edition published in 2004

ISBN 0–582–82300–5

British Library Cataloguing-in-Publication Data
A CIP catalogue record for this book is available from the British Library

10   9   8   7   6   5   4   3   2
09   08   07   06   05

Typeset in 10/12pt Sabon by 35
Printed in Great Britain by Henry Ling Ltd, at the Dorset Press, Dorchester, Dorset

The publisher's policy is to use paper manufactured from sustainable forests.

CONTENTS

Part One
GENERAL INTRODUCTION

Part Five
DISPUTE SETTLEMENT

Visit the *Carriage of Goods By Sea, fifth edition* Companion Website
www.pearsoned.co.uk/wilson_cgs to find updates in the field of
law governing the carriaage of goods by sea.

Companion Website and Instructor resources
Visit the Companion Website at **www.pearsoned.co.uk/wilson_cgs**

For students
- Updates in the field of law governing the carriage of goods by sea

For lecturers
- Updates for teaching law governing the carriage of goods by sea

PREFACE TO THE FIRST EDITION

The aim of this book is to provide a comprehensive and critical study of the principles of law governing the carriage of goods by sea in the compass of a medium-sized textbook. The need for such a book has become apparent with the recent introduction at a number of universities and polytechnics of courses, at both undergraduate and postgraduate level, on various aspects of maritime law. While the continuing authority of Scrutton and Carver is not open to challenge, the professionally orientated and encyclopaedic approach of both texts is not ideally suited to student use, while their respective costs are outside the range of the average student pocket.

The present volume is hopefully aimed at filling this gap, while also serving as an introductory work of reference for members of P and I Clubs and legal firms in the City engaged in cargo claims. It concentrates mainly on an exposition of the law relating to charterparties and bills of lading, but coverage is also devoted to the development of new forms of documentation and to problems arising from through and combined transport, in so far as they relate to the carriage of goods by sea. A final chapter describes the various factors involved in the prosecution of a cargo claim, ranging from the choice of forum and proper law, arbitration procedure, to the granting of a Mareva injunction.

The approach throughout is that of the normal textbook designed for use with a degree course. The legal principles involved are examined critically against a background of current documentation and contemporary practice in the shipping industry, while attention is paid to both existing problems and potential developments in the field. The emphasis throughout is primarily on the English common law approach, although an attempt has been made to incorporate references to international, Commonwealth and US material wherever appropriate. A more thorough comparative approach had, regretfully, to be abandoned as impractical when it threatened to run to the length of a second Benedict.

PREFACE

Developments in case law and practice since the publication of the fourth edition have not necessitated any basic restructuring of the text, although four of these developments are sufficiently significant to merit separate and more detailed treatment. Of these, an initiative with the greatest long-term potential is the project launched by the CMI, at the request of UNCITRAL, to seek international agreement on a new updated liability code designed to replace the Hague and Hamburg regimes. The CMI prepared a draft instrument, the detailed consideration of which was delegated to an UNCITRAL Working Group. Following a preliminary examination of the draft, the Working Group is currently concentrating on what its members consider to be the core issues raised by the instrument. An account is given of the present state of play but, as a number of controversial issues remain to be resolved, it may be some time before it is possible to report on the ultimate outcome of the Working Group's deliberations. In the meantime, national governments appear to have suspended their efforts to devise national or regional solutions to the many problems raised by bills of lading.

Recent changes in commercial practice have necessitated more detailed treatment being afforded to three further topics in the present edition. First, the development of electronic means of communication has provided the opportunity for the substitution of electronic alternatives for the traditional bills of lading. While a recent UNCTAD survey has revealed that the electronic bill has not yet achieved its full potential in commercial practice, the new draft carriage instrument, referred to above, seeks to make electronic and paper documents interchangeable. An account is given of the various types of electronic 'document' and of their current use in practice. Secondly, the increasing use of the straight bill of lading – to use US terminology – justifies treatment separate from that of the waybill. While the two documents have many features in common, and indeed are both classified as 'seawaybills' for the purposes of s. 1(3) of the Carriage of Goods by Sea Act 1992, the case of *The Rafaela S* indicates that they may also have significant differences in effect. In holding that a 'straight bill', drafted on a classic bill of lading form, qualified as a 'similar document of title' within s. 1(4) of the Carriage of Goods by Sea Act 1971, the Court of Appeal rejected a view long espoused by the majority of academic lawyers. Finally, the time seems appropriate to review the effects of the common practice of incorporating the Hague or Hague/Visby Rules into the standard charterparty. Problems of interpretation inevitably arise where a regime designed to deal with situations arising under a bill of lading contract is required to cope with an entirely different set of problems in the context of a charterparty.

The one significant legislative development to report is the coming into effect as from 13 May 2004 of the 1996 Protocol to the 1976 International Convention Relating to the Limitation of Liability of Sea Going Ships. The object of the Protocol is to introduce a substantial increase in liability limits to compensate for inflation since 1976 and also to raise the limits for smaller ships to bring them into line with the cost of claims in respect of such vessels.

In the field of case law, some seventy new cases have been incorporated into the new edition. In one of the more significant of these, the House of Lords, in *The Starsin*, clarified the law relating to identification of the carrier by reversing the decision of the Court of Appeal reported in the fourth edition. In their Lordships' view, the ultimate decision on identity must depend on a construction of the terms of the bill of lading as a whole and the presence in the bill of both an identity of carrier and a demise clause was not necessarily decisive. Members of the court took the practical view that users of a bill attached more importance to the facts recorded on the face of the bill than to the standard terms on the reverse. Elsewhere the doctrine of fundamental breach received a further blow when the Court of Appeal in *The Kapitan Petko Voivoda* overruled the decision in *The Chanda* by giving a literal interpretation to the phrase 'in any event' in Art IV, rule 5, of the Hague Rules. In their view the section entitled a carrier to limit its liability irrespective of the seriousness of any breach. *The Happy Day* illustrated the circumstances in which a premature notice of readiness to load cargo may still be effective, while *East West Corp* v *DKBS* highlighted the danger of transferring a bill of lading without ensuring that it is endorsed.

A copy of the text of the Hague Rules has been added to the documentation contained in the appendices. While this may appear to be somewhat of a venture into legal history it is hoped that it may be a useful source of reference in view of the number of recent leading cases dealing with different aspects of the Rules.

As always, I am much indebted to my colleagues in the Institute of Maritime Law for their encouragement and generous support and in particular to David Jackson for his invaluable advice on conflict of laws and to Nick Gaskell for his expertise in the field of limitation of liability. Any remaining errors or omissions in the text are entirely my responsibility.

My thanks are also due to Caroline Ciupek for the cheerful and competent way in which she handled an ever-changing manuscript and to my publishers for the speed and efficiency with which they produced this edition.

The law is stated in the light of reported cases and material available to me on 1 July 2004.

JFW
Southampton
July 2004

TABLE OF CASES

TABLE OF STATUTES

TABLE OF OVERSEAS STATUTES

ABBREVIATED BOOK TITLES

The following books are referred to in the text by means of the abbreviated forms shown in the following list in bold type.

Carver: Treitel, Sir Guenter and Reynolds, FMB, *Carver on Bills of Lading*, Sweet & Maxwell (2001)

Cheshire and Fifoot: Cheshire, GC, Fifoot, CHS and Furmston, MP, *Law of Contract*, 14th edn, Butterworths (2001)

Cooke: Cooke, J, Young, T, Taylor, A, Kimball, JD, Martowski, D and Lambert, L, *Voyage Charters*, 2nd edn LLP (2001)

Gaskell: Gaskell N, Asariotis, R, and Baatz, Y, *Bills of Lading – Law and Contracts*, LLP (2000)

Scrutton: Boyd, SC, Burrows, AS and Foxton, D, *Charter Parties and Bills of Lading*, 20th edn, Sweet & Maxwell (1996)

Tetley: Tetley, W, *Marine Cargo Claims*, 3rd edn, Blais (1988)

Tiberg: Tiberg, H, *Law of Demurrage*, 4th edn, Stevens (1995)

Treitel: Treitel, Sir Guenter, *The Law of Contract*, 11th edn, Sweet & Maxwell (2003)

Wilford: Wilford, M, Coghlin, T and Kimball, JD, *Time Charters*, 5th edn, LLP (2003)

LIST OF ABBREVIATIONS

ACL	Atlantic Container Line
c. and f.	cost and freight
c.i.f.	cost, insurance, freight
CIM	International Convention on Carriage of Goods by Rail
CMI	Comité Maritime International
CMR	International Convention on Carriage of Goods by Road
COGSA	Carriage of Goods by Sea Act
CTO	combined transport operator
f.a.s.	free alongside ship
EDI	electronic data interchange
FCA	free carrier (named place)
FCL	full container load
f.o.b.	free on board
f.i.o.	free in and out
f.i.o.s.t.	free in and out stowed trimmed
ICC	International Chamber of Commerce
LCL	less than container load
MTO	multimodal transport operator
NYPE	New York Produce Exchange
P and I Clubs	Protection and Indemnity Clubs
SDR	special drawing right
STC	said to contain
TCM	Transports Combinés des Marchandises (Multimodal Transport Convention)
UCP	Uniform Customs and Practice of Documentary Credits
UNCITRAL	United Nations Commission on International Trade Law
UNCTAD	United Nations Conference on Trade and Development

ACKNOWLEDGEMENTS

The publishers and author wish to acknowledge with thanks the permission given by the following bodies to reprint material from the copyright sources indicated below:

Association of Ship Brokers and Agents Inc.
  NYPE 46 and *NYPE 93* charterparties

The Baltic and International Maritime Council
  Baltime, Barecon 89 and *Gencon 94* charterparties; *Congenbill, Combiconbill* and *Conlinebill*

Comité Maritime International
  CMI Uniform Rules for Sea Waybills
  CMI Rules for Electronic Bills of Lading

P & O Nedlloyd Ltd
  Bill of Lading and *Sea Waybill*

Shell International Petroleum Co.
  Shelltime 4 and *Shellvoy 5* charterparties

SITPRO/General Council of British Shipping
  Common Short Form Bill of Lading and *Sea Waybill*

The Stationery Office
  Carriage of Goods by Sea Act 1971
  Carriage of Goods by Sea Act 1992

Part One

GENERAL INTRODUCTION

1

INTRODUCTION

When a shipowner, either directly or through an agent, undertakes to carry goods by sea, or to provide a vessel for that purpose, the arrangement is known as a contract of affreightment. Such contracts may take a variety of forms, although the traditional division is between those embodied in charterparties and those evidenced by bills of lading. Where the shipowner agrees to make available the entire carrying capacity of his vessel[1] for either a particular voyage or a specified period of time, the arrangement normally takes the form of a charterparty. On the other hand, if he employs his vessel in the liner trade, offering a carrying service to anyone who wishes to ship cargo, then the resulting contract of carriage will usually be evidenced by a bill of lading. The two categories of charterparty and bill of lading are not, however, mutually exclusive, since frequently the party chartering a vessel for a specific period of time may himself operate it as a general carrier.

1.1 THE CHARTERPARTY

A charterparty is a contract which is negotiated in a free market, subject only to the laws of supply and demand. While the relative bargaining strengths of the parties will depend on the current state of the market, shipowner and charterer are otherwise able to negotiate their own terms free from any statutory interference. In practice, however, they will invariably select a standard form of charterparty as the basis of their agreement, to which they will probably attach additional clauses to suit their own requirements. These standard forms have a variety of origins. Some have developed over a number of years in association with a particular trade, such as grain, coal or ore, while others have been designed by individual firms with a monopoly in a particular field, such as the transport of oil. A considerable number which have appeared during the past century, however, are the products of the documentary committees of such bodies as the United Kingdom Chamber of Shipping, the Baltic and International Maritime Conference and the Japanese Shipping Exchange, on many of which both shipowner and charterer interests are represented.

The existence of these standard forms is of considerable advantage in international trade where the parties may be domiciled in different countries and their negotiations hampered by language problems. In such circumstances, parties conversant with the terms of a standard form are unlikely to be caught by an unusual or unexpectedly onerous clause, and accordingly can concentrate their attention on the essential terms

---

[1] Or occasionally only part of the vessel, e.g. where liner companies charter space on each other's vessels.

covering such matters as freight, laytime and demurrage rates. The widespread international use of such forms also produces uniformity in the application of the law and its interpretation by the courts. Many of these advantages are, however, lost when in many instances the parties use the standard form merely as a framework for their contract. Depending on their relative bargaining positions, existing clauses are amended and extra clauses added until the final agreement bears little resemblance to the original form. As a result, clarity is lost and litigation encouraged.

There are essentially two basic forms of carriage charter,[2] depending upon whether the vessel is chartered for a period of time or for one or more voyages. In both instances the shipowner retains control of equipping and managing the vessel and agrees to provide a carrying service. In the case of the voyage charter he undertakes to carry a cargo between specified points, whereas in a time charter he agrees to place the carrying capacity of his vessel at the disposal of the charterer for a specified period of time. A typical example of a voyage charter is provided by a seller of goods under a c.i.f. contract who, having agreed to ship the goods to the buyer, then charters a vessel to carry them to their destination. Time charters, on the other hand, are often used by carriers who wish to augment their fleet for a particular period of time without the expense of buying or running the vessel.

Before briefly outlining the characteristics of these two basic charter forms, mention must be made of a variety of hybrids which are the inevitable product of a climate of freedom of contract. The first of these hybrids is the trip charter, which consists of a time charter of a vessel for a specific cargo voyage. Instead of the fixed freight payable per unit of cargo on the completion of a voyage charter, this device ensures that the shipowner is paid hire for the entire time spent on the voyage until the cargo has been discharged at its destination. A slight variation on this form, designed to protect the shipowner in cases where the port of discharge is in an isolated area where other cargoes are unlikely to be available, is to require payment of hire to continue until the vessel has returned to the normal trade routes.

While the trip charter falls into the category of time charters, the other two hybrids are treated as voyage charters despite the fact that in each case the contract involves the carriage of goods over a specified period of time. The first example is the consecutive voyage charter under which the vessel, having been chartered for a specific period of time, is required to complete a series of voyages between designated ports during that period.[3] An alternative form, with the same objective, is the long-term freighting contract under which the shipowner undertakes to transport specified quantities of a bulk product, such as coal or grain, between designated ports in a given time, using vessels of his own choice.[4]

The main distinctions between the two forms of voyage and time charter stem from their basic difference of function. While in both cases the shipowner remains

---

[2] There is also the demise or bareboat charter, which is not technically a carriage charter but a lease of the vessel transferring to the charterer not only the possession but also the management and navigation of the ship. See *infra* pp 7–8.

[3] For an example of a consecutive voyage charter in operation, see *Suisse Atlantique v Rotterdamsche Kolen Centrale* [1967] 1 AC 361.

[4] The actual vessels used are normally chartered under individual voyage charters.

responsible for the running of his own vessel and is merely providing a carrying service, in the case of the voyage charter he is undertaking to transport a specified cargo between designated ports, whereas in the time charter he is placing his vessel for an agreed time at the disposal of the charterer who is free to employ it for his own purposes within the permitted contractual limits. The time charterer thus controls the commercial function of the vessel and is normally responsible for expenditure directly resulting from compliance with his instructions, such as fuel costs, port charges and the cost of loading and discharging the cargo. He also undertakes to indemnify the shipowner against liabilities arising from bills of lading issued under his instructions. The voyage charterer, in contrast, takes little more part in the operation of the vessel than would a shipper under a bill of lading contract. His primary obligation is to provide a cargo and to arrange for its reception at the port of discharge. Normally he also has to bear the cost of any time used in loading or discharging the cargo in excess of the agreed lay days. Occasionally he may himself undertake responsibility for the loading or discharging operations, but otherwise he takes no part in the general running of the vessel.

A further difference to be found between the two types of charter is in the method by which the price is calculated for the services provided by the shipowner. In the case of a voyage charter, payment can take the form either of a lump sum for the voyage or can be fixed in proportion to the amount of cargo carried. With a time charter, hire is payable according to the amount of time the vessel is placed at the disposal of the charterer. In either situation the crucial factor to be taken into consideration in calculating the appropriate rate is the basic time required to complete the particular operation and the likelihood of this time being extended by delays and hindrances beyond the control of the parties. From the shipowner's point of view the time charter is far more attractive in this respect, since the risk of delay caused by such factors as bad weather, congestion in port or strikes of stevedores, falls on the charterer who must pay a flat rate for the time he hires the vessel. His only relief is to be found in the 'off-hire' clause which, in essence, provides that he is not required to pay for time lost due to circumstances which are attributable to the shipowner or the vessel, such as engine failure or crew deficiencies. On the other hand, in a voyage charter the shipowner, by quoting a fixed rate per ton of cargo for the complete voyage, will himself bear the risk of delay arising from causes beyond the control of the parties.[5] In fixing the appropriate freight rate for such a charter, therefore, negotiations will centre on the estimated time required for completion of the voyage, the number of lay days allowed for loading and discharge, and the amount of demurrage to be paid by the charterer in the event of those lay days being exceeded.

1.2 THE BILL OF LADING CONTRACT

For shippers with only a small quantity of cargo available, the chartering of any vessel is hardly a practical proposition. Their requirements are normally catered for by

---

[5] NB It is possible to transfer the risk of such delay to the charterer by the inclusion of appropriate terms to that effect in the charterparty, see *infra* at pp 56–8.

the regular liner services which operate between major ports or alternatively they may make use of the services of tramp vessels which sail from port to port in search of cargo. In either case, once the cargo is loaded, a bill of lading will be issued which will act, not only as a receipt for the cargo shipped, but also as prima facie evidence of the terms of the contract of carriage. Most companies engaged in the liner trade will produce their own proprietary brand of bill, while smaller operators can adopt the standard forms drafted by the international shipping organisations.[6] With the development of international trade and documentary credits, bills of lading have acquired a third function, that of acting as negotiable documents of title in situations where the shipper requires to transfer the ownership of cargo while it is in transit. In such circumstances, the endorsement and transfer of the bill effectively transfers such rights in the goods as are held by the transferor and also enables the transferee to claim delivery of the goods on arrival at the port of discharge. Where such facilities are not, however, required by the shipper, the bill of lading will frequently be replaced by a non-negotiable receipt, known as a waybill. Such a document possesses all the attributes of the normal bill of lading with the exception that it is not a negotiable document of title.

Whereas the parties to a charterparty are free to negotiate their own terms, the inherent inequality of bargaining power as between the parties to a bill of lading contract has necessitated restrictions being imposed on the traditional principle of freedom of contract. International conventions have defined the basic obligations of the carrier towards the cargo and prescribed the maximum immunities and limitation of liability he can claim. The provisions of one of these conventions, the Hague/Visby Rules, are now incorporated into English law by the Carriage of Goods by Sea Act 1971 and any attempt contractually to exclude them is declared to be null and void. While the Rules establish the mandatory core of carrier liability, they are not intended as a comprehensive code, and the parties are free to reach agreement on all other aspects of the contract of carriage on their own terms.

The development of containerisation has introduced a further complication in that many of these contracts of carriage now envisage the participation of a succession of carriers. In such circumstances the normal procedure is to issue a through bill of lading which may provide either that the carrier issuing the bill undertakes responsibility for the entire carriage through to the destination, or that each successive carrier only accepts liability for the period during which the goods are under his control. Should these successive stages involve carriage by different modes of transport, then the through bill of lading is known as a combined (or multimodal) transport document. Unless the terms of the contract otherwise provide, the provisions of the Carriage of Goods by Sea Act 1971 will of course only apply to the sea leg of such a combined carriage operation. Accordingly a combined transport document will normally include a term to the effect that, while the party issuing the document undertakes to deliver the goods to the agreed destination, any responsibility for loss or damage will be governed by the law of the place where the loss occurred and of the mode of transport being used at the time.

---

[6] For example, the Baltic and International Maritime Conference, the UK Chamber of Shipping, etc.

1.3 CHARTERERS' BILLS OF LADING

Difficulties arise in distinguishing the effects of the two types of contract of carriage in situations where both charterparties and bills of lading are in use at the same time. Thus charterers shipping their own goods on a chartered vessel require at least an acknowledgement of the quantity of goods taken aboard and the condition in which they were shipped. Bills issued to a charterer in such circumstances act merely as receipts for the cargo shipped and as potential documents of title should the charterer decide to sell the goods while they are still in transit. But the bills provide no evidence of the terms of the contract of carriage between shipowner and charterer since their relationship is governed solely by the terms of the charterparty. Nor will the Hague or Hague/Visby Rules apply to the contract of carriage while the bill remains in the hands of the charterer, although they will apply as soon as the cargo is sold and the bill negotiated to a third party.

Time charters will also invariably confer on the charterer the right to issue bills of lading in favour of third party shippers, and to present them to the master for signature, in return for an indemnity from the charterer covering any additional liabilities incurred by the shipowner as a result. Such a right is, for example, essential where a ship has been chartered to augment the charterer's fleet with the result that he is to control the commercial function of the vessel. In such a case the operative contractual document, so far as the shipper is concerned, will be the bill of lading which, in his hands, will control the contract of carriage in exactly the same way as if the vessel had not been chartered. As between shipper and carrier, the terms of the charterparty will have no relevance unless they have been expressly incorporated into the bill of lading contract. There will, however, generally be the residual problem of deciding whether, under the bill of lading, the shipowner or charterer is to be treated as the carrier for the purposes of the Hague or Hague/Visby Rules.

1.4 THE DEMISE CHARTERPARTY

Finally, brief mention must be made of the demise or bareboat charter which must be distinguished from the types of charter already discussed in that it operates as a lease of the vessel and not as a contract of carriage. It differs from other charterparties in much the same way as a contract to hire a selfdrive car differs from a contract to engage the services of a taxi.[7] Whereas in an ordinary time charter the shipowner retains control over the operation of the vessel, under a demise charter the charterer displaces the owner and, for the period of the 'lease', takes possession and complete control of the ship. Under this type of contract, the charterer mans and equips the vessel and assumes all responsibility for its navigation and management. For all practical purposes he acts

---

[7] An alternative method of expressing the distinction is to be found in the judgment of Mackinnon LJ in *Sea & Land Securities* v *Dickinson* [1942] 2 KB 65 at p 69: 'The distinction between the demise and other forms of charter contract is as clear as the difference between the agreement a man makes when he hires a boat in which to row himself and the contract he makes with a boatman to take him for a row.'

as owner for the duration of the charter and is responsible for all expenses incurred in the operation of the vessel, and also for insuring her.

The demise charter is suitable for use in connection with government shipping activities, particularly in time of war or other emergency. In the private sector it is available to the shipowner who wishes to supplement his fleet for a limited period of time without incurring the financial commitments associated with actual ownership, but at the same time requiring to have full control of the chartered vessel. It can also be used as a form of 'hire-purchase' contract, providing security for the financing company while the purchase price of the vessel is being repaid by instalments.[8] Demise charters are not so frequently encountered as the other two forms of carriage charter, although there has been an increase in their use over recent years, particularly in the oil tanker trade and in government hire.

As the charterer by demise is virtually acting as owner of the vessel, he will be regarded as the 'carrier' for the purposes of the Hague and Hague/Visby Rules.[9] He will be responsible for damage to the cargo and liable under bills of lading signed by the master. Conversely, he will be entitled to any salvage earned by the vessel.[10] As the shipowner is not in possession, he cannot exercise a lien over cargo as security for the charter hire.

---

[8] For an early example, see *Baumwoll* v *Furness* [1893] AC 8. See also Part II Barecon 89 charter form.

[9] See Art I(a). See also *The Stolt Loyalty* [1995] 1 Lloyd's Rep 598 where demise charterer is described as 'owner'.

[10] *Elliott Tug Co* v *Admiralty Commissioners* [1921] 1 AC 137.

2

IMPLIED OBLIGATIONS IN A CONTRACT OF AFFREIGHTMENT

In addition to the express clauses agreed by the parties, every contract of affreightment is negotiated against a background of custom and commercial usage from which a series of obligations are implied which are automatically incorporated into the contract in the absence of agreement to the contrary. Since such obligations are derived from a common source in the law merchant, a similar result follows at common law irrespective of whether the terms of the contract are enshrined in a charterparty or evidenced by a bill of lading. There is, however, one important proviso. In contracts of carriage which are governed by the Hague or Hague/Visby Rules the scope and application of some of these implied obligations have been modified while the ability of the parties to exclude their operation by mutual agreement has been considerably restricted. In the following pages each of these implied obligations will be considered separately and a final section will be devoted to the effect of frustration on a contract of affreightment.

2.1 THE UNDERTAKING AS TO SEAWORTHINESS

In every contract of affreightment there is an implied obligation to provide a seaworthy vessel 'fit to meet and undergo the perils of the sea and other incidental risks to which of necessity she must be exposed in the course of a voyage'.[1] In the majority of charterparties this implied undertaking is reinforced by an express term to the same effect, such as the requirement in the preamble to the NYPE form that the vessel be 'tight, staunch, strong and in every way fitted for the service'. The obligation covers not only the physical state of the vessel but also the competence and adequacy of the crew, the sufficiency of fuel and other supplies, and the facilities necessary and appropriate for the carriage of the cargo.

2.1.1 NATURE OF THE OBLIGATION

At common law the obligation of the owner to provide a seaworthy ship is absolute and, in the event of breach, he will be liable irrespective of fault. It amounts to an undertaking 'not merely that they should do their best to make the ship fit, but that the ship should really be fit'.[2] On the other hand, the owner is not under a duty to provide

---

[1] Field J in *Kopitoff* v *Wilson* (1876) 1 QBD 377 at p 380.
[2] Lord Blackburn in *Steel* v *State Line Steamship* Co (1877) 3 App Cas 72 at p 86.

a perfect ship but merely one which is reasonably fit for the purpose intended. The standard required 'is not an accident-free ship, nor an obligation to provide ship or gear which might withstand all conceivable hazards. In the last analysis the obligation, although absolute, means nothing more or less than the duty to furnish a ship and equipment reasonably suitable for the intended use or service.'[3] The test would appear to be objective in that 'the vessel must have that degree of fitness which an ordinary careful and prudent owner would require his vessel to have at the commencement of her voyage having regard to all the possible circumstances of it'.[4] The standard required will therefore be variable depending on the nature of the voyage, the type of cargo to be carried and the likely dangers to be encountered en route. This common law obligation can, however, be excluded by an appropriate clause in the contract of affreightment, although the courts are inclined to treat such clauses in the same way as all exceptions and apply a restrictive interpretation to them. Thus in *Nelson Line* v *Nelson*[5] a clause exempting the shipowner from liability for any damage to goods 'which is capable of being covered by insurance' was held not to be effective in excluding liability for damage to cargo resulting from unseaworthiness.[6] To be effective any such clause must be expressed in clear and unambiguous language.

Where the contract of affreightment is governed by the Hague or Hague/Visby Rules, the absolute obligation at common law is replaced by a duty to exercise due diligence to make the ship seaworthy.[7] Accordingly, while the carrier will no longer be strictly liable in the absence of any fault, he will be liable not only for his own negligence but also for the negligence of any party, even including an independent contractor, to whom he has delegated responsibility for making the vessel seaworthy.[8] This reduction in liability is, however, accompanied by a provision invalidating any attempt by the carrier further to reduce or exclude his responsibility under the rules to provide a seaworthy ship.[9]

Many modern standard charter forms have now adopted the Hague Rules formula with regard to the requirement of seaworthiness. Thus the NYPE charter, by the use of a 'clause paramount', expressly incorporates into the charterparty the provisions of the US Carriage of Goods by Sea Act 1936, while the Baltime form excludes the liability of the shipowner for loss or damage to cargo unless such 'loss has been caused by want of due diligence on the part of the Owners or their Manager in making the vessel seaworthy and fitted for the voyage'.[10] In both of these cases it would appear that the common law absolute obligation to provide a seaworthy ship has been replaced by a duty to exercise due diligence.

---

[3] District Judge Kilkenny in *President of India* v *West Coast Steamship Co* [1963] 2 Lloyd's Rep 278 at p 281.

[4] Channell J in *McFadden* v *Blue Star Line* [1905] 1 KB 697 at p 706 quoting with approval a passage from an early edition of *Carver on Carriage by Sea*.

[5] [1908] AC 16.

[6] See also *Ingram* v *Services Maritime* [1914] 1 KB 541; *The Rossetti* [1972] 2 Lloyd's Rep 116.

[7] See Art III rule 1.

[8] *The Muncaster Castle* [1961] AC 807. For further treatment, see *infra* at pp 189–91.

[9] See Art III rule 8.

[10] See clause 13. See *The Gundulic* [1981] 2 Lloyd's Rep 418.

2.1.2 INCIDENCE OF OBLIGATION

The requirement for the shipowner to provide a seaworthy vessel comprises a two-fold obligation. On the one hand, the vessel must be suitably manned and equipped to meet the ordinary perils likely to be encountered while performing the services required of it, while at the same time it must be cargoworthy in the sense that it is in a fit state to receive the specified cargo.

So far as the first aspect of the seaworthiness concept is concerned, the implied undertaking at common law covers not only the physical condition of the vessel and its equipment, but also extends to the competence of the crew and the adequacy of stores and documentation.[11] Thus a vessel will clearly be unseaworthy where it has defective engines[12] or a defective compass,[13] or where deck cargo is stowed in such a way as to render the vessel unstable.[14] But the shipowner will be equally in breach where he employs an incompetent engineer or other officer,[15] where inadequate bunkers are taken on board for the voyage,[16] or even where the documentation for the voyage is inadequate.[17] Once these legal requirements are satisfied, however, the implied undertaking does not extend to cover such matters as recommended manning levels and conditions of employment formulated by extra-legal organisations such as trade unions.[18]

In the case of a voyage charter the obligation to provide a seaworthy vessel in the above sense attaches at the time of sailing on the charter voyage. It is immaterial that defects exist rendering the vessel unseaworthy during the preliminary voyage to the loading port, or even during the loading operation, provided that they can be rectified by the time of sailing.[19] Similarly the obligation is discharged if the vessel is seaworthy at the time of sailing, irrespective of what happens afterwards either during the voyage or at an intermediate port. 'The warranty . . . is a warranty only as to the condition of a vessel at a particular time, namely, the time of sailing; it is not a continuing warranty in the sense of a warranty that she shall continue fit during the voyage. If anything happens whereby the goods are damaged during the voyage, the shipowner is liable because he is an insurer, except in the event of the damage happening from some cause in respect of which he is protected by the exceptions . . .'[20] It follows that, in the case of a

---

[11] The position is identical under the Hague and Hague/Visby Rules, see Art III rule 1. The US view is expressed in the following terms in *The Framlington Court* [1934] AMC 272 at p 277: 'Seaworthiness is a relative term depending for its application upon the type of vessel and the character of the voyage. The general rule is that the ship must be staunch and strong and well equipped for the intended voyage. And she must also be provided with a crew, adequate in number and competent for the voyage with reference to its length and other particulars, and have a competent and skilled master of sound judgment and discretion.'

[12] *Hong Kong Fir Shipping Co v Kawasaki* [1962] 2 QB 26; *The Amstelslot* [1963] 2 Lloyd's Rep 223.

[13] *Paterson Steamships Ltd v Robin Hood Mills* (1937) 58 LlLR 33.

[14] *Kish v Taylor* [1912] AC 604; *The Friso* [1980] 1 Lloyd's Rep 469.

[15] *The Makedonia* [1962] 1 Lloyd's Rep 316; *Hong Kong Fir Shipping Co v Kawasaki* [1962] 2 QB 26; *The Farrandoc* [1967] 2 Lloyd's Rep 276; *Heinrich C Horn v Cia de Navegacion Fruco* [1969] AMC 1495.

[16] *McIver v Tate Steamers* [1903] 1 KB 362; *Northumbrian Shipping Co v Timm* [1939] AC 397.

[17] *The Madeleine* [1967] 2 Lloyd's Rep 224.

[18] See *The Derby* [1985] 2 Lloyd's Rep 325, where a vessel was delayed in port for 21 days by a strike of stevedores resulting from failure of the vessel to comply with manning levels, rates of pay and conditions of employment of the crew as recommended by the International Transport Workers Federation.

[19] Cf. *Stanton v Richardson* (1875) LR 9 CP 390.

[20] Channell J in *McFadden v Blue Star Line* [1905] 1 KB 697 at p 703.

consecutive voyage charter, the obligation arises at the beginning of each voyage under-taken in performance of the charter.[21] Again, in the case where a voyage charter is divided into stages by agreement between the parties, there will be a duty to make the vessel seaworthy at the commencement of each stage of the voyage.[22] The position is, however, different in respect of the time charter where the obligation attaches only at the time of delivery of the vessel under the charterparty. In this case the initial sea-worthiness undertaking is normally supplemented by some form of maintenance clause under which the shipowner is required to 'keep the vessel in a thoroughly efficient state in hull, machinery and equipment for and during the service'.[23] But this express under-taking to maintain the vessel throughout the charter is entirely distinct from any obligation as to seaworthiness.

The second aspect of the common law undertaking as to seaworthiness relates to the cargoworthiness of the vessel. The shipowner is under an obligation to ensure that his ship is in a fit state to receive the contractual cargo. This requirement would not be satisfied where the vessel's holds needed fumigating or cleaning before being in a fit state to receive cargo,[24] where frozen meat was to be shipped and there was a defect in the vessel's refrigeration plant,[25] or where the pumps were inadequate to drain surplus water from the cargo.[26] In each case the implied undertaking as to cargoworthiness is operative as from the commencement of loading. 'The warranty is that, at the time the goods are put on board, she is fit to receive them and encounter the ordinary perils that are likely to arise during the loading stage; but . . . there is no continuing warranty after the goods are once on board that the ship shall continue fit to hold the goods during that stage and until she is ready to go to sea, notwithstanding any accident that may happen to her in the meantime.'[27] So in *McFadden* v *Blue Star Line*,[28] after cargo had been safely loaded, the ship's engineer opened a sluice door on a watertight bulkhead and on clos-ing it, failed to secure it properly with the result that water percolated through and damaged the plaintiff's cargo. It was held that, since the defective closure of the sluice door occurred after the cargo had been loaded, it did not constitute a breach of the cargoworthiness undertaking.

It has already been noted that many modern charter forms expressly include the pro-visions of either the Hague or Hague/Visby Rules and this practice may affect the operation of the implied seaworthiness obligation. Thus in the case of *Adamastos Shipping Co* v *Anglo-Saxon Petroleum*[29] the voyage charter involved included a clause

---

[21] See *Adamastos Shipping* v *Anglo-Saxon Petroleum* [1958] 1 Lloyd's Rep 73.
[22] *The Vortigern* [1899] P 140.
[23] NYPE 93 form, clause 6.
[24] *Tattersall* v *National Steamship Co* (1884) 12 QBD 297; *The Tres Flores* [1973] 2 Lloyd's Rep 247.
[25] *Cargo per Maori King* v *Hughes* [1895] 2 QB 550.
[26] *Stanton* v *Richardson* (1874) 9 CP 390.
[27] Channell J in *McFadden* v *Blue Star Line* [1905] 1 KB at p 704. Cf. the position under the Hague and Hague/Visby Rules where the Privy Council has held that the obligation to exercise due diligence to pro-vide a seaworthy ship under Art III rule 1 covers 'the period from at least the beginning of the loading until the vessel starts on her voyage'. *Maxine Footwear Co Ltd* v *Canadian Government Merchant Marine* [1959] AC 589 at p 603. See *infra* at pp 188–9.
[28] [1905] 1 KB 697.
[29] [1958] 1 Lloyd's Rep 73.

paramount incorporating the provisions of the US Carriage of Goods by Sea Act 1936 which were treated by the court as if written verbatim into the charter. In these circumstances a majority of the House of Lords was prepared to give full effect to the provisions of the Hague Rules in respect of all voyages under the charter irrespective of whether they were to or from ports in the United States, or whether they were in ballast or with cargo. Some writers have been prepared to go further by suggesting that, as the seaworthiness provisions of the Hague Rules[30] are applicable 'before and at the beginning of the voyage', the obligation to exercise due diligence to provide a seaworthy ship would arise in respect of each voyage under the time charter.[31] A note of caution has, however, been sounded by Mustill J in *The Hermosa*[32] where he pointed out that 'there are in most time charters express terms as regards initial seaworthiness and subsequent maintenance which are not easily reconciled with the scheme of the Hague Rules, which create an obligation as to due diligence attaching voyage by voyage. It cannot be taken for granted that the interpretation adopted in [the *Adamastos* case] in relation to voyage charters applies in all respects to time charters incorporating the Hague Rules.'

2.1.3 BURDEN OF PROOF

The burden of proof of unseaworthiness will rest on the party alleging it, although in many cases he may be assisted by inferences drawn by the court. Thus the presence of seawater in the hold will normally be treated by the courts as prima facie evidence of unseaworthiness. Having established breach of this undertaking, however, it will then be incumbent on the claimant to establish that the unseaworthiness caused the loss of which he complains.[33] In the case of *International Packers* v *Ocean Steamship Co*[34] a cargo of tinned meat shipped from Brisbane for Glasgow was damaged by seawater during the voyage as the result of tarpaulins being stripped from the hatch covers during a storm. On hearing that the vessel was equipped with locking bars designed to secure the hatches, the trial judge held that the loss was caused not by the unseaworthiness of the vessel but by the negligence of the crew in failing to make use of the equipment provided. Similarly, the cargo owner will fail to discharge the burden of proof if it is clear that the damage resulted from bad stowage rather than from any unfitness of the vessel to receive the contract cargo.[35]

2.1.4 EFFECT OF BREACH

Having established a breach, the next question is to decide what remedies are available to the charterer. Are the courts prepared to apply the traditional classification of terms into conditions or warranties and treat the obligation to provide a seaworthy ship

---

[30] See Art III rule 1.
[31] See Wilford, 34.15. Cf. obligation in context of a contract of affreightment: *The Kriti Rex* [1996] 2 Lloyd's Rep 171.
[32] [1980] 1 Lloyd's Rep 638 at p 647.
[33] See *The Europa* [1908] P 84.
[34] [1955] 2 Lloyd's Rep 218.
[35] *The Thorsa* [1916] P 257; *Elder Dempster* v *Paterson, Zochonis & Co* [1924] AC 522.

as either a condition, any breach of which would entitle the charterer to repudiate his obligations under the contract, or as a warranty, sounding only in damages? In the event the courts have taken the view that neither of these alternatives is appropriate. The shipowner's obligation to provide a seaworthy vessel was classified as an innominate or intermediate term by the Court of Appeal in *Hong Kong Fir Shipping Co v Kawasaki*.[36] In refusing to categorise the term once and for all as either a condition or a warranty, Diplock LJ pointed out that such an undertaking 'can be broken by the presence of trivial defects easily and rapidly remediable as well as by defects which must inevitably result in a total loss of the vessel'.[37] As the results of a breach could be so variable it would be as unreasonable to permit a party to repudiate a charter because a few rivets were missing as it would be to prevent him from doing so in the event of the defects in the vessel being irremediable.[38] Thus, while objectively a compass defect was a serious matter, it would be illogical to permit the rejection of a 24-month charterparty if the defect could be repaired by a compass adjuster within a matter of hours. While damages would always be available for breach of the undertaking, a charterer should only be allowed to repudiate his obligations under the charterparty where the breach deprived him 'of substantially the whole benefit which it was intended that he should obtain from the contract'.[39] Everything would depend on the effects of the breach in each individual case and, in the view of Diplock LJ, the test as to whether a party had been deprived of substantially the whole benefit of the contract should be the same whether it resulted from breach of contract by the charterer or from the operation of the doctrine of frustration.[40]

What remedies are then available to the charterer in the event of a breach of this intermediate obligation by the shipowner? A distinction has to be drawn between the situation where the breach is discovered before performance of the charterparty has commenced and the position where the breach only comes to light after the vessel has sailed. In the former case the charterer will be able to treat his obligations under the contract as discharged if the breach deprives him of substantially the whole benefit of the contract and it is a breach which cannot be rectified within such time as would prevent the object of the contract from being frustrated. Thus in the case of *Stanton* v *Richardson*,[41] where the pumping equipment on the chartered vessel was inadequate to deal with the surplus water from a cargo of wet sugar, the charterer was held entitled to repudiate the contract when it was established that new pumps could not be installed within a reasonable time. On the other hand, if the effects of the breach are less severe, the charterer will be restricted to his remedy in damages. In this respect it must be remembered that the permissible time allowance in which to remedy the defect will vary as between a voyage and a time charter. While a relatively brief delay may be sufficient

---

[36] [1962] 2 QB 26. The US courts take a similar view: see *Aaby v States Marine Corp (The Tento)* [1950] AMC 947.

[37] [1962] 2 QB at p 71.

[38] See *Bunge Corp v Tradax Export* [1981] 1 WLR 711.

[39] [1962] 2 QB at p 69.

[40] For an example of a court applying an identical test to a situation which involved both a breach of the seaworthiness undertaking and an alleged frustrating event, see *The Hermosa* [1982] 1 Lloyd's Rep 570.

[41] (1875) LR 9 CP 390. See also *Snia v Susuki* (1924) 18 LlLR 333.

to frustrate the object of the former, the Court of Appeal held in the *Hong Kong Fir* case that the absence of a vessel for five months undergoing repairs was insufficient to frustrate the objects of a 24-month time charterparty.

The provisions of the time charter itself may, however, provide the charterer with an opportunity for escape if the shipowner cannot make good the defect before the cancelling date, even though the breach would not otherwise have entitled the charterer to repudiate. Thus under clause 22 of the Baltime form the charterer is entitled to cancel the charterparty unless the vessel is delivered to him by a specified date, 'she being in every way fitted for ordinary cargo service'. The charterer in *The Madeleine*[42] was able to take advantage of this clause when the shipowner was unable to produce the required deratisation certificate by the cancelling date. In the words of Roskill J, 'there was here an express warranty of seaworthiness and unless the ship was timeously delivered in a seaworthy condition, including the necessary certificate from the port health authority, the charterers had the right to cancel'.[43] Such right to cancel is not, however, dependent on any breach of obligation by the shipowners.

Where the unseaworthy state of the vessel is not discovered until after it has set sail, mere acceptance of the vessel does not amount to a waiver of the charterer's right to damages.[44] Nor does it necessarily amount to a waiver of the right to repudiate the charter provided that the breach, when discovered, is sufficiently fundamental. This is particularly true of the time charter[45] though, in the case of the voyage charter, if the breach is not apparent before the vessel sails, for all practical purposes the charterer may have little opportunity to discover it before the vessel arrives at its destination and performance of the contract is complete.

2.2 OBLIGATION OF REASONABLE DISPATCH

A second undertaking inherent in every contract of carriage requires the shipowner or carrier to perform his contractual obligations with reasonable dispatch. Whenever no time is specified for a particular obligation there is an implied obligation to complete the performance within a reasonable time. Thus in a voyage charter there is an implied undertaking that the vessel will proceed on the voyage, load and discharge at the time agreed or within a reasonable time. Likewise in a time charter, the master is expected to prosecute each voyage with the 'utmost dispatch'.[46] Performance of this obligation is judged, not on a strictly objective basis, but in relation to what can reasonably be expected from the shipowner under the actual circumstances existing at the time of performance. 'When the language of the contract does not expressly, or by necessary implication, fix any time for the performance of a contractual obligation, the law implied that it shall be performed within a reasonable time. The rule is of general application, and is not confined to contracts for the carriage of goods by sea. In the case

---

[42] [1967] 2 Lloyd's Rep 224.
[43] *Ibid* at p 241. For a more detailed account of the effects of a cancellation clause, see *infra* at pp 66–7.
[44] *The Democritos* [1975] 1 Lloyd's Rep 386 at p 397.
[45] Cf. *Hong Kong Fir Shipping Co* v *Kawasaki* [1962] 2 QB 26.
[46] See Baltime, clause 9; NYPE 46, clause 8.

of other contracts the condition of reasonable time has been frequently interpreted; and has invariably been held to mean that the party upon whom it is incumbent duly fulfils his obligations notwithstanding protracted delay, so long as such delay is attributable to causes beyond his control, and he has neither acted negligently nor unreasonably.'[47]

2.2.1 EFFECT OF BREACH

As with the seaworthiness undertaking the obligation to exercise reasonable dispatch appears to fall into the category of innominate or intermediate terms. Accordingly, the remedy available in any particular case will be dependent on the effects of the relevant breach. While the injured party will always be able to recover compensation in the form of damages for any unreasonable delay, he will only be able to repudiate the contract if the delay is so prolonged as to frustrate its object. In *Freeman* v *Taylor*[48] a vessel had been chartered to take her cargo to Cape Town and, after discharging it, to proceed with all convenient speed to Bombay in order to load the charterer's cargo of cotton. After discharging at the Cape, however, the master for his own account took on board a cargo of mules and cattle for carriage to Mauritius en route to Bombay. As the result of this diversion, the vessel was some six or seven weeks late in arriving in Bombay and the court held the delay sufficiently long to frustrate the object of the charter. In cases where the delay is not so prolonged, however, the injured party will be restricted to a claim for damages.[49] Even such a claim may be barred if the particular delay is covered by an excepted peril.[50]

2.3 OBLIGATION NOT TO DEVIATE FROM THE AGREED ROUTE

The owner of a vessel, whether operating a liner service or under charter, impliedly undertakes that his vessel, while performing its obligations under the contract of carriage, will not deviate from the contract voyage. Deviation has been defined as 'an intentional and unreasonable change in the geographical route of the voyage as contracted'.[51] In order to determine whether such a deviation has occurred it is first necessary to ascertain the precise route envisaged by the contract of affreightment. A few standard charter forms make express provision for the route to be followed[52] but, in the absence of such provision, the presumption is that the proper route is the direct geographical route between the ports of loading and discharge. This presumption can,

---

[47] Lord Watson in *Hick* v *Raymond* [1893] AC 22 at p 32. For a modern example in the context of a contract of affreightment, see *The Kriti Rex* [1996] 2 Lloyd's Rep 171.
[48] (1831) 8 Bing 124.
[49] *MacAndrew* v *Chapple* (1866) LR 1 CP 643.
[50] *Barker* v *MacAndrew* (1865) 18 CB (NS) 759.
[51] Tetley p 737. While English courts have restricted the concept of deviation to geographic deviations, US courts have extended it to other departures from the terms of the contract which materially increase the risks to cargo such as unauthorised deck carriage (*Jones* v *Flying Clipper* (1954) 116 Fed Supp 386) or over-carriage (*The Silver Cypress* [1944] AMC 895).
[52] For example, Austral, clause 2; Austwheat, clause 2.

however, be rebutted by the shipowner adducing evidence as to the customary route in the trade, or even as to the route previously followed by the particular shipping line involved.[53] So in *Reardon Smith Line* v *Black Sea and Baltic General Insurance*[54] a vessel chartered to proceed from a Black Sea port 'to Sparrow Point' in the United States, departed from the direct geographical route to bunker in Constanza, where cheap supplies of oil fuel were available. On proof that vessels engaged in that trade invariably put into Constanza and that 25 per cent of ocean-going oil-burning vessels passing through the Bosphorus followed a similar practice, the House of Lords held that there had been no deviation from the normal route. The relevant law was neatly summarised by Lord Porter:

> 'It is the duty of a ship, at any rate when sailing upon an ocean voyage from one port to another, to take the usual route between those two ports. If no evidence be given, that route is presumed to be the direct geographical route but it may be modified in many cases, for navigational or other reasons, and evidence may always be given to show what the usual route is, unless a specific route be prescribed by the charterparty or bill of lading.'[55]

To constitute an unjustifiable deviation the departure from the contractual voyage must be the result of a deliberate act on the part of the owner or the ship's officers. Consequently, there will be no breach of this implied undertaking if the vessel is blown off course during a storm, or is set on a wrong course as the result of the illness of its navigation officer or reliance on a defective compass.[56]

2.3.1 JUSTIFIABLE DEVIATIONS

(I) AT COMMON LAW

A departure from the proper route is permissible at common law in the following circumstances:

1 To save human life or to communicate with a vessel in distress in case lives may be in danger. 'Deviation for the purpose of saving life is protected and involves neither forfeiture of insurance nor liability to the goods' owner in respect of loss which would otherwise be within the exceptions of "perils of the seas". And, as a necessary consequence of the foregoing, deviation for the purposes of communicating with a ship in distress is allowable, inasmuch as the state of the vessel in distress may involve danger to life. On the other hand, deviation for the sole purpose of saving property is not thus privileged, but entails all the usual consequences of deviation.'[57]

In the case from which this quotation is drawn, the vessel, having deviated to answer a distress call, could easily have taken off the crew from the stricken ship, but decided to take the latter in tow in order to earn salvage. While the vessel was engaged in this operation it was driven ashore in a gale with the loss of her cargo. The deviation in order

---

[53] *Frenkel* v *MacAndrews* [1929] AC 545.
[54] [1939] AC 562.
[55] *Ibid* at p 584.
[56] *Rio Tinto Co* v *Seed Shipping Co* (1926) 24 LlLR 316.
[57] Cockburn CJ in *Scaramanga* v *Stamp* (1880) 5 CPD 295 at p 304.

to salve the ship was held not to be justified and the shipowners were held liable for loss of cargo despite the fact that such loss was covered by the exception of perils of the sea in the charterparty. The position would have been otherwise had the weather been such that it had been necessary to take the disabled ship in tow in order to save the lives of the crew.

2   To avoid danger to the ship or cargo. The master is under an obligation to exercise reasonable care and skill in ensuring the success of the joint enterprise and accordingly is entitled to deviate from the proper course in order to ensure the safety of the vessel and its cargo. Indeed, in the majority of cases, he will be under a duty to take such action.[58] The risks may arise from natural causes such as storms, ice or fog, or they may involve political factors such as the outbreak of war or the fear of capture by hostile forces.[59] In either case, however, the danger must be of a reasonably permanent nature, since a master would not be justified in substituting a substantially different voyage in order to avoid a risk arising from a merely temporary obstruction such as a shortage of tugs or a neap tide.[60]

One of the most frequently encountered examples of this type of justifiable deviation is the vessel which, for safety reasons, has to put into port for repairs to damage sustained on the voyage.[61] Nor is it apparently material that the damage has resulted from the initial unseaworthiness of the vessel. Thus in *Kish v Taylor*[62] a vessel had been chartered to load a full and complete cargo of timber at two ports in the Gulf of Mexico for carriage to western Europe. On the charterer failing to provide a full cargo, the master procured further timber from other shippers, some of which he loaded on deck in such a way as to render the vessel unseaworthy. Heavy squalls were encountered during the voyage which caused the deck cargo to shift and endanger the safety of the vessel. Accordingly the master put into Halifax for the necessary repairs before proceeding to Liverpool where he discharged the cargo. When the shipowner sought to exercise the contractual lien for dead freight and demurrage, the cargo owner contended that the right to rely on the lien had been forfeited as the result of what was alleged to be an unjustifiable deviation to Halifax. The House of Lords rejected this argument and held the deviation to be justified even though it resulted from initial unseaworthiness. In their view justification was to be sought in the existence of a danger and not in its cause. Lord Atkinson indicated the policy considerations involved:

> 'It is the presence of the peril and not its cause which determines the character of the deviation, or must the master of the ship be left in this dilemma that, whenever, by his own culpable act or a breach of contract by his owner, he finds his ship in a perilous position, he must continue on his voyage at all hazards, or only seek safety under the penalty of forfeiting the contract of affreightment?'

---

[58] See *Notara v Henderson* (1870) LR 5 QB 346.
[59] *The Teutonia* (1872) LR 4 PC 171.
[60] *Hand v Baynes* (1839) 4 Wharton 204.
[61] *Phelps, James & Co v Hill* [1891] 1 QB 605.
[62] [1912] AC 604. US courts have held deviation not to be justified where the shipowner was aware of the unseaworthy condition of the vessel before it sailed: *The Louise* [1945] AMC 363.

In such a dilemma the master must clearly be given the benefit of the doubt, since:

> 'Nothing could, it would appear to me, tend more to increase the dangers to which life and property are exposed at sea than to hold that the law of England obliged the master of a merchant ship to choose between such alternatives.'[63]

It would appear that a deviation may be justified although the risk to be avoided affects only the ship and not the cargo.[64] On the other hand, in the reverse situation, the position is far from clear. There is authority for suggesting that where continuation of the voyage would result in substantial damage to the cargo, the master might be under a duty to deviate to protect the interests of the cargo owners,[65] but it is doubtful whether such an obligation arises where the apprehended damage is slight or only affects part of the cargo. While the master is expected to take into account the interests of both ship and cargo, 'I am not prepared to hold that the instant it becomes clear that by going on some mischief will be done to some portion of the cargo that it becomes the duty of the captain to go back, and perhaps put all concerned to a very enormous expense . . . '.[66] Presumably the decision as to whether a deviation is justified in such circumstances will depend upon a comparison between the gravity of the danger and the inconvenience and expense of taking avoiding action.

3   Where the deviation is made necessary by some default on the part of the charterer. Thus it may be justifiable to put into port to discharge dangerous cargo which has been loaded by the charterer without the knowledge of the shipowner. Again, a master may be permitted to deviate to obtain more cargo in a situation where the charterer has breached his contractual obligation to load a full cargo.[67]

(II) UNDER THE HAGUE AND HAGUE/VISBY RULES

In addition to the types of justification recognised at common law, Art IV rule 4 of the Hague/Visby Rules[68] provides two further heads: 'deviation in saving or attempting to save . . . property at sea', and 'any reasonable deviation'. The interpretation of these provisions is discussed elsewhere,[69] but it is relevant to note at this point that courts in the United Kingdom have given an extremely restricted interpretation to the term 'reasonable deviation' with the result that there are few reported cases in which the concept has been successfully invoked.

---

[63] [1912] AC at pp 618–19. Compensation in the form of damages would of course be available for any loss (including delay) resulting from the initial unseaworthiness.

[64] *The Teutonia* (1872) LR 4 PC 171.

[65] *The Rona* (No 2) (1884) 51 LT 28.

[66] Sir John Hannen in *The Rona* (1884) 51 LT 28 at p 30. See also Cockburn CJ in *Notara v Henderson* (1870) LR 5 QB 346 at p 354.

[67] *Wallems v Muller* [1927] 2 KB 99. Problems would, however, arise in this situation if cargo owned by third parties was already on board.

[68] The Hague Rules are identical on this point.

[69] See *infra*, pp 208–10.

2.3.2 LIBERTY CLAUSES

Most standard charter forms include a clause giving the master a liberty to deviate for specified reasons. A good example is provided by clause 3 of the Gencon form:

> 'The vessel has liberty to call at any port or ports in any order, for any purpose, to sail without pilots, to tow and/or assist vessels in all situations, and also to deviate for the purpose of saving life and/or property.'

Clauses in other charters specify a variety of reasons for which deviation is permissible, including for bunkering purposes,[70] for adjusting compasses or radio equipment,[71] or for landing and embarking crew members.[72] If such clauses were applied literally, they would have far-reaching effects, but, as they are inserted predominantly for the shipowner's benefit, the courts apply the principle of *contra proferentem* and where possible give them an extremely restricted interpretation. Thus in the case of *Glynn* v *Margetson*[73] a cargo of oranges was loaded in Malaga on a vessel bound for Liverpool on a bill of lading which gave the owner 'liberty to proceed to and stay at any port or ports in any rotation'. Despite the breadth of this clause, it was held not to protect the shipowner when the vessel called at ports not on the geographical route to Liverpool with the result that the oranges arrived at their destination in a damaged state. In a case involving a similar clause, Lord Esher expressed the view that such a term 'has always been interpreted to mean that the ship may call at such ports as would naturally and usually be ports of call on the voyage named. If the stipulation were only that she might call at any ports, the invariable construction has been that she would only be entitled to call at such ports in the geographical order; and therefore the words "in any order" are frequently added; but in any case it appears to me that the ports must be ports substantially on the course of the voyage.'[74]

Such principles of interpretation are ultimately at the mercy of a skilled draftsman and can be defeated by the use of appropriate words. Thus clause 13 of the Nubaltwood form gives the shipowner a liberty to call 'at any port or ports whatsoever in any order in or out of the route or in a contrary direction to or beyond the port of destination . . .' Clauses of this type have been given full effect by the courts which have described them as conferring on the ship a liberty to go where she pleased, subject only to the restriction that the essential purpose of the voyage must not be frustrated.[75]

A further problem arises in the not infrequent case where the standard charterparty form expressly incorporates the Hague or Hague/Visby Rules.[76] As these regimes prescribe the minimum protection for the cargo owner which is incapable of being reduced by agreement between the parties,[77] to what extent are such liberty clauses affected by

---

[70] Polcoalvoy, clause 26; Shellvoy 5, clause 31.

[71] Grainvoy, clause 20.

[72] Polcoalvoy, clause 26.

[73] [1893] AC 351.

[74] *Leduc* v *Ward* (1888) QBD 475 at p 482.

[75] Branson J in *Connolly Shaw* v *Nordenfjeldske SS Co* (1934) 50 TLR 418. See also *Hadji Ali Akbar* v *Anglo-Arabian SS Co* (1906) 11 Com Cas 219; *Frenkel* v *MacAndrews* [1929] AC 545.

[76] For example, Polcoalvoy, clause 28; Nuvoy 84, clause 43.

[77] Article III rule 8.

the requirement in Art IV rule 4 that a deviation, other than to save life or property, has to be reasonable? The US courts have taken a strict view in such circumstances, holding that liberty clauses in the charter only take effect to the extent that the deviation is reasonable.[78] English courts, on the other hand, regard the express liberty clause as defining the scope of the contractual voyage rather than as a provision seeking to excuse the shipowner should he depart from it. On this view there is no conflict between such a clause and Art IV rule 4 of the Hague/Visby Rules. In the words of Hodson LJ, 'the object of the Rules is to define not the scope of the contract of service, but the terms on which that service is to be performed'.[79] Presumably the same result would follow where a bill of lading, issued under a charterparty, included a provision expressly incorporating a liberty clause in the charter.

2.3.3 THE EFFECT OF BREACH

At common law any unjustifiable deviation from the proper route has been traditionally regarded as a fundamental breach of the contract of affreightment.

> 'The true view is that the departure from the voyage contracted to be made is a breach by the shipowner of his contract, a breach of such a serious character that, however slight the deviation, the other party to the contract is entitled to treat it as going to the root of the contract, and to declare himself as no longer bound by any of the contract terms.'[80]

A fundamental breach was traditionally distinguished from a condition by the fact that, on a breach of the former, the innocent party was entitled to repudiate his obligations under the contract and sue for damages at large irrespective of any exceptions or limitation of liability provisions in the contract of carriage.

The importance attached to the breach stems from the fact that, in earlier marine insurance practice in Great Britain and the United States, cover under a cargo insurance policy was lost in the event of deviation. The strict liability imposed on the shipowner was therefore designed to afford protection to the cargo owner. Under present insurance practice, however, such a policy will normally include a 'held covered' clause under which cover can be extended in the event of deviation in return for the payment of an additional premium. This change in procedure, together with the practice of incorporating widely drafted liberty clauses into the contract of carriage, has greatly reduced the practical importance of the deviation concept.

There is now some doubt as to whether the strict view of the concept of deviation, operating as a rule of law, can survive the combined effect of the strictures of members of the House of Lords in the two cases of *Suisse Atlantique*[81] and *Photo Production* v

---

[78] *The Nancy Lykes* 706 F2d 80 (1983); see also, 561 Fed Supp 1077 (1977).

[79] *Renton* v *Palmyra Trading Corp* [1956] 1 QB 462 at p 510. (Hodson LJ was referring to an identical provision in the Hague Rules.) See also *Foreman & Ellams* v *Federal SN Co* [1928] 2 KB 424; *Stag Line* v *Foscolo Mango* [1932] AC 328.

[80] Lord Atkin in *Hain SS Co* v *Tate & Lyle* (1936) 41 Com Cas 350 at p 354. See also Carver 9.043 ff; Gaskell 6.51 ff.

[81] [1967] 1 AC 361.

Securicor.[82] In their opinion, the doctrine of fundamental breach, conceived as a substantive rule of law, had been a judicial aberration initially designed to protect the consumer against the effects of exclusion clauses. Such protection is no longer required after the Unfair Contract Terms Act 1977. So far as the commercial world is concerned, a reversion to a strict application of the construction approach would leave them free to negotiate their own contracts and allocate risks as they see fit.

What effect will these judgments have on the traditional approach to the concept of deviation?[83] On the one hand, Lord Wilberforce in *Photo Production* v *Securicor* extended a possible lifeline to retaining the concept of deviation as a rule of law when he remarked that 'it may be preferable that [the deviation cases] should be considered as a body of authority *sui generis* with special rules derived from historical and commercial reasons'.[84] The alternative view would be that deviation, as one facet of the wider doctrine of fundamental breach, survives not as a rule of law, but as a sub-species of construction. This was the approach adopted by the Court of Appeal in *The Antares*,[85] where Lloyd LJ was of the opinion that deviation cases 'should now be assimilated into the ordinary law of contract'. Such an approach would require the courts to take into consideration the entire terms of the contract, including both exceptions and liberty clauses, with a view to discovering whether, on their true construction it was clear that the parties intended them to apply to the new situation, i.e. the substituted voyage.[86] With such formidable weapons at the disposal of the court it is doubtful whether there is any need to retain the rule of law approach to the problem raised by deviation. In the words of a modern writer, 'All the common law methods of control are retained and these are strengthened by the requirement of reasonableness. The rules of construction still weigh very heavily against the *proferens*. A competent judge should find little difficulty in ousting an unwelcome exemption clause.'[87]

What then is the effect of deviation on the contract of carriage? The traditional view is that, in the event of an unjustified deviation, however slight, the charterer or cargo owner is permitted an election. He is entitled either to treat the breach as a repudiation of the contract of carriage or to waive the breach with the result that he will be restricted to an action for damages. A similar approach would presumably be adopted by a court which found that, as a matter of construction, the terms of the contract of carriage were not intended to be applicable to the substituted voyage. The following account of the traditional view must, however, be treated with some reserve until the full implications of the decision in *Photo Production* v *Securicor* become evident.

---

[82] [1980] AC 827. The strict view was reaffirmed in the United States in *The Nancy Lykes* 706 F 2d 80 (1983). See also *Nemeth* v *General Steamship Corp* [1983] AMC 885. Judge LJ in *The Kapitan Petko Voivoda* [2003] 2 Lloyd's Rep 1 at p 16 refers to it as a 'moribund if not defunct principle'.

[83] In this respect it is important to note that contracts of carriage by sea will not normally be subject to the provisions of the Unfair Contract Terms Act (see Schedule 1) and so their terms will rarely be required to conform to the standard of reasonableness imposed by that statute.

[84] [1980] AC 827 at p 845. An approach still left open by Longmore LJ in *The Kapitan Petko Voivoda* [2003] 2 Lloyd's Rep 1, at p 10.

[85] [1987] 1 Lloyd's Rep 424 at p 430. See Mills, C P, 'The Future of Deviation in the Law of Carriage of Goods' [1983] LMCQ 587 at p 596.

[86] See Kerr LJ in *George Mitchell* v *Finney Lock Seeds* [1983] 1 All ER 108 at p 123. See also the New Zealand case of *The Pembroke* [1995] 2 Lloyd's Rep 290.

[87] Mills [1983] LMCQ at p 595. See also Gaskell 6.73 ff.

(I) EFFECT OF TREATING THE CONTRACT AS REPUDIATED

If the injured party elects to treat the contract as at an end, the shipowner can no longer rely for protection on the terms of the charterparty or bill of lading. Henceforth his liability will be equivalent to that of a common carrier in that he will be subject to the strict liability imposed by the common law. In the event of being sued for loss or damage sustained during or subsequent to the deviation, he cannot invoke the contractual exceptions or the provisions for limitation of liability. Only three exceptions are recognised at common law, namely, those relating to act of God, act of the Queen's enemies and inherent vice. Even these are not available as a defence to the shipowner unless he can prove that the relevant loss would have been sustained irrespective of the deviation. In the majority of cases this is no easy task. In *Morrison* v *Shaw, Savill*[88] the exception of King's enemies was held not to be applicable to a case where a vessel had been sunk by an enemy submarine after having deviated from her course without justification. The owner was unable to establish that the loss would have been sustained even if the vessel had not deviated. In practice the common law exceptions will rarely offer any protection to the deviating carrier except possibly in the case where damage to cargo results from inherent vice.[89]

Deviation was followed by equally drastic consequences even where the contract of carriage was covered by a bill of lading governed by the Hague Rules. The carrier could not in such an event rely on the Art IV exceptions as a defence to a cargo claim. 'The provisions of the Act import into the agreement compulsorily certain exceptions, but there is nothing in the Act to show that these exceptions can be relied upon while the vessel is not pursuing the contract voyage, but is pursuing a voyage, or part of it, which is not covered by the contract at all.'[90] This result was the inevitable consequence of the common law approach which apparently regarded the provisions of the Hague Rules, when applicable, as little more than compulsory terms of the contract of carriage. Doubts have, however, been expressed as to whether deviation would deprive the carrier of his right to limit liability under Art IV rule 5, or invoke the time bar under Art III rule 6, of the Hague Rules, since both provisions are expressly made applicable 'in any event'. In recent decisions involving unauthorised deck carriage the Court of Appeal has taken the view that the decisive factor in such cases is not the seriousness or otherwise of the breach, but a straightforward construction of the relevant provisions.[91] Adopting this approach, they held that the words 'in any event' meant what they said. 'They are unlimited in scope and I can see no reason for giving them any other than their natural meaning.'[92] The carriers were accordingly entitled to rely on the respective Hague Rules defences irrespective of the seriousness of the breaches involved.[93] The introduction in

---

[88] [1916] 2 KB 783.

[89] See *Internationale Guano* v *MacAndrew* [1909] 2 KB 360.

[90] Greer LJ in *Foscolo Mango* v *Stag Line* [1931] 2 KB 48 at p 69.

[91] See *The Kapitan Petko Voivoda* [2003] 2 Lloyd's Rep 1 (limitation of liability); *The Antares* [1987] 1 Lloyd's Rep 424 (time bar).

[92] Longmore LJ in *The Kapitan Petko Voivoda* at p 18 quoting Tuckey LJ in *The Happy Ranger* [2002] 2 Lloyd's Rep 357 at p 364.

[93] Cf. the opposite view adopted by the US courts. See *Jones* v *Flying Clipper* (1954) 116 Fed Supp 386; *Encyclopaedia Britannica* v *Hong Kong Producer* [1969] 2 Lloyd's Rep 536.

the United Kingdom of the Hague/Visby Rules has reinforced this approach since their provisions are expressly given 'the force of law'.[94] If they are to be effective as rules of law then presumably they will survive any repudiation of contractual obligations by the parties concerned.[95]

In the event of the charterer treating the deviation as a repudiation of the contract of carriage, to what extent can the shipowner rely on exceptions in the charterparty or bill of lading in respect of losses occurring before the deviation? Alternatively, can he sue for demurrage or dead freight incurred at the port of loading? The traditional view relating to breaches of condition in general was expressed by Lord Sumner: 'Though a party may exercise his right to treat the contract as at an end, as regards obligations *de futuro*, it remains alive for the purpose of vindicating rights already acquired under it on either side.'[96] Opinions are divided as to whether a similar rule applies in the case of fundamental breach,[97] but there seems no reason in principle why deviation should affect accrued rights, and this is the standpoint adopted by US courts.[98]

One final point relates to the effect of deviation on the shipowner's right to recover freight. There still appears to be some doubt on this point. While it is clear that there will be no right to recover the charter freight once the deviation has been accepted as a repudiation of the contract of carriage,[99] there seems no reason why, in appropriate circumstances where the cargo safely reaches its destination, the shipowner should not be entitled to reasonable freight on a *quantum meruit* basis.[100]

(II) EFFECT OF WAIVING THE BREACH

Despite deviation constituting a fundamental breach of contract, the cargo owner may elect to ignore it and treat the contract as still subsisting since 'however fundamental is the condition it may still be waived by the goods owner'.[101] The adoption of such a course of action is hardly surprising in the substantial number of cases where deviation results in little or no loss to the cargo owner. In the event of such affirmation, all the terms of the contract continue to apply including the exceptions and the provisions relating to the limitation of liability. Similarly, the shipowner is entitled to claim freight and general average contributions, the cargo owner being restricted to a remedy of damages for any loss attributable to the deviation and not covered by an exception.

A good example of the options open to the cargo owner is provided by the facts of the case of *Hain SS Co v Tate & Lyle*.[102] A vessel had been chartered to proceed to the West

---

[94] Carriage of Goods by Sea Act 1971, s 1(2). For the effects of the change of wording, see *The Morviken* [1983] 1 Lloyd's Rep 1. See *infra* at pp 184–6.

[95] This was the view taken by the Court of Appeal in *The Antares* [1987] 1 Lloyd's Rep 424 in respect of the Hague/Visby time limit.

[96] *Hirji Mulji* v *Cheong Yue SS Co* [1926] AC 497 at p 511. See also Lord Maugham in *Hain SS Co v Tate & Lyle* (1936) 41 Com Cas 350 at p 371.

[97] See, to the contrary, Pickford J in *Internationale Guano* v *MacAndrew* [1909] 2 KB 360; Scrutton p 259. Cf. Colinvaux, RP, *Carver's Carriage by Sea*, 13th edn, 1982, para 1200.

[98] See *The Poznan* (1922) 276 Fed Rep 418. See also Cooke 12.33 ff; Gaskell 6.58 ff.

[99] See Collins LJ in *Thorley* v *Orchis SS Co* [1907] 1 KB 660 at p 667.

[100] See Lord Wright in *Hain SS Co v Tate & Lyle* [1936] 41 Com Cas 350 at pp 368–9.

[101] Lord Wright in *Hain SS Co v Tate & Lyle* [1936] 2 All ER 597 at p 608.

[102] [1936] 2 All ER 597.

Indies and load a cargo of sugar at two ports in Cuba and one port in San Domingo to be nominated by the charterer. The charterer made the required nominations but, owing to a failure of communication by the owner's agents, the master was not informed of the nominated port in San Domingo. Consequently, when the relevant cargoes had been loaded at the two Cuban ports, the master proceeded to Queenstown for orders. Shipowners and charterers quickly discovered the mistake, whereupon the master was ordered back to San Domingo to load the remaining cargo. On subsequently leaving the latter port, however, the vessel ran aground and part of the cargo was lost, the remainder being transhipped on another vessel for completion of the voyage to the United Kingdom. Shortly before the vessel arrived at its destination the bills of lading covering the cargo of sugar were endorsed to Tate & Lyle who took delivery of the cargo in ignorance of the deviation.

The court had little doubt that the deviation constituted a fundamental breach of contract entitling the cargo owners to treat the contract as repudiated. So far as the charterers were concerned, however, with full knowledge of the facts they had elected to waive the breach by ordering the vessel back to San Domingo. As the aggrieved party, 'the cargo owner can elect to treat the contract as subsisting; and if he does this with full knowledge of his rights he must in accordance with the general law of contract be held bound'.[103] In these circumstances the shipowners, in the event of any claim being made by the charterers, would be entitled to rely for protection on the charter exception of perils of the sea. The position with regard to the bill of lading holders was, however, entirely different. There could be no waiver without knowledge of the breach and, on the principle enunciated in *Leduc* v *Ward*,[104] the bill of lading holders were not bound by any waiver on the part of the charterers. Consequently, the shipowners were unable to rely on the bill of lading exceptions as a defence to any cargo claim brought by the consignees.

The burden of proving waiver will always rest with the deviating shipowner, and as it will rarely be in the interest of the consignee to waive the breach once the cargo has reached its destination, 'A waiver to be operative so that a party's claim is estopped, must be unequivocal, definite, clear, cogent and complete.'[105] In this respect there appears to be some doubt as to whether mere reference of a dispute to arbitration in accordance with a clause in the charterparty would constitute such a waiver.[106] The better view is that it would not.

2.4 THE OBLIGATION TO NOMINATE A SAFE PORT

Whenever a charterer has the right to nominate a port, whether under a time or voyage charter he is under an implied obligation to nominate a safe port. In the majority of charters this implied obligation is reinforced by an express term to the same effect.

---

[103] *Ibid* Lord Atkin at p 601.
[104] (1888) 20 QBD 475; See *infra* pp 130–2.
[105] Slesser LJ in *McCormick* v *National Motor Insurance* (1934) 40 Com Cas 76 at p 93.
[106] See *US Shipping Board* v *Bunge y Born* (1924) 41 TLR 73 at pp 74–5.

An example of such a term is provided by clause 2 of the Baltime 1939 form which provides:

'The vessel to be employed in lawful trades for the carriage of lawful merchandise only between good and safe ports or places where she can safely lie always afloat.'

What then constitutes a safe port for the purpose of such warranties? The case law would suggest that the basic concept of a safe port remains the same irrespective of whether it relates to an express or implied warranty or to a time or voyage charter. The classic definition was provided by Sellers LJ in *The Eastern City*:[107]

'a port will not be safe unless, in the relevant period of time, the particular ship can reach it, use it and return from it without, in the absence of some abnormal occurrence, being exposed to danger which cannot be avoided by good navigation and seamanship.'

2.4.1 THE PERIOD COVERED BY THE WARRANTY

The 'relevant period of time' mentioned in the definition clearly covers the entire period during which the vessel is using the port from the moment of entry to the time of departure. In certain circumstances the coverage may be extended to incorporate risks encountered in the approaches to a port, as, for example, ice in the Elbe preventing safe access to the port of Hamburg,[108] while in exceptional cases it may even cover dangers encountered on the open sea, such as the risk of submarine activity around British ports during wartime.[109] Conversely, when the loading or discharging operation has been completed, the vessel must be able to leave the port in safety. So Manchester was held an 'unsafe' port for the ship involved in a case where, after discharge of the cargo, the masts of a vessel were too high to pass under bridges on the ship canal linking the port with the sea.[110] It is essential, however, that the danger must be linked with the use of the nominated port since, in the words of Devlin J in *Grace* v *General SN Co*,[111] 'It is obvious in point of fact that the more remote it is from the port, the less likely it is to interfere with the safety of the voyage. The charterer does not guarantee that the most direct route or any particular route to the port is safe, but the voyage which he orders must be one which an ordinarily prudent and skilful master can find a way of making in safety.'

Nevertheless, the majority of cases are concerned with the safety of the vessel while in the port itself where a similar variety is evident in the range of risks encompassed by the warranty. The most frequently encountered danger in an unsafe port is the risk of physical damage to the vessel. This may arise from an insufficient depth of water[112] or from

---

[107] [1958] 2 Lloyd's Rep 127 at p 131. For an alternative US definition, see Bond Smith J in 49 Tulane LR 861: 'A safe port is a place where a chartered vessel may enter, load or discharge, and leave without legal restraint and at which the vessel will encounter no perils greater than those of the sea. Whether a port is safe is a fact to be determined in each case having regard to the vessel concerned.'

[108] *Grace* v *General SN Co* [1950] 2 KB 383. See also *The M/V Naiad* [1978] AMC 2049.

[109] *Palace Shipping Co* v *Gans SS Line* [1916] 1 KB 138. See also *The Saga Cob* [1992] 2 Lloyd's Rep 545 (vessel attacked by Eritrean guerillas while anchored four miles off port).

[110] *Limerick* v *Stott* [1921] 2 KB 613.

[111] [1950] 2 KB at p 391.

[112] *The Alhambra* (1881) 6 PD 68; *Reynolds* v *Tomlinson* [1896] 1 QB 586.

the presence of ice or periodic silting[113] which hinders access to the port. Alternatively an exposed or rocky anchorage may render a port unsafe, particularly one which is liable to the onset of unpredictable gales or other bad weather.[114] On the other hand, the risks may have a political origin, as for example in the event of the imposition of a blockade or the outbreak of hostilities.[115] Finally, there are the organisational risks arising from faulty administration by the port authorities.[116] These may range from the lack of adequate safety equipment such as marker buoys, warning lights and radar, to the absence of suitable weather reports[117] or the provision of unsafe berths.[118]

2.4.2 THE NATURE OF THE RISKS COVERED

Whether or not a port is 'safe' is a question of fact depending on the circumstances of each individual case.[119] Regard must be paid to the type of vessel involved, the work to be done and the conditions pertaining in the port at the relevant time. Thus a port may be safe for one type of vessel but not for another as, for example, where the draught of a 250,000 ton tanker is too deep to allow it access to many ports which are otherwise perfectly safe for normal vessels. It must also be remembered that some risk is attached to the use of any port and a port will not be rendered unsafe by the presence of risks which can be avoided by good navigation and competent seamanship. Accordingly, a port is not necessarily unsafe because it is liable to the occasional storm even though vessels may be required to leave it in the event of bad weather.[120] On such occasions, however, adequate weather forecasts must be available and the organisation of the port must be such as to enable a competent master to take the necessary avoiding action. Thus, in the case of *The Khian Sea*,[121] the Court of Appeal held a port unsafe when, although the master obtained adequate warning of an approaching storm, he was prevented from leaving his berth by the presence of two other vessels anchored close by. Lord Denning MR took the opportunity of enumerating the requirements which had to be satisfied in such circumstances under the safe port warranty. 'First there must be an adequate weather forecasting system. Second, there must be an adequate availability of pilots and tugs.[122] Thirdly, there must be adequate sea room to manoeuvre. And fourthly, there must be an adequate system for ensuring that sea room and room for manoeuvre is always available.'[123]

It is not every hazard, however, which will render a port unsafe. Where the obstruction is only of a temporary nature as, for example, when caused by high winds, neap

---

[113] *The Hermine* [1979] 1 Lloyd's Rep 212.
[114] *The Eastern City* [1958] 2 Lloyd's Rep 127.
[115] *The Evia (No 2)* [1982] 2 Lloyd's Rep 307; *The Teutonia* (1872) LR 4 PC 171.
[116] See *The Marinicki* [2003] 2 Lloyd's Rep 655 (no proper system in place to investigate reports of underwater obstructions and to find and remove them).
[117] *The Dagmar* [1968] 2 Lloyd's Rep 563.
[118] *Reardon Smith Line* v *Australian Wheat Board* [1956] AC 266.
[119] See Morris LJ in *Compania Naviera Maropan* v *Bowaters* [1955] 2 QB at p 105.
[120] See *The Heinrich Horn* [1971] AMC 362.
[121] [1979] 1 Lloyd's Rep 545.
[122] See *The Universal Monarch* [1988] 2 Lloyd's Rep 483.
[123] *The Khian Sea*, at p 547.

tides or silting, the master is expected to wait a reasonable time until the danger has disappeared or been removed. Only where the resultant delay is 'inordinate', i.e. such as to frustrate the object of the charterparty, will it constitute a breach of the safe port warranty. Thus a port on the Mississippi was not unsafe because the departure of a vessel had been delayed for some 21 days as the result of fog and the periodic silting of the river downstream. In the words of Roskill LJ,[124] 'a shipowner cannot throw up a charterparty merely because there has been . . . "commercially unacceptable delay", that is to say, delay exceeding a reasonable time. The delay in such a case must, before he can rescind and treat the charterer's conduct as a repudiation of the charterer's obligation to load, be such as will frustrate the adventure.' He added that 'if you substitute any other test than frustration, you use a yardstick which is extremely difficult to apply in any given case. How do you judge whether a particular delay is commercially acceptable?'

As every case is decided on its own facts, it is probable that in normal circumstances a shorter period of delay would be required to frustrate a voyage charterparty than that necessary to frustrate a time charter.

2.4.3 THE NATURE OF THE UNDERTAKING – REMEDIES AVAILABLE FOR BREACH

There is little authority as to whether the safe port undertaking constitutes a condition or a warranty. In view of the fact that breach of a term which is technically classified as a condition entitles the innocent party to repudiate all further obligations under the contract, it is unlikely that the parties to a time charter envisage the term as constituting more than a warranty sounding in damages. The position may well be different in the case of a voyage charter, but everything would turn on the wording of the particular contract.

What does, however, appear clear is that a shipowner can refuse a nomination if he is aware that the port is inherently unsafe.[125] Indeed, if he ignores the obvious danger and proceeds to enter the nominated port, his conduct may well amount to a *novus actus interveniens* which prevents him from recovering compensation for any damage subsequently suffered by his vessel. The existence of the safe port warranty 'does not mean that a master can enter ports that are obviously unsafe and then charge the charterers with damage done'.[126] On the other hand, the courts recognise that, in such a situation, the master is in a dilemma and will often give him the benefit of the doubt where the choice lies between a loss of freight or a scratch to the paintwork.[127]

In the majority of cases the master, on receiving the nomination, will be unaware of the potential danger and, in any event, is entitled to presume that the charterer is fulfilling his obligation by nominating a safe port. Consequently, by sailing to the nominated port the master is not regarded as having waived any breach by the charterer. 'It

---

[124] *The Hermine* [1979] 1 Lloyd's Rep 212 at p 218.
[125] But if a shipowner with full knowledge of the danger unequivocally accepts a nomination, he cannot subsequently repudiate his election although he may retain his right to claim damages for breach of contract: *The Kanchenjunga* [1990] 1 Lloyd's Rep 391.
[126] *Per* Devlin J in *The Stork* [1955] 2 QB at p 77.
[127] See *American President Lines v USA* [1968] AMC 830.

does not lie in the mouth of the promisor to say that a promisee has no right to assume that a promise has been faithfully carried out and should make his own enquiries to see whether it has or not. If everything done under contract has to be scrutinised and tested by the other party before he can safely act upon it, many transactions may be seriously held up – in doubtful cases, perhaps indefinitely.'[128] Consequently, when, on arrival at the port, the master discovers the potential hazard, he is still entitled to refuse to enter. Whether or not the charterer is then entitled to make an alternative nomination is uncertain, although he will certainly be liable to compensate for any loss of time involved. The cases suggest that such alternative nomination is possible in the case of a time charter where the vessel has been chartered for a specified period of time during which the owner has undertaken to carry out the charterer's instructions. The position is different with regard to a voyage charter, since here the agreement is to charter the ship for a voyage between specified ports. Even where a charterer is given the right to nominate the ports, the cases suggest that, once nominated, the ports are to be treated as if they had been specified in the original charter.[129] No substitutions may therefore be permitted, in which case the safe port undertaking may be regarded as a condition precedent entitling the shipowner to repudiate further performance of the charterparty in the event of its breach. In practice, however, there may be specific provision for such an eventuality in the contract, or it may be covered by the proviso 'or as near as she can safely get'.[130]

Any claims for breach of the safe port undertaking will be limited by the rules of causation and remoteness of damage. They may take one, or more, of three possible forms:

(i)   Normally it will consist of a claim for physical damage to the vessel.
(ii) Alternatively, where no physical damage has been suffered, the shipowner may seek to recover the cost of avoiding the danger by, for example, engaging tugs or lightening the vessel where the draught is too great.
(iii) In cases where the vessel is trapped in a port for an 'inordinate' period of time by, for example, silting or the outbreak of hostilities, the claim will be for damages for detention. In order to constitute breach in such circumstances, the delay must be such as to frustrate the object of the contract, but the charterer is not allowed to avoid liability by pleading frustration, since his breach renders the frustration self-induced.

2.4.4 THE SCOPE OF THE UNDERTAKING

A final question, which has provoked some debate in recent years, relates to the precise scope of the undertaking given by the charterer. One point is, however, clear. The undertaking refers to the safety of the port at the time it is to be used, rather than to its safety at the time of nomination. Thus a port may be unsafe at the time of its nomination in January, because of the presence of ice which will have disappeared by the time

---

[128] Devlin J in *Compania Naviera Maropan v Bowaters* [1955] 2 QB 68 at p 77.
[129] See *infra* p 62.
[130] See *infra* pp 63–4.

of its intended use in the following June. Conversely, a port may be safe at the time of its nomination in June, but will be blocked by ice when used in the following January.

Beyond this point of agreement, however, there was, prior to the decision in *The Evia (No 2)*[131] a divergence of opinion as to the nature of this undertaking. On one view it imposed on the charterer a strict contractual liability for all loss suffered by the shipowner resulting from unsafe conditions in the port, irrespective of whether such conditions were foreseeable at the time of nomination. In essence, this would amount to a continuing guarantee of the safety of the port during the period it was to be used, subject of course to the normal rules of causation and remoteness of damage outlined above. Such an approach was justified on the grounds that it was in line with the express wording of the time charter clauses requiring the vessel to be employed only between good and safe ports, and also because it resulted in an equitable allocation of risk – the shipowner undertaking for a specified period to comply with the charterer's orders in return for a guarantee from the charterer to use the vessel only between safe ports.[132] The contrary view favoured an obligation which was 'limited to a warranty that the nominated port of discharge is safe at the time of nomination and may be expected to remain safe from the moment of a vessel's arrival until her departure'.[133] This approach would link the undertaking to the inherent characteristics of the port at the time of nomination and would involve an objective test to be applied irrespective of the knowledge of the charterer. In brief, such an obligation would relate to the prospective safety of the port at the time of nomination and would not extend to 'abnormal occurrences' which were not within the reasonable expectations of the parties at that time.

This difference of opinion was finally resolved by the House of Lords in *The Evia (No 2)*.[134] In this case *The Evia* had been chartered on a Baltime form which included an express undertaking that she be employed 'only between good and safe ports'. In March 1980 she was ordered by the charterers to load a cargo in Cuba for carriage to Basrah at a time when there was no reason to believe that Basrah was unsafe, or was likely to become so in the foreseeable future. *The Evia* arrived in the Shatt al Arab on 1 July but, owing to congestion, had to wait until 20 August before a berth was available in Basrah. Discharge was not completed until 22 September, the very day on which navigation on the Shatt al Arab ceased due to the outbreak of the Iran–Iraq war. *The Evia* being indefinitely trapped, the umpire in the subsequent arbitration held that the charterparty was frustrated as from 4 October. Being thus deprived of any further payments of hire, the shipowner appealed on the ground that any frustration was self-induced since it had resulted from a breach of the express undertaking to nominate a safe port. In rejecting the appeal, the Lords were unanimously of the view that the warranty did not amount to a continuing guarantee of the port's safety but referred only to the prospective safety of the port at the time of nomination. In the words of Lord

---

[131] [1982] 2 Lloyd's Rep 307.

[132] For a summary of the case law to this effect, see the judgment of Mustill J in *The Mary Lou* [1981] 2 Lloyd's Rep 272.

[133] Donaldson J in *The Evaggelos Th* [1971] 2 Lloyd's Rep at p 205. See also Sir Owen Dixon CJ in *Reardon Smith Line* v *Australian Wheat Board* [1954] 2 Lloyd's Rep 44.

[134] [1982] 2 Lloyd's Rep 307.

Diplock, 'It is with the prospective safety of the port at the time when the vessel will be there for the loading or unloading operation that the contractual promise is concerned, and the contractual promise itself is given at the time when the charterer gives the order to the master or other agent of the shipowner to proceed to the loading or unloading port.'[135]

In rejecting the 'continuing guarantee' approach, the Lords affirmed that the charterer would be liable for the prevailing characteristics of the port irrespective of whether they were known to him. On the other hand, he would not have to accept responsibility for such 'unexpected and abnormal' events as the outbreak of the Iran–Iraq war. 'I cannot think that if . . . some unexpected or abnormal event thereafter occurs which creates conditions of unsafety where conditions of safety had previously existed . . . that contractual promise extends to making the charterers liable for any resulting loss or damage, physical or financial. So to hold would make the charterer the insurer of such unexpected and abnormal risks which in my view, should properly fall upon the ship's insurers.'[136]

If the correct test to be applied in the future is to be based on the prospective safety of the port at the time of nomination, this cannot be the end of the story. What happens if the port becomes actually or prospectively unsafe to the knowledge of the charterer while the vessel is sailing towards it, or even after it has berthed within the port? In the view of their Lordships, the solution to this problem is to place on the time charterer a secondary obligation, in such circumstances, to cancel the original nomination and order the ship out of the danger. Where the vessel is already inside the port, as in *The Evia* case itself, such an obligation will only arise where it is still possible for the vessel to leave.[137]

The decision in *The Evia* clearly caught the market by surprise – in particular the rejection of the continuing guarantee formula as a 'heresy' by Lord Diplock,[138] in favour of a more complicated test based on a combination of primary and secondary obligations. As regards the new 'secondary obligation' concept two points require further clarification. First, how diligent is the charterer required to be in discovering any subsequent unexpected threat to the safety of the nominated port? Is the obligation to take avoiding action absolute, or based on due diligence, or on the actual knowledge of the charterer? Secondly, there is some uncertainty as to whether a secondary obligation can arise in the case of a voyage charter. Once the voyage charterer has exercised his right to nominate a port, the normal understanding is that no subsequent variation is permissible.[139] Their Lordships in *The Evia* refused to commit themselves on this point.

The two subsequent illustrations of the operation of Lord Roskill's secondary obligation have provided no elucidation on either problem. The facts in *The Lucille*[140] were practically identical with those in *The Evia* except for the fact that the vessel in the

---

[135] *Ibid* at p 310. See Lord Roskill at p 315 to the same effect.
[136] Lord Roskill at p 315.
[137] *Ibid* at p 320 *per* Lord Roskill.
[138] *Ibid* at p 310.
[139] See *infra* at p 62.
[140] [1983] 1 Lloyd's Rep 387. See also *The Concordia Fjord* [1984] 1 Lloyd's Rep 385.

former case was prevented by congestion from entering Basrah until 20 September, i.e. two days before the outbreak of the Iran–Iraq war. By that time the court found that Basrah was no longer prospectively safe and that consequently the charterer should have ordered the ship to escape while there was still an opportunity to do so. In failing to take such action, as a result of which the vessel was indefinitely trapped in Basrah, the charterer was in breach of his safe port undertaking.

2.5 THE OBLIGATION NOT TO SHIP DANGEROUS GOODS

At common law the shipper impliedly undertakes not to ship dangerous goods without first notifying the carrier of their particular characteristics. A similar obligation arises irrespective of whether the goods are shipped under a contract of affreightment governed by a bill of lading or a charterparty although, in the latter case, the implied undertaking will often be reinforced by an express clause in the charterparty itself.[141] No requirement of notification will, however, arise where the carriers, or members of their crew, knew or ought reasonably to have been aware of the dangerous nature of the cargo.

2.5.1 MEANING OF DANGEROUS GOODS

No definition of dangerous goods is provided by the common law and two alternative approaches to the concept are possible. On the one hand, a traditional view might be to regard dangerous goods as a category the extent of which is to be developed by precedent or statutory regulation. Certainly a number of substances such as explosives and radioactive materials are inherently unsafe, and it would not be difficult to compile a substantial list on this basis. Such an attempt is to be found in s 446 of the Merchant Shipping Act 1894 which refers to 'aquafortis, vitriol, naphtha, benzine, gunpowder, lucifer-matches, nitro-glycerine, petroleum, any explosive within the meaning of the Explosives Act 1875, and any other goods of a dangerous nature'.[142] The most recent example of such a 'list' is provided by regulation 1(2) of the Merchant Shipping (Dangerous Goods) Regulations 1981 which defines 'dangerous goods' by reference as any 'goods classified in the Blue Book, the IMDG Code or any other IMO publication specified below as dangerous for carriage by sea . . .'

   Such an approach, however, constitutes only half the story since the courts have defined the concept in far wider terms to embrace cases in which the danger is to be found in the surrounding circumstances rather than in the inherent nature of the goods themselves. Thus, while it may be thought inaccurate to categorise grain as an inherently dangerous cargo, a hazardous situation might well arise if grain shipped in bulk is allowed to overheat in transit. Similarly, liquids which are otherwise safe may nevertheless create problems if permitted to leak from their containers and damage other

---

[141] See Baltime form clause 2.
[142] The final phrase is presumably to be construed *eiusdem generis* with what has gone before.

cargo.[143] In these circumstances the danger lies rather in the overall situation than in the particular category of goods involved. In approaching such cases it is important, in the opinion of Mustill J, 'to find a general test which will permit the identification of those cargoes whose shipment is a breach of contract in the absence of a specific warning as to their characteristics. In my view, it is essential when looking for such a test to remember that we are here concerned, not with the labelling in the abstract of goods as "dangerous" or "safe" but with the distribution of risk for the consequences of a dangerous situation arising during the voyage. The character of the goods does, of course, play an important part in creating such a situation. But it is not the only factor. Equally important are the knowledge of the shipowner as to the characteristics of the goods, and the care with which he carries them in the light of that knowledge.'[144] In the case at issue, the vessel had been damaged by an explosion caused by the ignition of a mixture of air and methane gas emitted by a cargo of coal after loading. While it was impossible to categorise coal as either an inherently dangerous or safe cargo, it was common knowledge that it had a propensity to emit methane gas which might result in an explosion in the appropriate circumstances. The trial judge took the view that, 'In such a case, I consider that it is not correct to start with an implied warranty as to the shipment of dangerous goods and try to force the facts within it; but rather to read the contract and the facts together and ask whether, on the true construction of the contract, the risks involved in this particular shipment were risks which the [shipowners] contracted to bear.'[145]

The concept has also been extended to cases in which the goods themselves were in no way physically dangerous. So in *Mitchell, Cotts v Steel*[146] the shippers were aware that the cargo could not be discharged at Piraeus without the permission of the British Government and were held liable for the resulting delay when such consent was not forthcoming. In the view of Atkin J the loading of unlawful cargo which may involve the vessel in the risk of seizure or delay 'is precisely analogous to the shipment of a dangerous cargo which might cause the destruction of the ship'.[147]

2.5.2 NATURE OF LIABILITY

Where goods are shipped without notice of their dangerous qualities the shipper will be liable for any damage resulting either to the vessel or to any other cargo on board.[148] The orthodox view is that such liability is strict and in no way dependent on the knowledge available to the shipper as to the nature of the goods. This view stems from the majority decision in *Brass v Maitland*[149] where a consignment of 'bleaching powder'

---

[143] See Sellers J in *Ministry of Food v Lamport & Holt* [1952] 2 Lloyd's Rep 371 at p 382. The goods may be dangerous even though they constitute no risk to the vessel itself. See *The Giannis NK* [1998] 1 Lloyd's Rep 337.

[144] *The Athanasia Comninos* [1990] 1 Lloyd's Rep 277 at p 282. See also *Westchester Fire Ins Co v Buffalo Salvage Co* [1941] AMC 1601.

[145] [1990] 1 Lloyd's Rep 277 at p 283.

[146] [1916] 2 KB 610. See also, the shipment of contraband cargo: *The Donald* [1920] P 56.

[147] [1916] 2 KB at p 614.

[148] *Great Northern Rly Co v LEP Transport* [1922] 2 KB 742; *Micada v Texim* [1968] 2 Lloyd's Rep 742.

[149] (1856) 26 LJQB 49.

containing chloride of lime had been shipped in casks. During the voyage the chloride of lime corroded the casks and damaged other cargo in the hold. The majority of the court took the view that the shipper would be liable even though he was unaware of the dangerous nature of the goods, having shipped the casks immediately after receiving delivery from a third party, without any intermediate inspection. In the absence of knowledge on either side, the majority dealt with the issue purely as a question of allocation of risk. 'It seems much more just and expedient that, although they were ignorant of the dangerous qualities of the goods, or the insufficiency of the packing, the loss occasioned by the dangerous quality of the goods and the insufficient packing should be cast upon the shippers than upon the shipowners.'[150]

On the other hand, there was a strong dissenting judgment from Crompton J who felt that there was no authority to support an absolute obligation on the part of the shipper. 'It seems very difficult that the shipper can be liable for not communicating what he does not know . . . I entertain great doubt whether either the duty or the warranty extends beyond the cases where the shipper has knowledge, or means of knowledge, of the dangerous nature of the goods when shipped or where he has been guilty of some negligence as shipper, as by shipping without communicating danger, which he had the means of knowing and ought to have communicated.'[151] There has been little further authority on this point in the intervening years. Opinions still differ,[152] but in obiter dicta in *The Athanasia Comninos*, Mustill J supported the strict liability approach.[153] This approach has now been confirmed in the recent case of *The Giannis NK* where the House of Lords expressed the view obiter that both limbs of the common law undertaking were absolute.[154]

The distinction may not be of great practical importance since the issue will only arise on the rare occasion when neither shipper nor shipowner knows, or ought reasonably to be aware, of the dangerous nature of the goods. If the shipowner is aware of the nature of the cargo or reasonable means of knowledge are available to him, then the shipper will be under no obligation to give notice. Thus in *Brass* v *Maitland* where the cargo had been described as 'bleaching powder' the shipper was eventually held not liable since the shipowner ought to have known that the powder contained chloride of lime. Similarly, it might be argued that owners of vessels designed for the carriage in bulk of grain or coal ought to be aware of the propensities of the goods in such conditions even though the goods themselves may not be inherently dangerous.[155]

In essence, the object of the obligation imposed on the shipper to give notice is to provide the carrier with the opportunity either to refuse to carry the goods or to take the necessary precautions to protect his vessel and any other cargo on board. Once notice has been given, then, at common law, the shipper's obligation has been discharged and if the carrier subsequently consents to carry the cargo, the shipper will not be liable for

---

[150] *Ibid* at p 54, *per* Lord Campbell.
[151] *Ibid* at p 57. A similar view was taken by a US court in *Sucrest Corp* v *M/V Jennifer* [1978] AMC 2520.
[152] See Fletcher Moulton LJ in *Bamfield* v *Goole Transport Co* [1910] 2 KB 94 at p 110. Cf. Atkin J in *Mitchell, Cotts* v *Steel* [1916] 2 KB 610 at p 614.
[153] *The Athanasia Comninos* [1990] 1 Lloyd's Rep 277 at p 282.
[154] [1998] 1 Lloyd's Rep 337 at pp 344–5 *per* Lord Lloyd.
[155] *The Athanasia Comninos* [1990] 1 Lloyd's Rep 277; *The Atlantic Duchess* [1957] 2 Lloyd's Rep 55.

any resulting damage.[156] The only exception to this rule is where the shipper, in shipping dangerous goods, is in breach of a term of the charterparty. In such a case, even though the carrier accepts the cargo with full knowledge, the shipper will normally be liable for any damage caused by it.[157] Nor will the shipper be liable, even in the absence of notice, if the carrier knew, or ought reasonably to have been aware of, the hazardous nature of the cargo.[158] Presumably in the latter case, the carrier is treated as if his decision to carry the goods had been made in full knowledge of the risks involved. In the rare situation where the means of knowledge are available to neither party, there may be much to be said for Lord Campbell's view of treating the issue purely as a question of allocation of risk.

2.5.3 LIABILITY UNDER THE HAGUE/VISBY RULES

Express provision for the carriage of dangerous goods is to be found in Art IV rule 6 of the Hague/Visby Rules:[159]

'Goods of an inflammable, explosive or dangerous nature to the shipment whereof the carrier, master or agent of the carrier, has not consented, with knowledge of their nature and character, may at any time before discharge be landed at any place or destroyed or rendered innocuous by the carrier without compensation, and the shipper of such goods shall be liable for all damages and expenses directly or indirectly arising out of or resulting from such shipment.

If any such goods shipped with such knowledge and consent shall become a danger to the ship or cargo, they may in like manner be landed at any place or destroyed or rendered innocuous by the carrier without liability on the part of the carrier except to general average, if any.'

It will be noted that this section makes provision for two separate and distinct contingencies. In the first situation the carrier's consent to the shipment of the cargo has been obtained in ignorance of its inflammable, explosive or dangerous nature. In such an event the carrier is not only entitled to land, destroy or render the goods innocuous without paying compensation but he is also able to hold the shipper liable for all damages and expenses arising from such shipment. The second provision covers the alternative situation where cargo initially shipped with the knowledge and consent of the carrier, subsequently becomes a danger to ship or cargo. In such an event the carrier is entitled to take similar action to avoid the danger as in the first case, without liability to the shipper except possibly by way of general average. On this occasion, however, the shipper will not be liable for the damage and expenses involved.[160]

After some doubt as to the exact nature and scope of this provision, the situation has been greatly clarified by the recent decision of the House of Lords in *The Giannis*

---

[156] See Cooke 6.5 (i.e. 6.51).
[157] *Chandris* v *Isbrandtsen-Moller* [1951] 1 KB 240.
[158] *Brass* v *Maitland* (1856) 26 LJQB 49.
[159] The provision is identical in Art IV rule 6 of the Hague Rules.
[160] Provided that he is not in breach of a term of the contract not to ship dangerous goods: *Chandris* v *Isbrandtsen-Moller* [1951] 1 KB 240.

NK.[161] A cargo of groundnut extraction meal pellets had been shipped in Dakar for carriage to the Dominican Republic under a bill of lading incorporating the Hague Rules. On arrival at the port of discharge the cargo was found to be infested with Khapra beetle, although the infection had not spread to a cargo of wheat in an adjacent hold. The reaction of the health authorities in the Dominican Republic and in neighbouring US ports was such that the shipowner had little alternative but to jettison both cargoes at sea. He then commenced proceedings against the shippers of the groundnut cargo under Art IV rule 6 of the Hague Rules for damages for delay and other costs, together with an indemnity to cover any claims by the owners of the cargo of wheat.

The House of Lords, having accepted the finding of the trial judge that the infestation of Khapra beetle had originated with the shipment of the groundnut cargo, established two important markers with regard to the interpretation of Art IV rule 6:

1 The expression 'goods of a dangerous nature' should be given a broad interpretation and not be restricted *eiusdem generis* to goods of an 'inflammable' or 'explosive' nature. Nor should its application be confined to goods which are liable to cause direct physical damage to the vessel or other cargo. 'What made the cargo dangerous [in this case] was the fact that the shipment and voyage was to countries where the imposition of a quarantine and an order for the dumping of the entire cargo was to be expected. In that sense the Khapra-infested cargo posed a physical danger to the other cargo.'[162]

2 Liability under Art IV rule 6 was strict. In reaching this decision the Court declined to adopt the view taken by US courts that there should be no liability without fault.[163] The US interpretation was based on the alleged overriding effect of Art IV rule 3 of the Hague Rules which provides that:

> 'The shipper shall not be responsible for loss or damage sustained by the carrier or the ship arising or resulting from any cause without the act, fault or neglect of the shipper, his agents or his servants.'

In the view of the US courts, the word 'act' in this context must be read as connoting a positive intentional act on the shipper's part if it is to be reconciled with the alternative requirement of 'fault or neglect'. The majority of members of the House of Lords, however, reached a different conclusion and, while declining to comment on the US interpretation of the word 'act',[164] held that Art IV rule 6 was an independent provision in no way subject to Art IV rule 3. In the words of Lord Lloyd, 'Art IV rule 6 is a freestanding provision dealing with a specific subject-matter. It is neither expressly, nor by implication, subject to Art IV rule 3. It imposes strict liability on shippers in relation to the shipment of dangerous goods irrespective of fault or neglect on their part.'[165]

---

[161] [1998] 1 Lloyd's Rep 337. See Gaskell 15.38 ff.

[162] Lord Steyn at p 346.

[163] See *Serrano* v *US Lines Co* [1965] AMC 1038 (SDNY 1965); *The Stylianos Restis* [1974] AMC 2343 (SDNY 1972).

[164] Only Lord Cooke supported the more pragmatic approach of the Court of Appeal that the word 'act' in Art IV rule 3 would be triggered by the mere act of shipment itself, irrespective of any specific intent.

[165] Lord Cooke objected to the term 'free-standing provision', and preferred to justify his decision that Art IV rule 6 was not subject to Art IV rule 3 on the basis of the maxim *generalia specialibus non derogant*.

2.5.4 STATUTORY REGULATION

The position at common law has been reinforced by a series of statutes designed to control the shipment of certain categories of goods. In the main they seek to establish codes of procedure for the marking, packing and stowage of goods, the provisions of which are enforced by fines and other penalties. One of the earliest examples of such legislation is provided by s 446 of the Merchant Shipping Act 1894 which requires shippers of a specified list of goods to provide the master or shipowner with notice of their characteristics before shipment and also to indicate clearly on the outside of any package or container the nature of such goods. On failure to take such action the shipper is liable to a penalty of £100 for each offence. Should unmarked goods be loaded without the required notice being given to the carrier, s 448 further provides that, on discovery, the master or owner may have such goods thrown overboard without incurring any civil or criminal liability.

More recent legislation has taken the form of regulations issued by the Secretary of State for Trade and Industry under the authority of s 85 of the Merchant Shipping Act 1995 which are designed to implement the provisions of succeeding international conventions for the safety of life at sea. The current set of Merchant Shipping (Dangerous Goods and Marine Pollutants) Regulations 1997[166] give effect to the provisions of the 1974 SOLAS Convention and its 1978 Protocol as amended. After defining 'dangerous goods' as those classified in the IMDG Code and other specified IMO publications, the regulations proceed to formulate a detailed code for their documentation, marking, packaging and stowing. More specialised codes also exist for the carriage of bulk cargoes such as grain, meat and oil.[167]

2.6 THE EFFECT OF FRUSTRATION

In concluding the present chapter devoted to implied terms, it may not be inappropriate to make reference to the effect of frustration on a contract of affreightment. In the words of Lord Radcliffe, 'frustration occurs whenever the law recognises that without default of either party, a contractual obligation has become incapable of being performed because the circumstances in which performance is called for would render it a thing radically different from that which was undertaken by the contract. *Non haec in foedera veni.* It was not this that I promised to do.'[168] In its origins in the mid-nineteenth century the doctrine of frustration was justified on the basis of a term to be implied in order to give effect to the presumed intention of the parties, although in more recent years it has come to be treated more as a question of construction of the terms of the contract. It has pertinently been remarked that the implied term theory has never been acted on by the court as a ground of decision, but is merely cited as a theoretical

---

[166] Effective as from 1 November 1997.
[167] For fuller treatment, see Colinvaux RP, *Carver's Carriage by Sea*, 13th edn, 1982, paras 1114–35.
[168] *Davis Contractors* v *Fareham UDC* [1956] AC 696 at p 728. See Cheshire and Fifoot, Chapter 20; Treitel, Chapter 20.

explanation.[169] The more generally accepted view is that of Lord Wright that 'the court decides the issue and decides it *ex post facto* on the actual circumstances of the case. The data for decision are on the one hand the terms and construction of the contract, read in the light of the then existing circumstances, and on the other hand the events which have occurred. It is the court which has to decide what is the true position between the parties.'[170] In its operation the doctrine is potentially applicable to all forms of contracts of carriage by sea, although in practice the decided cases refer almost exclusively to charterparty disputes.

2.6.1 TYPES OF FRUSTRATION

In the context of shipping contracts, frustration can take a variety of forms ranging from impossibility of performance or supervening illegality to inordinate delay. The decision on frustration in each case appears to be a mixed question of fact and law. While in the ultimate analysis the decision as to whether or not a contract is frustrated is a question of law,[171] this decision has to be taken after an assessment of the relevant facts. Thus 'while the application of the doctrine of frustration is a matter of law, the assessment of a period of delay sufficient to constitute frustration is a question of fact'.[172] The distinction is particularly important in cases where a court is considering an appeal from an arbitration award, since courts will generally not disturb an arbitrator's decision on a point of fact. In the most recent ruling on this issue, Lord Roskill expressed the view that 'For the future I think that in those cases which are otherwise suitable for appeal,[173] the courts should only interfere with the conclusion on issues such as those which arise in cases of frustration expressed by arbitrators in reasoned awards either if they are shown to have gone wrong in law and not to have applied the right legal test or if, while purporting to apply the right legal test, they have reached a conclusion which no reasonable person could, on the facts which they have found, have reached.'[174]

(I) IMPOSSIBILITY OF PERFORMANCE

The most obvious example of this type of frustration occurs when a chartered ship is either actually lost or becomes a constructive total loss.[175] Indeed, in some time charters[176] there is an express clause providing that in such an event hire paid in advance, but not earned, is returnable. In the converse situation, however, destruction of the cargo intended to be shipped by a charterer will rarely result in frustration of the contract of affreightment. The reason is that a charterer is normally regarded as being under an

---

[169] Lord Wright in *Denny, Mott & Dickson v Fraser* [1944] AC 265 at p 276. 'The theory of the implied term has now been discarded by everyone, or nearly everyone, for the simple reason that it does not represent the truth': Lord Denning MR in *The Eugenia* [1964] 2 QB 226 at p 238.

[170] *Denny, Mott & Dickson v Fraser* [1944] AC at p 274.

[171] *Tsakiroglou v Noblee Thorl* [1962] AC 93.

[172] Devlin J in *Universal Cargo Carriers v Citati* [1957] 1 Lloyd's Rep 174.

[173] For requirements for appeal from arbitration award, see *infra* at pp 328–31.

[174] *The Nema* [1981] 2 Lloyd's Rep 239 at p 254.

[175] See *Blane Steamships v Minister of Transport* [1951] 2 Lloyd's Rep 155; *Asphalt International v Enterprise* 667 F 2d 261 (1982).

[176] For example, NYPE 93 clause 20.

absolute obligation to procure a cargo[177] and the only occasion on which he may be excused is where the contract is construed as constituting an agreement to load a specific cargo and the cargo, without any fault on the part of the charterer, has been destroyed before loading has commenced.[178] A similar result may follow where a vessel is chartered to ship a specific commodity, the export of which is subsequently prohibited by government decree.[179]

(II) SUPERVENING ILLEGALITY

A contract will also be frustrated when a subsequent change in the law renders further performance illegal. The implication is that parties contract on the assumption that they will be able legally to perform their obligations, with the result that when this assumption proves to be false, they will be discharged from further performance. It would appear to be immaterial whether such illegality results from a change in English law or from a change in the law of a foreign country in which performance is to take place.[180] Frustration will also occur where the outbreak of war renders further performance of the contract illegal. Such a situation may arise when a vessel is owned or chartered by a person who subsequently becomes an enemy alien, or where performance of the contract involves dealings with parties resident in enemy occupied territory.[181] In such circumstances the supervening illegality has the effect of automatically discharging the contract irrespective of its terms or the presumed intentions of the parties.

(III) DELAY

Where performance of the contract is delayed due to the occurrence of some event or change of circumstances, the contract may be frustrated if the resulting delay is likely to be so prolonged as to defeat the object of the parties in entering the contract of affreightment. Whether or not this test is satisfied will depend upon the facts of the particular case, but in general it is likely that a shorter delay will be sufficient to frustrate a voyage charterparty than would be required to discharge a time charter. In *Jackson v Union Marine Ins*[182] the shipowner contracted to pick up a cargo at Newport with all possible dispatch, 'dangers and accidents of navigation excepted'. When the ship ran aground in Caernarvon Bay en route for Newport, and suffered damage which would take six months to repair, all further liability under the contract was discharged despite the exception clause. In the opinion of the court the parties had not intended this clause to cover such a fundamental alteration in the nature of the contract.[183] It would appear to be immaterial whether the relevant event occurs before performance has commenced or after the contract has been partly executed, providing that its effect is to frustrate the

---

[177] See *infra* pp 68–72.
[178] See *Aaby's Rederi v LEP Transport* (1948) 81 LlLR 465.
[179] See *Société Co-opérative Suisse v La Plata* (1947) 80 LlLR 530. Cf. *The Zuiho Maru* [1977] 2 Lloyd's Rep 552.
[180] *Ralli v Compania Naviera Sota y Aznar* [1920] 2 KB 287; *Société Co-opérative Suisse v La Plata* (1947) 80 LlLR 530.
[181] See *Fibrosa v Fairbairn Lawson* [1943] AC 32.
[182] (1874) LR 10 CP 125.
[183] See Bramwell B at p 141.

intention of the parties in entering the contract.[184] The frustrating event may take a variety of forms as, for example, the length of time required to complete repairs after a collision,[185] detention by a foreign government,[186] or persistent strikes.[187]

From a survey of the decided cases the most frequent cause of delay results from the requisitioning of ships during an emergency or the trapping of vessels on the outbreak of hostilities. In the former case the decision as to whether to claim frustration may well hinge on the compensation being offered by the Government during the period of requisition. Should the amount of compensation exceed the hire rate under a time charter, then it is likely that the owner will allege frustration, whereas the position will be reversed should a lower rate be offered.[188] In *Tamplin SS Co v Anglo-Mexican Petroleum Products Co*[189] a tanker had been chartered for a period of five years to carry oil as the charterers should direct. When the charterparty had still three years to run the tanker was requisitioned by the Admiralty, whereupon the owners claimed that the contract was discharged. The charterers, however, were still willing to pay freight and they argued that the basis of the contract had not disappeared since no definite commercial adventure had been contemplated. This view was upheld on appeal by a majority of the Lords, who were possibly influenced by the fact that the owners were no doubt attempting to avoid the contract in order to obtain a higher degree of compensation from the Admiralty. As was later pointed out by Lord Finlay,[190] the principles of law enunciated by the majority and the dissentients were identical, the only divergence appearing in their respective application of those principles to the facts of the particular case.[191] A contrast is to be found in the case of *Bank Line v Capel*[192] where the plaintiffs had chartered a vessel for 12 months from the time when she should have been delivered to them, but, before that time arrived, the steamer was requisitioned by the Government. On these facts, the Lords held that the charter had been frustrated, even though the steamer had been released after only three months, for otherwise 'the whole character of the adventure would be changed'.[193] Lord Sumner pointed out that the early release of the ship was immaterial since, at the time when the requisitioning took place, it was envisaged that its duration would be indefinite.

Other examples of delay resulting in frustration are to be found in the numerous cases where, through no fault on the part of owner or charterer, vessels have been trapped on

---

[184] *Embiricos v Reid* [1914] 3 KB 45.
[185] *The Hermosa* [1980] 1 Lloyd's Rep 638.
[186] *Scottish Navigation v Souter* [1917] 1 KB 222; *Tatem v Gamboa* [1939] 1 KB 132.
[187] *The Nema* [1981] 2 Lloyd's Rep 239; *The Penelope* [1928] P 180. These cases appear somewhat exceptional in that, as strikes are potentially capable of being settled overnight, courts are reluctant to hold contracts frustrated in such circumstances.
[188] As to whether the charterer is, in any event, entitled to such compensation, see Scrutton p 29.
[189] [1916] 2 AC 397.
[190] In *Bank Line v Capel* [1919] AC 435 at p 443.
[191] For a similar decision see *Port Line v Ben Line* [1958] 1 Lloyd's Rep 290, where a vessel under a 30-month charter was requisitioned with 10 months of the charter still to run. The court refused to hold the charter frustrated in view of the fact that it was estimated that the requisition might last for not more than three to four months.
[192] [1919] AC 435.
[193] Lord Finlay at *ibid* p 442.

an unexpected outbreak of hostilities.[194] A spate of such litigation resulted from the closure of the Shatt al Arab in 1980 on the outbreak of war between Iran and Iraq.[195]

Whether an intervening event involves such delay as to frustrate the commercial object of the venture must obviously be decided on the facts of each individual case. As regards time charters, the decision will invariably be reached on the basis of a comparison between the period of interruption or delay and the overall length of the charterparty. The test is an objective one and must be applied without the benefit of hindsight. In the words of Bailhache J, 'the parties must have the right to claim that the charterparty is determined by frustration as soon as the event upon which the claim is based happens. The question will then be what estimate would a reasonable man of business take of the probable length of withdrawal of the vessel from such service with such materials as are before him, including, of course, the cause of the withdrawal and it will be immaterial whether his anticipation is justified or falsified by the event.'[196] Thus in *Bank Line v Capel*[197] it was immaterial that by the time the issue came for trial, it was clear that the requisition had lasted for a mere three months. The decision as to frustration had to be taken on the basis of information available at the time the requisition commenced. 'Rights ought not to be left in suspense or to hang on the chances of subsequent events. The contract binds or it does not bind, and the law ought to be that the parties can gather their fate then and there. What happens afterwards may assist in showing what the probabilities really were if they had been reasonably forecasted, but when the causes of frustration have operated so long or under such circumstances, as to raise a presumption of inordinate delay, the time has arrived at which the fate of the contract falls to be decided.'[198]

2.6.2 FACTORS TO BE TAKEN INTO CONSIDERATION

The burden of proving frustration will fall on the party alleging it. He must satisfy the court that the intervening event has rendered performance of the contract either impossible or radically different from that envisaged at the time of its formation. In reaching a conclusion on the basis of the evidence submitted, there are a number of factors which the court is required to take into consideration.

(I) FRUSTRATION OF THE COMMERCIAL OBJECT

In order to establish frustration it is necessary to prove that performance has been rendered either impossible or so radically different that it would be unjust to hold the parties bound to the terms of the contract.[199] 'It is not hardship or inconvenience or material loss itself which calls the principle of frustration into play. There must be as well such a change in the significance of the obligation that the thing undertaken would,

---

[194] See *Court Line v Dant* (1939) 44 Com Cas 345.
[195] See *The Evia (No 2)* [1982] 2 Lloyd's Rep 307; *The Wenjiang* [1982] 1 Lloyd's Rep 128.
[196] *Anglo-Northern Trading Co v Emlyn Jones* [1917] 2 KB 78 at p 84.
[197] [1919] AC 435.
[198] Lord Sumner at *ibid* p 454.
[199] *Per* Lord Denning MR in *The Eugenia* [1963] 2 Lloyd's Rep 381 at p 390.

if performed, be a different thing from that contracted for.'[200] Thus in *Tsakiroglou* v *Noblee Thorl*[201] sellers had agreed to sell a quantity of Sudanese groundnuts c.i.f. Hamburg. Shortly after the conclusion of the contract, the outbreak of hostilities in Egypt resulted in the closure of the Suez Canal to navigation. The only option open to the seller was to ship the groundnuts via the Cape of Good Hope at substantially enhanced freight rates and he accordingly pleaded frustration. The Lords rejected this contention on the ground that shipment via the Cape, while being more expensive 'was not commercially or fundamentally different' from shipment by the intended route. Similar decisions were reached in cases where vessels had been voyage chartered,[202] and time chartered for a trip.[203] In such circumstances it would appear that frustration is only likely to arise either where a specific route has been indicated which has subsequently been rendered impossible,[204] or where the vessel is carrying perishable cargo which is unlikely to survive the alternative route.

(II) EXPRESS PROVISION IN THE CONTRACT

In its origins the doctrine of frustration envisaged the occurrence of some unexpected event which radically transformed the contractual obligations. By implication if the particular event was foreseeable and no provision for it had been included in the contract, then it was presumed that the parties had intended to create an absolute obligation. Later cases have suggested that such an assumption is fallacious and that the doctrine will only be excluded where provision is made to cover the event in the express terms of the contract.[205] So in *Tatem* v *Gamboa*,[206] where a vessel which had been chartered to evacuate refugees from Spain during the Civil War was seized by the Nationalists, the contract was held frustrated even though such an outcome must have been foreseeable from the outset.[207]

Even where express provision is made in the contract to cover a particular event, such a term is normally subjected to strict interpretation by the courts. The attitude adopted is not dissimilar to the *contra proferentem* approach applied when construing clauses seeking to exclude liability for fundamental breach.[208] Thus in *Jackson* v *Union Marine Ins*[209] the contract was held frustrated when the vessel ran aground even though the charter included a provision excepting 'dangers and accidents of navigation'. In the opinion of the court the parties had not intended this clause to cover such a fundamental alteration in the nature of the contract. Again, in *Bank Line* v *Capel*[210] the

---

[200] Lord Radcliffe in *Davis Contractors* v *Fareham UDC* [1956] AC 696 at p 729. Frustration will accordingly not result from unexpected fluctuations in market rates of hire or the cost of bunkers: *Occidental* v *Skibs A/S Avanti* [1976] 1 Lloyd's Rep 293 at p 325.

[201] [1962] AC 93.

[202] *The Captain George K* [1970] 2 Lloyd's Rep 21.

[203] *The Eugenia* [1963] 2 Lloyd's Rep 381.

[204] Cf. *The Massalia* [1960] 1 Lloyd's Rep 594 overruled in *The Eugenia*.

[205] See *Bangladesh Export Import Co* v *Sucden Kerry* [1995] 2 Lloyd's Rep 1; *The Safeer* [1994] 1 Lloyd's Rep 637.

[206] (1938) 61 LlLR 149.

[207] See also *The Eugenia* [1963] 2 Lloyd's Rep 381.

[208] See *Suisse Atlantique* v *Rotterdamsche* [1967] 1 AC 361.

[209] (1874) LR 10 CP 125.

[210] [1919] AC 435.

House of Lords was prepared to hold that an express provision in the charter granting the charterer, but not the owner, the option of cancelling should the ship 'be commandeered by Government during this charter' did not prevent the shipowner from successfully pleading frustration when the vessel was subsequently requisitioned in wartime. In the view of Lord Haldane, 'what is clear is that, where people enter into a contract which is dependent for the possibility of its performance on the continued availability of the subject matter, and that availability comes to an unforeseen end by reason of circumstances over which its owner had no control, the owner is not bound unless it is quite plain that he has contracted to be so'.[211] In his Lordship's opinion no such contractual intention existed in this case.

(III) SELF-INDUCED FRUSTRATION

Where the event which is alleged to have interfered with performance arises from the act or election of one party, such a person cannot rely on his own default to excuse him from liability under the contract. So in *Maritime National Fish* v *Ocean Trawlers*,[212] the defendants had chartered a fishing trawler with knowledge that it could only be operated with an otter trawl, and that the use of such trawls was prohibited without a licence from the Newfoundland government. The defendants, who operated four other vessels equipped with otter trawls, eventually applied for five licences. When only three licences were granted, the defendants allocated them to their other vessels and claimed that this particular charter was frustrated since it was illegal to operate a trawler without a licence. The Privy Council rejected this argument on the ground that any frustration was self-induced having resulted from a deliberate election on the part of the defendant.

The burden of proving that frustration is self-induced lies on the party who makes the allegation,[213] and there appears to be some uncertainty as to the precise extent of the concept. On the one hand, it seems clear that a party cannot invoke frustration where the situation has been created by a breach of contract on his part. Thus where further performance of a charterparty has been rendered impossible as the result of breach of the safe port warranty,[214] or the seaworthiness obligation,[215] the defence is not available to the defaulter. The same may be true where the supervening event results from negligent conduct, as, for example, where the vessel is seriously damaged as the result of a negligent act on the part of the owner or a member of the crew.[216] It has been pointed out, however, that self-induced frustration involves deliberate choice and that in the majority of cases mere negligence may not suffice. Lord Russell noted that such cases 'can range from the criminality of the scuttler who opens the sea-cocks and sinks his ship, to the thoughtlessness of a prima donna who sits in a draught and loses her voice.

---

[211] *Ibid* at p 445. See also Viscount Simon in *Fibrosa* v *Fairbairn Lawson* [1943] AC 32 at p 40.

[212] [1935] AC 524. See also *The Super Servant Two* [1990] 1 Lloyd's Rep 1.

[213] *Constantine* v *Imperial Smelting Corp* [1942] AC 154.

[214] *The Lucille* [1983] 1 Lloyd's Rep 387.

[215] *Monarch SS Co* v *Karlshamns* [1949] AC 196; see also *The Eugenia* [1963] 2 Lloyd's Rep 381.

[216] See *Constantine* v *Imperial Smelting Corp* [1942] AC 154. But presumably not where the alleged breach of contract or negligent act is covered by an exception, e.g. negligence in the navigation or management of the ship under Art IV rule 2(a) of the Hague/Visby Rules.

I wish to guard against the supposition that every destruction of corpus for which a contractor can be said, to some extent or in some sense, to be responsible, necessarily involves that the resultant frustration is self-induced within the meaning of the phrase.'[217]

2.6.3 EFFECT OF FRUSTRATION

The effect of frustration at common law is automatically to discharge the parties from all further liability under the contract. 'Frustration brings the contract to an end forthwith, without more and automatically.'[218] The parties are given no option to treat the contract as at an end for it is discharged by operation of law, irrespective of their volition. A contract has, however, come into existence which is perfectly valid until the occurrence of the frustrating event. All rights and obligations which have accrued before that time are unaffected. On the other hand, the contract ceases to bind from the moment frustration intervenes, and rights which accrue after that time are unenforceable.[219] So freight paid in advance under a contract for the carriage of goods by sea or a voyage charterparty is irrecoverable even though the entire object of the contract is subsequently frustrated and the goods are not delivered at their destination. Conversely, freight payable on the completion of the voyage is not recoverable unless the contract is performed by the delivery of the cargo to the consignee at the agreed discharge point. It is believed that a similar rule operated in relation to the payment of hire under a time charter, prior to the Frustrated Contracts Act 1943.[220] Some amelioration of the strict common law rule resulted from the decision of the House of Lords in *Fibrosa* v *Fairbairn Lawson*[221] where it was held that an advance payment was recoverable in circumstances where the entire consideration provided in return for it had failed. The general view is that this decision in no way affected the well-established mercantile usage that freight payable in advance is irrecoverable,[222] although in such circumstances it would rarely be the case that there had been a total failure of consideration.

The legislature finally intervened in an attempt to remove the remaining anomalies. The Frustrated Contracts Act of 1943 provides no definition of a frustrating event but merely seeks to secure a reasonable apportionment of the loss resulting from frustration. Its provisions are applicable only to contracts governed by English law and, in the maritime sphere, only to time charters and charterparties by demise. Contracts for the carriage of goods by sea and voyage charterparties are still governed by the old common

---

[217] *Constantine* v *Imperial Smelting Corp* [1942] AC at p 179. 'Mere negligence seems never to have been suggested as sufficient to constitute "fault" in this connection', *per* Lord Wright at p 195. Cf. Bingham LJ in *The Super Servant Two* [1990] 1 Lloyd's Rep 1 at p 10.

[218] Lord Sumner in *Hirji Mulji* v *Cheong Yue SS Co* [1926] AC 497 at p 505.

[219] Some doubt exists as to whether an arbitration clause in a charterparty will survive its frustration. See *Heyman* v *Darwins* [1942] AC 356 at pp 366, 383; *Kruse* v *Questier* [1953] 1 QB 669. Cf. *Hirji Mulji* v *Cheong Yue SS Co* [1926] AC 497.

[220] See *French Marine* v *Compagnie Napolitaine* [1921] 2 AC 494; *Civil Service Co-operative Soc* v *General SN Co* [1903] 2 KB 756.

[221] [1943] AC 32.

[222] See [1943] AC 32, *per* Lord Wright at p 67, Lord Porter at p 79.

law rules although the risks involved are invariably covered by insurance. The distinction between time and voyage charters accordingly becomes increasingly important.

Two fundamental changes were introduced by the Act. Section 1(2) provides that all sums paid or payable before the frustrating event shall, if paid, be recoverable and, if not paid, shall cease to be payable. This provision confirms the *Fibrosa* decision, but extends its operation by allowing a party to recover sums paid even though there has been only a partial failure of consideration. The section is, however, subject to a proviso giving the court a discretionary power to grant compensation, out of the money so paid or payable, for expenses incurred before the frustrating event. Thus, where a time charter has been frustrated after the payment in advance of a monthly instalment of hire, such sum is recoverable by the charterer subject to the court's discretionary power to deduct an appropriate amount to cover the owner's running costs prior to frustration. In no circumstances may the amount recoverable by the owner exceed the actual expenses incurred, nor may it exceed the amount paid or payable under the contract before the frustrating event.

Section 1(3) further provides that where, prior to frustration, a valuable benefit has been conferred on one party by partial performance of the contract, the party conferring the benefit may recover as compensation such sum as the court considers just in the circumstances. The amount recoverable must not exceed the value of the benefit conferred, taking into account any expenses which the benefited party may himself have incurred in performing his side of the contract and any circumstances connected with the frustration which may have affected the value of the benefit.[223] In the case of frustration of a time charter this provision may enable the court, in an appropriate case, to order the payment of a sum equivalent to the full amount of the hire for the actual days on which the charterer had use of the vessel prior to the frustrating event. Such remedy would, of course, be an alternative to the recovery by the owner of running costs under s 1(2).

---

[223] For an illustration of the operation of this section, see *BP Exploration Co v Hunt* [1982] 1 All ER 925.

Part Two

CHARTERPARTIES

3

THE VOYAGE CHARTERPARTY

3.1 AN OVERVIEW OF THE CHARTER

There is a variety of standard voyage charter forms tailored for different trading routes and the carriage of different cargoes. In a free contracting situation the parties are also able to construct their own contracts or at least modify the terms of existing forms. Nevertheless, there is a certain uniformity in the basic framework of a voyage charter, the main elements of which it might be useful to identify at this stage.

3.1.1 INTRODUCTORY CLAUSES

All standard voyage forms will include an introductory clause identifying the contracting parties, the vessel, and the agreed voyage. The only aspect of the vessel's description which is of any serious concern to the charterer is its cargo capacity, since otherwise any deficiency in the vessel's performance is at the risk of the shipowner. Cargo capacity will normally be expressed in terms of deadweight tonnage which, when translated, means the weight of cargo the vessel is capable of carrying when loaded down at its maximum permitted draught. Such statements refer to the maximum weight of cargo that a vessel can carry and do not amount to a guarantee that it will be able to carry that amount of any cargo, since much will depend on the stowage factor of the particular cargo selected.[1] Thus, while the ship may be able to cope with the stated weight of a compact cargo, such as coal, it may not have the necessary stowage capacity to carry an equivalent weight of a bulky cargo, such as cotton or wool. In the latter case it will normally be of more assistance to the charterer if the cubic capacity of the cargo space is specified. Generally the stated deadweight tonnage in a voyage charter is not intended to include fuel, stores etc required for the voyage, but many of the standard forms, such as Gencon, are silent on the point.

So far as details of the voyage are concerned, the charter may identify the ports of loading and discharge, or the charterer may be given the right to nominate such ports, either from a specified list or from a designated geographical area. In the latter case an additional clause usually requires the charterer to nominate a safe port.

3.1.2 CARGO CLAUSES

When the vessel is chartered by a seller for the delivery of an export order, then the description of the type and quantity of cargo is likely to be specific, e.g. 10,000 metric

---

[1] See *Millar v Freden* [1918] 1 KB 611.

tonnes of Welsh anthracite. On the other hand, where the object of the charter is a more general trading venture, then the charterer may be permitted to select one or more from a specified range of cargoes, e.g. 'wheat and/or maize and/or rye', or may even be entitled to ship 'any lawful cargo'. In these latter cases he will probably be required to ship 'a full and complete cargo', that is the maximum amount of that particular cargo that the vessel can carry. Should a fixed amount of cargo be specified, such as 10,000 metric tons, it is usual to qualify the figure with a permitted allowance of plus or minus 5 per cent.

Should the charterer fail to supply the required quantity of cargo, he will be liable to pay compensation for the shortfall in the form of dead freight.

3.1.3 FREIGHT CLAUSES

The charterparty normally records the agreed rate of freight, the unit of measurement of cargo to which it applies, and the time and place of payment. The calculation of freight is usually a straightforward operation, although it is important to indicate in the charter whether the assessment has to be made on the quantity of cargo shipped or on the quantity discharged. The reason is that where cargo is weighed both on loading and on discharge, discrepancies between the recorded figures frequently arise which are caused either by defects in the weighing machinery or by natural factors. Thus certain cargoes are liable to spillage or evaporation which will reduce their weight on discharge, while other cargoes may increase in weight during the voyage as a result of absorbing moisture.

Many of these problems will be avoided if the freight is quoted as a lump sum for the voyage, regardless of the quantity of cargo shipped. This procedure will normally be adopted in cases where adequate facilities are not available at the relevant ports for weighing the cargo, or where the parties are uncertain as to the amount of cargo that will be available. There would seem to be little advantage in not invoking the lump sum procedure when cargo is shipped in bulk and the charterer is responsible for providing a 'full and complete cargo', since in such an event any shortfall has to be paid for in the form of dead freight.

Provision is also made in the standard form for indicating whether the freight is payable in advance on signing bills of lading, or only on delivery of the goods at their destination. In the latter event it is usual to protect the interests of the shipowner by including a clause granting him a lien on the cargo until the freight is paid. It is also, of course, possible to require part of the freight to be paid in advance and the balance on delivery of the cargo. Additional clauses will normally make provision for the currency in which the freight is to be paid. In a period of fluctuating exchange rates this is a matter of particular importance to the shipowner, especially where the expenses of the voyage are likely to be incurred in a different currency.

One final matter requiring clarification is whether the quoted freight rate includes the cost of loading and discharging the cargo, or whether these costs are an additional expense to be borne by the charterer. Where bulk cargoes are loaded at private wharves, or where it is otherwise difficult to estimate port handling charges in advance, freight is more conveniently quoted on 'net' terms and the handling costs are left to be paid directly by the charterer or consignee. Even where 'gross' terms are quoted, and the port handling charges are for the shipowner's account he will often protect himself with a clause stipulating that he is only liable for such charges providing that they do not exceed a specified rate per tonne of cargo. Should they do so, then the charterer will be liable to pay the excess.

3.1.4 LAYTIME PROVISIONS

One of the most important clauses in a voyage charterparty is that which specifies the amount of time allowed for loading and unloading the cargo. These agreed 'lay days' are available free of charge to the charterer, who is regarded as having paid for them in the freight. If these lay days are exceeded, however, then the charterer has to pay compensation to the shipowner either in the form of agreed damages (known as demurrage) or unliquidated damages (known as damages for detention). In the negotiations leading up to signing the charter, therefore, the charterer will be anxious to secure an adequate number of lay days to cover unexpected contingencies which might arise during the loading or discharging operations, while the shipowner will seek to restrict the number in order to have his vessel free as soon as possible for employment elsewhere. In view of the financial implications involved, it is essential that laytime provisions are precisely defined, otherwise litigation will invariably result.

The most intractable problem in this regard is to define the point of time at which laytime will commence to run. The normal formula which is applied requires two conditions to be satisfied. First, the vessel must become an 'arrived ship'[2] by reaching the destination point specified in the charter – which might be a berth, a dock, or a port – after which the shipowner must give the charterer notice of readiness to load. Congestion in the port might prevent the vessel from reaching its agreed destination and becoming an 'arrived ship' in which case the risk of the resulting delay will fall on the shipowner unless he has had foresight and bargaining strength to have a clause inserted in the charterparty providing that time waiting for a berth is to count as laytime. Once the vessel becomes an arrived ship, then laytime will begin to run within a specified period of the shipowner giving notice of readiness to load as, for example, 'at 1 p.m. if notice of readiness to load is given before noon and at 6 a.m. next working day if notice is given during office hours after noon'.[3]

As laytime will run against the charterer from that time, it is essential that the charter provides him with a reasonably accurate indication of the time at which the vessel is likely to reach the loading port, in order that he can ensure that the cargo is available. Only rarely, however, will the shipowner be prepared to agree to a specific date as, for example, when his vessel is already lying idle at the loading port. In the majority of cases charters are negotiated well in advance and shipowners are reluctant to be too specific about arrival dates in view of unforeseen contingencies which might arise during the intervening period. The normal procedure which is adopted is for the charter to name a date at which the vessel is expected to be ready to load at the loading port and to couple with it a cancelling date after which the charterer has the option of terminating

---

[2] For full consideration of the concept of an arrived ship, see *infra* pp 53 ff.
[3] Gencon form, clause 6(c).

the charter if the vessel has still not arrived. It is naturally in the shipowner's interest to have as long a period as possible between these two dates, whereas the charterer will seek to secure the shortest interval in order to minimise storage costs at the port.

The second aspect of laytime relates to its duration. The parties normally stipulate a specific number of days or hours to be allowed for the loading or discharge operation and this is a far preferable practice to the use of vaguer phrases such as 'fast as can' or 'according to custom of port', which invariably lead to disputes. An alternative method is to specify a loading rate such as 2,000 tons per day, from which the period of laytime can be calculated once the overall weight of cargo is known. Further refinements are to indicate whether the specified laytime is to run without interruption or whether it is to be suspended on Sundays and public holidays or in the event of bad weather. All these are matters for negotiation between the parties.

Additional clauses deal with the situation which arises when the loading or discharging operation is not completed within the specified period of laytime. Extra time has to be paid for by the charterer and, as this is a common occurrence, provision is normally made in the charter for the payment of demurrage at a fixed rate for such extra time. Demurrage is regarded as agreed damages for breach of contract and is recoverable without proof of loss by the shipowner. The demurrage rate is usually fixed in relation to current freight rates and the courts will not interfere with its recovery unless the amount recoverable is 'extravagant and unconscionable' with regard to the greatest loss that could have resulted from the delay.[4] In that event the clause will be struck down as a penalty, although a similar result does not follow where the demurrage rate is fixed at a low rate which bears no relationship to the potential loss.[5] Where there is no demurrage clause, or the provision for demurrage is for a fixed period (e.g. 10 days) which has expired, the shipowner is entitled to recover unliquidated damages for detention as compensation for the loss resulting from the delay.

As an inducement to the charterer to complete the loading operation as quickly as possible, the charter may provide for the payment of despatch money by the owners for any laytime saved. Normally the rate for despatch money is fixed at 50 per cent of the agreed demurrage rate, and it is important for the parties to specify whether it is payable for all time saved or only for working time saved.

3.1.5 OTHER CLAUSES

The clauses outlined above form the characteristic framework of the voyage charterparty but to them will be added a selection of other provisions covering such matters as the shipowner's responsibility for the care of cargo, the conditions under which the vessel may be entitled to deviate from the agreed route, and a group of clauses dealing with the effect on performance of the contractual obligations of such factors as ice, war or strikes. These clauses tend to vary as between the various standard forms of voyage charter and are frequently modified by the parties themselves. It will therefore be more convenient to defer their consideration until after the basic obligations of shipowner and charterer have been examined.

---

[4] See Lord Dunedin in *Dunlop* v *New Garage* [1915] AC 79 at p 86.
[5] See *Suisse Atlantique* v *NV Rotterdamsche Kolen Centrale* [1967] AC 361.

3.1.6 PERFORMANCE OF THE CHARTERPARTY

The performance of a voyage charterparty falls into four separate and distinct stages:

1 The preliminary voyage to the place specified as the loading point;
2 The loading operation, covering both loading and stowage;
3 The carrying voyage to the place specified for delivery of the cargo; and
4 The discharging operation.[6]

In normal circumstances the performance of stages 1 and 3 will be the sole responsibility of the shipowner, while stages 2 and 4 will be joint operations, though primarily under the control of the charterer. While the charterparty will specify in some detail the respective obligations of the parties in relation to each particular stage, one matter of overriding concern to them both is the question as to which of them will have to bear the risk of loss resulting from delay in performance of the charter which is beyond the control of either party. Voyage charters are particularly exposed to the risk of delay caused by such factors as bad weather or engine trouble on the voyage, or by adverse tides, strikes or the unavailability of berths on arrival at the designated port. As a general rule, in the absence of specific terms in the charter, the risk of any such accidental delay has to be borne by the party responsible for performing the particular stage during which the delay occurs. It is, of course, possible for the parties to include a clause in the charter transferring this risk, such as, for example, incorporating an exception suspending the running of laytime in the event of a strike. Nevertheless, it remains important to be able to establish with precision the time at which one stage ends and the next stage begins. Little practical difficulty has been experienced in establishing a workable test for identifying the conclusion of the loading and discharging stages,[7] but the courts have found it no easy task to devise a simple formula for identifying the point in time when the respective voyage stages are completed and laytime begins to run. There is general agreement that three requirements need to be satisfied before laytime can commence: the chartered vessel must have become an 'arrived ship' at the agreed destination, notice of readiness to load must have been given, and the vessel must in fact be ready to load.[8] The problem has been to devise an acceptable definition of an 'arrived ship'.

Before proceeding to consider in detail the respective obligations of the parties in relation to each of the four stages, it might therefore be useful to examine more closely the concept of the 'arrived ship'.

3.2 THE ARRIVED SHIP[9]

In seeking to establish when a vessel becomes an 'arrived ship' it is important to recognise that voyage charters are of three types, depending on whether the loading point is specified as a berth, a dock, or a port. The position with regard to berth and dock charters is relatively straightforward, it having been established that the vessel only

---

[6] See Lord Diplock in *The Johanna Oldendorff* [1973] 2 Lloyd's Rep 285 at p 304.
[7] See *infra* at pp 75–6.
[8] NB No notice of readiness to unload is required on arrival at the port of discharge. N.B. In certain circumstances provision of letter of credit may also be condition precedent to obligation of seller to load cargo. See *Kronos Worldwide Ltd* v *Semora Oil Trading* [2004] 1 Lloyd's Rep 260.
[9] On the whole subject see Davies, D, *Commencement of Laytime*, 3rd edn, 1997, Chapter 1.

becomes an arrived ship when it enters the specified berth[10] or dock[11] respectively. In both cases the risk of delay in reaching the specified berth or dock must be borne by the shipowner. The same rule also applies in cases where the charterer, having an express right to nominate the berth or dock, nominates a busy one, with the result that delay is inevitably incurred. The courts have taken the view that there would be little value to the charterer in having such an option if he was obliged to consult the convenience of the shipowner before exercising it.[12]

More difficulties arise, however, in formulating the test for an 'arrived ship' in the case of a port charterparty. This is partly due to the larger area involved and partly to the variety of definitions of a port, dependent on whether it is regarded from a geographical, administrative or commercial standpoint. After a series of earlier conflicting decisions,[13] the position was clarified by the House of Lords in the case of the *Johanna Oldendorff*.[14] Here the charterer, under a port charter, had nominated the port of Liverpool/Birkenhead. At the time the vessel reached the port no berths were available and it was ordered to anchor at the Mersey Bar, a point some 17 miles from the dock area but within the administrative limits of the port. The point at issue was whether the *Johanna Oldendorff* was an arrived ship at the Mersey Bar, or whether laytime only began to run 16 days later when she was eventually admitted to a berth. In reviewing the cases, the House of Lords criticised a test based on arrival within the 'commercial area' of a port advanced in the earlier case of *The Aello*[15] on the grounds that such an area was difficult to define and caused unnecessary uncertainty in the law, with no regard for practical commercial implications. Their Lordships were in favour of a more practical test based on the following propositions:

1   The vessel must be within the geographical and legal area of the port in the sense commonly understood by its users. Consequently, a vessel could never be considered to have 'arrived' if the port authorities ordered it to stay outside this area.

2   The decisive test is whether the vessel at this point is immediately and effectively at the disposal of the charterer in the sense that it can reach the berth quickly when informed that one is vacant. In view of improved radio communication and the increased speed of modern ships, a vessel could satisfy this test even if anchored at some distance from the specified berth, since it would usually be given advance warning of the time at which the berth was likely to become available.

3   The vessel is presumed to be effectively at the disposal of the charterer when anchored at a place where ships usually lie while waiting for a berth at that port, proof of the contrary resting with the charterer. Even if the vessel is anchored elsewhere, the shipowner is allowed to prove that it is equally at the effective disposal of the charterer, though in this case the burden of proof rests with him.

---

[10] *Stag Line Ltd* v *Board of Trade* [1950] 2 KB 194. See also *The Isabelle* [1984] 1 Lloyd's Rep 366; *The Mass Glory* [2002] 2 Lloyd's Rep 244.

[11] *Thorman* v *Dowgate SS Co* [1910] 1 KB 410. For the US position, see *The Ionia (No 2)* 135 Fed Rep 317.

[12] *Reardon Smith Line* v *Ministry of Agriculture* [1963] AC 691.

[13] *Leonis* v *Rank* [1908] 1 KB 499; *The Aello* [1960] 1 Lloyd's Rep 623.

[14] [1973] 2 Lloyd's Rep 285.

[15] [1961] AC 135: Parker LJ in the Court of Appeal expressed the view that the commercial area was that part of a port 'where a ship can be loaded when a berth is available, albeit she cannot be loaded until a berth is available'. [1958] 2 QB 385 at p 401.

As the Mersey Bar was within the administrative limits of the port of Liverpool/ Birkenhead and as it was the normal anchorage for vessels waiting for a berth at that port, the *Johanna Oldendorff* was held to be an arrived ship.

Within four years their Lordships were provided with an opportunity for second thoughts. In the *Maratha Envoy*[16] the charterer had nominated Brake, a river port on the Weser, as the port of loading but, as no berths were available there, the vessel had been instructed not to proceed upstream but to wait at the Weser Light. This lightship was stationed in the Weser estuary at a point some 25 miles downstream from Brake, and was the normal waiting place at that port for vessels the size of the *Maratha Envoy*, since there were no suitable anchorages on the river within the port itself at which vessels could lie while waiting for a vacant berth. In reviewing the criteria for an 'arrived ship' enumerated in the *Johanna Oldendorff*, the Court of Appeal took the view that the decisive factor was whether or not the vessel was 'immediately and effectively at the disposal of the charterer'. There was no reason why a vessel should not be regarded as an 'arrived ship' merely because she was outside the strict port limits, provided that she had reached the normal waiting place for that port and was effectively at the disposition of the charterer.[17] On appeal, the House of Lords had no hesitation in rejecting this heresy and restoring the position established in the *Johanna Oldendorff*. The *Maratha Envoy* was not an arrived ship while anchored at the Weser Light, since she was not within the limits of the port of Brake.

While this decision has undoubtedly clarified the position, it has not met with universal approval in the shipping world.[18] Nor is it in line with the more flexible approach adopted in other jurisdictions. What is required of any test for an arrived ship, in practical terms, is that it should clearly define the precise point at which the risk of time lost is transferred from shipowner to charterer. The possible weakness of the *Johanna Oldendorff* approach is that it fails to provide any really effective formula for identifying the port area in a specific case, despite the fact that the entire test hinges on this requirement. Despite Lord Diplock's assertion that little difficulty has been experienced in applying the *Oldendorff* test,[19] it is arguable that, for the purposes of such a test it would be found easier to identify the usual waiting place at a particular port rather than the precise limits of the port itself. Moreover, it might be argued that, for this particular purpose, a shipowner should be regarded as having fulfilled his obligation under a port charter when he has brought his vessel as close as possible to its destination at a congested port, the vessel being anchored at a point from which any further movement into a vacant berth is under the control of the port authorities. In such circumstances can it really be the intention of the parties that the incidence of risk of further delay

---

[16] *Federal Commerce & Navigation Co v Tradax Export* [1977] 2 All ER 849. Cf. *Puerto Madrin v Esso Standard Oil Co* [1962] AMC 147, where vessel was halted outside port but not at a normal waiting place.

[17] In reaching this conclusion the Court of Appeal followed an American arbitration award in *Maritime Bulk Carriers v Carnac Grain Co* [1975] AMC 1826.

[18] See Berlingieri: The allocation of risk in voyage charter parties [1977] 8 JMLC 497. Also Davies D, *Commencement of Laytime*, 3rd edn, 1997, Chapter 1.

[19] 'I am not aware that in practice the Reid test has proved difficult of application because of any doubt whether the usual place where ships wait their turn for a berth at a particular port lies within the limits of that port or not.' *Maratha Envoy* [1977] 2 All ER 849 at p 853. In the view of the US courts 'the port is ordinarily the place where the port authorities are exercising jurisdiction'. See *Yoni Suzuki v Central Argentine Rly Co* [1928] AMC 1521 at p 1534.

should be solely dependent on whether the port authorities have directed it to wait at a point inside or outside the port limits? No doubt we have not heard the last word on this subject.

3.2.1 CHARTERPARTY PROVISIONS SHIFTING RISK OF DELAY

So far we have been considering the position at common law where there are no provisions in the charterparty covering delay resulting from congestion in the port. In many cases, however, the shipowner is not prepared to bear the risk of such loss and takes appropriate action. On the one hand, he will, if possible, opt for the port charter rather than the berth or dock charter, since in the former it is easier to become an 'arrived ship' even if there is congestion in the port. Alternatively, he will demand the inclusion in the charterparty of a specific clause shifting the risk of such loss. There are three main types of clause designed to achieve this object:

(I) CLAUSES DESIGNED FOR SPECIFIC PORTS

In the case of ports which are frequently congested, or where the normal waiting place is outside the port limits, standard clauses are usually available which provide that laytime is to run from the time when a vessel reaches a specific point but is unable to proceed further because of a shortage of berths or other obstruction.[20] Such a clause will be effective even though the vessel does not become an arrived ship at that point. Thus in *Compañia Naviera Termar* v *Tradax Export*,[21] where a vessel was chartered to carry a cargo of corn from the United States to Hull, the charter provided that, if the vessel was unable to berth at Hull because of congestion, 'time to count from next working period after vessel's arrival at Spurn Head anchorage'. The fact that a similar 'Weser light' clause was available in respect of the port of Brake, but had not been incorporated into the charter, was one of the reasons why the House of Lords in *The Maratha Envoy* felt justified in adopting a strict construction of the arrived ship concept in that case.

(II) CLAUSES REQUIRING CHARTERER TO NOMINATE A 'REACHABLE BERTH'

Many charterparties include a clause requiring the charterer to nominate 'a reachable berth' on the vessel's arrival at her destination. As a matter of construction it was held in *The Angelos Lusis*[22] that such a clause transferred the risk of delay to the charterer if he could not nominate a vacant berth because of congestion in the port. Recent decisions at first instance have suggested, however, that the application of the clause is not restricted to cases of physical obstruction but will also cover situations where a berth is available but is not 'reachable' because of bad weather or fog.[23] In either case the vessel

---

[20] The time taken by the vessel when it eventually moves from the specified point into a vacant berth (the so-called 'shifting time') does not count as laytime.

[21] [1966] 1 Lloyd's Rep 566.

[22] [1964] 2 Lloyd's Rep 28.

[23] *The Fjordaas* [1988] 1 Lloyd's Rep 336; *The Sea Queen* [1988] 1 Lloyd's Rep 500. Doubt has been thrown on the views expressed in these cases by the decision of the House of Lords in *The Kyzikos* [1989] 1 Lloyd's Rep 1, see *infra* at p 58. Cf. the view of Webster J, at first instance, in *The Kyzikos* [1987] 1 Lloyd's Rep 48 at p 58, when he held that a vacant berth was still 'accessible', as opposed to 'reachable', even though a vessel was prevented by fog from entering it.

does not need to be an 'arrived ship' in the technical sense – all that is required is that it should have reached a point either inside or outside the port, where it would be held up in the absence of the nomination of a berth. From that point the charterer will have to bear the risk of any delay in that he will be liable for damages for breach of contract in failing to nominate a reachable berth.[24]

If, however, the vessel should also be an arrived ship at that point, with the result that laytime commenced to run, then the charterer cannot be required to pay twice for the same time. So in *The Delian Spirit*[25] it was held that once laytime began to run the charterer could trade off time saved in loading against the initial time lost while he was prevented from nominating 'a reachable berth'. On the other hand, if the vessel is not an arrived ship at that point, then the two periods of time run independently. Consequently, time saved on discharge cannot be credited against time lost while waiting for a reachable berth to be nominated.[26]

(III) 'TIME LOST WAITING FOR A BERTH' CLAUSE

Perhaps the most common of these clauses designed to shift the risk of delay is the Gencon clause which provides that 'Time lost in waiting for berth to count as loading (or discharging) time'.[27] The object of this clause is to shift the risk *before* the vessel becomes an arrived ship, i.e. from the time when it could have entered a berth had one been available. Thus in the case of a berth charter, it will cover the period while the vessel is waiting in port until a berth is available. Alternatively, in the case of the port charter, it will apply while the vessel is waiting outside the port and even while it is waiting inside the port in circumstances where, according to *The Johanna Oldendorff* criteria, it is not 'immediately and effectively' at the disposal of the charterer. The crucial question in each case is whether the basic reason for the delay is the unavailability of a berth.

The clause in its origins was essentially a berth charter clause which, because of its popularity and effectiveness, was later included in port charters. In fact this extension of use led to confusion since, in the case of port charters, there was the possibility of an overlap between waiting time and the laytime provisions, in that a vessel could be an arrived ship and still be waiting for a berth. For many years the courts held that the 'time lost' clauses should be given precedence and treated independently of the laytime provisions with the result that the charterer had to pay for all time lost irrespective of whether it occurred on a Sunday or public holiday, or whether a laytime exception might otherwise have been applicable.[28] The fallacy of this interpretation was finally recognised by the House of Lords in *The Darrah*[29] when the previous decisions on this point were overruled. Whether the clause provides that all time lost waiting for a berth is to count as 'loading time' or 'laytime' the result is the same. All such time lost is to be

---

[24] See also *The Laura Prima* [1982] 1 Lloyd's Rep 1.
[25] [1971] 1 Lloyd's Rep 506.
[26] *The President Brand* [1967] 2 Lloyd's Rep 338.
[27] Events causing delay which are covered by an appropriately worded exception will not trigger the operation of the clause. See *The Radauti* [1988] 2 Lloyd's Rep 416; *The Amstelmolen* [1961] 2 Lloyd's Rep 1.
[28] See *The Loucas N* [1971] 1 Lloyd's Rep 215.
[29] [1977] AC 157.

treated as laytime in the same way as if the vessel had become an arrived ship. There is no rule of law that 'time lost' clauses and laytime clauses constitute two independent and unrelated codes for computing the amount of permitted laytime that has been used up. In the words of Lord Diplock, 'the vessel is to be treated as if during that period she were in fact in berth and at the disposition of the charterer for carrying out the loading or discharging operation . . . and . . . in the computation of time lost in waiting for a berth there are to be excluded all periods which would have been left out in the computation of permitted laytime used up if the vessel had actually been in berth'.[30] In circumstances where waiting time and laytime overlap (i.e. the vessel while waiting for a berth is also an arrived ship), laytime provisions take precedence and the 'time lost' clause is regarded as surplusage.

(IV) 'TIME TO COUNT WHETHER IN BERTH OR NOT'

The so-called WIBON clause has a similar effect to the 'time lost' clause, being designed to deal with the problem of a ship, chartered under a berth charterparty, arriving at her destination and finding no berth available for her. In such circumstances the clause enables the shipowner to give a valid notice of readiness to load as soon as the vessel arrives in port, provided that the other conditions for a valid notice are satisfied.[31] In the view of Roskill LJ, the effect of the clause is to convert a berth charterparty into a port charterparty for purposes of applying the *Johanna Oldendorff* test[32] and starting the laytime clock.

An attempt was recently made in *The Kyzikos*[33] to extend the application of the clause to cover a situation where a vessel, on entering the discharging port, was delayed for three days in proceeding to a vacant berth by fog which resulted in the pilot station being closed. Their Lordships were unanimously of the opinion that there was no authority in earlier case law to support such an argument. The clause 'should be interpreted as applying only to cases where a berth is not available and not to cases where a berth is available but is unreachable by reason of bad weather'.[34]

3.2.2 READINESS TO LOAD OR DISCHARGE

Before laytime will begin to run, not only must the vessel become an 'arrived ship' at the designated port of loading, but two further requirements must be satisfied. First, the shipowner must have given the prescribed notice of readiness to load and secondly, the vessel must in fact be ready to load.[35] In the absence of special agreement in the charterparty, English law does not require the master to give notice of readiness to unload to the consignee at the port of discharge.

---

[30] *Ibid* at p 166.
[31] See *infra* at pp 59–60.
[32] [1972] 2 Lloyd's Rep 292 at p 312.
[33] [1989] 1 Lloyd's Rep 1.
[34] *Ibid* at p 8. Cf. the decision in *The Fjordaas* [1988] 1 Lloyd's Rep 336, where the application of the 'reachable berth' clause was extended to cover bad weather. See *supra* p 56–7.
[35] See Kennedy LJ in *Leonis v Rank* [1908] 1 KB 499 at p 518.

(I) NOTICE OF READINESS TO LOAD

The purpose of such notice is to inform the charterer that loading may commence and to provide a starting point for the calculation of laytime.[36] At common law the notice can be in any form, providing that it is communicated, but if a particular form is prescribed in the charter, such as notice in writing, then that form must be adopted. From the standpoint of business convenience, advance notice of expected readiness would be particularly helpful to the charterer and many standard forms require the giving of such notice at a specified time before arrival. For example, clause 2 of the Polcoalvoy charter requires at least 10 running days' written notice of the approximate date of readiness to load. On the other hand, many charter forms prefer certainty and the requirement at common law is for a simple notice of actual readiness to load. Such notice is, however, only effective in respect of an 'arrived ship' which is actually ready to load at the time notice is given.[37] In this respect English law takes a strict view and a notice of anticipated readiness is ineffective even though the vessel was in fact ready to load at the time the notice was given.[38] Problems arise, however, in such a case where, despite the invalid notice, the vessel proceeds to berth and to load or discharge cargo without a further notice of readiness being given. According to the strict legal view, laytime will not commence in the absence of a valid notice of readiness with the result that, not only will the owners have no claim for demurrage but they may also be obliged to pay the charterers despatch money for the whole of the agreed laytime.[39] This result, while legally impeccable, does not make commercial sense. Nevertheless, the courts have been reluctant to hold that a premature notice of readiness becomes automatically effective when the vessel is ready to discharge and proceeds to discharge with the co-operation of the charterers.[40] In their view mere awareness by the charterers of the vessel's readiness to discharge is not sufficient. Something extra is required in the form either of an implied or express agreement to dispense with the need for notice, or a waiver or estoppel binding on the charterers in respect of the necessity for a further valid notice.[41]

The Court of Appeal considered that these requirements were met in the case of *The Happy Day*,[42] where the vessel, having missed the tide, was unable to enter port but nevertheless gave a premature notice of readiness to discharge. The vessel berthed the following day and commenced discharge. The issues before the court were twofold: was a further notice of readiness required to commence laytime and, if not, when did laytime commence? On the facts of the case the charterers were aware of the arrival of

---

[36] See Moore-Bick J in *The Mass Glory* [2002] 2 Lloyd's Rep 244, at p 250.

[37] *Christensen v Hindustan Steel Ltd* [1971] 1 Lloyd's Rep 395; *The Tres Flores* [1973] 2 Lloyd's Rep 247 at p 249: 'Readiness is a preliminary existing fact which must exist before you can give a notice of readiness.' For a similar US position, see *Puerto Madrin SA v Esso Standard Oil Co* [1962] AMC 147.

[38] *Christensen v Hindustan Steel Ltd* [1971] 1 Lloyd's Rep 395 at p 400. See also *The Agamemnon* [1998] 1 Lloyd's Rep 675 (at time notice given vessel had not reached point at which notice contractually required to be given).

[39] See *The Mass Glory* [2002] 2 Lloyd's Rep 244.

[40] Despite reservations expressed by the court, the charterers in two cases conceded that, despite a premature NOR, laytime began to run when discharge of the cargo actually began. See *The Mexico 1* [1990] 1 Lloyd's Rep 507 and *The Agamemnon* [1998] 1 Lloyd's Rep 675.

[41] See Mustill LJ in *The Mexico 1* [1990] 1 Lloyd's Rep 507 at p 510.

[42] [2002] 2 Lloyd's Rep 487.

the vessel and of its readiness to discharge while, through their agents, they had accepted instructions to discharge the vessel without any reservation of their position as to the validity of the notice of readiness which they had earlier received. In these circumstances, Potter LJ was of opinion that 'the doctrine of waiver may be invoked and applied in such a case and the commencement of loading [*sic*] by the charterer or receiver without rejection of or reservation regarding the notice of readiness can properly be treated as the "something else" which Lord Justice Mustill[43] indic-ated was required to be added to mere knowledge of readiness on the part of the charterers, in order for a finding of waiver or estoppel to be justified.'[44] On the facts of the case, the notice of readiness previously tendered was treated as having been accepted at the time discharge commenced.

Such problems are avoided in some European jurisdictions, such as in Scandinavia and West Germany, where an anticipatory notice of readiness is effective provided that the vessel is ready by the time the notice expires.[45] Many charters have an additional requirement that notice of readiness be given during specified office hours, e.g. between 0600 and 1800 hours. The question then arises as to whether notice given outside these hours is a complete nullity, thus necessitating the rendering of a second notice within the required period. A recent decision has held that, provided the vessel is ready to load at the time the contractually invalid notice is given, there is no good reason why such notice should not take effect as from the time fixed by the contract for it to be ten-dered.[46]

If it is subsequently discovered that the vessel is not ready to load, then the notice will be wholly ineffective and laytime will not commence to run.[47] On the other hand, should the charterer in such circumstances waive the default by proceeding to load without protest, then he will not be allowed to invoke the lack of readiness at a later stage in the absence of proof of fraud.[48]

As noted earlier, English law does not require notice of readiness to be given at the port of discharge, where it is the responsibility of the consignee to keep a lookout for the arrival of the vessel. This rule probably stems from the situation in liner contracts where the obligation to notify a range of consignees might impose an unjustifiable burden on the shipowner particularly in cases where the bill of lading has been assigned during the voyage. It is, however, more difficult to justify the rule in the case of char-terparties and accept the view taken by Donaldson J that 'once his cargo has been loaded . . . [the charterer] may be expected to take an interest in the movements of the vessel which he would not take prior to loading'.[49] The problem of identifying the ulti-mate consignee can be avoided by a provision in the charter requiring the master to give notice to specified agents at the port of discharge.[50]

---

[43] See Mustill LJ in *The Mexico 1* [1990] 1 Lloyd's Rep 507 at p 510.
[44] *Ibid* at p 509.
[45] See UNCTAD: *Report on Charterparties*, p 37.
[46] *The Petr Schmidt* [1998] 2 Lloyd's Rep 1.
[47] *The Tres Flores* [1973] 2 Lloyd's Rep 247; *The Massalia (No 2)* [1960] 2 Lloyd's Rep 352.
[48] *The Helle Skou* [1976] 2 Lloyd's Rep 205. Cf. *The Mexico 1* [1990] 1 Lloyd's Rep 507.
[49] *Christensen v Hindustan Steel Ltd* [1971] 1 Lloyd's Rep 395 at p 398.
[50] Where notice of readiness is required, it can be validly given even though the shipowner is exercising a lien for general average. *Gill & Duffus v Rionda Futures* [1994] 2 Lloyd's Rep 67.

(II) ACTUAL READINESS TO LOAD

Whether or not a vessel is in fact ready to load depends on a variety of factors including the position of the vessel, whether it is physically capable of receiving the cargo, and whether it has complied with all the port health and documentary requirements.[51]

So far as the vessel's physical position is concerned, it is now clear that notice of readiness to load can be given even though it is impossible to commence the loading operation because the vessel is not in berth. Thus, providing the other requirements are met, a vessel may be ready to load when it becomes an 'arrived ship' under a port charterparty or where the charter provides that laytime shall begin to run 'whether the ship is in berth or not'.[52]

From the physical standpoint, 'a vessel is not ready to load unless she is discharged and ready in all her holds so as to give the charterer complete control of every portion of the ship available for cargo, except so much as is reasonably required for ballast to keep her upright'.[53] The charterer is entitled to immediate access to all the cargo space and consequently the vessel is not ready to load so long as even the smallest proportion of the previous cargo remains to be discharged,[54] or ready to unload if overstowed cargo has to be removed before access can be gained to the charterer's cargo.[55] A further facet of physical readiness is the requirement that the vessel must be 'cargoworthy in the sense that it must be fit to receive the agreed cargo'. Thus the holds must be clear and free from contamination,[56] the required loading gear must be fixed, and any special equipment required for particular cargoes must be available and in position.[57] But where the charterer is given the choice between a range of cargoes, the vessel may legally be ready to load even though not fit to receive the particular cargo selected by the charterer.[58]

The requirement of readiness to load is, however, subject to the principle of *de minimis* and here, it would appear, a less stringent test is applied in respect of port charters than in the case of berth charters. Thus, while berthed vessels have normally to be prepared in all respects to receive cargo before notice of readiness can be given, it has been held that an 'arrived ship' under a port charter could give notice of readiness even though the hatches had not been removed or the discharging gear rigged, provided that such work could be completed by the time the vessel berthed.[59]

The final aspect of readiness requires that the vessel has complied with the port regulations by satisfying the health requirements and obtaining the necessary

---

[51] In case of repudiation by charterer, burden of proof that vessel is ready to load rests on shipowner: *The Simona* [1986] 1 Lloyd's Rep 171; upheld on other grounds by the Court of Appeal [1987] 2 Lloyd's Rep 236.

[52] *The Kyzikos* [1989] 1 Lloyd's Rep 1; see also *The Notos* [1987] 1 Lloyd's Rep 503.

[53] Cozens Hardy MR in *Lyderhorn v Duncan, Fox* [1909] 2 KB 929 at p 938.

[54] *Lyderhorn v Duncan, Fox, supra.*

[55] *The Massalia (No 2)* [1960] 2 Lloyd's Rep 352; *The Mexico 1* [1990] 1 Lloyd's Rep 507. See also *The Virginia M* [1989] 1 Lloyd's Rep 603 (winches lacked power to discharge all cargo).

[56] *The Tres Flores* [1973] 2 Lloyd's Rep 247. See also *The Nikmary* [2004] 1 Lloyd's Rep 55 (tanks needed cleaning before fit to receive gasoil).

[57] For example, shifting boards for grain cargo: *Sun Shipping Co v Watson & Youell* (1926) 24 LlLR 28.

[58] *Vaughan v Campbell* (1885) 2 TLR 33; *Noemijulia v Minister of Food* (1950) 84 LlLR 354.

[59] *Armement Adolf Deppe v Robinson* [1917] 2 KB 204. The parties may also vary the readiness requirement by agreement: *The Linardos* [1994] 1 Lloyd's Rep 28. See Cooke 19.15 ff.

documentation. Here again, several of these requirements have been regarded as mere formalities and shipowners have been allowed to give notice of readiness even though they have not received free pratique,[60] or a police permit to move up river.[61] Presumably such notice would be ineffective if the master did not obtain the required documentation by the time, or shortly after, the vessel berthed.[62]

3.3 THE PRELIMINARY VOYAGE

3.3.1 NOMINATION OF PORT OF LOADING

The port of loading may be specified in the charterparty or the charterer may be given the right to nominate a port either from a given geographical area, for example 'One safe port East Coast of United States', or from a list of ports named in the charter.[63] Where the port is specified in the charter then, subject to the usual exceptions, the shipowner is under an absolute obligation to go there and there is no implied warranty by the charterer as to the safety of the port.[64]

Where the charterer has a right to nominate the port, he must exercise his election within the time specified, or otherwise within a reasonable time. If he fails to do so, the shipowner is not permitted to withdraw his vessel but must wait for instructions unless the delay is so prolonged as to result in frustration of the charterparty. The charterer is, however, liable for any loss to the shipowner resulting from the delay in giving the necessary instructions.[65] Once the charterer has exercised his election, the selected port is treated as though it had been named in the charter and the choice is irrevocable.

In selecting a port, the charterer has a free choice within the indicated range and is under no obligation to consult the shipowner's convenience. Accordingly, he may nominate a busy or strike-bound port and the shipowner will have no grounds for complaint unless the resulting delay is so prolonged as to frustrate the object of the charterparty. Thus in the case of *Reardon Smith Line Ltd* v *Ministry of Agriculture*[66] the charterers nominated the port of Vancouver where a strike of elevator men was already in progress. Loading of a cargo of wheat was prevented for a period of over six weeks, yet the court held that the delay was not so unreasonable as to frustrate the adventure. Not only were the charterers entitled to nominate a strike-bound port, but they could invoke a strike exception in the charter to avoid liability for demurrage accruing during the waiting period. Indeed, the opinion was expressed that charterparties would rarely be frustrated by strikes since, from their very nature, they were of uncertain duration and might be settled overnight. On the other hand, there is evidence to suggest that, in

---

[60] *The Delian Spirit* [1972] 2 QB 103.
[61] *The Aello* [1961] AC 135. See also *The Antclizo (No 2)* [1992] 1 Lloyd's Rep 558.
[62] *The Tres Flores* [1973] 2 Lloyd's Rep 247.
[63] The following rules are, of course, equally applicable to the situation when the charterer is entitled to nominate the port of discharge.
[64] See *M/V Naiad* [1978] AMC 2049 at p 2056. But compare case where charter also includes an express safe port warranty: *The Helen Miller* [1980] 2 Lloyd's Rep 95 at p 101 *per* Mustill J.
[65] *The Timna* [1971] 2 Lloyd's Rep 91.
[66] [1963] AC 691.

certain circumstances, the courts may be prepared to restrain a completely unfettered choice. In a recent case, where a charterer had the right to nominate '1/2 safe ports all India' the court held that he was not entitled to nominate them in other than their geographical order.[67]

The right to nominate is invariably accompanied by a clause in the charterparty requiring any nominated port to be 'safe'.[68] Such a clause is a natural corollary to the right to nominate if the interests of the shipowner are to be adequately protected and there are dicta to suggest that, in the absence of such a clause, the common law will imply an obligation to the same effect.[69] In the event of the charterer failing to nominate a safe port, damages recoverable will extend to cover such items as actual physical injury to the vessel, losses resulting from any delay, and additional expenses arising from discharging the cargo at an alternative port.[70] Where an obstruction has prevented the charterer from loading a full cargo, he may also be liable to a claim for dead freight.[71]

3.3.2 'OR SO NEAR THERETO AS SHE MAY SAFELY GET'

While the shipowner's primary obligation on the preliminary or carrying voyage is to bring his ship to the port named in the charter or nominated by the charterer, this obligation is frequently qualified by the words 'or so near thereto as she may safely get'. If this clause is successfully invoked, the contractual voyage is treated as being complete on arrival at the alternative port, with the result that the shipowner can then claim the full freight and the consignee must bear the cost of transporting the goods to the originally intended destination. Clauses of this type have accordingly been narrowly construed and considerable litigation has ensued concerning the circumstances in which they can be invoked and the appropriateness of any alternative port selected by the shipowner.

The cases would suggest that the shipowner can only rely on such a clause when he is prevented from entering a port by a hazard or obstruction of a permanent nature or one which, from a commercial standpoint, would delay him for an unreasonable length of time. Such temporary obstacles as high winds or unfavourable tides would clearly not qualify. In *Metcalfe* v *Britannia Ironworks*[72] a vessel had been chartered to ship a cargo to Taganrog, a port in the Sea of Azov, or as near thereto as she could safely get. On arrival in mid-December, the Sea of Azov was found to be closed by ice and it was unlikely that a passage would be free before the following April. Nevertheless, the shipowner was not allowed to invoke the clause and unload the cargo at a port at the mouth of the Sea of Azov, since the obstruction was regarded by the court as being a merely temporary one. While this might appear to be an extreme case, it is partly explained by the fact that Taganrog was named in the charter and the court took the view that the shipowner should have been aware of conditions in the Sea of Azov at

---

[67] *The Hadjitsakos* [1975] 1 Lloyd's Rep 356.

[68] For definition of safe port, see *supra* pp 25 ff.

[69] See Morris LJ in *Compania Naviera Maropan* v *Bowaters Ltd* [1955] 2 QB 68 at p 105.

[79] For a full discussion of the rights and obligations of the parties following a breach of this undertaking by the charterer, see *supra* at pp 28–9.

[71] See *Garcia & Diaz* v *Maguire Inc* [1936] AMC 584.

[72] (1877) 2 QBD 423.

that time of year.[73] On the other hand, in the more recent case of *The Athamas*,[74] the pilotage authorities on the Mekong River refused to allow the vessel to proceed upstream to the port of Pnom Penh while strong river currents persisted. The Court of Appeal allowed the master to invoke the clause to justify unloading the cargo at Saigon, when it was established that the river passage would not have been 'safe' for a further five months.

With regard to the choice of an alternative discharging port, there is likely to be a conflict of interest between consignee and shipowner. The consignee will be anxious to have the cargo discharged at a point as near as possible to the intended destination in order to minimise additional transport costs. On the other hand, the shipowner will not be attracted by the nearest safe port unless it has adequate facilities for discharging the cargo. In these circumstances the courts have imposed the so-called 'ambit' test, requiring the selected alternative port to be within an area or zone in close proximity to the original port. In the interests of the charterer, some restriction must clearly be applied to the general wording of the 'so near thereto' clause. Taken literally it might even be invoked to justify the shipowner discharging the cargo at the loading port should some obstruction of a permanent nature prevent him leaving that port. Even so, the 'ambit' test has been somewhat restrictively applied as in the case of *Metcalfe v Britannia Ironworks*[75] where it was held that a port at the mouth of the frozen Sea of Azov was not within the 'ambit' of Taganrog, some 300 miles away. Recent cases have suggested, however, that a more flexible approach may be adopted towards the 'ambit' test and it has been recognised that distance is relative. Charterers and shipowners must be presumed to be endowed with normal commercial knowledge and experience and to realise that some parts of the world are more sparsely provided with ports than others. Consequently, while only a very restricted scope can be given to the 'ambit test' in respect of ports in northern Europe, a distance of 250 miles may be justified in the South China Sea where ports are few and far between.[76]

In interpreting the phrase 'so near thereto as she may safely get', the word 'safely' refers to the safety of the ship and not to the safety of the cargo. It covers not only hazards arising from physical obstructions and weather conditions, but extends to political dangers[77] and even delay caused by congestion in the port.[78]

A number of variations may be added to the clause to provide extra protection for the shipowner. The addition of the words 'always afloat' protects him from possible damage to the vessel by grounding and entitles him to unload at the nearest safe port if unreasonable delay would otherwise result.[79] The alternative variation of 'at all times of the tide always afloat' removes the necessity for the shipowner to wait for a favourable tide.[80]

---

[73] See also *Schilizzi v Derry* (1855) 4 E & B 873.
[74] [1963] 1 Lloyd's Rep 287.
[75] (1877) 2 QBD 423.
[76] *The Athamas* [1963] 1 Lloyd's Rep 287. See also Cooke 5.103 ff.
[77] *Nobel's Explosives v Jenkins* [1896] 2 QB 326.
[78] *Dahl v Nelson* (1881) 6 App Cas 38.
[79] *Treglia v Smith's Timber Co* (1896) 1 Com Cas 360.
[80] *Horsley v Price* (1883) 11 QBD 244.

3.3.3 THE VOYAGE TO THE LOADING PORT

It will rarely be the case that at the time when a vessel is chartered it will already be in berth at the port of loading ready to perform the charter. In the great majority of cases it will be at some distance from that port and will in all probability be trading under a prior charter. It will therefore be necessary for the vessel to undertake a preliminary voyage to the agreed port of loading, and this will form the first stage in the performance of the charterparty. In these circumstances there will be a basic conflict of interest between charterer and shipowner. The charterer will require to know at least the approximate time of arrival of the vessel at the loading port in order that he can make the necessary arrangements to have the cargo available at that time. It will be to his advantage to have the arrival time indicated as precisely as possible since he will be anxious to avoid unnecessary storage costs by having the cargo at the loading port too early, or unnecessary demurrage costs by having it there too late. The shipowner, on the other hand, will be reluctant to commit himself to a firm date in order to avoid liability for breach of contract should unforeseen circumstances delay the arrival of the vessel.

The starting point for any estimate of arrival time is to be found in information relating to the current position of the vessel and the time at which it will be free from any existing commitments. Most standard forms include a clause indicating the position of the vessel at the time the charter is signed,[81] and the courts attach considerable importance to the accuracy of such information. Any substantial error in the stated position of the vessel is treated as a breach of condition entitling the charterer to rescind the contract.[82] In the absence of any more specific undertaking on the part of the shipowner, the common law implies an obligation to proceed on the preliminary voyage with reasonable dispatch. Breach of this obligation will entitle the charterer to claim damages for any loss attributable to the undue delay, but he will not be permitted to rescind the charterparty unless the result of the breach is such as to frustrate the entire object of the contract.[83]

Clearly the charterer would prefer greater precision but rarely will the shipowner commit himself to a specific time of arrival at the loading port or even to a specific date for setting sail on the preliminary voyage to that port. By doing so he could make time of the essence of the contract, in which case the courts would tend to treat any failure to meet the agreed date as a breach of condition entitling the charterer to repudiate the contract.[84]

The solution to the problem in the majority of charter forms is to insert a clause requiring the shipowner to indicate a date at which the vessel is expected to be ready to load and to couple with it a further clause entitling the charterer to cancel the charter should the vessel not have arrived by a specified later date.[85] The combined practical effect of these clauses is to indicate the earliest date at which the charterer may be

---

[81] For example, Gencon clause 1; Polcoalvoy box 12.
[82] *Behn* v *Burness* (1863) 3 B & S 751.
[83] *Jackson* v *Union Marine Insurance* Co (1874) LR 10 CP 125. The US position is similar, see *Hildebrand* v *Geneva Mills* Co [1929] AMC 971.
[84] *Glaholm* v *Hays* (1841) 133 ER 743.
[85] And be in a seaworthy state: *The Madeleine* [1967] 2 Lloyd's Rep 224.

required to commence loading the cargo[86] and the latest date on which he is bound to accept the vessel for loading. It is naturally in the interest of the charterer that the gap between these dates should be as short as possible if he is to avoid unnecessary storage costs, whereas the shipowner would prefer the longest possible interval to avoid the risk of losing the charter should the vessel be delayed on the preliminary voyage. In practice the length of the interval will tend to vary in proportion to the time lapse between the signing of the charter and the expected time of arrival at the loading port.

A statement by the shipowner as to the date of expected readiness to load does not amount to an undertaking on his part that the chartered vessel will be ready to load at that date. Consequently, its arrival after that date will not *per se* amount to a breach of contract entitling the charterer to damages.[87] Indeed, in the absence of an express cancelling clause, the charterer would not be able to repudiate the charter unless the delay was so substantial as to frustrate the object of the enterprise. On the other hand, such a statement is not entirely without effect. The shipowner 'is undertaking that he honestly and on reasonable grounds believes at the time of the contract that the date named is the date when the vessel will be ready to load'.[88] If, therefore, when he makes the prediction he knows that the vessel cannot reach the loading port by that date, or there are no reasonable grounds for such a belief, then he commits a breach of condition entitling the charterer to repudiate the contract.[89]

The presence of a cancelling clause is of particular value to a charterer since it indicates a time beyond which he is no longer obliged to wait for the arrival of the chartered vessel. Once this date has been reached, he can safely repudiate the charter and make alternative provisions for the carriage of his cargo. As this is a contractual right of cancellation, he is relieved of the onus of proving that the object of the charterparty has been frustrated or even that he has suffered loss as a result of the delay. But he is not allowed to prejudge the issue by repudiating the charter before the cancelling date even though it is physically impossible for the chartered vessel to arrive at the loading port by that date.[90] A further point to note is that the cancelling clause merely affords the charterer an opportunity to repudiate any further obligations under the charter, it does not entitle him to claim any damages for loss which he has suffered as a result of the delay.[91] Only if a shipowner has breached his obligation to proceed to the loading port with reasonable dispatch are any damages recoverable.

The cancelling clause provides the charterer with an option to rescind the contract which he is not bound to exercise until the vessel reaches the loading port and notice of

---

[86] In order to minimise the uncertainty attached to an estimated time of arrival clause, many forms also indicate a specific date before which the charterer will not be required to load, e.g. 'lay days not to count before . . .': Polcoalvoy, clause 2.

[87] The late arrival may, of course, be due to breach by the shipowner of his obligation to use reasonable dispatch.

[88] Megaw LJ in *The Mihalis Angelos* [1971] 1 QB 164 at p 204.

[89] *Sanday & Co v Keighley, Maxsted & Co* (1922) 27 Com Cas 296; *The Mihalis Angelos, supra*.

[90] *The Mihalis Angelos* [1971] 1 QB 164. In such circumstances the charterer might only be liable for nominal damages for breach of contract: Denning MR at p 196. Cf. situation where premature cancellation is accepted by the shipowner: *The Helvetia-S* [1960] 1 Lloyd's Rep 540.

[91] See *The Democritos* [1976] 2 Lloyd's Rep 149 at p 152.

readiness to load is given. It may be in his interest to delay any decision on exercising the option until the last possible moment in order to test the current state of the market. If freight rates are rising there will be little incentive to cancel, whereas if they are falling an opportunity to renegotiate the charter would be attractive. Until the option has been exercised, however, the shipowner remains under a duty to proceed to the loading port with reasonable dispatch, even if there is no possibility of arriving there before the cancelling date.[92] Nor is the charterer under any obligation at common law in these circumstances to indicate to the shipowner how he intends to exercise his option, and failure to respond to an enquiry from the shipowner will not amount to a waiver of his rights under the option.[93] In order to minimise the resulting loss to the shipowner, many forms require the charterer to declare his option at a specified time prior to the vessel's arrival at the port of loading, for example, 'if demanded, at least 48 hours before vessel's expected arrival at port of loading'.[94] Even in the absence of such a clause, it may be of advantage to the shipowner to indicate to the charterer that he will be unable to reach the loading port before the cancelling date. Should he be in breach of his obligation to proceed with reasonable dispatch, he will provide the charterer with an opportunity to mitigate his loss by enabling him to delay delivery of the cargo to the port and thus avoid unnecessary warehouse charges.

Finally, it must be noted that the right to cancel on the specified date is an absolute right and can be exercised irrespective of whether the late arrival was due to the fault of the shipowner, or whether the cause of the delay was covered by an exception.[95] While the exception may protect the shipowner from any claim for damages, it will not protect him from the exercise of the cancelling option by the charterer.

Mention has already been made of the fact that, at the time a vessel is chartered, it might have existing commitments under previous charters. Any outstanding obligations of this type are usually listed in the charterparty and linked with an 'expected ready to load clause' in respect of the new charter. Indeed, there is no objection to the shipowner taking on additional intermediate commitments after signing a new charter, provided that the vessel will be ready at the loading point on the 'expected' date.[96] In both cases, however, he will have to take the risk of unexpected delays in fulfilling prior obligations which prevent him from reaching the loading port on time. Exceptions in the charterparty designed to cover the preliminary voyage do not extend to cover events occurring under previous charters.[97] In the words of Greer LJ, 'people who have to make engagements in advance necessarily run the risk of the engagements clashing with one another so as to prevent the performance of one or other of their contracts, and they have to take the consequences by paying damages to the party whose contract they, in the result, have failed to perform'.[98]

---

[92] *Moel Tryvan Ship Co Ltd* v *Weir* [1910] 2 KB 844.
[93] *Ibid.*
[94] Gencon 1976, clause 10.
[95] *Smith* v *Dart* (1884) 14 QBD 105. See also *The North Sea* [1999] 1 Lloyd's Rep 21 at p 26.
[96] *Monroe Bros* v *Ryan* [1935] 2 KB 28.
[97] *Evera* v *North Shipping Co* [1956] 2 Lloyd's Rep 367.
[98] *Monroe Bros* v *Ryan* [1935] 2 KB 28 at p 38. See also *The Almare Seconda* [1981] 2 Lloyd's Rep 433.

3.4 THE LOADING OPERATION

3.4.1 DIVISION OF RESPONSIBILITY

The traditional division of responsibility at common law for the loading operation between shipowner and charterer is based on the 'alongside rule'. It is the responsibility of the charterer to bring the cargo alongside the vessel and within reach of the ship's tackle after which it is the duty of the shipowner to load it. A similar rule operates in reverse in relation to the discharging operation when the consignee is under an obligation to receive the cargo after it has been put over the side by the shipowner and is free of the ship's tackle. The 'alongside rule' represents an appropriate division of labour in the basic situation where the loading and discharging is to be performed by means of the ship's tackle, since it results in the charterer being responsible for the cost of the work done on land, and the carrier for the work done on board. In modern conditions, however, it bears little resemblance to reality since the loading operation both on shore and aboard is often performed by professional stevedores engaged by a shipbroker acting on behalf of both parties. Again, bulk cargoes are loaded, not by the ship's tackle, but generally by shore-based mechanical equipment such as elevators, grabs or cranes which are often owned or controlled by the charterers. In such circumstances the charter party may provide that the goods are carried on f.i.o. terms,[99] i.e. that the charterer will perform and pay the cost of both the loading and discharging operations.[100]

In the absence of express agreement to the contrary, however, the common law implies the 'alongside rule' and the charterer is merely responsible for the cost of bringing the cargo within the reach of the ship's tackle. Where the vessel is unable to berth in a particular port, this obligation will extend to cover the cost of the necessary lighters to transport the cargo to the ship's side. The charterer must also bear the risk of any delay during the performance of this obligation and, on the principle established in *Grant* v *Coverdale*,[101] will not be able to claim the protection of exceptions which are only applicable to the loading operation.

3.4.2 PROVISION OF CARGO

While the charterparty will normally specify the type and amount of cargo to be provided by the charterer at the port of loading, the arrangements for procuring that cargo are outside the scope of the contract. The shipowner is in no way concerned with the methods by which the charterer intends to acquire the cargo, and his sole interest is whether it will be available at the loading port at the required time. The charterer, on the other hand, is under an absolute duty to provide the cargo and it will be no excuse that he is prevented from doing so by reasons which are entirely beyond his control. Thus it will be no defence to an action for breach of contract that cargo was not available

---

[99] 'Free in and out'. Another variation is that the charterer will bear the cost of loading and the shipowner the cost of discharging. Such an arrangement is common in the transport of oil.

[100] 'Once it is established that the loading and stowage are the responsibility of the merchant, it must follow that the merchant must do the operation of loading and stowing with reasonable care.' See *The Apostolis (No 2)* [1999] 2 Lloyd's Rep 292 at p 300 *per* Longmore J.

[101] (1884) 9 App Cas 470. See *infra* p 69.

because of crop failure, government controls on exporting[102] or transport delays on the way to the loading port caused by strikes[103] or bad weather.[104] While it is true that many charters include exceptions covering delay in loading, there is a strong presumption that such clauses apply only to the actual process of loading the cargo when ready, and not to delay in providing the cargo.[105] Thus in *Grant* v *Coverdale*[106] where a vessel had been chartered to proceed to Cardiff and load a cargo of iron, there was an exception covering 'hands striking work, or frost or floods, or any other unavoidable accidents preventing the loading'. The charterer sought to rely on this exception when he was prevented from lightering part of the cargo from the wharf, where it had been stored, to the loading dock because an intervening canal had been blocked by ice and it was impracticable to transport it by any other means. The court held that the exception had reference only to the loading operation and did not cover delays in transporting the goods to the loading point. Where, however, the only available storage facilities in a particular port are at some distance from the loading berths, the carriage of the cargo between these two points will be regarded as part of the loading process and covered by the exceptions. Such a situation might arise in the case of container stores which are often located outside the dock area, and it has even been held that movement of grain from storehouses sited some 110 miles from the loading port was part of the loading operation.[107] Where difficulties are foreseen in procuring a particular cargo, then the charterer may gain relief from his absolute obligation if he ensures inclusion in the contract of an appropriate and clearly worded exception.[108]

The cargo to be provided by the charterer will normally be expressly agreed in the charterparty. It may take the form of a specific cargo, e.g. 10,000 tonnes of wheat, or it may consist of a series of alternative cargoes, e.g. wheat and/or barley and/or rye, from which the charterer may select one or more. Occasionally it may appear in the more general form of 'any lawful cargo'. The charterer is under an obligation to provide a cargo of the type or types specified and any attempt on his part to load a different cargo amounts to a serious breach of contract entitling the shipowner to repudiate the charterparty. Should the shipowner waive this breach by accepting the substituted cargo, then an obligation will be implied that the charterer will pay the current rate of freight for cargo of that description.[109]

Where the charterparty specifies a range of alternative cargoes, the charterer will normally have a free choice between them, even though the respective freight rates may vary.[110] On the other hand, he is under an obligation to load a full cargo from the range open to his selection and, if some of the cargoes later prove not to be available, he must load an alternative from such a range. The fact that he intends to load one particular

---

[102] *The Aello* [1961] AC 135.
[103] *Bunge y Born* v *Brightman* [1925] AC 799.
[104] *Grant* v *Coverdale* (1884) 9 App Cas 470.
[105] *Ardan Steamship Co* v *Weir* [1905] AC 501. See also *The Nikmary* [2004] 1 Lloyd's Rep 55 at p 60 *per* Mance LJ.
[106] (1884) 9 App Cas 470. See also *Bunge y Born* v *Brightman* [1925] AC 799.
[107] *Hudson* v *Ede* (1868) LR 3 QB 412.
[108] *Gordon Steamship Co* v *Moxey, Savon & Co* (1913) 18 Com Cas 170.
[109] *Steven* v *Bromley* [1919] 2 KB 722.
[110] *Moorsom* v *Page* (1814) 4 Camp 103.

cargo does not amount to a decisive election and he cannot plead frustration because the intended cargo is not available. Even though failure to load that particular cargo is covered by an exception, he is not relieved from his obligation to load an alternative cargo.[111] In the words of Viscount Radcliffe, 'If a shipper has undertaken to ship a full and complete cargo made up of alternative commodities as in the terms "wheat and/or maize and/or rye", his obligation is to have ready at the port of shipment a complete cargo within the range of those alternatives. Consequently the fact that he is prevented from loading one of the possible types of cargo by a cause within the exceptions clause, even though that is the type that he has himself selected and provided for, is not an answer to a claim for demurrage.'[112] This right of selection of the charterer, with its correlative duty, continues 'until the final ton is put on the ship'.[113] On the other hand, where the charterer is prevented from loading his original choice of cargo, he is entitled to a reasonable time in which to make alternative arrangements.[114]

Occasionally a charterer is given a true election between a range of cargoes, but it would appear to be a rare occurrence. So in *Reardon Smith Line* v *Ministry of Agriculture*[115] the vessel was chartered to receive 'a full and complete cargo . . . of wheat in bulk', the charterer having an option to substitute barley for wheat, in respect of one third of the cargo, on payment of additional freight. When a strike of elevator men prevented the loading of any wheat, the House of Lords held that the charterer could rely on the strike clause in the charter and was not obliged to load an alternative cargo of barley. On the wording of the charterparty, the charterer had a 'true option' between the two cargoes and, in the event of one cargo not being available, he was not obliged to load the other.

(I) AMOUNT OF CARGO

The amount of cargo required to be provided by the charterer may be indicated in the charterparty in a variety of different ways. Where a vessel has been chartered to fulfil an export order or to carry any other specific consignment, the description of the cargo in the charterparty will be precise, e.g. 200 Ford Escort cars, and the charterer's obligation will thus be clearly defined. It is, however, more common for the standard forms to include a clause requiring the charterer to provide a 'full and complete cargo'.[116] Under this clause his obligation is assessed in relation to the actual capacity of the vessel and not that stated in the charterparty, should the two differ. Thus in one case a ship chartered to load a full and complete cargo of sugar was 'guaranteed by owners to carry 2,600 tons dead weight, excluding bunkers'. When it was later discovered that the vessel could in fact safely carry 2,950 tons of this particular cargo, the Court of Appeal held the charterer bound to ship a cargo of 2,950 tons.[117] It should be noted, however, that the capacity of the ship in this respect refers to the holds and those other parts of the

---

[111] *South African Dispatch Line* v *Owners of Steamship Niki* [1960] 1 KB 518.
[112] *Reardon Smith Line* v *Ministry of Agriculture* [1963] AC 691 at p 716.
[113] Per Atkin LJ in *Brightman* v *Bunge y Born* [1924] 2 KB 619 at p 637.
[114] *South African Dispatch Line* v *Owners of Steamship Niki* [1960] 1 QB at p 530.
[115] [1963] AC 691.
[116] For example, Gencon, clause 1.
[117] *Heathfield SS Co* v *Rodenacher* (1896) 1 Com Cas 446.

vessel normally used for the carriage of cargo. The charterer is not obliged to provide ballast or to supply cargo to fill space in cabins, bunkers or on deck unless expressly agreed in the contract.

In an attempt to be more precise, the obligation to load a 'full and complete cargo' is often accompanied by a clause stipulating maximum and minimum quantities. This has been interpreted by the courts as imposing a liability on the charterer to load either a full cargo or the specified maximum, whichever is less.[118] It also amounts to a warranty by the shipowner that the vessel is able to carry the stipulated quantity.[119] A slight variation on this formula provides that the quantity is to be at the shipowner's option to be declared by the master at the commencement of loading. In such an event the master must declare a figure between the specified maximum and minimum quantities, which then establishes the precise amount to be loaded.[120] A third possibility is provided by some modern charter forms which require a precise quantity of cargo to be stated either as a specific tonnage, cubic capacity or other relevant measurement. Often the stated quantity is accompanied by an allowance of, e.g., '5 per cent more or less', or is qualified by a term such as 'about'[121] or 'thereabouts'.[122] The courts have generally interpreted the latter phrases as permitting an allowance of from 3 to 5 per cent either way.[123]

Failure of the charterer to load all the agreed cargo will naturally result in a loss of freight for the shipowner, for which he will be able to recover damages in the form of 'dead freight'. He may also incur additional expenses as, for example, where he has to ship extra ballast to compensate for the shortage of cargo. Such costs would generally be recoverable as damages for breach of contract. One particular problem arises in relation to the obligation to provide a 'full and complete cargo' when the charterer is entitled to ship a variety of different cargoes. Where the particular goods are of different shapes and sizes, he is not allowed to leave broken stowage but must fill the gaps left between individual items with other cargo.[124] Failure to do so will render him liable for the payment of dead freight unless the method of loading adopted is covered by local custom.[125] When a charterer fails to provide a full cargo, the shipowner is entitled to take reasonable steps to acquire alternative cargo in order to minimise his loss and is allowed a reasonable time in which to make the necessary arrangements.[126]

Should the charterer fail to provide a cargo on the arrival of the vessel at the loading port, the shipowner must wait until the laytime has expired and even then it would appear that he is not entitled to withdraw his ship until either it is clear that the charterer has no intention of loading a cargo or the delay is such as to frustrate the object of the charterparty.[127] If, however, the charterer expressly or by conduct refuses to load the

---

[118] *Carlton SS Co Ltd v Castle Mail Packets Co Ltd* (1897) 2 Com Cas 173; *Jardine Matheson & Co v Clyde Shipping Co* [1910] 1 KB 627.

[119] *Louis Dreyfus v Parnaso Cia Naviera* [1960] 1 Lloyd's Rep 117 at p 123.

[120] *Ibid* at p 121.

[121] *Morris v Levison* (1876) 1 CPD 155.

[122] *The Resolven* (1892) 9 TLR 75.

[123] *Louis Dreyfus, supra.*

[124] *Cole v Meek* (1864) 15 CB (NS) 795.

[125] *Cuthbert v Cumming* (1855) 11 Ex 405.

[126] *Wallems Rederi A/S v Muller & Co* [1927] 2 KB 99.

[127] *Universal Cargo Carriers v Citati* [1957] 2 Lloyd's Rep 191.

vessel, then the shipowner can treat this as an anticipatory breach and withdraw his vessel even before the expiration of the lay days. Should he do so, he will be required to take reasonable steps to mitigate his loss if cargoes are available at that port from other shippers. If the shipowner does not accept the refusal to load as final, then the contract will continue and he will have no claim if the charterer subsequently decides to load a cargo or a supervening event frustrates further performance of the contract.[128]

3.4.3 LAYTIME

The period of time within which the loading or discharging operation is required to be completed will be prescribed in the charterparty and is known as laytime. It is at the charterer's free disposal in that he is regarded as having paid for it in the freight. In the words of Salmon LJ, 'Laytime is a sort of bogey for the course.'[129] If such period is exceeded, he will have to pay compensation to the shipowner in the form of demurrage or damages for detention. It is obviously in the charterer's interest for the laytime period to be as extensive as possible in order to allow for unforeseen contingencies, whereas it is to the economic advantage of the shipowner to have a speedy turnround of his vessel and, with this object in view, he is often prepared to offer an inducement to the charterer in the form of dispatch money if the operation can be completed in a shorter time.

(I) CALCULATION OF LAYTIME

The period of laytime may be stipulated in the charterparty either as a specific number of days or hours or in relation to a fixed rate of loading or discharge. Occasionally the wording is less specific, as when the charterer undertakes to load his cargo with 'customary dispatch' or 'as fast as the ship can receive'. Such phrases are interpreted as imposing an obligation to load within a reasonable time according to the custom of the port and the charterer is expected to exercise reasonable dispatch in conducting the operation.[130]

Where laytime is expressed as a certain number of 'days' or 'running days', this is construed by the courts as meaning consecutive periods of 24 hours running without interruption except in the case where specific days are excluded, e.g. 'Sundays and holidays excepted'. In the absence of any such excepted periods, time would run continuously through Sundays, holidays and other periods such as Saturday afternoons, during which it was not customary to work in the port. As this wording is merely regarded as an abstract formula for the calculation of average loading time, it is immaterial that it may be illegal to work on some of these days at a particular port.[131] Traditionally such periods of 24 hours were regarded as calendar days running from midnight, but under modern forms of charterparty they will be treated as artificial or

---

[128] *Avery v Bowden* (1856) 6 E & B 953.
[129] *The Theraios* [1971] 1 Lloyd's Rep 209 at p 210. Modern golfing parlance requires this dictum to be rephrased as 'par for the course'.
[130] *Good v Isaacs* [1892] 2 QB 555. The same implication is drawn when the contract makes no express or implied reference to the period of laytime. *Hick v Raymond* [1893] AC 22.
[131] *Hain SS Co v SA Commercial de Exportacion y Importacion* (1934) 49 LlLR 86.

conventional days of 24 hours starting from the time when the notice of readiness to load expires.[132]

An alternative method of describing laytime is in the form of 'working days'. A working day is a day on which work is ordinarily done in the particular port, excluding Sundays and holidays (Fridays in Muslim countries). The term describes the character of the day as a whole, and consequently the day will count even though the charterer does not intend to load on that day or is prevented from doing so by bad weather, unless the latter is covered by an exception.[133] The number of hours in a particular working day on which a ship is required to load will depend on the custom of the port, and Saturday will normally count as a whole day although it may not be customary to work in the afternoon.[134]

The phrase 'weather working day' is a further refinement, excluding from the calculation of laytime those working days on which loading would have been prevented by bad weather, had any loading been envisaged at that time. It is immaterial that the charterer had no intention of loading during such periods, since 'the status of a day as being a weather working day, wholly or in part or not at all, is determined solely by its own weather and not by extraneous factors such as the actions, intentions and plans of any person'.[135] Where only a part of the working day is affected by bad weather, an appropriate deduction from the laytime will be made in proportion to the length of the interruption.[136] The term 'weather' is widely construed by the courts and has been held to cover not only rain and gales but also accumulations of ice which prevented loading.[137] On the other hand, the weather must affect the loading process and not merely the safety of the vessel, with the result that the mere threat of bad weather, which resulted in a ship being ordered from the berth by the harbour master, did not prevent the period in question from counting as weather working days.[138]

A different method of assessment which is increasingly used in modern standardised forms is to base the calculation of laytime on a specified daily rate of loading or discharging, e.g. 120 tonnes per weather working day. The number of lay days is then ascertained by dividing the total amount of cargo by the daily rate and it would appear that any resulting fraction must be treated as an appropriate fraction of the working day and will not, as formerly, entitle the charterer to an extra full day.[139] Often this formula is qualified by being expressed as a daily rate 'per hatch' or 'workable hatch'. In the former case, the overall rate is calculated by multiplying the daily rate by the number of hatches, but the assessment in the latter case is not so straightforward. The term

---

[132] Lord Devlin in *Reardon Smith Line* v *Ministry of Agriculture* [1963] AC 691 at p 738. Thus in charters, which provide that laytime will commence at 1 p.m. when notice of readiness is given before noon, the 'conventional day' will run from 1 p.m. An appropriate adjustment will have to be made when Sundays are excepted. See Mackinnon J in *Hain SS Co* v *SA Commercial* (1934) 49 LlLR 86 at p 88.

[133] *The Sandgate* [1930] P 30 at p 34 per Scrutton LJ; *The Rubystone* [1955] 1 QB 430.

[134] *Reardon Smith Line* v *Ministry of Agriculture* [1963] AC 691.

[135] Pearson J in *Compañia Naviera Azuero* v *British Oil & Cake Mills Ltd* [1957] 2 QB 293.

[136] *Alvion SS Co* v *Galban Lobo Trading Co* [1955] 1 QB 430 at p 447. For the possible formulae for calculating broken days, see Colinvaux, RP, *Carver's Carriage by Sea*, 13th edn, 1982, paras 1849–56.

[137] *Dampskibsselskabet Botnia SA* v *Bell* [1932] 2 KB 569.

[138] *Compania Crystal de Vapores* v *Herman* [1958] 2 QB 196. Cf. term 'working days, weather permitting'. *Gebr Broere* v *Saras Chemica* [1982] 2 Lloyd's Rep 436.

[139] See Tiberg p 381. Cf. *Houlder* v *Weir* [1905] 2 KB 267.

'working hatch' is used to 'denote a hatch which can be worked either because under it there is a hold into which cargo can be loaded or a hold out of which cargo can be discharged. Once the hold has been loaded or discharged it ceases to be a working hatch . . . Therefore the average daily quantity to be loaded into or discharged from the ship cannot be ascertained until the loading or discharging operations have begun, and may vary as those operations proceed.'[140] Only if all the hatches remain 'workable' throughout the loading or discharging operation will the calculation be reasonably straightforward, since it can then be assessed in relation to the time taken to load the largest hold.[141]

(II) SUSPENSION OF LAYTIME

To what extent will hindrances and obstructions encountered during the loading or discharging operation interrupt the running of laytime? Where no specific period of laytime is fixed, or the charterer is required to load 'with customary dispatch', it would appear that any obstruction which effectively interrupts the loading will excuse the charterer, provided that it is outside his control and that otherwise he has conducted the operation with reasonable dispatch. Thus laytime will be suspended during such time as the loading or discharging operation is interrupted by a strike of dock labourers,[142] by the lack of an available berth due to congestion in the port[143] or by the arrest of the vessel.[144]

On the other hand, when the agreed laytime is specified in the contract, the charterer is under a strict obligation to load within the prescribed time limit and must bear the risk of any intervening obstructions unless they are covered by exceptions in the charterparty or arise through the fault of the shipowner. Thus charterers have been held liable to pay for time lost as a result of congestion in the port,[145] strikes of stevedores employed by the shipowner,[146] the need to take on ballast to keep the ship upright during loading,[147] and the need to remove the vessel temporarily from the port for her own safety during bad weather.[148] However, time will not run against the charterer if the delay is attributable to the fault of the shipowner[149] or results from action taken entirely in his own interest as, for example, when the vessel is removed from a loading berth for bunkering purposes.[150] In the majority of cases, however, the charterparty will include exceptions

---

[140] Salmon LJ in *The Theraios* [1971] 1 Lloyd's Rep 209 at pp 211–12, see also *The Sandgate* [1930] P 30; *The Giannis Xilas* [1982] 2 Lloyd's Rep 511. See Charterparty Laytime Definitions 1980.

[141] *Compania de Navigacion Zita SA v Louis Dreyfus* [1953] 2 Lloyd's Rep 472 at p 475.

[142] *Hick v Raymond* [1893] AC 22.

[143] *Good v Isaacs* [1892] 2 QB 555.

[144] *The Dynamic* [2003] 2 Lloyd's Rep 693 (but not where vessel arrested by charterer).

[145] *The Johanna Oldendorff* [1974] AC 479.

[146] *Budgett v Binnington* [1891] 1 QB 35.

[147] *Houlder v Weir* [1905] 2 KB 267.

[148] *Compañia Crystal de Vapores v Herman* [1958] 2 QB 196. But not where shipowner had no intention of returning to port: *Petrinovic & Co v Mission Française des Transports Maritimes* (1941) 71 LlLR 208 at pp 215, 216.

[149] For example, removing vessel from loading berth without due cause: *The Fontevivo* [1975] 1 Lloyd's Rep 339.

[150] In *Re Ropner Shipping Co* [1927] 1 KB 879. See also *Stolt Tankers v Landmark Chemicals* [2002] 1 Lloyd's Rep 786.

providing for the suspension of laytime on the occurrence of the more frequent causes of delay in loading or discharge such as congestion in port,[151] strikes, bad weather, civil commotions[152] or even 'any other cause beyond the control of the charterers'.[153]

(III) COMPLETION OF LOADING

Laytime is at the free disposal of the charterer since he is regarded as having paid for it in the freight.[154] He is entitled to use it in the way which suits him best and, provided that the agreed period is not exceeded, the shipowner is not entitled to complain that the cargo could have been loaded in a shorter time. 'The method of loading and discharging the ship is entirely a matter for the charterers to decide . . . Nor is it of any consequence to the owners whether the loading or discharge proceed very slowly on some days and exceptionally fast on others or at an even pace. All that matters to the owners is the actual time occupied by those operations.'[155] The most striking example of this principle in operation is to be found in the case of *Margaronis Navigation Agency* v *Peabody*[156] where a vessel had been chartered to load a full and complete cargo of maize at an average rate of 1,000 tons per weather working day of 24 hours, Sundays and holidays excepted. The charterers were required by the master to provide a cargo of 12,600 tons and when, by 5 p.m. on Friday, 27 December, all but 11 tons 16 cwts. of this amount had been loaded, they instructed the stevedores to stop work as they were anxious for business reasons to obtain January bills of lading. Loading was resumed at 8 a.m. on Tuesday, 2 January, the next working day in the port, and was completed in 40 minutes, after which the vessel sailed. Although the operation had been completed within the agreed laytime, the shipowners nevertheless claimed damages for detention on the ground that the charterers had wrongfully detained the vessel for their own purposes after a full cargo had been loaded. While admitting that the charterer's obligation 'was to load a full and complete cargo subject to the *de minimis* rule',[157] the Court of Appeal nevertheless upheld the decision of the arbitrator that, in view of the accuracy of the loading equipment being used, a shortage of approximately 12 tons (i.e. less than 0.01 per cent) was not a commercially insignificant amount and so the charterers were entitled to detain the vessel until the balance of the agreed cargo was loaded.[158]

---

[151] *The Amstelmolen* [1961] 2 Lloyd's Rep 1.

[152] See e.g. Gencon General Strike Clause.

[153] *The Loch Dee* [1949] 2 KB 430. Some charters require notice of the specified event to be given to the shipowner before the exception will operate: see *The Mozart* [1985] 1 Lloyd's Rep 239; *The Chanda* [1985] 1 Lloyd's Rep 563.

[154] *The Delian Spirit* [1971] 1 Lloyd's Rep 506 at p 509.

[155] Salmon LJ in *The Theraios* [1971] 1 Lloyd's Rep 209 at p 211. See also *The Ulyanovsk* [1990] 1 Lloyd's Rep 425; *The World Navigator* [1991] 2 Lloyd's Rep 23.

[156] [1965] 1 QB 430.

[157] Pearson LJ at *ibid* p 446.

[158] Contrast the case of *Williams* v *Manisselian Freres* (1923) 17 LlLR 72, where the charterer, under an obligation to load 'minimum one-half cargo' at a particular port, had loaded an amount 34 tons short of this quantity (i.e. 1–1½ per cent) and successfully relied on the defence of *de minimis*. The Court of Appeal in *Margaronis* differentiated this case on the ground of the uncertainty involved in the assessment of half a cargo.

In contrast, once the loading operation has been completed, the charterer has no right to detain the vessel further, even though the laytime has not expired. In *Nolisement (Owners)* v *Bunge y Born*[159] the loading was completed some 19 days before the expiration of the lay days, but the charterers delayed a further three days before presenting bills of lading to the master since they were unable to decide on the port of discharge. They were held liable for damages for two days' detention. It would seem a little inconsistent for the charterer to be penalised for detaining the vessel after the completion of loading if he could retain complete freedom of action by withholding a minimal amount of cargo.[160]

Finally, it must be noted that the loading stage is not complete until the cargo is aboard the vessel and also stowed.[161] Although stowage of the cargo is normally the responsibility of the shipowner and the cost is usually borne by him, it is nevertheless regarded as part of the loading operation and the charterer is under an obligation to bring the cargo alongside the vessel in sufficient time to enable the shipowner to complete the stowage within the lay days.[162]

With the completion of the loading operation, the end of the second stage of the voyage charterparty is reached and the risk of subsequent delay due to accidental hindrances and obstructions reverts to the shipowner. Consequently, if after the cargo has been stowed the vessel is prevented from embarking on the carrying voyage by reason of ice or bad weather, the cost of the delay must be borne by the shipowner.[163]

3.4.4 DEMURRAGE AND DAMAGES FOR DETENTION

(I) DEMURRAGE

If a charterer detains the vessel beyond the agreed lay days, then he is in breach of contract. The majority of charterparties, however, include a clause providing that he may retain the vessel for additional days in order to complete the loading or discharging operation on payment of a fixed daily amount, known as demurrage. In the late nineteenth century this additional period was judicially referred to as 'lay days that have to be paid for'.[164] This is a misleading description since it conceals the fact that, in reality, the charterer is in breach of contract even though he is entitled, on payment of the agreed rate, 'to detain the ship for the purpose of enabling him, if possible, to perform his broken contract and so mitigate any further damage'.[165] Nevertheless, it is an anoma-

---

[159] [1971] 1 KB 160.

[160] Yet this appears to be the view advanced by Roskill J in *Margaronis Navigation Agency* v *Peabody* [1965] 1 QB 300 at p 324, when distinguishing the *Nolisement* case. 'The distinction between such a case and the Nolisement case, in my judgment, lies in this. A charterer is entitled to have that time to load but, once he has loaded, he must not use that time for some other purpose. But, so long as he has not completed loading, that time is his, and he is under no obligation to accelerate that rate of loading so as to shorten the time to which he is otherwise entitled.'

[161] *Argonaut Navigation Co* v *Ministry of Food* [1949] 1 KB 572; *Svenssons Travaruaktiebolag* v *Cliff Steamship Co* [1932] 1 KB 490.

[162] *Harris* v *Best* (1892) 68 LT 76 at p 77.

[163] *Williams* v *Manisselian Freres* (1923) 17 LlLR 72; *The Hermine* [1979] 1 Lloyd's Rep 212.

[164] Lord Trayner in *Lilly* v *Stevenson* [1895] 22 Sess Cas (4th Series) 278 at p 286. In civil law countries demurrage is often referred to as 'supplementary freight'.

[165] Atkin LJ in *A/S Reidar* v *Arcos* [1927] 1 KB 352 at p 363.

lous position since, despite the breach, the shipowner is unable to rescind the contract and withdraw his ship during the demurrage period unless the failure of the charterer to load amounts to a repudiation of the contract on his part, or the delay is so substantial as to frustrate the object of the charterparty.[166] This principle applies whether the charter stipulates for a fixed number of days on demurrage or no time limit is expressed as, e.g., 'eight days for loading, after which demurrage at £2,000 *per diem*'.

At common law a demurrage clause is purely a creation of contract and is in the nature of a provision for agreed damages for detention of the vessel beyond the agreed lay days. The stipulated sum is recoverable by the shipowner irrespective of proof of damage, and represents the maximum amount recoverable for loss resulting from the detention. Demurrage will thus cover losses of freight arising under subsequent charterparties affected by the delay, or from the consequent reduction in the number of voyages possible under a consecutive voyage charterparty.[167] On the other hand, it will not extend to limit claims for losses arising from causes other than detention as, for example, from failure to load a full cargo.[168]

As with any other provision for liquidated damages, a demurrage clause may be struck down by the courts as a penalty if the rate is fixed so high as to be 'extravagant and unconscionable' in comparison with the greatest possible loss that could flow from the breach.[169] In such circumstances the courts would consider the shipowner adequately compensated by being allowed to recover his actual loss. A similar principle would not appear to be applicable in reverse in cases where the rate is fixed at an unreasonably low level. In such an event the shipowner is unable to recover his actual loss but is limited to the specified demurrage rate even though the delay has been deliberately caused by the charterer for his own benefit.[170] Such a situation may be open to abuse at times when costs and freight rates are rising and the shipowner may be left without an effective remedy should excessive delay result in him losing a subsequent charter.

The actual rate of demurrage will be stated in the charterparty and will normally be fixed at a figure in line with current freight rates at the time of the conclusion of the charter. As such fixtures are often made well in advance, the figure may bear little resemblance to prevailing freight rates by the time demurrage becomes payable. Liability for the payment of demurrage accrues immediately on the expiration of the lay days and runs continuously through Sundays, holidays and other periods normally excluded from laytime, e.g. bad weather working days. The rule is 'once on demurrage, always on demurrage'. For a similar reason, laytime exceptions are held not to be applicable to a demurrage period unless expressly worded to that effect. Thus in a case in which the House of Lords had refused to allow a charterer to invoke a strike exception after laytime had expired, Lord Reid justified the decision on the grounds that 'the [ship]owner might well say: true, your breach of contract in detaining my ship after the end of laytime did not cause the strike, but if you had fulfilled your contract the strike

---

[166] *Inverkip SS Co v Bunge y Born* [1917] 2 KB 193 at p 201.
[167] *Suisse Atlantique v NV Rotterdamsche Kolen Centrale* [1967] AC 361.
[168] *A/S Reidar v Arcos* [1927] 1 KB 352.
[169] *Dunlop v New Garage* [1915] AC 79.
[170] *Suisse Atlantique v NV Rotterdamsche Kolen Centrale* [1967] AC 361. A demurrage clause was held not to be an exception or limitation clause in these circumstances.

would have caused no loss because my ship would have been on the high seas before it began: so it is more reasonable that you should bear the loss than that I should'.[171] Nevertheless, the 'once on demurrage' rule may still apply even though the event covered by the exception occurs before the expiry of laytime.[172] Of course, an exception can be expressly worded so as to cover the demurrage period as, for example, where it was provided that demurrage was to be paid 'at 12s 6d per hour unless detention arises from a lock-out, strikes etc'.[173] Similarly, demurrage will not accrue during a period where delay was due to the fault of the shipowner or resulted from action taken by him for his own convenience.[174] It will, however, accrue where the delay is accidental and not due to the fault of either shipowner or charterer.[175] Even where the delay results from a breach of contract by the shipowner, demurrage may still be payable if the length of such delay is beyond the reasonable contemplation of the parties as a possible consequence of the breach.[176]

(II) DAMAGES FOR DETENTION

When there is no provision in the charterparty for the payment of demurrage, a charterer will be liable for damages for detention for all the time he detains the vessel after the expiration of the lay days.[177] In this situation damages are at large and will be assessed by the court in relation to the actual loss suffered by the shipowner, and in accordance with the normal principles governing remoteness of damage in contract.[178] Damages for detention is also the appropriate remedy where a charterparty stipulates a fixed number of days for the payment of demurrage, and those days have expired. In the latter case, however, the court will normally assess the damages at a figure corresponding to the agreed demurrage rate, though it is open to either party to prove that such a rate does not represent the actual loss suffered by the shipowner.

It has already been noted that a shipowner is not allowed to withdraw his vessel during any period for which the payment of demurrage has been agreed, unless the delay is such as to frustrate the object of the charterparty.[179] On the other hand, once the specified demurrage period has expired he is no longer obliged to remain in port to complete the loading operation and to be restricted to a claim for damages for detention.

---

[171] *Compañia Naviera Aeolus* v *Union of India* [1964] AC 868 at p 882. See also *Dias Compañia Naviera SA* v *Louis Dreyfus* [1978] 1 All ER 724; *The Saturnia* [1984] 2 Lloyd's Rep 366; *The Altus* [1985] 1 Lloyd's Rep 423; *The Anna CH* [1987] 1 Lloyd's Rep 266; *The Kalliopi A* [1988] 2 Lloyd's Rep 101.

[172] *The Lefthero* [1992] 2 Lloyd's Rep 109, followed in *The Solon* [2000] 1 Lloyd's Rep 292.

[173] *Lilly* v *Stevenson* (1895) 22 Sess Cas (4th Series) 278. See also *The John Michalos* [1987] 2 Lloyd's Rep 188.

[174] In *Re Ropner* [1927] 1 KB 879 (vessel removed from loading berth by shipowner for bunkering purposes); *The Union Amsterdam* [1982] 2 Lloyd's Rep 432 (vessel grounded while moving into berth); *Stolt Tankers* v *Landmark Chemicals* [2002] 1 Lloyd's Rep 786 (to load or unload other cargo).

[175] See *The Nordic Navigator* [1984] 2 Lloyd's Rep 182 (delay in discharging cargo of oil due to defect in shore pipeline and subsequent shortage of capacity in storetanks). Cf. *The Siam Venture* [1987] 1 Lloyd's Rep 147 where, in absence of bills of lading, shipowners refused to deliver to receivers, who were not known to them, without bank guarantee.

[176] *The Forum Craftsman* [1991] 1 Lloyd's Rep 81.

[177] Where no lay days are specified, damages will be payable on the expiration of what the court considers to be a reasonable time for the loading or discharging of the vessel.

[178] See *infra* at pp 343 ff.

[179] See *supra*, pp 76–7.

If part of the cargo has been loaded, he may sail and claim compensation in the form of dead freight, or, if the charterer has failed to ship any cargo, he may rescind the charter and sue for damages at large. If, however, the delay occurs at the discharging port, he has little option except to complete the unloading operation and claim damages for detention.

(III) DISPATCH MONEY

While laytime is at the free disposal of the charterer, he is entitled to no reward at common law if he completes the loading or discharging operation in a shorter time. As it is usually of considerable advantage to a shipowner to have his vessel free as quickly as possible, an incentive is often provided by the insertion in the charterparty of a dispatch money clause. This clause entitles the charterer to payment at an agreed rate – usually fixed at half the demurrage rate – for time that is saved. Problems of construction frequently arise, however, in the calculation of such time. Is dispatch money payable only for laytime saved, or is it payable for Sundays, holidays and other periods normally excluded from the calculation of laytime? There is a strong argument for treating 'time saved' in this context as 'time saved to the ship in the same way as time lost on demurrage is time lost for the ship'.[180] There are, however, conflicting decisions in the cases on this point,[181] and much depends on the construction of the particular clause at issue. Thus at one extreme is the clause providing that dispatch money is payable for 'all time saved',[182] while at the other is the provision for payment only for 'laytime saved'.[183]

Normally the periods for which demurrage or dispatch money are payable are calculated separately at the ports of loading and discharge. Consequently, it is of little benefit to the charterer to be paid dispatch money at one port if he is liable for demurrage at the other, since the latter is normally fixed at double the rate of the former. He would prefer to set off time saved at one port against time lost at the other. This result can be achieved in one of two ways, either by providing that laytime shall be 'reversible' or that time for loading and discharge shall be 'averaged'.[184] Where laytime is 'reversible', the charterer is entitled to add together the time used at each port and deduct these periods from the overall laytime until the latter is exhausted. Due allowance will, of course, be made for Sundays, holidays and other periods excepted from the calculation of laytime. Under the averaging system, the amount of laytime used at each port is calculated separately, after which time saved at one port is set off against excess time used at the other. The only practical difference between the two systems is that in the latter the charterer

---

[180] Tiberg p 509. It would appear that dispatch money can be claimed even though the saving of time has been achieved by loading during Sundays, holidays or other 'free' time. See *Pteroti Compañia Naviera SA v NCB* [1958] 1 Lloyd's Rep 245.

[181] *The Glendevon* [1893] P 269. Cf. *Re Royal Mail Steam Packet Co* [1910] 1 KB 600. In *Mawson SS Co v Beyer* [1914] 1 KB 304 at p 312 Bailhache J attempted a statement of principle in the following terms: 'Prima facie, the presumption is that the object and intention of these dispatch clauses is that the shipowners shall pay to the charterers for all time saved to the ship, calculated in the way in which, in the converse case, demurrage would be calculated; that is, taking no account of the lay day exceptions.'

[182] Centrocon clause 16. *Mawson SS Co v Beyer* [1914] 1 KB 304.

[183] Polcoalvoy clause 24(b). *Thomasson SS Co v Peabody* [1959] 2 Lloyd's Rep 296.

[184] See Charterparty Laytime Definitions approved by BIMCO and the General Council of British Shipping in 1980.

might obtain credit for time saved, e.g. Sundays, which would not have counted as lay-time. It would appear that the charterer has an option whether or not to invoke such provisions and will be presumed to have opted against doing so if he claims dispatch money at the port of loading.[185]

3.5 THE CARRYING VOYAGE

On completion of the loading operation, the responsibility for continued performance of the charterparty will be transferred to the shipowner. His obligation will be to proceed with reasonable dispatch and convey the cargo to the designated port of discharge. As freight once calculated has reference to the cargo carried rather than to the time expended on performance of the charter, it is in the shipowner's interest to complete the voyage as speedily as possible, although he will be protected by the usual exceptions from liability for loss arising from delay due to factors beyond his control. While the ship-owner will normally indicate to the consignee the estimated time of arrival at the dis-charging port, there will be no cancelling clause for this voyage since the cargo owner, for obvious reasons, will have little interest in cancelling the charterparty at this stage.

The carrying voyage will terminate on the vessel having become an 'arrived ship' at the port of discharge and being ready to unload the cargo. These two requirements are identical with those outlined above with respect to the preliminary voyage[186] and, once they have been fulfilled, laytime will begin to run at the risk of the charterer.

Only one point calls for further comment. It will be remembered that where the char-terer is given an express right to nominate a berth, the vessel will not become an 'arrived ship' until it reaches the specific berth nominated by him. In exercising this option, the charterer is under no obligation to consult the convenience of the shipowner and may even nominate a congested berth so long as the resultant delay is not so prolonged as to frustrate the object of the charter.[187] In the absence of an express right to nominate, it would appear that the charterer is still entitled to select the berth, though in this case he must bear the risk of any delay resulting from his choice.[188]

English law does not, as we have noted earlier, require notice of readiness to unload to be given at the port of discharge.[189] It is the responsibility of the consignee to keep a lookout for the arrival of the ship. In practice few problems result for the charterer, since modern standard forms invariably contain an express provision requiring the shipowner to give notice of readiness.

Even at common law notice must be given in cases where the shipowner fails to reach the designated port but invokes the 'so near thereto as she can safely get' clause.[190] Similarly, the charterer will not have to bear the risk of any resultant delay where his failure to learn of the vessel's arrival is due to the fault of the shipowner.[191]

---

[185] See *Fury Shipping Co Ltd* v *The State Trading Corp of India Ltd* [1972] 1 Lloyd's Rep 509.
[186] For 'arrived ship', see *supra* pp 53 ff; for 'readiness to load', see *supra* pp 58 ff.
[187] *Tharsis Sulphur Co* v *Morel* [1891] 2 QB 647.
[188] *Leonis* v *Rank (No 1)* [1908] 1 KB 499.
[189] See *supra* p 60.
[190] *The Varing* [1931] P 79 at p 87.
[191] *Bradley* v *Goddard* (1863) 3 F & F 638.

3.6 THE DISCHARGING OPERATION

Laytime will run from the moment the vessel arrives at the port of discharge and is ready to unload. The respective obligations of shipowner and charterer are similar to those at the port of loading except for the fact that the operation is conducted in reverse. Discharge is a joint operation, the shipowner being responsible for moving the cargo from the hold to the ship's side and the consignee for taking it from alongside. Where lighters are required for receiving the cargo alongside, the cost will normally fall on the charterer.[192] This division of responsibility may of course be modified by the custom of the port or by express provision in the charterparty. Thus it may be agreed that the shipowner will be responsible for the cost of discharging, in which case he will have to bear such incidental expenses as the cost of any necessary rebagging of the cargo.[193] Alternatively, the charter may provide that discharge is 'to be free of expense to vessel', with the result that the charterer will be liable for stevedoring costs.[194] The discharging operation must, of course, be completed within the specified lay days, otherwise the charterer will incur the same liability for demurrage or damages for detention as if a similar delay had occurred during the loading operation.[195]

3.6.1 DELIVERY

The shipowner is under a contractual obligation to deliver the cargo to a specified, or identifiable, person. Normally the requirement is to deliver to the consignee named in the bill of lading or to any person to whom the consignee has validly endorsed the bill. In the event of no bill having been issued, the consignee will normally have been designated either in the charterparty itself or in a non-negotiable receipt.

(I) FAILURE OF CONSIGNEE TO ACCEPT DELIVERY

The first problem confronting the shipowner on arrival at the port of discharge may be the absence of any consignee ready to receive the cargo. As the shipowner is under a duty to make personal delivery of the cargo, he cannot discharge that obligation at common law merely by unloading the goods and leaving them on the dockside.[196] In such a situation he is required to allow the consignee a reasonable time in which to collect the cargo, after which he may land and warehouse it at the consignee's expense. Even so, it is doubtful whether the shipowner can divest himself of his strict liability as a carrier merely by warehousing the goods although to counterbalance any such potential liability he will retain the protection of the carriage exceptions.

Personal delivery may be excused by the custom of the port or by express provisions of the contract. Thus in certain ports delivery to a dock company or to harbour porters may be treated as equivalent to personal delivery to the consignee. In the case of *Chartered Bank of India* v *British India Steam Navigation Co*[197] such a clause was

---

[192] *Petersen v Freebody* [1895] 2 QB 294.
[193] *Leach & Co v Royal Mail Steam Packet Co* (1910) 16 Com Cas 143.
[194] *The Azuero* [1967] 1 Lloyd's Rep 464.
[195] See *supra*, pp 76–9.
[196] *Bourne v Gatliffe* (1841) 133 ER 1298.
[197] [1909] AC 369. But see *infra* pp 157–8.

accompanied by a provision that the shipowners' liability was to cease absolutely as soon as the goods were free of the ship's tackle. These clauses were held effective in excluding the shipowners from liability when landing agents employed by them fraudulently delivered the cargo without presentation of the bill of lading.

For any further protection, shipowners must rely on the terms of the individual contract of carriage. Many standard forms of bill of lading include a selection of remedies available to the shipowner in the event of a cargo owner failing to take delivery at the port of discharge. These range from the basic right to discharge and warehouse the cargo to the right, after the expiry of a stated period of time, to auction the goods and recoup any outstanding freight or other charges from the proceeds of sale.[198]

(II) DELIVERY TO THE PERSON ENTITLED

The shipowner is also under a duty to ensure that the cargo is handed over at the port of discharge to the person entitled to delivery. Few problems arise where the charterer is also the consignee since his identity will be known and, in any event, the cargo will normally be covered by a non-negotiable receipt, presentation of which is not required in order to obtain delivery.[199] Where bills of lading are issued, however, the situation is more complex. The shipowner's basic obligation is then to deliver to the consignee named in an unindorsed bill of lading, or to the person to whom the bill has been validly indorsed. If he makes delivery accordingly on presentation of the bill, he will normally be protected, provided that he is not aware of any other claims or of any circumstances which should put him on enquiry. Thus in *Glyn, Mills & Co* v *East and West India Dock Co*[200] where goods were deliverable 'to Cottam & Co or assigns' Cottam deposited one bill of the set with the plaintiff bank as security for a loan. He later obtained delivery of the cargo at the port of discharge on presentation of the second unindorsed bill of the set. It was held that delivery had been made bona fide and in ignorance of the bank's claim, and that no liability for wrongful delivery arose, even though only one bill of the set had been presented.

If the shipowner is aware of adverse claims, he may run the risk of liability in conversion for the full value of the goods should he deliver to anyone other than the person rightfully entitled. In case of doubt he should interplead and refuse to deliver the goods until the rival claimants have resolved the issue in court at their own expense. Finally, a shipowner who delivers goods without the presentation of a bill of lading does so at his own peril, even though delivery is made to the person named as consignee in the bill.[201] Such delivery has traditionally been regarded as a fundamental breach of contract, and, if made to the wrong person, may even prevent the shipowner from relying for protection on the bill of lading exceptions.[202]

---

[198] See the Conlinebill, clauses 8 and 12; The P & O Nedlloyd bill clause 20. Sections 492–8 of the Merchant Shipping Act 1894, which provided somewhat similar rights on a statutory basis, have now been repealed by the Statute Law (Repeals) Act 1993, Sch 1 Part XV.

[199] See *infra* pp 160 ff.

[200] (1882) 7 App Cas 591.

[201] *The Stettin* (1889) 14 PD 142.

[202] *Sze Hai Tong Bank* v *Rambler Cycle Co* [1959] AC 576. For a fuller discussion of these presentation problems, see *infra*, pp 155 ff.

(III) DELIVERY OF MIXED OR UNIDENTIFIABLE CARGO

The shipowner is under an obligation to deliver to the consignee at the port of discharge the appropriate quantity of goods consigned to him in the condition in which they were shipped. Problems arise where such goods are shipped along with similar goods destined for other consignees and lose their identity during the course of the voyage. Such loss of identity may result either from the obliteration of leading marks or from the goods themselves becoming irretrievably intermixed with other cargo on the vessel. In the latter event it is apparently immaterial whether the cargoes involved are liquid or consist of grain particles or their equivalent since, in the majority of cases, it would be commercially impracticable to separate them.[203]

The liability of the shipowner in such circumstances depends on whether or not the event causing the loss of identity is covered by an exception. Thus the mixing of the cargo may result from a peril of the sea, or the charterparty may include a clause excluding the shipowner from liability for 'obliteration or absence of marks'. In such an event while the shipowner will avoid liability, the unidentifiable cargo will become the property of the bill of lading holders who will hold as tenants in common of the whole, in the proportions in which they severally contributed to it. In *Spence v Union Marine Ins Co*[204] cotton belonging to different holders had been shipped in specifically marked bales from Mobile to Liverpool. During the voyage the vessel was wrecked on the Florida Keys and a quantity of the cotton was lost. The remainder was transhipped to another vessel and conveyed to Liverpool where, on arrival, it was discovered that the marks on 1,645 of the 2,262 bales were unidentifiable. The plaintiff, who had received only two of the 43 bales consigned to him was suing his insurers alleging a total loss of the remaining 41 bales. In rejecting this argument, the court felt unable to 'assume that the whole of the plaintiff's 41 bales were amongst those that were destroyed, any more than we can assume that they all formed part of the 1645 which were brought home'.[205] Bovill J formulated the relevant principle in the following terms: 'When goods of different owners become by accident so mixed together as to be undistinguishable, the owners of the goods so mixed become tenants in common of the whole in the proportions which they have severally contributed to it.'[206]

The position is different where the occurrence is not covered by an exception. The shipowner will be in breach of his obligation to deliver the specified goods to the consignee and will not be able to reduce his liability by requiring the consignee to accept an appropriate proportion of the mixed goods.[207] The position is further complicated where part of the cargo is lost at sea, while a portion of the remainder arrives at the port of discharge in an unidentifiable state. In such circumstances it may be impossible to establish what proportion of the claimant's missing cargo fell into either category. So in

---

[203] See Bovill CJ in *Spence v Union Marine Ins Co* (1868) LR 3 CP 427 at p 438.

[204] (1868) LR 3 CP 427.

[205] *Ibid* at p 439.

[206] *Ibid* at p 437. For the formula on which such an allocation may be made, see Scrutton p 294; *Gill & Duffus v Scruttons* [1953] 1 WLR 1407.

[207] The position may be different if the consignee chooses to accept part of the mixed cargo: see Lord Moulton in *Sandeman v Tyzack* [1913] AC 680 at p 697.

Sandeman v *Tyzack*[208] a quantity of bales of jute were shipped to various consignees under bills of lading which recorded the appropriate identification marks. The bills expressly excluded the shipowner's liability for 'obliteration or absence of marks'. On discharge 14 bales were missing and a further 11 were not labelled as indicated in the bills and could not be identified as belonging to any particular consignment. In reply to the plaintiff's claim for short delivery of six bales from his consignment, the shipowner argued that he should be required to accept an appropriate proportion of the 11 unidentifiable bales in mitigation of his loss. The House of Lords rejected this contention on the grounds that the shipowner could only succeed if he could prove that the plaintiff's missing bales were to be found among the 11 unidentifiable bales. Only in such an event could he rely on the exception covering 'obliteration or absence of marks'. In the words of Lord Loreburn, 'Apart from the 11 unidentifiable bales, there were 14 missing bales. It may be that the six which the appellants complain have not been delivered to them were among these 14. So the shipowners cannot prove, at least they have not proved, that the failure to deliver these six was due to any absence or obliteration of marking of such bales.'[209]

Reference must finally be made to the situation where part of a cargo shipped in bulk is lost or damaged during the voyage as the result of an excepted peril. In such a case the shipowner is not required to apportion the loss or damage between the various consignees but can deliver the full quantity of sound goods due to the first consignee to take delivery.[210]

---

[208] [1913] AC 680.
[209] *Ibid* at p 689.
[210] *Grange* v *Taylor* (1904) 20 TLR 386.

4

THE TIME CHARTERPARTY

4.1 GENERAL LEGAL OVERVIEW

The terms of a time charter differ radically from those of a voyage charter because of the difference of function. In the time charter the shipowner is placing his vessel for an agreed period at the disposal of the charterer who is free to employ it for his own purposes within the permitted contractual limits. As the charterer controls the commercial function of the vessel, he is normally responsible for the resultant expenses of such activities and also undertakes to indemnify the shipowner against liabilities arising from the master obeying his instructions. While there is a variety of standard forms of time charter, the following clauses are usually found to constitute the core of the contract.

4.1.1 CLAUSE DESCRIBING VESSEL

The efficiency of the chartered vessel is of vital importance to the time charterer since the entire success of the commercial enterprise may depend on it. The preamble to the charter therefore sets out in detail the specifications of the vessel, the most important of which are normally those relating to speed, loading capacity and fuel consumption. There are differing views as to the legal significance of such statements and the remedies available in the event of them proving inaccurate. Thus, while New York arbitrators generally regard specifications as to speed and fuel consumption as constituting continuing warranties that the vessel will maintain such capabilities throughout the charter, English courts treat them merely as warranties as to the state of the vessel at the time of delivery under the charter. In the event of breach of any of these warranties, it would appear that the appropriate measure of damages would be the difference in the market rate of hire between a vessel with the indicated specifications and the chartered vessel. In the case of a breach of the speed warranty, it has been suggested that an alternative remedy might be to treat the vessel as off-hire for the appropriate period.[1]

4.1.2 THE CHARTER PERIOD

A clause in the charter will normally specify the precise length of the charter period in days, months, or years. It is, however, recognised that in practice a vessel's movements under a time charter cannot be so accurately planned as to ensure that it arrives at the

---

[1] See *infra* p 90.

agreed port for redelivery on the exact date fixed for termination of the charter. Inevitably the vessel will arrive earlier (underlap) or later (overlap), in which event litigation is likely to ensue during a period in which there have been fluctuations in freight rates. The courts recognise the problem and are prepared to imply a margin of tolerance of some 5 per cent on the period stated in the charter unless the parties themselves have made express provision for overlap. Should the charterer return the vessel to its owner after the stated charter period has expired but within the permitted margin of overlap, he will be required to pay for the extra time at the normal charter rate. Only in the event of exceeding the overlap allowance will he be guilty of breach of contract and liable to damages based on the current market rate of hire.[2]

4.1.3 OFF-HIRE

Hire is payable throughout the charter period irrespective of whether the charterer has any use for the vessel. On the other hand, provision is normally made in an off-hire clause that no hire shall be payable during periods when the full use of the vessel is not available to the charterer because of some accident or deficiency which falls within the owner's sphere of responsibility. The clause specifies the occasions on which the vessel will go off-hire and is normally triggered by the mere occurrence of the event, irrespective of any fault on the part of the shipowner.

Should the clause operate, the charterer will, of course, be entitled to an adjustment of the hire to compensate for the time lost. Many off-hire clauses include express provision designed to enable the charterer to deduct the appropriate amount from the next instalment of hire and, even in the absence of such an express right, the courts are apparently prepared to imply a right to deduct, provided that such deductions are made in good faith and on reasonable grounds.[3]

4.1.4 PAYMENT OF HIRE – RIGHT TO WITHDRAW FOR NON-PAYMENT

Hire is the price paid for the use of the vessel and is usually calculated on the basis of a fixed sum per ton of the vessel deadweight for a specific period of time, such as 30 days or a calendar month. It is normally payable in advance at monthly or semi-monthly intervals. Where vessels are chartered for relatively long periods of time, there is constant exposure to the risks of currency devaluations, fluctuations in the market rate of hire, and the effects of inflation on the operating costs of the vessel defrayable by the shipowner. It is, therefore, common for the parties to make express provision in the charter for such contingencies by the use of such devices as a 'currency clause', providing for a fixed rate of exchange between the currency stipulated for payment of hire and any other relevant currency, and an 'escalator' clause providing for a periodic revision of the hire rate.[4]

---

[2] See *infra* pp 92–4.
[3] See *infra* pp 100–2.
[4] See *infra* p 94.

At common law time is not of the essence of a charter of this type with the result that a shipowner cannot repudiate the contract for late payment of hire unless the delay is such as to frustrate the object of the contract. It is consequently standard practice for a specific clause to be included in the charter giving the shipowner the right to withdraw his vessel in default of payment of an instalment of hire on the due date. While the original object of the clause was to enable a shipowner to put pressure on the recalcitrant charterer, or to recover the vessel from an incipient bankrupt, it has been used in recent years to take advantage of fluctuations in the market rates of hire. Vessels have accordingly been immediately withdrawn by their owners on a default in payment of the hire and then offered back to the identical charterers for the residue of the charter period at the current enhanced market rate. The courts have adopted a strict approach in the interpretation of such withdrawal clauses and have refused to exercise their discretion by extending towards the charterer any form of equitable relief against forfeiture. This problem can, however, be avoided by including in the charter an 'anti-technicality clause' requiring the shipowner, on default in payment of hire, to give the charterer a specified period of notice before exercising his right to withdraw the vessel.[5]

4.1.5 EMPLOYMENT AND INDEMNITY CLAUSE

Most charters include a clause entitling the charterer to have full use of the vessel within the limits stipulated in the charter and undertaking that the master will comply with the charterer's orders and instructions to this end. The limits imposed on the charterer's trading activities will depend on individual agreement between the parties but may extend to cover the types of cargo to be carried and the geographical limits of permitted trading. There will also invariably be included an express requirement that the charterer will only employ the vessel between safe ports. Probably one of the most important rights conferred on the charterer is the right to issue bills of lading which are to be signed by the ship's master on demand even though the terms of these bills may differ radically from the terms of the charterparty. As the master, in signing, is normally acting as agent of the shipowner, the terms of such bills are enforceable against the shipowner by any indorsee for value of the bill who takes in good faith.[6] Nor is the shipowner protected against such claims by the fact that the charterparty includes a clause providing that the shipowner is not to be liable for loss or damage to cargo except where it results from a 'want of due diligence on the part of the Owners or their Manager in making the Vessel seaworthy and fitted for the voyage, or any other personal act or omission or default of the Owners or their Manager'.[7] In the absence of a suitable incorporation clause in the bill of lading, such terms in the charterparty are only binding as between shipowner and charterer.

It will be evident that the commercial use of the vessel by the charterer, coupled with his right to issue bills of lading, may result in a substantial increase in the shipowner's liability. To meet this problem it is normal practice to include in the charterparty an express clause under which the charterer undertakes to indemnify the owner against any

---

[5] See *infra* pp 107–8.
[6] See *infra* pp 235 ff.
[7] Baltime, clause 13.

additional liability incurred by him as a consequence of the exercise of these powers by the charterer. Even where the charter fails to incorporate such a provision, the courts are prepared to imply a term to the same effect.[8]

4.1.6 RETURN OF THE VESSEL

The charterparty will normally require the charterer to maintain the vessel in 'an efficient state' during the period of hire, while the redelivery clause will expect the vessel to be returned 'in the same good order as when delivered to the charterers (fair wear and tear excepted)'.[9] Clearly the charterer will be liable for damage to the vessel resulting from negligence on the part of himself or his agents, but it is not clear whether accidental damage to the vessel incurred during loading and discharge is covered by the 'fair wear and tear' proviso. In this respect the 'fair wear and tear' exception conflicts with the charterer's obligation to indemnify the shipowner for the consequences of complying with his instructions.[10]

It may now be appropriate to consider these clauses individually in more detail.

4.2 DESCRIPTION OF THE VESSEL

As the time charterer is in control of the commercial operation of the vessel and is obliged to pay hire at a fixed rate throughout the charter period, the profit margin he derives from the enterprise will be largely dependent on the characteristics and performance of the chartered ship. Accordingly, standard time charter forms include in the preamble a detailed description of the vessel covering such matters as its name and flag, ownership, class, gross and net registered tonnage, cargo capacity, speed, and fuel consumption. The success of the adventure may depend on the accuracy of these particulars, since the risk of efficient vessel performance will fall largely on the charterer. It is therefore in his interest to secure as detailed a description as possible and, in cases of doubt, to have the vessel inspected by qualified staff. In the majority of cases, however, the reputation of the shipowner may be a more reliable guide.

While any facet of a vessel's description might be of importance on a particular occasion, as, for example, a vessel's flag in time of war, the bulk of litigation tends to centre on the three characteristics of cargo capacity, speed, and fuel consumption. In order to minimise the possibility of disputes in the event of minor discrepancies in such particulars, it is usual to qualify any statement by the addition of 'about' or some similar phrase, which is normally interpreted as permitting a tolerance of approximately 5 per cent.[11] Similarly, when reference is made to a vessel's speed, it is normal to add the proviso 'in good weather conditions', thus enabling arbitrators to ignore checks made on days when prevailing winds range above force 4 or 5 on the Beaufort Scale.

---

[8] See *infra* pp 108 ff.
[9] Baltime, clause 7.
[10] See *infra* pp 111–12.
[11] For a definition of the terms 'about' and 'on average', see *The Al Bida* [1987] 1 Lloyd's Rep 124. See also *Hurley Lumber Co v Cia San Gerassimo* [1958] AMC 2502.

There can be little doubt that specifications of this type incorporated in a charterparty are intended to have contractual effect and amount to undertakings by the shipowner as to the performance of his vessel.[12] Opinions have, however, been divided as to their precise legal effect. Are they merely factual statements as to the vessel's capabilities at the time of signing the charter, or are they contractual undertakings that the vessel will maintain that capability throughout the period of the charter, or at least until it has been delivered to the charterer? While New York arbitrators generally regard statements as to a vessel's speed and fuel consumption as continuing warranties throughout the charter, British courts have taken a more restrictive view. In the late nineteenth century the Court of Appeal held that a statement as to a vessel's classification was not a continuing warranty, but was only applicable to the time at which the charter was signed.[13] This rather extreme view has been modified more recently in the case of *Cosmos Bulk Transport Inc* v *China National Foreign Trade Transportation Co*[14] where Mocatta J held that a speed warranty referred to the capability of the vessel at the date of delivery under the charterparty. In that case the vessel concerned was capable of steaming at the speed warranted when the charterparty was signed but her capability was subsequently affected as the result of her hull becoming encrusted with molluscs while calling at a tropical port during the completion of a previous charter. In holding the shipowners liable for breach, Mocatta J expressed the view that 'commercial considerations require this description as to the vessel's speed to be applicable as at the date of her delivery, whether or not it is applicable at the date of the charter'.[15] In his opinion similar considerations applied to representations as to fuel consumption and cargo capacity, although he distinguished earlier cases involving classification warranties on the ground that, as changes in classification were outside the control of the parties, the shipowner should only be responsible for the accuracy of statements as to classification at the time they were made.[16] The shipowner is not, however, taken to have guaranteed the accuracy of these specifications throughout the period of the charter, although some oil charter forms contain express undertakings to that effect.[17] In practice, with the notable exception of those relating to speed and fuel consumption, few of the specifications are likely to vary between the signing of the charter and the delivery of the vessel in the absence of some deliberate act on the part of the shipowner as, for example, a decision to sell the vessel which would result in a change of ownership and possibly of flag.

The burden of proving failure to comply with the specifications rests on the charterer and, in the circumstances of ocean transport, proof may be difficult to obtain. Breach of such an undertaking may, in the extreme case, give the charterer a right to cancel the charter,[18] but in practice he will normally be restricted to claiming compensation for the

---

[12] But this presumption may be rebutted where the specification is stated to be made in good faith but 'without guarantee': *The Lipa* [2001] 2 Lloyd's Rep 17 (fuel consumption).

[13] *French* v *Newgass* (1878) 3 CPD 163; see also *Lorentzen* v *White & Co* [1943] 74 LlLR 161 at p 163.

[14] [1978] 1 Lloyd's Rep 53. US courts take the same view that the warranty 'speaks from the time of delivery'. See *Denholm Shipping Co* v *Hedger* [1931] AMC 297.

[15] [1978] 1 Lloyd's Rep at p 64. See also Wilford 3.104 ff.

[16] [1978] 1 Lloyd's Rep at p 62.

[17] For example, Shelltime 3, clause 24.

[18] See *The Aegean Dolphin* [1992] 2 Lloyd's Rep 178.

vessel's failure to meet the relevant specification. According to basic contractual principles, the appropriate measure of damages recoverable would be calculated on the difference between the respective market rates of hire for a vessel with the required contractual specifications and one with the specifications of the vessel delivered. In practice such a test may be extremely difficult to operate and, in any event, may result in the award of a derisory amount of damages. It is, therefore, interesting to note that in the *Cosmos Bulk Transport* case the court adopted an alternative formula to cover breach of a speed warranty, allowing the charterer to treat the vessel as off-hire for the extra time taken on the relevant voyage.[19]

Occasionally alternative remedies for errors in description may be derived from other clauses in the charterparty.[20] Thus the obligation in many charters to prosecute 'all voyages with the utmost dispatch'[21] might provide a remedy for a speed deficiency, while an off-hire clause may specifically cover a reduction in speed caused by 'defect in or breakdown of any part of her hull, machinery or equipment'.[22] An alternative approach to the question of a reduction in speed caused by the fouling of a vessel's bottom is provided by the New York Produce Exchange form which allows the charterer to request the vessel to be taken off-hire into dry dock for cleaning at the owner's expense.[23]

4.3 PERIOD OF HIRE

A specific clause in the charterparty will state the length of the charter period, and this may be expressed in days, months or years, or a combination of them.[24] In recent years it has also become a frequent practice for the period to be expressed as the time required for a specified voyage or a round trip between named ports. For all practical purposes such arrangements are treated as time charters,[25] though the charterer will be in breach if he does not send the vessel on the specified voyage.[26]

It is, however, recognised that a vessel's movements under a time charter cannot be so accurately planned as to ensure that it arrives at the redelivery port on the exact date fixed for the expiration of the charter. Problems inevitably arise, when scheduling the final voyage under the charter, as to whether it will fall short of the time limit (underlap) or exceed it (overlap). The object of the charterer in hiring the vessel is to raise income either by using it in the liner trade or, more frequently, subchartering it for specific voyages. His aim is to design a combination of voyages which will make maximum

---

[19] Cf. *The Al Bida* [1987] 1 Lloyd's Rep 124 (on breach of fuel consumption warranty, damages were assessed on basis of cost of extra fuel consumed).

[20] A remedy may also be barred where the charterparty includes a Paramount Clause incorporating either the Hague or Hague/Visby Rules and the cause of the failure to meet the speed warranty falls within one of the convention exceptions: *The Leonidas* [2001] 1 Lloyd's Rep 533.

[21] For example, Baltime, clause 9.

[22] NYPE 46 form, clause 15. See also Baltime, clause 3.

[23] NYPE 46 clause 21.

[24] When the vessel is redelivered in a different time zone, the period of hire is calculated on the actual time which has elapsed since the charterer took delivery under the charterparty and not by a comparison of the respective local times at the ports of delivery and redelivery: *The Arctic Skou* [1985] 2 Lloyd's Rep 478.

[25] See *The Democritos* [1976] 2 Lloyd's Rep 149.

[26] *Temple SS Co v V/O Sovfracht* [1945] 79 LlLR 1. See also *The Kalma* [1999] 2 Lloyd's Rep 374.

profitable use of the vessel and still return it to the redelivery port on time. Litigation results whenever there are substantial fluctuations in hire rates and is encouraged by the wide variations in the wording of overlap clauses. When market rates are high, the charterer is keen to make use of every minute of the charter period, whereas the owner is anxious to regain possession of the vessel. When market rates have fallen, the position is reversed. Invariably clauses are inserted into the charterparty to provide for this situation and, in examining such clauses, attention must be paid first to the precision with which the time limit is specified and, secondly, to the rate to be paid for the overlap period.

4.3.1 SPECIFIC CLAUSES

Where the charter is for a stated flat period of time, such as 'six months' or 'two years' without qualification, the courts generally take the view that time is not of the essence of the contract and are prepared to imply a reasonable and commercially acceptable margin of error – usually in the region of 4 to 5 per cent, which amounts to two weeks on a 12-month charter.[27] An alternative approach is preferred by US arbitrators who apply the so-called 'overlap/underlap rule' in deciding whether the charterer is entitled to send the vessel on a final voyage under the charter. Under this rule the charterer may, in a choice between underlap and overlap, select whichever of the two alternatives brings the time of redelivery nearer to the end of the charter period.[28]

The insertion of the word 'about' before the charter period, as in the New York Produce Exchange form, is taken as an express incorporation of the otherwise implied reasonable allowance.[29]

In many cases, however, express provision is made for a specified leeway in the charter clause itself. Clauses of this type take a variety of forms such as 'a period of 6 months, 20 days more or less in charterer's option'[30] or 'minimum 11/maximum 13 months'.[31] Such clauses are regarded as fixing the maximum permissible tolerance, and the charterer who redelivers the vessel outside these limits will be regarded as in breach of contract.[32] Alternatively, further leeway may be afforded by an estimate drafted in the form, 'duration about 11/12 months without guarantee'. Liability for any overrun beyond the 12 months will depend on whether or not the original estimate was made in good faith and on reasonable grounds.[33]

---

[27] *Gray* v *Christie* (1889) 5 TLR 577; *The Berge Tasta* [1975] 1 Lloyd's Rep 422.

[28] See *Britain Steamship Co* v *Munson Line* (1929) 31 F 2d 530, *per* Swan CJ at p 531.

[29] *The Democritos* [1976] 2 Lloyd's Rep 149. See also *The Federal Voyager* [1955] AMC 880; *The Adelfoi* [1972] AMC 1742.

[30] *The Dione* [1975] 1 Lloyd's Rep 115.

[31] *The Johnny* [1977] 2 Lloyd's Rep 1.

[32] *The Dione, supra*; *The Johnny, supra*. In a case where the charter period was '6 months, 30 days more or less' and the charterer had an option to extend for a further period of '6 months, 30 days more or less' which he exercised, the court held that he was only entitled to an overall period of twelve months '30 days more or less'. In the opinion of Orr LJ, 'it can hardly have been the intention of the parties that the charterers, in the circumstances of this case, should have the benefit of two tolerance periods in respect of only one delivery'. *The Aspa Maria* [1976] 2 Lloyd's Rep 643 at p 645.

[33] See *The Lendoudis Evangelos II* [1997] 1 Lloyd's Rep 404. See also *Benship International Inc* v *Deemand Shipping Co* (unreported, 14 May 1988).

In contrast it is open to the parties, by express words or by implication, to make time of the essence of the contract. Thus in *Watson* v *Merryweather*,[34] where the charter provided for 'redelivery to owners between 15 and 31 October', it was held that this clause made time of the essence with the result that failure to redeliver the vessel on 31 October amounted to a breach of contract. It is believed that the deliberate deletion of the word 'about' before the stated charter period in the NYPE form will, by implication, have a similar effect.[35]

Where the vessel is returned to the owner before the expiry of the stated minimum period of hire, it would appear that the charterer is not entitled to a refund but must pay the full hire for the agreed period.[36] If such early redelivery be regarded as a breach of contract, then it is arguable that the owner is under a duty to mitigate his loss by rehiring the vessel should this be commercially possible within the balance of the charter period.[37] On the other hand, where the charter specifically provides a tolerance of '30 days more or less', presumably the charterer may redeliver the vessel within this period without having to pay hire for the balance of the charter period.[38]

4.3.2 EFFECT OF OVERLAP

In the event of overlap, the liability of the charterer will vary, depending on whether or not he is in breach of contract. Where redelivery is made within the period of tolerance, and so the charterer is not in breach, he will have to pay for the extra time at the normal charter rate.[39] On the other hand, where redelivery is made outside this period, damages will be assessed in relation to the current market rate of hire.

In recent years the courts have applied the 'legitimate last voyage' test in deciding whether a charterer is in breach of contract. Under this test the charterer is not in breach if, when the vessel was dispatched on its final voyage he could reasonably have expected the voyage to be completed within the charter period plus the permitted leeway. The legitimacy of the voyage is consequently judged at the time of the vessel's departure and not at the time the order was given.[40] Even though the order for the final voyage is legitimate, however, the charterer is still under an obligation to redeliver the vessel on time. Consequently, if supervening events prevent him from doing so, he will be liable for breach of contract even though the failure was due to circumstances beyond his control.[41] In such an event he will remain liable for hire at the charter rate

---

[34] (1913) 12 Asp 353.

[35] See *The London Explorer* [1972] AC 1. See also Wilford 4.29.

[36] *Reindeer SS Co* v *Forslind* [1908] 13 Com Cas 214. See also *Trechman SS Co* v *Munson Line* (1913) 203 F 692.

[37] See Cheshire and Fifoot pp 682 ff. Cf. *White & Carter (Councils) Ltd* v *McGregor* [1962] AC 413.

[38] See *Trechman SS Co* v *Munson Line* (1913) 203 F 692.

[39] See *Britain Steamship Co* v *Munson Line* (1929) 31 F 2d 530. But the charter itself may expressly provide that any overlap is to be paid at the market rate if higher than the charter rate. See Baltime, clause 7.

[40] *The Democritos* [1976] 2 Lloyd's Rep 149; *The Gregos* [1995] 1 Lloyd's Rep 1. In both cases orders were given well in advance but delays intervened, and it was evident, by the time the vessel set sail on the final voyage, that the voyage could not be completed in time. The voyages were held not to be legitimate.

[41] *The Gregos* [1992] 2 Lloyd's Rep 40 at p 43 *per* Evans J. *The Peonia* [1991] 1 Lloyd's Rep 100 at p 116 *per* Bingham LJ; at pp 117–18 *per* Slade LJ disapproving dicta to the contrary of Donaldson J in *The Berge Tasta* [1975] 1 Lloyd's Rep 422 at p 424, and of Kerr J in *The Mareva AS* [1977] 1 Lloyd's Rep 368 at p 378.

until redelivery, together with damages to cover any excess period when the market rate of hire is higher than the charter rate.[42] Charterparty clauses may, however, relieve charterers from such liability and require owners to complete a legitimate last voyage, free of any liability in damages for late delivery, provided the unexpected delay does not involve any fault on the part of the charterer.[43] Such clauses do not confer a right to require the owners to embark on an illegitimate last voyage unless the clause is so worded as to override the charterer's obligation to redeliver the vessel on time. An example of such a clause is provided by clause 18 of the Shelltime 3 form which states that, 'notwithstanding' the stated charter period, 'should the vessel be upon a voyage at the expiry of the period of this charter, charterers shall have the use of this vessel at the same rate and conditions for such extended time as may be necessary for the completion of the round voyage on which she is engaged . . .' The Court of Appeal in *The World Symphony*[44] held that these words clearly overrode the clause specifying the charter period and entitled the charterers at any time during that period to give orders for a final voyage in the knowledge that it would overrun the time otherwise stipulated for re-delivery of the vessel. Throughout the whole of such a voyage the charterer would be entitled to the use of the vessel at the normal charter hire rate.

The contrasting position was outlined by Lord Denning MR in *The Dione*.[45] If the charterer sends the vessel on an illegitimate last voyage, that is, a voyage which it cannot be expected to complete within the charter period, then the shipowner is entitled to refuse that direction and call for alternative instructions for a legitimate last voyage. If the charterer refuses to give it, the shipowner can accept his conduct as a breach going to the root of the contract, fix a fresh charter for the vessel, and sue for damages.[46] If the shipowner accepts the direction and goes on the illegitimate last voyage, he is entitled to be paid, for the excess period, at the current market rate when higher than the charter rate. In *The Dione* the vessel had been chartered for a period of '6 months, 20 days more or less in charterer's option'. When sent on its final voyage the charterers could not reasonably have expected redelivery by the expiry of this period on 28 September. The vessel was eventually redelivered on 7 October. The charterers were held liable to pay hire at the contract rate up to 28 September and at the market rate thereafter.[47]

When assessing damages for breach of contract in such circumstances, the relevant 'market rate' is taken to be the current rate for a time charter of equivalent length to the one breached, and not the rate for a theoretical voyage charter based on the illegitimate last voyage. So in *The Johnny*[48] a vessel had been chartered on a Baltime form for

---

[42] The charterer is under an obligation to pay hire at the charter rate until redelivery even where, on breach, the market rate is lower than the charter rate: *The London Explorer* [1972] AC 1.

[43] *The Peonia* [1991] 1 Lloyd's Rep 100.

[44] [1992] 2 Lloyd's Rep 115. Followed in *Kriti Akti Shipping Co v Petroleo Brasilero* [2004] EWCA 116, where the Court of Appeal held that the instructions for the 'illegitimate' final voyage could even be given during the optional extensions to the basic charter period, e.g. 15 days *more* or less at charterer's option.

[45] [1975] 1 Lloyd's Rep 115 at p 118.

[46] The giving of an illegitimate order does not in itself constitute a repudiatory breach – only if the charterer persists in repeating the order. *The Gregos* [1995] 1 Lloyd's Rep 1 at pp 9–10; *The Peonia* [1991] 1 Lloyd's Rep 100.

[47] See also *The Democritos* [1976] 2 Lloyd's Rep 149; *The Black Falcon* [1991] 1 Lloyd's Rep 77.

[48] [1977] 2 Lloyd's Rep 1.

'minimum 11/maximum 13 months', which period expired on 7 November 1974. On 19 September the vessel was sent on a last voyage to Karachi, as the result of which she was redelivered to the owners 29 days late. In assessing the appropriate market rate for those 29 days[49] the court held that the calculation should be based on the current rate for an 11/13-month time charter and not, as the owners argued, on the current rate for a voyage charter to Karachi.

4.4 PAYMENT FOR HIRE

An express term of the charterparty normally specifies the time, place and frequency of payments of hire, together with the currency in which the hire is to be paid. The amount of hire payable is normally fixed at a certain rate for a specified period of time, ranging from 24 hours to 30 days or a calendar month. Instalments of hire are then expressly made payable every 15 or 30 days. In view of the fact that such instalments of hire are intended to be paid over a lengthy period of time they are particularly susceptible to the risk of inflation and currency fluctuations. In an attempt to minimise these risks it is not uncommon for time charters to include 'currency clauses', providing for a fixed rate of exchange between the currency of payment and other relevant currencies[50] and 'escalator clauses' which enable the hire rate to be adjusted in line with rises in vessel operating costs.[51]

A typical example of a basic hire clause is provided by clause 6 of the Baltime (1939) form:

'The charterers to pay as hire: . . . per 30 days, commencing in accordance with clause 1 until her redelivery to the owners. Payment of hire to be made in cash, in . . . without discount, every 30 days, in advance.'

4.4.1 PAYMENT IN CASH

Time charters invariably require payment of hire to be made in cash. In the view of Brandon J in *The Brimnes*,[52] 'these words must be interpreted against the background of modern commercial practice. So interpreted it seems to me that they cannot mean only payment in dollar bills or other legal tender of the US. They must . . . have a wider meaning, comprehending any commercially recognised method of transferring funds, the result of which is to give the transferee the unconditional right to the immediate use of the funds transferred.' Thus banker's drafts and 'banker's payment slips'[53] appear to have been accepted by commercial usage as equivalent to cash, although opinion appears to be divided as to whether 'payment orders' under the London Currency Settlement

---

[49] Under the Baltime charter any extra time has to be paid for at the market rate if higher than the contract rate, irrespective of whether the charterer is in breach.

[50] For examples see Gram, P, *Chartering Documents*, 2nd edn, 1988, pp 32–3. See also *The Lips* [1987] 1 Lloyd's Rep 131.

[51] See UNCTAD: *Report on Charterparties*, p 61.

[52] [1972] 2 Lloyd's Rep 465 at p 476.

[53] As in *The Georgios C* [1971] 1 Lloyd's Rep 7.

Scheme fall into this category.[54] While the latter are regarded in the banking world as being equivalent to cash, a customer has no right to draw on a payment order until after the document has been processed. On the other hand, the need for internal processing did not deter Lloyd J in *The Afovos*[55] from expressing the view that payment by telex transfer from one bank to another constituted 'payment in cash' for this purpose. He was prepared to hold that 'when payment is made by telex transfer from one bank to another for the account of a customer, the payment is complete when the telex is received and tested by the receiving bank; so that if the owners were to make an enquiry at their bank they would be told "Yes, the money has arrived for your account". It is unnecessary that the funds should have been credited to the owners' account. Still less is it necessary that the owners should have been in a position to transfer the funds out of the account. It is enough that the funds should have been received for the owners' account.'[56] This view is in marked contrast to the attitude adopted by the House of Lords in *The Chikuma*[57] where the monthly instalments of hire had been paid into the owner's bank in Genoa on the due date, but the telex transfer included a 'value date' four days later. Under Italian banking practice this meant that the money in the owner's account did not attract interest until the 'value' date and should the owner have attempted to withdraw it, he could only have done so 'subject to a (probable) liability to pay interest'. In substance it was the equivalent of an overdraft facility, which the bank was bound to make available.[58] In these circumstances the House of Lords had no hesitation in holding that such a payment was not 'equivalent to cash'. Again, in *The Brimnes*[59] itself, where owner and charterer had accounts in the same branch of the same bank, the receipt of a telex instruction from the charterer to transfer the amount of the monthly instalment of hire into the owner's account did not operate as a payment in cash. Not until the appropriate amount had been credited to the owner's account so that he could draw on it was payment effective.

4.4.2 PAYMENT IN ADVANCE

A further requirement is that payment should be made in advance at monthly (or 30 days[60]) or semi-monthly[61] intervals. Payment is therefore required before performance and may be made on or before the date due. Where the due date falls on a Sunday or other non-banking day, then payment must be made not later than the immediately preceding banking day,[62] otherwise the charterer will be in default. On the other hand, the charterer is permitted the full period up to midnight of the day on which the instalment of hire

---

[54] *The Laconia* [1977] 1 Lloyd's Rep 315; see Lord Salmon p 327, Lord Russell p 333, and compare Lord Fraser p 330.
[55] [1980] 2 Lloyd's Rep 469.
[56] *Ibid* at p 473. The decision of Lloyd J in this case was overruled by the Court of Appeal on other grounds. In the House of Lords, Lord Roskill reserved his opinion on this point. [1983] 1 Lloyd's Rep 335 at p 342.
[57] [1981] 1 Lloyd's Rep 371.
[58] *Ibid* at p 376 *per* Lord Bridge.
[59] [1974] 2 Lloyd's Rep 241.
[60] For example, Baltime form, clause 6.
[61] NYPE 46 form, clause 5.
[62] *The Laconia* [1977] 1 Lloyd's Rep 315. Some charters provide that in such circumstances the hire shall be paid on the next banking day, e.g. BP Time 3, clause 8.2.

is due in which to make payment.[63] In the words of Lord Hailsham LC in *The Afovos*,[64] 'I take it to be a general principle of law not requiring authority that where a person under an obligation to do a particular act has to do it on or before a particular date he has the whole of that day to perform his duty.' As the charterer is not in default until the expiry of that period, it is immaterial that payment can only be effected during banking hours. In the view of Griffiths LJ, it is 'far preferable that so important an obligation . . . should be fixed at the certain time of midnight rather than it should depend upon the particular hours of business of a particular bank named in the charterparty which are likely, of course, to vary from country to country and even from bank to bank and to be a ready source of confusion'.[65]

In the absence of provision to the contrary, the final instalment of hire due under the charter is payable in full even though it is clear that the vessel will be redelivered to its owner before the expiry of the relevant period.[66] Any overpayment will be refunded by the owners after the return of the vessel.[67]

The obligation to pay hire punctually in advance is strictly construed and the charterer is in default if he fails to make payment on or before the specified date even though only a matter of hours or minutes is involved. Nor is it material that the default was not intentional. 'Apart from some special circumstances excusing performance, it is enough to constitute default that payment has not in fact been made; neither deliberate non-performance nor negligence in performing the contract is required.'[68]

4.5 THE OFF-HIRE CLAUSE

Standard forms of time charter invariably include a clause providing that hire is not payable by the charterer during any period when full use of the vessel is not available to him because of an accident or deficiency falling within what might broadly be termed the shipowner's sphere of responsibility. The precise events which take the vessel off-hire and the period for which hire is not payable vary with each form of charter and are dependent on the wording of the relevant off-hire clause. A typical example is provided by clause 11A of the Baltime form:

'In the event of drydocking or other necessary measures to maintain the efficiency of the vessel, deficiency of men or owner's stores, breakdown of machinery, damage to hull or other accident, either hindering or preventing the working of the vessel and continuing for more than twenty-four consecutive hours, no hire to be paid in respect of any time lost thereby during the period in which the vessel is unable to perform the service immediately required. Any hire paid in advance to be adjusted accordingly.'

---

[63] *Startup* v *MacDonald* (1843) 6 Man & G 593; *The Mihalios Xilas* [1979] 2 Lloyd's Rep 303; *The Afovos* [1983] 1 Lloyd's Rep 335.

[64] [1983] 1 Lloyd's Rep at p 340.

[65] *The Afovos* [1982] 1 Lloyd's Rep 562 at p 567.

[66] *Tonnelier* v *Smith* (1897) 2 Com Cas 258. Cf. NYPE 46 clause 5 which provides 'for the last half month or part of the same the approximate amount of hire, and should same not cover the actual time, hire is to be paid for the balance day by day as it becomes due, if so required by owners, unless bank guarantee or deposit is made by the charterers'.

[67] *Stewart* v *Van Ommeren* [1918] 2 KB 560.

[68] *Per* Lord Porter in *Tankexpress* v *Compagnie Financière Belge des Petroles* (1948) 82 LlLRep 43 at p 51.

Normally the range of events which will take a vessel off-hire are listed in an off-hire clause of this type.[69] Occasionally, however, a series of mini off-hire clauses covering particular events such as speed deficiency or dry-docking, are scattered throughout the charterparty and these may cause inconsistencies and apparent contradictions unless clearly cross-referenced to the main off-hire clause. The operation of the standard clause is triggered merely by the occurrence of one of the specified events irrespective of any fault on the part of the shipowner. Being a 'no fault' clause, its provisions are strictly construed by the courts, and the burden of proof rests firmly with the charterer when seeking a suspension of the hire. In the words of Bucknill LJ, 'I think he must bring himself clearly within the exceptions. If there is a doubt as to what the words mean, then I think those words must be read in favour of the owners because the charterer is attempting to cut down the owners' right to hire.'[70] On the other hand, the operation of the clause is unaffected by exceptions or *force majeure* clauses in the charterparty.[71] There is some authority for suggesting that the clause will not operate where the specified event results from a breach of contract by the charterer[72] though, even if the vessel did go off-hire in such an event, presumably the owner could include the loss of hire in his claim for damages for breach.

The standard off-hire clause frequently concludes with the phrase, 'or by any other cause preventing the full working of the vessel'.[73] Authority restricts such 'other causes' to those which directly affect the efficient running of the vessel, and excludes external events which, while delaying performance of the contract, do not relate to the physical condition of the vessel or its crew. Thus delays caused respectively by an obstruction on the Yangtse river,[74] or by a vessel too heavily loaded for entry to the Panama canal,[75] were not caught by the clause; while delay in obtaining free pratique, caused by the suspicion that a member of the crew was suffering from typhus, was sufficiently closely related to the vessel's performance to take it off-hire.[76] The general view is that the phrase 'any other cause' is not caught by the *eiusdem generis* rule, since in the majority of cases it would not be possible to isolate a distinct genus from the various items listed in the clause. In any event, the rule would clearly be inoperative in the frequent case where the clause is amended to read 'any other cause whatsoever'.[77] It also appears to be restricted to fortuitous events, so as not to include those naturally resulting from the use of the vessel.[78]

---

[69] The clause will operate even though the incident causing the time loss occurred before the beginning of the charter period: *The Apollonius* [1978] 1 Lloyd's Rep 53.

[70] *Royal Greek Government v Minister of Transport* (1948) 82 LlLR 196 at p 199. Cf. where delay caused by charterer's fault excepted: *The Berge Sund* [1993] 2 Lloyd's Rep 453.

[71] *Meling v Minos Shipping Co* [1972] 1 Lloyd's Rep 458.

[72] See *Nourse v Elder, Dempster* (1922) 13 LlLR 197; *Lensen v Anglo-Soviet Shipping Co* (1935) 52 LlLR 141. The charter may provide that the off-hire clause is excluded by 'fault of charterer'. See *The Berge Sund* [1993] 2 Lloyd's Rep 453, where it was held that 'fault' required proof of conscious wrongdoing or negligence on the part of the charterer.

[73] For example, NYPE 1946 15; BP Time 3, clause 19.1.4.

[74] *Court Line v Dant* (1939) 44 Com Cas 345. See also *The Mareva AS* [1977] 1 Lloyd's Rep 368.

[75] *The Aquacharm* [1982] 1 Lloyd's Rep 7. See also *The Laconian Confidence* [1997] 1 Lloyd's Rep 139 (refusal of port authorities to allow vessel to work).

[76] *The Apollo* [1978] 1 Lloyd's Rep 200.

[77] See *The Roachbank* [1987] 2 Lloyd's Rep 498.

[78] *The Rijn* [1981] 2 Lloyd's Rep 267.

4.5.1 PERIOD OF OFF-HIRE

In normal circumstances the charterer will be unable to rely on the clause unless he is deprived of the use of the vessel by the occurrence of one of the specified events. Thus, while an engine breakdown at sea might take the vessel off-hire, it would not have the same effect if it occurred while the vessel was discharging in port, provided that the vessel was otherwise efficient for carrying out that operation. Similarly, the installation of new equipment by the owner at the charterer's request while the vessel was waiting for a berth, did not activate the off-hire clause since the charterer was not, in the circumstances, deprived of the use of the vessel.[79] Everything depends, however, on the precise wording of the clause and the strict standards of interpretation adopted by the courts have resulted in superficially similarly drafted clauses producing radically different effects.

The majority of standard off-hire clauses fall into one of two distinct categories: they are either 'period' or 'net loss of time' clauses. The 'period clause' is distinguished by the fact that it designates the start and end of any period for which hire is suspended by linking them to the occurrence of specified events. Thus, while any one of a selection of events (e.g. deficiency of men or stores, drydocking etc.) might activate the clause, it would normally only cease to operate when the vessel was restored to a fully efficient state, capable of providing the service immediately required of it.[80] Restoration of partial efficiency of the vessel is generally insufficient to satisfy this requirement.[81] Such a clause involves little difficulty in application, provided that the occurrence of the specified events is readily ascertainable.[82] In a case where time was lost as the result of defective loading equipment, it was held that the operation of a 'period clause' was not limited to working hours, but that no hire was payable for the entire time the charterers were deprived of the use of the equipment and that it was immaterial that loading would not have taken place because of strikes, bad weather or unavailability of cargo.[83]

The 'net loss of time clause' on the other hand, merely provides that hire is not payable for time lost as the result of the occurrence of one of the specified events. In the words of clause 11A of the Baltime form, 'no hire to be paid in respect of any time lost thereby during the period in which the vessel is unable to perform the service immediately required'.[84]

Prima facie such wording should mean that hire does not cease to be payable merely on the occurrence of one of the specified events but only if, and to the extent that, time is lost as a result. This is particularly important in the case of partial efficiency of a vessel

---

[79] *Sea & Land Securities Ltd* v *Dickinson & Co Ltd* [1942] 2 KB 65.
[80] So in *Tynedale* v *Anglo-Soviet Shipping Co* (1936) 41 Com Cas 206 the relevant clause provided that 'hire to cease from commencement of such loss of time until steamer is again in efficient state to resume service'.
[81] See *Hogarth* v *Miller* [1891] AC 48.
[82] See *The Bridgestone Maru (No 3)* [1985] 2 Lloyd's Rep 62 where Hirst J strongly favoured construing off-hire clauses as 'period' clauses 'to avoid calculating minutiae of lost time under the [net loss of time] approach' (at p 84).
[83] *The HR Macmillan* [1974] 1 Lloyd's Rep 311.
[84] See also NYPE (1946) clause 15: 'the payment of hire shall cease for the time thereby lost'. For an example of the practical application of this clause, see *The Ira* [1995] 1 Lloyd's Rep 103.

as, for example, in the event of the breakdown of one of several loading cranes,[85] or on the discovery of a speed deficiency.[86]

Under the 'period' type of off-hire clause, the obligation to pay hire will resume once the vessel becomes efficient and full use is restored to the charterer. Consequently, where a vessel has been compelled to deviate for repairs, the expense of making up lost ground once the repairs have been completed will fall on the charterer in the absence of provision to the contrary in the charterparty.[87] A similar result apparently follows in English law in the case of the 'net time lost' type of clause, despite the fact that the time taken to make up lost ground would appear to fall within the concept of 'any time lost' as the result of the occurrence of the specified event.[88] Indeed, recent cases would suggest the existence of a wider principle preventing the deduction of any time lost under such a clause, once the full operating efficiency of the vessel has been restored. Thus in *The Marika M*[89] where a vessel went off-hire on running aground, it was held that the charterer could not deduct time lost waiting for a berth after she had been refloated, even though it was the direct consequence of the original grounding. Express provision for such contingencies can, of course, be made in the off-hire clause itself. So clause 20 of the Intertanktime 80 form provides that 'hire shall cease to be payable from the commencement of such deviation [for repairs] until the time when the vessel is again ready to resume her service from a position not less favourable to charterers than that at which the deviation commenced'.[90]

4.5.2 EFFECTS OF THE OPERATION OF THE OFF-HIRE CLAUSE

Many off-hire clauses include a *de minimis* provision and are not activated until a period of 24 or 48 hours has elapsed from the occurrence of the specified event.[91] Once the clause operates, however, all time lost will count, including the initial 24 or 48 hours.[92] In the absence of provision to the contrary, the suspension of the obligation to pay hire under this clause does not relieve the charterer of his other obligations arising under the charterparty during that period, for example his obligation to pay for bunkers[93] or other port services during the off-hire period, or to pay the crew for

---

[85] See Lord Denning MR in *The HR Macmillan* [1974] 1 Lloyd's Rep 311 at p 314.

[86] *The Apollonius* [1978] 1 Lloyd's Rep 43.

[87] *Smailes* v *Evans* [1917] 2 KB 54.

[88] *Vogemann* v *Zanzibar* (1902) 7 Com Cas 254; see also Lord Roche in *Tynedale* v *Anglo-Soviet Shipping Co* (1936) 41 Com Cas 206 at p 220.

[89] [1981] 2 Lloyd's Rep 622. See also *The Pythia* [1982] 2 Lloyd's Rep 160. Cf. the position in the US where such time would appear to be deductible: *The Chris* SMA No 199 (Arb at NY 1958); *The Chrysanthi GL* SMA No 1417 (Arb at NY 1980).

[90] See also Shelltime 4, clause 21; Texacotime 2, clause 9; BP Time 3, clause 19.2. See *The Trade Nomad* [1998] 1 Lloyd's Rep 57.

[91] Loss of time for this period must be continuous: *The Fina Samco* [1994] 1 Lloyd's Rep 153. See also BP Time 3, clause 19.1.

[92] Texacotime 2, clause 9, provides: 'hire shall cease to be due or payable from the commencement of such loss of time'. Some charters require no qualifying time (e.g. Shelltime 4, clause 21), while others have cumulative clauses providing for a recurrent series of short delays (e.g. STB Time, clause 11(b)).

[93] *Arild* v *Hovrani* [1923] 2 KB 141.

overtime.[94] Occasionally the clause will give the charterer an option to extend the charter for an equivalent period[95] but, since such a provision can be unfair to owners on a rising market or where subsequent charters have already been arranged, it is more normal practice to require the off-hire period to be counted as part of the basic charter term.[96] Should the off-hire event arise from breach of an owner's warranty, or some other act or neglect not covered by the exceptions, then the charterers may also have a claim for damages in addition to their right to suspend payment of hire.[97]

4.6 DEDUCTIONS FROM HIRE

A charterer may be entitled to an overall adjustment of hire for a variety of reasons including, *inter alia*, advances for disbursements made on the shipowner's behalf, deductions for off-hire periods, allowances for speed deficiency or other failure of the vessel to meet charter specifications, or compensation for damage to cargo. In such circumstances most charterers prefer self-help in the form of making appropriate deductions from future payments of hire rather than the danger of running the risk of having to collect an arbitration award from an insolvent owner, or from a single ship-owning company with its head office in a distant country. Conversely, shipowners resist an interruption to their cash flow.

Certain charters make express provision for the charterer to make deductions from future payments of hire for disbursements made on the owners' behalf or for periods of off-hire.[98] Some charters do not allow deductions in the event of a disputed claim,[99] while others suspend the obligation to pay instalments of hire which fall due at a time when the vessel is off-hire.[100]

Where no express right to deduct is given in the charter, British courts have been reluctant to allow self-help. It has long been established that a claim in respect of cargo cannot be asserted by way of deduction from freight,[101] and the initial reaction of the courts was to extend a similar rule to deductions from hire. So Donaldson J in *Seven Seas Transportation* v *Atlantic Shipping*[102] held that there was no general equitable right of set-off for time lost under an off-hire clause. In his view, arguments against the existence of such a right to deduct centred on the problem which would result should the shipowner deny liability or dispute the amount of the claim. Any exercise of a right to deduct in such circumstances would involve the risk of the vessel being withdrawn

---

[94] *Court Line Ltd* v *Finelvet* [1966] 1 Lloyd's Rep 683. Some charters do, however, expressly relieve the charterer of such obligations during an off-hire period, e.g. Texacotime 2, clause 9.

[95] For example, Texacotime 2, clause 12; BP Time 3, clause 19.3.

[96] For example, Intertanktime 80, clause 20.

[97] See Lord Denning MR in *HR Macmillan* [1974] 1 Lloyd's Rep 311 at p 314. See also Kerr J in *The Democritos* [1975] 1 Lloyd's Rep 380 at p 401.

[98] For example, Shelltime 4, clause 9; Texacotime 2, clause 7; Intertanktime 80, clause 3.

[99] Fonasbatime, clause 16.

[100] Standtime, clause 10. See also *The Lutetian* [1982] 2 Lloyd's Rep 140, where Bingham J held that clause 15 of the NYPE 46 form had the same effect. But the charterer is not entitled to make deductions in advance for prospective periods of off-hire. *The Noto* [1979] AMC 116.

[101] *The Brede* [1973] 2 Lloyd's Rep 333; *The Aries* [1977] 1 Lloyd's Rep 334.

[102] [1975] 2 Lloyd's Rep 188.

for non-payment of hire, should the claim later prove to be unjustified in whole or in part.[103] A radically different approach, however, was advocated by Parker J in *The Teno*[104] who expressed the opinion that 'it would be grossly unjust to allow an owner to recover hire in respect of a period during which he had, in breach of contract, failed to provide that for which the hire was payable'. Accordingly, he favoured the existence of an equitable right of set-off under which the charterer was entitled to make deductions from future payments of hire to cover disbursements made on the owner's behalf and to cover periods while the vessel was off-hire due to a breakdown of machinery. Moreover, he held that the right of set-off extended not only to total but also to partial withdrawal of the use of the ship.

These conflicting views were considered by the Court of Appeal in *The Nanfri*[105] where the charterers had made a deduction in paying an instalment of hire for an earlier alleged loss of speed by the chartered vessel. In the view of Lord Denning MR, the line of authority holding that deductions from freight were not permissible was not applicable to payment of hire under a time charter. 'So different are the two concepts that I do not think the law as to "freight" can be applied indiscriminately to "hire".'[106] A clear distinction had to be drawn between a defensive right of set-off, and a cross-claim or counter claim. For 'it is not every cross-claim which can be deducted. It is only cross-claims that arise out of the same transaction or are closely connected with it. And it is only cross-claims which go directly to impeach the plaintiff's demand, that is, so closely connected with his demands that it would be manifestly unjust to allow him to enforce payment without taking into account the cross-claim.'[107] Accordingly, on the facts of the case under review, Lord Denning was of the opinion that 'if the shipowner wrongly and in breach of contract deprives the charterer for a time of the use of the vessel, the charterer can deduct a sum equivalent to the hire for the time so lost'.

While this decision has not yet been reviewed by the House of Lords, the members of which have recently tended to apply an increasingly strict interpretation to charter clauses,[108] its underlying philosophy has been endorsed by the lower courts.[109] In the view of Mocatta J the decision is more 'in accord with what commercial considerations demand'.[110] Nevertheless, the operation of the set-off is limited to claims 'which go directly to impeach the plaintiff's demand' for hire and the better view is that it does not extend to claims for cargo damage,[111] or to other claims which do not involve loss

---

[103] See *The Mihalios Xilas* [1979] 2 Lloyd's Rep 303. On the subject of the right to withdraw for non-payment of hire, see *infra* at pp 102 ff.

[104] [1977] 2 Lloyd's Rep 289 at p 296.

[105] [1978] 2 Lloyd's Rep 132. When the case ultimately went to the Lords, [1979] 1 Lloyd's Rep 201, it was decided on other grounds without any reference to the point at issue.

[106] [1978] 2 Lloyd's Rep 132 at p 139.

[107] *Ibid* at p 140. For the attitude of the US courts to an alleged implied right to deduct, see *The Miriam* [1952] AMC 1625.

[108] See e.g. *infra* at pp 103, 106–7. In particular, the House of Lords has rejected the introduction of equitable principles of construction. See *The Scaptrade* [1983] 2 Lloyd's Rep 253.

[109] See *The Aliakmon Progress* [1978] 2 Lloyd's Rep 499; *Santiren Shipping Ltd* v *Unimarine* [1981] 1 Lloyd's Rep 159; *The Kostas Melas* {1981] 1 Lloyd's Rep 18.

[110] *Santiren Shipping Ltd* v *Unimarine* [1981] 1 Lloyd's Rep 159 at p 164.

[111] See *per* Lord Denning MR in *The Nanfri* [1978] 2 Lloyd's Rep at p 140. A similar view is taken by US courts: see *The Uranus* [1977] AMC 586.

of use of the vessel.[112] Nor is the charterer entitled to deduct for claims in excess of the amount of hire otherwise payable for the period during which the required services were not provided.[113] The courts have also recognised that it would be unreasonable to expose the charterer to the risk of withdrawal of the vessel should he make a marginal error in calculating the precise amount to be deducted. All that is required is a 'reasonable assessment made in good faith. . . . Then the actual figures can be ascertained later: either by agreement between the parties or, failing agreement, by arbitration. . . . If it subsequently turns out that he has deducted too much, the shipowner can of course recover the balance. But that is all.'[114] To hold otherwise would render valueless the express right to deduct conferred by many off-hire clauses.

4.7 RIGHT TO WITHDRAW VESSEL FOR NON-PAYMENT OF HIRE

At common law time is not of the essence of the contract and a shipowner cannot repudiate the charterparty and withdraw his vessel for late payment of an instalment of hire unless the circumstances show a clear intention on the part of the charterer not to perform the contract as, for example, by an express repudiation of his obligations or by repeated non-payment.[115] However, the terms of the charterparty invariably provide an express contractual right of withdrawal, an example of which is provided by clause 6 of the Baltime form:

> 'In default of payment the Owners to have the right of withdrawing the Vessel from the service of the Charterers, without noting any protest and without interference by any court or any other formality whatsoever and without prejudice to any claim the Owners may have on the Charterers under the Charter.'

Clause 5 of the New York Produce Exchange form makes similar provision for self help on the part of the shipowner 'failing the punctual and regular payment of the hire'.[116] The original object of such clauses was to enable pressure to be exerted on a persistent defaulter or to recover possession of the vessel before becoming embroiled in proceedings attending the bankruptcy of an impecunious charterer. In periods of fluctuating market rates of hire, these clauses have afforded a lifeline to the owner involved in a long-term charter at fixed rates. By invoking the clause and withdrawing the vessel on

---

[112] *The Aliakmon Progress* [1978] 2 Lloyd's Rep 499 (loss of cargo due to vessel going off-hire); *The Leon* [1985] 2 Lloyd's Rep 470 (misappropriation of bunkers by master and failure to keep accurate logs). See also Wilford 16.25 ff.

[113] See *The Aditya Vaibav* [1991] 1 Lloyd's Rep 573.

[114] *Per* Lord Denning MR in *The Nanfri* [1978] 2 Lloyd's Rep at p 141. See also *Santiren Shipping Ltd* v *Unimarine* [1981] 1 Lloyd's Rep 159. Cf. *The Kostas Melas* [1981] 1 Lloyd's Rep 18 where Robert Goff J held the deductions excessive.

[115] See *Cochin Refineries* v *Triton Shipping* [1978] AMC 444.

[116] Clause 5 of NYPE 46 also permits withdrawal 'on any breach of this charter'. This phrase is construed restrictively by the courts: see *The Antaios (No 2)* [1984] 2 Lloyd's Rep 235 at p 241, where Lord Diplock expressed the view that it only applied to repudiatory breaches. See also *The Athos* [1983] 1 Lloyd's Rep 127. The NYPE 93 form clause 11A now substitutes 'on any fundamental breach whatsoever of this charterparty'.

any default in payment of hire, he has been enabled to recharter the vessel at current market rates even, in many instances, by offering it back to the original charterer. In the inimitable prose of Lord Denning MR,[117] 'when market rates are rising, the shipowners keep close watch on payments of hire. If the charterer makes a slip of any kind – a few minutes too late or a few dollars too little – the shipowners jump on him like a ton of bricks. They give notice of withdrawal and demand thenceforward full payment of hire at the top market rate. Very rarely is the vessel actually withdrawn. Arrangements are made by which she continues in the service of the charterer just as if nothing had happened. Then there is a contest before the arbitrators or in the courts. It is as to whether the notice of withdrawal was justified or not.' Although such conduct is entirely without merit, the courts 'do not suggest . . . that the owners [are] guilty of any sharp practice . . . it [is] just a matter of business – a matter of very hard business'.[118]

4.7.1 REQUIREMENTS FOR EXERCISE OF RIGHT OF WITHDRAWAL

The charterer must be in default by failing to pay an instalment of hire, or failing to pay it on time. He will be equally in default if only part payment is made on the date due,[119] hence the importance of deciding whether or not he has an implied right to make deductions in specified events. Payments cannot satisfy the requirements of being 'punctual' or made 'in advance' unless they are effected on or before the specified date. In cases where an instalment of hire falls due on a day when banks are closed, payment must be effected before the close of trading on the immediately preceding day of business.[120] These requirements are strictly construed and it is immaterial whether late payment involves a matter of days or merely hours. A late tender of hire made before the shipowner has exercised his right to withdraw the vessel will not rectify the default unless the shipowner is willing to accept such payment as if made on time and waive the breach. A decision of the Court of Appeal to the contrary in *The Georgios C*[121] was expressly overruled by the Lords in *The Laconia*.[122] Clear notice of withdrawal of the vessel must be given to the charterers or their agents. Notice to the master of the chartered vessel is not sufficient.[123] 'No particular form of words or notice is required, but the charterers must be informed that the owner is treating the non-payment of hire as having terminated the charter party.'[124]

---

[117] *The Tropwind* [1982] 1 Lloyd's Rep 232 at p 234.

[118] *Per* Griffiths LJ in *The Afovos* [1982] 1 Lloyd's Rep 562 at p 566.

[119] See *The Mihalios Xilas* [1979] 2 Lloyd's Rep 303.

[120] *The Laconia* [1977] 1 Lloyd's Rep 315.

[121] [1971] 1 All ER 193. Lord Denning MR at p 197 expressed the view that the phrase 'in default of payment' in clause 6 of the Baltime form had to be construed as 'in default of payment and so long as the default continues'.

[122] [1977] 1 Lloyd's Rep 315. The law of the United States with respect to the withdrawal clause is more liberally applied and New York arbitrators regard withdrawal as a drastic remedy which they will rarely sanction unless the charterer has been placed on notice, or otherwise warned, that failure to make prompt payment will result in withdrawal. See *The Noto* [1979] AMC 116 and, on the subject generally, Healy, NJ, Jr, 'Termination of Charter Parties', 49 *Tulane Law Review* 845 at p 851.

[123] *The Georgios C* [1971] 1 Lloyd's Rep 7.

[124] Donaldson J in *The Aegnoussiotis* [1977] 1 Lloyd's Rep 268 at p 275.

4.7.2 WAIVER OF RIGHT TO WITHDRAW

The shipowner may lose his right of withdrawal by waiver of the breach. But to constitute waiver his conduct must amount to a clear and unequivocal act showing acceptance of late payment as though it had been made on time or such a delay in refusing the late tender of payment as might reasonably cause the charterer to believe that it had been accepted.[125] Receipt of late payment by an agent will not amount to waiver by the shipowner unless the agent has express authority to take such decisions on the shipowner's behalf. Thus in *The Laconia*, where payment of hire was due on a Sunday, the charterer's bankers delivered by hand to the shipowner's bank at 3 p.m. the following day a payment order for the appropriate sum under the London Currency Settlement Scheme. The bankers took delivery of the payment order over the counter but, on subsequently informing the shipowners of its receipt, were immediately instructed to refuse the money and return it to the charterer's bank. In these circumstances the House of Lords held that the shipowners were still entitled to withdraw the vessel since, in taking delivery of the payment order, their bankers were merely performing a ministerial act and had no authority to make business decisions on behalf of their principals as to the continuance or otherwise of the charterparty. 'Certainly it was not within the bankers' express or implied authority to make commercial decisions on behalf of their customers by accepting or rejecting late payments of hire without taking instructions. They did take instructions and were told to reject the payment. They did so and returned it to the charterers on the following day which in any view must have been within a reasonable time.'[126]

Acceptance of part of the hire on or before the date due does not amount to a waiver of the owner's right to withdraw the vessel if the balance of the hire is not paid by midnight on the due date. In *The Mihalios Xilas*[127] the charterers had the right, on payment of the final month's hire under the charterparty, to deduct bunker cost and owner's disbursements. In the erroneous belief that the ninth month was the final month of the charterparty, the charterer indicated his intention of deducting $31,000 from the instalment due on 22 March, though without disclosing the basis on which the deductions had been calculated. On 20 March the shipowners objected to the proposed deductions, but did not instruct their bankers to refuse payment of the balance of the hire, which was made on 21 March. The following day the shipowners were supplied with details of the deductions from which it was evident that the charterers were treating the ninth month as the last month of the charterparty. The shipowners then requested further details and supporting vouchers which were not supplied by the charterers. Eventually the owners withdrew the vessel on 26 March, whereupon the charterers claimed damages for wrongful withdrawal, arguing that by accepting the payment tendered on 21 March the owners had waived their right to withdraw the vessel. The House of Lords held that acceptance of part of the hire on 21 March did not amount to a waiver since, as the charterer had at least until the end of trading on 22 March in which to make payment, there was no default of payment for the owner to waive at that stage. As

---

[125] See Lord Wilberforce in *The Laconia* [1977] 1 Lloyd's Rep at p 320.
[126] *Ibid* at p 326, *per* Lord Salmon.
[127] [1979] 2 Lloyd's Rep 303.

to the delay of four days before withdrawing the vessel, Lord Diplock took the view that 'Waiver requires knowledge, and I agree with the umpire that the owners were entitled to a reasonable time to make enquiries of the charterers and of the master of the vessel (as they did) with a view to ascertaining whether [the right to withdraw the vessel under clause 7 had accrued] before electing whether to withdraw or not. That being so, his finding that from 21 March to noon on 26 March was a reasonable time to do so is one of fact which cannot be disturbed.'[128] Nor did the retention of the advance payment of hire during this period amount to an unequivocal act of waiver.[129]

Subsequent cases have suggested that a delay of from four to five days after the failure to make payment on the due date is not unreasonable and will not constitute waiver of the breach. In the view of Lloyd J in *The Scaptrade*,[130] 'what is the shortest time reasonably necessary will depend upon all the circumstances of the case. In some cases it will be reasonable for the owners to take time to consider their position, as withdrawal under a time charter is a serious step not lightly to be undertaken. In other cases it may be reasonable for owners to seek legal advice . . . it would be quite wrong in cases of this kind to require owners to grasp at the first opportunity to withdraw or to hold that they act at their peril by giving charterers two or three days grace.'

4.7.3 POSSIBLE BARS TO EXERCISE OF THE RIGHT OF WITHDRAWAL

There is authority to suggest that repeated failure by a shipowner to insist on his strict legal rights in respect of payment of instalments of hire might establish a course of conduct which would prevent him from exercising his right of withdrawal in the event of a subsequent breach by the charterer, at least until the shipowner had given adequate warning of his intention to revert to his strict legal rights on future occasions.

In *Tankexpress* v *Compagnie Financière Belge des Petroles*[131] a seven-year time charter required hire to be paid in cash, monthly in advance, with the proviso that the owners could withdraw the vessel 'in default of such payment'. In fact, from the outset, the charterers had regularly posted a cheque for the relevant amount, addressed to the owner's bank in London, two days before the hire was due. The owners had accepted this mode of payment for two years without complaint but, when payment of the September 1939 instalment arrived late having been delayed in the post by the outbreak of war, they sought to exercise their right to withdraw the vessel. The House of Lords held that they were not entitled to do so. In the words of Lord Porter, 'In these circumstances I think the true inference to be drawn is that the method of performance of the contract was varied by an arrangement for payment to Hambros bank by cheque posted at such time as would in the ordinary course of post reach London on the 27th of the month . . . No doubt the owners could at any time have insisted upon a strict performance of the contract after due notice, but they were not, in my view, entitled suddenly

---

128 *Ibid* at p 307.
129 See Lord Scarman, *ibid* at p 316.
130 [1981] 2 Lloyd's Rep 425 at p 429; see also *The Balder London* [1980] 2 Lloyd's Rep 489.
131 (1948) 82 LlLR 43.

to vary the accepted mode of performance without first notifying the charterers in time to enable them to perform the contract in the manner demanded.'[132] On the other hand, it would appear that a distinction has to be drawn between such an 'accepted mode of performance' and the situation where the shipowner accepts late payment on a number of occasions without complaint. In the latter case such conduct will rarely constitute an unequivocal representation that the right to withdraw will not be exercised on a future occasion in the event of a late payment of hire. So in *The Scaptrade*[133] the Court of Appeal held that such an estoppel did not arise when only six of the previous 22 instalments had been paid on time. In the opinion of Robert Goff LJ, 'it is not at all easy to infer, from the mere fact that late payments had been accepted in the past by the owners without protest, an unequivocal representation by them not to exercise their strict legal right of withdrawal in the event of late payment by the charterers of a subsequent instalment of hire – if only because the circumstances prevailing at the time when the earlier late payments were accepted may not be the same as those prevailing in the future'.[134]

For a while it was thought that the equitable doctrine of relief against forfeiture might be invoked to mitigate the effects of a strict application of the withdrawal clause. However, attempts to enlist the aid of the doctrine found little support in *The Laconia*. In the Court of Appeal Lord Denning MR commented that 'on reflection I do not think that equity would have intervened in a commercial case of this kind. It would have left the parties to have their rights determined by law. In commercial matters certainty is of the essence, as well as time and speed, and equity provides none of these.'[135] In the House of Lords, Lord Wilberforce took a similar view, pointing to the clear distinction between contracts of charterparty and leases of land, in the context of which the equitable doctrine had been developed.[136] Lord Simon could, however, 'conceive of circumstances where failure to make punctual payment might be due to some pure accident and might occasion no real detriment to the owners whereas withdrawal might cause very heavy loss to the charterers; so that reasonable commercial people might think it unconscionable for the owners to take advantage of the failure'.[137] Even so, he admitted that such cases would be extremely rare. This possible loophole now appears to have been finally closed by the decision in *The Scaptrade* where it was held that the courts had no jurisdiction to grant equitable relief in such cases. The judgment of Robert Goff LJ in the Court of Appeal epitomises the current attitude of the courts to the interpretation of charterparty clauses:

> 'It is of the utmost importance in commercial transactions that if any particular event occurs which may affect the parties' respective rights under a commercial contract, they should know where they stand. The Court should so far as possible desist from placing obstacles in the way of either party ascertaining his legal position, if necessary with the aid of advice from a

---

[132] *Ibid* at pp 51–2.
[133] [1983] 1 Lloyd's Rep 146.
[134] *Ibid* at p 150. This point was not argued when the case went on appeal to the House of Lords: [1983] 2 Lloyd's Rep 253.
[135] [1976] 1 Lloyd's Rep at p 400.
[136] [1977] 1 Lloyd's Rep at p 319.
[137] *Ibid* at p 322.

qualified lawyer: because it may be commercially desirable for action to be taken without delay, action which may be irrecoverable and which may have far-reaching consequences. . . . The policy which favours certainty in commercial transactions is so antipathetic to the form of equitable intervention invoked by the charterers in the present case that we do not think it would be right to extend that jurisdiction to relieve time charterers from the consequences of withdrawal. We consider that the mere existence of such a jurisdiction would constitute an undesirable fetter upon the exercise by parties of their contractual rights under a commercial transaction of this kind . . . for the mere possibility that it may be exercised can produce uncertainty, disputes and litigation.[138]

The reluctance of the courts to invoke equitable relief in such cases stems partly from the fact that a number of 'anti-technicality clauses' are available for inclusion in a charterparty if the parties so desire. These clauses normally provide that, in the event of default in payment of hire, the shipowner must give specific notice to the charterer before invoking the withdrawal clause. So in *The Libyaville*[139] a clause in the charterparty provided that 'where there is any failure to make punctual and regular payment . . . Charterers shall be given by Owners two banking working days' written notice to rectify the failure'.[140] These anti-technicality clauses have, in their turn, been equally strictly applied by the courts. Thus an enquiry as to the reason for failure to pay an instalment of hire has been held not to constitute notice of intention to exercise the right of withdrawal.[141] Again, it has been held that notice under such a clause cannot be given until after midnight on the day an instalment of hire is due, with the result that notice given before midnight but after the banks had closed on the due date was ineffective.[142] The practical reasons behind the strict adherence to the terms of an anti-technicality clause were explained by Griffiths LJ in *The Afovos*.[143] 'Payments of [hire] are normally made by telex through a number of banks and it may well be that, through some slip up, the money does not arrive in the owner's account as quickly as the charterer has a right to expect. Once the charterer has instructed his bank to pay he has no further control over the payment which is now in the banking chain . . . therefore . . . charterers do require to be told by the owners that payment has not been received. There is little point in telling the charterer that payment has not been received until the time for payment has expired; if the charterer is told that payment has not been received before the time for payment has expired, he may not realise the urgency of the matter and continue to expect that the payment will be credited in time. On the other hand, if he is told after the

138 [1983] 1 Lloyd's Rep at pp 153–4. Lord Diplock, in expressly adopting this quotation from Robert Goff LJ as part of his judgment, stressed the importance of putting ' "a matter of such practical importance" to the shipping world . . . beyond reach of future challenge': [1983] 2 Lloyd's Rep 253 at p 256. In his view, granting an injunction restraining the owner from exercising his rights of withdrawal was tantamount to awarding a decree for specific performance of a contract to render services.

139 [1975] 1 Lloyd's Rep 537.

140 See also Texacotime 2, clause 7 (10 days' notice); STB Time, clause 3(t) (10 days); Intertanktime 80 (6 days); NYPE 93, clause 11(b) (grace period left blank).

141 *The Rio Sun* [1982] 1 Lloyd's Rep 404. See also *The Pamela* [1995] 2 Lloyd's Rep 249.

142 *The Afovos* [1983] 1 Lloyd's Rep 335. Such notice, sent by telex, has been held to take effect not from the time of dispatch, but only from the time of receipt during normal office hours. *The Pamela* [1995] 2 Lloyd's Rep 249.

143 [1982] 1 Lloyd's Rep 562 at p 567.

time for payment has expired, he will realise that he is in breach and has only 48 hours in which to save himself.'

4.7.4 EFFECT OF EXERCISE OF RIGHT TO WITHDRAW

The exercise of the right to withdraw the vessel for default in payment of hire terminates the charterparty. The shipowner has no right temporarily to withdraw the vessel in an attempt to put pressure on the charterer to pay the hire unless there is an express term in the charterparty to that effect. Such action by the owner amounts to a breach of contract for which damages are recoverable.[144] Nor is the owner entitled to take any other action as, for example, withdrawing the charterer's contractual authority to sign bills of lading or instructing the master not to sign pre-paid bills of lading.[145] In *The Nanfri*[146] such conduct was held to amount to a repudiatory breach of contract entitling the charterers to determine the charterparty. Practical problems would, however, arise where an attempt was made to withdraw the vessel after cargo had been loaded and bills of lading had been issued, particularly where those bills had been issued to parties other than the charterer. In such circumstances any withdrawal would be subject to the completion of the voyage covered by the relevant bills of lading.[147] In practice, however, 'after the notice of withdrawal is given, in nine cases out of ten the parties agree to go on just as before. If it turns out that notice of withdrawal was rightly given, the charterer will pay the increased market rate. If it was wrongly given, the rate remains the same.'[148]

The effect of exercising the right to withdraw the vessel is to terminate the contract from that point and the shipowner is not entitled to any hire for the remainder of the charter period.[149] Nor is he entitled to retain any unearned hire already paid in advance.[150] Damages for the unexpired period of the charter can only be recovered where default in payment of hire amounts to a repudiation of the contract by the charterer.[151] As time is normally not of the essence of a time charter, default in payment of hire by the charterer will rarely amount to repudiation of the contract and the owner wishing to withdraw the vessel will invariably have to rely on the contractual withdrawal clause.

4.8 EMPLOYMENT AND AGENCY CLAUSE

The majority of time charters will include a clause entitling the charterer to have full use of the vessel during the charter and undertaking that the master will comply with

---

[144] See *The Aegnoussiotis* [1977] 1 Lloyd's Rep 268; *The Mihalios Xilas* [1978] 2 Lloyd's Rep 186.
[145] See *The Agios Giorgis* [1976] 2 Lloyd's Rep 192, where the owners instructed the master to suspend discharge of cargo.
[146] [1979] 1 Lloyd's Rep 201.
[147] *The Alev* [1989] 1 Lloyd's Rep 138; *The Irina A (No 2)* [1999] 1 Lloyd's Rep 189. See possible resultant liability of shipowners to pay for bunkers: *The Saetta* [1993] 2 Lloyd's Rep 268.
[148] Lord Denning MR in *The Afovos* [1982] 1 Lloyd's Rep 562 at p 564.
[149] *The Sun* [1997] 2 Lloyd's Rep 314; see also Lord Goff in *The Trident Beauty* [1994] 1 Lloyd's Rep 365 at p 368.
[150] *The Mihalios Xilas* [1979] 2 Lloyd's Rep 303 at p 308, *per* Lord Diplock.
[151] *Overstone* v *Shipway* [1962] 1 WLR 117; *The Sun* [1997] 2 Lloyd's Rep 314.

the charterer's orders and instructions to this end. One of the most important rights conferred on the charterer by such a clause is the right to issue bills of lading which the master is required to sign on demand, and which can be enforced by a third party holder against the shipowner even though their terms differ radically from the terms of the charterparty.[152] In return, the charterer undertakes to indemnify the shipowner against any additional liability incurred by him as a consequence of the exercise of these powers. A typical example of such a provision is found in clause 9 of the Baltime form:

'The master to prosecute all voyages with the utmost despatch and to render customary assistance with the vessel's crew. The master to be under the orders of the charterers as regards employment, agency, or other arrangements. The charterers to indemnify the owners against all consequences or liabilities arising from the master, officers or agents signing bills of lading or other documents or otherwise complying with such orders, as well as from any irregularity in the vessel's papers or for overcarrying goods . . .'

The justification for the inclusion of such a clause was clearly stated by Devlin J: 'If [the shipowner] is to surrender his freedom of choice and put his master under the orders of the charterer, there is nothing unreasonable in his stipulating for a complete indemnity in return.'[153] The express indemnity is designed to reimburse the shipowner for any additional expenditure or liability incurred as the result of placing his vessel at the disposal of the charterer. Such liability may result either from complying with the charterer's instructions regarding the employment of the vessel or from the master signing bills of lading at the request of the charterer. So far as the employment aspect is concerned, the shipowner is thus able to recover for physical damage to the vessel resulting from it being despatched to an unsafe port[154] or from the charterer loading dangerous cargo.[155] Again, he will be indemnified against financial liability to third parties on releasing cargo, at the charterer's request, without requiring presentation of the relevant bills of lading.[156] On the other hand, the shipowner will be covered if additional liability is incurred by the master signing bills of lading at the charterer's request. The crucial test is whether such bills impose more onerous terms on the shipowner than would have arisen under the charterparty.[157] This would occur where the bills fail to incorporate a charterparty exception,[158] or where they become automatically subject to the operation of the Hague or Hague/Visby Rules.[159]

At first sight it might appear that an indemnity clause of this type would entitle the shipowner to recover from the charterer for any additional liability or expenditure

---

[152] For a full discussion of this aspect, see *infra* Chapter 8.

[153] *Royal Greek Govt v Ministry of Transport* (1950) 83 LlLR 228 at p 234.

[154] *Lensen v Anglo Soviet Shipping Co* (1935) 40 Com Cas 320; *Vardinoyannis v Egyptian Petroleum Co* [1971] 2 Lloyd's Rep 200.

[155] *Chandris v Isbrandtsen-Moller* (1950) 83 LlLR 385; *Royal Greek Govt v Ministry of Transport* (1950) 83 LlLR 228; *Deutsche Ost-Afrika Linie v Legent Maritime Co* [1998] 2 Lloyd's Rep 71.

[156] *Strathlorne SS Co v Andrew Weir & Co* (1935) 50 LlLR 185.

[157] See McNair J in *The Brabant* [1965] 2 Lloyd's Rep 546 at p 552. See also *Field Line (Cardiff) Ltd v South Atlantic Line* 201 F 301.

[158] *Kruger v Moel Tryvan Shipping Co* [1907] AC 272; *Milburn v Jamaica Fruit Co* [1900] 2 QB 540; *The Imvros* [1999] 1 Lloyd's Rep 848.

[159] *The Brabant* [1965] 2 Lloyd's Rep 546.

arising during the currency of the charter since, in the absence of employment of the vessel, the particular loss would not have been incurred. There are, however, a number of limitations on the shipowner's right to recover.

First, it must be remembered that under a time charter, as opposed to a charter by demise, the shipowner retains responsibility for all matters relating to navigation and ship management.[160] Consequently, he will not be able to claim reimbursement for loss attributable to negligent navigation or unseaworthiness, even though incurred while carrying out the charterer's instructions, since these matters fall within the shipowner's sphere of responsibility. In the words of Lloyd J in *The Aquacharm*,[161] 'It is not every loss arising in the course of the voyage that can be recovered. For example, the owners cannot recover heavy weather damage merely because, had the charterers ordered the vessel on a different voyage, the heavy weather would not have been encountered. The connection is too remote. Similarly, the owners cannot recover the expenses incurred in the course of ordinary navigation, for example, the cost of ballasting, even though in one sense the cost of ballasting is incurred as a consequence of complying with the charterer's orders . . .'

Secondly, while a master is expected to comply with the charterer's instructions within a reasonable time,[162] he is not entitled to act on orders which are clearly beyond the authority of the charterer. 'I cannot think that a clause in a time charterparty which puts the master under the orders of the charterers as regards employment is to be construed as compelling him to obey orders which the charterers have no power to give.'[163] Consequently, if the master accepts instructions to proceed to a port that is obviously unsafe[164] or signs a bill of lading, presented by the charterer, which is manifestly inconsistent with the terms of the charterparty,[165] the shipowner will not be entitled to rely on the indemnity clause to claim reimbursement for any resulting loss. In practice, however, the courts recognise the dilemma confronting the master in such circumstances and will invariably give him the benefit of the doubt provided they are of the opinion that he acted reasonably and in good faith.

Finally, of course, there is the question of causation. 'A loss may well arise in the course of compliance with the charterer's orders, but this fact does not, without more, establish that it was caused by, and is in law a consequence of, such compliance, and in the absence of proof of such causation there is no right of indemnity.'[166] Thus the indemnity will not operate when the chain of causation is broken by some act of

---

[160] But, subject to safety considerations, the choice of ocean route is primarily a question of employment and not navigation. See *The Hill Harmony* [2001] 1 Lloyd's Rep 147, at p 153.

[161] [1980] 2 Lloyd's Rep 237 at pp 244–5. See also *The Erechthion* [1987] 2 Lloyd's Rep 180.

[162] *Midwest Shipping Co v Henry* [1971] 1 Lloyd's Rep 375.

[163] Devlin J in *Grace v General Steam Nav Co* (1950) 83 LlLR 297 at p 307. See also *Larrinaga SS Co v R* [1945] AC 246. Again, the circumstances in which an order is given, or the nature of it, may make it unreasonable for the master to comply without further investigation or enquiry. *The Houda* [1994] 2 Lloyd's Rep 541.

[164] *Grace v General Steam Nav Co, supra.*

[165] *Kruger v Moel Tryvan Shipping Co* [1907] AC 272, at pp 278, 282. See also *The Nogar Marin* [1988] 1 Lloyd's Rep 412 where goods damaged on shipment but master negligently signed clean bill presented by charterer.

[166] Donaldson J in *The White Rose* [1969] 2 All ER 374 at p 382.

negligence on the part of a member of the crew.[167] Nor has it been held applicable to cover a situation where a cargo of coal, loaded on the charterer's instructions, gave off methane gas which was ignited by a spark emitted during repairs to the vessel's water tanks. In the opinion of the court, the loading of the cargo was not the direct cause of the explosion.[168] The crucial test in such cases would appear to be whether the loss to the shipowner was the inevitable result of complying with the orders of the charterer.

Recent cases have established that, in the absence of an express provision, a right to indemnity may be implied where, in a time charter, a shipowner places the master under the orders of a charterer.[169] Such an implication is justified on the grounds of business efficacy, 'in the sense that if the charterer requires to have the vessel at his disposal, and to be free to choose voyages and cargoes and bill of lading terms also, then the owner must be expected to grant such freedom only if he is entitled to be indemnified against loss and liability resulting from it'.[170] The implied indemnity will be subject to all the qualifications already outlined in respect of the express indemnity[171] and will be excluded by the presence of a conflicting provision in the charterparty.[172]

4.9 REDELIVERY OF THE VESSEL

Provision is normally made in the charter for the vessel to be redelivered to its owner at a specified port or range of ports 'in like good order and condition, ordinary wear and tear excepted'.[173] On failure to fulfil this obligation, the charterer will be liable in damages should such failure result from a breach of any of his obligations under the charterparty.[174] Moreover, the obligation will extend to cover any damage to the vessel for which the charterer is responsible under the employment and indemnity clause.[175] Opinions are, however, divided as to whether or not the clause imposes a strict obligation on the charterer to return the vessel in good order.[176] In view of the fact that the owner normally undertakes to maintain the vessel in a thoroughly efficient state throughout the charter, it is arguable that the charterer's responsibility does not extend beyond damage caused by himself or resulting from compliance with his orders.[177]

---

[167] *Portsmouth SS Co v Liverpool & Glasgow Salvage Assoc* (1929) 34 LlLR 459 at p 462.
[168] *Royal Greek Govt v Minister of Transport* (1949) 83 LlLR 228. See also *Portsmouth v Liverpool & Glasgow Salvage Assoc (supra)*.
[169] *The Berge Sund* [1993] 2 Lloyd's Rep 453; *The Island Archon* [1994] 2 Lloyd's Rep 227.
[170] *The Island Archon* [1994] at p 237 *per* Evans LJ. See also *Newcastle P & I v Gard* [1998] 2 Lloyd's Rep 387.
[171] [1994] 2 Lloyd's Rep at p 238.
[172] *The Berge Sund* [1993] 2 Lloyd's Rep 453.
[173] *Royal Greek Govt v Minister of Transport* (1949) 83 LlLR 228. See also *Portsmouth v Liverpool & Glasgow Salvage Assoc (supra)*.
[174] For example, failure to nominate a safe port.
[175] See 4.8, *supra*.
[176] See Acton J in *Chellew Navigation v Appelquist* (1933) 45 WLR 190. Cf. Viscount Cave in *Canadian Pacific Rly v Board of Trade* (1925) 22 LlLR 1 at p 3. Scrutton LJ in *Limerick v Stott* (1921) 7 LlLR 69 reserved his opinion on the point.
[177] See Wilford 15.9.

Although the charterer is required to return the vessel in good order, the owner is not entitled to refuse redelivery until any defect has been remedied.[178] In the words of Lord Denning MR, the requirement is 'not a condition precedent to the right to redeliver, but only a stipulation giving a remedy in damages'.[179] Consequently, in a case where the cost of repairs would have substantially exceeded the value of the vessel when repaired, the owner was not permitted to claim hire until the repairs had been completed, but was required to accept redelivery and sue for damages.[180] 'Both legal and commercial considerations demand that the charter shall come to an end, even if the condition of the vessel on redelivery is unsatisfactory.'[181]

So far as 'ordinary wear and tear' is concerned, this is purely a question of fact and, in reaching a decision on the point, account must be taken of the particular use for which the vessel was chartered. Thus in a case where damages were claimed for refitting a liner which had been chartered for troop carrying during the First World War, Lord Buckmaster remarked, 'I find it difficult to see how the charterparty of a vessel which is expressly stated to be hired for the purposes of conveying troops and similar objects can have that fact excluded from the consideration of what are the expenses which are to be incurred in the course of the running.'[182] It is arguable that if a vessel is chartered to engage in a particular trade, and is so employed without negligence, then any resulting damage must be attributable to fair wear and tear.[183]

The final obligation of the charterer is to redeliver the vessel at the port or place named in the charter. In the event of redelivery elsewhere, the owner 'has a contractual right to have the ship kept in employment at the charter rate of hire until the service is completed. This does not happen until the ship reaches the redelivery range and the voyage to that range forms part of the chartered service . . . and full compensation for the breach requires the charterer to restore to the owner the hire which he would have earned if the voyage had in fact been performed.'[184] In practice this means that the assessment of damages will be based on the net profit to be made from a notional voyage to the agreed delivery point, less the net profit derived from any alternative employment during the period required to complete the notional voyage.

---

[178] *Wye Shipping Co v Compagnie Paris-Orleans* [1922] 1 KB 617.
[179] *The Puerto Buitrago* [1976] 1 Lloyd's Rep at p 253. See also *The Rozel* [1994] 2 Lloyd's Rep 161. 'In a commercial context a plaintiff will not recover damages on a "cost of cure" basis if that cost is disproportionate to the financial consequences of the deficiency': Philips J at p 168.
[180] *The Puerto Buitrago* [1976] 1 Lloyd's Rep 250.
[181] *The Rijn* [1981] 2 Lloyd's Rep at p 270 *per* Mustill J.
[182] *Canadian Pacific Rly v Board of Trade* (1925) 22 LlLR 1 at p 4.
[183] Cf. Acton J in *Chellew Navigation v Appelquist* (1933) 45 LlLR 190.
[184] *Per* Mustill J in *The Rijn* [1981] 2 Lloyd's Rep 267 at p 270.

Part Three

BILLS OF LADING

5

BILLS OF LADING AND
THEIR FUNCTIONS

5.1 HISTORICAL INTRODUCTION

A contract of affreightment is normally evidenced by a bill of lading when the goods to be shipped form only part of the cargo which the ship is to carry. This situation will arise when a shipowner, or other person authorised to act on his behalf, employs his vessel as a general ship by advertising that he is willing to accept cargo from allcomers for a particular voyage. Such carriage forms part of the liner trade in cases where vessels of a particular shipping line regularly ply an advertised route, year in year out. Once cargo has been accepted and shipped by such a carrier, a bill of lading will be issued on his behalf acknowledging that the goods have been received for carriage or shipped, as the case may be.

The bill of lading originated around the fourteenth century as a non-negotiable receipt issued by a shipowner, for cargo received, to a merchant who did not intend to travel with his goods. It would contain statements as to the type and quantity of goods shipped and the condition in which they were received. Subsequent experience led to the incorporation into the document of the terms of the contract of carriage in order to resolve the disputes which inevitably arose between cargo owners and carrier. Finally by the eighteenth century the bill of lading had acquired its third characteristic, that of being negotiable by indorsement in order to meet the needs of those merchants who wished to dispose of their goods before the vessel reached its destination.

Historically the liability of the carrier under a bill of lading contract to transport the cargo safely to its destination was strict, subject only to what were known as the common law exceptions, namely, act of God, public enemies, or inherent vice. Even though the loss was covered by one of these exceptions, the carrier remained liable if his negligence or other fault had contributed to it. In this respect it is important to note that the carrier's liability under a bill of lading contract for safe custody of the cargo was identical with the shipowner's corresponding liability under a charterparty. With the development of the concept of freedom of contract during the nineteenth century, however, the bill of lading carrier was able to take advantage of his superior bargaining power by introducing clauses into the contract of carriage which, to an increasing extent, excluded his common law liability. The ultimate point in this development was reached when some carriers sought to exempt themselves from liability even for loss resulting from their own negligence in the care of cargo. The resultant combined resistance from shippers, bankers and underwriters led to the production in some countries of model bills of lading to cover certain trades, while in others it led to the introduction of legislation designed to curb the excesses of an unbridled laissez faire. A typical example of such legislation is provided by the Harter Act 1893 in the USA, which in essence sought to ban the exclusion of carrier liability for loss resulting from fault in the care and custody of cargo, while similar legislation was passed in some Commonwealth countries.[1]

Eventually it came to be recognised that such piecemeal legislation was insufficient, but many shipowning countries feared that an abandonment of a policy of freedom of contract would inevitably lead to an increase in freight rates which would place their carriers at a disadvantage. Clearly any solution, if it was to be of practical value in international trade, would have to be based on international agreement. Discussions were initiated between representatives of shipowners, shippers, underwriters and bankers drawn from the major maritime nations, which finally led to the drafting of a set of rules by the Maritime Law Committee of the International Law Association at a meeting held in the Hague in 1921. These draft rules (henceforth known as the 'Hague Rules') were the subject of negotiation and amendment which culminated in them being incorporated in an international convention which was signed in Brussels on 25 August 1924 by the major trading nations.

The declared objective of the Convention was to unify certain rules relating to bills of lading and to establish a minimum degree of protection for the cargo owner. The Rules were not intended to provide a comprehensive and self-sufficient code regulating the carriage of goods by sea, but were designed merely to define the basic obligations of the carrier and to prescribe the maximum protection he could derive from the insertion of exception and limitation clauses in the contract of carriage. The parties retained the power to negotiate their own terms as regards those aspects of the contract not specifically covered by the Rules. The major maritime nations introduced legislation to give effect to the Hague Rules which, in the case of the United Kingdom, took the form of the Carriage of Goods by Sea Act 1924.[2]

Over the years dissatisfaction grew at the limited nature of the protection afforded to cargo owners by the Hague Rules. Criticism mainly centred on the narrow area of operation of the Rules, since in the majority of countries they only applied to outward bills,[3] and covered only the tackle-to-tackle period. Again, they were only applicable to certain aspects of the contract of carriage rather than providing a comprehensive code, and cargo owners alleged that their underlying philosophy was still biased in favour of the carrier.[4]

Opinions were, however, divided as to how progress could be achieved. On the one hand, the major shipowning nations were opposed to any radical change in the regime and favoured selective adjustments to the Hague Rules in order to remove the most obvious blemishes. This approach resulted in a series of draft amendments to the Rules which were incorporated into a document known as the Brussels Protocol, the text of

---

[1] For example, the Australian Carriage of Goods by Sea Act 1904, the New Zealand Shipping and Seamen Act 1908, and the Canadian Water Carriage Act 1910.

[2] Prior to 1977 the Convention had secured more than 60 ratifications and accessions while several other states implemented legislation to similar effect.

[3] Compare the position in US and Scandinavia where the relevant legislation also applied to inward bills.

[4] For fuller details, see UNCTAD: *Report on Bills of Lading*, 1971, pp 11–22.

which was agreed at an international conference held in Brussels in February 1968. The revised rules incorporating the amendments contained in the Brussels Protocol are known as the 'Hague/Visby Rules'. On the other hand, more radical reform was advocated by some leading cargo providing countries, the majority of whom are drawn from the so-called Third World. Under their sponsorship lengthy negotiations were conducted through UNCTAD and a specialised UNCITRAL Working Party, which resulted in the drafting of a new comprehensive code covering all aspects of the contract of carriage by sea. This code was incorporated in a Convention (known as the 'Hamburg Rules') which was signed at an international conference held in Hamburg in March 1978. This new code finally came into force on 1 November 1992 having collected the required total of 20 ratifications and accessions from different states, irrespective of tonnage.[5]

In the meantime, the United Kingdom and a number of other western European governments decided to adopt the Hague/Visby approach and consequently implemented legislation to give effect to the Convention. In the case of the United Kingdom this took the form of the Carriage of Goods by Sea Act 1971 which did not, however, become effective until 23 June 1977, by which date the Convention had collected the required number of accessions and ratifications. While 30 states have so far formally adopted the Hague/Visby Rules, their provisions have been incorporated into the maritime codes of several other states where they tend to be applied in international trade on a reciprocal basis.[6]

The consequence is that the overall international situation with regard to contracts of carriage by sea exhibits a certain degree of complexity. While many states still remain loyal to the original Hague Rules, 30 have adopted the Hague/Visby amendments, a further 29 have adopted the Hamburg code, while a fourth group has implemented, or is in the course of implementing, hybrid systems based on a combination of provisions drawn from both the Hague/Visby and Hamburg regimes.[7] The position is further complicated by the application of varying conflict of laws principles with the result that a decision as to which Convention is applicable may well depend on the choice of country in which the action is brought. Such legal complexity hardly encourages the development of international trade and a greater degree of uniformity would be desirable.

5.2 FUNCTIONS OF A BILL OF LADING

An individual wishing to ship a consignment of goods overseas approaches a shipping line, either directly or more often through a forwarding agent, with a view to reserving space on a vessel. He is then instructed by the carrier when and where to deliver the goods and, having done so, is issued with a receipt indicating the type and quantity of goods handed over and the condition in which they were received by the carrier's agent.

---

[5] The signatories, which now number 29 states, represent a total of little more than 5 per cent of world trade, none of the major maritime states having as yet ratified the convention.

[6] Mainly in the former socialist states of eastern Europe.

[7] For example, Australia. The US Senate is also discussing a Bill to similar effect. See *infra* at pp 229–30.

From that point the carrier normally has control of the goods and is ultimately responsible for loading aboard. In the meantime the shipper will normally acquire a copy of the
carrier's bill of lading form which is obtainable either direct from the carrier's agents or
from stationers throughout the country. On the form he will enter details of the type and
quantity of goods shipped, together with any relevant marks, and *inter alia* will specify
the port of destination and the name of the consignee.[8] On receipt of the completed bill,
the carrier's agent will check the cargo details against the tallies at the time of loading
and, if correct, will acknowledge them if so requested. After calculating the freight and
entering it on the bill, the master or his agent will sign the bill and release it to the shipper in return for delivery of the mate's receipt or equivalent and payment of any advance
freight due. The shipper is then free either to dispatch the bill directly to the consignee
or to deliver it to a bank if the shipment forms part of an international sales transaction
involving a documentary credit. In either case, the consignee may decide to sell the
cargo while in transit, in which case he may indorse the bill of lading in favour of the
purchaser. Eventually the ultimate consignee or indorsee of the bill will surrender it at
the port of discharge in return for delivery of the goods.

   This brief outline indicates the vital importance of the bill of lading to the performance of the carriage contract and it is now necessary to consider the various functions of
the bill in more detail.

5.2.1 AS RECEIPT FOR GOODS SHIPPED

Originally the bill of lading started life as a mere bailment receipt which was required to
obtain delivery of the goods at the port of discharge. Even when used in this capacity it
would normally include statements as to the quantity and description of the goods
shipped together with the condition in which they were received by the carrier. Such
representations of fact had important commercial effects. First they formed the basis of
any cargo claim by the receiver should the goods be short delivered or damaged on discharge. Secondly, where goods had been sold c.i.f., under the terms of which contract
payment had to be made against delivery of documents, the buyer was entitled to reject
the documents if the description of the goods in the bill of lading did not correspond
with their description in the sales invoice. Similarly, the terms of the c.i.f. contract
might entitle the buyer or bank to insist on the production of a 'clean' bill, i.e. a bill containing an unqualified statement that the goods had been shipped in good order and
condition. Thirdly, such statements of fact might seriously affect the negotiability of the
bill in the hands of a consignee, since the goods would not readily be saleable in transit
if the bill disclosed that they had been shipped in a damaged condition.

   In these circumstances it is vitally important for the shipper or consignee that the carrier should be required to make accurate and unambiguous statements as to the quantity
and condition of the goods shipped. In the absence of such statements in the bill, a consignee seeking to recover for goods short delivered or damaged on discharge would have
the burden of proving the quantity or condition of the goods when shipped. While it is

---

[8] Alternatively, in the liner trade the bill of lading may have been prepared on the carrier's computer from
written details supplied by the shipper when he reserved space.

true that such details are normally entered onto the bill by the shipper himself, the natural reaction of the carrier's agent would be to protect his principal by inserting a clause to the effect that 'weight, quantity and condition unknown' or 'shipper's count' before adding his signature to the bill.[9] In view of the fact that the carrier is normally in the stronger bargaining position, there is little the shipper can do to prevent him adding clauses of this type. In order to deal with this problem, Art III rule 3 of the Hague/Visby Rules entitles the shipper to demand the issue of a bill of lading containing certain specified information:

> 'After receiving the goods into his charge the carrier or the master or agent of the carrier shall, on demand of the shipper, issue to the shipper a bill of lading showing among other things –
> a) The leading marks necessary for identification of the goods as the same are furnished in writing by the shipper before the loading of such goods starts, provided such marks are stamped or otherwise shown clearly upon the goods if uncovered, or on the cases or covering in which such goods are contained, in such a manner as should ordinarily remain legible until the end of the voyage.
> b) Either the number of packages or pieces, or the quantity, or weight, as the case may be as furnished in writing by the shipper.
> c) The apparent order and condition of the goods.'

In return, the shipper is 'deemed to have guaranteed' to the carrier the accuracy of any information supplied by him in writing for incorporation in the bill,[10] and is required to indemnify the carrier against all loss arising in the event of any inaccuracies. The carrier is under no obligation to issue a bill containing such information unless specifically requested by the shipper[11] and, even then, he can refuse if either he has reasonable grounds for believing the information supplied to be inaccurate, or has no reasonable means of checking it.[12]

The Hague/Visby Rules further provide that such statements in a bill of lading shall be prima facie evidence of the receipt by the carrier of the goods as so described, but conclusive evidence against him once the bill has been transferred to a third party acting in good faith.[13] The common law had earlier reached much the same position with regard to the evidentiary value of statements in a bill of lading, although it is noticeable that, in the case of third parties, the Hague/Visby formulation dispenses with the need for action in reliance which was an essential requirement for triggering the estoppel mechanism at common law.[14] There is, however, some ambiguity as to the effect of the failure of a carrier to comply with a request from the shipper to provide information required by Art III rule 3. The obvious answer in such circumstances would be to invoke Art III rule 8 and render any expression such as 'weight unknown' null, void and of no

[9] Indeed, printed clauses to this effect appear in many of the standard forms, such as the Conlinebill and the Congenbill. Such a qualification greatly reduces the evidentiary value of the statement so far as the shipper is concerned. See *The Atlas* [1996] 1 Lloyd's Rep 642.
[10] Article III rule 5.
[11] *The Mata K* [1998] 2 Lloyd's Rep 614.
[12] See *The Esmeralda* [1988] 1 Lloyd's Rep 206.
[13] Article III rule 4.
[14] See *Compania Naviera Vascongada v Churchill* [1906] 1 KB 237 at p 249.

effect. Clarke J, however, expressed the view obiter in *The Mata K*[15] that the operation of rule 8 was restricted to contractual provisions which removed or reduced the liability of a carrier for failure to fulfil his obligations under Art III, i.e. to breaches of Art III rules 1 and 2. 'The inclusion of the provision "weight unknown" does not have the effect of relieving the carrier from such a liability or lessening such a liability. It merely means . . . that the provisions of Article III rule 4 as to prima facie evidence cannot come into effect.'[16] Such a conclusion would appear to defeat the object intended by the draftsmen of Art III rule 3, and it is to be hoped that the position will be reviewed in subsequent cases.[17]

   Should the bill of lading contain a clause to the effect that statements as to the quantity and condition of the goods shipped 'shall be conclusive evidence' of the facts stated as against the carrier, then no evidence will be admitted to rebut such statements even where the claim has been brought by the shipper and even though the carrier can prove, for example, that the goods were not shipped.[18]

   It is now necessary to consider each of the three facets of the receipt function in more detail. They will be examined first from the point of view of the common law and secondly from the standpoint of the Hague/Visby Rules. This dual approach is still necessary since, as will be indicated later, there are a considerable proportion of carriage contracts to which the Hague/Visby Rules are inapplicable.

(I) RECEIPT AS TO QUANTITY

(a) Position at common law

In the hands of the shipper, the bill of lading is prima facie evidence at common law of the weight or quantity of goods shipped. To avoid liability, the carrier has the burden of proving that the goods were not shipped as stated in the bill. His burden is no light one since he must clearly establish that the goods were not in fact shipped, not merely that it is unlikely on a balance of possibilities. Thus in *Smith* v *Bedouin Steam Navigation Co*,[19] a case in which 988 bales of jute had been delivered under a bill which stated that 1,000 bales had been shipped, Lord Shand indicated that for the carrier to succeed, 'the evidence must be sufficient to lead to the inference not merely that the goods may possibly not have been shipped, but that in point of fact they were not shipped'.[20] Such a burden may be difficult to discharge in practice since, if the carrier was unaware that the goods were not shipped at the time when he signed the bill, he is unlikely to be able to establish the fact several weeks later unless, for example, the goods are found still lying in the warehouse at the port of loading. On the other hand, if he can discharge this burden of proof there is no reason why the shipper should profit at his expense, since the shipper can hardly be said to have suffered loss by relying on the statement in the bill.

---

[15] [1998] 2 Lloyd's Rep 614.

[16] At p 620. See also the comments of Longmore J in *The Atlas* [1996] 1 Lloyd's Rep at p 646.

[17] See Gaskell 7.79; Carver 2.003.

[18] See *Fisher, Renwick & Co* v *Calder* (1896) 1 Com Cas 456. Such clauses are rarely used at the present day. For a recent example, see *The Herroe and Askoe* [1986] 2 Lloyd's Rep 281.

[19] [1896] AC 70.

[20] *Ibid* at p 79. See also *Att Gen of Ceylon* v *Scindia Steam Navigation Co* [1962] AC 60.

More questionable, however, was the fact that at common law until recently a shipowner could escape liability, even towards a bona fide transferee of the bill for value, if he could establish that the goods were not in fact shipped. This situation would seem ideally suited for the application of an estoppel, as in the case of statements as to condition,[21] but the anomaly was judicially justified on the ground that the master had no ostensible authority to bind the shipowner by such statements in the bill. The earliest case on this point was *Grant* v *Norway*[22] where the master signed a bill acknowledging the shipment of 12 bales of silk, none of which had been loaded. The court held that the plaintiffs, who were indorsees of the bill for value, had no remedy when the carrier established that no bales had been shipped. Jervis CJ justified this finding on the grounds that 'It is not contended that the captain had any real authority to sign bills of lading unless the goods had been shipped; nor can we discover any ground upon which a party taking a bill of lading by indorsement would be justified in assuming that he had authority to sign such bills, whether the goods were on board or not.'[23] A similar principle would appear to apply to statements in a bill indicating that a larger quantity of goods had been shipped than had actually been loaded.[24]

While this decision was cited with approval in a number of later cases,[25] the result was unsatisfactory in that a consignee or assignee will rely as much on a statement as to quantity in a bill as on a statement as to the condition of the goods shipped, although only in the latter case will he have the protection of estoppel. Such a result also defeats the object of requiring the master to acknowledge the quantity of cargo shipped, though it is true that, if the master is not a man of straw, he can arguably be sued for damages to cover any loss resulting from the breach of his warranty of authority in making the statement.[26]

Fortunately the practical effects of this common law anomaly were largely circumvented by Art III rule 4 of the Hague/Visby Rules,[27] which provides that statements as to quantity in a bill of lading are conclusive evidence in favour of a consignee or indorsee who takes the bill in good faith. Not all bills, however, are governed by the Rules,[28] and in those situations to which they did not apply, the anomaly persisted until the legislature finally intervened in the form of s 4 of the Carriage of Goods by Sea Act 1992. This statute came into force on 16 September 1992, and from that date representations in a bill of lading as to the quantity of goods shipped or received for shipment are conclusive evidence against the carrier in favour of a lawful holder of the bill, i.e. a transferee in

---

[21] See pp 124–5 *infra*.

[22] (1851) 10 CB 665.

[23] *Ibid* at p 688.

[24] See *Rasnoimport* v *Guthrie & Co* [1966] 1 Lloyd's Rep 1.

[25] *Russo-Chinese Bank* v *Li Yan Sam* [1910] AC 174; *Kleinwort Sons & Co* v *Associated Automatic Machines Corp Ltd* (1935) 151 LT 1 (HL); *Uxbridge Permanent Building Soc* v *Pickard* [1939] 2 KB 248 (CA). The rule is also apparently recognised in Australia. See *Rosenfeld, Hillas & Co* v *Port Laramie* (1923) 32 CLR 25. In later cases the rule was questioned and the courts refused to extend the principle: see *The Nea Tyhi* [1982] 1 Lloyd's Rep 606; *The Saudi Crown* [1986] 1 Lloyd's Rep 261.

[26] See *Rasnoimport* v *Guthrie & Co* [1966] 1 Lloyd's Rep 1. But this remedy will apparently not be available in the event of failure to ship any cargo, since there would then be no contract and the bill of lading would be a nullity. In the absence of any remedy against the shipowner on the bill, no damages would be recoverable from the agent. See *Heskell* v *Continental Express* [1950] 1 All ER 1033.

[27] See *infra* p 123.

[28] See *infra* pp 174 ff.

good faith. The Act therefore brings the position at common law broadly into line with that under the Hague/Visby Rules. The Act is not retrospective, however, and consequently this provision does not apply to bills of lading issued before the statute came into force, nor does it provide protection for the person entitled to delivery under a sea waybill.[29] In both these cases, the effect of the representations contained in the respective documents is still governed by the old common law rule in *Grant* v *Norway*.[30]

Contracting out. As freedom of contract exists at common law, the shipowner can destroy even the prima facie evidentiary effect of a representation of quantity in the bill by a suitable indorsement, such as 'weight and quantity unknown', 'shipper's count', or 'said to weigh 50 tonnes'. Indeed, where the quantity of cargo written in the bill conflicts with a printed clause to the effect that 'weight etc. unknown', the normal interpretation adopted by the courts is that the figure appearing on the bill is merely a statement made by the shipper which has not been verified by the owner's agent.

In the case of *New Chinese Antimony Co Ltd* v *Ocean Steamship Co*[31] a bill of lading covering a cargo of antimony oxide stated that 937 tons had been shipped. In the body of the bill was a printed clause in ordinary type to the effect that 'weight, measurement, contents and value (except for the purpose of estimating freight) unknown'. In these circumstances the Court of Appeal held that the written statement in the bill did not provide even prima facie evidence of the quantity shipped. In the opinion of Viscount Reading LJ, 'the true effect of this bill of lading is that the words "weight unknown" have the effect of a statement by the shipowners' agent that he has received a quantity of ore which the shippers' representative says weighs 937 tons but which he does not accept as being of that weight, the weight being unknown to him, and that he does not accept the weight of 937 tons except for the purpose of calculating freight and for that purpose only'.[32]

(b) Position under the Hague/Visby Rules

Article III rule 3 of the Rules provides that the shipper can demand that the carrier issue a bill of lading showing 'either the number of packages or pieces, or the quantity or weight, as the case may be, as furnished in writing by the shipper'. The carrier is under no obligation to issue a bill or, presumably to acknowledge the quantity of cargo shipped, unless requested by the shipper.[33] If no such request is made, then consignees

---

[29] Section 4 of the 1992 Act refers specifically to 'bills of lading', from the definition of which in s 1(2)(a) seaway bills are excluded. The Law Commission recommended that s 4 should not apply to sea waybills on the ground that s 1(6)(b) of the Carriage of Goods by Sea Act 1971, while giving the force of law to the Hague/Visby Rules where they were expressly incorporated into a sea waybill, nevertheless specifically excluded the application of the relevant sentence in Art III rule 4 to representations contained in such a document. There was no mandate to extend the protection offered by the 1971 Act.

[30] In the case of waybills, this result can be avoided by the incorporation into the waybill contract of the CMI Rules for Sea Waybills. Rule 5 provides that statements in a sea waybill as to the quantity or condition of goods shall be conclusive evidence of the receipt of goods as so stated in favour of a consignee in good faith. In return, the shipper warrants the accuracy of the particulars furnished by him. For a full discussion of the Rules, see *infra* at p 162.

[31] [1917] 2 KB 664. See also *The Atlas* [1996] 1 Lloyd's Rep 642.

[32] *Ibid* at p 669. See also *The Esmeralda* [1988] 1 Lloyd's Rep 206.

[33] The burden of proving such a request rests with the shipper. See *The Atlas* [1996] 1 Lloyd's Rep 642; *The Mata K* [1998] 2 Lloyd's Rep 614.

or assignees of the bill are prejudiced, since they have no right to demand compliance with the rule. In practice, however, the carrier will almost always want to issue a bill for reasons of his own.

The choice of which of the three methods of quantifying cargo to acknowledge rests with the carrier, though presumably his choice could be influenced by the nature of the information supplied by the shipper. The carrier is, however, not obliged to acknowledge more than one and can disclaim knowledge of the others. So in *Oricon v Intergraan*[34] the bills of lading acknowledged the receipt of 2,000 packages of copra cake 'said to weigh gross 105,000 Kgs . . . for the purposes of calculating freight only'. Roskill J was of the opinion that 'while each of the bills of lading, being Hague Rules bills of lading, acknowledged the number of packages shipped, and are prima facie evidence of those numbers, neither bill of lading is any evidence whatever of the weight of the goods shipped'. In these circumstances the burden of proof rested with the consignee to establish the weight of cargo shipped before he could succeed in his action for short delivery.[35]

So far as the evidentiary value of the bill of lading is concerned, the Hague/Visby Rules follow the common law in regarding the bill in the hands of the shipper as prima facie evidence of the amount of cargo shipped. Where they differ, however, is in treating the bill as conclusive evidence once it has been transferred to a third party acting in good faith.[36] It is noticeable that there is no requirement that the third party should have given value to raise the estoppel, only good faith is needed on his part. It would also appear that where the Hague/Visby Rules are applicable the anomalous principle in *Grant v Norway* would be excluded.[37]

(II) RECEIPT AS TO CONDITION

The second type of statement traditionally included in a bill of lading is a representation by the shipowner as to the condition in which the goods were shipped.[38] This refers merely to their apparent condition in so far as the carrier or his agent is able to judge by a reasonable outward inspection.[39] At a time when an increasing proportion of cargo is containerised, such statements are only of limited value since, in the majority of cases, they will refer merely to the outward appearance of the container or other packaging, and not to the condition of the goods inside. The shipowner's agent will naturally

---

[34] [1967] 2 Lloyd's Rep 82. In such circumstances US courts take the view that carriers are entitled to acknowledge either the quantity or weight of cargo shipped but, if they acknowledge both, they should be liable for both. See *Spanish American Skin Co v MS Ferngulf* [1957] AMC 611.

[35] The courts are prepared on many occasions to assist the claimant in establishing his case by allowing the introduction of alternative evidence, e.g. by calculating the weight of missing sacks from the average weight of sacks actually delivered: *Att Gen of Ceylon v Scindia Steam Navigation Co* [1962] AC 60; by allowing the plaintiff to rely on tally records compiled by persons acting under duty to port authorities: *The Atlas* [1996] 1 Lloyd's Rep 642.

[36] Article III rule 4. For a discussion as to who may be regarded as a 'third party' see Gaskell 7.23.

[37] See Scrutton p 433. Cf. the judgment of Sheen J in *The Nea Tyhi* [1982] 1 Lloyd's Rep 606 at p 610.

[38] Cf. the position where goods were damaged by fire after shipment but before the bill of lading was issued: *The Galatia* [1980] 1 Lloyd's Rep 453.

[39] There would appear to be no authority to suggest that the master contractually warrants the absolute accuracy of statements as to condition entered by him in the bill of lading. It suffices if he has an honest belief in their accuracy and it is a belief that could properly be held by a reasonably observant master. See the judgment of Colman J in *The David Agmashenebeli* [2003] 1 Lloyd's Rep 92 at pp 104 ff.

catalogue on the bill of lading any damage which is observed during such examination and will be under an obligation to deliver the goods at their destination in the same condition as that received, subject to the contractual exceptions. In many cases the shipper will be anxious to avoid any such indorsements on the bill since the shipment is being financed by a documentary credit from a bank under which he is required to produce a 'clean bill of lading', i.e. a bill containing an unqualified statement that the goods were shipped 'in good order and condition'.[40]

(a) Effect at common law

As with representations as to quantity, statements as to the condition in which goods are shipped are prima facie evidence in favour of the shipper, but conclusive evidence once the bill comes into the hands of a bona fide purchaser for value. Thus in *Compania Naviera Vascongada* v *Churchill*[41] where timber became badly stained with petroleum while awaiting shipment, the master nevertheless issued a bill acknowledging that the timber had been shipped in good order and condition. Channell J held that, in these circumstances, the shipowners were estopped as against an assignee of the bill from denying the truth of the statement. The justification for the estoppel was detrimental reliance by the assignee. 'In order to make the statement in the bill of lading binding as an estoppel it is of course necessary that it would have been acted on to the prejudice of the person so acting. The defendants here allege that they are prejudiced because, on the faith of the statement that the timber was in good condition when shipped, they accepted the bills of lading as a good tender under a contract for clean timber, and paid their vendors the full contract price.'[42]

Such detrimental reliance will invariably be present either because the shipment formed part of an international sale and the purchaser was induced to pay the contract price by the presentation of the clean bill of lading, or because the consignee of the bill obtained delivery of the goods by presenting the bill and paying the required freight. The estoppel has even been held effective in favour of a party who had advanced money to the shipper on the security of the bill and subsequently obtained delivery of the goods from the carrier on presentation of the bill and payment of the freight even though technically he was not a party to the contract of carriage.[43] It must be remembered, however, that the estoppel will only be effective in respect of defects which would be apparent on a reasonable inspection by the carrier or his agents. Thus in *Silver* v *Ocean Steamship Co*[44] the shipowners had issued clean bills of lading covering a cargo of Chinese eggs shipped in 42-lb square tins which were not covered with any cloth or packing. When the goods arrived at their destination in a damaged condition, the Court of Appeal held that, while the shipowners were estopped from contending either that the cargo was insufficiently packed or that the tins were gashed on shipment, they were not estopped from alleging that pin-hole perforations in the tins were present on shipment, since the latter would not necessarily be apparent on a reasonable inspection.

---

[40] Uniform Customs and Practice for Documentary Credits 500 (1993 edn) Art 32.
[41] [1906] 1 KB 237.
[42] *Ibid* at p 249.
[43] *Brandt* v *Liverpool Steam Navigation Co* [1924] 1 KB 575. See also pp 145 ff.
[44] [1930] 1 KB 416.

It is, of course, possible at common law for the shipowner to exclude responsibility for the truth of such statements or to indorse the bill with a clause to the effect 'condition unknown'. On the other hand, representations as to condition purport to be statements made by the shipowner after a reasonable inspection of the goods, and differ basically from representations as to quantity or leading marks, which are merely acknowledgments by the shipowner of information supplied by the shipper. Consequently, the courts tend to construe any attempts by the shipowner to negate the effectiveness of such representations fairly strictly. Thus in the case of *The Peter der Grosse*[45] a marginal indorsement to the effect that 'weight, contents and value unknown' did not displace a positive statement in the bill that the goods were shipped in good order and condition. There would also appear to be an established convention that a clear statement by the shipowner that the goods were shipped in good order and condition will override any standard printed clause in the body of the bill indicating that the state of goods on shipment was unknown.[46]

If the goods are damaged on shipment, the shipowner can, of course, qualify his representation by listing the observed damage on the bill in the form of a marginal indorsement. Such indorsements normally specify the precise damage but can be so worded as to render the representation as to condition too ambiguous to found an estoppel. A good example is provided by the case of *Canada & Dominion Sugar Co Ltd v Canadian National Steamships Ltd*[47] which involved the shipment of a cargo of sugar. The shipper was anxious to obtain a clean bill of lading and, in order to facilitate his business arrangements, the carrier agreed to issue a bill of lading before the completion of loading on receiving an assurance that there was nothing wrong with the cargo. Against the statement in the bill that the goods had been 'shipped in apparent good order and condition', the shipowners entered a marginal indorsement 'signed under guarantee to produce ship's clean receipt'. In fact, the sugar had been damaged while lying on the wharf awaiting shipment, and the mate's receipt eventually recorded 'many bags stained, torn and resewn'. When assignees of the bill subsequently brought an action, the Privy Council held that they could not rely on an estoppel unless the statement as to condition in the bill was unambiguous and unqualified. In the opinion of the court, 'the bill did in fact on its face contain the qualifying words "Signed under guarantee to produce ship's clean receipt"; that was a stamped clause clear and obvious on the face of the document and reasonably conveying to any business man that, if the ship's receipt was not clean, the statement in the bill of lading as to apparent order and condition could not be taken to be unqualified'.[48] In view of this qualification, and the fact that the mate's receipt was available to a prospective buyer, the court held that the assignee could not rely on the estoppel.

(b) Position under the Hague/Visby Rules

As we have already noted, under Art III rule 3 of the Rules, the shipper is entitled to demand the issue of a bill of lading incorporating a statement as to the apparent order

---

[45] (1875) 1 PD 414.
[46] *The Skarp* [1935] P 134.
[47] [1947] AC 46. See also *Tokio Marine & Fire Ins Co v Retla* [1970] 2 Lloyd's Rep 91.
[48] [1947] AC 46 at p 54.

and condition of the goods when received by the carrier. Such bill is prima facie evidence of receipt by the carrier of the goods as therein described, but conclusive evidence when the bill has been transferred to a third party acting in good faith. In the latter respect there is once more no requirement for detrimental reliance, as at common law.

The master will, of course, enter marginal indorsements on the bill to indicate the actual condition of the goods, but otherwise he is not entitled to introduce clauses relieving him of obligations imposed by Art III of the Rules.[49] It is therefore somewhat surprising to find that the courts are prepared to countenance such qualifications of liability on the part of the shipowner on what appear to be purely technical grounds. Thus in the case of *Canada & Dominion Sugar Co Ltd* v *Canadian National Steamships Ltd*[50] it was argued that the provisions of the Hague Rules rendered void the shipowner's qualification that the bill had been 'signed under guarantee to produce ship's clean receipt'. Lord Wright responded by pointing out that Art III rule 3 of the Hague Rules[51] 'expressly applies only if the shipper demands a bill of lading showing the apparent order and condition of the goods. There is no evidence that the shipper here made such a demand: indeed, no demand of this nature is alleged. The condition of the rule is thus not fulfilled.'

The US Court of Appeals adopted a similar line in *Tokio Marine & Fire Ins Co* v *Retla Steamship Co*[52], a case which involved the shipment of a cargo of galvanised and ungalvanised pipes from Yokohama to Los Angeles. Despite the fact that rust and wetness was noted on the tallysheets and the mate's receipt, a clean bill of lading was issued. The bill, however, incorporated a qualifying clause to the effect that, 'apparent good order and condition when used in this bill of lading . . . does not mean that the goods, when received, were free of visible rust or moisture. If the shipper so requests, a substitute bill of lading will be issued omitting the above definition and setting forth any notations as to rust or moisture which may appear on the Mate's or Tally Clerks' receipts.' As the shipper had not requested the issue of a substitute bill, the court held that the consignee was caught by the qualification which, in its view, was not invalid under the Hague Rules. It would seem unreasonable that consignees or assignees should be deprived of their protection by the device of a clause of this type.[53]

The carrier will often be under considerable pressure from the shipper to issue a clean bill of lading, since otherwise the shipper may be unable to complete a sale or draw on a documentary credit. In these circumstances the carrier may be induced to ignore defects in the condition of the cargo tendered in return for the express promise of an indemnity from the shipper to cover losses resulting to the shipowner from any action subsequently brought by a receiver of the goods. Such an indemnity will provide illusory protection for the shipowner since it will be ineffective as a defence to any claim brought by a third party on the clean bill, and may even be unenforceable against the shipper on the ground that its object is to defraud the consignee or his bank. This situation arose in the case of *Brown, Jenkinson & Co Ltd* v *Percy*

---

[49] See Art III rule 8 which renders such clauses 'null and void and of no effect'.

[50] [1947] AC 46. See discussion of this case *supra* at p 125.

[51] NB The provisions of the Hague/Visby Rules are identical in this respect.

[52] [1970] 2 Lloyd's Rep 91.

[53] See Tetley pp 291–3; Gaskell 7.74 ff; Carver 9.149.

Dalton[54] where the plaintiff shipping agents had arranged for the carriage of 100 barrels of orange juice from London to Hamburg. On delivery to the dock, many of the barrels were found to be old and leaking but the defendant shippers were anxious to obtain clean bills of lading and accordingly undertook to indemnify the plaintiffs for any resulting loss if they would refrain from indorsing the bills. Clearly the plaintiffs had no defence when sued for damages by the consignees at Hamburg, but they then sought to recover this loss from the defendants by enforcing the indemnity. The Court of Appeal (Evershed LJ dissenting) held the indemnity to be illegal and void on the grounds of fraud. Even though there was no intention that anyone should be out of pocket as a result of the transaction, nevertheless 'at the request of the defendants the plaintiffs made a representation which they knew to be false and which they intended should be relied on by persons who received the bill of lading, including any banker who might be concerned. In these circumstances, all the elements of the tort of deceit were present.'[55]

Such indemnities are not uncommon in international trade and, providing no fraud is involved, there would appear to be no legal bar to their enforcement. Thus, even in the case itself, it was suggested that such indemnities might be useful where there was a bona fide dispute as to the condition or packing of the goods in order to avoid the necessity of rearranging a letter of credit which might cause difficulty where time was short. Similarly under the Hague/Visby Rules the carrier is entitled to refuse to acknowledge the condition in which the goods are received in circumstances where there is no reasonable opportunity to inspect them. This would provide another occasion for the use of an indemnity where the shipper was anxious to obtain a clean bill. Only in the case where the carrier was actually aware of the falsity of the declaration would the indemnity be ineffective.

While dealing with indemnities, it might be relevant to recall that under Art III rule 5 of the Hague/Visby Rules the carrier is provided with a statutory implied indemnity to cover losses resulting from being required to acknowledge the quantity or leading marks of the goods received on the basis of information supplied by the shipper, which later turns out to be false.[56] This rule is not applicable to statements as to the condition of the goods shipped.[57] There is no mention in this Article of the validity of such an indemnity in a situation where the carrier knows that the information supplied is false, nor does any obligation appear to be imposed on the carrier to inspect the cargo before acknowledging such a statement in the bill. In such circumstances, if the carrier is in any doubt, it would clearly be in his interest not to enquire, provided of course that the shipper is solvent and the carrier can rely on his ability to meet the indemnity.

(III) RECEIPT AS TO LEADING MARKS

Any identification or quality marks appearing on the goods shipped will normally be recorded in the bill of lading. The shipowner will not, however, be estopped at common

---

[54] [1957] 2 QB 621. See also *Standard Chartered Bank v Pakistan National Shipping Corp* [1995] 2 Lloyd's Rep 365 (knowingly issuing antedated bills of lading).

[55] *Ibid* at p 632, *per* Morris LJ.

[56] See *supra* p 119.

[57] Nor will there be an implied indemnity at common law if the master was negligent in not checking the condition of the goods: *The Nogar Marin* [1988] 1 Lloyd's Rep 412.

law from denying that goods were shipped under the marks as described in the bill unless such marks are essential to their identity or description. Thus in *Parsons v New Zealand Shipping Co*[58] a consignment of frozen carcasses of lamb had been exported from New Zealand under a bill which stated that 608 carcasses had been shipped, each bearing the leading mark 622X. In fact, 507 carcasses bore this mark, but the remaining 101 carried the mark 522X. On arrival of the cargo at the port of discharge, the indorsees for value of the bill refused to accept delivery of these 101 carcasses, arguing that the shipowners were estopped from denying that all 608 carcasses shipped bore the 622X mark. The trial judge found that all the carcasses were of equal quality and value and that the sellers had merely attached the marks for their own bookkeeping purposes. In these circumstances a majority of the Court of Appeal held that, as the marks were not material to the identity of the goods, there was no estoppel.

In the view of Collins LJ, 'It is the identity of the goods shipped with those represented as shipped which is the pith of the matter; that is the subject of the misrepresentation referred to, and nothing which would not be material to such identity need be embraced in the estoppel. It is obvious that where marks have no market meaning, and indicate nothing whatever to a buyer as to the nature, quality, or quantity of the goods which he is buying, it is absolutely immaterial to him whether the goods bear one mark or another.'[59] Later in the judgment he adds that 'a mistaken statement as to marks of this class merely makes identification more difficult; it does not affect the existence or identity of the goods'.[60]

On the other hand, leading marks may refer to the identity or description of the goods as, for example, to the type of liquid in a container or the type of fruit packed in a crate. In such circumstances the marks recorded in the bill follow the normal common law rule in providing prima facie evidence against the carrier and conclusive evidence when the bill is in the hands of a bona fide indorsee for value.

The same pattern in relation to leading marks is adopted by the Hague/Visby Rules and the presumptions raised by Art III rule 4 are only applicable to 'leading marks necessary for identification of the goods'. The shipper can demand that such marks are acknowledged by the shipowner provided 'they are stamped or otherwise shown clearly upon the goods . . . in such a manner as should ordinarily remain legible until the end of the voyage'.[61]

It must finally be noted that, unless they are essential to the identity of the goods, there is no obligation on the shipowner under the Rules to acknowledge in the bill any quality marks attached to the goods. Even if the master should voluntarily do so, it has long been established at common law that the shipowner is not estopped from subsequently proving that goods of a different quality were shipped. As against the shipowner, the master has no apparent authority to insert such marks since, in the majority of cases, he clearly does not possess the commercial knowledge or expertise necessary to conduct an adequate check on their accuracy. When such a situation arose

---

[58] [1901] 1 KB 548.
[59] *Ibid* at p 564.
[60] *Ibid* at p 564.
[61] Article III rule 3(a).

in the case of *Cox* v *Bruce*,[62] the Court of Appeal held that a shipowner was not estopped from establishing, as against an indorsee for value, that the quality marks on a consignment of jute had been incorrectly entered on the bill of lading by the master: 'It was no part of the master's duty to insert these quality marks at all . . . and, therefore, he had not authority to make such a representation and I do not think that any man of business was entitled to assume that he had such authority.'[63]

(IV) EFFECT OF OTHER REPRESENTATIONS IN THE BILL OF LADING

While the Hague/Visby Rules contain no requirement for additional information to be incorporated into bills of lading, the parties themselves or their agents may include statements of fact which are capable of raising an estoppel in favour of future transferees for value of the bill. One such relevant fact is the date on which the bill was issued. Thus it was held in *The Saudi Crown*[64] that where a master or other agent has been authorised to sign bills of lading on behalf of shipowners, this carries with it the authority to insert in the bill the date and place at which the bill was issued. The contract of sale in this case required the goods to be shipped under bills dated between 20 June and 15 July. Although loading was not in fact completed until 26 July, bills dated 15 July were issued on the faith of which the buyer authorised payment for the goods. When the goods arrived later than expected and the buyer had to acquire replacements in order to meet his existing commitments, he was held entitled to recover damages for misrepresentation from the shipowner. The shipowner's argument, based on *Grant* v *Norway*[65] that the agent had no authority to enter an incorrect date on the bill, was firmly rejected. 'It cannot be said that the nature and limitations of the agent's authority are known to exclude authority to insert the dates on the grounds that the ascertainment of the correct date is obviously quite outside the scope of the functions or capacities of those agents.'[66] In appropriate circumstances a similar estoppel might apply to statements in the bill as to the date on which the cargo was shipped.[67]

5.2.2 AS EVIDENCE OF THE CONTRACT OF CARRIAGE

On the reverse side of every standard liner bill of lading form is to be found a detailed set of printed contractual terms or a reference to the 'long form' bill in which they are set out in full. The accepted view is that, at least so far as the shipper is concerned, these terms do not constitute the contract of carriage itself, but merely provide evidence of it. The contract is normally concluded orally long before the bill is issued, and the terms are inferred from the carrier's sailing announcements and from any negotiations with loading brokers before the goods are shipped. Consequently, should the goods be lost or damaged before a bill of lading is issued, the shipper will not be deprived of a remedy for

---

[62] (1886) 18 QBD 147.
[63] *Ibid* p 154 *per* Lopes LJ.
[64] [1986] 1 Lloyd's Rep 261. Cf. *The Almak* [1985] 1 Lloyd's Rep 557.
[65] See *supra* at pp 121–2.
[66] [1986] 1 Lloyd's Rep at p 265. For the power to amend incorrect dates inserted in bills of lading by error, see *The Wilomi Tanana* [1993] 2 Lloyd's Rep 41.
[67] See *Westpac Banking Corp* v *South Carolina Nat Bank* [1986] 1 Lloyd's Rep 311; *Alimport* v *Soubert Shipping Co Ltd* [2000] 2 Lloyd's Rep 447.

breach of contract.[68] Similarly, if the printed terms of the bill of lading which is subsequently issued do not comply with those of the earlier oral agreement, the shipper is not debarred from submitting oral evidence to establish the precise terms of that agreement. This view was expressed as early as 1879 by Lush J in the following terms: 'A bill of lading is not the contract but only the evidence of the contract and it does not follow that a person who accepts the bill of lading which the shipowner hands him necessarily, and without regard to circumstances, binds himself to abide by all its stipulations. If a shipper is not aware when he ships them, or is not informed in the course of the shipment, that the bill of lading which will be tendered to him will contain such a clause, he has a right to suppose that his goods are received on the usual terms, and to require a bill of lading which shall express those terms.'[69]

Surprisingly, however, the only actual decision on this point arose at first instance in the case of *The Ardennes*.[70] Here the plaintiff exporter wished to ship a consignment of mandarin oranges from Cartegena to London, where he was anxious they should arrive before 1 December in order to avoid a threatened rise in import duty. He explained the position to shipping agents who gave an oral assurance that if the cargo was loaded on 22 November, the vessel would sail direct to London. In fact, the vessel on which the oranges were shipped already had cargo on board destined for Antwerp, while the bill of lading which was eventually issued included a liberty entitling the vessel to call at intermediate ports on the voyage to London. As the result of calling in at Antwerp, the vessel did not reach London until 4 December by which time there had been an increase in import duty and a considerable fall in the market price of oranges due to an influx of other cargoes. When the plaintiff sought to recover damages for breach of contract, the shipowner pleaded in defence the liberty clause in the bill of lading. In holding that oral evidence was admissible to establish the original terms of the contract, Lord Goddard CJ had no doubts about the status of the bill of lading:

'It is, I think, well settled that a bill of lading is not, in itself, the contract between the shipowner and the shipper of goods, though it has been said to be excellent evidence of its terms . . . The contract has come into existence before the bill of lading is signed. The bill of lading is signed by one party only and handed by him to the shipper, usually after the goods have been put on board. No doubt if the shipper finds that it contains terms with which he is not content, or that it does not contain some term for which he has stipulated, he might, if there were time, demand his goods back, but he is not in my opinion thereby prevented from giving evidence that there was a contract which was made before the bill of lading was signed and that it was different from that which is found in the document or contained some additional term. He is not a party to the preparation of the bill of lading, nor does he sign it.'[71]

If this statement is correct, two reservations still need to be made. First, the bill of lading will clearly provide prima facie evidence of the terms of the contract of carriage and in many cases it may not be easy for the party challenging its accuracy to discharge the burden of proof. Secondly, it is inaccurate to state in general terms that the shipper

---

[68] *Pyrene* v *Scindia Navigation Co* [1954] 2 QB 402.
[69] *Crooks* v *Allan* (1879) 5 QBD 38 at p 40. See also Lord Bramwell in *Sewell* v *Burdick* (1884) 10 App Cas 74 at p 105.
[70] [1951] 1 KB 55. See now *Cho Yang Shipping Co Ltd* v *Coral (UK) Ltd* [1997] 2 Lloyd's Rep 641.
[71] *Ibid* at pp 59–60.

is no party to the preparation of the bill of lading. In the majority of cases he will be responsible for filling in the details of the cargo to be shipped at which time he will have an opportunity to check the remaining terms of the document.

There can be no doubt, however, that once indorsed for value to a bona fide third party, the bill of lading becomes conclusive evidence of the terms of the contract of carriage. In *Leduc* v *Ward*[72] the indorsees of a bill of lading sought to recover damages for a consignment of rape seed, shipped from Fiume to Dunkirk, which had been lost off the mouth of the Clyde. They argued that as the vessel had made an unjustifiable deviation to Glasgow, the shipowners could not rely on the perils of the sea exception in the bill. The shipowners on their part contended that the deviation was not unjustified since the shippers were aware at the time of shipment that the vessel intended to call at Glasgow. In rejecting this argument, the Court of Appeal held that, in the circumstances, the bill provided conclusive evidence of the terms of the contract. The decision was in essence based on an interpretation of s 1 of the Bills of Lading Act 1855[73] which provides that the indorsee of a bill 'shall have transferred to, and vested in, him all rights of suit, and be subject to the same liability in respect of such goods, as if the contract contained in the bill of lading had been made with himself'.[74] Fry LJ preferred to rest his judgment 'on the view that the provision of the statute, making the contract contained in the bill of lading assignable, is inconsistent with the idea that anything which took place between the shipper and the shipowner and not embodied in the bill of lading, could affect the contract'.[75]

Up to this point the case appears to be no more than another example of the application of the estoppel doctrine in favour of a bona fide indorsee of the bill for value, and in line with the reaction of the courts towards the receipt function of the bill outlined in 5.2.1, *supra*. The argument was, however, taken a stage further by an alternative justification for the decision advanced by Lord Esher:[76]

'it may be true that the contract of carriage is made before [the bill] is given because it would generally be made before the goods are sent down to the ship: but when the goods are put on board the captain has authority to reduce that contract into writing; and then the general doctrine of law is applicable by which, where the contract has been reduced into writing, which is intended to constitute the contract, parol evidence to alter or qualify the effect of such writing is not admissible, and the writing is the only evidence of the contract'.

A writer[77] has rightly pointed out that this latter argument is equally applicable to the bill in the hands of the shipper and argues that this throws some doubt on the authority of the decision in *The Ardennes*.[78] His thesis is strengthened by the fact that s 1

---

[72] (1888) 20 QBD 475.

[73] Now repealed. See s 6 of the Carriage of Goods by Sea Act 1992.

[74] With respect to this particular point, s 3(3) of the Carriage of Goods by Sea Act 1992, replacing s 1 of the Bills of Lading Act 1855, is drafted in more general terms. It provides that any lawful holder of a bill of lading who seeks to enforce the contract of carriage shall 'become subject to the same liabilities under that contract as if he had been a party to that contract'. It is submitted, however, that the repeal of the Bills of Lading Act should not affect the validity of the decision in *Leduc* v *Ward* which is a clear case of estoppel.

[75] *Leduc* v *Ward* at p 484.

[76] *Ibid* at p 479.

[77] Debattista, C (1982) 45 MLR 652.

[78] *Supra* p 130.

of the Bills of Lading Act 1855 specifically refers to 'the contract contained in the bill of lading', a point taken up by Fry LJ in *Leduc* v *Ward*:[79] 'Here is a plain declaration of the legislature that there is a contract, contained in the bill of lading, and that the benefit of it is to pass to the indorsee under such circumstances as exist in the present case. It seems to me impossible, therefore, now to contend that there is no contract contained in the bill of lading, whatever may have been the case before the statute.'[80]

To hold *The Ardennes* to be wrongly decided, and to restore the full vigour of the parol evidence rule at this stage, would clearly not conform to the expectations of the reasonable businessman. It must be remembered that the parol evidence rule has itself been much modified since the decision in 1888 in *Leduc* v *Ward*,[81] while a plea of rectification can be raised where the written document is out of line with the terms of a prior oral agreement.[82] It is also noticeable that Lord Goddard, before giving judgment in *The Ardennes* had given full consideration to *Leduc* v *Ward* and had come to the conclusion that it 'was a case between shipowner and indorsee of the bill of lading between whom its terms are conclusive by virtue of the Bills of Lading Act 1855 s 1 . . . Between those parties the statute makes it the contract.'[83] In these circumstances it might seem preferable to regard *The Ardennes* principle as still being good law since it conforms with commercial practice and is in line with the attitude adopted towards the receipt function of the bill.

Bills of lading issued to charterers.   Where the shipper of goods is also charterer of the vessel, the master will still issue a bill of lading. In such circumstances the bill will merely operate as a receipt for the goods shipped, but will not provide evidence of the contract of carriage. The terms of the contract of carriage between shipowner and charterer are exclusively to be found in the charterparty. Should the charterer, however, subsequently indorse the bill to a bona fide purchaser for value, then the bill will become conclusive evidence of the contract of carriage so far as the indorsee is concerned. The situation then will be identical with that in *Leduc* v *Ward*.

5.2.3 AS A DOCUMENT OF TITLE

Negotiable bills of lading originated in sea transport because the voyages were normally lengthy, and invariably slow. The owners of cargo therefore required a document of title in order to raise credit for an international sale or to take advantage of an opportunity to sell the goods in transit. A bill will only operate as a document of title, however, if it is drafted as an 'order' bill, i.e. a bill under which the carrier agrees to deliver the goods at their destination to a named consignee or to his 'order or assigns'. If the document only makes provision for delivery to a named consignee, it is known as a 'straight' bill

---

[79] (1888) 20 QBD 475 at p 483.

[80] Cf. the diametrically opposed interpretation of Lord Bramwell in *Sewell* v *Burdick* (1884) 10 App Cas 74 at p 105 to the effect that s 1 'speaks of the contract contained in the bill of lading. To my mind there is no contract in it. It is a receipt for goods stating the terms on which they were delivered to and received by the ship and therefore excellent evidence of those terms but it is not a contract. That has been made before the bill of lading was given.'

[81] See *Couchman* v *Hill* [1947] KB 554; *City of Westminster Properties* v *Mudd* [1959] Ch 129.

[82] *Roberts* v *Leicestershire County Council* [1961] Ch 555.

[83] [1951] 1 KB at p 60.

of lading or waybill, and lacks the negotiable quality required to qualify it as a document of title.[84] Such a document is not so attractive as security for a commercial credit, nor can the holder of the bill transfer a good title to the goods during transit.

While order bills are transferable by indorsement they are not technically negotiable instruments, since a bona fide transferee gets no better title to the goods covered by the bill than was held by the transferor.[85] The bill merely 'represents' the goods and possession of the bill of lading is treated as equivalent to possession of the goods covered by it – no more, no less. In the colourful words of Bowen LJ in *Sanders v Maclean*:[86]

> 'A cargo at sea while in the hands of the carrier is necessarily incapable of physical delivery. During this period of transit and voyage the bill of lading, by the law merchant, is universally recognised as its symbol and the indorsement and delivery of the bill of lading operates as a symbolic delivery of the cargo. Property in the goods passes by such indorsement and delivery of the bill of lading whenever it is the intention of the parties that the property should pass, just as under similar circumstances the property would pass by an actual delivery of the goods . . . it is the key which, in the hands of the rightful owner, is intended to unlock the door of the warehouse, floating or fixed, in which the goods may chance to be.'

There are three purposes for which possession of the bill may be regarded as equivalent to possession of the goods covered by it:

a) The holder of the bill is entitled to delivery of the goods at the port of discharge.

b) The holder can transfer the ownership of the goods during transit merely by indorsing the bill.

c) The bill can be used as security for a debt.

The development of the bill as a document of title has been so successful that, over the years, it has come to exercise a tripartite function in relation to the contract of carriage, to the sale of goods in transit, and to the raising of a financial credit. There is a general feeling that this multiplicity of roles is not always compatible and that the present form of the bill of lading is somewhat of an anachronism. The feeling is particularly strong among shipowners who believe that the three roles should be separated in order to prevent the carrier being burdened by the incidents of transactions which are none of his concern. The three roles of the bill will now be examined separately:

(I) FUNCTION IN CONTRACT OF SALE

Indorsement and delivery of the bill of lading will normally transfer the ownership in the goods covered by it to the indorsee, provided that four requirements are met:

1   The bill must be transferable on its face. That is, it must be an order bill expressly deliverable to the 'order or assigns' of the shipper or consignee. This is not the case

---

[84] See *The Chitral* [2000] 1 Lloyd's Rep 529.

[85] 'It is well settled that "Negotiable", when used in relation to a bill of lading, means simply transferable. A negotiable bill of lading is not negotiable in the strict sense; it cannot, as can be done by the negotiation of a bill of exchange, give to the transferee a better title than the transferor has got, but it can by endorsement and delivery give as good a title.' Lord Devlin in *Kum v Wah Tat Bank* [1971] AC 439 at p 446. See also Scrutton p 185.

[86] (1883) 11 QBD 327 at p 341.

where the bill makes the goods deliverable only to a specified person, or where the bill is stated to be 'non-negotiable'. Bills are normally issued in sets of three to six originals and, in the absence of any special agreement to the contrary, the indorsement of one bill of a set is sufficient to transfer the ownership in the goods covered by it. No subsequent indorsement of any of the remaining originals will have any effect on the ownership of those particular goods. This was the decision reached in *Barber* v *Meyerstein*[87] where the consignee of a cargo of cotton had sold the goods to Meyerstein, indorsing two of the set of bills to him, and had subsequently sought to use the third bill of the set to gain an advance from a third party. In holding that Meyerstein had a good title to the cotton, Lord Westbury was of the view that:

> 'There can be no doubt . . . that the first person who for value gets the transfer of a bill of lading, though it be only one of a set of three bills, acquires the property, and all subsequent dealings with the other two bills must in law be subordinate to that first one and for this reason, because the property is in the person who first gets a transfer of the bill of lading. It might possibly happen that the shipowner, having no notice of the first dealing with the bill of lading, may, on the second bill being presented by another party, be justified in delivering the goods to that party. But although that may be a discharge to the shipowner, it will in no respect affect the legal ownership of the goods, for the legal ownership of the goods must still remain in the first holder for value of the bill of lading, because he had the legal right in the property.'[88]

2 The goods must be in transit at the time of the indorsement. This does not mean that the cargo need be at sea, but it must be in the possession of a forwarding agent or carrier for the purposes of carriage and not yet be handed over to the party entitled to delivery at the destination port. The right to assign is lost once delivery has been made, a warrant for delivery has been issued or an order for delivery has been accepted.

3 The bill must be initiated by a person with good title. As has been noted earlier, possession of the bill is equivalent to no more than possession of the goods, with the result that an indorsee acquires no better title than that held by the indorser. The bill of lading does not possess the attributes of a negotiable instrument. In essence, indorsement of a bill of lading merely assigns the right to receive the goods described at their destination and operates to discharge the shipowner. It does not transfer an ownership which the shipper never possessed, otherwise possession of the bill would be more effective than possession of the goods.

4 The indorsement must be accompanied by an intention to transfer the ownership in the goods covered by it. Only such interest will be transferred as the parties intended at the time of the indorsement. Three different solutions are possible:

a) The parties intend to pass property absolutely as, for example, in performance of a normal contract of sale.

b) There is no intention to pass any property in the goods to the indorsee. Thus, for example, the shipment may amount to no more than an in-house movement of

---

[87] (1870) LR 4 HL 317.
[88] *Ibid* at p 336.

goods between two branches of the same firm located in different countries. Such shipments are becoming increasingly common with the development of multi-national corporations and clearly no shift in ownership is envisaged in such trans-actions. Alternatively, a seller, when shipping goods under a contract of sale, may wish to retain ownership as security for payment of the price. In the case of the sale of unascertained goods, ownership will normally pass to the buyer when goods are unconditionally appropriated to the contract with the assent of both parties, whether express or implied.[89] Such an implied appropriation will usually take place in the case of export sales when the seller unconditionally delivers the goods to a carrier for transmission to the buyer.[90] Were this to happen, an unpaid seller would be placed at a considerable disadvantage and so, in order to protect him, s 19 of the Sale of Goods Act 1979 confers on him the right, exercisable at the time of shipment, to reserve the right of disposal of the goods, i.e. to prevent the ownership from passing until the price has been paid. The right can be exercised in a variety of ways, either expressly, by naming the seller or his agent as consignee, or by sending the bill of lading to the buyer with a draft bill of exchange attached.[91] In none of these cases will there be any intention that the mere transfer of the bill will effect any change in the ownership of goods.

c) The indorsement may merely be intended to effect a pledge as temporary security for a loan. In such circumstances there will be no intention that the creditor become owner of the goods although, of course, there may be provision for him to assume ownership later, should the loan not be repaid. Indorsements in blank are frequently made in favour of banks as security for money advanced.[92]

(II) FUNCTION IN FINANCING CONTRACT OF SALE

A considerable proportion of international trade is financed by banks through a system of documentary credits. Under this system the prospective buyer requests his bank to open a credit in favour of the seller. In order to draw on this credit the seller is required to ship the contract goods and then to submit appropriate documents in the required form to the bank. The precise obligations of the parties will depend on the terms of the individual credit but standard formats for such arrangements are recommended by the International Chamber of Commerce under the title 'Uniform Customs and Practice for Documentary Credits'.[93] Thus under the normal c.i.f. contract, once the goods are shipped the seller is required to submit to the bank the bill of lading together with the original sales invoice, and a policy of insurance covering the goods during transit. On the presentation of these documents in the form required by the bank, he is then entitled to payment of the contract price.[94]

---

[89] Sale of Goods Act 1979 s 18 rule 5(1).
[90] Sale of Goods Act 1979 s 18 rule 5(2).
[91] See Sale of Goods Act 1979 s 19(3). See *Mitsui* v *Flota Mercante* [1988] 2 Lloyd's Rep 208 (f.o.b. contract); *The Antares III* [2002] 1 Lloyd's Rep 233 (f.a.s. contract).
[92] See *Sewell* v *Burdick* (1884) 10 App Cas 74.
[93] 1993 edition.
[94] *Horst* v *Biddell Bros* [1912] AC 18.

There can be no doubt as to the vital importance of the bill of lading to any system of documentary credits. At the initial stage the bank is able to check the information on the bill to ensure that the seller has complied with all the conditions imposed by the bank for granting the credit, before it makes any advance. Thus statements on the bill indicating the quantity and description of the goods shipped will be checked with the corresponding details on the sales invoice to see if there is any discrepancy. Of equal importance to the bank will be the date on which the goods were shipped, whether they were shipped in good order and condition[95] and whether or not they were loaded on deck.[96] The credit will normally call for a shipped bill of lading rather than one merely acknowledging that the goods have been 'received' by the carrier, while banks are usually reluctant to accept clauses in a bill incorporating terms from any charterparty that may be operative in relation to the carrying vessel.[97]

In addition to the information contained in the bill, the bank is interested in its attribute as a negotiable document of title, capable of providing the required security for the credit. In the event of the creditor defaulting, the bank can thus assume control of the goods through the bill and so recoup its loss. There is, however, one possible security weakness in that bills are normally issued in sets of several originals. There is always a risk that the holder of one of the other originals may obtain delivery of the goods at the port of discharge before the bank.[98] In order to avoid this eventuality the terms of the credit normally provide for the delivery of all bills in the set before any money is advanced by the bank.

(III) FUNCTION IN CARRIAGE CONTRACT

It must be remembered that the prime function of a bill of lading as a document of title is in relation to the contract of carriage and that the two functions already outlined are merely parasitic, at least so far as the carrier is concerned. In the context of the contract of carriage, however, the fact that the bill is a symbol representing the goods during transit has the following consequences:

a) The holder of the bill controls the goods during transit.

b) A lawful holder of the bill, by s 2(1) of the Carriage of Goods by Sea Act 1992, has title to sue under the contract of carriage as if he had been an original party to it. He becomes subject to liabilities under the contract only when he takes or demands delivery of the goods from the carrier, or initiates a claim for loss or damage.

c) The holder is entitled to delivery of the cargo at the port of discharge on presentation of the bill of lading.

The second proposition requires further consideration.

While indorsement and delivery of a bill of lading will normally transfer ownership of the goods covered by it, such indorsement has always been ineffective at common law in transferring to the indorsee the rights and obligations arising under the contract of

---

[95] See Uniform Customs and Practice for Documentary Credits (UCP) 500 (1993 edn) Art 32.
[96] UCP 500 Art 31.
[97] UCP 500 Art 23(a)(vi) and Art 25(a)(i).
[98] See *Glyn, Mills & Co v E & W India Dock Co* (1882) 7 App Cas 591.

carriage. The reason is to be found in the traditional doctrine of privity of contract, which prescribes that only the original parties to the contract can sue or be sued on it. Over the years English law has sought to bridge this gap by a variety of statutory and judicial devices which have enabled receivers of cargo, in the majority of cargo disputes, to acquire title to sue the carrier. Initially the legislature sought to solve the problem by the introduction of a statutory form of assignment by s 1 of the Bills of Lading Act 1855. Under this statute, title to sue was linked to the property in the goods and a consignee or endorsee of the bill of lading acquired title to sue provided that property in the goods passed to him 'upon or by reason of such consignment or endorsement'.[99] To reinforce this statutory provision, the common law subsequently developed two complementary remedies. First, the courts were prepared to imply a contract between consignee or indorsee and the carrier – a contract separate and distinct from the original contract of carriage between shipper and carrier – from delivery of the goods at the port of discharge against presentation of the bill of lading.[100] Secondly, in appropriate cases, a remedy in tort was available where the damage or loss had resulted from the negligence of the carrier or his servants.[101]

Court decisions over the years, however, highlighted the inherent limitations of these stratagems and indicated the necessity for more fundamental reform. The Law Commission responded by proposing a radical solution to the problem which was given statutory force in the Carriage of Goods by Sea Act 1992. Title to sue on a carriage contract is now governed by the provisions of this statute,[102] although the implied contract approach is still available should the need arise for an alternative remedy.[103]

(a) THE CARRIAGE OF GOODS BY SEA ACT 1992

This Act, drafted by the Law Commission, came into force on 16 September 1992 and governs all contracts of carriage concluded on or after that date.[104] Unlike its predecessor, the Bills of Lading Act 1855 which applied only to bills of lading, the provisions of the 1992 Act also cover sea waybills and ship's delivery orders.[105] In the case of bills of lading, it is immaterial whether the document is a shipped or received for shipment bill.[106] The Secretary of State is also empowered to draft regulations extending the provisions of the Act to cover any electronic transmission of information which might in the future replace written documentation.[107]

---

[99] For the full text of this section, see *infra* at p 355.

[100] See *infra*, pp 140 ff.

[101] See *infra*, pp 143 ff.

[102] Contracts for the carriage of goods by sea are expressly excluded from the operation of s 1 of the Contracts (Rights of Third Parties) Act 1999 which, subject to satisfying the requirements of the Act, confers a right to enforce a term of a contract on a person who is not a party to that contract. Under s 6(5)(a) of the Act, third parties to a carriage contract acquire no rights other than an entitlement to avail themselves of an exclusion or limitation of liability clause contained in such a contract. For a full discussion of the effects of this statute, see *infra* pp 154 ff.

[103] For a detailed account of the law prior to the 1992 Act, see the second edition of this book, pp 148–55.

[104] The Act repealed its predecessor, the Bills of Lading Act 1855.

[105] Section 1(i).

[106] This provision disposes of the questionable argument that received for shipment bills do not constitute documents of title and so fall outside the ambit of the Bills of Lading Act 1855. See Debattista, C, *Sale of Goods Carried by Sea*, 2nd edn, 1998, pp 40 ff.

[107] Section 1(5).

The legislation envisages two significant departures from existing law:

a) title to sue is no longer linked to property in the goods;

b) the transfer of rights under a contract of carriage is effected independently of any transfer of liabilities.

The new law can be stated as follows:

1 Title to sue is now vested in the lawful holder of a bill of lading, the consignee identified in a sea waybill or the person entitled to delivery under a ship's delivery order, irrespective of whether or not they are owners of the goods covered by the document.[108]

2 The 'lawful holder' of a bill of lading is defined[109] as a person in possession of the bill in good faith who is either:

a) identified in the bill as consignee, or

b) an indorsee of the bill,[110] or

c) a person who would have fallen within categories a) or b) if he had come into possession of the bill before it ceased to be a document of title.

The final provision will cover a situation such as that where goods are delivered against a bank guarantee before the bill comes into the possession of a consignee or an indorsee.[111] By the time such a bill eventually comes into their possession, it is no longer a transferable document of title in the sense of entitling its holder to possession of the goods.[112] The provision will also cover the case where goods are lost in transit before the bill comes into the hands of a consignee or ultimate indorsee.[113] In both cases, however, the ultimate holder of the bill will obtain title to sue only provided that he became holder of the bill in pursuance of contractual or other arrangements made before the bill ceased to be a transferable document of title.[114]

3 The transfer of the right to sue under s 2(1) of the Act, from one lawful holder of a bill to another, will extinguish the contractual rights of the shipper or of any intermediate holder of the bill.[115] This result will follow even if the shipper retains the property in the

---

[108] Section 2(1). See *East West Corp v DKBS 1912* [2003] 1 Lloyd's Rep 239.

[109] Section 5(2).

[110] But not where bill indorsed by mistake and never delivered by indorser to indorsee. *The Aegean Sea* [1998] 2 Lloyd's Rep 39. This category also includes the holder of a bearer bill which is transferable by delivery without the necessity for a specific indorsement. See *Keppel Tatlee Bank v Bandung Shipping* [2003] 1 Lloyd's Rep 619.

[111] See *The Delfini* [1990] 1 Lloyd's Rep 252.

[112] No provision is made for the situation where the bill never comes into the possession of the ultimate indorsee, either because it is lost or because an intermediate holder considers there is little point in transferring it once the goods have been delivered.

[113] Section 5(4).

[114] Section 2(2)(a).

[115] Section 2(5). Transfer of the right to sue will not, however, affect the rights of the original parties to a contract evidenced by a sea waybill, or to the contract under which the delivery order was issued. While indorsement of the bill of lading will transfer the contractual rights of the shipper, it will not necessarily transfer any possible rights in bailment. See Mance LJ in *East & West Corp v DKBS 1912* [2003] 1 Lloyd's Rep 239 at p 253: 'The 1992 Act does not expressly modify any rights other than contractual rights. The definition of the holder is in terms of possession of the bill, not in terms of any possessory rights in respect of the goods that such possession may bring with it.'

goods after such indorsement and he will not regain title to sue even though he regains possession of the relevant documents unless they have been reindorsed back to him. Thus in *East West Corp* v *DKBS*[116] bills of lading had been indorsed to bankers in connection with documentary credits and, on the buyer failing to pay the price for the goods, the bills were returned to the shipper without further indorsement. In these circumstances the shipper had no title to sue.[117] The operation of this provision also raises a practical problem which is specifically dealt with by the Act. The problem relates to the situation where, under a contract of sale, goods are shipped by a seller and eventually delivered to an overseas buyer on presentation of the relevant bill of lading. On transfer of the bill to the buyer, the seller will lose his right to sue on the contract of carriage while, on delivery of the goods to the buyer, the bill of lading will cease to be a document of title. What, then, is the position if the goods have been damaged in transit and are subsequently rejected by the buyer? The seller is the only person with an interest in suing the carrier, but has apparently lost his right of suit on transfer of the bill. In these circumstances the Act specifically confers on him title to sue when he regains lawful possession of the bill.[118]

4 Since title to sue is divorced from property in the goods, a person with rights of suit under s 2(1) may not have suffered personal loss or damage resulting from the carrier's breach of contract. In such an event he is entitled to exercise rights of suit for the benefit of the party who has actually suffered the loss, and will then hold any damages recovered from the carrier for the account of such person.[119] Unfortunately, while the Act empowers the holder of the bill to sue on another's behalf, it apparently does not place him under any obligation to do so. Parties such as banks or other financial institutions, who are looking to the bill for purposes of security, may therefore prefer to be named as consignees, with a consequent right to sue, rather than to rely on the goodwill of future holders of the bill.

5 As mentioned earlier, liabilities under the contract of carriage are no longer transferred simultaneously with title to sue. Under s 3 of the new Act they will only attach to persons in whom rights of suit are vested when they either:

a) take or demand delivery of the goods,[120] or

b) make a claim under the contract of carriage, or

c) took or demanded delivery of the goods before rights of suit vested in them under s 2(1) of the Act.

The final provision covers the situation where the receivers took delivery of the goods against a bank indemnity before they became 'lawful holders' of the relevant bills within the meaning of the Act.[121]

---

[116] [2003] 1 Lloyd's Rep 239.

[117] See also *Keppel Tatlee Bank Ltd* v *Bandung Shipping Ltd* [2003] 1 Lloyd's Rep 619.

[118] Section 2(2)(b).

[119] Section 2(4). This appears to be a statutory enactment of a common law principle laid down in *Dunlop* v *Lambert* (1839) 6 Cl&F 600.

[120] But demand for delivery reversible until indorsee takes actual delivery of cargo, *The Berge Sisar* [1998] 2 Lloyd's Rep 475; see also *The Aegean Sea* [1998] 2 Lloyd's Rep 39.

[121] See *The Delfini* [1990] 1 Lloyd's Rep 252.

The clear division of rights from liabilities will effectively protect a bank which is holding the bill as security for a credit from incurring liabilities under the contract of carriage until it seeks to enforce its security by claiming delivery of the goods or instituting proceedings against the carrier.[122]

Lastly, the Act provides that such transfer of liabilities is without prejudice to the existing liabilities of the original party to the contract.[123] Intermediate holders of the bill will presumably no longer incur liability under the contract of carriage once they have transferred title to sue to a subsequent holder of the bill.

6 The provisions outlined above apply equally, so far as appropriate, to the consignee identified in a sea waybill or the person entitled to delivery under a ship's delivery order. The former is entitled to sue on the contract evidenced by the sea waybill,[124] and the latter to enforce the terms of the undertaking contained in the delivery order,[125] but only in relation to the goods covered by that order.[126] Both will incur liability only when they seek to enforce the respective contractual undertakings.

Sea waybills are by definition non-negotiable,[127] but they often contain provision for an alternative consignee to be nominated by the shipper. In such a case, title to sue will be transferred on the shipper instructing the carrier to deliver to a person other than the consignee named in the sea waybill.[128]

(b) THE IMPLIED CONTRACT APPROACH

While most of the problems associated with title to sue have been resolved by the Carriage of Goods by Sea Act 1992, the well-established common law device of the implied contract remains available should the remedies provided by the Act prove deficient or inappropriate in any particular case. In adopting this approach the courts have been prepared, in appropriate circumstances, to imply a contract between a consignee or indorsee of a bill of lading and the carrier, which is separate and independent of the original contract of carriage between shipper and carrier. This new contract was implied from delivery of the goods against presentation of the bill of lading, the consideration being provided by the payment by the receiver of the goods of any outstanding freight or other charges due under the original contract of carriage. It was then a short step for the courts to presume that the terms of the implied contract were those of the bill against which delivery had been obtained. An example of the application of this principle is provided by *Cremer* v *General Carriers*[129] where a cargo of tapioca chips had been shipped in bulk under two bills of lading which were issued to the consignee.

---

[122] Cf. the earlier solution in *Sewell* v *Burdick* (1884) 10 App Cas 74.

[123] Section 3(3). This provision will clarify the uncertainty which existed in relation to the operation of s 1 of the Bills of Lading Act 1855. See *The Athanasia Comninos* [1990] 1 Lloyd's Rep 277 at p 281 *per* Mustill J. Cf. Bills of Lading Act s 2.

[124] Section 2(1)(b).

[125] Section 2(1)(c).

[126] Section 2(3).

[127] Section 1(2)(a) and 1(3). For the purposes of the Act, the term 'sea waybill' would appear to include the 'straight' bill of lading, i.e. a non-negotiable bill of lading under which goods are to be delivered to a named consignee. The definition of 'bill of lading' in s 1(2)(a) specifically excludes non-negotiable documents.

[128] Section 5(3).

[129] [1973] 2 Lloyd's Rep 366. See also *Brandt* v *Liverpool SN Co* [1924] 1 KB 575.

Both bills were clean despite the fact that the mate's receipts recorded that the tapioca was damp on shipment. The consignee then indorsed one of the bills to the plaintiff and handed it over together with a ship's delivery order for part of the remainder of the cargo. After the plaintiff had taken delivery of his share of the cargo against production of these documents, he subsequently sued the carrier for cargo damage caused by moisture, seeking to rely on the estoppel created by the clean bills. Even though he had no rights under the original contract of carriage, since property in the goods had not been transferred by indorsement of the bill, the trial judge held that he could recover. In his view, 'A contract incorporating the terms of the bill of lading was to be implied between the plaintiffs and the defendants by reason of the payment of the freight by the plaintiffs and the delivery of the goods by the defendants against the bill of lading.'[130] Furthermore, it was held that where the plaintiff had taken delivery against a *ship's* delivery order (as opposed to a delivery order issued by the seller), he was entitled to the same rights as if he had taken delivery under a bill of lading. In both cases, however, it was essential that delivery was taken against payment of freight or other outstanding charges, since the latter provided the consideration necessary to make the implied contract enforceable. Presumably in cases where the freight was prepaid and there were no other charges outstanding, the indorsee would be unable to invoke this principle.

The limits of this doctrine have not been clearly defined, although it has been established that the decision as to whether or not a contract is to be implied in any particular case is one of fact and not of law.[131] While some judges have urged restraint,[132] others have been prepared to extend its application as a general panacea. Thus in *The Elli 2*[133] the Court of Appeal held that, where cargo had reached the port of discharge in advance of the documentation, a guarantee to present the bill when it arrived was as effective as actual presentation in raising the inference of a contract. Again, where, in the circumstances of a particular case, there has been a degree of mutual cooperation between carrier and receiver of the cargo which is only explicable on the existence of some form of contractual relationship between them, the courts have been prepared to imply a contract to give 'business reality' to the transaction. Thus in *The Captain Gregos (No 2)*[134] a consignment of oil, which had been the subject of a series of chain sales, was delivered to the ultimate purchaser in Rotterdam. The appropriate documentation not being available, the shipowner made delivery against a letter of indemnity. The available evidence suggested to the court that the cargo could not have been discharged into the purchaser's refinery complex in Rotterdam without the active cooperation of the purchaser and the crew of the vessel. In these circumstances the Court of Appeal found 'very powerful grounds for concluding that it is necessary to imply a contract between BP and the shipowners to give business reality to the transaction between them and create the obligations which, as we think, both parties believed to exist'.[135] The same

---

[130] At p 371 *per* Kerr J, citing with approval the Court of Appeal in *Brandt v Liverpool SN Co, supra.*
[131] See Parke B in *Möller v Young* (1855) 25 LJQB 94 at p 96.
[132] For example, Staughton J in *The Kelo* [1985] 2 Lloyd's Rep 85 at p 87; May LJ in *The Elli 2* [1985] 1 Lloyd's Rep 107 at p 118.
[133] [1985] 1 Lloyd's Rep 107.
[134] [1990] 2 Lloyd's Rep 395.
[135] *Ibid* at p 403.

court was, however, less accommodating in the subsequent case of *The Gudermes*[136] where a quantity of oil sold to the plaintiffs was shipped on a vessel which was subsequently discovered to have no operative heating coils. The oil having cooled in transit, the plaintiff's sub-purchasers refused delivery in Ravenna, fearing the oil might clog their underwater sealine. The plaintiffs accordingly arranged for the oil to be transhipped into another vessel off Malta, had it reheated on board and thereafter delivered at Ravenna. In an attempt to recover the cost of transhipment, the plaintiffs argued that, as a result of the dealings between themselves and the carrier in respect of the transhipment, there was to be implied a *Brandt* v *Liverpool*[137] contract on the terms of the bill of lading which expressly incorporated the Hague/Visby Rules. The Court of Appeal rejected this contention and stressed that, before any contract could be implied, the conduct of the parties must be explicable only on the basis of the contract sought to be implied. In its opinion, the final decision must be one of fact and, in the circumstances of this particular case, the facts did not support the contention that any new contract between the parties should be implied.

There are clearly limits to the extent to which the fiction can be taken. No contract was implied in *The Aramis*[138] where there was a complete failure by the carrier to deliver any cargo. In this case a quantity of goods covered by several bills of lading had been shipped in bulk but, by the time the final bill was presented at the port of discharge, the supply of cargo had been exhausted. The Court of Appeal refused to imply a contract from the mere act of presentation of a bill of lading in the absence of any corresponding response from the carrier which could be interpreted as an 'acceptance' of the plaintiff's 'offer'. This decision effectively denied any remedy for non-delivery.

Again, mere presentation of a bill of lading followed by part delivery will not constitute sufficient evidence to found an implied contract in circumstances where the conduct of the parties is equally explicable as constituting performance of obligations and rights under the original contract.[139] The absence of any consideration provided by the party presenting the bill of lading may be an important factor in reaching such a conclusion, but it does not appear to be decisive.[140]

Lastly, there are two practical problems resulting from the implied contract concept. The first raises doubts as to whether the device will provide a remedy for the consignee under a waybill. As waybills were designed to avoid the problems arising from the late arrival of shipping documents, and consequently are not normally presented to obtain delivery of the cargo, the implied contract device fails to provide a practical solution to the problem of the consignee's title to sue under such a document. The second query relates to the proper law of the implied contract. In the absence of any choice of law clause in the bill of lading, the proper law of a contract implied from the conduct of the parties at the port of discharge might differ from that appropriate to the original contract of carriage.

---

[136] [1993] 1 Lloyd's Rep 311.
[137] [1924] 1 KB 575.
[138] [1989] 1 Lloyd's Rep 213.
[139] [1989] 1 Lloyd's Rep 213 at p 224 *per* Bingham LJ, at p 230 *per* Stuart-Smith LJ.
[140] [1989] 1 Lloyd's Rep 213 at pp 224, 225 *per* Bingham LJ. Cf. *The Captain Gregos (No 2)* [1990] 2 Lloyd's Rep 395.

5.3 BILLS OF LADING AND THIRD PARTIES

While the 1992 Act has resolved most of the difficulties associated with the doctrine of privity of contract in so far as they affect the relationship between the holder of a bill of lading and the contractual carrier, a number of residual problems still remain. For example, to what extent may the holder of a bill of lading sue persons other than the contractual carrier for loss or damage to the goods caused by their acts or omissions, and to what extent may such individuals, when sued, rely for protection on the terms of a contract of carriage to which they were not parties? The following is a review of the strategies adopted by the common law in an attempt to find a solution for the various problems arising from a strict application of the privity doctrine.

5.3.1 LIABILITY IN TORT

Where a claim for loss or damage is based on the negligence of the carrier or his servants, an alternative to the contractual remedy might be to sue the party responsible for the loss in tort. There would be little advantage to a bill of lading holder in pursuing such an action against the contractual carrier,[141] but there are a number of other situations where a tortious action might provide an effective remedy. Thus, in appropriate circumstances, it might be advantageous to sue an agent or servant of the carrier who was personally responsible for the loss. Again, many bill of lading contracts include an express provision entitling the contractual carrier to sub-contract the whole or part of the carriage. In the event of such delegation of performance, where the goods are damaged or lost while in the possession of the sub-contractor, the bill of lading holder may, for a variety of reasons, prefer to sue such sub-contractor in tort rather than to rely on his remedies against the contractual carrier. On the one hand, the latter may not be financially sound; on the other, the bill of lading holder may be attracted by a right of recovery in tort free from the exceptions and limitation of liability provisions contained in the bill of lading. In the majority of the above cases there will be no contractual relationship between the claimant and the actual tortfeasor with the result that the doctrine of privity would normally prevent the latter from invoking any of the defences available under the contract of carriage.[142]

There is, however, one serious qualification to the availability of this right of action in tort. Roskill J held in the case of *Margarine Union* v *Cambay Prince*[143] that an action in negligence would not succeed unless the plaintiff was, at the time of the commission of the tort, the owner of the goods in question or the person entitled to immediate

---

[141] In circumstances where the Hague/Visby Rules are applicable, Art IV *bis* rule 1 provides that the defences and limits of liability provided for in the Rules can be invoked by the carrier irrespective of whether the action against him is founded in contract or in tort.

[142] The remedy in tort might also be the solution to the problem where a bill of lading holder has suffered no personal loss or damage but is unwilling to exercise rights of suit under s 2(4) of the Carriage of Goods by Sea Act 1992 for the benefit of the party who has actually suffered the loss.

[143] [1969] 1 KB 219.

possession of them.[144] The facts of the case were that a cargo of copra, shipped in bulk, had been seriously damaged by giant cockroaches as the result of the negligence of the shipowner in failing to have the holds of his ship fumigated before the commencement of the voyage. The plaintiff was the holder of a delivery order for part of the cargo issued by the seller under a c.i.f. contract. As the plaintiff did not become owner of the goods in question until they had been ascertained on discharge, Roskill J held that an action in negligence would not lie.

The decision met with considerable criticism and attempts were made to circumvent it;[145] one judge in 1981 going so far as to express the view that if *Margarine Union* v *Cambay Prince* 'were being decided today, it would be decided differently'.[146]

This more liberal approach was firmly rejected a few years later by a unanimous House of Lords in *The Aliakmon*[147] who restored the full vigour of the principle laid down in *Margarine Union* v *Cambay Prince*. In this case a cargo of steel suffered damage in transit due *inter alia* to negligent stowage at a time when the risk but not the property in the goods had passed to a c. and f. buyer. In denying the buyer any remedy in the tort of negligence on the ground that he was not the owner of the steel at the time the damage was inflicted, Lord Brandon asserted that the decision in the *Margarine Union* case 'was good law at the time it was decided and remains good law today'.[148] In their Lordships' view there was no lacuna in the law relating to carrier liability which required to be filled by extending the range of duty of care in negligence. If for some reason the indorsee of a bill of lading could not sue, because the property in the goods remained with the indorser after indorsement of the bill, this merely meant that the indorser rather than the indorsee retained the right to sue the carrier for negligent damage to the goods. In such circumstances buyers under a c.i.f. or c. and f. sale could gain adequate protection by ensuring that the contract of sale contained provision that 'the sellers should either exercise this right for their [the buyers'] account . . . or assign such right to them to exercise for themselves'.[149]

There can be little doubt that this decision was to a great extent influenced by policy considerations. On the one hand, the courts have a long-standing reluctance to extend the right of recovery in negligence for what amounts to pure economic loss. On the other, there is evident concern that by allowing the indorsee to sue in negligence – free

---

[144] For an example of a non-owner who nevertheless has an immediate right to possession, see *The Hamburg Star* [1994] 1 Lloyd's Rep 399. But the tort of negligence requires both a breach of duty and resulting damage. What is the position where title in the goods is transferred after the breach of duty occurred but before the resulting loss? The House of Lords in *The Starsin* [2003] 1 Lloyd's Rep 571 held that, while such loss might in principle be recoverable, once 'more than insignificant damage' had resulted from such breach of duty, the tort was complete and that further damage arising from the same negligent act, after the claimant acquired title, would not give rise to a separate cause of action.

[145] See *The Irene's Success* [1981] 2 Lloyd's Rep 635, a decision which was overruled in *The Aliakmon*. Judicial opinion was, however, divided, and support for the views expressed in the *Margarine Union* case was to be found in *The Elafi* [1981] 2 Lloyd's Rep 679; Cf. Sheen J in *The Nea Tyhi* [1982] 1 Lloyd's Rep 606.

[146] Lloyd J in *The Irene's Success* [1981] 2 Lloyd's Rep at p 639.

[147] [1986] 2 Lloyd's Rep 1. Followed in New Zealand case of *The Seven Pioneer* [2001] 2 Lloyd's Rep 57. See also *The Starsin* [2003] 1 Lloyd's Rep 571; Gaskell 8.73 ff; Carver 5.111 ff.

[148] [1986] 2 Lloyd's Rep 1 at p 11, *per* Lord Brandon.

[149] See *The Albazero* [1976] 2 Lloyd's Rep 467.

from any constraints imposed by the contract of carriage – there is the danger that the carrier would lose the protection afforded by the terms of that contract and the relevant provisions of the Hague/Visby Rules.[150]

5.3.2 THIRD PARTY RELIANCE ON BILL OF LADING TERMS

Any unfettered right of action available to a cargo owner as against an actual tortfeasor creates its own problems. A shipper of goods, when negotiating a contract of carriage, will be aware that the obligations arising from that contract will rarely be performed personally by the contractual carrier but will be delegated to employees of the carrier or to independent contractors engaged to carry out a particular function, such as stevedores engaged to load or discharge the cargo. A brief glance at the printed terms of the bill of lading will also alert the shipper to the fact that, in many cases, the carrier will reserve the right to delegate performance of the carriage itself to a sub-contractor, although the contractual carrier will normally retain primary responsibility for due performance of the contractual obligations involved.[151] In these circumstances it would seem reasonable to expect that the carriage would be undertaken on the agreed terms, including exceptions and limitation of liability provisions, irrespective of the identity of the party who actually performed the contract, or of the party who sought to claim for loss or damage to the cargo: provided, of course, that there was an identity of interest between the respective parties, and that any party seeking the protection of the contractual terms was providing the identical services stipulated in the contract.

Unfortunately, this desirable result is often defeated by the intervention of the doctrine of privity of contract with the consequence that, where performance of obligations under a contract of carriage is delegated to an employee or a sub-contractor, the shipper can ignore the provisions of that contract and sue the employee or sub-contractor directly in tort where the loss or damage to cargo resulted from their negligence. The latter cannot rely on the protection afforded by the terms of that contract since they were not parties to it.

Such results are undesirable for a number of reasons. On the one hand, they do not correspond with commercial reality. Once the parties have agreed on the terms on which a contract of carriage is to be performed and the overall risk and insurance liability has been allocated, it does not make commercial sense for the resultant balance of interest to be disturbed. Again, there are policy reasons rendering it undesirable for a party to invoke the privity doctrine in an attempt to circumvent the terms of an agreement to which he has freely and expressly consented. Thirdly, while it may be possible to avoid some of the more objectionable results of the privity rule by the introduction of a variety of indemnity and cross-indemnity clauses into the respective carriage contracts, such devices are not always successful and, in any event, result in unnecessary complications in the relevant law.

---

[150] Their lordships rejected the suggestion of Goff LJ in the Court of Appeal ([1985] 1 Lloyd's Rep 199 at p 225 that under his so-called principle of transferred loss if the buyer were allowed to sue the carrier in negligence he should have no more extensive right of recovery than the seller would have had under the provisions of the contract of carriage. Cf. Art IV *bis* rule 1 of the Hague/Visby Rules.

[151] See P & O Nedlloyd Container Bill, cl 6. Cf. Conlinebill, cl 6 where 'the responsibility of the carrier shall be limited to the part of the transport performed by him on vessels under his management . . .'

When faced with this dilemma, the courts have used considerable ingenuity in devising a variety of strategies to extend the protection afforded by the terms of the contract of carriage to litigants who were clearly not parties to it.

(a) BAILMENT ON TERMS

One method of achieving this objective was advanced by the Privy Council in the recent case of *The Pioneer Container*.[152] A variety of plaintiffs had contracted with freight carriers for the carriage of their goods from Taiwan to Hong Kong either as a complete voyage or as part of a through transport to other ports. In each case the bill of lading issued to the shipper included a clause entitling the carrier to sub-contract 'on any terms the whole, or any part, of the carriage, loading, unloading, storing, warehousing or handling' of the goods. The carriage was in fact sub-contracted to the defendant shipowners, who issued feeder bills acknowledging receipt of the goods and including an exclusive Taiwan jurisdiction clause. On the voyage to Hong Kong the defendants' vessel was involved in a collision and sank with the loss of the plaintiffs' cargo. The latter then sought to recover their loss by the issue of a writ *in rem* in Hong Kong against a sister ship of the defendants' vessel. In reply, the defendants sought a stay of proceedings based on the exclusive Taiwanese jurisdiction clause in the feeder bills.

On these facts the weak link in the defendants' argument was that the jurisdiction clause appeared in their sub-contract with the freight carrier, whereas it was acknowledged that there was no contractual relationship between the defendants and the plaintiffs. The Privy Council sought to bridge this gap by invoking the doctrine of bailment on terms, the possibilities of which had been explored in earlier cases, though largely in obiter dicta.

There could be no doubt that the original contract of carriage concluded between the plaintiffs and the freight carriers created a relationship of bailor and bailee, while Pollock and Wright in the late nineteenth century had taken the view that, if in such a situation the bailor had authorised the bailee to enter into a sub-bailment of the goods, while there would be no privity of contract between the original bailor and the sub-bailee, 'it would seem that both the owner and the first bailee have concurrently the rights of a bailor against the [sub-bailee] according to the nature of the sub-bailment'.[153] To what extent, therefore, could the head bailor be bound by the terms of the sub-bailment? In the view of the Privy Council,[154] 'if the effect of the sub-bailment is that the sub-bailee voluntarily receives into his custody the goods of the owner and so assumes towards the owner the responsibility of a bailee, then to the extent that the terms of the sub-bailment are consented to by the owner, it can properly be said that the owner has authorised the bailee so to regulate the duties of the sub-bailee in respect of the goods entrusted to him, not only towards the bailee but also towards the owner'.

On the facts of *The Pioneer Container* there could be no doubt that the plaintiffs had consented to the sub-bailment and, by authorising the carrier to sub-contract 'on any terms', such consent would encompass all contractual provisions other than those which

---

[152] [1994] 2 AC 324. See also *East West Corp v DKBS 1912* [2003] 1 Lloyd's Rep 239; Gaskell 12.46 ff; Carver 7.094 ff.

[153] Pollock and Wright: *Possession* (1888) p 169.

[154] [1994] 2 AC 324 at p 339.

were unreasonable or unexpected in their context. Moreover, in the view of the Privy Council,[155] the inclusion of a jurisdiction clause, of the type in question, in the sub-bailment 'would be in accordance with the reasonable commercial expectations of those who engage in this type of trade and that such incorporation will generally lead to a conclusion which is eminently sensible in the context of the carriage of goods by sea, especially in a container ship, in so far as it is productive of an ordered and sensible resolution of disputes in a single jurisdiction, so avoiding wasted expenditure in legal costs and an undesirable disharmony of consequences where claims are resolved in different jurisdictions'. Accordingly, the Privy Council granted the stay, holding that the plaintiffs were bound by the jurisdiction clause, even though no contractual relationship existed between them and the sub-bailees.[156]

What then are the characteristics and effects of such a bailment on terms and what potential does it have for use in other carriage situations?[157] It is clear that the relationship between owner of the goods and sub-bailee is independent of contract and is created by the voluntary taking possession of goods with knowledge that they are the property of persons other than the immediate bailor. The result is that such sub-bailees owe the duty of a bailee[158] not only towards their immediate bailor but also towards the owner of the goods.[159] In fulfilling such duties, to what extent can the sub-bailee call in aid the exceptions, limitation of liability provisions and time bars contained in his sub-contract with the intermediate bailor, as reinforced by the Hague or Hague/Visby Rules?

The key requirement would appear to be the consent of the owner of the goods to the sub-bailment on the terms in question. In the words of Lord Denning MR, in the earlier case of *Morris* v *CW Martin & Sons Ltd*,[160] 'The answer to the problem lies, I think, in

---

[155] *Ibid* 347.

[156] While there is no equivalent authority in English case law, the Court of Appeal had to adjudicate on a remarkably similar factual situation in *Dressler UK Ltd* v *Falcongate Freight Management Ltd (The Duke of Yare)* [1992] QB 502. On the hypothesis (which was not admitted) that the cargo owner in that case was bound by the terms of a sub-bailment to which he had consented, the Court of Appeal held that he was nevertheless not caught by an exclusive jurisdiction clause in a bill of lading issued by the sub-bailee since, on its true construction, the clause was only applicable to the parties to the contract covered by that bill of lading. As no contractual relationship existed between the cargo owner and the sub-bailee, the former was accordingly not bound by the clause. Two members of the court, however, expressed regret in reaching this conclusion since, in their view, 'the doctrine of bailment on terms is . . . a pragmatic legal recognition of commercial reality': *Ibid*, 524 *per* Ralph Gibson LJ.

[157] For an outline of the basic principles of bailment and bailment on terms, see Mance LJ in *East West Corp* v *DKBS 1912* [2003] 1 Lloyd's Rep 239, at p 248 ff.

[158] In the case of a carriage contract, the duty owed will invariably be that of a bailee for reward where value is provided by the contractual carrier who subsequently delegates performance to the sub-bailee. No consideration is required moving from the owner of the goods to the sub-bailee. In the words of Lord Goff in *The Pioneer Container* [1994] 2 AC 324, 338: 'Their Lordships . . . consider that, if the sub-bailment is for reward, the obligation owed by the sub-bailee to the owner must likewise be that of a bailee for reward notwithstanding that the reward is payable not by the owner but by the bailee.'

[159] The duty of a bailee towards the owner of the goods involves not only a duty to take reasonable care of the goods while in his possession but also to ensure that, if he transfers possession of the goods to a third party, he does so on a basis consistent with the bailment he himself has undertaken. See Mance LJ in *East West Corp* v *DKBS 1912* [2003] 1 Lloyd's Rep 239, at p 257. A carrier who warehoused goods with a third party was liable when he failed to contract for or insist upon the presentation of original bills of lading prior to delivery of the goods by the warehouse operator.

[160] [1966] 1 QB 716 at p 729.

this: the owner is bound by the conditions if he has expressly or impliedly consented to the bailee making a sub-bailment containing those conditions, but not otherwise.' Although this opinion was expressed obiter, it was adopted by the Privy Council as the basis of its judgment in *The Pioneer Container*.[161] On the facts of that case there could be little doubt as to the owner's consent. The bill of lading provided that the carrier should be entitled to sub-contract 'on any terms' the whole or any part of the carriage. 'Where, as here, the consent is very wide in its terms only terms which are so unusual that they could not reasonably be understood to fall within such consent, are likely to be held to be excluded.' In the opinion of the Privy Council, there was nothing unusual or unreasonable in an exclusive jurisdiction clause which would commonly be found in the container trade.

Once one accepts the premise of a sub-bailment on terms, then the facts of *The Pioneer Container* are reasonably clear cut. To what extent, however, will this principle be applicable in other carriage situations? Bills of lading for sea carriage frequently incorporate clauses entitling the carrier to sub-contract the carriage of the goods, while for bills covering combined transport, sub-contracting is virtually a necessity. Some bills follow *The Pioneer Container* pattern and allow sub-contracting 'on any terms'[162] or 'on any terms whatsoever',[163] others 'on any terms which are reasonable in the circumstances'.[164] More difficulty may be caused by bills which include a general authority to sub-contract, though without reference to the terms.[165] Here again, it could be argued that the shipper has consented to the bailment on terms subject only to the aforementioned test of reasonableness.

What, however, is the position where the bill of lading makes no reference to the possibility of sub-contracting? Lord Denning MR indicated in *Morris v Martin*[166] that implied consent by the shipper of the goods to a sub-bailment on terms might be sufficient and this view was adopted by the Privy Council in *The Pioneer Container*: 'Such consent may, as Lord Denning pointed out, be express or implied; and in this context the sub-bailee may also be able to invoke, where appropriate, the principle of ostensible authority.'[167] A typical example of implied consent might arise when the shipper of goods contracts for their carriage with a freight forwarder or other person known to him to operate as a non-vessel owning carrier. In such a case the shipper must be presumed to be aware that performance of the contract is to be sub-contracted.[168]

Even though consent to a sub-bailment may be implied, it does not automatically follow that there is therefore consent to all the terms of that sub-bailment. Here again the test of reasonableness may be an appropriate guide, particularly if the terms involved

---

[161] [1994] 2 AC 324 at p 346.
[162] Combicon bill cl 6(i). See also *Jarl Tra AB v Convoys Ltd* [2003] 2 Lloyd's Rep 459.
[163] P & O Nedlloyd Container bill cl 4(i).
[164] Visconbill cl 9(a).
[165] Conlinebill cl 6.
[166] [1966] 1 QB 716.
[167] [1994] 2 AC 324 at p 341.
[168] See *Singer (UK) Ltd v Tees & Hartlepool Port Authority* [1988] 2 Lloyd's Rep 164 at p 168. See also *Spectra International plc v Hayesoak Ltd* [1997] 1 Lloyd's Rep 153 where consent was implied to a freight forwarder sub-contracting on the standard conditions of the Road Haulage Association; *Sonicare International v East Anglia Freight Terminal Ltd* [1997] 2 Lloyd's Rep 48 (implied consent to sub-contracting on standard conditions of National Association of Warehouse Keepers).

are standard conditions in the particular trade. Thus, it has been suggested that the terms of a sub-bailment might satisfy the reasonableness test where the exclusions and limitations of liability were no wider than their counterparts in the contract of carriage concluded between the shipper of the goods and the contractual carrier. Certainly it is arguable that, where carriage by sea is envisaged, a sub-bailee should be entitled to rely on the defences provided by the Hague or Hague/Visby Rules where such rules were mandatorily incorporated into the contract of sub-bailment. Different conditions might apply where the effect of such rules was dependent on contractual incorporation.

What is, however, clear is that the sub-bailee cannot rely on the terms of a sub-bailment to which the owner of the goods did not consent.[169] Any argument to the contrary was rejected by the Privy Council in *The Pioneer Container* as being inconsistent with the reasoning of Lord Denning MR in *Morris v Martin*.[170] 'As [their Lordships] see it, once it is recognised that the sub-bailee, by voluntarily taking the owner's goods into his custody, ipso facto becomes the bailee of those goods *vis-à-vis* the owner, it must follow that the owner's rights against the sub-bailee will only be subject to terms of the sub-bailment if he has consented to them, i.e. if he has authorised the bailee to entrust the goods to the sub-bailee on those terms.'[171]

(B) THE VICARIOUS IMMUNITY APPROACH

The *Pioneer Container* establishes that, in appropriate circumstances, a sub-bailee may invoke the terms of the sub-bailment as a defence to an action brought by the owner of the goods. The courts have, however, been more reluctant to allow him to rely on defences contained in the head contract between the shipper of the goods and the head bailee, to which he is obviously not a party. There are two main reasons why the sub-bailee might prefer to adopt this approach rather than to seek the protection of the terms of the sub-bailment. On the one hand, the court might find it impossible to infer any consent by the owner of the goods to the terms of the sub-bailment. On the other, the sub-bailment may take the form of a charterparty, the terms of which might offer protection to the sub-bailee inferior to that available under the bill of lading.

The first sub-bailee to adopt this approach was, however, successful. In *Elder Dempster & Co v Paterson Zochonis Co*,[172] cargo shipped on board the defendant's vessel was damaged as the result of bad stowage which was covered by an exception in the bill of lading. The bills had, however, been issued by charterers of the vessel, who were held to be the contractual carriers. When sued for negligence by the owners of the cargo, the defendant shipowners sought to rely on the stowage exception in the bill of

---

[169] A contrary view was advanced by Donaldson J in *Johnson Matthey & Co v Constantine Terminals Ltd* [1976] 2 Lloyd's Rep 215 at p 222 to the effect that consent of the owner of the goods was not relevant in such a situation. In his opinion, the owner could not rely on the sub-bailment to establish his case without accepting the entire terms of the sub-bailment, whether or not he had consented to them. 'Consent seems to me to be relevant only between the bailor and the head bailee. If the sub-bailment is on terms to which the bailor consented, he has no cause of action against the head bailee. If it was not, the sub-bailee is still protected but, if the bailor is damnified by the terms of the sub-bailment, he has a cause of action against the head bailee.'

[170] [1966] 1 QB 716.

[171] [1994] 2 AC 324 at p 341. See also *Garnham, Harris & Elton Ltd v Alfred W Ellis (Transport) Ltd* [1967] 1 WLR 940.

[172] [1924] AC 522. See Carver 7.014 ff.

lading, despite the fact that they were not parties to that contract. A majority of the House of Lords, supporting the dissenting opinion of Scrutton LJ in the Court of Appeal, held that the shipowners were entitled to do so, though the reasons for this decision are far from clear. Only Lord Summer[173] hinted at a solution based on a bailment on terms similar to that subsequently advanced by the Privy Council in *The Pioneer Container*. The majority of the court, together with Scrutton LJ in the Court of Appeal, preferred to base their decision on a principle of vicarious immunity, pointing to the fact that the bill of lading was signed by the master of the ship, a servant of the shipowner, and that the exception in question specifically stipulated that the 'shipowners' should not be liable for damage resulting from bad stowage. In the words of Scrutton LJ in the Court of Appeal,[174] 'The real answer to the claim is in my view that the shipowner is not in possession as a bailee, but as the agent of a person, the charterer, with whom the owner of the goods has made a contract defining his liability, and that the owner as servant or agent of the charterer can claim the same protection as the charterer.'

This decision has met with far from universal approval and has not been followed in subsequent cases. When the case eventually came to be considered by the House of Lords in *Scruttons Ltd* v *Midland Silicones Ltd*,[175] only Lord Denning, a noted opponent of the doctrine of privity, was prepared to support the arguments advanced by Scrutton LJ. The appellants in this case were stevedores who had damaged a drum of chemicals during the unloading operation. When sued by the owners in negligence they unsuccessfully sought to rely on the limitation of liability provision in the Hague Rules, which had been incorporated into the bill of lading. The House of Lords strictly applied the privity rule. As the stevedores were not parties to the bill of lading contract, they could not rely on its provisions for their protection. In this case stevedores engaged as independent contractors to discharge the cargo were clearly not bailees of the goods since there was no intention that they should acquire legal possession of them. Would the result have been different if, as in *Elder Dempster*, there had been a sub-bailment of the goods? Such a situation might, for example, arise where independent contractors are engaged not only to discharge cargo but also to store it awaiting collection by a consignee.[176]

Unfortunately the combination of facts encountered in the *Elder Dempster* case has not come up for reconsideration by an English court, although it has been the subject of judicial decision in the Australian case of *Gadsden* v *Australia Coastal Commission*.[177] Cargo shipped under a charterer's bill of lading was damaged while in the course of transit on board the defendant's vessel. When sued by the cargo owner for negligence, the shipowner sought to rely on the Hague Rules time limitation, which had been expressly incorporated into the relevant bill of lading. The New South Wales Court of Appeal had little hesitation in applying the privity rule and holding that, as the shipowner was not party to the bill of lading contract, he could not rely on its terms for protection.[178]

---

[173] *Ibid* 564.
[174] [1923] 1 KB 420 at p 441.
[175] [1962] AC 446.
[176] See *Gilchrist Watt* v *York Products* [1970] 1 WLR 1262. Cf. *Lee Cooper* v *Jeakins* [1964] 1 Lloyd's Rep 300.
[177] [1977] 1 NSWLR 575.
[178] See also *The Forum Craftsman* [1985] 1 Lloyd's Rep 291.

(C) THE HIMALAYA CLAUSE

While the House of Lords strictly applied the privity rule in *Scruttons v Midland Silicones* in refusing to allow stevedores, engaged as independent contractors, to invoke the protection of a limitation clause in the contract of carriage, Lord Reid threw out a lifeline by suggesting that an agency relationship might provide the answer to such a problem. In his view such a relationship might have been created on the facts of that case if four basic requirements were satisfied: 'first, the bill of lading makes it clear that the stevedore is intended to be protected by the provisions in it which limit liability, (secondly) the bill of lading makes it clear that the carrier in addition to contracting for those provisions on his own behalf, is also contracting as agent for the stevedore that those provisions should apply to the stevedore, (thirdly) the carrier has authority from the stevedore to do that or perhaps later ratification by the stevedore would suffice, and (fourthly) that any difficulties about consideration moving from the stevedore were overcome'.[179]

This invitation was gladly accepted by the draftsman of the bill of lading which came up for consideration by the Privy Council in *The Eurymedon*.[180] A drilling machine had been shipped from Liverpool to New Zealand under a bill of lading which incorporated the Hague Rules. The bill included an express clause stipulating that any servant, agent or independent contractor employed by the carrier should be entitled to the protection of every exemption available to the carrier and that, in respect of this clause, the carrier was contracting not only on his own behalf but also as agent or trustee on behalf of the parties named. When a stevedore was later sued in negligence for damage caused to the drilling machine during discharge, he sought to rely on the Hague Rules, Art III rule 6, which barred any action brought more than 12 months after the damage occurred. The Privy Council with two members dissenting, held that the stevedore was entitled to do so since the carrier, in concluding the contract of carriage, had been acting as agent on his behalf. Overall the terms of the contract were considered to fulfil the four criteria suggested by Lord Reid.[181]

Once the validity of the agency device had been confirmed, its potential was quickly recognised. Not only could it be used to extend the protection afforded by the carriage contract to employees of a contractual carrier, and to independent contractors engaged in its performance, but it could also provide similar protection for an actual carrier where performance of the carriage itself had been delegated to a sub-contractor[182] or where it formed part of a combined transport operation. Clauses incorporating this

---

[179] [1962] AC 446 at p 474.

[180] *New Zealand Shipping Co Ltd v AM Satterthwaite & Co (The Eurymedon)* [1975] AC 154; see also *The New York Star* [1980] 2 Lloyd's Rep 317.

[181] For the reasoning behind the judgment, see Lord Wilberforce [1975] AC 167–9. See also Tetley Ch 36. For the policy underlying the agency device, see Lord Goff in *The Mahkutai* [1996] 2 Lloyd's Rep 1 at p 8. The resulting contract involving the servant, agent or independent contractor has been held to be neither a covenant not to sue nor an independent contract of carriage, but merely a contract of exemption entitling the beneficiary to rely on the defences available to the contractual carrier. See *The Starsin* [2003] 1 Lloyd's Rep 571 at p 580

[182] See *The Starsin*. [2003] 1 Lloyd's Rep 571 where the House of Lords held that the actual carrier (shipowner) fell within the definition of an 'independent contractor' for the purposes of the clause.

formula soon began to appear in many standard forms of bill of lading. Its usefulness depended, of course, on the foresight of the contracting parties and their mutual consent to its incorporation into their agreement.

As with all such stratagems, the use of the Himalaya clause has its limitations, as was exemplified in the recent case of *The Starsin*.[183] Charterers' bills had been issued which included a Himalaya clause purporting to exclude the independent contractor from any liability to the shipper resulting from, *inter alia*, negligent damage to the goods. The majority of the Court of Appeal held that, in so far as the clause sought to extend to the independent contractor a wider exemption than that available to the contractual carrier under the Hague Rules, it was rendered void by Art III rule 8. Again in *The Mahkutai*[184] the relevant charterer's bills had been issued which included both a Himalaya clause and an Indonesian choice of jurisdiction clause. When sued for cargo damage by the cargo owners, the shipowner unsuccessfully sought to rely on the jurisdiction clause in the bill of lading. In the view of the Privy Council, the accepted function of a Himalaya clause was to prevent cargo owners from avoiding the effect of contractual defences available to the carrier by suing the actual tortfeasor in negligence. Such defences were designed to benefit only one party whereas, in contrast, jurisdiction clauses were intended to create mutual rights and obligations. In expressing regret in reaching this conclusion, Lord Goff noted that 'it is inevitable that technical points of contract and agency law will continue to be invoked by cargo owners seeking to enforce tortious remedies against stevedores and others uninhibited by the exceptions and limitations in the relevant bill of lading contract'.[185] In so far as this decision turns on the precise wording of the Himalaya clause, its effect can presumably be nullified by appropriate draftsmanship.

(D) THE DIRECT APPROACH

All of the above examples of judicial creativity have their limitations and none deals effectively with the basic problem. Inevitably the ultimate solution must be to meet the issue of privity head-on. This tactic was adopted by the Supreme Court of Canada in 1993 in the case of *London Drugs Ltd* v *Kuehne & Nagel*.[186] The plaintiff in this case had delivered a transformer to a warehouseman for storage under a contract which specified that his liability was limited to $40 per package unless the owner declared the true value of the goods and paid an additional charge. The plaintiff elected not to exercise this option. Subsequently, employees of the warehouseman damaged the transformer while, contrary to express instructions, attempting to lift it with a fork-lift truck. When sued for damages in negligence, the employees sought to invoke the limitation of liability clause in the contract between the plaintiff and their employer, even though they were clearly not parties to that contract.

In these circumstances, the Supreme Court of Canada was prepared to make an exception to the privity rule and allow the employees to limit their liability to $40. The

---

[183] [2003] 1 Lloyd's Rep 571.
[184] [1996] 2 Lloyd's Rep 1. See also *Bouygues Offshore SA* v *Caspian Shipping Co* [1997] 2 Lloyd's Rep 485. For a further limitation, see *Raymond Burke Motors* v *Mersey Docks & Harbour Co* [1986] 1 Lloyd's Rep 155; *The Rigoletto* [2000] 2 Lloyd's Rep 532.
[185] *Ibid* 8.
[186] (1993) 97 DLR (4th) 261. See Carver 7.019 ff.

majority of the court indicated that they had no intention of abolishing the privity rule but were merely creating a new exception to it, which represented only an 'incremental change'. The justification for this new exception was outlined by Iacobucci J[187] in presenting a judgment in which three of his five colleagues concurred. 'When an employer and a customer enter into a contract for services and include a clause limiting the liability of the employer for damages arising from what will normally be conduct contemplated by the contracting parties to be performed by the employer's employees, and in fact so performed, there is simply no valid reason for denying the benefit of the clause to employees who perform the contractual obligations.'

In the view of the majority of the court, it did not make commercial sense to allow a plaintiff to invoke the doctrine of privity in such circumstances in order to circumvent a contractual exclusion or limitation clause to which he had freely consented.

Two requirements must be satisfied before such an exception will operate. First, the limitation of liability clause must either expressly or impliedly extend its benefit to the employees seeking to rely on it; and, secondly, such employees 'must have been performing the very services provided for in the contract between their employer and the customer when the loss occurred'.[188]

While this decision centred on the existence of an employer–employee relationship, the Canadian Supreme Court indicated in the subsequent case of *Fraser River* v *Can-Dive Services*[189] that there was no intention to limit the exception to situations involving such a relationship. In this case the charterer of a barge, when sued in negligence for the loss of the vessel, sought to rely on a waiver of subrogation clause in the hull subscription policy taken out by the owner of the barge. While he was clearly not a party to the insurance contract, the Supreme Court, in finding in his favour, was satisfied that the two basic requirements for the operation of the exception had been met. On the one hand, the parties to the insurance policy had clearly expressed an intention to extend the benefit of the waiver of subrogation clause to any 'charterer' of the vessel, while the third-party beneficiary in this case was engaged in the very activities envisaged by the clause on which he sought to rely.

On this occasion the Supreme Court was also required to address the question as to whether the original contracting parties could unilaterally revoke the provision in favour of the third-party beneficiary. In its view, such a revision of the contract was no longer possible, without the third party's consent, once the benefit had 'crystallised' by the occurence of the event envisaged by the contract.[190]

To what extent are English courts likely to follow a similar path? Lord Goff in *The Mahkutai*[191] recognised that 'the time may well come when, in an appropriate case, it will fall to be considered whether the courts should take what may legitimately be perceived to be the final, and perhaps inevitable, step in this development and recognise in these cases a fully-fledged exception to the doctrine of privity of contract, thus escaping from all the technicalities with which courts are now faced in English law'. For a

---

[187] *Ibid* 361.
[188] *Ibid* 366.
[189] [2000] 1 Lloyd's Rep 199 at p 206.
[190] *Ibid* 207.
[191] [1996] 2 Lloyd's Rep 1 at p 8.

variety of reasons, however, he did not consider that the appeal in *The Mahkutai* was an appropriate occasion on which to follow the lead given by the Canadian court.

(E) CONTRACTS (RIGHTS OF THIRD PARTIES) ACT 1999

The challenge has, however, been accepted by the legislature in enacting the Contracts (Rights of Third Parties) Act 1999, the provisions of which came into effect on 11 May 2000.[192] The statute provides that a third party is entitled to enforce a contractual provision in his or her own name where either the contract contains an express term to that effect[193] or where the contract purports to confer a benefit on a third party[194] unless, in the latter case, it is clear on a true construction of the contract that the contracting parties did not intend the third party to have a personal right to enforce such benefit.[195] In both cases the right of enforcement is dependent on the third party being expressly identified in the contract by name, class or description.[196] There is, however, one proviso in relation to contracts for the carriage of goods by sea.[197] In such a context the statutory right to 'enforce' a contractual provision is not intended to confer positive rights on a third party, its effect being expressly restricted to enabling a third party to avail himself of an exclusion or limitation of liability provision in such a contract.[198]

The first limb of the new statutory enforceability test would appear to provide an alternative solution to the use of a Himalaya clause. Thus, in the typical situation covered by such a clause, the agency device is specifically designed to extend the protection afforded by the provisions of the carriage contract to cover a third party while performing the obligations envisaged by the contract. Such third parties are invariably identified by description.[199] The direct relief provided by the new statutory remedy might be expected in time to supplant the more cumbersome agency device in the Himalaya clause, although the Act specifically preserves existing common law remedies.[200] Much will depend on the relative effectiveness in practice of the new statutory provisions.

One possible defect of the new legislation in this context is the retention of the right of the original parties to vary or rescind the contract without the consent of the third-party beneficiary.[201] The exercise of such a right of revision, which could effectively remove the protection otherwise afforded to the third party, is, however, subject to certain qualifications. The parties to the contract cannot vary or rescind the contract without the third party's consent once the third party has communicated to the

---

[192] That is, six months after its enactment on 11 November 1999.

[193] Section 1(1)(a).

[194] Section 1(1)(b).

[195] Section 1(2).

[196] Section 1(3).

[197] A contract for the carriage of goods by sea is defined as a contract of carriage 'contained in or evidenced by a bill of lading, sea waybill or a corresponding electronic transaction'. The definition also covers analogous undertakings 'contained in a ship's delivery order or a corresponding electronic transaction' (s 6(6)).

[198] Section 6(5)(a).

[199] The standard modern Himalaya clause expressly extends the protection afforded by the terms of the contract of carriage to any 'servant or agent of the carrier (including every independent contractor from time to time employed by the carrier)'.

[200] Section 7(1).

[201] Section 2(1).

promisor his assent to the provisions in the contract to his benefit,[202] or where he has relied on such provisions and the promisor is either aware of such reliance[203] or could reasonably be expected to have foreseen it.[204]

All three potential bars presume that the third party is aware of the contractual provision in his favour when he either accepts or acts in reliance on it. Indeed, the Law Commission in its report advocating the legislation expressly states that 'Reliance on a promise, in our view, means "conduct induced by the belief (or expectation) that the promise will be performed or at least, that one is legally entitled to performance of the promise".'[205] The only problem is that, in many cases, the stevedore or sub-contractor may be unaware of the Himalaya clause in the bill of lading at the time when he performs what would otherwise be an act of reliance. Would the absence of intentional reliance in this context defeat the object of the legislation?[206] In practice it may have little significance since any variation in the terms of the contract requires the agreement of both of the original contracting parties and a carrier is unlikely to consent to such a change if it would leave him exposed to an indemnity claim by the third party. So in *Scruttons v Midland Silicones* the carrier, in engaging stevedores to discharge the cargo, had contracted to provide them with the same protection as was afforded to the carrier in the bill of lading. On falling victim to the privity rule, and being held liable for the full value of the damaged cargo, the stevedores were subsequently able to recoup their loss from the carrier as damages for breach of contract.

5.4 PRESENTATION OF A BILL OF LADING

The unique characteristic of the bill of lading is that delivery of the goods has to be made against surrender of the document.[207] This rule has a twofold purpose. On the one hand, it protects the holder of the bill in that it is a basic term of the contract of carriage that the carrier must only deliver the goods against presentation of the bill of lading. On the other hand, such delivery serves to discharge the carrier from further obligations under the contract of carriage. The only problem so far as the carrier is concerned is that, while he is aware of the identity of the shipper, he is not aware of the identity of the party entitled to delivery at the port of discharge in cases where the goods have been sold and resold in transit. As the carrier is liable to substantial damages in the event of misdelivery, he would obviously prefer a 'straight' or non-negotiable bill under which his obligation is to deliver only to the named consignee. In the case of export sales, the use of such a non-negotiable bill is often not commercially practicable. The carrier's problems are compounded by the fact that bills of lading are traditionally issued in sets

---

[202] Section 2(1)(a). Such assent may be by words or conduct (s 2(2)(a)).

[203] Section 2(1)(b).

[204] Section 2(1)(c).

[205] Law Commission Report No 242: *Reforming Privity of Contract* (1996) para 9.14.

[206] Compare the alternative solution to this problem advanced by the Supreme Court of Canada in *Fraser River v Can-Dive Services* [2000] 1 Lloyd's Rep 199. In its view, the provision in favour of the third-party beneficiary could not be unilaterally revoked once the benefit had crystallised. See *supra* at p 153.

[207] NB The terms of the contract of carriage or a custom of trade might require delivery of cargo without production of the bill of lading: *Chilewich Partners v MV Alligator Fortune* [1994] 2 Lloyd's Rep 314.

of from three to six originals and that delivery of the cargo can be required against the presentation of a single original from such a set. This practice dates back to the sixteenth century and is designed to enable one original to be retained by the shipper, a second by the carrier as part of the ship's papers, and the remainder despatched to the consignee, often by different methods, for example, one by seamail and another by airmail. The justification for the practice is somewhat obscure and its usefulness was queried as early as 1882 by Lord Blackburn, who commented 'I should have thought that . . . every purpose would be answered by making one bill of lading only, which should be the sole document of title, and taking as many copies certified by the Master to be true copies, as it is thought convenient.'[208] If, however, the object of the exercise is to protect the interests of the various parties in the event of other originals going astray, or the shipper defaulting in payment, then an original would be required in order to secure delivery from the carrier.

In order to protect the carrier there is frequently a provision in the bill that 'one being accomplished, the others to stand void'. The carrier is thus protected if he makes delivery against a single unindorsed original bill or alternatively against a single validly indorsed bill. Liability here is, however, strict and the carrier will be liable if he makes delivery against a forged indorsement even though he is unlikely to be able to detect it.[209] In such circumstances the opportunity for fraud is obvious and it is somewhat surprising to find so few recorded cases of the misuse of an original bill. One such case was that of *Glyn Mills* v *East & West India Dock Co*[210] in which a cargo of sugar was shipped in Jamaica and consigned to Cottam and Co, a firm of London merchants. A set of three bills of lading was issued by the master in which Cottam and Co were named as consignees and freight was made payable on delivery of the cargo in London. While the goods were in transit, Cottam indorsed one bill to Glyn Mills as security for a loan. On arrival of the goods in London they were deposited in a warehouse from which Cottam obtained delivery on paying the freight due and presenting the second unindorsed original bill. In an action brought by Glyn Mills, the House of Lords held the warehouseman not liable for misdelivery as he had acted bona fide on the presentation of an unindorsed bill of lading and without notice of the bank's claim. In the opinion of Lord Selborne LC, 'It would be a matter neither reasonable nor equitable nor in accordance with the terms of such a contract, that an assignment, of which the shipowner has no notice, should prevent a bona fide delivery under one of the bills of lading produced to him by the person named on the face of it as entitled to delivery (in the absence of assignment) from being a discharge to the shipowner.'[211]

On the other hand, if the warehouseman had been aware of the claim from Glyn Mills before making delivery on the bill, he would have acted at his peril. In such circumstances the correct procedure would be to interplead.[212]

---

[208] *Glyn Mills* v *East & West India Dock Co* (1882) 7 App Cas 591 at p 605. See also Earl Cairns at *Ibid* p 599.
[209] *Motis Exports Ltd* v *Dampskibsselskabet* [2000] 1 Lloyd's Rep 211, *per* Stuart Smith LJ at p 216: 'A forged bill of lading is in the eyes of the law a nullity; it is simply a piece of paper with writing on it, which has no effect whatever.'
[210] (1882) 7 App Cas 591.
[211] *Ibid* at p 596. In the circumstances in question, the position of the warehouseman was identical to that of the carrier, had the latter retained possession of the cargo.
[212] *Ibid* at p 611 *per* Lord Blackburn.

Should the carrier, or his agent, deliberately disregard the basic obligation to make delivery of the cargo only against presentation of the bill, he will be guilty of a fundamental breach of the contract of carriage and could lose the protection of all exceptions and limitation of liability clauses.[213] So in *Sze Hai Tong Bank Ltd* v *Rambler Cycle Co Ltd*[214] the respondents shipped a consignment of bicycle parts under a bill which included a clause providing that 'the responsibility of the carrier shall be deemed to cease absolutely after the goods are discharged from the ship'. On the vessel's arrival at Singapore the goods were discharged and subsequently the carrier's agents released them to the consignee without production of a bill of lading, after receiving a form of indemnity from the appellant bank. Although it was alleged that such procedure was common practice in Singapore, the Privy Council held that, by knowingly delivering goods without production of the bill, there had been a breach of a basic obligation of the contract which deprived the carrier of the protection of the cesser clause. In the opinion of the Court:

'If such an extreme width were given to the exemption clause, it would run counter to the main object and intent of the contract. For the contract, as it seems to their Lordships, has as one of its main objects, the proper delivery of the goods by the shipping company, "unto order or his or their assigns", against production of the bill of lading. It would defeat this object entirely if the shipping company was at liberty at its own will and pleasure to deliver the goods to somebody else, to someone not entitled at all, without being liable for the consequences.'[215]

This judgment represents the traditional view of the effect of fundamental breach. Following the decision in *Photo Production* v *Securicor*,[216] however, fundamental breach no longer operates as a rule of law but must be approached as a question of construction. The evidence suggests, however, that similar results may be achieved by the courts applying strict rules of interpretation to exception clauses in such circumstances.[217] Thus, in a recent case in which the Court of Appeal refused to interpret an exception clause as covering delivery of cargo against a forged bill of lading, Stuart-Smith LJ expressed the view that 'even if the language was apt to cover such a case, it is not a construction which should be adopted, involving as it does excuse from performing an obligation of such fundamental importance. As a matter of construction the

---

[213] See *The Stettin* (1889) 14 PD 142.

[214] [1959] AC 576.

[215] *Ibid* at p 587 *per* Lord Denning. The Court at p 588 distinguished the earlier Privy Council decision in *Chartered Bank of India* v *British India Steam Navigation Co* [1909] AC 369 where effect had been given to an almost identical cesser clause in somewhat similar circumstances. In the latter case however, the contract also gave the carrier the option of landing the cargo at its destination at the risk and expense of the shipper or consignee, and in the event the goods had been misdelivered as the result of fraud on the part of the landing agents. In the view of Lord Denning, 'the action of the fraudulent servant there could in no wise be imputed to the shipping company. His act was not its act. His state of mind was not its state of mind ... Whereas in the present case the action of the shipping agents at Singapore can properly be treated as the action of the shipping company itself.' See also *The Stone Gemini* [1999] 2 Lloyd's Rep 255 (shipowner also liable in conversion).

[216] See *supra* at pp 21ff.

[217] See *The Sormovskiy 3068* [1994] 2 Lloyd's Rep 266; *The Ines* [1995] 2 Lloyd's Rep 144; *Kamil Export (Aust) Pty Ltd* v *NPL (Australia) Ltd* (1992) Unreported – see *Davies* [1994] LMCLQ 407–9.

Courts lean against such a result if adequate content can be given to the clause.'[218] On the other hand, it is now possible, by an appropriately drafted clause, to exclude all liability for the consequences of ignoring the presentation rule. So in *The Antwerpen*,[219] the New South Wales Court of Appeal held that a carrier was afforded complete protection by a clause providing that 'the exemptions limitations terms and conditions in this bill of lading shall apply whether or not loss or damage is caused by . . . actions constituting fundamental breach of contract'. Paradoxically an effectively drafted clause of this type will destroy the entire purpose of the rule.

5.5 PROBLEMS IN PRESENTATION

In recent years the unique characteristic of the bill of lading, which requires delivery of the goods only against presentation of the document, has been causing serious practical problems.[220] The speeding up of transport through containerisation and similar devices has coincided with banking delays and a universal slowing up of postal services, with the result that in an increasing number of cases the cargo will reach its destination before the documentation. This is particularly true of the carriage of bulk cargoes, such as oil or gas, on the short sea routes. In such an event the carrier is placed in somewhat of a dilemma. If he insists on presentation of the bill, a number of problems will arise. As he will be unaware of the identity of the current holder of the bill, or the reason for the delay in the bill's arrival, he will be unable to make any assessment of the time at which it will ultimately be available. On many occasions there may be no place available to store the cargo, pending the arrival of the bill, except on board ship. In such an event a charterer may face liability for demurrage or damages for detention, while the shipowner may run the risk of losing the next charter should it contain a cancelling clause. Similarly, in the liner trade the carrier will be worried about his schedule. Again there are the obvious risks to the cargo owner should the goods be perishable or subject to fluctuating market prices.

Alternatively, if the carrier is reasonably sure of the identity of the receiver, he may risk delivering the goods without presentation of the bill of lading. In such a case, as we have seen earlier,[221] he acts at his peril since such action amounts to wilful misconduct and a deliberate breach of his contractual obligations. Should he deliver to the wrong party, even though in good faith, he may lose the entire protection afforded by the contract of carriage together with, where relevant, the Hague exceptions and limitations of liability.[222] Moreover, he may also lose the protection of the liability insurance provided by his Protection and Indemnity (P & I) Club.

---

[218] *Motis Exports Ltd* v *Dampskibsselskabet* [2000] 1 Lloyd's Rep 211 at p 216.

[219] [1994] 1 Lloyd's Rep 213.

[220] For a survey of the most recent cases on the subject, see Wilson [1995] LMCLQ 289.

[221] See p 157, *supra*.

[222] It is doubtful whether a carrier in similar circumstances would lose the protection afforded by the Hague/Visby Rules which are given the 'force of law'. See *The Morviken* [1983] 1 Lloyd's Rep 1; *The Antares* [1987] 1 Lloyd's Rep 424.

A third possibility is for the carrier to require an indemnity before agreeing to deliver without presentation of the bill of lading.[223] Normally a bank indemnity would be demanded, but occasionally a charterparty may require the shipowner to deliver against personal guarantees only,[224] but clearly an indemnity is only as good as the financial standing of the guarantor. The problem is that bank indemnities tend to be expensive since they invariably require more than adequate cover both in time and amount.

None of the three methods outlined provides an ideal solution to the problem raised by the absence of the bills at the material time.[225] Over recent years various proposals have been advanced to deal with the problem and have met with varying degrees of success. One obvious solution is for the sales contract or bill of lading to make express provision for the eventuality as, for example, the standard GAFTA 100 form in the grain trade. This provides that 'In the event of the shipping documents not being available on arrival of the vessel at destination, sellers may provide other documents or an indemnity entitling Buyers to obtain delivery of the goods and payment shall be made by Buyers in exchange for same.'[226] Alternatively, procedures can be adopted to speed up the transmission of the current forms of documentation. Thus the documents can be produced at the destination of the cargo or at a point close to the consignee, where the relevant information can be supplied by telex or photographic telefax. Again, arrangements can be made for the presentation of the bill to a bank or other agent of the carrier at a convenient place other than the discharging port. Much has also been done to speed up the production of documents by the development of uniform layouts such as the data aligned formats designed by the International Chamber of Shipping, SITPRO and other similar bodies. By the use of such uniform formats the entire documentation required can be produced with economy, accuracy and speed. The master document contains all the information while, by the use of blocking mechanisms, the various copies produced will provide only the relevant material required. The elimination of the need for transcription considerably reduces the opportunities for mistakes.

5.5.1 SHORT FORM BILL OF LADING[227]

One of the earliest of the data aligned documents to appear was the short form bill of lading. First introduced in Sweden, it is now widely used, and a common form was produced by the General Council of British Shipping in 1979. The object of the exercise was to simplify documentation and increase the speed of production by reducing the amount of information on the bill. This result was achieved by removing the printed terms of the contract of carriage from the reverse of the bill and substituting a straightforward

---

[223] See *The Delfini* [1990] 1 Lloyd's Rep 252. In the absence of a provision in the contract to the contrary, a carrier is not obliged to accept a letter of indemnity if the bill of lading is not forthcoming: *The Houda* [1994] 2 Lloyd's Rep 541. Cf. The Scandports Bill of Lading clause in *The Delfini* [1990] 1 Lloyd's Rep 252.

[224] See *The Stone Gemini* [1999] 2 Lloyd's Rep 255. NB Acceptance of a letter of indemnity does not exonerate the shipowner from liability. Its object is to indemnify him from the consequences of conduct which amounts to a breach of contract. See also *Sze Hai Tong Bank Ltd* v *Rambler Cycle Co* [1959] AC 576.

[225] For a review of other possible defences open to the carrier, see *The Sormovskiy 3068* [1994] 2 Lloyd's Rep 266.

[226] GAFTA 100, line 100.

[227] See Appendix 18.

clause incorporating the carrier's standard terms and conditions. This short form bill can be produced either in a proprietary form with the carrier's name printed at the head, or in a common form in which the name of the selected carrier is inserted in the bill by the shipper. The latter type has considerable advantages since it is available for universal use and dispenses with the need for the shipper to carry separate stocks of bills appropriate to each individual carrier.

The most important characteristic of the short form bill is that it possesses all the qualities of the standard long form in that it acts as a receipt, provides evidence of the contract of carriage, and constitutes a transferable document of title enabling the holder to sell the goods in transit or pledge them with a bank. It is thus available as a direct substitute for the long form bill in any context and has received the final accolade by being recognised as acceptable in the banking world as security for documentary credits.[228] As with the long form, it will be subject to the Hague/Visby Rules where applicable in the United Kingdom.

The main problem associated with the short form bill is the effectiveness of the incorporation clause in different jurisdictions. There would appear to be little doubt as to its validity in the common law world, since it would comply with all the requirements of the doctrine of notice developed in the series of ticket cases.[229] On the other hand, there may be more doubt as to the reaction of courts in civil law jurisdictions, particularly if a copy of the carrier's standard terms is not readily available. Similarly, the courts may be more sympathetically disposed towards the assignee of a short form bill who may be prejudiced by lack of access to a copy of the standard terms, in contrast to the shipper who will no doubt have a copy in his office. For this reason some shippers feel safer to type the crucial provisions of the contract on the short form, thus to some extent defeating the object of the exercise. Such terms include jurisdiction and choice of law clauses (of vital importance to the consignee), arbitration clauses and clauses expressly incorporating the Hague/Visby Rules. It must also be remembered that the short form bill is basically a 'received for carriage' document, whereas banks providing for documentary credits normally call for a 'shipped' bill. While facilities exist for adding a 'shipped' notation, the delay involved will naturally defeat the time-saving objective.

5.5.2 THE WAYBILL[230]

In situations where a negotiable document of title is not required, the presentation problem can be solved by the substitution of a waybill for the normal bill of lading. These documents were first developed for use in land and air transport in which negotiable documents of title were not required since the journeys involved were normally so brief that little opportunity was provided for the consignee to sell the goods in transit. Since negotiation of a waybill is not possible, the obligation of the carrier

---

[228] The Uniform Customs and Practice for Documentary Credits (1993 edn) provide that the short form is acceptable to banks 'unless otherwise stipulated in the credit': Arts 23(a)(v) and 24.

[229] See *Parker* v *South Eastern Rly Co* (1877) 2 CPD 416 at pp 422–3; *Thompson* v *London Midland and Scottish Rly Co* [1930] 1 KB 41.

[230] See Appendices 20 and 21.

is to deliver to the named consignee and, provided the latter can identify himself, there is no requirement for presentation of the waybill before he can obtain delivery of the goods.

The waybill differs from the bill of lading in that, while it acts as a receipt and provides evidence of the contract of carriage, it lacks the third characteristic in that it does not constitute a negotiable document of title. For this reason it is not so acceptable where documentary credits are involved or where there is a possibility that the consignee might wish to sell the goods in transit. Nevertheless, increasing use is being made of the waybill and it is reported that at the present time as much as 85 per cent of the trans-Atlantic trade in containerised cargo could be carried on waybills.[231] Typical examples are provided by in-house movements of goods between different branches of a multi-national firm, the shipment of household or personal effects, and open account trading with long-standing and trusted overseas buyers where security is not needed. It must also be remembered that general cargo is rarely sold in transit, while cargo of mixed ownership in containers packed by freight forwarders is never so sold. All these shipments provide opportunities for the use of waybills since they are destined for delivery solely to the named consignee.

The modern waybill follows the pattern of the short form bill of lading in that it is a short form document with a blank back but with a specific clause incorporating the carrier's standard terms and conditions. As with the bill, the waybill is available either in a proprietary or common form. Again, it is generally a 'received for carriage' document, although facilities are available for 'shipped' notation. Unlike the bill of lading, however, it is not subject to the Hague/Visby Rules in the United Kingdom,[232] although most standard versions include a clause expressly incorporating the Rules except in the case of deck cargo and live animals.

The obvious advantage of the waybill is that it avoids the problems arising from the late arrival of documentation. The consignee has merely to identify himself at the port of discharge in order to obtain delivery of the cargo since the presentation rule does not apply. As no negotiation of the document is envisaged, the contents of the waybill can be telexed to the destination, thus speeding up the receipt of the required information by the carrier. The major drawback, however, is that, as the waybill is neither negotiable nor a document of title, it is not well suited to transactions involving documentary credits, where banks tend to place greater emphasis on security than simplification. For them the negotiable document of title endorsed in blank is the ideal solution, since it provides the required security for the credit without involving the bank in any liability under the contract of carriage.[233] The only method by which an equivalent security could be acquired through the use of a waybill would be for the bank to be designated as consignee in the document. This would not necessarily be an attractive solution for the bank for two reasons. First, as the bank is not a party to the contract of carriage, the shipper is free to change his instructions and order the carrier to deliver to a party other than the consignee designated in the waybill.[234] Secondly, in the event of default

---

[231] Gronfors, K, *Cargo Key Receipt and Transport Document Replacement*, 1982, p 13.
[232] See s 1(4) of the Carriage of Goods by Sea Act 1971.
[233] See *Sewell* v *Burdick* (1884) 10 App Cas 74.
[234] This eventuality is covered by s 5(3) of the Carriage of Goods by Sea Act 1992.

in repayment of the credit, the cargo would not readily be disposable in the absence of a document of title. A further potential problem arising from doubt as to whether the consignee under a waybill had title to sue the carrier, has now been resolved by s 2(1) of the Carriage of Goods by Sea Act 1992.[235]

In an attempt to remove some of the above anomalies associated with the use of a waybill, the CMI recently formulated a set of rules for voluntary incorporation into any contract of carriage covered by such a document.[236] Recognising that neither the Hague nor the Hague/Visby conventions are applicable to waybills, the Rules provide that a contract of carriage covered by a waybill shall be governed by whichever international convention or national law, if any, would have been compulsorily applicable if the contract had in fact been covered by a bill of lading or similar document of title.[237] The Rules then proceed to incorporate a provision relating to representations in a waybill as to the quantity or condition of goods received for shipment similar in effect to Art III rules 3 and 4 of the Hague/Visby Rules.[238] Accordingly, such representations, if not qualified by the carrier, shall be prima facie evidence in favour of the shipper and conclusive evidence in favour of a consignee in good faith.

The Rules further confirm the right of the shipper, as original party to the contract of carriage, to change the name of the consignee at any time before the consignee claims delivery of the goods after their arrival at the contractual destination. Such right is subject to the proviso that the shipper gives the carrier adequate warning and indemnifies him against any additional expenditure involved.[239] The shipper can, however, relinquish such right of control to the consignee at any time not later than the receipt of the goods by the carrier, provided that such transfer of control is recorded on the waybill. Banks prepared to accept a waybill as security for a commercial credit will presumably insist on such a transfer of control. Finally, the Rules, while requiring the carrier to deliver the goods to the consignee on production of proper identification, absolve him from liability for wrong delivery on proof that he exercised reasonable care in seeking to identify the consignee.[240]

5.5.3 THE STRAIGHT BILL OF LADING

The straight bill of lading is a document in less frequent use than a waybill but which, being non-negotiable, is capable of fulfilling similar functions. It differs from the waybill in that it employs the standard bill of lading form which is available for use as either a negotiable or non-negotiable document. When the form is drafted as a straight bill, the goods are consigned to a specific person without reference to order or assigns. As a shipping document it possesses all the attributes of the standard bill of lading except that,

---

[235] For a full discussion of this point, see *supra* pp 138–9.
[236] The CMI Uniform Rules for Sea Waybills.
[237] Rule 4.
[238] Rule 5. Thus closing the gap left by s 1(6)(b) of the Carriage of Goods by Sea Act 1971, and s 4 of the Carriage of Goods by Sea Act 1992. See *supra*, pp 121–2.
[239] Rule 6.
[240] Rule 7. The Rules also seek to provide the consignee, where necessary, with title to sue by use of the agency device sanctioned in *The Eurymedon* [1974] 1 Lloyd's Rep 534. This contractual provision has been largely superseded by s 2(1) of the Carriage of Goods by Sea Act 1992.

being non-negotiable, the straight bill exhibits the same deficiencies as a waybill when security is required for documentary credits or similar financial arrangements.

The absence of the attribute of negotiability raises questions similar to those already considered in relation to waybills. First is the question as to whether the Hague or Hague/Visby Rules are compulsorily applicable to the contract of carriage covered by it. Lacking any authoritative caselaw on the point, academic writers came to the almost unanimous conclusion that such regimes were not applicable because a straight bill could not be regarded as a document of title.[241] This approach was decisively rejected by the Court of Appeal in the recent case of *The Rafaela S.*[242] A consigned straight bill of lading had been issued for the carriage of four containers of printing machinery from Durban to Felixstowe with a final indicated destination of Boston. In the event the cargo was discharged at Felixstowe and reshipped on a second vessel owned by the same carrier for carriage to Boston. No new bill of lading was issued. On the voyage to Boston the cargo suffered severe damage and the point at issue was whether the carrier could invoke the Hague/Visby Rules to limit any claim by the cargo owner. Despite the fact that both the initial carriage and the on-carriage were performed by the same carrier, the Court of Appeal held that two separate contracts were involved. The on-carriage from Felixstowe to Boston constituted a separate contract with a separate port of shipment, thus entitling the shipper to demand the issue of a new bill of lading. Had such a document been issued, the court presumed that it would have followed the same pattern as that used for the initial carriage, i.e. a straight bill drafted on an other-wise classic bill of lading form. With Felixstowe as the port of shipment, this second contract would be subject to the Hague/Visby Rules provided that the straight bill con-stituted 'a bill of lading or similar document of title' within s 1(4) of the Carriage of Goods by Sea Act 1971. Such authority as existed was opposed to such a conclusion on the ground that a straight bill, being non-negotiable, did not constitute a document of title.

The Court of Appeal took the view, however, that a straight bill, drafted on a classic bill of lading form,[243] could constitute a document of title even though non-negotiable. Rix LJ gave three reasons for reaching this conclusion. First, the Hague and Hague/Visby Rules, in his opinion, were primarily concerned with the content of a contract of carriage rather than with its negotiability. Their object was to create an international regime of minimum standards and, by so doing, protect any third party into whose hands the bill of lading might be transferred and who, not being a party to the original contract, could not otherwise influence its terms. While the standard nego-tiable bill could be transferred to a succession of transferees, the straight bill could only be transferred once – i.e. to the named consignee – but 'unless he is the same person as the shipper [he] is as much a third party as a named consignee under a classic bill . . . [and] prima facie within the concern of the rules'.[244] Secondly, a straight bill, while transferable on only one occasion may still, in a sales context, be withheld by the ship-per against payment of the price. Similarly, as with a classic bill, transfer of a straight bill

---

[241] See Scrutton art 2 pp 1–2; Carver 6.007, 6.014; Benjamin, 5th edn, para 18.007; Cf. Tetley p 949.

[242] [2003] 2 Lloyd's Rep 113.

[243] I.e. one available as either a negotiable or non-negotiable document.

[244] [2003] 2 Lloyd's Rep at p 143 (para 136).

may mark the intended transfer of the property in the goods. 'In these circumstances, the shipper and his bankers and insurers need the same protection as the shipper under a classic bill; and the consignee and his insurers in turn need to have rights against the carrier under the contract of carriage'.[245] Finally, in practice the straight bill, unlike the waybill, is written on the classic bill of lading form which invariably includes a provision requiring presentation of the bill in order to obtain delivery of the goods from the carrier. Such a clause was present in *The Rafaela S* bill, but it was argued that where a document has alternative uses, not all the terms are necessarily applicable in both contexts. In particular, the provision requiring presentation is not relevant when the document is used as a straight bill. The Court of Appeal rejected this argument, holding that on its true interpretation the attestation clause in *The Rafaela S* was applicable whether the bill of lading was used as a negotiable or non-negotiable document. If the parties had intended otherwise, they had every opportunity to have said so. In the opinion of the court, a document which had to be produced in order to obtain possession of the goods should be regarded as a document of title and one which qualified as the 'similar document of title' required by s 1(4) of the Carriage of Goods by Sea Act 1971. Taking the above three factors into consideration, the court reached the conclusion that 'the straight bill of lading is in principle, function and form much closer to a classic negotiable bill than to a non-negotiable receipt'.[246] Accordingly, the straight bill was held to be a document of title and the Hague/Visby Rules were applicable to the contract of carriage covered by it. In the opinion of Rix LJ this conclusion was consistent with the *travaux préparatoires* of the Hague Rules and in line with the decisions of the courts of various European states.

The second point of comparison with the waybill relates to the question of title to sue in the event of loss or damage to cargo. The straight bill is classified as a sea waybill for the purposes of s 1(3) of the Carriage of Goods by Sea Act 1992, with the result that title to sue vests in the consignee identified in the bill.[247] The Court of Appeal indicated in *The Rafaela S* that, while a straight bill is not a bill of lading for the purposes of the 1992 Act, it does not necessarily follow that its status is the same for purposes of the Hague or Hague/Visby Rules.[248]

The final question is whether a straight bill confers the advantage available to the holder of a waybill that a named consignee can require delivery of the cargo without presentation of the bill of lading. The Court of Appeal in *The Rafaela S* answered this question in the negative, at least in the situation where the straight bill is in the form of a classic bill of lading which includes an attestation clause requiring surrender of the bill against delivery of the goods.[249] In the absence of such an attestation clause, or its equivalent, Rix LJ expressed the view obiter that the bill should still be regarded as a document of title requiring presentation before delivery.[250]

---

[245] *Ibid* at p 143 (para 137).
[246] [2003] 2 Lloyd's Rep at p 143 (para 139) *per* Rix LJ.
[247] Section 2(1)(6).
[248] [2003] 2 Lloyd's Rep at p 134 (para 94) *per* Rix LJ.
[249] *Ibid* at p 143 (para 142). This conclusion was anticipated by the Singapore Court of Appeal in *Voss* v *APL Ltd* [2002] 2 Lloyd's Rep 707.
[250] [2003] 2 Lloyd's Rep at p 143 (para 145).

5.5.4 A REGISTRY SYSTEM[251]

Carriers are coming under increasing pressure to release goods without production of documents and, while it would be possible for carriers to insure themselves against the risks involved, P & I Clubs at present do not think it appropriate to offer such cover. The existing practice of using letters of indemnity is expensive and banks are increasingly reluctant to tie up credit in this way. The attitude of the carrier tends to be that 'presentation is the cargo-owners' problem' – a problem resulting from the business practices adopted by the cargo owner for his own benefit. In the view of the carrier, therefore, the cargo owner should bear the cost of any resultant changes required in the documentation.

One radical solution to the problem involves the development of some form of registry system. This proposal, which has never been developed beyond an experimental stage, envisages the establishment of a central registry at which the bill of lading will be deposited by the shipper immediately after being issued by the carrier. The bill will be issued at the port of loading in the normal negotiable form but, once deposited at the registry, there will be no further physical transfer of the document. Instead, all subsequent transactions involving the bill will be recorded at the registry on notification by the consignee of record. Facilities will also be available for the carrier to register unpaid charges under the contract of carriage and for any bank involved to register its security interest under a documentary credit. Each of the parties will have access to the registry through an appropriately coded key which will not only enable them to register charges against the bill, but also to have access to relevant information it contains such as the quantity and condition of the cargo shipped. Under the scheme the carrier is required to notify the registry of his estimated time of arrival when not less than 48 hours sailing time from the port of discharge. The registry will then contact the party currently recorded as consignee requesting notification, not less than 24 hours before the estimated time of arrival of the vessel, of the identity of the person entitled to delivery of the goods. Once the registry is informed of the name of the receiver, no further transactions involving the bill can be registered, and the carrier will be instructed to deliver the cargo to him. Such instructions from the registry will be treated as equivalent to the presentation of the bill to the carrier and will operate as a discharge of the carrier's obligations under the contract of carriage.

This system has obvious attractions in that it uses existing documents and procedures and requires no change in the existing body of case law. Thus it is envisaged that notification of any transaction involving the bill to the registry will have the same effect as a physical transfer of the bill, in that it will operate to pass the property in the goods to the party recorded as assignee, and also entitle him to rely on the representations in the bill as to the quantity and condition of the goods shipped. No transaction will be binding on the parties until it has been notified to the registry for registration but, once registered, it will be secure against subsequent assignees who will be provided with access to the current state of the documents. Possibly the greatest attraction of the

---

[251] A project originally sponsored by Intertanko in collaboration with the Chase Manhattan Bank. For details see Gram, P, *Delivery of Tanker Cargoes without Presentation of Bills of Lading*, 1985. The proposal is not being actively pursued at the present time.

scheme is that it will solve the problem of the late arrival of documents in that the carrier will obtain his discharge by delivering to the party specified by the registry, who should have no difficulty in identifying himself in normal circumstances. There would be no danger of competing claims from holders of different original bills, since no bill would be in circulation. Indeed, there would be little purpose in producing more than one original although, if the practice were retained, it would be essential that the registry should require the deposit of the entire set.

A number of formidable obstacles need to be surmounted before a registry system of this type could be successfully introduced. Banks and P & I Clubs need to be convinced that it would provide watertight security for their interests so that there could be no doubt as to the identity of the receiver entitled to delivery. Again, a registry would be expensive to set up and there is the obvious problem of who is to bear the cost. No doubt running costs could be met from users' fees, but there is still the problem of the substantial initial outlay necessary to establish the registry. Carriers and their P & I Clubs argue that the major costs should be borne by cargo owners since the presentation problem stems solely from the methods they adopt to conduct their business. There is also the question as to whether it would be preferable to establish one central registry or a series located at strategic points throughout the world. In either case it would be essential for the bill to contain a choice of law clause since problems would clearly arise as to the applicability of the Hague or Hague/Visby Rules to bills deposited in such a registry. Finally, there is the problem of who is to bear the risks of mistakes or negligence on the part of the staff of the registry which result in a misdelivery of the cargo. Presumably the registry will be an independent body separate from carrier or cargo interests and possibly established by a consortium of banks. If such a body did not seek contractually to exclude liability, then the resultant insurance costs might lead to a substantial rise in fees. Merely to enumerate the main queries raised concerning the registry would suggest that some time may elapse before the proposals are implemented.[252]

5.5.5 A POSSIBLE PRACTICAL SOLUTION

Mention must finally be made of one practical solution to the problem of the late arrival of documents which has recently been developed. There is an increasingly common practice, particularly in the oil trade, for a shipper to give one original bill of lading to the Master with the instruction to deliver it to a specified person at the port of discharge and, on receiving that original bill of lading back, to deliver the cargo against it. The bill may either contain the name of the consignee or be made out to 'Order' and indorsed by the bank. While this practice certainly disposes of the problem of the late arrival of documents, there are certain doubts as to its desirability and legal validity. On the one hand, the master is exposing the carrier to the risk of an action in conversion should he deliver

---

[252] A number of queries have also been raised concerning the practical operation of such a system, which clearly depends on the registry being able to maintain contact with the carrier. Even if a central registry is prepared to offer a 24-hour service, it is unlikely that shipowners' offices will reciprocate. Will this mean that the registry can only give notice during office hours, which will obviously vary in different time zones? Again, how will the registry get a message through to a master at an isolated port where electronic data processing facilities are non-existent?

to the wrong party, a risk which is considerably increased if the other original bills are allowed to remain in the hands of the shipper, thus providing the opportunity for a fraudulent indorsement. While the carrier may be able to raise an estoppel against the shipper, so long as the master is carrying out the latter's instructions, he may not be protected against bona fide indorsees for value of other original bills in the set. As against third parties there is no certainty that, in these circumstances, delivery of cargo against presentation of the bill will act as a discharge for the carrier.[253]

5.6 ELECTRONIC BILLS OF LADING

The developments already considered are merely modifications of existing documentary procedures, but in recent years there has been a call for a more radical approach to the problem which would make full use of modern technology. Electronic means of communication are already widely used in the industry for the transmission of various types of information, ranging from vessel manifests to bill of lading data. The question is whether such facilities could be used for the development of electronic alternatives to the traditional paper documents. For any new system of 'documentation' to be effective, however, it must involve and be acceptable to a wide variety of interests including shippers, carriers, consignees, banks, underwriters and P & I Clubs. Several of these groups are traditionally conservative in their reaction to innovation, while the interests of others clearly conflict.

A recent wide-ranging survey of the market conducted by UNCTAD[254] revealed that electronic alternatives to traditional transport documents do not currently play as significant a role in commercial practice as might be expected. The respondents to a questionnaire circulated by UNCTAD indicated that, to be acceptable in the market, an electronic bill must satisfy two basic requirements. On the practical side it must replicate the functions of the traditional bill of lading in an electronic environment while at the same time enjoying the same legal recognition as its paper equivalent. There appears to be little doubt that an electronic bill could adequately fulfil two of the functions of the paper document, namely, that of receipt and of evidence of the terms of the contract of carriage.

There should be little difficulty, therefore, in substituting an electronic record for a paper waybill.[255] The key question is whether it could replicate the third function, unique to traditional bills of lading, of acting as a document of title. From the legal standpoint, however, the position is far from clear. There is doubt, for example, as to whether an electronic bill would qualify as a 'document' so as to trigger the operation of the Carriage of Goods by Sea Acts 1971 and 1992.[256] Both statutes are expressly

---

[253] For further comment, see Professor Jan Schultz and Mr RJL Thomas: *CMI Colloquium on Bills of Lading*, June 1983, p 22. For an example of this procedure in operation, see *The Mobil Courage* [1987] 2 Lloyd's Rep 655.

[254] UNCTAD report: The use of transport documents in international trade (September 2003) UNCTAD/SDTE/TLB/2003/3. See para 78.

[255] UNCTAD Report (2003) paras 87–9.

[256] See Clarke, M, 'Transport documents: their transferability as documents of title; electronic documents' [2002] LMCLQ 356 at p 359.

made applicable to 'bills of lading' or 'other documents', while the wording of the relevant statutory provisions appears to assume the use of a paper document. Again, although s 1(5) of the 1992 Act provides for regulations to be made by the relevant Secretary of State for the application of the Act's provisions where 'information technology is used,' no such regulations have yet appeared.[257] More hope may be derived from the current draft of CMI/UNCITRAL proposals for a carriage regime designed to supercede the Hague and Hague/Visby Rules.[258] These proposals seek to establish a general principle of equivalence between electronic and paper communications subject only to the proviso that the use of an electronic bill must have the express or implied consent of the carrier and shipper involved.[259] The means by which this objective is to be achieved is, however, left to rules of procedure agreed by the parties to the relevant transaction.[260]

In view of the uncertain outcome of such a process, it is doubtful whether the proposal, as it stands, will provide a universally acceptable solution to the problem in the long term. Ultimate success may be dependent on the drafting of a set of uniform rules of procedure by an internationally recognised body.

Against this background it is possible to assess the relative effectiveness of the three main types of electronic documentation currently in use.

5.6.1 ATLANTIC CONTAINER LINE DATAFREIGHT SYSTEM[261]

The first venture into the electronic field took the form of the Atlantic Container Line datafreight system which has been tried on an experimental basis in Sweden. This system is designed to make full use of the possibilities of electronic data processing by dispensing with the need for the traditional documentation. The basic information concerning the shipment is supplied by the shipper and fed into the carrier's computer at the port of loading when the cargo is received by him. The carrier will add supplementary information pertinent to himself, including the amount of freight due, 'clean bill' notation if appropriate or otherwise the relevant clausing. The computer will then print out a datafreight receipt containing all the information fed into it, and this will be certified as a first printout and handed to the shipper. All the particulars in the computer will then be transferred to the carrier's second computer at the destination port, where advance notice of the arrival of the cargo will be despatched to the consignee together with a further copy of the datafreight receipt. As the procedure is based on the waybill model, problems relating to the disposal of the goods during transit will not arise and consequently the consignee will only be required to identify himself in order to obtain delivery of the cargo.

The new computerised procedure exhibits many attractive features. It solves the problems posed by delay in the arrival of the bill of lading in that no presentation of

---

[257] *Ibid* p 360.
[258] See *infra* at p 000.
[259] UNCITRAL Working Group III: Draft paper for Twelfth Session Oct. 2003: Draft instrument on the carriage of goods by sea, A/CN.9/WG III/WP32. See Ch 2 Art 3.
[260] UNCITRAL Working Paper Ch 2 Art 6.
[261] See further Gronfors, K, *supra* note 231.

documents is required, while it conforms to existing business practices and involves no basic change in the underlying body of law. Moreover, the computer fulfils the majority of legal functions required of the bill of lading. Thus the information fed into the computer as to the quantity and condition of goods shipped enables it to fulfil the receipt function, while similarly it can provide evidence of the contract of carriage. The obvious weakness of the system, however, is that it does not provide a document of title and consequently, in its original form, is unsuited to situations where the consignee intends to sell the goods during transit. It is nevertheless envisaged that the procedure will provide adequate security for a commercial credit if the financing bank is identified as the consignee. In such a situation the seller of the goods would obtain payment from the corresponding bank on shipment of the goods followed by presentation of the certified computer printout of the datafreight receipt, provided that the latter satisfied the requirements imposed by the bank. In particular, the receipt should name the buyer's bank as consignee, include a 'clean bill' notation, and also a declaration irrevocably transferring the right of disposal of the goods during transit to the consignee. Following the procedure outlined above, advance notice of the arrival of the cargo at its destination would be sent to the buyer's bank as consignee, together with a second copy of the datafreight receipt. In addition, a similar notification of arrival would be sent to the buyer's address, in order to enable him to pay off the loan before the arrival of the cargo. Once the bank has received payment, it will release the cargo receipt, thus enabling the buyer to take delivery of the goods.

There is nevertheless still some doubt as to the effectiveness of the bank's security in a commercial credit situation, particularly where the buyer becomes insolvent while the goods are still in transit.[262] Banks have traditionally been wary of the waybill formula which requires them to be named as consignee, since they wish to avoid being involved in the obligations arising under the contract of carriage. Thus, if the buyer is eventually unable to refund the loan, they will be left with the problem of disposing of the cargo. In the meantime, they may well delay in giving the carrier instructions as to the delivery of the cargo and thereby duplicate the problem originally caused by the late arrival of the bill of lading.

5.6.2 ELECTRONIC DATA EXCHANGE SYSTEMS

A more sophisticated system of electronic data interchange (EDI) has been developed which is designed to dispense entirely with any form of documentation. This system aims at replicating the functions of the negotiable bill of lading and thus permitting successive sales of the goods while they are in transit. Under this procedure the information normally contained in the bill of lading is fed into the carrier's computer, as described above, and the shipper is provided with a 'private key' to access such material and control the goods during transit. He can relinquish the right of control by giving irrevocable instructions to the carrier to hold the goods for a named consignee, who will accordingly be entitled to delivery at the contractual destination. The named consignee can

---

[262] In order to provide added security, it is recommended that the following declaration be included in the datafreight receipt: 'Carrier to hold this consignment (which has been pledged by the buyer as owner) in security and as collateral for the bank named as consignee.'

then, if he so wishes, give similar irrevocable instructions to the carrier requiring him to make delivery to an alternative consignee. The mechanism for securing such transfers is the 'private key' originally issued to the shipper in substitution for the paper bill of lading. On each transfer the existing private key is cancelled and replaced by a new key issued to the transferee. Under this system the person currently holding the 'private key' would be the person otherwise entitled to possession of the bill of lading under the normal documentary procedure. The carrier is required to take instructions regarding the disposition of the goods exclusively from the current key holder, and delivery at destination is made to the party referring to the code valid at that time.

The adoption of such an EDI system is dependent on the mutual agreement of the parties, and a procedure for its operation has been formulated in the CMI Rules for Electronic Bills of Lading[263] which can be incorporated into contracts of carriage. In order to conform with the various mandatory carriage conventions, the Rules contain provision for the parties to opt out of the system should the shipper, for example, exercise his right to demand an original bill of lading for purposes of obtaining a documentary credit, or because a subsequent transferee does not have EDI facilities available. In such an event the private key would be cancelled, and the procedures under the Rules terminated.

5.6.3 BOLERO

A final word must be devoted to Bolero,[264] the most recent experiment in the use of electronic bills of lading.[265] In seeking to take advantage of the potential of electronic data interchange outlined above, and to produce a 'document' capable of replicating the three main functions of the traditional bill of lading, the architects of Bolero foresaw two main legal obstacles to the achievement of this objective. On the one hand, doubt existed as to whether such an electronic document would fall within the legal definition of a 'bill of lading' so as to trigger the relevant maritime legislation and conventions. A contractual solution was sought to this potential problem by requiring all users of Bolero to become parties to a multilateral contract designed to replicate contractually the functions of the paper document. So the basic contract, or 'rule book', to which all parties to the contract of carriage subscribe, could specifically incorporate the Hague/Visby Rules or other relevant maritime convention, while electronic messages processed through Bolero could be required to conform to the CMI Rules for Electronic Bills of Lading. The second potential difficulty stemmed from the fact that, in the absence of legislation or an established mercantile custom, an electronic document would not attract the negotiable characteristic of the traditional bill of lading. Bolero seeks to circumvent this problem of privity of contract by use of the device of novation of the contract of carriage. On notification to Bolero of 'indorsement' of the electronic bill of lading, the existing contract between carrier and shipper is extinguished and

---

[263] See Appendix 7, pp 388–91.
[264] Bills of Lading Electronic Registry Organisation.
[265] Bolero is a joint initiative sponsored by SWIFT, an interbank communications network, and the Through Transport Club. See Gaskell 1.57 ff for fuller discussion.

a new contract on identical terms is created between the carrier and the named con-signee. A similar procedure is followed in regard to any subsequent indorsement. By such means the indorsee will obtain control of the goods and title to sue the carrier.

One practical point requires mention. All 'indorsements' or other transactions relat-ing to the electronic document are communicated through Bolero to the receiving party and not directly between the parties themselves. In transmitting such messages, Bolero checks the unique 'private key' allotted to the sender against its register of keys and authenticates the message by the addition of its own digital signature. By this means it is hoped that the security and integrity of the transaction will be preserved together with the authentication of the electronic document. Facilities are also available for users to switch to paper documentation where, for example, the current holder wishes to 'indorse' the electronic bill in favour of an indorsee who is not a member of the Bolero club and thus not a party to the 'rule book' . Bolero clearly has many advantages in accelerating and simplifying transactions and in successfully replicating the functions of the traditional bill of lading. On the other hand it is a 'closed' subscription system based on contract and relies on all parties to the carriage transaction being members of the club. Unless a sufficient proportion of the market has 'signed up' to Bolero, there will be a frequent need to switch to paper documentation. Because of the need for sophist-icated equipment, it is suggested that the system will be unsuitable for trade with under-developed or developing countries, nor will it function effectively in states where the national legislation requires paper documentation for customs or other purposes.[266] It remains to be seen whether Bolero will prove to be the ultimate solution to the problems of electronic documentation.

5.6.4 CONCLUSIONS

There are many advantages to be derived from the use of an electronic bill. Among these are an increase in the speed and a reduction in the cost of transactions together with the elimination of the problem of late arrival of documents.[267] The recent survey of the market by UNCTAD has, however, revealed a lack of confidence in the use of electronic bills on the grounds, *inter alia*, that existing systems are not secure and that the under-lying legal framework is either unclear or inadequate.[268] Traditional bills are acceptable in the trade because users are satisfied that they give merchants the rights and protection they need. Any electronic equivalent must engender similar confidence.

Certain requirements must be met by an electronic system to achieve such an object-ive.[269] First, the originality and genuineness of the electronic record must be capable of being established. This requirement is uniquely satisfied in the case of a paper document by the production of the original bill of lading. An electronic alternative may probably achieve this objective by the creation of a central registry exercising control through an independent electronic network, as in the case of Bolero. A private key may play a

---

[266] UNCTAD Report (2003) paras 78 ff.
[267] *Ibid* paras 83–6.
[268] *Ibid* para 79.
[269] See Clarke M, 'Transport documents: their transferability as documents of title; electronic documents' [2002] LMCLQ 356. The author is much indebted to this article for the views expressed in this section.

part, though not necessarily a decisive part, in such a process. Secondly, there must be confidence in the security of both the method of communication and the central registry. There must be no fear of any leakage of confidential business information. Finally, the electronic bill must replicate all the functions of the traditional bill of lading and have the same legal effect as its paper counterpart.

In particular it must provide the security inherent in a document of title for the protection of banks and unpaid sellers. Similarly, it must qualify as a 'document' for purposes of the UK Carriage of Goods by Sea Act 1992 and its users must be afforded the protection of the relevant transport conventions. Unfortunately, at the present time there is some doubt as to the extent to which the provisions of these conventions are applicable to the electronic bill. It is to be hoped that any new carriage convention will deal explicitly with the issue.

5.7 SWITCH BILLS

In concluding the survey of the functions of bills of lading, brief mention must be made of the modern practice of issuing switch bills. Under this procedure, the original set of bills of lading under which the goods have been shipped is surrendered to the carrier, or his agents, in exchange for a new set of bills in which some of the details, such as those relating to the name and address of the shipper, the date of issue of the bills or the port of shipment, have been altered. This practice may be adopted for a variety of commercial reasons. On the one hand, the object may be to conceal the source of the goods where such source is politically sensitive;[270] alternatively the practice may be adopted for fraudulent purposes, for example to avoid customs duties at the port of loading or discharge, or to misrepresent the date of shipment where such date controls the purchase price of the goods shipped.[271] Whatever the motive, 'it is a practice fraught with danger, not only does it give rise to obvious opportunities for fraud but also, if it is intended that the bills of lading should constitute contracts of carriage with the actual owner of the ship (as opposed to any disponent owner) the greatest care has to be taken to ensure that the practice has the shipowner's authority'.[272] Thus the provision in an employment and agency clause in a time charter entitling the charterer to issue bills of lading does not automatically authorise him to issue a second set of switch bills. Again, while there may be express authority in a sub-charter for the sub-charterer to issue switch bills, such bills will not bind the shipowner in the absence of a similar provision in the head charter.[273]

The greatest risk associated with this practice is of the carrier failing to ensure that the original set of bills is surrendered before the new set is issued. In such an event the circulation of two competing sets of bills not only increases the opportunities for fraud but also creates problems for the carrier, aware of the existence of two sets, in ensuring that

---

[270] *The Atlas* [1996] 1 Lloyd's Rep 642 (sellers of steel billets to buyers in Taiwan obtained switch bills because they did not want the receivers to know the identity of their Russian suppliers); *The Irini A (No 2)* [1999] 1 Lloyd's Rep 189 (switch bills were issued to show actual destination of goods where different from that stated in original bill).

[271] See, for example, *The Almak* [1985] 1 Lloyd's Rep 557.

[272] Longmore J in *The Atlas* [1996] 1 Lloyd's Rep 642 at p 645.

[273] *The Atlas* [1996] 1 Lloyd's Rep 642. Cf. *The Irini A (No 2)* [1999] 1 Lloyd's Rep 189.

the goods are delivered to the rightful claimant.[274] As it would be the shipowner or his agent, in the normal case, who was responsible for the issue of the bills, it would seem appropriate that he should bear the cost of any resulting loss.[275]

Problems will also arise where the terms of the two sets of bills are not identical. It is arguable that a subsequent indorsee of a switch bill will have no complaint on discovering that the terms of the original bill were more favourable to his interests. From the contractual point of view, the surrender of the original set of bills in consideration of the issue of the switch bills could be regarded as a bilateral variation of the terms of the contract of carriage by the parties currently involved. Difficulties might, however, arise where the two sets of bills were issued in different jurisdictions and the Hague/Visby Rules were applicable in one but not the other. In such circumstances, would the Rules be applicable throughout the carriage or, if applicable to the original bills, would they be displaced by the issue of the switch bills?[276] Again, a number of issues remain to be resolved where the carriage forms part of an international sale contract, particularly where the latter is financed by a documentary credit. To what extent will the terms and representations in the switch bill satisfy the documentary requirements of the credit, or will the bill provide the buyer with the continuous documentary cover required from port of shipment to the destination?[277] Despite the increasing use of switch bills, there has been little litigation on the subject and many of these questions remain to be answered.[278]

---

[274] It is arguable which, if either, of the sets of bills should have priority.

[275] *The Lycaon* [1983] 2 Lloyd's Rep 548. (A shipowner who had issued a second set of bills while the first set was still in circulation was denied the costs and charges involved in interpleading since the necessity of interpleading was due to his own default.)

[276] The situation would not seem to be analogous with transhipment in *Mayhew Foods v OCL* [1984] 1 Lloyd's Rep 317.

[277] See Debattista, C, *Sale of Goods Carried by Sea*, 2nd edn, 1998, pp 141 ff.

[278] For a comprehensive survey of the problems raised by switch bills, see Toh, KS, 'Of Straight and Switch Bills of Lading' [1996] LMCLQ 416.

6

APPLICATION OF THE
HAGUE/VISBY RULES

At common law the parties to a contract of affreightment covered by a bill of lading or similar document had complete freedom to negotiate their own terms as had the parties to a charterparty. Abuse of the carrier's stronger bargaining position during the nineteenth century, however, resulted in the curtailment of this freedom and the formulation in 1924 of the Hague Rules. The object of these Rules, and of their successors the Hague/Visby Rules, was to protect cargo owners from widespread exclusion of liability by sea carriers. This objective was achieved by requiring standard clauses to be incorporated into bills of lading, defining the risks which must be borne by the carrier and specifying the maximum protection he could claim from exclusion and limitation of liability clauses. Any attempt further to exclude or lessen such basic liability was declared to be null and void and of no effect.[1] There is, of course, no bar to prevent the carrier from undertaking to assume a more extensive liability than the minimum prescribed by the Rules.

The Hague/Visby Rules accordingly envisage a basic and mandatory framework of contractual clauses for incorporation in a contract of carriage outside of which the parties are free to negotiate additional terms of their own. The Rules are attached as a schedule to the Carriage of Goods by Sea Act 1971 and became effective in the United Kingdom on 23 June 1977.[2]

6.1 APPLICATION OF THE RULES

6.1.1 TYPES OF CARRIAGE COVERED BY THE RULES

The basic formula for application of the Rules focuses on the document covering the carriage contract rather than on the contract of carriage itself.[3] Thus Art I(b) states that the Rules are applicable 'only to contracts of carriage covered by a bill of lading or any similar document of title in so far as such document relates to the carriage of goods by sea'. This approach is reinforced by s 1 of the Carriage of Goods by Sea Act 1971,

---

[1] Article III rule 8.
[2] In the succeeding pages attention will be directed almost exclusively to the provisions of the Hague/Visby Rules. In interpreting these provisions, however, illustrations will be drawn from cases decided on the basis of the earlier Hague Rules where the provisions of the two sets of Rules are identical.
[3] Compare the position with regard to the Hamburg Rules, see *infra* Chapter 7.

which gives legislative effect to the Rules and provides in subsection (4) that 'Subject to subsection (6) . . . nothing in this section shall be taken as applying anything in the Rules to any contract for the carriage of goods by sea unless the contract expressly or by implication provides for the issue of a bill of lading or any similar document of title.'[4]

From the above quotations it would appear that the Rules are not designed to cover contracts of carriage which envisage the issue of a waybill or other non-negotiable document since these do not constitute documents of title.[5] Nor would the Rules apply to charterparties, or even bills of lading issued under charterparties, at least so long as such bills remain in the hands of the charterer. In such circumstances the bill merely acts as a receipt and does not 'cover' the contract of carriage, the terms of which are to be found exclusively in the charterparty. Once the bill is assigned to a third party, however, the position will change and the Rules will operate 'from the moment at which such bill of lading or similar document of title regulates the relations between a carrier and a holder of the same'.[6]

On the other hand, if the parties envisage that the contract of carriage will be covered by a bill of lading, it would appear that the Rules will take effect even though, in the event, no such document is in fact issued. This was established in the case of *Pyrene Co Ltd* v *Scindia Navigation Co*[7] where a consignment of fire tenders had been delivered alongside the vessel for shipment. While one of the tenders was being lifted aboard by the ship's tackle it fell back onto the dockside and was seriously damaged. The remaining tenders were loaded safely and the bill of lading which was eventually issued made no reference to the damaged tender. When the carrier sought to limit his liability under Art IV rule 5 of the Hague Rules, the shipper argued that he was unable to do so because the carriage of the damaged tender was not 'covered by a bill of lading'. The trial judge held that the important factor was whether the parties, in contracting, envisaged the issue of a bill of lading and not whether one was in fact actually issued. Contracts of carriage were invariably concluded long before the issue of the relevant bill and, in his opinion, 'Whenever a contract of carriage is concluded and it is contemplated that a bill of lading will, in due course, be issued in respect of it, that contract is from its creation "covered" by a bill of lading and is, therefore, from its inception a contract of carriage within the meaning of the Rules and to which the Rules apply.'[8]

While the operation of the Hague Rules was restricted by the Carriage of Goods by Sea Act 1924 to bills of lading issued in respect of outward voyages from the United Kingdom,[9] Art X of the Hague/Visby Rules has a considerably wider ambit extending to:

---

[4] Subsection (6) refers *inter alia* to the case where a non-negotiable receipt expressly incorporates the Rules.

[5] But the straight bill of lading is an exception to this rule. See *supra* pp 162–4.

[6] Article I(b) of the Hague/Visby Rules.

[7] [1954] 2 QB 402.

[8] *Per* Devlin J at p 419. See also the Canadian case of *Anticosti Shipping Co* v *Viateur St Armand* [1959] 1 Lloyd's Rep 352, where Rand J expressed the view that 'if, as the respondent's agent, he did not see fit to demand a bill of lading – as by Article III rule 3 he had the right to do – it cannot affect what on both sides was contemplated'.

[9] In the United States and several other countries, the Hague Rules are applicable to both inward and outward bills.

'every bill of lading relating to the carriage of goods between ports in two different states if:

a)   the bill of lading is issued in a contracting State, or

b)   the carriage is from a port in a contracting State, or

c)   the contract contained in or evidenced by the bill of lading provides that these Rules, or legislation of any State giving effect to them, are to govern the contract,

whatever may be the nationality of the ship, the carrier, the shipper, the consignee, or any other interested person.'

The wording of Art X clearly envisages an international contract of carriage 'between ports in different states', although s 1(3) of the Carriage of Goods by Sea Act 1971 extends the operation of the Rules, so far as the United Kingdom is concerned, also to cover the coastal trade.[10]

Two of the situations specified in Art X satisfy the basic requirement that a bill of lading be issued, namely, where the bill is issued in a contracting state and also where the bill expressly incorporates the Rules, irrespective of the geographical location of the port of loading in either case. The third alternative refers simply to carriage from a port in a contracting state. Here there is a latent ambiguity since, unless the outward shipment itself automatically triggers the operation of the Rules, their application could be avoided by the carrier issuing some form of non-negotiable document[11] in place of the required bill of lading. While Art III rule 3 undoubtedly confers a right on the shipper to demand the issue of a bill on receipt of the cargo by the carrier or his agent, such right would only be effective if the Rules were already in operation. As the main objective of the draftsmen of both the Hague and Hague/Visby Rules was to make their application mandatory in respect of outward shipments of cargo from contracting states, a rational resolution of this ambiguity is essential. Perhaps the most logical interpretation would be to hold the Rules applicable in all cases of outward shipments from the United Kingdom except in circumstances where the shipper was not entitled to demand the issue of a bill or other document of title, since such issue was not in accordance with the custom of a particular trade or the intention of the parties.[12] Such an interpretation would account for the prevalence of the use of waybills in the container trade and for roll on/roll off traffic and would be in line with the spirit of s 1(4) of the Carriage of Goods by Sea Act 1971 which provides that 'nothing in this section shall be taken as applying anything in the Rules to any contract for the carriage of goods by sea unless

---

[10] Section 1(3) provides that 'Without prejudice to subsection (2) . . . the said provisions shall have effect (and have the force of law) in relation to and in connection with the carriage of goods by sea in ships where the port of shipment is a port in the United Kingdom, whether or not the carriage is between ports in two different States within the meaning of Article X of the Rules.' Subsection (2) is the provision giving legislative effect to the Hague/Visby Rules.

[11] Such a document might include a sea waybill or a straight bill of lading. See *The Happy Ranger* [2002] 2 Lloyd's Rep 357 at p 361, where the majority of the Court (Rix LJ dissenting) took the view that, in order to trigger the operation of the Hague/Visby Rules, the claimant had not only to satisfy Art X but also Art I(b), i.e. to establish that the contract was 'covered' by a bill of lading or other similar document of title.

[12] Cf. the view of Steyn J in *The European Enterprise* [1989] 2 Lloyd's Rep 185 at p 188: 'Shipowners, if they are in a strong enough bargaining position, can escape the application of the rules by issuing a notice to shippers that no bills of lading will be issued by them in a particular trade.'

the contract expressly or by implication provides for the issue of a bill of lading or any similar document of title'.[13]

It is only fair to add, however, that a number of writers are of the opinion that the parties have no power to exclude the operation of the Rules, where otherwise applicable, either by mutual agreement or by the shipper accepting a waybill and refraining from exercising his right under Art III rule 3 to demand the issue of a bill.[14] Such a power of exclusion by agreement would be essential for the implementation of the new documentary procedures outlined in a previous chapter.[15]

This problem of interpretation is further complicated by the wording of Art VI, which, in essence, permits the carrier and shipper to avoid the provisions of the Hague/Visby Rules and to negotiate their own terms in respect of the carriage of 'particular goods'.[16] Such goods are envisaged as 'one-off' cargoes not in the usual course of trade, where either the particular character or condition of the goods or the circumstances in which they are to be carried, justifies a special contract. Obvious examples are experimental cargoes or contracts for the carriage of nuclear waste. The Article further requires that such cargoes should be covered by a non-negotiable receipt. The object is to prevent the peculiar incidents of such a contract being transferred to anyone other than the original shipper. A final proviso specifies that the provisions of Art VI 'shall not apply to ordinary commercial shipments made in the ordinary course of trade'. This proviso may be interpreted merely as an attempt to emphasise the fact that the special provisions are applicable only to the carriage of 'particular goods'. Some commentators, however, construed it as ruling out any possibility of excluding the operation of the Hague/Visby Rules in respect of normal commercial cargoes by shipping them under waybills or other non-negotiable receipts.[17]

---

[13] See also the cases of *Pyrene Co v Scindia Navigation Co* [1954] 2 QB 402 and *Anticosti Shipping Co v Viateur St-Amand* [1959] 1 Lloyd's Rep 352 where the Hague Rules were held applicable even though no bill of lading had been issued. See *supra* at p 175.

[14] See Colinvaux, RP, *Carver's Carriage by Sea*, 13th edn, 1982, paras 470–1. Cf. Scrutton p 423.

[15] See pp 160 ff *supra*.

[16] 'Notwithstanding the provisions of the previous articles, a carrier, master or agent of the carrier and a shipper shall, in regard to any particular goods, be at liberty to enter into any agreement in any terms as to the responsibility and liability of the carrier for such goods, and as to the rights and immunities of the carrier in respect of such goods, or his obligation as to seaworthiness, so far as this stipulation is not contrary to public policy, or the care or diligence of his servants or agents in regard to the loading, handling, stowage, carriage, custody, care and discharge of the goods carried by sea, provided that in this case no bill of lading has been or shall be issued, and that the terms agreed shall be embodied in a receipt which shall be a non-negotiable document and shall be marked as such.

   Any agreement so entered into shall have full legal effect: Provided that this article shall not apply to ordinary commercial shipments made in the ordinary course of trade, but only to other shipments where the character or condition of the property to be carried, or the circumstances, terms and conditions under which the carriage is to be performed are such as reasonably to justify a special agreement.' See Carver 9.265, who suggests that Article VI may have reduced significance after s 1(4) of COGSA 1971 permitted the issue of waybills.

[17] See Colinvaux, *Carver's Carriage by Sea*, 13th edn, 1982, para 471; Cf. Scrutton p 423; Carver 9.138, quoting s 1(4) of COGSA 1971. This argument would lead to the conclusion that, at least in some circumstances, the Hague/Visby Rules are applicable to waybills. Tetley justifies this conclusion largely on the public order nature of the Rules. In his view overriding authority is given to Art VI by Art II which provides that 'subject to the provisions of Article VI, under every contract for the carriage of goods by sea the carrier . . . shall be subject to the responsibilities and liabilities, and entitled to the rights and immunities hereinafter

Finally, it is important to note that the operation of the Hague/Visby Rules has been further extended by s 1 of the Carriage of Goods by Sea Act 1971. Not only does s 1(3) extend coverage to the coastal trade in the United Kingdom, but under s 1(6)(b) the Rules are given the force of law in relation to 'any receipt, which is a non-negotiable document marked as such, if the contract contained in or evidenced by it is a contract for the carriage of goods by sea which expressly provides that the Rules are to govern the contract as if the receipt were a bill of lading'. It would appear that the object of this sub-section is to indicate the legal effect of a clause in a non-negotiable receipt expressly incorporating the Rules, rather than any attempt to delimit the circumstances in which the Rules will be applicable to such a document.[18]

6.1.2 THE CARGOES EXCLUDED

Two types of cargo are expressly excluded from the application of the Rules in Art I(c). These consist of live animals and 'cargo which by the contract of carriage is stated as being carried on deck and is so carried'. In both cases the parties are free to negotiate their own terms of carriage for such cargoes. The exclusion is justified by the peculiar risk attached to the carriage of both categories of cargo, arising in the first case from the nature and inherent propensities of the animals involved and in the second from the exposed position in which the cargo is stowed. As has already been noted, the parties are also entitled to contract on their own terms in relation to the carriage of 'particular goods', provided that these terms are incorporated into a non-negotiable receipt and no bill of lading is issued.[19]

(I) DECK CARGO – EXCLUSION OF HAGUE/VISBY RULES

Two requirements need to be satisfied in order to avoid the operation of the Rules. First, the cargo must actually be stowed on deck and, secondly, this fact must be clearly stated on the bill of lading. Unless both requirements are met, the contract of carriage will still be controlled by the Rules. So they will continue to be applicable where the bill makes no reference to deck carriage but the goods are nevertheless stowed on deck, or where the bill contains a statement that the goods are to be carried on deck but in fact they are stowed in the hold.

Whether or not the goods are stowed on deck is a question of fact which can be easily ascertained. It is, however, more difficult to satisfy the requirement that a statement to that effect should appear on the bill of lading. The acid test appears to be whether an innocent transferee can ascertain, merely by scrutinising the provisions of the bill, whether the cargo has been stowed on deck. For this reason, a clause in the bill conferring a liberty on the carrier to stow cargo on deck would be insufficient, since the transferee would not know whether that liberty had been exercised. So in the case of

---

set forth'. This construction may be questioned on the ground that the primary object of Article VI would appear to be to define the conditions subject to which the parties may contract on their own terms for the shipment of particular goods rather than to define the circumstances in which non-negotiable receipts are not subject to the provisions of the Hague/Visby Rules (14 JMLC (1983) at pp 471–3).

[18] *The European Enterprise* [1989] 2 Lloyd's Rep 185.

[19] For a discussion of the operation of Art VI, see *supra* p 177.

Svenska Traktor v *Maritime Agencies*[20] a consignment of tractors had been shipped from Southampton under a bill which conferred a liberty on the carrier to stow the cargo on deck. When one of the tractors was washed overboard during the voyage, the shipowner sought to rely on a clause in the bill excluding his liability for loss or damage to deck cargo. The court held that he was unable to do so since 'A mere general liberty to carry goods on deck is not, in my view, a statement in the contract of carriage that the goods are in fact being carried on deck.'[21] The trial judge pointed to the fact that 'Such a statement on the face of the bill of lading would serve as a notification and a warning to consignees and indorsees of the bill of lading, to whom the property in the goods passed under the terms of s 1 of the Bills of Lading Act 1855, that the goods which they were to take were being shipped as deck cargo. They would thus have full knowledge of the facts when accepting the documents and would know that the carriage of goods on deck was not subject to the Act.' Without such warning, the transferee of the bill would presume the Rules to be applicable. Accordingly, the carrier was held liable for a breach of Art III rule 2 in failing to look after the cargo properly and carefully during transit.

Nor is the requirement satisfied by a clause in the bill providing that the carrier is entitled to carry the cargo on deck unless the shipper objects. Here again the transferee of the bill is not to know whether or not the shipper has lodged an objection. This situation arose in the US case of *Encyclopaedia Britannica* v *Hong Kong Producer*[22] in which a consignment of encyclopaedias was shipped in containers under a bill which authorised the carrier to stow the cargo on deck 'unless shipper informs carrier in writing before the delivery of goods to carrier that he requires under deck stowage'. A further clause in the bill then excluded the carrier from all liability for loss or damage to the goods during transit. When the goods arrived at their destination, and were found to have been damaged by seawater, the carrier sought to rely on the exclusion clause. In these circumstances the US Court of Appeals held Art I(c) not to be applicable since 'it nowhere states that the cargo is *being carried on deck*. Clause 13 says it *may* be so carried but not that it is being so carried. No consignee or assignee could tell from the bill whether it was below deck or on deck cargo.'[23]

Finally, it must be noted that the mere fact that it is customary in the trade for certain cargoes, such as timber or inflammable goods, to be carried on deck is irrelevant to the question of the applicability of the Hague/Visby Rules. If a carrier wishes to take advantage of Art I(c) and avoid their operation, it is essential that the bill contains an express statement that the goods have been shipped on deck.

(II) CONSENT TO DECK CARRIAGE

It may be appropriate at this point to raise another matter which is linked, and often confused, with the circumstances in which deck cargo is not subject to the provisions of the Hague/Visby Rules. This relates to the effect on the contract of carriage of the carrier deciding to stow the cargo on deck without first obtaining the consent of the shipper. The traditional view was that such conduct amounted to a fundamental breach

---

[20] [1953] 2 QB 295.
[21] At p 300 *per* Pilcher J.
[22] [1969] 2 Lloyd's Rep 536.
[23] At p 542 *per* Anderson Ct J.

of the contract of carriage which prevented the carrier, in the event of loss or damage to the cargo, from relying for protection on any of the contractual terms and exceptions. The US Court of Appeals even went so far as to hold in *Encyclopaedia Britannica* v *Hong Kong Producer*[24] that, in the event of such a breach, the carrier was not allowed to take advantage of the protection afforded by the Hague Rules and, in particular, the limitation of liability provisions. Neither of these assumptions would appear now to be justified so far as English law is concerned. On the one hand, it is doubtful whether the doctrine of fundamental breach can survive the decision of the House of Lords in *Photo Production* v *Securicor Transport.*[25] Secondly, the Court of Appeal has now held in *The Kapitan Petko Voivoda*[26] that carriage of cargo on deck, in breach of an express under-taking for underdeck carriage, will not prevent a carrier from relying for protection against a cargo claim on the limitation of liability provisions in the Hague Rules. Longmore LJ took the view that 'the seriousness of the breach is no longer a self-sufficient yardstick for determining whether exemption or limitation clauses apply to particular breaches'.[27] Approaching the problem 'purely as a question of construction, the words "in any event"[28] become very important. Their most natural meaning to my mind is "in every case" (whether or not the breach of contract is particularly serious; whether or not the cargo was stowed under deck).'[29] Accordingly, the carrier was able to limit his liability despite having committed what had been previously regarded as a 'fundamental breach' of contract.[30]

If such a breach of contract is to be avoided, the shipper must have consented, either expressly or impliedly, to the stowage of his cargo on deck. In this respect it would appear that the inclusion of a general liberty clause in the bill of lading might suffice for this purpose, or even a clause to the effect that 'carrier permitted to stow on deck unless shipper objects', provided that the shipper has sufficient notice of the clause at the time of shipment.[31] Thus in the *Svenska Traktor* case, the Court of Appeal, while refusing to permit the carrier to exclude the provisions of the Hague Rules in the absence of a state-ment in the bill that the goods had been shipped on deck, nevertheless held that, in view of the inclusion of a liberty clause in the bill, deck stowage did not amount to a breach of the contract of carriage. Accordingly, the court was prepared to allow the carrier to take advantage of the defences provided by the Rules. Similarly, consent would normally be implied where it is customary in the trade to ship certain types of goods on

---

[24] [1969] 2 Lloyd's Rep 536. See also *Jones* v *Flying Clipper* [1954] 1 AMC 259. See also Gaskell 6.46 ff.

[25] [1980] AC 827. For a full discussion of the possible implications of this judgment, see *supra* p 22.

[26] [2003] 2 Lloyd's Rep 1.

[27] *Ibid* at p 10.

[28] In Art IV rule 6.

[29] [2003] 2 Lloyd's Rep at p 13.

[30] In reaching this conclusion, the Court of Appeal expressly overruled an earlier decision of Hirst J in *The Chanda* [1989] 2 Lloyd's Rep 494, where, on similar facts, the trial judge had reached the opposite con-clusion. See also *The Antares* [1987] 1 Lloyd's Rep 424, where the Court of Appeal held that unauthorised carriage on deck did not prevent a carrier from invoking the Hague/Visby time limitation. Cf. the New Zealand case of *The Pembroke* [1995] 2 Lloyd's Rep 290 at p 295.

[31] Cf. *Encyclopaedia Britannica* v *Hong Kong Producer* [1969] 2 Lloyd's Rep 536 where the US Court of Appeals held that a general reference in a short form bill of lading to the carrier's standard terms did not con-stitute adequate notice of a liberty clause contained in the carrier's long form bill.

deck. Examples of such cargoes include timber, certain types of inflammable or other dangerous goods and, more importantly, containers carried on a specially designed container ship.[32]

This view is strongly contested by Tetley[33] who argues that the presence of a printed liberty clause in a bill of lading is insufficient to constitute implied consent unless it is accompanied by a clear statement on the face of the bill that the goods have in fact been shipped on deck. In his view the liberty clause is no more than an option, while the absence of a clear statement in the bill amounts to an assurance that the option has not been exercised. Any resultant ambiguity is undesirable when the carrier can obtain complete protection by a clear statement on the face of the bill that the cargo has been stowed on deck. There is always the suspicion that the carrier's reluctance stems from the fear that such a statement might result in a bank or a consignee refusing to accept the bill. In these circumstances Tetley is prepared to treat shipment on deck as a 'fundamental' breach of contract.

There seems little support for this approach in the British cases as is exemplified by the Court of Appeal decision in *Svenska Traktor*. Moreover, there are often good commercial reasons for the absence of any clear statement as to deck carriage on the face of the bill of lading. Thus in the container trade some 30 per cent of containers are normally carried on the deck of a container ship in an efficient operation. Rarely will the carrier be aware until the last moment of the identity of the containers which will eventually travel on deck. The final location of each container will be dependent on a variety of factors including the possible dangerous nature of its contents, the trim of the ship, or merely the time of its arrival at the dockside. In these circumstances the carrier will rarely have the time or the opportunity to notate each bill, but will in practice rely in each case on the inclusion of a liberty clause.

6.1.3 PERIOD OF COVERAGE OF THE RULES

Even though the Rules are applicable to a particular contract of carriage covered by a bill of lading, they do not necessarily govern performance of the contract in its entirety, but are merely relevant to that part of the contract relating to sea transport. Thus, for the purpose of the Rules, the term 'contract of carriage' is defined as constituting 'the period from the time when the goods are loaded on to the time they are discharged from the ship'.[34] This is normally construed as covering the 'tackle to tackle' period in

---

[32] See *The Mormacvega* [1974] 1 Lloyd's Rep 296. See also *Insurance Co of N America v Blue Star Ltd* [1997] AMC 2434.

[33] Tetley pp 658–61.

[34] Article I(e). Devlin J in *Pyrene Co v Scindia Navigation Co* [1954] 1 Lloyd's Rep 321 stresses that the 'operation of the Rules is determined by the limits of the contract of carriage by sea and not by any limits of time. The function of Art I(e) is, I think, only to assist in the definition of "contract of carriage".' In his opinion, it is fallacious to believe that rights and liabilities under the Rules attach to a period of time. 'I think they attach to a contract, or part of a contract. I say "part of a contract" because a single contract may cover both inland and sea transport; and in that case the only part of it that falls within the Rules is that which, to use the words in the definition of "contract of carriage" in Art I(b), "relates to the carriage of goods by sea".' But an appropriate clause in the bill of lading may extend the application of the Rules, e.g. to the inland leg of an intermodal contract of carriage. See *The OOCL Bravery* [2000] 1 Lloyd's Rep 394.

circumstances where the carrier is responsible for loading and discharge, that is, from the time when the ship's tackle is hooked onto the cargo at the port of loading until the hook of the tackle is released at the port of discharge.[35] It is therefore clear that carrier liability is subject to the Rules, not only during the actual carriage, but also during the loading and discharging operations as, for example, where the cargo falls back on the dockside while being lifted aboard with the ship's tackle,[36] or where it falls into the sea while being discharged into lighters.[37] On the other hand, the Rules do not apply to any additional time during which the goods are under the control of the carrier outside the tackle-to-tackle period. Under modern trading conditions such periods of time may be extensive since cargo for shipment, delivered to shipping agents nominated by the carrier, will frequently be discharged into a designated warehouse at its destination. Since Art VII provides that the parties are free to negotiate their own terms in respect of care of cargo before loading and after discharge, the carrier will seek, where possible, to exclude responsibility during this period. This has come to be known as the 'before and after problem' and is an obvious weakness in the Rules which cargo interests now seek to rectify.

A further problem arises where goods are shipped under a through bill of lading or a combined transport document which envisages that they will be transhipped at an intermediate port. In such circumstances will the Rules govern the operation throughout, or only until the goods reach the port of transhipment? One factor to be taken into consideration in answering this question is the wording of Art I(c) which, in defining the term 'contract of carriage' for the purpose of the Rules, specifies contracts of carriage covered by bills of lading 'in so far as such document relates to the carriage of goods by sea'. There can accordingly be little doubt that the Rules will be inapplicable to any segment of the through transport which involves carriage by land or air, but a Canadian court has given a wider construction to this clause by holding that, even where sea carriage is envisaged throughout the transit, the Rules will not cover any period during which the cargo is lying on the dockside awaiting transhipment. Thus in *Captain* v *Far Eastern Steamship Co*[38] goods were shipped from Madras to Vancouver under a contract which envisaged that the cargo would be transhipped at some point on the route. The bill of lading contained a term providing that the responsibility of the carrier should be limited to that part of the transport performed by him on vessels under his

---

[35] Where shore tackle is used, the operative period will normally be from the time the cargo crosses the ship's rail during loading until it recrosses the rail during discharge. See Tetley p 14; UNCTAD: *Report on Bills of Lading*, p 34.

[36] *Pyrene Co* v *Scindia Navigation* [1954] 2 QB 402. In the view of Devlin J, 'Even if "carriage of goods by sea" were given by definition the most restricted meaning possible, for example, the period of the voyage, the loading of the goods (by which I mean the whole operation of loading in both its stages and whichever side of the ship's rail) would still *relate* to the carriage on the voyage and so be within the "contract of carriage".' See also *Thermo Engineers* v *Ferrymasters* [1981] 1 Lloyd's Rep 200.

[37] *Falconbridge Nickel Mines* v *Chimo Shipping Co* [1973] 2 Lloyd's Rep 469. The Rules have also been held applicable where cargo has been damaged, after being released from the ship's tackle, by other cargo being discharged into the same lighter: *Goodwin Ferreira & Co* v *Lamport & Holt Ltd* (1929) 34 LlLR 192. While the latter is a questionable decision, it has been followed in the US case of *Hoegh* v *Green Truck Sales Inc* [1962] AMC 431.

[38] [1979] 1 Lloyd's Rep 595.

management. When the cargo was eventually transhipped at Singapore, the container vans were stored in the open for three weeks during which time they suffered rainwater damage amounting to some $32,000. The court held that the carrier was entitled to rely on the contractual clause excluding liability during this period since the Hague Rules did not apply to the period during which the goods were stored on the dock, 'because it does not relate to the carriage of goods by water'.[39]

This decision, however, has since been distinguished by Bingham J in *Mayhew Foods v OCL*,[40] a case where the contract provided for the carriage of a consignment of frozen poultry from Sussex to Jeddah. The intention was that the poultry would be transported by road from Uckfield to a south coast port and there shipped on one of the defendant's vessels for Jeddah. The bill which was eventually issued provided for the carrier to accept liability for loss or damage to the goods from the time of receipt in Sussex to the time of delivery in Jeddah, although such liability was limited to US $2 per kilo of the gross weight of the goods – an amount significantly below the Hague/Visby limit. In the event the goods were shipped from Shoreham, and not Southampton as originally intended, and the carrier subsequently took advantage of a liberty in the combined transport document to tranship the goods in Le Havre. The poultry eventually arrived in Jeddah in a putrefied state due to the fact that the temperature control on the container had been set at plus 2 to 4 degrees centigrade instead of the required temperature of minus 18 degrees centigrade. On the basis that the evidence suggested that the damage had occurred while the cargo was lying ashore at Le Havre awaiting transhipment, the carrier contended, on the basis of *Captain v Far Eastern Steamship Co*, that the Hague/Visby Rules were not applicable during this period and that he could therefore limit his liability to the contractual figure of US $2 per kilo.

In rejecting this argument Bingham J distinguished *Captain v Far Eastern Steamship Co* on the grounds that 'the shipper there was told when the contract was made that there would be transhipment and there were separate bills of lading for the two legs of the journey'.[41] In *Mayhew Foods v OCL* on the other hand the bill of lading when issued covered the entire journey from Shoreham to Jeddah and the shipper had no knowledge of the carrier's intention to invoke the liberty to tranship the container in Le Havre. In the view of the trial judge, 'It would . . . be surprising if OCL could, by carrying the goods to Le Havre and there storing the goods before transhipment, rid themselves of liabilities to which they would have been subject had they, as contemplated, shipped the goods at Southampton and carried them direct to Jeddah.'[42] Moreover, if the carrier decided to exercise his contractual right to discharge, store and tranship the goods en route, these were still operations 'in relation to and in connection with the carriage of goods by sea' within the meaning of the Hague/Visby Rules definition.

The result of the decision in *Mayhew Foods v OCL* would therefore appear to be that, whenever goods are shipped from a contracting state under a bill of lading which

---

[39] At p 602 *per* MacDonald J.
[40] [1984] 1 Lloyd's Rep 317.
[41] *Ibid* at p 320.
[42] At p 320.

covers the entire sea-carriage through to the ultimate destination then, despite any intermediate transhipment, the requirements of Art X will be satisfied and the Hague/Visby Rules will control the operation throughout.[43]

6.2 LEGAL EFFECT OF THE RULES

When statutory force was given to the original Hague Rules, it was provided by s 1 of the Carriage of Goods by Sea Act 1924 that the Rules 'shall have effect in relation to and in connection with "certain types of contract for the carriage of goods by sea" '. The phrase 'shall have effect' appears to have been interpreted by the courts as, in practice, conferring little more than contractual force on the Rules. This view is to some extent reinforced by the fact that s 3 of the Act required bills of lading issued in pursuance of such contracts to contain 'an express statement that it is to have effect subject to the provisions of the said Rules as applied by this Act'.[44] Thus the Privy Council in the case of *Vita Food Products* v *Unus Shipping Co*[45] held that bills of lading issued in Newfoundland, which did not contain a paramount clause and which otherwise would have been subject to the Hague Rules by virtue of local legislation corresponding to the English COGSA, were taken outside the ambit of the Rules by the simple expedient of including an English choice of law clause.[46] A similar approach is also reflected in earlier decisions which suggest that a fundamental breach of contract by the carrier as, for example, deviation from the agreed course,[47] or stowage of the cargo on deck without the shipper's consent,[48] will debar him from invoking the Hague Rules exceptions or limitation of liability provisions.[49]

A radically different approach was adopted by the legislature in implementing the provisions of the Hague/Visby Rules. The 1971 Carriage of Goods by Sea Act drops the requirement for the inclusion in every bill of lading of a paramount clause expressly incorporating the Rules but provides that they shall have 'the force of law'.[50] An opportunity for the House of Lords to consider the legal effect to be attributed to this phrase was provided in *The Morviken*.[51] In this case a substantial piece of machinery had been

---

[43] A similar conclusion was reached by the High Court of Hong Kong in *The Anders Maersk* [1986] 1 Lloyd's Rep 483, where boilers had been shipped from Baltimore to Shanghai under through bills of lading incorporating the Hague Rules (as enacted in the US COGSA) and which permitted the carriers to tranship the cargo en route. The court rejected the argument that, after transhipment of the boilers in Hong Kong, the remainder of the carriage to Shanghai was controlled by the Hague/Visby Rules in accordance with Hong Kong law. In the court's view, the through bills issued in the United States were intended to govern the contract of carriage throughout.

[44] The so-called paramount clause which appears in the majority of standard forms of bill of lading.

[45] [1939] AC 277.

[46] Cf. *The Torni* [1932] P 78. It is only fair to add that the Privy Council in the *Vita Food* case indicated that the decision might well have been different if the case had been tried by a Newfoundland court. See also Tetley pp 5–6.

[47] See *Stag Line* v *Foscolo Mango & Co* [1932] AC 328.

[48] See *Encyclopaedia Britannica* v *Hong Kong Producer* [1969] 2 Lloyd's Rep 536.

[49] For the present law relating to fundamental breach, see *supra* pp 21 ff.

[50] Section 1(2).

[51] [1983] 1 Lloyd's Rep 1.

shipped aboard a Dutch vessel at Leith for carriage to the Dutch Antilles under a bill of lading which included a Dutch choice of law clause and provided that the Court of Amsterdam should have exclusive jurisdiction over any dispute arising under the bill. The machinery was subsequently transhipped at a Dutch port but on arrival at the Dutch Antilles was severely damaged during the discharge operations. When the shippers commenced proceedings *in rem* in the Admiralty Court claiming negligence on the part of the carrier's servants, the carrier sought a stay of action based on the exclusive jurisdiction clause in the bill of lading. The material point at issue concerned the respective limitation of liability provisions in the two jurisdictions. Under Dutch law, where the Hague Rules were still in operation at the time of the relevant litigation, the carrier's liability based on the package or unit formula would have been limited to approximately £250. On the other hand, under the Hague/Visby Rules operative in the United Kingdom, the shipper would have been entitled to a higher sum calculated on the gross weight of the damaged cargo which would have amounted to some £11,000.

The House of Lords was unanimous in refusing to apply the *Vita Food Products* approach by granting primacy to the intention of the parties as demonstrated by the choice of law clause. In the opinion of Lord Diplock, the draftsmen of the 1971 Act had deliberately abandoned the 'clause paramount' technique of 1924 by giving the Hague/Visby Rules the force of law, with the result that they must now 'be treated as if they were part of directly enacted statute law'.[52] The Hague/Visby Rules were clearly applicable to the bill of lading in question since it fell within both paragraphs a) and b) of Art X, having been issued in a contracting state and also covering a shipment from a port in a contracting state. To give effect to the choice of law clause in these circumstances would, in Lord Diplock's view, clearly contravene Art III rule 8 which renders void any attempt to lessen the carrier's liability as enshrined in the Hague/Visby Rules. Accordingly, the House of Lords refused to grant a stay of action. To reach any other conclusion 'would leave it open to any shipowner to evade the provisions of Art III rule 8 by the simple device of inserting in his bills of lading issued in, or for carriage from a port in, any contracting state a clause in standard form providing as the exclusive forum for resolution of disputes what might aptly be described as a court of convenience, viz. one situated in a country which did not apply the Hague/Visby Rules'.[53]

The decision in *The Morviken* has attracted considerable criticism from legal commentators, many of whom adopt a different interpretation of the phrase 'force of law' and argue that effect should be given to the intentions of the parties as expressed in the choice of law clause.[54] The reasoning of their Lordships has, however, been cited with approval and followed in subsequent cases,[55] in one of which the trial judge recalled 'the guidance of Lord Diplock in *The Morviken* that, in their interpretation, the words

---

[52] *Ibid* at p 5.
[53] *Ibid* at p 7. It is interesting to note that a Singapore court reached a similar result in *The Epar* [1985] 2 MLJ 3 even though s 3(1) of the Singapore COGSA 1972 merely gives 'effect' to the Hague/Visby Rules. Would the decision in *The Morviken* have been different if the document involved had been not a bill of lading but a non-negotiable receipt?
[54] See Jackson [1980] LMCLQ 159; Mann (1983) 99 LQR 397 ff. Cf. Diamond [1978] 2 LMCLQ 225; Morris (1979) 95 LQR 57; Carver 9.076 ff.
[55] See *The Vechscroon* [1982] 1 Lloyd's Rep 301; *The Antares* [1987] 1 Lloyd's Rep 424.

should be given a purposive rather than a narrow legalistic construction, particularly whenever the adoption of a literalistic construction would enable the stated purpose of the International Convention, viz. the unification of domestic laws of the contracting states relating to bills of lading, to be evaded by the use of colourable devices that, not being expressly referred to in the rules, are not specifically prohibited'.[56] There is considerable force in this argument and it is pertinent to note that the legislature in Australia achieved an identical result more directly by incorporating an express provision in the Australian Sea-Carriage of Goods Act 1924 rendering void any attempt to evade the application of the Hague Rules by the use of an exclusive jurisdiction or choice of law clause.[57]

On the other hand, the decision in *The Morviken* will only be relevant in a situation where the application of the Hague/Visby Rules is mandatory. In circumstances where the Rules are not otherwise applicable, the courts are not prepared to interpret a choice of English law as indicating an intention to incorporate the Rules into the contract of carriage within the meaning of Art X. Thus, in *The Komninos S*,[58] a cargo of steel coils was shipped from Thessaloniki to Ravenna under bills of lading which provided that any disputes arising under the contract of carriage were 'to be referred to British courts'. In the view of the Court of Appeal, this express choice of forum also involved an implied choice of law. In response to a claim for cargo damage, the shipowner sought to rely on exclusion clauses in the contract which would be rendered null and void by the Hague/Visby Rules, if the latter were applicable. As Greece was not a contracting state, the Rules were not mandatorily applicable since shipment was not from a port in a contracting state, nor had the bill of lading been issued in a contracting state. Accordingly, the Rules would only be relevant if it was the intention of the parties that they should be incorporated into the contract of carriage within the meaning of Art X(c). The Court of Appeal refused to infer such an intention merely from the inclusion in the contract of a choice of forum clause. The shipowner was therefore able to invoke the protection of the contractual exceptions.

Finally, it must be remembered that the parties are free expressly to incorporate the Hague/Visby Rules into a bill of lading or non-negotiable receipt in situations where the Rules would not otherwise be applicable. Formerly, when similar action was taken with respect to the Hague Rules, the incorporation was treated purely as a matter of contract and, in the event of any conflict between the provisions of the Rules and the remaining terms of the contract, the courts attempted to resolve the issue as a matter of construction.[59] Now s 1(6) of COGSA 1971 provides that in the event of any conflict,

---

[56] *The Benarty* [1983] 2 Lloyd's Rep 50 at p 56 *per* Sheen J. The decision at first instance was reversed by the Court of Appeal [1984] 2 Lloyd's Rep 244 on other grounds.

[57] Sea-Carriage of Goods Act 1924, s 9. See *Wilson* v *Compagnie des Messageries Maritimes* [1954] 2 Lloyd's Rep 544; *John Churcher* v *Mitsui* [1974] 2 NSWLR 179. Cf. *The Amazonia* [1990] 1 Lloyd's Rep 236. The substance of this provision has been re-enacted in s 11 of the Australian Carriage of Goods by Sea Act 1991, which repeals the 1924 Act and substitutes the provisions of the Hague/Visby Rules, to which it also gives the 'force of law' (s 8). New Zealand has a similar provision in s 11A of its Sea Carriage of Goods Act 1940.

[58] [1991] 1 Lloyd's Rep 371.

[59] A similar attitude was adopted by the courts where the Rules were expressly incorporated into a charterparty. See *Adamastos Shipping Co* v *Anglo-Saxon Petroleum Co* [1958] 1 Lloyd's Rep 73. Cf. *Overseas Tankship (UK)* v *BP Tanker Co* [1966] 2 Lloyd's Rep 386.

the provisions of the Rules will override express terms of the contract which are inconsistent with them. The object of the subsection is 'to confer on a voluntary contractual tie a statutory binding character'.[60] This result will follow, however, only where the non-negotiable receipt purports to incorporate the Hague/Visby Rules in their entirety. Thus, in *The European Enterprise*[61] a consignment of meat, packed in a refrigerated tractor trailer unit, was shipped from Dover to Calais under a non-negotiable consignment note. The note expressly incorporated the Hague/Visby Rules subject to a number of provisos, including a limitation of liability provision 'substantially less generous' than that contained in Art IV rule 5 of the Rules. When the goods were damaged in transit, the cargo owner argued that the lower contractual limit was rendered null and void by s 1(6)(b) of the Carriage of Goods by Sea Act 1971 which gave to the Rules the force of law. In rejecting this argument, the trial judge pointed out that as the Rules were not mandatorily applicable to non-negotiable receipts, the parties had freedom to negotiate their own terms and to decide whether or not to incorporate the Rules, in whole or in part, into their contract. In his opinion, 'it would be curious if a voluntary paramount clause, which reflected only a partial incorporation of the Rules, had a result that a statutory binding character was given to *all* the rules, even where there was no primary contractual bond'.[62]

Perhaps more debatable is the further conclusion drawn by Steyn J in this case that, before the Rules will acquire the force of law on incorporation into a non-negotiable receipt, it is necessary literally to comply with two formal requirements contained in s 1(6)(b). First, the receipt must specifically state that it is non-negotiable and, secondly, it must expressly provide that the Rules are to govern the contract 'as if the receipt were a bill of lading'. Failure to incorporate the latter phrase will result in the Rules being denied statutory force.

6.3 BASIC PROVISIONS OF THE HAGUE/VISBY RULES

The Hague/Visby Rules were 'not conceived as a comprehensive and self-sufficient code regulating the carriage of goods by sea',[63] but merely designed to provide a basic, but compulsory, framework for the contract of carriage, outside of which the parties were free to negotiate the remaining terms. As the title of the Convention indicates, the object was merely 'to unify certain rules relating to bills of lading' and so achieve a substantial degree of uniformity in the protection afforded to carriers and cargo interests. The provisions of the Hague/Visby Rules fall broadly into two main categories: first, those establishing the minimum obligations of the carrier and, secondly, those defining the maximum immunities to which he is entitled and the extent to which he can limit his liability.

---

[60] *The European Enterprise* [1989] 2 Lloyd's Rep 185 at p 188.
[61] [1989] 2 Lloyd's Rep 185. See also the New Zealand case of *The Tasman Discoverer* [2002] 2 Lloyd's Rep 528.
[62] [1989] 2 Lloyd's Rep 185 at p 191. In reaching this conclusion Steyn J refused to follow a decision to the contrary of Lloyd J in *The Vechscroon* [1982] 1 Lloyd's Rep 301.
[63] UNCTAD: *Report on Bills of Lading*, p 15.

6.3.1 DUTIES OF THE CARRIER

(I) OBLIGATION TO PROVIDE A SEAWORTHY SHIP – ART III RULE 1

At common law the carrier was under an absolute obligation to provide a seaworthy ship subject only to the common law exceptions of act of God, Queen's enemies or inherent vice. Such liability is now abrogated by s 3 of COGSA 1971 and replaced by an obligation to use due diligence.

Article III rule 1 provides that:

'The carrier shall be bound before and at the beginning of the voyage to exercise due diligence to –

a)   Make the ship seaworthy.

b)   Properly man, equip and supply the ship.

c)   Make the holds, refrigerating and cool chambers, and all other parts of the ship in which goods are carried, fit and safe for their reception, carriage and preservation.'

As defined in Art III, the obligation embraces the three distinct aspects of seaworthiness recognised at common law, namely, the physical condition of the ship, the efficiency of the crew and equipment, and the cargoworthiness of the vessel.[64]

(a) Duration of obligation

The Article requires the carrier to exercise due diligence to provide a seaworthy ship 'before and at the beginning of the voyage'. The phrase has been interpreted as covering 'the period from at least the beginning of the loading until the vessel starts on her voyage . . .'.[65] In the case from which this quotation is drawn the plaintiff's cargo was lost when the defendant's vessel had to be scuttled before it could set sail on the contractual voyage. After the cargo had been loaded an attempt was made, under the supervision of a ship's officer, to thaw ice in three scupper holes by the use of an oxyacetylene lamp. The cork insulation on the pipes ignited and the fire rapidly spread, with the result that the vessel had to be scuttled. The owners sought to rely on the fire exception in Art IV rule 2(b) under which they would not be responsible for the

---

[64] For examples see:
  a) Physical condition of vessel: *The Muncaster Castle* [1961] AC 807 (faulty replacement of inspection covers on storm valves); *The Amstelslot* [1963] 2 Lloyd's Rep 223 (fatigue crack in engine); *The Hellenic Dolphin* [1978] 2 Lloyd's Rep 336 (gash in plating letting in seawater); *The Friso* [1980] 1 Lloyd's Rep 469 (bad stowage rendering vessel unstable); *The Theodegmon* [1990] 1 Lloyd's Rep 52 (breakdown of steering gear).
  b) Efficiency of crew and equipment: *The Makedonia* [1962] 1 Lloyd's Rep 316 (inefficient chief engineer – lack of plan of fuel system); *The Star Sea* [1997] 1 Lloyd's Rep 360 (incompetence of master); *The Farrandoc* [1967] 2 Lloyd's Rep 276 (incompetence of crew); *The Eurasian Dream* [2002] 1 Lloyd's Rep 719 (incompetence of master and crew – lack of training and equipment for fire-fighting); *Northumbrian Shipping Co* v *Timm & Son Ltd* [1939] AC 397 (insufficiency of bunkers). Cf. *President of India* v *West Coast Steamship Co* [1963] 2 Lloyd's Rep 278 (lack of radar and loran).
  c) Cargoworthiness: *The Fehmarn* [1964] 1 Lloyd's Rep 355 (failure to clean vessel's storage tanks); *The Benlawers* [1989] 2 Lloyd's Rep 51 (defective ventilation system).
[65] Lord Somervell in *Maxine Footwear Co Ltd* v *Canadian Government Merchant Marine* [1959] AC 589 at p 603.

consequences of fire unless it resulted from 'the actual fault or privity' of the owners,[66] which it clearly did not in this case. The Privy Council held, however, that the loss resulted from a breach of the seaworthiness obligation in Art III rule 1 since the carrier's obligation to exercise due diligence continued throughout the entire period from the beginning of loading until the ship sailed. The negligence of the carrier's servants which caused the fire occurred during this period and constituted a failure to exercise due diligence for which the carrier was liable. In the view of the Privy Council, the implied undertaking as to seaworthiness in Art III rule 1 constituted an overriding obligation, any breach of which deprived the carrier of the protection of the exceptions listed in Art IV in respect of any resulting damage.[67]

Should the shipowner have exercised due diligence to make his ship seaworthy in all respects before she sails on her voyage, he will not be liable under this Article should defects develop on the voyage or arise during a call at an intermediate port. The term 'voyage' in Art III has been construed as covering the entire voyage covered by the bill of lading, irrespective of calls at intermediate ports. The charterparty doctrine of stages, under which the vessel is required to be seaworthy at the commencement of each stage, does not apply. So in the case of *Leesh River Tea Co v British India Steam Nav Co*[68] a vessel was held not to be unseaworthy within the meaning of Art III when cargo was damaged by the surreptitious removal of a storm valve cover plate by a person unknown while the vessel was calling at an intermediate port.

(b) Meaning of due diligence

In imposing on the carrier an obligation to exercise 'due diligence' the draftsmen of the Hague Rules adopted a term first used in the US Harter Act in 1893. The standard imposed by this obligation has been interpreted by the courts as being roughly equivalent to that of the common law duty of care,[69] but with the important difference that it is a personal obligation that cannot be delegated. In the words of Tetley, 'The carrier may employ some other person to exercise due diligence, but, if the delegate is not diligent, then the carrier is responsible.'[70] Consequently, the carrier will remain liable if the person to whom performance of the obligation is delegated is negligent, whether that person be a servant of the carrier, an independent contractor, or even a Lloyd's surveyor.[71] It will be no defence for the carrier to argue that he engaged competent or reputable experts to perform the task, or that he lacked the necessary expertise to check their work.[72] In these circumstances it is perhaps not surprising to discover that carriers have frequently claimed that their liability under the Rules differs little from that at common law, which imposed on them an absolute duty to provide a seaworthy ship.

---

[66] See *infra* pp 268 ff.
[67] Breach of the Art IV rule 1 obligation might also override the shipowner's right to an indemnity for damage caused by the shipment of dangerous cargo under Art IV rule 6: *The Fiona* [1994] 2 Lloyd's Rep 506.
[68] [1966] 2 Lloyd's Rep 193.
[69] *The Amstelslot* [1963] 2 Lloyd's Rep 223 at p 235 *per* Lord Devlin.
[70] Tetley p 391.
[71] *The Amstelslot* [1963] 2 Lloyd's Rep 223.
[72] *The Muncaster Castle* [1961] 1 Lloyd's Rep 57.

There is, however, this important distinction, that the carrier will not be liable under the Rules if neither he nor his delegate has been negligent.[73]

The definitive interpretation of the concept of due diligence is provided by the case of *The Muncaster Castle*[74] in which a consignment of ox tongue had been shipped from Sydney under a bill of lading which incorporated the Hague Rules. During the voyage the cargo was damaged by water entering the hold via the inspection covers on the storm valves. Some months earlier, a load line survey of the vessel had been undertaken in Glasgow by a reputable firm of ship repairers, during which there had been an inspection of the storm valves under the supervision of a Lloyd's surveyor. After the inspection had been completed, the task of replacing the inspection covers on the storm valves had been delegated to a fitter employed by the ship repairers. Owing to negligence on his part in tightening the nuts holding the covers, they loosened during the subsequent voyage allowing water to enter the hold and damage the cargo. Despite the fact that there had been no negligence on the part of the carrier in that he had delegated the work to a reputable firm, the House of Lords held the carrier liable for breach of the obligation to exercise due diligence. In the words of Viscount Simonds, 'no other solution is possible than to say that the shipowner's obligation of due diligence demands due diligence in the work of repair by whomsoever it may be done'.[75]

This interpretation of the carrier's obligation appears to be generally acceptable in most jurisdictions since it is always open to the shipowner to cover himself by claiming an indemnity from the independent contractor involved. Lord Radcliffe in *The Muncaster Castle*[76] also advanced a practical reason in support of this solution:

> 'I should regard it is as unsatisfactory, where a cargo owner has found his goods damaged through a defect in the seaworthiness of the vessel that his rights of recovering from the carrier should depend upon particular circumstances in the carrier's situation and arrangements with which the cargo owner has nothing to do; as, for instance, that liability should depend on the measure of control that the carrier had exercised over persons engaged on surveying or repairing the ship, or on such questions as whether the carrier had or could have done whatever was needed by the hands of his own servants or had been sensible or prudent in getting done by other hands. Carriers would find themselves liable or not liable according to circumstances quite extraneous to the sea carriage itself.'

The carrier will not, of course, be held responsible for the seaworthy condition of a vessel until it comes under his control. Consequently if he commissions the construction of a new ship, or charters or purchases a ship from another party, he will not be liable for existing defects rendering the vessel unseaworthy unless such defects were reasonably discoverable by the exercise of due diligence at the time of takeover. The carrier can hardly be held responsible for the negligence of shipbuilders or their employees who were not acting as his servants or agents at the material time. On the other hand, if the defect should have been apparent on a reasonable inspection of the vessel at the time of

---

[73] 'I can find nothing in the Hague Rules or at common law to make a carrier responsible for the unseaworthiness of its vessel resulting from a shipper's misconduct of which it, the carrier, has not been put on notice.' Auld LJ in *The Kapitan Sakharov* [2000] 2 Lloyd's Rep 255 (shipment of undeclared dangerous cargo in sealed container).

[74] [1961] 1 Lloyd's Rep 57.

[75] *Ibid* at p 71. See also *Dow Europe v Novoklav Inc* [1998] 1 Lloyd's Rep 306.

[76] [1961] 1 Lloyd's Rep 57 at p 82.

take-over, the carrier cannot in that event rely for protection even on the certificate of a Lloyd's surveyor.

Thus in the case of *The Amstelslot*[77] the delivery of a cargo of wheat was delayed by an engine breakdown which was subsequently attributed to a fatigue crack. The vessel in question had been built in 1922 but had only been acquired by the defendant in 1956 at which time the engines had been inspected by a Lloyd's surveyor. The cargo owner having claimed that the vessel was unseaworthy within the meaning of Art III rule 1, Lord Reid formulated the issue for the Court in the following terms: 'if the appellants [the carrier] are to escape from liability they must prove that due diligence had been exercised not only by themselves and their servants, but by the Lloyd's Register of Shipping surveyor who surveyed this gear but failed to discover the crack'.[78] On the facts of the case the House of Lords held that the Lloyd's surveyor had taken reasonable care in conducting the survey, thus discharging the burden of proof on the carrier that due diligence had been exercised.[79]

(c) Burden of proof

Some difference of opinion exists as to the incidence of the burden of proof relating to the exercise of due diligence. Article IV rule 1 provides that the carrier shall not be liable for loss or damage arising or resulting from unseaworthiness unless caused by want of due diligence on his part to make the ship seaworthy, as defined in Art III rule 1. The section then continues: 'Whenever loss or damage has resulted from unseaworthiness the burden of proving the exercise of due diligence shall be on the carrier or other person claiming exemption under this article.' The phraseology of this article has led to the general assumption that no onus is cast on the carrier in relation to proof of due diligence until the other party has first established that the vessel was unseaworthy and that his loss was attributable to that fact.[80] An alternative view is provided by Tetley who argues that on policy grounds the burden of proof in both cases should rest with the carrier, who is usually the only party to have access to the full facts. In his opinion such a construction is contrary to the spirit of the Rules and to the express wording of Art III rules 1 and 2.[81] The case law, on balance, tends to favour the majority view. Thus in *The Hellenic Dolphin*[82] a cargo of asbestos was found, on discharge, to have been damaged by seawater. It was later established that the seawater had gained access to the hold through a four-feet long indent in the ship's plating, of which the shipowner had previously been unaware. No evidence was available as to whether the damage to the vessel had been inflicted before or after the cargo had been loaded. In these circumstances the trial judge allowed the shipowner to rely on the exception of perils of the sea since, in his opinion and in the absence of evidence to the contrary, the type of damage involved was

---

[77] [1963] 2 Lloyd's Rep 223.

[78] *Ibid* at p 229.

[79] See also *Angliss & Co v P & O Steam Nav Co* [1927] 2 KB 457; *The Muncaster Castle* [1961] 1 Lloyd's Rep 57 at pp 86–7 *per* Lord Keith.

[80] See Scrutton p 442. See also *The Toledo* [1995] 1 Lloyd's Rep 40 at p 50; *The Fjord Wind* [2000] 2 Lloyd's Rep 191; *The Kamsar Voyager* [2002] 2 Llyd's rep 57.

[81] Tetley pp 375–6.

[82] [1978] 2 Lloyd's Rep 336. See also *The Antigoni* [1991] 1 Lloyd's Rep 209; *The Subro Valour* [1995] 1 Lloyd's Rep 509; *The Apostolis* [1997] 2 Lloyd's Rep 241.

a classic example of damage caused by a peril of the sea. The shipowner would only be prevented from relying on the exception if the shipper could prove that the loss resulted from the vessel being unseaworthy 'before and at the beginning of the voyage'.[83]

The facts of this case tend to support the thesis advanced by Tetley that it is often extremely difficult for the cargo owner to discharge the burden of proof of unseaworthiness. In practice, however, the problem is frequently solved by the readiness of the court to treat the presence of seawater in a vessel's hold as prima facie evidence of unseaworthiness.

(II) CARE OF CARGO

The second duty imposed on the carrier by the Hague/Visby Rules relates to the care of the cargo. Article III rule 2 provides that:

> 'Subject to the provisions of Article IV, the carrier shall properly and carefully load, handle, stow, carry, keep, care for and discharge the goods delivered.'

This Article has been construed as requiring from the carrier the exercise of a standard roughly equivalent to that of reasonable care. So much is apparent from the inclusion of the word 'carefully' in the definition, but the addition of 'properly' raises the question as to whether the draftsmen of the Rules intended a higher duty of care. The point was considered by the House of Lords in *Albacora* v *Westcott and Laurance Line*,[84] a case in which a consignment of wet salted fish had been shipped at Glasgow for Genoa. The crates were marked 'keep away from engines and boilers', but otherwise no special instructions for carriage were given by the shippers. It was subsequently established that fish of this type could not be safely carried on such a voyage without refrigeration, although this fact was unknown to the carrier. On arrival at Genoa the cargo was found to have deteriorated substantially in quality as a result of bacterial action and the question was whether it had been carried 'properly' within the meaning of Art III. In answering this question in the affirmative, Lord Reid expressed the view that 'properly' meant in accordance with a sound system. 'In my opinion, the obligation is to adopt a system which is sound in light of all the knowledge which the carrier has or ought to have about the nature of the goods. And if that is right, then the Respondents did adopt a sound system. They had no reason to suppose that the goods required any different treatment from that which the goods received.'[85] In concurring with this view, Lord Pearce added the qualification that 'A sound system does not mean a system suited to all the weaknesses and idiosyncrasies of a particular cargo, but a sound system under all the circumstances in relation to the general practice of carriage of goods by sea. It is tantamount, I think, to efficiency.'[86] In the absence of any breach of duty under this Article, the carrier was accordingly allowed to rely on the defence of inherent vice.[87]

---

[83] [1978] 2 Lloyd's Rep 336 at p 339 *per* Lloyd J. See also *Minister of Food* v *Reardon Smith Line* [1951] 2 Lloyd's Rep 265. Cf. *The Farrandoc* [1967] 1 Lloyd's Rep 232 at p 234.
[84] [1966] 2 Lloyd's Rep 53.
[85] *Ibid* at p 58.
[86] *Ibid* at p 62.
[87] See also *Shipping Corp of India* v *Gamlen Chemical Co* (1980) 55 ALJR 88, a decision of the High Court of Australia.

The wording of Art III rule 2 implies a continuous obligation on the carrier running from 'tackle to tackle', i.e. from the commencement of loading to the completion of discharge. This presupposes that the carrier has undertaken to load and discharge the cargo, whereas occasionally the contract may provide that these operations are to be performed by shore based tackle at the responsibility of the shipper or consignee. The Court of Appeal has held in the case of *Jindal Iron & Steel Co* v *Islamic Solidarity Shipping Co*[88] that Art III rule 2 does not oblige the carrier to perform these obligations but merely provides that, if he has undertaken to do so, he must perform them properly and carefully. In effect, such a transfer of responsibility does not contravene the Rules, since it is intended merely to define the scope of the contract of carriage and not the terms on which the cargo is to be carried. Clear words are, however, needed to effect such a transfer and the fact that the shipper undertakes to perform the loading and discharging operations free of expense to the carrier (e.g. f.i.o.s.t.) does not raise the presumption that the carrier is thereby relieved of liability for their proper performance.

It will be noted that the duty of care required to be exercised by the carrier is made expressly subject to the provisions of Art IV. This reference to the catalogue of exceptions listed in Art IV rule 2 raises a query as to the incidence of the burden of proof. In the event of the cargo being damaged in the course of transit, does the onus rest with the carrier to establish that the goods were carried 'properly and carefully', or does the burden of proving negligence remain with the cargo owner? The better view appears to be that once the cargo owner has proved that the goods have been lost or damaged in transit (e.g. by the production of a clean bill of lading acknowledging the shipment in apparent good order or condition of a specified quantity) the onus shifts to the carrier to bring the cause of damage within one of the exceptions listed in Art IV rule 2(a)–(p). If he fails to do so he will be held strictly liable unless he can prove that the damage or loss occurred 'without the actual fault or privity of the carrier, or without the fault or neglect of the agents or servants of the carrier'.[89] Should he succeed in bringing the loss within an exception, the carrier will escape liability unless the cargo owner can then establish a breach of the carrier's duty of care within Art III rule 2.[90]

(III) OBLIGATION TO ISSUE A BILL OF LADING

Article III rule 3 provides that:

> 'After receiving the goods into his charge the carrier or the master or agent of the carrier shall, on demand of the shipper, issue to the shipper a bill of lading showing among other things –

---

[88] [2003] 2 Lloyd's Rep 87. In reaching this conclusion the court adopted an opinion expressed by Devlin J in *Pyrene & Co* v *Scindia Navigation Co* [1954] 2 QB 402 at pp 417–18. See also Cooke paras 14.53–14.55 and Scrutton p 175.

[89] See Art IV rule 2(q).

[90] This interpretation is in line with the decision in *The Glendarroch* [1894] P 226 and with the dicta of Viscount Simon LC and Lord Wright in *Constantine SS Co* v *Imperial Smelting Corp* [1942] AC 154 at pp 164 and 194. In the latter case Lord Wright expressed the view that 'If the carrier pleads an exception the goods-owner may counter by pleading the fault of the carrier, but the onus of proving that . . . is . . . on the goods-owner who makes it.' (At p 164.) The High Court of Australia adopted a similar approach in *Shipping Corp of India* v *Gamlen Chemicals* (1980) 55 ALJR 88. See also Cadwallader in *Current Legal Problems* (1969) p 41. Cf. *Gosse Millard* v *Canadian Mercantile Marine* [1927] 2 KB 432, 436.

a) The leading marks necessary for identification of the goods as furnished in writing by the shipper before the loading of such goods starts, provided such marks are stamped or otherwise shown clearly upon the goods if uncovered, or on the cases or coverings in which such goods are contained in such a manner as should ordinarily remain legible until the end of the voyage;

b) Either the number of packages or pieces, or the quantity, or weight, as the case may be, as furnished in writing by the shipper;

c) The apparent order and condition of the goods.'

The obligation imposed on the carrier is, however, subject to two provisos. First, he is not bound to acknowledge the above facts if either he has reasonable grounds for suspecting that the information supplied by the shipper is inaccurate, or he has no reasonable means of checking it, as for example if the goods are delivered to him in a sealed container. Secondly, the shipper in return is deemed to have guaranteed the accuracy of the information supplied by him and is required to indemnify the carrier in the event of the latter suffering loss as a result of its inaccuracy.[91]

It will be noted that the right to demand the issue of a bill containing the specified information is restricted solely to the shipper and no equivalent right is conferred on the consignee or a subsequent endorsee.[92] Consequently, it would appear that the carrier is not bound to issue a bill or provide the required information in the absence of a request from the shipper, and the insertion of the words 'weight and condition unknown' tends to be a not uncommon occurrence.[93] The resultant effect is to defeat the object of Art III of providing the consignee with a bill of lading which will operate as an effective receipt for the goods.

Article III further provides that the bill of lading shall be prima facie evidence of the receipt by the carrier of the goods as therein described, which shall become conclusive when the bill has been transferred to a third party acting in good faith.[94] There is no mention of any requirement that the transfer should be for value as was previously the case under the common law estoppel rule. Bills issued under this provision, however, will normally be 'received for shipment' bills and will merely testify as to the quantity and condition of the cargo at the time of its receipt by the carrier. They will not provide even prima facie evidence of its quality or condition at the time of shipment – information which is vital in the event of a commercial credit being involved. This gap is filled by Art III rule 7 which confers on the shipper the right to demand, after the goods are loaded, the issue of a shipped bill of lading containing the relevant information.[95]

---

[91] Article III rule 5. See *The Boukadoura* [1989] 1 Lloyd's Rep 393.

[92] See Colinvaux, *Carver's Carriage by Sea*, 13th edn, 1982, para 518.

[93] *Vitafood Products* v *Unus Shipping Co* [1939] AC 277 at p 294. Different versions of such clauses are frequently to be found in the printed conditions of standard forms of bill of lading e.g. Conlinebill, Congenbill and Nuvoybill.

[94] Article III rule 4.

[95] In the case of documentary credits, the gap is also filled by the requirements imposed by the UCP for Documentary Credits.

6.3.2 RIGHTS AND IMMUNITIES OF THE CARRIER

(I) THE CATALOGUE OF EXCEPTIONS

Article IV rule 2 lists the exceptions which are available to the carrier under the Hague/Visby Rules. He is permitted to surrender the protection afforded by these exceptions in whole or in part,[96] but he is not allowed to add to the list.[97] The full catalogue reads as follows:

'Neither the carrier nor the ship shall be responsible for loss or damage arising or resulting from –

a) Act, neglect, or default of the master, mariner, pilot or the servants of the carrier in the navigation or in the management of the ship.

b) Fire, unless caused by the actual fault or privity of the carrier.

c) Perils, dangers and accidents of the sea or other navigable waters.

d) Act of God.

e) Act of war.

f) Act of public enemies.

g) Arrest or restraint of princes, rulers or people, or seizure under legal process.

h) Quarantine restrictions.

i) Act or omission of the shipper or owner of the goods, his agent or representative.

j) Strikes or lockouts or stoppage or restraint of labour from whatever cause, whether partial or general.

k) Riots and civil commotions.

l) Saving or attempting to save life or property at sea.

m) Wastage in bulk or weight or any other loss or damage arising from inherent defect, quality or vice of the goods.

n) Insufficiency of packing.

o) Insufficiency or inadequacy of marks.

p) Latent defects not discoverable by due diligence.

q) Any other cause arising without the actual fault or privity of the carrier, or without the fault or neglect of the agents or servants of the carrier, but the burden of proof shall be on the person claiming the benefit of this exception to show that neither the actual fault or privity of the carrier nor the fault or neglect of the agents or servants of the carrier contributed to the loss or damage.'

The meaning and effect of these exceptions are discussed fully elsewhere,[98] but certain points are worth noting at this stage. All but two of the exceptions listed involve no fault on the part of the carrier or his servants or agents. Indeed, as we have already seen, the presence of fault will normally prevent the carrier from relying on the protection of the exceptions.[99] The two anomalous cases are the exceptions covering navigational or

---

[96] Article V.
[97] Article III rule 8.
[98] See *infra* Chapter 10.
[99] See *supra* p 193.

management error, and the liability of the carrier for damage caused by fire. Both have been strongly criticised by cargo interests and the exception covering navigational error is unique in that no equivalent is to be found in any other transport convention. The second comment relates to the final exception on the list. If the carrier is unable to establish that the cause of loss falls within one of the specific exceptions, he can still avoid liability by proving that whatever the cause, it involved no fault on the part of himself or his servants or agents. This is a difficult though not impossible burden of proof to discharge[100] and it is not surprising to discover that carriers seek, wherever possible, to rely on one of the other 16 exceptions.

(II) LIMITATION OF LIABILITY

The concept of limitation of liability in its various forms has a history dating back to the sixteenth century and was originally designed to encourage investment in shipping. While the justification for its continued retention in the context of the package limitation in the contract of carriage is less evident, it does still serve two useful purposes. It protects the carrier from the risks associated with cargoes of high undisclosed value and, by establishing a standard level of liability, enables him to offer uniform and cheaper freight rates. There is the obvious danger that, left to his own devices, the carrier might limit his liability to a derisory amount, and it was to obviate this risk that the draftsmen of the Hague Rules, and succeeding conventions, sought to prescribe a minimum standard. The option was still left open for the shipper to obtain full cover by declaring the full value of the cargo to the carrier before shipment, and having this amount entered on the bill of lading. Evidence has shown, however, that this option is rarely used since declaration of the cargo's value invariably attracts an *ad valorem* increase in freight rates which is normally more expensive than the cost to the cargo owner of obtaining his own insurance cover.[101]

Two problems face the draftsmen of an international convention seeking to establish a formula for limitation of liability. First, selection of an appropriate quantitative unit of goods by which to calculate the carrier's overall liability and, secondly, agreement on a monetary unit on which to base the minimum liability.

(a) Under the Hague Rules

Article IV rule 5 of the Hague Rules limited the liability of the carrier to £100 gold value[102] per package or unit. The United Kingdom in implementing the Hague Rules in COGSA 1924 initially interpreted the figure as £100 sterling, while many other signatories to the Convention converted the amount into equivalent sums in their own currencies.[103] Inflation over succeeding years has resulted in these limits now bearing

---

[100] See e.g. *Goodwin, Ferreira v Lamport & Holt* (1929) 34 LlLR 192; *Leesh River Tea Co v British India Steam Nav Co* [1967] 2 QB 250.

[101] See Selvig: Unit Limitation of Carrier's Liability (1960) p 200. The US courts have, however, held that the limitation provisions will not apply unless the shipper is provided with an opportunity to declare the full value of the goods: see *General Electric Co v Lady Sophie* [1979] 2 Lloyd's Rep 173; *Sommer Corp v Panama Canal Co* [1974] 1 Lloyd's Rep 287. See also *The OOCL Bravery* [2000] 1 Lloyd's Rep 394.

[102] Article IX.

[103] For example, USA $500; Australia $200; Federal Republic of Germany 1,250 marks; India £100; Greece 800 drachmas; Norway 1,800 kroner.

little relation to the actual damage suffered by cargo owners, but few states have seen fit to amend their respective figures in the light of this development. The problem was to some extent solved in the United Kingdom by successive Gold Clause Agreements drawn up by the British Maritime Law Association in 1950 and 1977 under which the signatories undertook to waive the 'gold value' criterion and substitute the sums in sterling of £200 and £400 respectively.[104]

Problems have also arisen in many countries in interpreting the terms 'package' and 'unit' as used in the formula. What constitutes a 'package'? Is size relevant and is it essential that the article carries some form of wrapping? Again, is the term 'unit' intended to refer to a shipping unit, such as a crate, package, or container, or would it equally apply to a freight unit, i.e. the unit of measurement used to calculate the freight? The latter interpretation would be particularly appropriate when dealing with bulk cargo such as grain or oil.[105] There is little authority on these points in English law, where the issue has attracted little litigation probably due to the fact that the terms 'package' and 'unit' have been used interchangeably, the word 'unit' having been interpreted as meaning 'shipping unit'.[106] This approach has obviated the need to provide a definition for the word 'package', though it is perhaps surprising to find an absence of any formula to cope with the problem of bulk cargo.

The interpretation of these terms has, however, caused difficulties elsewhere, and nowhere more so than in the United States where the case law on the subject is prolific. The fact that US legislation[107] expresses the unit of measurement in the alternative as 'package' or 'customary freight unit' inevitably creates a need for a definition of the term 'package'. On this point the case law is not decisive. While it would appear that US courts do not regard it as essential that 'packages' should be fully covered or wrapped, they are nevertheless hesitant to treat unboxed vehicles or machinery as 'packages' for this purpose.[108] On many occasions the cargo owner will find it more profitable to invoke the 'freight unit' alternative, as, for example, in circumstances where the freight units exceed the number of shipping units,[109] but this is not invariably the case.[110]

---

[104] The Gold Clause Agreement ceased to be effective as from midnight on 31 May 1988 except with regard to claims arising under bills dated before then. Parties suing under bills of lading specifically incorporating the Hague Rules Convention have received an unexpected windfall in recent cases. The limit of '£100 sterling gold value' in the original text has been defined as the quantity of gold which was the equivalent of £100 sterling in 1924. In the case of *The Rosa S* [1988] 2 Lloyd's Rep 574, a calculation based on this definition produced the sum of £6,630.50 sterling. A similar construction was applied to the phrase by the NSW Court of Appeal in *The Nadezhda Krupskaya* [1989] 1 Lloyd's Rep 518.

[105] See *The Pioneer Moon* [1975] 1 Lloyd's Rep 199. This interpretation never appears to have been accepted in the UK. See Carver 9.234.

[106] As also in Canada: *Falconbridge Nickel Mines Ltd v Chimo Shipping Co* [1973] 2 Lloyd's Rep 469. See now the comment of Colman J in *The River Gurara* [1996] 2 Lloyd's Rep 53.

[107] US COGSA 1936 Art 4(5).

[108] See *Gulf Italia v American Export Lines* [1958] AMC 439. Cf. *Whaite v Lancs & Yorks Rly Co* (1874) LR 9 Ex 67 where an open railway wagon and its contents, consisting of 10 paintings, were held to be a 'package' for the purposes of the Carriers Act 1830. See also *Studebaker Distributors Ltd v Charlton SS Co* [1938] 1 KB 459; *Middle East Agency v Waterman* [1949] AMC 1403; *Pannell v American Flyer* [1958] AMC 1428.

[109] As in *Gulf Italia v American Export Lines (supra)*.

[110] See *The Edmund Fanning* [1953] AMC 86.

A further problem arose in applying the Hague Rules package formula to containers, pallets and other devices for the consolidation of goods. Such methods of handling cargo were not envisaged by the draftsmen of the Rules, but to limit the liability of the carrier to $500 for the entire contents of a container at the present day would be to provide the cargo owner with a derisory remedy. Again until recently there was little authority on the point in English law,[111] although it has been a constant source of litigation across the Atlantic. Over the years, the US courts developed three separate and distinct methods of dealing with the problem:

1 Where the contents of a container are listed as separate items in the bill of lading, then each item should be treated as an individual package for limitation purposes. Thus in *The Mormaclynx*,[112] where the cargo was described in the bill of lading as 'one container said to contain 99 bales of leather', the court held that each bale constituted a separate 'package'. Conversely, where the bill of lading merely refers to the container without listing its contents then the container itself will be treated as the package.[113]

2 An alternative solution advanced was the so-called 'functional packing' test. The crucial question for the court in this instance was whether the contents of the container could be transported in the individual wrappings or cartons in which they had been packed by the shipper or whether the presence of the container was essential for their preservation. If their individual packing was adequate to withstand the hazards of transport, then each would count as a separate package for limitation purposes. The leading case in which the theory was advanced was *The Kulmerland*[114] where a consignment of 350 adding machines had been shipped inside a container in individual corrugated cartons sealed with thin paper tape. In the view of the US Court of Appeals (2nd Circuit) these cartons did not satisfy the functional packing test since, until they were packed into containers, they were not suitable for ocean transportation. In consequence, it was the container and not the individual carton which constituted the package. The only disadvantage of this solution is that it is contrary to normal business practice and does not make economic sense. One of the main objectives of containerisation is to reduce the cost of transport by *inter alia* removing the necessity for expensive and elaborate packing of individual items of cargo.

3 The third approach concentrated on the identity of the party responsible for stuffing the container and the reasons underlying its use. Thus, if the shipper or his agent selects, packs and seals the container without any supervision or participation by the carrier, it is more likely that the courts will treat the container as the package rather than its contents. This is particularly true where the shipper fails to enumerate the contents in the bill of lading.[115] On the other hand, if the carrier for his own purposes

---

[111] See infra pp 199–200.

[112] [1971] 2 Lloyd's Rep 476. See also the Canadian case of *The Tindefjell* [1973] 2 Lloyd's Rep 253; the Australian case of *Chellaram v China Ocean Shipping Co* [1989] 1 Lloyd's Rep 413; and the English case of *The River Gurara* [1998] 1 Lloyd's Rep 225.

[113] *Standard Electrica S/A v Hamburg Sudamericanische* [1967] 2 Lloyd's Rep 193.

[114] [1973] 2 Lloyd's Rep 428. See also *The American Legion* [1975] 1 Lloyd's Rep 295; *The Brooklyn Maru* [1975] 2 Lloyd's Rep 512.

[115] *Lucchese v Malabe Shipping Co* [1973] AMC 979 (cargo listed as one container of household goods). See also *Sperry Rand Corp v Norddeutscher Lloyd* [1974] 1 Lloyd's Rep 119 at p 126; *The American Legion* [1975] 1 Lloyd's Rep 295 at p 304.

consolidates cargo received from a variety of individual shippers into a single container, the courts will not entertain the argument that the container constitutes the 'package' for purposes of limitation. Indeed, it is arguable that they are prohibited from so holding by Art III rule 8 which renders void any attempt by the carrier to reduce his liability below the prescribed limits.[116]

US courts have not regarded the above three tests as mutually exclusive and frequently more than one test has been invoked in a particular case.[117] In recent years, however, the courts have sought to evaluate these tests and attempt some form of rationalisation. In *The Aegis Spirit*[118] a consignment of television sets and various stereophonic equipment had been shipped from Japan to the United States in containers supplied by the carriers. The equipment was contained in double-walled cardboard cartons which had been packed into sealed containers by the shippers in the absence of any representative of the carrier. Elements relevant to all three tests were present in the facts which the trial judge had to consider in reaching a decision as to whether the container or the carton constituted the Hague Rules 'package'. In his opinion any acceptable test 'must reflect the realities of the maritime industry of today, while remaining faithful to the express language and legislative policy embodied in the pertinent COGSA provisions'.[119] The functional packing test did not meet these criteria and must be rejected as being 'commercially impracticable and unwise'. The trial judge stressed that the function of the court was not to create a fair and equitable rule for allocating risks with respect to containerised cargo, but to provide a fair and sensible interpretation of existing legislation. Approaching the construction of Art IV from this angle, the judge considered that containers should be treated as detachable compartments of the ship and the master should insist on their contents being listed in the bill. Whether or not these contents constituted individual packages should be decided in accordance with the plain and accepted meaning of the term.[120] In his view, on the facts of the case, the unit of measurement was the individual carton and not the container.

Until recently English courts had not been called upon to adjudicate on this issue, but the opportunity arose in 1998 in the case of *The River Gurara*.[121] A vessel on a voyage from West Africa had run aground on the coast of Portugal and later sank with total loss of cargo. Much of the cargo was containerised and was shipped under bills of lading incorporating the Hague Rules. Many of the containers had been stuffed privately by the shippers and were covered by bills stating that they were 'said to contain' a given number of items such as pallets, crates, cartons or bags. The point at issue was whether the cargo owner's right of recovery was limited to £100 per container or £100 per individual item listed on the bill.

---

[116] See *The Mormaclynx* [1971] 2 Lloyd's Rep 476. See also *The River Gurara* [1998] 1 Lloyd's Rep 225. 'If carriers alone, or even carriers and shippers together, are allowed to christen something a "package" which distorts or belies the plain meaning of the word as used in the statute, then the liability floor becomes illusory and negotiable.' Phillips LJ at p 231 quoting Beeks DS in *The Aegis Spirit* [1977] 1 Lloyd's Rep 93, at p 100.

[117] The *American Legion* [1975] 1 Lloyd's Rep 295.

[118] [1977] 1 Lloyd's Rep 93. See also *Mitsui* v *American Export Lines* [1981] AMC 331.

[119] *The Aegis Spirit* at p 99.

[120] See also *Hartford Fire Ins* v *Pacific Far East Line* [1974] 1 Lloyd's Rep 359.

[121] [1998] 1 Lloyd's Rep 225.

The Court of Appeal adopted the US approach in holding that, where the contents of the container were individually listed in the bill, each item would prima facie constitute a 'package' for limitation purposes. The court then proceeded to consider the effect of the carrier failing to confirm the number of items listed in the bill by the shipper. Any such reservation could take one of two forms. On the one hand, the carrier could deny all knowledge of the contents of the container by the use of a phrase such as 'weight, number and contents unknown'.[122] The majority of the Court of Appeal took the view that the inclusion of such a clause destroyed the evidential value of any statement in the bill detailing the contents of the container.[123] In such circumstances the cargo owner would have to seek alternative evidence extrinsic to the bill in order to establish the number of items for limitation purposes. Alternatively, the carrier could indicate that any statement in the bill as to the contents of the container was the sole responsibility of the shipper by the use of such phrases as 'shipper's count' or 'said to contain'. Although the effect of such reservations did not arise for decision in *The River Gurara*, Phillips LJ expressed the view that such a phrase did not necessarily destroy the evidential value of the bill. 'It seems . . . at least arguable that the words 'said to contain' do no more than make plain that the carrier is, as required by Art III rule 3, stating on the bill the "number of packages . . . as furnished in writing by the shipper" without dissenting from the description, so that the description can be relied upon as providing prima facie evidence as to what was within the containers.'[124]

(b) Under the Hague/Visby Rules

The Hague/Visby Rules retained the 'package or unit' limitation of liability for individual items of cargo of high value, but also introduced an alternative formula based on the weight of the cargo, the shipper being entitled to invoke whichever alternative produces the higher amount.[125] Presumably the old case law interpreting the terms 'package or unit' will still be applicable, while the alternative limitation 'per kilo of the gross weight' will be particularly relevant in the case of bulk cargo.[126]

The problem of the conflict of opinion surrounding the appropriate container test has been solved, at least so far as the United Kingdom and the other states implementing the Hague/Visby Rules are concerned, by the new Art IV rule 5(c). The section reads:

> 'Where a container, pallet or similar article of transport is used to consolidate goods, the number of packages or units enumerated in the bill of lading as packed in such article of transport shall be deemed the number of packages or units for the purpose of this paragraph as far as these packages or units are concerned. Except as aforesaid such article of transport shall be considered the package or unit.'

---

[122] This is the approach adopted by such standard forms as the Congenbill or the Conlinebill.

[123] 'Where the bill of lading is so qualified it does not even constitute prima facie evidence that the goods detailed by the shipper have been shipped.' Phillips LJ at p 234.

[124] [1998] 1 Lloyd's Rep at p 234. Although this view was expressed obiter, it appears also to be the approach generally adopted by US courts as evidenced by the decisions in the leading cases of *The Mormaclynx* [1971] 2 Lloyd's Rep 476 and *The Aegis Spirit* [1977] 1 Lloyd's Rep 93. See Gaskell 16.36.

[125] Article IV rule 5(a).

[126] There was some controversy as to whether the Hague Rules 'package or unit' formula was applicable to bulk cargo. Certainly there was no authority in the UK case law on the subject. Scrutton p 451; Gaskell 16.33.

The adoption of this formula is certainly a move in the right direction, but certain ambiguities remain which still require clarification. First, what is meant by a 'similar article of transport . . . used to consolidate goods'? Would a roll on/roll off lorry or wagon fall within this category? Secondly, an interpretation of the phrase 'units enumerated in the bill of lading' will be required. Does this mean units as listed by the shipper or only those acknowledged by the carrier as required by Art III rule 3(b)? In respect of the latter it will be remembered that no acknowledgment as to quantity of cargo shipped is required from the carrier unless he has a reasonable opportunity to check. As a substantial proportion of containers are now packed and sealed by the shipper before delivery to the carrier, it is only to be expected that the carrier will take advantage of this proviso for his own protection by indorsing the bill 'said to contain', or 'contents unknown'.[127] If the container in question should subsequently be lost overboard without any further opportunity of inspecting its contents, what is the extent of the carrier's liability? The wording of the Article suggests that, even in such an event, the units of limitation will be the items listed on the bill and not the container itself,[128] and this should certainly be the result in cases where the carrier has adjusted the freight in response to such itemisation. In conclusion, there remains a doubt as to whether the new container formula will be of any material benefit to the cargo owner. It has already been noted that the provision enabling the shipper to declare the full value of the cargo in the bill of lading is rarely invoked because it invariably results in an increase in the freight rate which exceeds the cost to the shipper of insuring the balance.[129] It remains to be seen whether the itemisation of the contents of the container produces a similar result.

So far as the monetary unit of limitation is concerned, the draftsmen of the Hague/Visby Rules abandoned the pound sterling in favour of the Poincaré franc in an attempt to devise a 'currency' which would retain its value during a period of inflation. The franc was defined in Art IV rule 5(d) as 'a unit consisting of 65.5 milligrammes of gold of millesimal fineness 900' and it was further provided that the date of conversion of the sum awarded into national currencies should be governed by the law of the court seised of the case. So far as the United Kingdom was concerned, the problems of conversion were simplified by s 1(5) of the COGSA 1971 which empowered the Secretary of State periodically to specify the conversion amount in sterling by statutory instrument.

The Poincaré franc has in turn been replaced as the unit of account by the special drawing right, as defined by the International Monetary Fund, as the result of s 2(4) of the Merchant Shipping Act 1981.[130] The prescribed limitation amounts are 666.67 units of account per package or unit or 2 units of account per kilo of the gross weight of the goods lost or damaged, whichever is the higher. The special drawing right has been preferred to the Poincaré franc since the unit is based on a basket of currencies, the value of which is probably more sensitive to the trends of inflation than the fluctuating market price of gold.

---

[127] See *The Esmeralda I* [1988] 1 Lloyd's Rep 206.
[128] See Scrutton p 451 fn 60. See the comments of Phillips LJ in *The River Gurara* [1998] 1 Lloyd's Rep 225 at p 234.
[129] See *supra* p 196.
[130] Giving legislative effect to the Brussels Protocol of December 1979 to which the United Kingdom and 21 other nations are parties.

(c) Problems of limitation

Two further problems associated with the operation of the Hague/Visby limitation rules remain to be discussed. The first relates to the scope of application of the rules. What types of claim are they intended to cover and are their provisions designed to afford protection not only to the carrier but also to other parties engaged by him in performance of the contract of carriage? Secondly, in what circumstances, if any, will the carrier's conduct prevent him from invoking the protection of the limitation provisions?

Scope of application.   The common law doctrine of privity of contract prevents a person who is not a party to a contract from relying on its provisions for protection against any claim brought against him. Consequently, it was held in *Adler* v *Dickson (The Himalaya)*[131] that a member of a ship's crew sued in negligence for causing injury to a passenger, could not rely on an exception clause in the contract of carriage concluded between the passenger and the shipowners. On similar grounds the House of Lords refused to allow a firm of stevedores engaged by the carrier in *Scruttons* v *Midland Silicones*[132] to invoke the protection of the Hague Rules limitation of liability provisions when sued for negligently damaging the cargo during the discharging operations. In neither case could the party being sued be regarded as a party to the contract of carriage.

A partial solution to this problem is now to be found in Art IV *bis* rule 2 of the revised Hague/Visby Rules which provides that 'a servant or agent of the carrier (such servant or agent not being an independent contractor)' can, in the event of an action being brought against him, avail himself of the same defences and limits of liability provided by the Rules as could be invoked by the carrier himself. The provision clearly reverses the effect of the decision in *Adler* v *Dickson*, thus enabling an employee of a carrier to rely on the protection of the Hague/Visby Rules to the same extent as his employer. On the other hand, it does not extend the cover to independent contractors engaged by the carrier, such as the stevedores in *Scruttons* v *Midland Silicones* who have to look elsewhere for their protection. There would seem to be no logical commercial basis for this distinction but it is only fair to add that the problems associated with privity of contract and the concept of an independent contractor seem almost exclusively confined to the common law world. Even so, there are two possible avenues of escape open to the independent contractor. First, he can insist on obtaining from the carrier an indemnity to cover this extended liability before embarking on the work. Secondly, he can require the carrier to ensure that he is specifically made a party to the contract of carriage, at least so far as the Hague/Visby provisions relating to excepted perils and limitation of liability are concerned. This object can be achieved by the inclusion in the contract of carriage of the so-called 'Himalaya clause', the effectiveness of which stems from the decision of the Privy Council in *New Zealand Shipping Line* v *Satterthwaite*.[133] Thirdly, he may be able to invoke the protection of the limitation of liability provisions in the contract of carriage if he satisfies the requirements of the Contracts (Rights of Third Parties) Act 1999.[134]

---

[131] [1954] 2 Lloyd's Rep 267.
[132] [1962] AC 446.
[133] *New Zealand Shipping Line* v *Satterthwaite (The Eurymedon)* [1975] AC 154. For the reasoning behind the judgment, see Lord Wilberforce at pp 167–9. See also *supra* at p 151.
[134] For a full discussion of these requirements, see *supra* p 154–5.

In conclusion, it should be noted that Art IV *bis* rule 1 provides that the overall defences and limits of liability provided by the Rules apply whether the action brought against the carrier is founded on contract or tort, while rule 3 stipulates that should the cargo owner institute separate proceedings against the carrier and his servant or agent in respect of the same damage, the aggregate amount recoverable shall not exceed the limit provided by the Rules.

Breaking the limits. Under Art IV rule 5 of the Hague Rules, the limits of liability therein prescribed were to be applicable 'in any event'. Despite this wording, the view persisted that carriers could not rely on the limitation provisions if they were in fundamental breach of the contract of carriage as, for example, where they had deviated from the agreed course or stowed the goods on deck without the shipper's consent.[135] This approach was, however, challenged by the Court of Appeal in the recent case of *The Kapitan Petko Voivoda*,[136] where a number of excavators had been stowed on deck contrary to an express undertaking in the contract of carriage for underdeck stowage. Subsequently, on the voyage, several of the excavators had been washed overboard in heavy weather, while others had suffered salt water damage. When the carrier sought to limit his liability under Art IV rule 5 of the Hague Rules, the cargo owner pleaded fundamental breach. The Court of Appeal rejected this argument, taking the view that 'the seriousness of the breach is no longer a self-sufficient yardstick for determining whether exception or limitation clauses apply to particular breaches'.[137] Longmore LJ pointed out that breach of the seaworthiness obligation might on occasion result in far more serious loss than unauthorised carriage on deck, yet there was little doubt that the Hague limitation was applicable to such a situation.[138]

Adopting the construction approach advocated in *Photo Production* v *Securicor Transport*,[139] the Court of Appeal reached the conclusion that the words 'in any event' meant what they said and were applicable to a breach irrespective of the seriousness of its nature.[140]

This decision leaves two outstanding issues. On the one hand, in reaching the conclusion that the carrier was entitled to limit his liability, the court appears to have attached no particular significance to the express undertaking in the contract of carriage to ship the cargo underdeck. As the same decision would presumably have been reached in the absence of such an express undertaking, it is difficult to appreciate the benefit to the cargo owner of its inclusion in the contract. Secondly, in reaching their decision, members of the Court of Appeal resisted the argument that the application of the limi-

---

[135] *Jones* v *Flying Clipper* (1954) 116 Fed Supp 386; *Encyclopaedia Britannica* v *Hong Kong Producer* [1969] 2 Lloyd's Rep 536; *Foscolo, Mango* v *Stag Line* (1932) 41 LlLR 165 at p 170.
[136] [2003] 2 Lloyd's Rep 1.
[137] Longmore LJ at p 10.
[138] See *The Happy Ranger* [2002] 2 Lloyd's Rep 357.
[139] See *supra* at p 122.
[140] Longmore LJ cited with approval the dicta of Tuckey LJ in *The Happy Ranger* [2002] 2 Lloyd's Rep at p 364 that 'the words "in any event" are unlimited in scope and I can see no reason for giving them any other than their natural meaning'. In reaching this decision the Court of Appeal expressly overruled an earlier contrary decision of Hirst J on similar facts in *The Chanda* [1989] 2 Lloyd's Rep 494 on the ground that in reaching his conclusion he had taken no account of the words 'in any event'.

tation provision in the present case would amount to a virtual exclusion of carrier liability.[141]

In justification, members of the court drew attention to the fact that several practical methods of avoiding this result were available to the parties. First, the owner of cargo could declare its true value and insert this information in the bill of lading, as the result of which the full loss would be recoverable.[142] Secondly, the parties were at liberty to agree a higher limitation figure than the amount specified in rule 5[143] and, finally, the parties could specifically incorporate the Hague/Visby Rules into the contract of carriage since they prescribed higher limitation amounts than those contained in the original Hague Rules.[144] These suggestions, however, beg the question as to the relative bargaining power of the respective parties.

The phrase 'in any event' has been retained in the corresponding Art IV rule 5(a) of the Hague/Visby Rules and will presumably receive the same construction as its predecessor.[145] On this occasion, however, account must also be taken of s 1(2) of COGSA 1971, which provides that the Hague/Visby Rules 'shall have the force of law'. The effect of the latter provision is also believed to make the Rules applicable irrespective of any fundamental breach of the contract of carriage.[146] The position may be clarified by the fact that the Hague/Visby Rules themselves do now prescribe certain types of misconduct which will deprive the carrier of the protection of the limitation provisions.[147] Article IV rule 5(e) provides that:

> 'Neither the carrier nor the ship shall be entitled to the benefit of the limitation of liability provided for in this paragraph if it is proved that the damage resulted from an act or omission of the carrier done with intent to cause damage or recklessly and with knowledge that damage would probably result.'[148]

Similar conduct on the part of a servant or agent of the carrier will deprive him personally of the benefit, not only of the limitation provisions but also of any other defences provided for in the Rules.[149] It is not intended that misconduct by the servant or agent will break the limit so far as the carrier's personal liability is concerned.[150] It remains to be seen how the courts will interpret the phrase 'recklessly and with knowledge that damage would probably result' in this context. For example, will unauthorised stowage on deck or intentional deviation amount to 'reckless' conduct if there is a strong likelihood of damage resulting to the cargo?[151] A possible indicator is to be found in the approach adopted by the Court of Appeal in interpreting an identical phrase in Art 25

---

[141] [2003] 2 Lloyd's Rep at p 15.

[142] Article IV rule 5.

[143] Article IV rule 5.

[144] Hague/Visby Rules Art IV rule 5(a).

[145] See Tuckey LJ in *The Happy Ranger* [2002] 2 Lloyd's Rep 357 at p 364.

[146] See *The Antares* [1987] 1 Lloyd's Rep 424. Account must also be taken of the different approach adopted towards the doctrine of fundamental breach in *Photo Production v Securicor Transport* [1980] 1 Lloyd's Rep 545.

[147] Carrier may not even be allowed to rely on value declared by owner, where an underestimate: *Antwerp United Diamonds v Air Europe* [1995] 2 Lloyd's Rep 224 (a Warsaw Convention case).

[148] See Carver 9.241 ff.

[149] See Art IV *bis* rule 4.

[150] See *The European Enterprise* [1989] 2 Lloyd's Rep 185.

[151] See *The Pembroke* [1995] 2 Lloyd's Rep 290. Cf. *Jones v Bencher* [1986] 1 Lloyd's Rep 54.

of the Warsaw Convention. In the opinion of Dyson J, 'It is sufficient for recklessness that a person should act regardless of the *possible* consequences of his acts. What Art 25 requires is that there should be knowledge of the *probable* consequences.' Moreover, 'it is clearly established that knowledge in Art 25 is not imputed knowledge. It is not sufficient to show that, by reason of his training and experience, the pilot ought to have known that damage would probably result from his act or omission. The test is subjecive . . . Actual knowledge is required.'[152] If a similar test is applied in the context of Art IV rule 5(e) of the Hague/Visby Rules, the burden of proof on the claimant will be a formidable one.

Limitation of actions. Municipal law invariably prescribes a general time limit within which actions have to be brought for the recovery of compensation for lost or damaged goods. In the United Kingdom s 5 of the Limitation Act 1980 bars the initiation of a contractual claim after the expiration of six years from the time when the goods in question were delivered or should have been delivered. In an attempt to speed up the settlement of cargo claims, the Hague/Visby Rules impose a one-year time limit which can, however, be extended by agreement of the parties after the cause of action has arisen.[153]

Article III rule 6 provides that:

'Subject to paragraph 6 *bis*, the carrier and the ship shall in any event be discharged from all liability whatsoever in respect of the goods, unless suit is brought within one year of their delivery or of the date when they should have been delivered. This period may, however, be extended if the parties so agree after the cause of action has arisen.'

Several points relating to this provision call for comment. First, the limitation period runs from the time the goods were delivered, or should have been delivered. The selection of the word 'delivery' instead of 'discharge' appears deliberate on the part of the draftsmen of the Rules and presumably at least some form of constructive delivery to the consignee or his authorised agent will be required before time will begin to run.[154] In this respect paragraph 6 further provides that 'In the case of any actual or apprehended loss or damage the carrier and the receiver shall give all reasonable facilities to each other for inspecting and tallying the goods.'

Secondly, the Article provides for time to run either from the date of delivery or from the date when the goods should have been delivered without any reference to the respective timing of these events. Consequently, if it can reasonably be concluded that delivery has been made under the original contract, even though the terms of that contract may have been varied to some extent to accommodate problems encountered on a particular voyage, then it is irrelevant for purposes of the time bar that such delivery has been effected at a date significantly later than that on which the goods should have been

---

[152] *Nugent & Killick* v *Michael Goss Aviation Ltd* [2000] 2 Lloyd's Rep 222 at p 232. See also *SS Pharmaceutical Co* v *Qantas* [1991] 1 Lloyd's Rep 288.

[153] But it cannot be extended by a court exercising its discretion under s 27 of the Arbitration Act 1950. See *The Antares* [1987] 1 Lloyd's Rep 424. For rationale behind the rule, see comments of Judge Diamond QC in *The Leni* [1992] 2 Lloyd's Rep 48 at pp 52–3; see also *The Finnrose* [1994] 1 Lloyd's Rep 559 at p 572.

[154] For a consideration of what the concept of 'delivery' involves, see *The Seki Rolette* [1998] 2 Lloyd's Rep 638. See also Wilford para 85.189: 'Discharge is a purely physical act, whether performed by carrier, charterer or receiver, whereas delivery is a legal concept concerned with the passing of actual or constructive possession.'

delivered. Time will run from the date of actual delivery. Only in the event of failure to deliver the goods, or in a situation where delivery is made under what is held to be a separate and distinct contract, will the date on which the goods should have been delivered become relevant for purposes of the time bar.[155] Thus in *The Sonia*[156] a cargo of jet oil was shipped from a Saudi Arabian port for delivery in Lagos under a voyage charterparty incorporating specified provisions of the Hague/Visby Rules. On arrival at Lagos the cargo was rejected by receivers as being off specification due to contamination. After prolonged negotiations between shipowners and charterers, the vessel was eventually rerouted to a Greek port where delivery of the cargo was made some eight weeks later to a receiver nominated by the charterer. In response to a claim against the shipowners for failing to take proper care of the cargo resulting in its rejection in Lagos, the Court of Appeal held that time began to run under Article III rule 6 from the date of delivery in Greece rather than from the date on which the cargo should have been delivered in Lagos. In the opinion of the court, as the cargo had remained on the same vessel throughout and had been delivered by the same shipowner to the order of the same charterer, delivery had been made under the original contract of carriage and no separate and distinct contract was involved.

Thirdly, the carrier is 'discharged from all liability whatsoever in respect of the goods'. This provision has been interpreted as covering not only the normal claim for cargo damage or loss,[157] but also extending to claims arising from a fundamental breach of contract by the carrier or from the type of misconduct listed in Art IV rule 5(e). This view is justified on the grounds that the provision is expressly given 'the force of law'.[158]

Fourthly, the paragraph requires that 'suit' be brought within a period of 12 months. A narrow construction was applied to this requirement in *Compañia Colombiana de Seguros* v *Pacific Steam Nav Co*[159] where it was held that the suit must be brought within the relevant jurisdiction during this period. The bill of lading concerned provided for exclusive English jurisdiction, but the claimant brought his initial action in New York. By the time the error was discovered, the 12 months period had elapsed and the trial judge held that any action in an English court was then barred. This seems an unnecessarily restrictive interpretation if the object of the time limit is to encourage cargo owners to give prompt notice of their claims to carriers since an action brought in any jurisdiction will suffice for this purpose. The term 'suit' has also been construed as including both litigation and arbitration proceedings. Thus in *The Merak*[160] the bill of

---

[155] See *Western Gear Corp* v *States Marine Lines Inc* (1966) F 2d 328 (cargo lost overboard and, when later retrieved, shipped to destination on different vessel under new bill of lading). See also *Universal Ruma Co* v *Mediterranean Shipping Co* (2001) AMC 110.

[156] [2003] 2 Lloyd's Rep 201.

[157] Including financial loss arising from failure to load cargo; *The OT Sonya* [1993] 2 Lloyd's Rep 435 and from delay in loading caused by unseaworthiness of vessel: *Linea Naviera Paramaconi* v *Abnormal Load Engineering Ltd* [2001] 1 Lloyd's Rep 763. See also *The Marinor* [1996] 1 Lloyd's Rep 301 (effect where incorporated in time charter).

[158] See *The Antares* [1987] 1 Lloyd's Rep 424. The provision also covers claims in tort, e.g. for conversion of the cargo. See *The Captain Gregos* [1990] 1 Lloyd's Rep 310.

[159] [1965] 1 QB 101.

[160] [1965] P 223. See also *The Stolt Sydness* [1997] 1 Lloyd's Rep 273; *Thyssen Inc* v *Calypso Shipping Corp* [2000] 2 Lloyd's Rep 243. Cf. the position in US law where a US Circuit Court of Appeal held that the time bar applied only to litigation and not arbitration: *Son Shipping Co* v *DeFosse & Tanghe* 199 F 2d 687 (1952). See also Cooke p 663.

lading incorporated the terms of a charterparty which included an arbitration clause. Unaware of this fact, the plaintiff brought a court action for cargo damage and, by the time this action was stayed, the 12 months period had expired. It was held that the word 'suit' included arbitration proceedings and consequently the arbitration avenue was now time barred.[161] In view of the prevalence of bills of lading which incorporate charterparty terms, the problems raised by *The Merak* are likely to recur, with consequent hardship to the unwary consignee. On the other hand, if suit is brought within the required twelve months Art III rule 6 does not prevent the amendment of such a claim outside that period, provided that the amendment does not substantially alter the nature of the original claim.[162]

Fifthly, the case of *The Clifford Maersk*[163] has established that where the final day of the limitation period falls on a Sunday or other day on which the office of the Supreme Court is closed, suit will be brought in time if the claim form is issued on the next day on which the office is open.[164]

Finally, it is important to note the effect of the time bar on the substantive claim concerned. It is generally accepted that the provisions of the Limitation Act 1980 merely bar the relevant claim but do not extinguish it. Consequently, the party entitled to a statute barred debt, while not being able to recover it by action, may still obtain satisfaction if alternative methods of recovery are available to him.[165] The position is, however, different under Art III rule 6 which expressly provides that the carrier 'shall be discharged from all liability whatsoever' on the expiry of the time limit. In the case of *The Aries*[166] the House of Lords held that the effect of this provision was not only to bar the remedy but also to extinguish the right. Here the defendants, in paying freight on receipt of the cargo, had made a deduction to cover short delivery. Two years later they were sued by the carrier for the balance of the freight and sought to serve a defence based on a right of set-off. The court held that no such defence was admissible since any right on which it might initially have been based had been extinguished by the time lapse.[167]

Article III rule 6 makes express provision for the extension of the 12-month period 'if the parties so agree after the cause of action has arisen'.[168] Presumably an agreement

---

[161] The suit in arbitration is brought when one party to the dispute serves notice on the other requiring him to appoint an arbitrator: *The Sargasso* [1994] 1 Lloyd's Rep 162. See *Nea Agrex* v *Baltic Shipping Co* [1976] QB 933 (an informal letter requesting carrier to name an arbitrator sent within time limit satisfied requirement of 'suit brought').

[162] See *The Pioneer* [1995] 1 Lloyd's Rep 223; *The Kapetan Markos* [1986] 1 Lloyd's Rep 211; *Anglo-Irish Beef Processors* v *Federated Stevedores* [1997] 1 Lloyd's Rep 207.

[163] [1982] 2 Lloyd's Rep 251.

[164] The rule is similar in the United States: *Aron & Co* v *Sterling Navigation Co* [1976] AMC 311.

[165] For examples, see Cheshire and Fifoot p 713.

[166] *Aries Tanker Corp* v *Total Transport* [1977] 1 Lloyd's Rep 334.

[167] Lord Denning MR in *The Brede* [1973] 2 Lloyd's Rep 333 at p 336 had expressed the view that the defence to a claim, e.g. right of set-off, was distinguishable from a counter claim in that the former was not caught by a time bar. He held, however, that there was a long established rule that a cargo owner had no right to make deductions from freight in respect of short delivery or damage to cargo. The Lords took a similar view in *The Aries*. Cf. *The Fiona* [1995] 2 Lloyd's Rep 506 (cargo owner not caught by time bar when pleading breach of seaworthiness obligation under Art III rule 1 as defence to claim by carrier for loss caused by shipment of dangerous goods).

[168] NB, any attempt to reduce the period below twelve months will be void under Art III rule 8. *The Ion* [1971] 1 Lloyd's Rep 541 (Centrocon arbitration clause).

reached between the parties at an earlier date will also be effective since Art V allows a carrier to increase his obligations by surrendering a right or immunity to which he would otherwise be entitled, although here there is a requirement that any such provision should 'be embodied in the bill of lading issued to the shipper'.[169]

What has been said above naturally relates to the initial claim against the carrier. The Hague/Visby Rules, however, frequently provide for the carrier to be indemnified by a third party in the event of any successful claim being made against him (e.g. under Art III rule 5) and similar provisions may have been expressly incorporated into the contract of carriage. No such indemnity action can be launched until the initial claim against the carrier has been concluded by judgment or settlement and this is unlikely to occur within the limitation period. Accordingly, Art III rule 6 *bis* provides that an action for indemnity may be brought outside the 12-month period if it is initiated within the normal limitation period of the court seised of the case. In the case of the United Kingdom, the relevant period would be six years in respect of the normal claim based on contract or tort.[170] The paragraph provides that, in any event, a minimum period of three months shall be allowed from the time the party seeking the indemnity 'has settled the claim or has been served with process in the action against himself'.

6.3.3 OTHER PROVISIONS

(I) DEVIATION

The only provision in the Hague/Visby Rules specifically referring to deviation is to be found in Art IV rule 4, which provides:

> 'Any deviation in saving or attempting to save life or property at sea, or any reasonable deviation shall not be deemed to be an infringement or breach of these Rules or of the contract of carriage, and the carrier shall not be liable for any loss or damage resulting therefrom.'

The paragraph makes no attempt to define the concept of deviation, but merely specifies the types of deviation which are justifiable under the Rules. Presumably there is no intention to disturb well-established common law principles,[171] the object of the provision being to provide extended protection for shipowners by adding deviations

---

[169] In the United Kingdom provision to extend the period up to a maximum of two years was formerly to be found in clause 4 of the Gold Clause Agreement 1950 to which many shipowners, cargo associations and P & I Clubs were parties. This clause required the shipowner, if a party to the agreement, at the request of any party representing cargo, to extend the one-year period for a further 12 months 'unless (A) notice of the claim with the best particulars available has not been given within the period of 12 months, or (B) there has been undue delay on the part of consignees, receivers or underwriters in obtaining the relevant information and formulating the claim'. The request could be made either before or after the expiry of the initial 12-month period. The Gold Clause Agreement ceased to be effective from midnight on 31 May 1988.

[170] Section 5 of the Limitation Act 1980. See Lord Brandon in *The Xingcheng* [1987] 2 Lloyd's Rep 210 at p 213. See also Cooke p 742: 'The rule [6 bis] abolishes the rule 6 time bar altogether in case of indemnity claims, leaving the matter to the limitation rules of the forum in which the indemnity action is brought.' The Supreme Court of Israel held in *Bellina Maritime SA v Menorah Ins Co* [2002] 2 Lloyd's Rep 575 that a subrogation claim against a carrier by a shipper's insurer did not qualify as an indemnity action for this purpose. In the court's view (at p 577), 'the person having the right of subrogation has no greater rights than the assured at the time of subrogation'. Accordingly, the subrogation claim will be caught by the 12-month limit.

[171] See *supra* p 16.

to save property and reasonable deviations to the existing list of deviations which are justifiable at common law.

English courts have, however, experienced some difficulty in interpreting the phrase 'any reasonable deviation', although it appears to be generally accepted that whether or not a deviation is reasonable is to be treated as a question of fact. In *Stag Line* v *Foscolo, Mango & Co*[172] a vessel on a voyage from Swansea to Constantinople made a slight deviation into St Ives to land two engineers who had been taken on board for the purpose of testing her fuel-saving apparatus. On leaving St Ives, the vessel ran aground and the cargo was lost. The House of Lords held that this was not a reasonable deviation and refused to allow the shipowner to rely on the protection afforded by the Hague Rules. In an attempt to clarify the issue, Greer LJ in the Court of Appeal[173] had said: 'I think the words [reasonable deviation] mean a deviation whether in the interests of the ship or the cargo-owner or both, which no reasonably minded cargo-owner would raise any objection to.' In the Lords a variety of alternative definitions was advanced, the main difference of opinion turning on the question as to whether a deviation could be reasonable if it was not in the interests of both ship and cargo. Lord Atkin, who considered the point most fully, did not regard this as an essential requirement. In his opinion a deviation:

> 'may be reasonable, though it is made solely in the interests of the ship or solely in the interests of the cargo, or indeed in the direct interest of neither: as for instance where the presence of a passenger or a member of the ship or crew was urgently required after the voyage had begun on a matter of national importance; or where some person on board was a fugitive from justice, and there were urgent reasons for his immediate appearance. The true test seems to be what departure from the contract voyage might a prudent person controlling the voyage at the time make and maintain, having in mind all the relevant circumstances existing at the time, including the terms of the contract and the interests of all parties concerned, but without obligation to consider the interests of any one as conclusive.'[174]

Despite these attempts at clarification of the 'reasonable' deviation concept, there are remarkably few reported English cases in which a carrier has successfully invoked the defence.[175] A similar uncertainty surrounds the application of the concept in other jurisdictions and the majority of courts have tended to be strict in their interpretation of what amounts to reasonable conduct in this context. It is also interesting to note that the United States version of Art IV rule 4 of the Hague Rules includes the proviso that 'if the deviation is for the purpose of loading or unloading cargo or passengers, it shall, *prima facie*, be regarded as unreasonable'.[176]

A final point of uncertainty relates to the relationship between express liberties to deviate contained in the contract of carriage and the provisions of Art IV rule 4. If such liberties are not regarded by the courts as 'reasonable' within the meaning of Art IV, are they caught by Art III rule 8 which renders void any clauses which derogate from the

---

[172] [1932] AC 328. See also *Thiess Bros* v *Australian SS Pty Ltd* [1955] 1 Lloyd's Rep 459.
[173] (1931) 39 LlLR 101 at p 111.
[174] [1932] AC 328 at pp 343–4.
[175] A recent example occurred in *The Al Taha* [1990] 2 Lloyd's Rep 117. See also *The Iran Bohonar* [1983] 2 Lloyd's Rep 620.
[176] For a discussion of the effects of deviation, see *supra* at pp 21 ff.

protection offered by the Rules? The better view would appear to be that there is no conflict since the object of the liberty clause is to define the scope of the contract voyage and in such an event it is difficult to understand how a permissible 'deviation' can constitute a breach of contract. In holding that an express liberty to deviate is not affected by Art IV rule 4 Hodson LJ expressed the view that 'the object of the Rules is to define, not the scope of the contract of service, but the terms on which that service is to be performed'.[177]

(II) DANGEROUS CARGO

Article 4 rule 6 defines the liability for the shipment of dangerous cargo in the following terms:

> 'Goods of an inflammable explosive or dangerous nature to the shipment whereof the carrier, master or agent of the carrier has not consented with knowledge of their nature and character, may at any time before discharge be landed at any place or destroyed or rendered innocuous by the carrier without compensation, and the shipper of such goods shall be liable for all damages and expenses directly or indirectly arising out of or resulting from such shipment.
>
> If any such goods shipped with such knowledge and consent shall become a danger to the ship or cargo, they may in like manner be landed at any place or destroyed or rendered innocuous by the carrier without liability on the part of the carrier except to general average, if any.'

This specific provision in the Rules reinforces the implied term at common law that the shipper will not ship dangerous goods without the consent of the carrier.[178] Rule 6 provides that when such goods are shipped without the knowledge or consent of the carrier, not only is he entitled to neutralise them at the expense of the shipper, and without any obligation to compensate the cargo-owner, but the shipper is also liable for any loss or damage resulting from their shipment.[179] The latter liability will not normally arise in circumstances where the carrier consents to the shipment with full knowledge of the dangerous nature of the cargo.[180] Even though the carrier initially consents to the shipment of dangerous goods he may nevertheless dispose of them 'in like manner' should they subsequently endanger either the ship or the cargo, though presumably not in this case at the expense of the shipper.

6.4 INCORPORATION OF THE HAGUE/VISBY RULES IN CHARTERPARTIES

Although Art V of the Hague/Visby Rules provides that the rules do not apply mandatorily to charterparties, many standard form charters incorporate them on a voluntary

---

[177] *Renton* v *Palmyra* [1956] 1 QB 462 at p 510. See also *Stag Line* v *Foscolo, Mango & Co* [1932] AC 328; *Foreman & Ellams* v *Federal SN Co* [1928] 2 KB 424; Carver para 548; Scrutton p 452.

[178] For a full discussion of the effects of Art IV rule 6, see *supra* pp 35 ff.

[179] The shipowner's right to an indemnity might, however, be lost if negligence on his part was a contributory factor to the loss: *The Fiona* [1994] 2 Lloyd's Rep 506; *The Kapitan Sakharov* [2000] 2 Lloyd's Rep 255 (stowage of highly inflammable cargo in unventilated hold in breach of IMDG Code).

[180] *General Trades* v *Consorcio Pesquero Del Peru* [1974] AMC 2343. Cf. *Chandris* v *Isbrandtsen-Moller* [1951] 1 KB 240.

basis. This result is achieved either by specific reference to the legislation enacting the Rules in the country of shipment, by specific reference to the Rules themselves, or by a clause incorporating the substance of Arts III and IV.[181] Such incorporation is usually effected by the inclusion in the charterparty of a so-called Clause Paramount as, for example, clause 24 of the New York Produce Exchange 1946 form which specifically incorporates the provisions of the US Carriage of Goods by Sea Act 1936. Frequently, however, the charterparty refers simply to a 'Paramount Clause', without any words of qualification. In such circumstances shipowners have argued that, with so many possible interpretations available, the phrase is ambiguous and should be ignored. This approach was rejected by Denning LJ in *The Agios Lazarus*[182] as 'a counsel of despair', taking the view that the court 'should try to give effect to this incorporation, rather than render it meaningless'.[183] The Court of Appeal accordingly held that the intention of the parties in using the phrase was to incorporate the entire Hague Rules in their original form.[184]

Action of this type inevitably results in conflicts arising between provisions of the incorporated Rules and the existing terms of the charterparty. In many cases the relevant paramount clause will provide that in cases of conflict the provisions of the Hague Rules are to take precedence.[185] Where such an indication is absent, the courts tend to regard incorporation as a contractual issue and to approach such conflicts as matters of construction.[186] As the Rules are not mandatorily applicable in this context, the objective of the courts appears to be a desire to avoid technicalities and to give effect to the intentions of the parties. Thus in *Adamastos Shipping Co v Anglo-Saxon Petroleum*[187] the parties had written the US paramount clause verbatim into an oil tanker charter without noticing that the clause expressly provided for the incorporation of the Hague Rules into 'this bill of lading'. The House of Lords had little hesitation in holding that the intention of the parties was to incorporate the Rules into 'this charterparty'. Nor were they receptive to the argument that Art V of the Rules, once incorporated, expressly provided that they were not applicable to charterparties. In the view of Viscount Simonds:

'parties to a charterparty often wish to incorporate the Hague Rules in their agreement; and by that I do not mean, nor do they mean, that they wish to incorporate the *ipsissima verba* of those Rules. They wish to incorporate into the contractual relation between owners and charterers

---

[181] See *The Sonia* [2003] 2 Lloyd's Rep 201. See also Polcoalvoy charter, clause 28; Sovorecon, clause 32.

[182] [1976] 2 Lloyd's Rep 47. See also *Seabridge Shipping v Orssleff's EFTFS* [1999] 2 Lloyd's Rep 685.

[183] At p 50.

[184] See Shaw LJ at p 58; Goff LJ at p 53. See also *The Bukhta Russkaya* [1997] 2 Lloyd's Rep 744, where Thomas J was required to interpret the unqualified phrase 'general paramount clause'. In his view a clause 'described as "the general paramount clause" has the following essential terms: (1) if the Hague Rules are enacted in the country of shipment then they apply as enacted; (2) if the Hague Rules are not enacted in the country of shipment, the corresponding legislation of the country of destination applies or, if there is no such legislation, the terms of the Convention containing the Hague Rules apply; (3) if the Hague/Visby Rules are compulsorily applicable to the trade in question, then the legislation enacting those rules applies'. (at p 746). In the circumstances of the case he held that the Hague Rules were incorporated.

[185] See *The Agios Lazarus* [1976] 2 Lloyd's Rep 47. See Goff LJ at p 53.

[186] See *Sabah Flour v Comfez* [1988] 2 Lloyd's Rep 18; *The Leonidas* [2001] 1 Lloyd's Rep 533.

[187] [1959] AC 133. See also *The Miramar* [1984] 2 Lloyd's Rep 129. Cf *Sabah Flour v Comfez* [1988] 2 Lloyd's Rep 18.

the same standard of obligation, liability, right and immunity as under the rules subsists between carrier and shipper.'[188]

Again, in *The Satya Kailash*[189] a vessel had been time chartered to lighten a second vessel which, being too heavily laden, was unable to enter port. During the lightening operation the two vessels collided as the result of negligent navigation by the chartered vessel. In holding that the paramount clause in the charter, which incorporated the US Carriage of Goods by Sea Act 1936, entitled the shipowner to invoke the protection of the Hague Rules exception covering negligent navigation, the Court of Appeal decided that the provisions of the Act were applicable even though the charter involved no cargo-carrying voyage and no voyage to or from a US port was envisaged.[190] Presumably, the courts would adopt a similar attitude in interpreting clauses seeking to incorporate into charterparties the provisions of the Hague/Visby Rules, since the requirement that the latter Rules should have the force of law is apparently only applicable where they are expressly incorporated into a bill of lading or non-negotiable receipt.[191]

6.4.1 EFFECT OF INCORPORATION

The incorporation of the Hague or Hague/Visby Rules will affect many of the basic obligations arising under a charterparty.

(A) THE SEAWORTHINESS OBLIGATION

The strict obligation at common law to provide a seaworthy ship will be replaced by the duty to exercise due diligence to make the ship seaworthy 'before and at the beginning of the voyage'. Some difficulty may be encountered in interpreting the latter phrase in the context of a charterparty. Does the duty to exercise due diligence arise at the beginning of the initial voyage under the charterparty or at the beginning of each and every voyage? Little difficulty may arise in the cases of a voyage charter or a trip charter where the relevant contracts envisage only a single voyage. What is the position, however, with respect to a charter which involves a series of voyages? A majority of the House of Lords in *Adamastos Shipping Co v Anglo-Saxon Petroleum*[192] held that the duty applied to all voyages under a charterparty, irrespective of whether the vessel had cargo aboard or was in ballast.[193] The charterparty involved in the case was a consecutive voyage charter, but Scrutton is of the view that the obligation is equally applicable to each voyage under a time charter 'where the charter requires the master to sign bills of lading for each voyage which themselves incorporate the Hague/Visby Rules'. He adds the rider, however, that 'the question must also turn on the construction of the charter as a whole'.[194]

---

[188] At p 154. Compare the situation where the intention of the parties is ambiguous.
[189] [1984] 1 Lloyd's Rep 588.
[190] At p 594.
[191] See Carriage of Goods by Sea Act 1971, s 1(6).
[192] [1959] AC 133.
[193] See also Wilford para 34.13.
[194] Scrutton p 364; see also Wilford para 34.15. But Mustill J strikes a note of caution in *The Hermosa* [1980] 1 Lloyd's Rep 638 at p 647.

The House of Lords in the *Adamastos* case also held that the provisions in Art IV rules 1 and 2 relating to the recovery of compensation for 'damage or loss' resulting from breach of the seaworthiness obligation were not limited in their operation to physical damage or loss of the goods. Consequently, they allowed recovery of damages for the loss of freight resulting from the unseaworthy vessel completing fewer voyages than expected within the period of the charter. Recovery in such circumstances was, however, dependent on the damage or loss arising within the general context of the activities envisaged in Art II of the Rules.[195]

(B) EXCEPTIONS

Under a charterparty the shipowner is normally required to perform a wider range of activities than those involved in a bill of lading contract or envisaged by the exceptions listed in Art IV rule 2 of the Hague/Visby Rules. The question then arises as to whether, in a situation where the charter incorporates the Rules, the shipowner is entitled to invoke the immunities in Art IV to cover this wider range of activities. The Court of Appeal in the case of *The Satya Kailash*[196] answered this question in the affirmative. The shipowner's vessel had been chartered to lighten another ship which was too heavily laden to enter port. During the lightening operation the two vessels collided as the result of the shipowner's negligent navigation. Despite the fact that a lightening operation did not normally form part of a bill of lading contract, the shipowner was allowed to invoke in his defence the navigation exception contained in the US Carriage of Goods by Sea Act 1936, which had been incorporated into the charter. In the words of Goff LJ, 'general words of incorporation can be effective to give an owner the protection of the statutory immunities in respect not only of those matters specified in s 2,[197] but also of other contractual activities performed by him under the charter'.[198]

(C) TIME BAR

The incorporation of the Hague/Visby Rules into a charterparty will enable a shipowner to take advantage of the 12-month time bar in Art III rule 6. This provision will normally take precedence over any clause in the charterparty providing for a shorter period of limitation, even where that clause provides for the reference of disputes to arbitration.[199]

As with exceptions, there is a problem as to the extent to which a shipowner can rely on the time bar as a protection against claims for breach of any of the many obligations arising under a charterparty which are not of a type to be encountered in a bill of lading contract. Two factors are of importance in this context.

---

[195] Article II of the Hague Rules provides that the carrier is entitled to the rights and immunities set out in the Act with respect to activities 'in relation to the loading, handling, stowage, carriage, custody, care and discharge of the goods'.

[196] [1984] 1 Lloyd's Rep 588. See also *Australian Oil Refining Pty v Miller* [1968] 1 Lloyd's Rep 448.

[197] The reference is to s 2 of the US Carriage of Goods by Sea Act 1936, which enacts the immunities listed in Art IV rule 2 of the Hague Rules.

[198] [1984] 1 Lloyd's Rep at p 596. See also *The Hill Harmony* [2001] 1 Lloyd's Rep 147; *The Leonidas* [2001] 1 Lloyd's Rep 533.

[199] See *The Stolt Sydness* [1997] 1 Lloyd's Rep 273. While Art III rule 6 applies to both litigation and arbitration in English law (see *The Merak* [1964] 2 Lloyd's Rep 527), the time bar is not applicable to arbitration under US law: *Son Shipping v Defosse & Tanghe* 199 F2d 687 (1952).

First, Art III rule 6 requires the claim to be for loss or damage 'in respect of the goods'. Clearly, claims for any breach resulting in physical loss or damage to cargo will fall within this definition, but the courts have given the phrase a wider interpretation:

> 'Where there is incorporation by general words into a time charter of legislation enacting the Hague Rules or Hague/Visby Rules, the shipowners will be entitled to rely on the protection of the time bar against claims for breach of any of the terms of the charter, even if not coextensive with obligations under the rules, provided that (i) those claims assert (a) a liability involving physical loss or damage to goods, or (b) a liability for financial loss sustained in relation to goods[200] and (ii) the goods in question were either shipped or intended to be shipped pursuant to the charter. In order to operate the time bar provision in the case of goods intended to be shipped, it is clearly necessary for a particular voyage or voyages to have been in the contemplation of both parties at the time when the breach preventing shipment on that voyage occurred.'[201]

In the case from which this quotation is taken, a vessel (*The Marinor*) had been chartered for a period of ten years for the carriage of sulphuric acid from the charterers' plant in Quebec to East Coast ports in the United States. The charter included a paramount clause incorporating the Canadian Carriage of Goods by Water Act. During the course of the charter, cargo was discharged in a contaminated condition on four consecutive voyages, allegedly due to the unseaworthy condition of the vessel. At this point the charterers decided that the next cargo of acid destined for Savannah should be delivered by an alternative vessel but, in order to give *The Marinor* a final chance, they decided to use the vessel to ship a cargo of acid for Tampa where the acid could be used in the fertilizer industry even if it were discharged in a contaminated condition. When this shipment was also found to be contaminated on discharge, the charterers commenced arbitration proceedings claiming damages on three counts for breach of the time charter. First, the difference between the actual price received for the cargo in Tampa and the market price they would have received if the cargo had been delivered uncontaminated in Savannah; secondly, for the extra costs of the longer voyage to Tampa, and finally for the additional port costs in Tampa. Colman J upheld the shipowners' contention that all three claims were caught by the time bar in Art III rule 6 since all were 'sufficiently connected with the goods shipped'.[202] On the other hand, the time bar was not applicable to a claim for the cost of the substituted vessel since this was not a claim 'in respect of' any particular cargo.

Again, in *The Seki Rolette*[203] Mance J was of the opinion that 'it would be wrong to restrict the application of Art III rule 6 to goods being carried under a specific contract of carriage as distinct from goods "exposed to risk by reason of the charterers' involvement in the contractual adventure" '.[204] In this case, as the result of a collision involving the chartered vessel, the charterer had personally lost property including, *inter alia*, a fork-lift truck, lashing equipment and a Mercedes Benz truck. Mance J held that the

---

[200] See *The Stolt Sydness* [1997] 1 Lloyd's Rep 273.
[201] Colman J in *The Marinor* [1996] 1 Lloyd's Rep 301, at p 311.
[202] *Ibid* at p 312. Cf *The Standard Ardour* [1988] 2 Lloyd's Rep 159, where Saville J held that the claim for loss or damage related not to the goods shipped but to the relevant documents.
[203] [1998] 2 Lloyd's Rep 638.
[204] At p 648.

charterers' claims in respect of these items were caught by the time bar even though they did not form the subject-matter of the contract of carriage.

The second factor to be taken into consideration is that the 12-month period runs from the time at which the goods are delivered or should have been delivered. For the time bar to operate, the claim must therefore relate to breach of an obligation which involves some form of delivery. This requirement was satisfied in *The Seki Rolette*, since the charterers' property, on board for purposes of the charter, would presumably have been returned to them on its termination. On the other hand, the time bar would not operate in respect of the charterers' alternative claim for lost bunkers because the bunkers were not due for delivery or redelivery, but were intended to be consumed on the voyage. Clearly, much will depend on the courts' interpretation of the term 'delivery'. In the recent case of *The Sonia*,[205] a vessel had been chartered to carry a cargo of jet oil to Lagos under a charterparty which incorporated specific articles of the Hague Rules, including Art III rule 6. On arrival at Lagos the cargo was rejected as off-specification, whereupon the vessel was despatched to Abidjan to await orders. Eventually, the vessel was ordered to a Greek port, where the cargo was discharged some eight weeks later. In reply to the owners' contention that the charterers' claim for breach of charterparty was time-barred, the Court of Appeal held that the 12-month period ran from the time that the cargo was actually discharged in Greece rather than from the time it should have been delivered in Lagos.

---

[205] [2003] 2 Lloyd's Rep 201.

7

BILLS OF LADING – THE HAMBURG RULES

7. 1 INTRODUCTION

The modifications to the Hague Rules effected by the Brussels Protocol in 1968 did not gain universal approval. They were regarded by many cargo owning countries as constituting merely a temporary expedient and there was a growing demand for a thorough reappraisal of carrier liability designed to produce a comprehensive code covering all aspects of the contract of carriage. This movement culminated in the drafting of a new Convention which was adopted, at an international conference sponsored by the United Nations in Hamburg, in March 1978. The Convention, known as the 'Hamburg Rules', became effective on 1 November 1992 on the expiration of one year from the date of the deposit of the twentieth instrument of ratification, acceptance, approval or accession.[1] To date 29 states have adhered to the Convention,[2] although it has not yet been ratified by any major maritime nation.[3]

7.2 SCOPE OF APPLICATION OF THE RULES

The Hamburg Rules apply to contracts of carriage by sea which are defined as 'any contract whereby the carrier undertakes against payment of freight to carry goods by sea from one port to another'.[4] Where the contract envisages some form of multimodal carriage, the application of the Rules will be restricted to the sea leg. This approach differs from that of either the Hague or Hague/Visby Rules which concentrate on 'contracts of carriage covered by a bill of lading or any similar document of title'.[5] So far as the Hamburg Rules are concerned, it is immaterial whether a bill of lading or a non-negotiable receipt is issued, and the definition of 'bill of lading' in Art 1.7 is worded accordingly. The new Convention, however, follows its predecessors in that its provisions are not applicable to charterparties or to bills of lading issued pursuant to them

---

[1] Article 30.1
[2] As at 24 February 2004 these states are: Austria, Barbados, Botswana, Burkina Faso, Burundi, Cameroon, Chile, Czech Republic, Egypt, Gambia, Georgia, Guinea, Hungary, Jordan, Kenya, Lebanon, Lesotho, Malawi, Morocco, Nigeria, Romania, St Vincent and the Grenadines, Senegal, Sierra Leone, Syria, Tanzania, Tunisia, Uganda and Zambia. It is estimated that overall these states represent approximately 5 per cent of world trade by sea.
[3] For an analysis of the Hamburg Rules, see Mankabady, S, (ed) *The Hamburg Rules on the Carriage of Goods by Sea*, (1978); Tetley, W [1979] LMCLQ 1.
[4] Article 1.6.
[5] Article 1(b).

unless such a bill 'governs the relation between the carrier and the holder', i.e. it has been issued or negotiated to a party other than the charterer.

The application of the provisions of the new Convention is restricted to contracts of carriage by sea between ports in two different states (i.e. it does not apply to coastal trade) and the range of voyages covered is roughly similar to those enumerated in Art X of the Hague/Visby Rules, with one important exception. The Hamburg Rules govern both inward and outward bills – an important factor to be taken into account by shipowners who trade with countries in which the Convention is now effective. Provision is also made for the parties expressly to incorporate the Rules into the bill of lading or other document evidencing the contract.

Whereas the Hague and Hague/Visby Rules are only applicable from tackle to tackle, the Hamburg Rules are designed to operate throughout the entire period 'during which the carrier is in charge of the goods at the port of loading during the carriage and at the port of discharge'.[6] The duration of this period is then defined in detail and it is clear that this provision is designed to remedy the existing 'before and after' problem in the Hague/Visby Rules as the result of which the carrier is entitled to exclude all liability for the cargo when it is not physically aboard his vessel.[7]

7.3 BASIC CARRIER LIABILITY

(I) GENERAL DEFINITION

In framing a uniform and comprehensive test of carrier liability, the draftsmen of the Hamburg Rules have adopted the argument long advanced by cargo interests that carrier liability should be based exclusively on fault and that a carrier should be responsible without exception for all loss of, and damage to, cargo that results from his own fault or the fault of his servants or agents. They have accordingly chosen to state an affirmative rule of responsibility based on presumed fault and to abolish the catalogue of exceptions contained in Art IV rule 2 of the Hague and Hague/Visby Rules. This statement of basic liability is drafted in the following terms:

> 'The carrier is liable for loss resulting from loss of or damage to the goods, as well as from delay in delivery, if the occurrence which caused the loss, damage, or delay took place while the goods were in his charge as defined in Article 4, unless the carrier proves that he, his servants or agents, took all measures that could reasonably be required to avoid the occurrence and its consequences.'[8]

In so far as the majority of the exceptions listed in the Hague/Visby Rules do not in fact involve fault on the part of the carrier,[9] the effect of the abolition of the catalogue on carrier liability should be minimal as far as they are concerned. It might indeed even be beneficial from a legal standpoint in removing unnecessary uncertainty surrounding the definition and extent of such exceptions which are merely examples of circumstances in which fault cannot be attributed to the carrier. However, one major shift of

---

[6] Article 4.1.
[7] See *supra* pp 181–2.
[8] Article 5.1.
[9] See Art IV rule 2(c)–(p).

responsibility is envisaged by the abolition of the exception covering negligence in the navigation or management of the ship.[10] Cargo interests have long contended that it is invidious that a carrier, in complete control of vessel and cargo, should exclude such liability which is basic to the contract of carriage. Moreover, it is a form of protection which is not extended to the carrier in any other mode of transport. Carrier interests are naturally reluctant to forgo such traditional protection and argue strongly, *inter alia*, that such a change would result in a substantial increase in freight rates. Resistance to the abolition of the exception covering fault in the management of the ship is more muted since it is generally recognised that the conflict between this exception and the carrier's duty of care in relation to the cargo[11] has resulted in considerable uncertainty and litigation.

(a) Nature of liability

In imposing a uniform test of liability, the draftsmen of the Hamburg Rules were seeking to remove some of the incongruities and inconsistencies arising from ambiguous wording in the Hague/Visby Rules. Under the latter, the obligation of the carrier to provide a seaworthy ship was limited to a duty to exercise 'due diligence', while he was required to look 'properly and carefully' after the cargo throughout the carriage. The introduction of a uniform test of liability based on fault was designed to obviate these problems. The carrier's duty to provide a seaworthy ship under the Hamburg Rules is to be judged on the same basis as his duty towards the cargo, and both obligations are to run throughout the period of carriage. The only issue remaining to be resolved will be the construction to be placed by national courts on the carrier's duty to take 'all measures that could reasonably be required to avoid the occurrence and its consequences'. Would British courts construe this as indicating negligence liability or would they still hold the carrier liable for the negligence of independent contractors as in the case of *The Muncaster Castle*?[12] If they took the latter view, would they extend a similar duty of care towards the cargo?

Unfortunately the search for uniformity of construction is not assisted by the introduction of variations in phraseology such as occur later in Art 5 when reference is made to 'fault or neglect' of the carrier rather than to 'all measures that could reasonably be required'. Is an identical duty of care intended in both cases? Further confusion is caused by the annexing to the Convention of a Common Understanding 'that the liability of the carrier under this Convention is based on the principle of presumed fault or neglect'.

(b) Burden of proof

In a further attempt to achieve uniformity and simplicity, the Hamburg Rules adopt a unified burden of proof rule. The Hague and Hague/Visby Rules dealt specifically with questions of burden of proof in only a few limited situations with the result that courts have frequently reached conflicting conclusions in interpreting their provisions on this

---

[10] Article IV rule 2(a).
[11] That is, Art III rule 2.
[12] See *supra* p 190. On the facts of *The Muncaster Castle*, where the shipowner had engaged a reputable firm of ship repairers to conduct a survey under the supervision of a Lloyd's surveyor, it is arguable that they had satisfied the requirement of taking 'all measures that could reasonably be required'.

issue. Particular difficulty has been experienced in allocating the respective burdens of proof as between the carrier's duty of care towards cargo in Art III rule 2 and his reliance on the exceptions listed in Art IV rule 2.[13] The Hamburg Rules seek to remove this confusion by presuming fault in all cases of loss or damage to cargo and so imposing a uniform burden of proof on the carrier. This provision is justified on the desirability of placing the burden of proof on the party most likely to have knowledge of the facts. Only in the case of damage caused by fire is the burden shifted away from the carrier, presumably for the reason that it is difficult to establish the precise origin of a fire at sea, the majority of cases of which in any event tend to originate with the cargo. Article 5.4 accordingly provides that the carrier is only liable for loss caused by fire if the cargo owner proves either that the fire arose from fault or neglect on the part of the carrier, his servant or agents, or from their fault or neglect in not taking all measures that could reasonably be required to put out the fire and avoid or mitigate its consequences.

(II) SPECIFIC PROVISION FOR PARTICULAR CASES

Having outlined the basic liability of the carrier, Article 5 then proceeds to make special provision for certain eventualities. It is generally recognised that certain types of cargo, such as animals or deck cargo, present problems of assimilation to any set formula of carrier liability. The reaction of the draftsmen of the Hague Rules was to exclude such problem cases from the general formula and allow the parties to contract on their own terms for such carriage. While recognising the difficulties involved in the carriage of such cargo, cargo owners naturally saw this as no reason for excluding such cargo entirely from the operation of the code and allowing the carrier to impose his own terms for carriage. The draftsmen of the Hamburg Rules agreed with this view and felt that a more just solution was to include the problem cases initially in the general formula and then to make special provision to cover their peculiarities.[14]

(a) Carriage of live animals

While the carriage of live animals is subject to the general obligation of care outlined in Art 5.1, the carrier will not be liable for loss 'resulting from any special risks inherent in that kind of carriage'. Moreover, provided that the carrier can establish that he has complied with any instructions given to him by the shipper respecting the carriage of the animals in question, and the particular loss incurred could be attributed to such risks, it will be presumed that the loss was so caused 'unless there is proof that all, or a part of the loss, damage or delay in delivery resulted from fault or negligence on the part of the carrier, his servants or agents'.[15]

(b) Carriage of deck cargo

According to Art 9, deck cargo will be treated as normal cargo, and subject to the Rules, where it is shipped 'in accordance with an agreement with the shipper, or with

---

[13] See *supra* pp 192 ff.

[14] No special provision is made in the Hamburg Rules for the shipment of 'particular goods' as defined in Art VI of the Hague/Visby Rules. See *supra* at p 177. Liability for such goods is covered by the general test in Art 5.1.

[15] Article 5.5. Carriers will accordingly be encouraged to ask shippers for carriage instructions.

the usage of the particular trade or is required by statutory rules or regulations'. Where the cargo is shipped on deck by agreement with the shipper, such agreement must be recorded on the bill of lading, otherwise the carrier will have the burden of proving its existence, though he will not be allowed to invoke such agreement against a third party who has acquired the bill in good faith. Should the cargo be shipped on deck without consent or authority, this would no longer constitute a fundamental breach of contract, but the carrier's liability for loss, damage or delay in delivery would be restricted to that 'resulting solely from the carriage on deck'. Moreover, he would still be entitled to take advantage of the provisions limiting liability under Art 6 unless he had breached an express undertaking to stow the goods below deck.[16]

(c) Deviation

It will be remembered that under Art IV rule 4 of the Hague/Visby Rules a carrier will not be liable for loss resulting from 'any deviation in saving or attempting to save life or property at sea or any reasonable deviation'.[17] In discussions leading to the adoption of the Hamburg Rules, no real objection was voiced to continuing the carrier's freedom from liability while deviating to save life at sea. On the other hand, there was less support for the extension of protection to cover deviation to save property, particularly when such action was independent of any attempt to save life. Such exemption was criticised on the ground that it permitted a carrier to gain substantial profit from salvage, often to the detriment of the cargo carried on his own ship. So far as the Hague Rules exception covering 'reasonable deviation' was concerned, this had caused some problems of construction, but had rarely been invoked successfully in the courts.[18] In the view of the draftsmen of the Hamburg Rules, no special provision should be made for deviation but liability for resultant loss, damage or delay should be brought under the general umbrella of carrier liability. Accordingly, the carrier would be liable for loss resulting from deviation unless he could establish that he or his servants or agents had taken 'all measures that could reasonably be required to avoid the occurrence and its consequences'. It was, however, felt that specific reference should be made to loss resulting from attempts to save life, but that it was undesirable to provide an unqualified immunity for attempts to save property in view of possible abuse. The final draft appears in Art 5.6 in the following terms:

> 'The carrier is not liable, except in general average, where loss, damage or delay in delivery resulted from measures to save life or from reasonable measures to save property at sea.'

(d) Partial liability of carrier

Problems could arise under the Hague/Visby Rules where fault of the carrier combined with an Art IV exception to cause damage to the cargo. In some cases carrier negligence might have been the operative cause of the loss whilst in others it might only have been an aggravating factor. Where the carrier's fault has been responsible for the occurrence

---

[16] But 'request' for underdeck carriage may not be sufficient. See *Insurance Co of N America v Blue Star Ltd* [1997] AMC 2434.
[17] For the effects of deviation, see *supra* at pp 208 ff.
[18] See *supra* p 209.

of the excepted peril, as, for example, where his negligence has resulted in storm damage to the cargo, the general reaction of the courts is to hold that the exception will not exonerate the carrier. On the other hand, where the carrier's negligence combines with the exception to cause damage, for example where goods deteriorate as the result of a combination of delay caused by strikes and bad ventilation in the hold, the carrier in some jurisdictions will only be held responsible for that proportion of the loss which is attributable to his fault, provided that the amount of this loss can be identified.

In an attempt to clarify the position, the Hamburg Rules provide that the carrier shall be liable 'only to the extent that the loss damage or delay in delivery is attributable to his fault' provided that he can establish the proportion of loss attributable to other factors.[19] Presumably he is liable for the entire loss if he fails to discharge this burden of proof, which in most cases will be no light one.

(e) Loss caused by delay in delivery

The Hague/Visby Rules contain no specific provision for the recovery of loss caused by delay in delivery of the cargo. In so far as delay results in physical damage to the goods, e.g. by deterioration in quality, there seems little doubt that such loss is recoverable under Art III rule 2 which imposes a general duty of care in handling the cargo. The position is not so clear, however, with regard to purely economic loss, such as loss of market resulting from delay in delivery. Some countries expressly provide for the recovery of such loss in their maritime codes,[20] while in common law jurisdictions it usually falls within the ambit of the 'reasonable contemplation of the parties' test in *Hadley* v *Baxendale*.[21] Elsewhere the position is obscure and it is not uncommon to see clauses in liner bills either excluding or limiting liability for delay.

In order to remove all doubts and to bring carriage by sea in line with carriage by the three other modes of international transport,[22] the Hamburg Rules expressly provide that the carrier will be liable for loss resulting from delay in delivery unless he can discharge the standard burden of proof, i.e. that neither he nor his servants or agents were at fault.[23] Presumably such liability in English law will continue to be restricted to loss which was reasonably within the contemplation of the parties according to the *Hadley* v *Baxendale* test.

7.4 LIMITATION OF LIABILITY

Despite strong arguments to the effect that the retention of the principle of limitation of liability was no longer justifiable, the draftsmen of the Hamburg Rules favoured such retention on the ground that it was of benefit to both shipper and carrier in that it enabled the latter to calculate his risks in advance and so establish uniform and cheaper

---

[19] Article 5.7.
[20] See e.g. Art 130 of the Swedish Maritime Code and Art 149 of the Merchant Shipping Code of the USSR.
[21] (1854) 9 Ex 341. See *Renton v Palmyra Trading Corp* [1957] AC 149; *The Ardennes* [1951] 1 KB 55.
[22] See Art 19 of the Warsaw Convention 1929: 'The carrier is liable for damage occasioned by delay in the carriage by air of passengers, luggage or goods.' See similar provisions in Article 17(i) of the CMR (road) Convention 1956 and Article 27(i) of the CIM (rail) Convention 1962.
[23] Article 5.1.

freight rates. Any agreed new limits must, however, be fixed at a sufficiently high level to encourage the carrier to look after the cargo and, so far as possible, they should be inflation proof. As with the Hague Rules, two aspects of the formula required special consideration: namely, the appropriate unit of cargo and a suitable monetary unit of account. In the negotiations leading up to the adoption of the Hamburg Rules there was strong support for a formula based exclusively on weight in line with the policy adopted in the other three transport conventions, but in the event the dual system of limitation was retained in the interests of the owners of high value, light weight cargo. One particular change in the Hamburg draft is to be welcomed. The conflict between 'shipping' and 'freight' units[24] has been resolved by a clear statement that the unit at issue is a 'package or other *shipping* unit'.[25]

The above dual system relates exclusively to liability for loss or damage to the goods. Neither of these alternatives was considered an appropriate formula for limiting liability for delay in delivery. The preference was for a limitation based on an amount equivalent to two and a half times the freight payable for the goods delayed, provided that such sum did not exceed the total freight payable under the contract of carriage. In any event, the overall amount recoverable for any combination of loss, damage or delay must not exceed the sum recoverable on a total loss of the goods.[26] Whether or not it is satisfactory to limit the maximum compensation for loss resulting from delay to the amount of the bill of lading freight seems questionable. So far as container limitation is concerned, the Hamburg Rules have adopted the Hague/Visby solution preferring to construe the shipping units as the individual items listed in the bill of lading or other document evidencing the contract of carriage. If the contents of the container or pallet are not separately listed, then the container or pallet together with its contents are treated as a single shipping unit.[27] In the case of loss or damage to the container or pallet itself, this will be treated as a separate unit for limitation purposes, provided that it is not owned or supplied by the carrier.[28] If the carrier has cause to challenge the shipper's load and count as enumerated on the bill, either because he has reasonable grounds for believing them to be inaccurate, or because he has no reasonable opportunity of checking them, he is now required not only to insert a reservation in the bill, but also to specify the reasons for doing so.[29]

UNIT OF ACCOUNT

The draftsmen of the Hamburg Rules rejected the Poincaré franc as the unit of account in favour of the Special Drawing Right ('SDR') as defined by the International Monetary Fund. Article 26 provides that 'the relevant units of account be converted into the national currency of a State according to the value of such currency at the date of judgment or the date agreed upon by the parties'. Where states are members of the International Monetary Fund, the conversion of SDR units into the appropriate

---

[24] See *supra* p 197.
[25] Article 6.1(a).
[26] Article 6.1(c).
[27] Article 6.2(a).
[28] Article 6.2(b).
[29] Article 16.1.

national currency will be in accordance with the rules of the Fund but, where they are not members, the method of calculation will be determined by the state itself. It was recognised, however, that the law of certain states may not permit a calculation to be made on this basis, in which case such states may use the Poincaré franc as the basic unit of account.

In cases where the SDR is the appropriate unit of account, Art 6.1(a) provides that the carrier's liability is limited to an amount 'equivalent to 835 units of account per package or other shipping unit, or 2.5 units of account per kilogramme of gross weight of the goods lost or damaged, whichever is the higher'. Alternatively, in those states permitted to use the Poincaré franc, the corresponding limitation would be 12,500 and 37.5 monetary units respectively. These figures represent a 25 per cent increase on the limits presently prescribed in the Hague/Visby Rules.[30]

7.4.1 LOSS OF RIGHT TO LIMIT LIABILITY

While the Hague Rules entitled the carrier to limit his liability for cargo damage within the permitted amounts 'in any event',[31] this phrase has now disappeared from the corresponding limitation clause in the Hamburg Rules. In its place is the unqualified statement that the liability of the carrier 'is limited' to the amounts specified without any further reservation except that contained in Art 8. Should the Hamburg Rules when implemented be given 'the force of law' (as were the Hague/Visby Rules in s 1(2) of the Carriage of Goods by Sea Act 1971), it may well be that the carrier will be able to claim the benefit of limitation in all circumstances including deviation, except where the case falls within the purview of Art 8.

Article 8 specifically denies the carrier the right to limit his liability for any loss, damage or delay which results from an act or omission of the carrier 'done with intent to cause such loss, damage or delay, or recklessly and with knowledge that such loss, damage or delay would probably result'. A similar clause bars a servant or agent of the carrier from invoking the limitation clause to cover his personal liability where he has displayed a similar intent, or recklessness. These clauses merely reiterate the policy introduced by the Hague/Visby Rules except for the reference to 'such loss' etc which presumably limits the operation of Art 8, unlike its counterpart in the Hague/Visby Rules, to cases where the intent relates to the actual loss, damage or delay which occurred. Attempts by cargo interests to make the carrier vicariously responsible without limit for damage resulting from intent or recklessness on the part of his servants or agents were strongly resisted and reference to them was excluded from the final draft. It remains to be seen how the courts would interpret this formula for breaking the liability limits and to what extent it would extend to situations formerly covered by the doctrine of fundamental breach. It is doubtful, for example, whether deviation from the agreed course would constitute conduct appropriate to fulfil the requirements of this article, whereas it is clearly not the intention that unauthorised stowage on deck *per se* should have this effect.[32] The only guideline provided by the Rules is to be found in

---

[30] See *supra* p 201.
[31] See *supra* pp 203–4.
[32] See Art 9.

Art 9.1, which provides that 'Carriage of goods on deck contrary to express agreement for carriage under deck is deemed to be an act or omission of the carrier within the meaning of Article 8.'

7.5 OTHER PROVISIONS

(I) ISSUE OF BILL OF LADING

Once the carrier has taken the goods into his charge he is required[33] on demand of the shipper to issue a bill of lading containing a variety of information listed in Art 15. Among the particulars specified, he is required to state 'the general nature of the goods, the leading marks necessary for identification of the goods, an express statement, if applicable, as to the dangerous character of the goods, the number of packages or pieces and the weight of the goods or their quantity otherwise expressed, all such particulars as furnished by the shipper'. He is also required to acknowledge the apparent condition of the goods. After the goods have been loaded on board, the shipper is also entitled to demand the issue of a 'shipped' bill of lading which must state that the goods are on board a named ship or ships together with the date of loading.[34] In return, the shipper is required to indemnify the carrier against any loss resulting from inaccuracies in the particulars supplied by him.

These provisions covering the receipt function of the bill of lading generally follow the pattern established by the Hague and Hague/Visby Rules, but there are significant variations in detail. Thus, while the carrier is excused from acknowledging particulars which he knows or has reasonable grounds for suspecting are inaccurate, or which he has no reasonable means of checking, he is now required to 'insert in the bill of lading a reservation specifying these inaccuracies, grounds of suspicion or the absence of reasonable means of checking'.[35] Again, while such particulars in a bill are prima facie evidence against the carrier, they only become conclusive in favour of a bona fide transferee of the bill if he 'has *acted in reliance* on the description of the goods therein'.[36] It is also interesting to note that failure to indicate in the bill the amount of freight or demurrage incurred at the port of loading and payable by the consignee, is treated as prima facie evidence that no such demurrage or freight is payable by him. It becomes conclusive in the hands of a bona fide transferee of the bill who 'has acted in reliance on the absence in the bill of lading of any such indication'.[37]

Express provision is also made for the situation where the carrier, knowing the goods to be damaged, is induced to issue a clean bill of lading in return for an indemnity from the shipper. The solution favoured by the draftsmen of the Hamburg Rules is broadly in line with the decision of the Court of Appeal in *Brown, Jenkinson* v *Percy Dalton*.[38] The carrier will have no right of indemnity against the shipper if his intention in issuing the bill in this form was 'to defraud a third party, including a consignee, who acts in reliance

---

[33] Article 14.
[34] Article 15.2.
[35] Article 16.1.
[36] Article 16.3.
[37] Article 16.4.
[38] [1957] 2 QB 621.

on the description of the goods in the bill of lading'.[39] Moreover, when sued by such third party for loss incurred through reliance on the statement in the bill, the carrier will not be able to invoke the provisions relating to limitation of liability.[40]

(II) LIMITATION OF ACTION

Actions are time-barred under the Hamburg Rules if judicial or arbitral proceedings have not been instituted within a period of two years from the time the goods have been delivered or should have been delivered.[41] This limit applies irrespective of whether proceedings have been instituted by the cargo owner or the carrier. This compares with a period of 12 months under the Hague/Visby Rules, applicable only to proceedings against the carrier or the ship. The person against whom a claim is made may at any time, during the running of the limitation period, extend that period by a declaration in writing to the claimant.[42] Actions for indemnity may, of course, be instituted outside the basic limitation period and in this respect the Hamburg Rules follow their predecessors in specifying a minimum extension of 90 days from the date on which the party seeking the indemnity 'has settled the claim or has been served with process in the action against himself'.[43]

(III) DANGEROUS GOODS

The Hamburg Rules introduce three new requirements for the shipment of dangerous goods. First the shipper must mark or label the goods in such a way as to indicate that they are dangerous;[44] secondly he must inform the carrier of the dangerous character of the goods and of any necessary precautions to be taken[45] and, finally, the bill of lading must include an express statement that the goods are dangerous.[46] Otherwise the sanctions for failure to comply with these requirements appear to be practically identical with those provided in the Hague and Hague/Visby Rules. If the seller fails to disclose the dangerous nature of the goods, and the carrier is not otherwise aware, not only will the shipper be liable for any loss resulting from their shipment, but the carrier is empowered at any time to unload, destroy or render the cargo innocuous, 'as the circumstances may require' without payment of compensation.[47] Even though he has consented to their shipment, the carrier may take similar action should the cargo become an actual danger to life or property during the voyage.[48]

(IV) JURISDICTION

In the event of a claim being brought in respect of a contract for the carriage of goods governed by this convention, the plaintiff is given a wide choice of courts in which to

---

[39] Article 17.3.
[40] Article 17.4.
[41] Article 20.1.
[42] Article 20.4.
[43] Article 20.5.
[44] Article 13.1.
[45] Article 13.2.
[46] Article 15.1.
[47] Article 13.2.
[48] Article 13.4.

initiate judicial or arbitral proceedings.[49] Provided that the court selected is competent in terms of its own domestic law, the plaintiff has the option of instituting proceedings in any court:

'within the jurisdiction of which is situated one of the following places:

a) the principal place of business or, in the absence thereof, the habitual residence of the defendant; or

b) the place where the contract was made provided that the defendant has there a place of business, branch or agency through which the contract was made; or

c) the port of loading or the port of discharge; or

d) any additional place designated for that purpose in the contract of carriage by sea.'[50]

In addition, an action may be brought in the courts of any port or place in a contracting state at which the carrying vessel or a sister ship has been arrested in accordance with normal legal procedures. In such an event, however, the defendant can demand the removal of the hearing to one of the jurisdictions listed above in Art 21.1 provided that he is prepared to furnish security sufficient to cover any possible judgment against him.[51] No proceedings can be instituted under the convention in any other court.

(V) DEFINITION OF THE 'CARRIER'

The main purpose of the Hamburg Rules, as also of their predecessors the Hague and Hague/Visby Rules, is to provide the shipper with basic and inalienable rights against the carrier. Consequently, any attempt to derogate from the provisions of the Rules is declared to be null and void,[52] though the carrier is free to extend his obligations under the contract of carriage or waive rights conferred on him by the Convention.[53]

Who then is the carrier for the purposes of the Hamburg Rules? He is defined in Art 1 as 'any person by whom or in whose name a contract of carriage of goods by sea has been concluded with a shipper'.[54] This definition is somewhat wider than that provided by the Hague or Hague/Visby Rules, since it extends beyond the shipowner or charterer to include any person who has negotiated, as principal, a contract to carry goods by sea, even though he has no intention of carrying the goods himself. Accordingly, it could include a freight forwarder, a combined transport operator or any other type of non-vessel owning carrier. The Rules then proceed to distinguish the 'carrier' as already described, from the 'actual carrier' i.e. the party to whom actual performance has been entrusted.[55] In many cases, of course, 'carrier' and 'actual carrier' will be one and the same person.

---

[49] NB Under Art 22 the parties may provide by agreement evidenced in writing that any dispute be referred to arbitration.

[50] Article 21.1.

[51] Article 21.2(a).

[52] Article 23.1.

[53] Article 23.2. NB Where performance of the contract is delegated to an 'actual' carrier any special agreement extending the carrier's liability will not bind the actual carrier unless agreed to by him expressly in writing: Art 10.3.

[54] The name and principal place of business of such persons must be recorded on the face of the bill of lading: Art 15(1)(c).

[55] Article 1.2.

Having made this distinction, the Convention then makes clear that where the contracting carrier delegates performance of the contract of carriage he remains responsible throughout for the acts and omissions of the actual carrier and of his servants and agents acting within the scope of their employment.[56] At the same time, the provisions of the Convention equally govern the responsibilities of the actual carrier for that part of the carriage performed by himself, and, where the obligations of the two parties overlap, their liability is joint and several.[57] These provisions will greatly assist the cargo owner claimant who at present has the difficult task of unravelling the complicated relationship between owners, charterers and demise charterers in order to establish the identity of the carrier. The need to identify the carrier arises from the fact that the Hague and Hague/Visby Rules will only recognise a single carrier, i.e. the contractual carrier. In contrast, the Hamburg Rules dispense with the need for such identification since, where both types of carrier are involved, they impose identical obligations on contractual and actual carriers. In any event, a cargo claimant can safely institute proceedings against an actual carrier who will remain liable for loss, damage or delay incurred during that part of the carriage contract performed by himself, irrespective of whether or not he was also the contractual carrier at the time. There are many practical reasons for preferring to bring suit against the shipowner.

In one case only are contracting carriers permitted to exclude their liability. This arises in the situation where the contract of carriage provides explicitly that a specified part of the carriage covered by the contract is to be performed by a named person other than the contractual carrier.[58] In such circumstances the contractual carrier can expressly exclude his liability for the stage in question. This provision is ideally suited to cases of combined transport or through bills of lading, where performance of a particular leg has been delegated to an 'actual carrier', although it may not always be possible to take advantage of this concession since the name of the particular on-carrier is frequently not known at the time of shipment. On the other hand, there seems no reason why the phrase 'specified part of the carriage' should not be extended to cover the entire carriage period where the contract has been negotiated by a non-vessel owning contractual carrier. Thus the voyage or time charterer, in negotiating a contract of carriage, could identify the actual carrier and shift the entire liability to the shipowner.

7.6 PROSPECTS FOR ADOPTION OF THE HAMBURG RULES

Opposition from shipowning interests to the implementation of the Convention is based on a number of factors. First, there is strong objection to the abolition of the catalogue of exceptions, and in particular to the removal of the traditional exclusion of liability for negligent navigation. Secondly, fears have been expressed about the new formulation of the fire exception, while the extension of the limitation period for instituting proceedings to two years is far from popular. More general concern surrounds the adoption of the language and terminology of the new Convention. Whatever the merits of the draftsmanship of the Hague and Hague/Visby Rules, their provisions have been well

---

[56] Article 10.1.
[57] Articles 10.2, 10.4.
[58] Article 11.1.

tested in litigation and their effects are now reasonably clear. On the other hand, the introduction of new concepts phrased in ambiguous language, which is often the result of diplomatic compromise, presents the opportunity for endless litigation, the cost of which may well be prohibitive. With the burden of proof now resting firmly with the carrier, litigation may be encouraged to test the strength of the carrier's case. All these factors, together with the substantial rise in liability limits, lead the opponents of the Convention to the view that its implementation would inevitably result in a substantial increase in freight rates.

The response from advocates of the Rules' adoption is that all these arguments have been rehearsed before. Forecasts of steep rises in freight rates preceded the implementation of both the Hague and Hague/Visby Rules and on both occasions proved to be unfounded. In their view the time is long overdue for a more equitable redistribution of risk as between cargo owner and carrier and it is appropriate that the burden of proving the cause of loss should lie on the party in possession of the relevant facts. Nor is there any justification in their opinion for protecting the carrier by sea against the consequences of his own negligent navigation when no similar immunity is granted to carriers by any other mode of transport. Finally, the desirability was urged of achieving a uniform regime of carrier liability operative throughout the world. There is widespread agreement on the need for revision of the Hague Rules but the amendments proposed in the Brussels Protocol have not proved generally acceptable. In these circumstances it is argued that the adoption of the Hamburg Rules, which has strong support among some developing countries, offers the only hope of achieving the desired uniform regime in the foreseeable future.

In retrospect it is arguable that the main criticism of the Hamburg Rules is the failure of its draftsmen to grasp the nettle by imposing strict liability on the carrier and so concentrating all the risk on him. The failure to adopt this course, coupled with the retention of the principle of package limitation of liability, means that it will still be necessary to retain both cargo and carrier's liability insurance with all the resultant problems and expense attending the allocation of risk. The adoption of the more radical solution would not, however, be so attractive to cargo underwriters or maritime lawyers.

Some few years after the Rules came into effect, what are the chances of their widespread adoption? At present they have not been ratified by any major maritime nation but have been implemented in 29 states estimated to represent overall some 5 per cent of world trade. Despite such a modest start, there are several reasons for believing that their influence is likely to expand, apart from the likelihood of their being ratified by other trading nations in the not too distant future. First, in the states where they are operative, they are mandatorily applicable not only to outward cargoes, but also to inward cargoes irrespective of their port of origin. Secondly, they require bills of lading to include a paramount clause expressly incorporating the Rules and declaring null and void any provisions in the contract of carriage which seek to detract from them to the detriment of the cargo owner. Moreover, on failure to include such a clause in the bill, the carrier is liable to compensate the cargo owner for any loss resulting from its omission. Thirdly, the claimant has a wide choice of forum in which to litigate or arbitrate, which cannot be restricted by any express choice of forum clause in the contract of carriage.

In practice, therefore, a carrying voyage may be mandatorily subject to two conflicting conventions. To take, for example, a carrying voyage from a port in the United Kingdom to a port in a Hamburg state, the contract of carriage would be governed by the Hague/Visby Rules at the port of shipment, and by the Hamburg Rules at the port of discharge. Which set of Rules would actually be applied would depend on the forum in which the dispute was litigated. On the presumption that, as the cargo was destined for a Hamburg state, the bill of lading would incorporate the appropriate paramount clause, the cargo owner could exercise his option to litigate in the Hamburg state, irrespective of any choice of forum clause in the contract of carriage. Even if suit was brought in an English court, the paramount clause would still be effective, since Art V of the Hague/Visby Rules permits the enforcement of terms which are more favourable to cargo interests than its own provisions.[59] Should the English court enforce the Hague/Visby regime, however, because the carriage contract failed to incorporate a Hamburg paramount clause, then the cargo owner would be entitled in a subsequent action to claim an indemnity from the carrier to cover any resultant loss.

For the above reasons the Hamburg Rules may come to exert a wider influence than may be at first apparent. In particular, it may be difficult to draft a clause which effectively will exclude their application in circumstances other than where they are mandatorily applicable. Certainly, their operation cannot be excluded, as can the Hague/Visby regime, by the simple expedient of issuing a waybill instead of a bill of lading. The reaction of the international P & I clubs, however, has been to offer normal cover only where the Hamburg Rules are mandatorily applicable by operation of law. Where the liability of the carrier has been increased by the voluntary incorporation of the Rules into the carriage contract, the cover will be no more extensive than that required to compensate for obligations arising under the normal Hague or Hague/Visby regimes.

7.7 LATER DEVELOPMENTS

In recent years the overall situation has been further complicated by the fact that a number of states have unilaterally adopted a hybrid Hague–Hague/Visby–Hamburg regime, the details of which differ from state to state. The major maritime nations involved include China, Japan, the Scandinavian states and Australia,[60] while a draft bill to similar effect is currently before the US Senate.[61]

The respective approaches of both the Australian legislation and the US draft Bill are remarkably similar and are broadly in line with developments elsewhere. While the substantive law relating to carrier liability follows the Hague/Visby pattern, the scope

---

[59] In certain circumstances the Hamburg Rules may be less favourable to cargo interests than the provisions of the Hague/Visby Rules, e.g. the limit of liability for loss resulting from delay, the possible repeal of the rule in *The Muncaster Castle*, see *supra* p 218.

[60] The Australian legislation came into effect on 1 July 1998 and is enacted in the Carriage of Goods by Sea Act 1991, as amended by the Carriage of Goods by Sea Amendment Act 1997 and the COGSA Regulations 1998.

[61] Deliberations on the draft bill are currently in suspension pending the outcome of the CMI/UNCITRAL initiative described below.

of application of these provisions is expanded in line with Hamburg principles. Thus, both systems adopt the Hague–Hague/Visby formula for basic carrier liability, i.e. the duty to exercise due diligence to provide a seaworthy ship coupled with the requirement to take reasonable care of the cargo, subject to the catalogue of exceptions listed in Art IV rule 2. The only variation, although an important one, appears in the US draft, which abolishes the nautical fault exception.[62] Both regimes also retain limitation of liability based on the Hague/Visby formula and SDRs,[63] together with the one-year limit on court actions and arbitrations.[64]

The principal innovations, however, are to be found in the extended scope of application of the new regimes which largely follow the Hamburg pattern. Thus, the revised rules are applicable not only to contracts of carriage covered by negotiable bills of lading, but also to those covered by non-negotiable bills, waybills or by their electronic equivalents. Again, the carrier's period of responsibility is extended from tackle-to-tackle to cover the entire period during which the goods are 'in the charge' of the carrier. Deck carriage is brought within the rules for the first time, although the carriage of live animals is still excluded, as are 'particular goods' under Art VI, provided that their carriage is covered by a non-negotiable receipt marked as such. The two regimes do, however, differ on the range of contracts to which they are mandatorily applicable. In the case of the proposed US regime, the new provisions will apply to all contracts of carriage by sea, where the port of loading or port of discharge is in the United States, or where the goods are either received by the carrier or delivered to him in the United States (i.e. the rules will be applicable to combined transport). In contrast, the Australian legislation, while being mandatorily applicable to all outward shipments from Australia, is only applicable to inward shipments which are not covered by one of the three standard conventions.

The overall result of these developments is a further step away from the ultimate objective of international uniformity. A proliferation of such national regimes, especially when designed to govern both inward and outward bills, can only lead to increased confusion and uncertainty in international trade. In an attempt to prevent further fragmentation, the CMI, in conjunction with UNCITRAL, has launched a project seeking to gain international agreement on a new updated liability regime capable of meeting the requirements of modern commerce while promoting as great a degree of uniformity as possible. The hope is that, in the meantime, national governments will refrain from devising their own national or regional solutions to the problem.

7.8 THE CMI/UNCITRAL PROJECT

In an attempt to prevent further fragmentation, a new international initiative has been launched. At the request of UNCITRAL, the CMI prepared a 'Draft Instrument on

---

[62] The US draft bill substitutes a provision that any party alleging negligence in the navigation or management of a ship has the burden of proving such negligence.
[63] The Australian legislation also incorporates a separate limitation of liability for loss or damage caused by delay using the Hamburg formula.
[64] While broadly adopting the Hague/Visby formula for carrier liability, the US draft includes an extensive redrafting of the Hague/Visby provisions with the stated objective of obtaining greater clarity.

Transport Law' which it submitted to the UNCITRAL secretariat in December 2001. The detailed examination of this draft was delegated to a UNCITRAL Working Group which completed its first reading of the document in March 2003.[65] The Working Group then decided to concentrate its attention during 2003/2004 on what are thought to be the core subjects in the instrument.[66] The object of the exercise is to gain international agreement on a new updated liability regime for carriage, capable of meeting the requirements of modern commerce while promoting as great a degree of uniformity as possible. At the moment a number of controversial issues remain to be resolved and the current version of the draft includes not only alternative variants of individual articles but also suggested variations in the phraseology of the articles themselves.

While any conclusions must be tentative until the appearance of the final draft, certain major policy trends are already apparent.[67] Perhaps not surprisingly, these trends tend to mirror the pattern of the developments already described in Australia, the USA and elsewhere.

Although the draft instrument is drafted so as to cover either eventuality, the majority view appears to support a convention applicable from door-to-door rather than the port-to-port coverage favoured in previous conventions, provided only that the carriage includes a sea leg and that sea leg involves cross-border transport. Accordingly, the carrier's period of responsibility would run from the time of receipt of the goods to the time of delivery to the consignee and would include liability for loss, damage or delay during inland carriage preceding or subsequent to the sea leg. The draft does, however, incorporate a limited form of network liability in that its provisions would be overridden in circumstances where an international convention was mandatorily applicable to a particular leg and it was proved that the loss, damage or delay occurred solely in the course of carriage on that leg. The draft instrument follows the pattern of the Hamburg Rules, in that its provisions are applicable to contracts of carriage by sea irrespective of the type of documentation used.[68] Its provisions are also applicable in situations where electronic equivalents replace the traditional paper documents, provided that both carrier and shipper agree on their use.

Perhaps the most interesting and controversial development is the formula adopted to deal with the basic question of carrier liability. The current proposed solution is an amalgam of the respective approaches adopted by the Hague and Hamburg regimes. The definition of carrier liability is contained in a modified version of Art 5.1 of the Hamburg Rules, i.e. it is based on fault with a reversed burden of proof.[69] Accordingly, if the claimant can establish that the loss, damage or delay occurred during the carrier's period of responsibility, the carrier will be liable unless it can prove that neither its fault

---

[65] For report see UNCITRAL document A/CN.9/WGIII/WP32.

[66] The first of these special sessions was held in October 2003, when the Working Party discussed the core subjects of the scope of application of the draft instrument and the issue of 'performing parties'. For report see UNCITRAL document A/CN.9/544.

[67] In outlining the following proposals, reference is not made to specific numbered articles in the instrument as these tend to change with successive drafts.

[68] Charterparties are still excluded from the scope of the draft instrument.

[69] In the new draft instrument the carrier is specifically required to prove the absence of 'fault' rather than that 'he took all measures that could reasonably be required to avoid the occurrence and its consequences' (the Hamburg formula).

nor the fault of any other 'performing party'[70] caused or contributed to the loss, damage or delay. In seeking to discharge this burden of proof, the carrier can prove that the loss, damage or delay resulted from one of a list of events which act as presumptions of the absence of fault on his part. This list follows the general pattern of the exceptions set out in Art IV rule 2 of the Hague/Visby Rules, with the omission of the controversial nautical fault exception. On this occasion, however, the intention is that they should act merely as rebuttable presumptions of the absence of fault rather than, as previously, exonerations from liability.[71]

It might be thought that the above provisions provide an adequate definition of carrier liability, but the majority view favoured the introduction of an additional clause stating the obligations of the carrier as positive duties. Accordingly, the draft instrument reiterates the Hague/Visby obligations to exercise due diligence to provide a seaworthy ship coupled with the duty to deal properly and carefully with the cargo during the carrier's period of responsibility. In the case of the seaworthiness requirement, there is strong support for the view that this should be a continuous obligation throughout the voyage. It is envisaged that a claimant should be able to rebut the presumption of absence of fault, resulting from the carrier's reliance on an exception, by establishing that the operative cause of the loss was either the unseaworthy state of the vessel[72] or lack of due care on the part of the carrier.

Brief reference must also be made to other aspects of carriage covered by the draft instrument. First, the provisions on limitation of liability broadly follow the Hague/Visby pattern as modified by Hamburg. Thus the container clause is retained and liability for loss or damage is limited to specified numbers of units of account per package or other shipping unit or per kilo of the gross weight of the goods, whichever provides the higher amount. The limit for loss caused by delay is calculated as a multiple of the freight due on the goods delayed. SDRs are retained as the currency of account although the appropriate number of units in each case is left for future decision. On the question of a time limitation, the Hague/Visby one-year limit is preferred, although the option is left open as to whether the lapse of such time will merely bar the claim or extinguish the right.

The question has always been controversial as to whether a convention should in principle be applicable to all types of goods or whether certain problem cases should be excluded, leaving the parties free to negotiate their own terms for such carriage. The Hague regime adopted an exclusive approach to such problems, while the Hamburg regime preferred an inclusive formula though making special provision to cover the peculiarities of certain types of goods. The draft instrument adopts the Hamburg model in regard to the carriage of deck cargo while following the Hague/Visby approach

---

[70] A term intended to cover any person, other than the carrier, who physically performs any of the carrier's responsibilities under the contract at the carrier's request or under his supervision or control. The precise definition of this term is still under discussion.

[71] A minority view favours the retention of exceptions as exonerations of carrier liability, but the question is largely academic since, whichever approach is adopted, it is widely felt to be essential to preserve a rebuttable mechanism in the draft instrument.

[72] In such an event the carrier can still avoid liability by proving that it exercised due diligence.

towards the carriage of live animals and 'particular goods,' as described in Art VI.[73] In the latter case the carrier is permitted to exclude or limit his liability for loss or damage if the 'character and condition' of the goods reasonably justify a 'special contract', provided that no negotiable transport document or negotiable electronic record is issued for the carriage of the goods.

Finally, there are a number of topics ancillary to the carriage of goods which have traditionally been regulated by national law and not included in international conventions. The CMI has taken the view that on many of these subjects uniformity would be desirable. The precedent was set by the Hamburg Rules, which for the first time included provisions relating to jurisdiction, arbitration and general average. The new draft instrument seeks to consolidate this approach by introducing additional chapters devoted to freight, delivery, right of control, transfer of rights, and rights of suit against the carrier.

It is important to stress that the above account is a summary of the current state of proposals for a new convention on carriage of goods by sea. Many of the core issues involved are controversial and many of the provisions may be substantially redrafted in the course of future discussion. Some considerable time may elapse before agreement is reached on a final draft. The hope is that, in the meantime, national governments will refrain from devising their own national or regional solutions to the problem.

---

[73] The new draft does not use the term 'particular goods' as such.

8

BILLS OF LADING ISSUED
UNDER CHARTERPARTIES

It is the normal practice for bills of lading to be issued by the master or other agent of the shipowner even though the cargo has been shipped under a charterparty. Most standard charter forms make express provision to this effect while, in the event of the shipper being a party other than the charterer, he will normally be able to demand the issue of a bill under the provisions of the Hague/Visby Rules. The precise status and effect of such a bill will vary according to the identity of the holder, and problems arise where there is a conflict between the terms of the bill and the terms of the charterparty under which it was issued. Each of these possibilities requires separate consideration.

8.1 WHERE BILL OF LADING ISSUED TO CHARTERER

Where bills of lading are issued for cargo shipped by the charterer, they operate as receipts for the goods shipped and as potential documents of title, but do not constitute evidence of the contract of carriage. The relationship between shipowner and charterer is governed solely by the terms of the charterparty,[1] unless the latter contains provision that its terms can be modified or superseded by the subsequent issue of a bill.[2] A similar rule applies in the case where a bill, initially issued to a third party shipper, is subsequently indorsed to the charterer. So in *President of India* v *Metcalfe*[3] the charterer was caught by an arbitration clause in the charterparty even though there was no such clause in the bill indorsed to him by the shipper.

The second point to note is that neither the Hague nor Hague/Visby Rules are applicable to a bill of lading in the hands of a charterer since such bill does not 'regulate the relations between a carrier and the holder' as required by Art 1(b). As noted earlier, the relationship between shipowner and charterer is governed exclusively by the terms of the charterparty. There is, however, the slightly ambiguous provision in Art V that 'if bills of lading are issued in the case of a ship under a charterparty, they shall comply with the terms of these Rules'. From this it would appear that, while the charterer cannot invoke the Hague/Visby Rules to demand the issue of a bill of lading, should a

---

[1] *Rodocanachi* v *Milburn* (1886) 17 QBD 316.
[2] *The Jocelyne* [1977] 2 Lloyd's Rep 121.
[3] [1970] 1 QBD 289. See also *Love & Stewart Ltd* v *Rowtor Steamship Co* [1916] 2 AC 527. Cf. *Calcutta SS Co* v *Andrew Weir* [1910] 1 KB 759, where charterparty and bill related to different contracts.

bill nevertheless be issued, he can require it *inter alia* to list the information prescribed by Art 3 rule 3.[4] Many standard charter forms solve this problem by expressly incorporating either the Hague or Hague/Visby Rules into the charterparty.[5]

8.2 WHERE BILL ISSUED TO THIRD-PARTY SHIPPER

When goods are shipped on a chartered vessel by a party other than the charterer, two problems face the shipper in the event of the cargo being lost or damaged during transit. First he has to identify the carrier against whom the cargo claim can be pursued and, secondly, he has to establish the precise terms of the contract of carriage.

8.2.1 WHO IS THE CARRIER?

In practice the carrier is rarely identified in the bill of lading which may be issued in the name of the shipowner, the charterer, a sub-charterer or the agent of any one of them. The position is further complicated by the fact that in the majority of cases the bill will be signed by or on behalf of the ship's master, who is normally the agent of the shipowner. Faced with this conflicting evidence, it is important for the shipper to make the correct choice since the normal rule in English law is that only one party is liable as carrier under any individual carriage contract. The problem is even more acute where the contract is governed by the Hague/Visby Rules under which any cargo claim is barred if it is not instituted within the prescribed 12-month time limit. In such circumstances a wrong choice might be fatal since, by the time it is discovered, it may be too late to commence proceedings against the true defendant.[6]

In normal circumstances the shipowner would be regarded as the carrier since, despite the existence of the charterparty, he remains responsible for the management of the ship and the master signs any bills which are issued as his agent. This rule remains generally applicable even though the particular contract of carriage has been arranged by the charterer and even though the bills of lading have been issued in his name. The right of the charterer to issue such bills is dependent on an express term in the charter normally drafted to the following effect:

> 'The Captain (although appointed by the Owners) shall be under the orders and directions of the charterers as regards employment and agency; . . . the Captain . . . to sign the bills of lading as presented in conformity with mate's or tally clerk's receipts . . . All bills of lading shall be without prejudice to this charter.'[7]

---

[4] Cf. Scrutton p 412.

[5] See pp 193–4 *supra*.

[6] See *The Antares* [1987] 1 Lloyd's Rep 424. Cf. Tetley p 244 who recommends that suit should be brought against all possible contenders, but this might prove to be an expensive expedient. In certain circumstances US courts are prepared to hold the shipowner and charterer jointly liable: *The Quarrington Court* [1941] AMC 1234; *Nichimen Co v M/V Farland* [1972] AMC 1573 at p 1587; *International Produce Inc v Frances Salman* [1975] AMC 1521 at p 1535. Cf. the position under the Hamburg Rules, *supra* p 225.

[7] NYPE 46 charter clause 8.

Any bills presented by the charterer and signed by the master under the authority of such a clause will be binding on the shipowner. He will be regarded by law as the carrier for purposes of the resultant contract of carriage. Where such authority exists, it is apparently not even necessary to present such bills to the master for signature. The shipowner will be bound even though the bills are signed by the charterer himself, providing that he indicates on the bill that he is signing on behalf of the master and owners.[8] A similar result will also follow where the bills are signed to like effect by the charterer's agents.[9] Finally, there is the situation where the head charter authorises sub-letting. In such an event, 'by necessary implication the head charter authorised the charterer in the case of such sub-letting to put the sub-charterer in the same position as to signature of the bills of lading as the charterer was under the head charter, i.e. to authorise the sub-charterer to require the master to sign bills of lading, or to sign them himself'.[10]

To what extent are limits attached to the authority of the charterer to bind the shipowner by the issue of such bills of lading? Where the charterer is given the right, as in the New York Produce Exchange form already cited, to present bills for signature by the master 'without prejudice to this charterparty' then 'it is for the charterer, not the owner, to decide on the form of the bill of lading, always providing that the bill of lading does not encroach on the rights conferred on the owner by the charterparty'.[11] So, in the case from which this quotation is taken, the shipowner could not insist, before signature, on the inclusion in the bill of an additional clause clarifying his right to a lien over the cargo. Experience would suggest that there are few occasions on which the master can refuse to sign bills presented by the charterer, although there is authority for the view that he is entitled to do so where the terms of the bill are 'manifestly inconsistent with the charterparty'.[12] Nevertheless, there are few examples in the cases of successful reliance on this principle, and shipowners have been unable to resist the inclusion in the bill of, *inter alia*, a demise clause[13] or a jurisdiction clause which differed from its counterpart in the charterparty.[14] On the other hand, the shipowner would presumably be entitled to object if the bill named ports outside trading limits specified in the charterparty or if the bill referred to goods known not to have been shipped.[15] The shipowner would, however, be bound if such a bill were signed by the

---

[8] See *Tillmans* v *Knutsford* [1908] AC 406.

[9] *The Berkshire* [1974] 1 Lloyd's Rep 185 at p 188 *per* Brandon J. Expressly followed in the Australian case of *LEP International* v *Atlanttrafic Express* [1987] 10 NSWLR 614. See also *Alimport* v *Soubert Shipping Co Ltd* [2000] 2 Lloyd's Rep 447. NB In each case the authority in the employment and agency clause to submit bills of lading for signature will be accompanied by an undertaking to indemnify for any additional liability resulting from such signature. See *infra* pp 243–4. The value of such undertaking will, of course, be dependent on the financial position of the party giving it.

[10] *The Vikfrost* [1980] 1 Lloyd's Rep 560 at p 567 *per* Browne LJ.

[11] Mustill J in *Gulf Steel* v *Al Khalifa Shipping Co* [1980] 2 Lloyd's Rep 261 at p 265.

[12] Lord Halsbury in *Kruger* v *Moel Tryfan Ship Co* [1907] AC 272 at p 278. See also *The Berkshire* [1974] 1 Lloyd's Rep 185 at p 188.

[13] *The Berkshire* [1974] 1 Lloyd's Rep 185.

[14] *The Vikfrost* [1980] 1 Lloyd's Rep 560. See also *The C Joyce* [1986] 2 All ER 177.

[15] Cf. *The Garbis* [1982] 2 Lloyd's Rep 283 where master required to sign bills in a specified form.

master and issued to a third party who took in good faith and without knowledge of the lack of authority.[16]

So far we have concentrated on the more common situation where the shipowner is the carrier, but it is frequently the intention of the parties that the charterer should fill this role. Even where the contract of carriage is governed by the Hague/Visby Rules, it is possible for the carrier to be either the shipowner or the charterer.[17] Thus the charterparty itself may provide that the master is authorised to sign bills 'as agent on behalf of the charterers', in which event the charterer will clearly be bound.[18] Alternatively, the charterer will be regarded as the carrier where he contracts as principal, negotiating the contract of carriage in his own name and issuing his own bills of lading. He may also be caught where he merely signs the bills of lading without indicating that he is acting as the agent of the master and owners.[19] Everything will depend on the terms of the bill of lading and the construction of the documents as a whole.[20]

Even in the situation where the charterer is apparently a party to the bill of lading, he may still seek to transfer contractual liability to the shipowner. One method of achieving this object is to include a demise clause in the bill of lading, of which the following is a typical example:

> 'If the ship is not owned or chartered by demise to the company or line by whom this bill of lading is issued (as may be the case notwithstanding anything which appears to the contrary) the Bills of Lading shall take effect as a contract with the Owner or demise charterer, as the case may be, as principal made through the agency of the said company or line who act as agents only and shall be under no personal liability whatsoever in respect thereof.'

In essence the clause amounts to an express term in the contract of carriage to the effect that the party issuing the bill is not liable unless he is either the owner of the vessel or a charterer by demise. Unfortunately the clause fails to reveal whether or not he falls within one or other of these categories with the result that the holder of the bill is left in doubt as to the identity of the party with whom he is contracting. Tetley argues that such ambiguity is undesirable when the claimant has only a limited period in which to institute proceedings under the Hague/Visby Rules, while it contradicts the impression created by the presence of the charterer's name at the head of the bill of lading.[21] Many jurisdictions refuse to give effect to such a clause while in others it is strictly construed.[22] Its validity has, however, been recognised by the High Court in the case of *The*

---

[16] Compare the position where such a bill had been signed by the charterer himself 'as agent on behalf of the shipowner'. See Lord Dunedin in *Knutsford* v *Tillmans* [1908] AC 406 at p 411: 'Had the bill of lading contained stipulations of such an extraordinary character that the master might have refused to sign, then that defence would have been equally open upon the question of whether the signature of the charterers bound the owners.'

[17] Article I(a).

[18] Cf. position where master signs merely 'as agent'. Presumably the shipowner will be estopped unless the third party transferee is aware of the master's authority under the charter to sign only as agent for the charterer.

[19] *Gadsden* v *Australian Coastal Shipping Commission* [1977] 1 NSWLR 575.

[20] See *The Venezuela* [1980] 1 Lloyd's Rep 393; *The Rewia* [1991] 2 Lloyd's Rep 325; *The Hector* [1998] 2 Lloyd's Rep 287; *The Starsin* [2003] 1 Lloyd's Rep 571.

[21] Tetley, pp 248–51. See also UNCTAD: *Report on Bills of Lading*, pp 32–3. See Carver 9.096.

[22] *Andersons (Pacific) Trading* Co v *Karlander* [1980] 2 NSWLR 870.

Berkshire,[23] where effect was given to a demise clause included in a bill of lading issued by a sub-charterer. Brandon J commented:

> 'I see no reason not to give effect to the demise clause in accordance with its terms . . . it follows that the bill of lading is, by its express terms, intended to take effect as a contract between the shippers and the shipowners made on behalf of the shipowners by Ocean Wide as agents only . . . All the demise clause does is to spell out in unequivocal terms that the bill of lading is intended to be a shipowner's bill of lading . . . In my view, so far from being an extraordinary clause, it is an entirely usual and ordinary one.'

Nor does it apparently offend Art III rule 8 of the Hague/Visby Rules which renders null and void any attempt to exclude carrier liability as prescribed by the Rules. The clause is acceptable since rather than seeking to exclude liability, its aim is merely to identify the party liable under the Rules.

An alternative method by which the charterer can avoid liability is to insert an 'Identity of Carrier' clause in the bill of lading. A typical example of such a clause is the following:

> 'The contract evidenced by this bill of lading is between the Merchant and the Owner of the vessel named herein and it is, therefore, agreed that the said shipowner alone shall be liable for any damage or loss due to any breach or non-performance of any obligation arising out of the contract of Carriage.'[24]

Such a clause has much the same effect as a demise clause, but is perhaps more acceptable in that it removes any ambiguity by clearly designating the shipowner as the carrier.

The presence of one or other of the above clauses in a bill of lading is not necessarily conclusive. Thus in *The Starsin*[25] the House of Lords held that the bill of lading in question was a charterer's bill despite the fact that it contained both an identity of carrier clause and a demise clause. Their Lordships regarded as decisive the fact that the signature box on the face of the bill had been completed by shipping agents at the port of loading expressly as agents of the charterers who were described as 'The Carrier'. In their view, construction of the bill must be approached objectively in the way in which a reasonable person, versed in the shipping trade, would read the bill. In cases where individual terms conflict, such a person would attach greater weight to provisions which the contracting parties had themselves introduced into the document rather than to pre-printed terms 'in miniscule print' which were designed to cover a variety of different situations. They would also place greater reliance on provisions on the face of the bill rather than on terms on the reverse. In the present case the unequivocal statement on the face of the document identifying the charterer as carrier must take precedence over printed terms on the back of the bill. Lord Bingham found 'great difficultly in accepting that a shipper or transferee of a bill of lading would expect to have to resort to the detailed conditions on the reverse of the bill . . . when the bill of lading contains on its face an apparently clear and unambiguous statement of who the carrier is'.[26]

---

[23] [1974] 1 Lloyd's Rep 185 at p 188. See also Gaskell 3.66 ff.
[24] See Conlinebill, clause 17. See *The Ines* [1995] 2 Lloyd's Rep 144.
[25] [2003] 1 Lloyd's Rep 571, reversing the majority decision of the Court of Appeal [2001] 1 Lloyd's Rep 437, and overruling the decision of Moore-Bick J in *The Flecha* [1999] 1 Lloyd's Rep 612.
[26] [2003] 1 Lloyd's Rep at p 578.

8.2.2 WHAT ARE THE TERMS OF THE CONTRACT?

Where goods are shipped by a third party, the result will be much the same whether the bill of lading is issued by the shipowner or by a charterer. The bill of lading will provide prima facie evidence of the terms of the contract of carriage, though such evidence may be rebutted by proof of other terms specifically agreed by shipper and carrier.[27] Normally the third party will be unaffected by the terms of the charterparty even though he is aware of its existence. Certainly he will not be bound by any of its terms which conflict with the terms in his bill of lading or conflict with the provisions of the Hague/Visby Rules where they are applicable. Most shipowners, however, are anxious to ensure that their liability as carriers is not extended by the issue of bills of lading by the charterers and, to avoid this, insist on the inclusion in such bills of a clause incorporating the terms of the charterparty. By English law such an incorporation clause is effective provided that it satisfies the notice rules in that adequate steps have been taken to bring it reasonably to the attention of the shipper before or at the time he enters into the contract of carriage.[28] These requirements would normally be met since such a term would take the form of a printed clause in what is clearly a contractual document. Moreover, it would be a document which would normally be in the hands of the shipper before the goods were shipped for the purpose of filling in details of the cargo. The attitude of the courts, however, is to apply a strict interpretation to such incorporation clauses since they are reluctant to enforce against a third-party shipper the terms of a charterparty which he is unlikely to have seen.

The three conditions which have to be met in order to ensure the effectiveness of such incorporation clauses were articulated in a series of cases involving attempts to incorporate charterparty arbitration clauses into bills of lading. A strict *contra proferentem* approach has been adopted towards such attempts since, while arbitration clauses are common in charterparties, they are rarely found in bills of lading.

The first requirement is that effective words of incorporation must be found in the bill of lading itself without reference to the provisions of the charterparty. Where it is envisaged that bills of lading will be issued, shipowner and charterer normally make their intentions clear as to the status and form of such bills in the charterparty. Provision may be made for the use of a standard form of bill or the precise charterparty clauses to be incorporated may be specified. Such evidence of intention is, however, irrelevant so far as the bill of lading holder is concerned, since his contract is to be found exclusively in the bill of lading. A mere general reference in the bill to the incorporation of charterparty terms will not entitle the court to peruse the provisions of the charterparty in order to discover which precise clauses were intended to be incorporated. In the words of Sir John Donaldson MR:

> 'What the [shipowners] agreed with the charterers, whether in the charterparty or otherwise, is wholly irrelevant, save in so far as the whole or part of any such agreement has become part of the bill of lading contract. Such an incorporation cannot be achieved by agreement between the owners and the charterers. It can only be achieved by the agreement of the parties to the bill

---

[27] *The Ardennes* [1951] 1 KB 55. See *supra* p 130.
[28] Cheshire and Fifoot pp 173 ff; Treitel pp 216 ff. See *Gill & Duffus v Rionda Futures* [1994] 2 Lloyd's Rep 67.

of lading contract and thus the operative words of incorporation must be found in the bill of lading itself.'[29]

The second requirement is that the words of incorporation must be apt to describe the charterparty clause sought to be incorporated – the 'description issue'.[30] While the attitude of the courts has varied in the strictness of their approach over the years, the effectiveness of suitably drafted words of incorporation may be illustrated by the range of charterparty provisions which have been held enforceable against the bill of lading holder. These include liens for charterparty freight,[31] liens for dead freight[32] and liens for demurrage, even though such demurrage payments have been incurred at the port of loading and have not been indorsed on the bill.[33] More difficulty has, however, been experienced with attempts to incorporate arbitration clauses into bills of lading. Such clauses are regarded as ancillary to the main purpose of a contract of carriage and will not be incorporated in the absence of specific reference to the clauses themselves. So in *The Varenna*[34] it was held that the phrase 'all conditions and exceptions of which charterparty' was inadequate to describe an arbitration clause since the phrase means 'such conditions and exceptions as are appropriate to the carriage and delivery of goods and do not, as a matter of ordinary construction, extend to collateral terms such as an arbitration clause'.[35] Similarly, in *Siboti* v *BP France*[36] the phrase 'all terms whatsoever' was held insufficiently specific to incorporate a charterparty exclusive jurisdiction clause into a bill of lading. In the opinion of the trial judge the addition of the word 'whatsoever' did not convert an otherwise general into an explicit reference to the ancillary clause. Such a judicial approach, reminiscent of that adopted towards exception clauses, is likely to have only a limited effect in controlling the problem, since ultimately the draftsman will succeed in circumventing it. Nevertheless, the general rule remains that it is a matter of construction of the incorporation clause in each case, while there may also be a lingering doubt as to whether courts will enforce charterparty terms which are unusual or unexpected in the context of a bill of lading.

The final requirement is that the charterparty clause, when incorporated, must be consistent with the remaining terms of the bill of lading – the 'consistency issue'.[37] In the

---

[29] *The Varenna* [1983] 2 Lloyd's Rep 592 at p 594, overruling the contrary view expressed by Staughton J in *The Emmanuel Colocotronis (No 2)* [1982] 1 Lloyd's Rep 286 at p 293.

[30] See *per* Staughton J in *The Emmanuel Colocotronis (No 2)* at p 289.

[31] *Gardner* v *Trechman* (1884) 15 QBD 154. But not to cover the balance where the freight reserved in the bill is less than the charterparty freight (i.e. a case of conflict).

[32] *Kish* v *Taylor* [1912] AC 604.

[33] *Fidelitas Shipping* Co v *V/O Exportchleb* [1963] 2 Lloyd's Rep 113.

[34] [1983] 2 Lloyd's Rep 592. Cf. *The Nerano* [1996] 1 Lloyd's Rep 1; *The Rena K* [1978] 1 Lloyd's Rep 545 (where specific reference to incorporation of arbitration clause).

[35] *Ibid* at p 597. See also *The Delos* [2001] 1 Lloyd's Rep 703. The phrase 'all terms, conditions and exceptions as per charterparty' met with a similar fate in *The Federal Bulker* [1989] 1 Lloyd's Rep 103. Similar rules apply to attempts to incorporate charterparty terms into c.i.f. sales contracts: *OK Petroleum* v *Vitol Energy* [1995] 2 Lloyd's Rep 160.

[36] [2003] 2 Lloyd's Rep 364. A specific reference in the bill to the charterparty clause would, of course, suffice as would, for example, a mere reference to 'clause 35', even though such reference would provide the holder of the bill with no information as to the content of that clause: see *The Merak* [1964] 2 Lloyd's Rep 527. Cf. *The Oinoussin Pride* [1991] 1 Lloyd's Rep 126.

[37] *Per* Staughton J in *The Emmanuel Colocotronis (No 2)* [1982] at p 289.

event of any conflict, the provisions of the bill of lading will prevail. Thus in the case of *Hamilton* v *Mackie*[38] a clause providing that 'all disputes arising under this charterparty shall be referred to arbitration' was held, after incorporation, not to be applicable to disputes arising under the bill of lading. A similar result followed in *The Miramar*[39] where a shipowner, on the insolvency of the charterer, was seeking to invoke an incorporation clause in order to recover demurrage due under the charterparty from a bill of lading holder. While the House of Lords had no doubt that the incorporation clause was drafted sufficiently broadly to incorporate the charterparty demurrage provisions verbatim into the bill, the problem was that these provisions expressly stated that '*charterer* shall pay demurrage'. Their Lordships disapproved of a suggestion advanced by Lord Denning MR in an earlier case[40] that, where the object of an incorporation clause was to impose upon the bill of lading holder personal liability for nonperformance of the obligations undertaken by the charterer, and the clause incorporated was 'directly germane to the shipment, carriage and delivery of the goods' the court should be entitled to indulge in a degree of verbal manipulation in order to ensure that the words exactly fitted the bill of lading. In the case of *The Miramar* this would have involved substituting the words 'bill of lading holder' for 'charterer' in the clause.

In holding that, under the clause in question, only the charterer was liable for demurrage, Lord Diplock outlined the practical effect of any other construction. The suggested verbal manipulation would have the effect that 'every consignee to whom a bill of lading covering any part of the cargo is negotiated, is not only accepting personal liability to pay the owner's freight, as stated in the bill of lading, but is also accepting blindfold a potential liability to pay an unknown and wholly unpredictable sum for demurrage which may, unknown to him, already have accrued or may subsequently accrue without any ability on his own part to prevent it, even though that sum may actually exceed the delivered value of the goods to which the bill of lading gives title'.[41] In his view, 'no business man who had not taken leave of his senses would intentionally enter into a contract which exposed him to a potential liability of this kind'.

Lord Diplock's comment merely reflects the considerable body of criticism which has been levelled at the use of such incorporation clauses, particularly when they are invoked against an indorsee of a bill of lading who rarely has any knowledge of the charterparty terms.[42] Indeed, authority would suggest that such a holder might have no right to demand production of the charterparty even though reference is made to its terms in the bill of lading.[43] The result is that subsequent indorsees will have difficulty in establishing their legal position and, even where they do manage to obtain sight of the

---

[38] (1889) 5 TLR 677. See also *The Phonizien* [1966] 1 Lloyd's Rep 150; *The Nai Matteini* [1988] 1 Lloyd's Rep 452. A suitably worded clause can, however, easily surmount this difficulty as, for example, 'any dispute arising out of this charter or any bill of lading issued hereunder, shall be referred to arbitration': *The Merak* [1964] 2 Lloyd's Rep 527.

[39] [1984] 2 Lloyd's Rep 129. See also *The Spiros C* [2000] 2 Lloyd's Rep 319.

[40] *The Annefield* [1971] 1 Lloyd's Rep 1 at p 4. See also Russell LJ in *The Merak* [1964] 2 Lloyd's Rep 527 at p 537.

[41] *The Miramar* [1984] 2 Lloyd's Rep at p 132.

[42] See UNCTAD: *Report on Bills of Lading*, pp 51–3.

[43] See *Finska* v *Westfield Paper Co* (1940) 68 LlLR 75. See also *The Epsilon Rosa* [2003] 2 Lloyd's Rep 509, where the shipowner failed to produce the relevant charterparty on request.

charterparty, the arbitration clause cases suggest that it may still be difficult to establish which of the charterparty terms have been incorporated. *Prima facie* it is the bill of lading which normally governs the relationship between carrier and holder, and arguably it is unfair to allow the carrier to rely on claims and defences which are not apparent on the face of the bill. A further problem of construction arises where the incorporation clause in the bill of lading, while referring to a charterparty, fails to identify which charterparty is intended.[44] A not infrequent example is provided by the printed form of bill which expressly provides for the incorporation of the terms and conditions of 'the charterparty dated ____' and the parties omit to fill in the blank. Little difficulty is encountered where only one charterparty is involved and a single carrier is operating under both the charter and the bill of lading. In such case 'the effect is the same as if the reference was simply to "the charterparty" and the omission does not demonstrate an intention to negate the incorporation'.[45] The problem is more complex in the situation where a series of sub-charters is involved. In such circumstances the normal rule would be to construe the reference as relating to the head charter, since this would be the only charter to which the shipowner, as issuer of the bill of lading, would be a party.[46] The result might, however, be different in the case where the head charter was a time charterparty, the terms of which would generally be inappropriate to a voyage.[47]

    A final criticism is that the inclusion of such incorporation clauses affects the commercial value of the bill in that it reduces its transferability. Thus a c.i.f. buyer who is normally required to pay for the goods on presentation of the relevant documents, which include the bill of lading, is entitled to refuse payment if he considers that reference to the charterparty terms will endanger his security. Again where a bill of lading is presented in accordance with the requirements of a documentary credit, the bank may be entitled to reject a bill which is issued subject to the terms of a charterparty unless such a bill is expressly authorised in the credit.[48] Many of these problems could, however, be resolved by the introduction of a few basic reforms. Thus, where such a bill of lading is issued by a carrier, or tendered under a sale contract, there could be a requirement for a copy of the relevant charterparty to be attached to the bill as is now recommended by 'Incoterms'. Secondly, where the bill incorporates charterparty liens to cover demurrage, dead freight or other charges, any such charges already incurred

---

[44] See Carver 3. 002/3. A related problem of interpretation arose in *The Epsilon Rosa* [2003] 2 Lloyd's Rep 509, where the term sought to be incorporated appeared in a telex recap rather than in a formal charterparty document. In deciding that an arbitration clause was effectively incorporated into the bill of lading in such circumstances, the Court of Appeal held that the 'Charter Party' referred to in the bill was the agreement contained in the telex recap together with the standard form attached. These documents satisfied the requirement that the charterparty be reduced to writing, while (per Tuckey LJ at p 515) 'a quick look at the telex and the accompanying terms would have left the reader in no doubt that the charter required London arbitration'.

[45] *The Ikariada* [1999] 2 Lloyd's Rep 365 at p 373 *per* Cresswell J. See also Scrutton p 76; Gaskell 21.23.

[46] *Scrutton* p 76. See *The San Nicholas* [1976] 1 Lloyd's Rep 8; *The Sevonia Team* [1983] 2 Lloyd's Rep 640; *The Nai Matteini* [1988] 1 Lloyd's Rep 452. The position might well be different in the case of sub-charterer's bills, since the sub-charterer would not be a party to the head charter.

[47] *The SLS Everest* [1981] 2 Lloyd's Rep 389. Query where head time charter is for a trip.

[48] Uniform Customs and Practice for Documentary Credits 500 (1993 edn) Art 23(a)(vi) and Art 25(a)(i).

could be indorsed on the bill before it is handed over to the shipper. Similarly, potential liability for future charges could be clearly indorsed on the bill.[49]

8.3 WHERE BILL INDORSED BY CHARTERER TO A THIRD PARTY

Where a bill, initially issued to a charterer, is subsequently indorsed by him to a third party, then, in the hands of a bona fide purchaser for value, the terms of the bill of lading supplant the charterparty and become conclusive evidence of the contract of carriage. The position is apparently little different from the situation which arises when the bill is issued directly to a third party as outlined in the previous section. Yet such a result was difficult to justify on the basis of s 1 of the Bills of Lading Act 1855 which referred to the rights being transferred as those arising under the contract contained in the bill of lading. It could be argued that, as the charterer has no contractual rights under the bill of lading, there are no rights to transfer. Following the repeal of the 1855 Act, a similar problem of construction arises in relation to s 2(1) of the Carriage of Goods by Sea Act 1992. This section vests in a lawful holder of a bill of lading, by virtue of becoming holder, 'all rights of suit under the contract of carriage as if he had been a party to that contract'. Prior to the indorsement of the bill, the terms of the contract of carriage are to be found in the charterparty, the bill of lading constituting a mere receipt in the hands of the charterer. Perhaps the most acceptable rationalisation is that of Lord Atkin that, on indorsement of the bill by the charterer, 'the consignee has not assigned to him the obligations under the charterparty, nor in fact any obligation of the charterer under the bill of lading, for *ex hypothesi* there is none. A new contract appears to spring up between the ship and the consignee on the terms of the bill of lading.'[50]

As the bill of lading now 'regulates the relations between . . . carrier and . . . holder', the Hague/Visby Rules will bite, where applicable, and their provisions will apparently have retrospective effect.

8.4 SHIPOWNER'S RECOURSE AGAINST CHARTERER

The liability of the shipowner, as expressed in the terms of the charterparty, is likely to be extended considerably where the charterer has a right to issue bills of lading. This is particularly true in cases where the provisions of the Hague/Visby Rules become applicable after the bill has been indorsed to a third party. Shipowners who wish to exert some control over such extension of their liability may, as we have seen, require any bill to be issued in the standard form designed for use with a particular charterparty, or alternatively they may require the bill to include a clause specifically incorporating the terms of the charterparty.[51] Such devices afford only limited protection for the

---

[49] Problems would arise in implementing this proposal should the amount of such charges be in dispute. The Hamburg Rules now require, where relevant, outstanding loading port demurrage to be recorded on the bill. See *supra* p 224.

[50] *Hain SS Co v Tate & Lyle* (1936) 41 Com Cas 350 at p 356.

[51] See *supra* pp 239 ff.

shipowner and are more frequently replaced by clauses requiring the master to sign bills 'as presented . . . without prejudice to this charter'.[52]

On the other hand, clauses requiring the master to sign bills presented by the charterer are normally coupled with provisions requiring the charterer to indemnify the shipowner for any resulting increase in cargo liability. Thus clause 9 of the Baltime form provides: 'The charterers to indemnify the owners against all consequences or liabilities arising from . . . signing bills of lading.' Even in the absence of such an express clause, there is authority for the view that there is 'an implied term in the charterparty to the effect that, in case the charterers should present – or cause to be presented – bills of lading imposing a greater liability on the shipowners than that contained in the charterparty, the charterers would indemnify the shipowners in respect of that greater liability'.[53]

---

[52] NYPE 1993 clause 30.
[53] Lord Denning MR in *Coast Lines Ltd* v *Hudig* [1972] 1 Lloyd's Rep 53 at p 56. See also *The Garbis* [1982] 2 Lloyd's Rep 283 at pp 287–8 *per* Robert Goff J; *The Ikariada* [1999] 2 Lloyd's Rep 365 at p 372 *per* Cresswell J.

9

PROBLEMS OF COMBINED TRANSPORT

With the development of international trade and the increased use of containers, sea carriage may form only one leg of a combined transport contract. Modern contracts of carriage are frequently negotiated on a door-to-door basis and involve not only a series of different modes of carriage, but also a succession of different carriers. Such contracts may take a variety of forms:

1 A freight forwarder may act as the shipper's agent and create a series of individual carriage contracts with separate carriers by rail, road or sea. Each such contract will be independent and subject to the relevant unimodal terms and conventions. In such circumstances the freight forwarder will normally exclude any personal liability for damage or loss during carriage and transhipment from one mode to another will normally be stated to be at the cargo owner's risk.

2 An alternative arrangement would be for a specific carrier (or freight forwarder) to act as principal for one stage of the carriage and as agent for the shipper to negotiate independent contracts of carriage for the other stages. Thus a sea carrier may arrange for transport of the containers by road to the port of loading and for delivery by rail from the port of discharge. In such a case each carrier would only be responsible for his own stage and each of the series of contracts would be subject to its own relevant unimodal terms and conventions. Here again, provision would be made for any transhipment to be at the risk of the cargo owner.

3 A third possibility is for a combined transport operator to negotiate a single contract for multimodal transport on a door-to-door basis. Under such a scheme, the combined transport operator would remain solely responsible to the cargo owner for the safety of the goods during transit, having negotiated separate contracts for the different legs with individual unimodal carriers. The essence of such an arrangement is that the cargo owner would not be in contractual relations with individual 'actual carriers' and his rights and liabilities would depend solely on the terms of the combined transport contract.

Many modern shipping documents are now drafted in a form in which they can be used interchangeably for either combined transport, through transport or on a port-to-port basis, and include terms appropriate for each contingency.[1]

The main problem encountered by the parties to a multimodal contract stems from the potentially wide variety of terms and conditions of carriage in operation between the

---

[1] For example, P & O Nedlloyd bill, Conline bill, ACL bill.

different modes. The problem is aggravated by the existence of a series of mandatory transport conventions[2] imposing different liability regimes on the operators of the various modes of transport. Attempts to produce a uniform multimodal regime have so far been unsuccessful,[3] but the gap has been partially filled by the production of a set of Rules for a Combined Transport Document by the International Chamber of Commerce ('ICC') which are available to be incorporated by the parties into their individual contracts.[4] In the absence of any agreement on an international uniform regime, modified versions of the ICC rules have appeared in a variety of standard forms of bill.[5]

In approaching the formulation of a set of rules to govern multimodal transport, two alternative solutions have been advanced. Proponents of the 'uniform' approach advocate that a single uniform regime of liability should govern the contract from the point of dispatch to the final destination. Supporters of the alternative 'network' solution take a more pragmatic approach and argue that where it can be established at what stage of the transit the particular loss or damage occurred, then the liability of the carrier should be regulated by the appropriate convention or national law applicable to that particular mode of transport. While the former is obviously the more rational solution, the 'network' approach avoids any potential conflict with existing mandatory unimodal conventions.

Any attempt to solve the problem by agreement is similarly restricted, since contractual provisions are liable to be overruled where a unimodal convention is mandatory on a particular leg. This problem can, however, be overstated since, in general, unimodal conventions are only applicable where the leg in question is 'international', i.e. the points of departure and arrival are located in different states.[6] In practice this means that, outside Europe, conventions other than the Hague or Hague/Visby Rules are rarely relevant.

A brief account will now be given of the legal problems encountered in formulating and interpreting a multimodal contract for the carriage of goods.

9.1 THE LIABILITY OF THE CARRIER

In the absence of an applicable mandatory international convention, the parties to a combined transport contract are, of course, entitled to negotiate their own terms and can impose on the carrier a uniform liability throughout the period of transit. Even if an international convention is applicable on one leg, the parties may still agree on a

---

[2] That is, Warsaw convention (air), CIM convention (rail), CMR convention (road) and Hague, Hague/Visby, or Hamburg Rules (sea).

[3] The CMI draft TCM convention was abandoned in 1972 while the UNCTAD Convention on Multimodal Transport adopted in May 1980 has not yet received sufficient ratifications to bring it into operation. For main provisions, see *infra* pp 251–2.

[4] The ICC Rules for a Combined Transport Document (1975) were modelled on the provisions of the TCM convention.

[5] For example, P & O Nedlloyd, ACL, Combicon bills.

[6] Exceptions to the 'international' rule are provided by Art 2 of the CMR Convention (Convention applicable throughout journey where goods carried 'piggy-back', e.g. roll-on, roll-off) and Art 2 of the CIM Convention (covering ancillary collection and delivery services).

uniform liability throughout the remainder of the transit. In the majority of cases, however, the extent of the carrier's liability will be dependent on locating the place where the damage or loss occurred.

9.1.1 LOCATING DAMAGE OR LOSS

(I) WHERE KNOWN ON WHAT STAGE DAMAGE OR LOSS OCCURRED

Where the location of the damage or loss can be identified, then any unimodal international convention or mandatory national law applicable to that leg will operate to define the carrier's liability. Such international conventions may be applicable either by statute as, for example, the Hague/Visby Rules by the Carriage of Goods by Sea Act 1971, or may be incorporated into the contract by the use of an appropriate paramount clause.

Should no international convention or national law be applicable, however, the parties are then free to contract on their own terms and a wide variety of solutions is apparent from the standard forms. Some bills provide that a specific convention shall be applicable to a particular leg,[7] others include a formula to restrict the liability of the combined transport operator to the amount recoverable from any sub-contractor to whom he has delegated performance of the particular stage in question.[8] The ICC Rules, and many bills based on them, aim at achieving uniformity by providing that the same regime of carrier liability shall be applicable as if the location of the damage had not been identified.[9]

(II) WHEN NOT KNOWN ON WHAT STAGE DAMAGE OR LOSS OCCURRED

Here by definition no unimodal convention will be applicable and the parties will have freedom to draft their own contract. Once again, a variety of different solutions is evident from a perusal of the standard forms. In order to gain the maximum protection for the carrier, some bills raise the presumption that the loss occurred during the sea leg and thus invoke the Hague or Hague/Visby Rules as appropriate.[10] Other carriers devise their own code of liability, while many adopt the ICC Rules.[11]

The ICC code is based on the combined transport operator ('CTO') assuming liability for the goods throughout their transit from the time of taking them into his charge until the time of delivery at their destination.[12] Moreover, he accepts responsibility for the acts of his servants or agents 'acting within the scope of their employment'[13] and for the acts of other persons 'whose services he uses for the performance of the contract'.[14] The latter omnibus phrase would clearly embrace independent contractors, such as sub-contracting 'actual' carriers, and stevedores employed by him. The CTO is

---

[7] Combicon bill 11(2): Combidoc 11(i)(b).
[8] Tranztas bill 5(B)(2)(c).
[9] ICC Rules 13(d). See also Combidoc 11(i)c.
[10] ACL bill clause 3IV.
[11] ICC Rules for a Combined Transport Document.
[12] Rule 5(e). See also Combidoc 9(1); Multidoc 95, clause 10(a).
[13] Rule 5(b). See also Combidoc 9(2); Multidoc 95, clause 10(c).
[14] Rule 5(c). See also Combidoc 9(2); Multidoc 95, clause 10(c).

liable for such loss or damage occurring during transit unless he can bring it within a list of specific exceptions,[15] the burden of proof resting on him. It is permissible to extend the protection of the ICC Rules to any servant or 'other person' engaged by the CTO to perform the contract.[16]

9.1.2 LIMITATION OF LIABILITY

Contracts of carriage invariably contain a clause limiting the liability of the carrier though conventions, where mandatory, prescribe a baseline. Here again, the importance in combined transport of establishing precisely where the loss occurred is exemplified by the widely varying minimum limits imposed by the different conventions ranging from 17 SDRs per kilo for air transport to 2 per kilo under the Hague/Visby Rules.[17]

In an attempt at uniformity, the ICC Rules prescribe a minimum limit of 30 Poincaré francs (roughly equivalent to 2 SDRs) per kilo in situations where no specific convention is applicable, and in many modern combined transport documents this has been converted into 2 SDRs per kilo or into the more precise figure of 2 or 2.5 US dollars per kilo.[18]

The problem for the cargo owner in this situation is that it is impossible to predict before transit begins which limit will be applicable in the event of his goods suffering damage. Everything will depend on the stage on which the damage or loss was suffered and whether that stage can be identified. Only in cases where this fact cannot be established, or where no international convention is applicable, can the parties rely on the uniform limit prescribed by the carriage contract.[19]

9.1.3 CLAIMS IN TORT

In combined transport, performance of individual legs is frequently subcontracted by the CTO to independent carriers. In such an event there is no contractual relationship between the cargo owner and the actual carrier, the latter having concluded a unimodal contract with the CTO and being presumably bound by any relevant unimodal convention. There is, therefore, nothing to prevent the cargo owner from suing the actual carrier in negligence and thus circumventing any limitation clause in his contract with the CTO.

This loophole can, of course, be closed by any of the traditional methods employed in a similar situation by the draftsmen of ocean bills of lading. On the one hand, the introduction of a Himalaya clause into a bill of lading is designed to extend to servants, agents or independent contractors all the protection afforded to the carrier by the terms

---

[15] Rule 12.

[16] Rule 18.

[17] For a definition of SDR, see *supra* p 201. The precise limits per kilo of the gross weight of the cargo are 17 SDRs for air (Warsaw), 16⅔ for rail (CIM), 8⅓ for road (CMR) and 2 for sea (Hague/Visby). In sea transport alone, there is an alternative of 666.67 SDRs per package or unit.

[18] See e.g. Combicon bill 10(3).

[19] This situation may, however, frequently arise in the case of containerised cargo. Note that in certain bills there is a presumption that in such an event the loss occurred during the sea leg, thus invoking the low limit in the Hague or Hague/Visby Rules.

of the contract of carriage.[20] A similar result can be achieved by the use of a circular indemnity. This type of clause is based on the theory that, while no provision in a contract between A and B can regulate the conduct of X, who is not a party to that contract, it is possible to require B, should he subsequently enter into contractual relations with X, to use that opportunity to control X's activities in the required manner, or to compensate A for any loss suffered as the result of his failure to do so. Thus a time or voyage charter may require any bills of lading issued under it by the charterer to contain clauses prohibiting holders of the bill, in the event of cargo damage, from suing any other party than the carrier, with a proviso for the charterer to indemnify the shipowner in case of default. This device is of particular use where a number of container operators have decided to pool their carrying capacity by entering into a consortium agreement. Under such an arrangement, consortium members are entitled to exchange space[21] on their own vessels for space on the vessels of other members in order to provide a regular rationalised service. In practice this is done by a member either chartering space on another operator's vessel[22] or hiring his containers.[23] In either event the need is felt to protect the container operator from actions brought by the other member's customers. This result is achieved by constructing a chain of indemnity clauses originating in the Consortium Operating Agreement itself and carried through into the operator's bills of lading and contracts with sub-contractors.

The effectiveness of these circular indemnities was demonstrated in the case of *Nippon Yusen Kaisha* v *International Import and Export Ltd*[24] where a CTO obtained a perpetual injunction staying proceedings for cargo damage brought against a sub-contracting carrier by the indorsee of the bill of lading in contravention of an undertaking not to do so in the bill.

ICC Rules permit the CTO to extend the protection of the Rules to his servants or agents or any other persons 'whose services he uses for the performance of the contract'.[25]

9.2 COMBINED TRANSPORT AND DOCUMENTARY CREDITS

The need for documentary credits to finance international trade is as great when combined transport is used as when the goods are shipped by some form of unimodal carriage. From the banker's point of view, however, the security provided by the combined transport document is not as effective as that available under an ocean bill of lading. First, such a document covering the entire transit period is not statutorily recognised as a document of title. Secondly, as the goods normally originate from an inland point of shipment, the document is a 'received for shipment' bill rather than the 'shipped' bill desired by the banking fraternity.

---

[20] *The Eurymedon* [1974] 1 Lloyd's Rep 534. See *supra* at pp 151–2.
[21] Known as a 'slot'.
[22] A cross slot charterparty.
[23] A container hiring agreement.
[24] [1978] 1 Lloyd's Rep 204.
[25] ICC Rules for a Combined Transport Document: Rule 18.

Nevertheless, banking practice has had to adapt itself to the transport revolution and the first step was taken in 1969 when OCL and ACL combined transport bills of lading were recognised by the banks for port-to-port shipments but only provided that they were indorsed as 'shipped' bills. Since that time banking procedures have been considerably modified as is evidenced by the 1993 edition of the ICC's Customs and Practice for Documentary Credits. These rules now provide that, unless the credit stipulates an ocean bill of lading, a combined transport document is acceptable even in short or blank back form. This document may indicate a place of taking in charge different from the port of loading and/or a place of final destination different from the port of discharge, and may relate to cargoes in containers or pallets. Even though the credit does stipulate an ocean bill of lading, a combined transport document is acceptable, provided that on its face it has been issued and signed by a named carrier or his agent and contains a 'shipped' notation on a named ship. Finally, to complete the picture, unless the credit requires an 'on board' document, banks will accept a document which indicates merely that the goods have been taken in charge or received for shipment.[26]

9.3 EFFECT OF TRANSHIPMENT

By its very nature, combined transport consists of a series of unimodal stages, with transhipment taking place at the end of each stage. Such transhipment periods are not usually covered by any of the existing unimodal conventions[27] with the result that the parties have freedom of contract and the CTO is able to exclude liability during this operation. This problem is avoided in many of the standard combined transport bills by the CTO accepting liability from the time the goods come into his charge until they are delivered to the consignee.[28]

More difficulties arise, however, where provision is made for transhipment during a particular leg in the event of it not being convenient for the CTO to perform the contract himself. Such a situation would arise where the CTO undertakes to carry the goods for part of the journey but reserves the right to tranship in certain circumstances, as, for example, where he does not have an adequate consignment for a particular port.[29] Again, transhipment may be recognised as part of the system where a series of interconnecting services is involved. Here again, there will be no problem if such transhipment is permitted by the terms of the bill and the CTO accepts liability throughout the entire period of transit.

Where the transhipment takes place during the sea leg and the CTO falls within the definition of a carrier in Art I(a) of the Hague or Hague/Visby Rules, he is entitled to sub-contract but cannot exclude his own liability during the sea leg while the carriage is covered by a bill of lading.[30] Thus, even though the contract expressly provides him with

---

[26] See UCP 500 (1993 edn) Arts 23 and 26.
[27] A possible exception is under Art 2 of the CMR Convention.
[28] For example, Combidoc 9(1); Combicon bill 9(1); Multidoc 95, clause 10(a).
[29] Conline bill 6. A somewhat similar situation arises where the contract makes provision for sub-contracting, as, for example, chartering a substitute vessel: Conline bill 6.
[30] See Art III, rule 8.

an option to tranship, he will remain fully responsible under Art III for the safety of the goods during the transhipment period.[31] The only possible exception may be the case where transhipment during the sea leg is envisaged by the parties as constituting two separate contracts each covered by its own separate bill. In such circumstances the CTO may be permitted to exclude his personal liability under the Hague or Hague/Visby Rules for the on-carriage.[32] Arrangements of this type are rare since a single through bill is preferred where commercial credits are involved.

9.3.1 TRANSHIPMENT AND DOCUMENTARY CREDITS

The combined transport operation has two main disadvantages from the bankers' point of view where commercial credits are involved. First, banks normally require a 'shipped' document for security purposes, whereas the combined transport bill is a 'received for shipment' document. Secondly, bankers are reluctant to accept the risks of transhipment and in the past have been inclined to outlaw clauses permitting such practices. The problem is now largely solved by the modern combined transport document under which the CTO accepts responsibility for the goods from the time of receipt to the time of delivery.[33] This fact is now recognised in the 1993 edition of the ICC Rules which provide that, unless transhipment is prohibited by the terms of the credit, banks will accept transport documents which indicate that the goods will be transhipped, provided the entire carriage is covered by one and the same transport document.[34] Indeed, the Rules go even further by stating that even though transhipment is prohibited by the terms of the credit, transport documents making provision for transhipment will be accepted if specified requirements are satisfied.[35]

9.4 MULTIMODAL CONVENTION 1980

This brief survey of the problems raised by combined transport will be concluded by a summary of the main provisions of the Multimodal Convention signed in 1980. This Convention was drafted under the auspices of UNCTAD, and its provisions are broadly in line with the regime established by the Hamburg Rules. It remains to be seen whether its chances of being ratified have been increased by the coming into operation of the latter convention.

The Convention is made applicable to a single multimodal transport contract between a multimodal transport operator ('MTO'), acting as principal, and a consignor, for the through movement of goods from a place of receipt in one country to a place of delivery in another by more than one form of transport.[36] It is also essential that either the

---

[31] *Mayhew Foods* v *OCL* [1984] 1 Lloyd's Rep 317.
[32] *Captain* v *Far Eastern* [1979] 1 Lloyd's Rep 595. For a full discussion of the problem, see *supra* pp 182 ff.
[33] See Combidoc 9(1); Combicon bill 9(1); Multidoc 95, clause 10(a).
[34] ICC Customs and Practice for Documentary Credits 500 (1993 edn) Art 23(c).
[35] *Ibid* Art 29(c).
[36] Article 1.

place where the goods are taken in charge, or the place where they are delivered, is located in a contracting state.[37]

The MTO remains responsible for the goods throughout the period from the time he takes them in his charge until the time of their delivery.[38] His liability follows the pattern established by the Hamburg Rules, being based on the concept of presumed fault,[39] though subject to a similar limitation based on the higher of 920 units of account per package or unit or 2.75 per kilo of the gross weight of the goods.[40] An interesting innovation here is that if no sea leg is involved in the transit then the limitation is based solely on weight, i.e. 8.33 units of account per kilo.[41] Where the MTO delegates performance of the contract to a sub-contractor, such 'actual carrier' is entitled to invoke any of the Convention defences available to the MTO, including the limitation provisions.[42]

One of the perennial problems facing the draftsmen of a multimodal convention is whether to adopt a 'uniform' or 'network' solution to the problem of the multimodal operator's liability. Clearly there are advantages in imposing a liability which is uniform throughout the period of carriage, rather than one which varies with each leg; on the other hand difficulties may result from a conflict with existing unimodal conventions. In the event, the Multimodal Convention attempts a compromise, depending on whether or not the location of the damage can be ascertained. If it cannot be ascertained then the MTO's liability, based on presumed fault, will be uniform throughout, as will the limitation provisions outlined above. On the other hand, if the damage can be located on a particular leg, then, although liability will remain uniform throughout, network limitation will apply, provided that the relevant unimodal limitation is higher than the amount prescribed in the Convention.[43]

---

[37] Article 2.

[38] Article 14.1.

[39] Article 16. For a definition of 'presumed fault' and a discussion of the corresponding provisions of the Hamburg Rules, see *supra* Chapter 7.

[40] Article 18.1.

[41] Article 18.3. This is equivalent to the limitation amount prescribed by the CMR Convention governing road transport. There is an alternative limit provided for loss arising from delay in transit: Art 18.4.

[42] Article 20.2.

[43] Article 19.

Part Four

COMMON ASPECTS OF CONTRACTS OF AFFREIGHTMENT

10

EXCEPTIONS

Provisions are invariably to be found in contracts of affreightment exempting the parties from liability for damage or loss resulting from specified contingencies. In the unlikely event of the absence of any express stipulations in the contract, the carrier is allowed to invoke the four common law exceptions of act of God, Queen's enemies, inherent vice, and a general average sacrifice.[1] Otherwise in charterparties and bills of lading falling outside the ambit of the Hague/Visby Rules, the parties are entitled to negotiate their own terms and the range and extent of such exceptions will be dependent on their respective bargaining powers. In the context of bills to which the Rules are applicable, however, the protection afforded to the carrier is restricted to the catalogue of 17 exceptions listed in Art IV rule 2.

An almost limitless variety of exceptions is available ranging from perils of the sea to defective packing and even negligent navigation. While such clauses were originally introduced into charterparties for the protection of the shipowner, many modern forms provide that the various perils are 'always mutually excepted'.[2] In such cases the exceptions are equally available to the charterer, although many of them may not be relevant to the obligations which he is required to fulfil.[3] In the following pages an attempt will be made to describe some of the more widely used exceptions which are incorporated into the contract of carriage by the common law, by agreement or by statute.

10.1 COMMON LAW EXCEPTIONS

10.1.1 ACT OF GOD

This exception can only be invoked where the damage or loss is solely attributable to natural causes independent of any human intervention. In the words of James LJ in the early case of *Nugent* v *Smith*,[4] ' "Act of God" is a mere short way of expressing this proposition: A common carrier is not liable for any accident as to which he can show that it is due to natural causes, directly and exclusively without human intervention, and

---

[1] These are the exceptions available to the so-called 'common carrier', i.e. the carrier who operates a general ship and holds himself out as willing to carry goods for anyone who may wish to employ him. As contracts of carriage invariably include clauses expressly excluding liability, the concept is in practice important only where the carrier loses the protection of the contract as the result of a deviation or some other fundamental breach. See *supra*, at p 21.

[2] For example, NYPE 46 clause 16.

[3] See *The Kalliopi A* [1987] 2 Lloyd's Rep 263.

[4] (1876) 1 CPD 423 at p 444.

that it could not have been prevented by any amount of foresight and pains and care reasonably to be expected from him.'

Thus damage caused by storm, frost, lightning or high wind would fall within this exception even though they may be relatively common occurrences. On the other hand, the carrier will not be able to rely on the defence of 'act of God' if the damage could have been foreseen and reasonable steps could have been taken to prevent it. Accordingly, the shipowner in *Siordet* v *Hall*[5] could not plead the exception where cargo was damaged by water escaping from a burst pipe following a hard frost. In the opinion of the court he was aware of the likelihood of frost and should have drained the boiler while the vessel was lying in port.

Nor is the exception available where there is any human participation in the occurrence which causes the loss. The defence of act of God was, therefore, not available in a case where a vessel ran aground in fog.[6] The fact that the shipowner was in no way negligent was not material.

10.1.2 ACT OF THE QUEEN'S ENEMIES

While this is a common law exception, it is invariably to be found as an express term in contracts of carriage. It is designed to cover acts committed by states, or their subjects, with whom the Sovereign is at war[7] and is traditionally justified on the ground that otherwise the carrier would have no recourse since the parties involved are outside the jurisdiction of the national courts.[8] The exception also extends to reasonable steps taken by the carrier to avoid an imminent threat of such action as, for example, deviating into a neutral port to avoid capture.[9] It is, however, apparently confined to the activities of public enemies of the state and does not extend to robbers on land or pirates at sea.[10]

Where the carrier is a foreign national or company, the exception will cover the activities of enemies of the state to which the carrier owes allegiance.[11] In such an event the phrase 'Queen's enemies' 'means enemies of the sovereign of the carrier, whether that sovereign be an Emperor, or Queen, or a reigning Duke'.[12] Lest there should be any left out, it is usual in charterparties to add the words 'restraint of princes and rulers'. These include all cases of restraint or interruption by lawful authority.[13]

A somewhat similar exception is incorporated into bills of lading by Art IV rule 2(g) of the Hague/Visby Rules under the title of 'act of public enemies'. This presumably is intended to have the same overall effect as the common law exception, particularly when combined with the additional exception in the Rules covering 'act of war'.[14]

---

[5] (1828) 4 Bing 607.
[6] *Liver Alkali* v *Johnson* (1874) LR 9 Ex 338.
[7] Cf. *Spence* v *Chadwick* (1847) 10 QB 517 where no state of war existed and the exception did not apply.
[8] *Southecote's Case* (1601) Cro Eliz 815.
[9] *The Teutonia* (1872) LR 4 CP 171.
[10] See Byles J in *Russell* v *Niemann* (1864) 17 CB (NS) 163 at p 174.
[11] *Russell* v *Niemann* (1864) 17 CB (NS) 163.
[12] Today it would be more likely to be a President.
[13] Byles J in *Russell* v *Niemann* (1864) 17 CB (NS) at p 174. For the definition of 'restraint of princes', see *infra* at pp 260–3.
[14] Article IV rule 2(e).

10.1.3 INHERENT VICE

A carrier is not liable at common law for loss or damage which results exclusively from some inherent quality or defect of the cargo carried. The exception is most frequently invoked in the case of perishable goods such as fruit[15] or fish[16] which in the normal course of events are likely to deteriorate in quality during transit. It will also cover the inevitable wastage associated with the carriage of bulk cargo such as oil or grain, provided that such reduction in volume falls within the customary tolerance recognised in the trade. Again, certain liquids are known to ferment during carriage, while metal goods are susceptible to rust damage.[17]

Many of these characteristics are well known in the trade and the carrier, in accepting delivery of such cargo, is expected to exercise that degree of care which the nature of the goods demand. In such circumstances he is not obliged to accept the goods for carriage but if he does so, he is required 'to adopt a system which is sound in the light of all the knowledge which the carrier has, or ought to have, about the nature of the goods'.[18] The degree of care expected of the carrier will, of course, vary depending on the extent of his knowledge of the characteristics of the particular cargo. Thus in a case where a consignment of wet salted fish was shipped at Glasgow for Genoa, the carrier was not held liable for the deterioration in quality of the goods during transit since he had not been told by the shipper that the fish required refrigeration. He was allowed successfully to rely on the exception of inherent vice. 'It follows that whether there is an inherent defect or vice must depend on the kind of transit required by the contract. If this contract had required refrigeration there would have been no inherent vice. But as it did not, there was inherent vice because the goods could not stand the treatment which the contract authorised or required.'[19] Even though a clean bill of lading had been issued, the carrier would not be estopped from pleading the exception providing that the loss had resulted from the inherent unfitness of the cargo to withstand the ordinary incidents of the voyage and had in no way been aggravated by the conduct of the carrier.

The corresponding exception made applicable to bills of lading by Art IV rule 2(m) of the Hague/Visby Rules is expressed to cover: 'Wastage in bulk or weight or any other loss or damage arising from inherent defect, quality or vice of the goods.'

10.2 CONTRACTUAL EXCEPTIONS

There is a wide variety of exceptions to be found in the standard charter forms and these exceptions can be supplemented by the parties expressly incorporating the common law exceptions or the catalogue listed in Art IV rule 2 of the Hague/Visby Rules. The following is a selection of the more frequently used clauses.

---

[15] *The Hoyanger* [1979] 2 Lloyd's Rep 79.
[16] *Albacora v Westcott & Laurance Line Ltd* [1966] 2 Lloyd's Rep 53.
[17] *Tokio Marine & Fire Ins v Retla SS Co* [1970] 2 Lloyd's Rep 91.
[18] Lord Reid in *Albacora v Westcott & Laurance Line Ltd* [1966] 2 Lloyd's Rep 53 at p 58.
[19] *Ibid* at p 59.

10.2.1 PERILS OF THE SEA

This exception is broader in scope than 'act of God' in that it covers any damage to cargo caused by risks peculiar to the sea, or to the navigation of a ship at sea, which cannot be avoided by the exercise of reasonable care. Thus it extends to loss resulting from vessels running aground in fog, being driven onto rocks in a gale, or even colliding with other vessels,[20] provided that the owner of the vessel carrying the cargo was not at fault. On the other hand, the exception refers only to perils of the sea and not to perils which could equally be encountered on land or on any other form of transport. Accordingly, unlike 'act of God', it does not extend to damage caused by rain,[21] lightning or fire[22] or to loss resulting from rats or cockroaches contaminating the cargo.[23]

The exception can also be invoked to cover consequential loss arising from action taken to counteract a peril of the sea. In *Canada Rice Mills* v *Union Marine Ins*[24] a cargo of rice suffered heat damage as the result of periodic closing of ventilators and hatches during the voyage to prevent the incursion of seawater during a storm. In the view of Lord Wright, 'where weather conditions so require, the closing of the ventilators is not to be regarded as a separate or independent cause, interposed between the peril of the sea and the damage, but as being such a mere matter of routine seamanship necessitated by the peril that the damage can be regarded as the direct result of the peril'.[25]

For the exception to be applicable, the weather conditions do not need to be extreme or unexpected,[26] since storms and high seas are a relatively common occurrence in sea transit, although the shipowner is expected to exercise reasonable care in avoiding such perils where possible. On the other hand, the exception does not protect 'against that natural and inevitable action of the wind and waves which results in what may be described as wear and tear'.[27]

The exception is variously worded in different charter forms ranging from the basic 'perils of the sea' to 'dangers and accidents of the seas, rivers and navigation of whatsoever nature and kind'.[28] In the Hague/Visby Rules it appears as 'perils dangers and accidents of the sea or other navigable waters'.[29] The coverage afforded by the different versions is basically similar although, in the more extended form, it applies to navigation in inland waters in addition to on the high seas.

---

[20] *The Xantho* (1887) 12 App Cas 503.

[21] *Canada Rice Mills* v *Union Marine Ins* [1941] AC 55 at p 64 *per* Lord Wright, 'Rain is not a peril of the sea, but at most a peril on the sea.' Cf. *The Sabine Howaldt* [1971] 2 Lloyd's Rep 78 (violence of wind forcing seawater through hatch covers).

[22] *Hamilton* v *Pandorf* (1887) 12 App Cas 518 at p 527 *per* Lord Bramwell.

[23] *Ibid* at p 525 *per* Lord Watson.

[24] [1941] AC 55.

[25] *Ibid* at p 70.

[26] See *The Bunga Seroja* [1999] 1 Lloyd's Rep 512 at p 529 ('the foreseeability of the peril does not preclude the carrier from relying on the perils of the sea immunity'); cf. *The Tuxpan* [1991] AMC 2432 at p 2438 ('the test is one of foreseeability, i.e whether the conditions encountered were unusual and beyond reasonable expectation'). The two cases illustrate the difference between the Anglo-Australian and US approaches.

[27] Lord Herschell in *The Xantho* (1887) 12 App Cas 503 at p 509.

[28] See e.g. NYPE 16, STB Time 22(a) ('collision, stranding or peril, danger or accident of the sea or other navigable waters').

[29] Article IV rule 2(c).

10.2.2 COLLISIONS – BOTH-TO-BLAME CLAUSE

It has long been established that collision falls within the perils of the sea exception, although it still appears as a separate and distinct exception in many charter forms. The shipowner will not, however, be able to rely on the clause if the cargo owner can establish that the operative cause of the collision was fault on the part of the carrying vessel, since negligence overrides the exceptions.[30] Alternatively, the cargo owner will have a remedy in tort to recover the full loss if the owner of the other vessel involved was solely responsible for the collision. In the more frequent situation, where both vessels are to blame, he will be able to recover from each in proportion to their respective degrees of fault.[31]

The position is further complicated by the Hague and Hague/Visby Rules which contain a provision that, if a carrier has exercised due diligence to provide a seaworthy ship, he is not liable for loss resulting from negligent navigation.[32] Consequently, where these Rules are applicable,[33] the cargo owner will not be able to recover compensation from a carrier whether he is totally or only partially to blame for the collision. The cargo owner's remedies, if any, against the owner of the other vessel involved in the collision will, of course, be unaffected.

Problems have arisen in US courts with regard to the precise effect to be given to the exception covering navigational fault. Where cargo is lost or damaged in a collision in which both vessels are to blame, under US law the cargo owner can recover in full from the owner of the non-carrying vessel. The latter may then reclaim half of this sum from the owner of the carrying vessel under the 'divided damages' rule.[34] The overall result is that the navigational error exception is circumvented by the use of this procedure, but only where both parties are to blame for the collision. Where the owner of the carrying vessel is solely responsible, the exception bars any right of recovery by the cargo owner. The general view is that it is anomalous to exempt a carrier from all liability if he alone is guilty of negligent navigation but to hold him liable for half the loss if he is only partly to blame for the collision.

In order to avoid this 'anomaly' it is now customary to include in bills of lading or charterparties a both-to-blame clause which in effect provides that cargo owners will indemnify the carrier to the extent that he is indirectly required to pay any compensation for cargo damage under the 'divided damages' rule.[35] In view of the wide powers of

---

[30] See *infra* p 272.
[31] See Maritime Conventions Act 1911 s 1(1).
[32] Article IV rule 2(a).
[33] That is, mandatorily or by contractual incorporation into a bill of lading or charterparty.
[34] NB There is no legislation in the United States equivalent to the Maritime Conventions Act 1911.
[35] The standard form of a both-to-blame clause states: 'If the vessel comes into collision with another ship as a result of the negligence of the other ship and any act, neglect or default of the Master, Mariner, Pilot, or the servants of the Carrier in the navigation or in the management of the vessel, the Owners of the cargo carried hereunder will indemnify the Carrier against all loss or liability to the other or non-carrying ship or her Owners in so far as such loss or liability represents loss of, or damage to, or any claim whatsoever of the owners of the said cargo, paid or payable by the other or non-carrying ship or her Owners to the owners of said cargo and set-off, recouped or recovered by the other or non-carrying ship or her Owners as part of their claim against the carrying Vessel or Carrier. The foregoing provision shall also apply where the Owners, operators or those in charge of any ship or ships or objects other than, or in addition to, the colliding ships or objects are at fault in respect of a collision or contact.'

a US shipowner to attach in a US port any vessel in the same ownership as the one with which he collided, it is advisable for a shipowner to make use of this clause if it is likely that any of his vessels might call at a US port.

When tested in the US courts, however, such a clause in a bill of lading has been held invalid as conflicting with 'a general rule of law that common carriers cannot stipulate for immunity from their own or their agents' negligence'.[36] In response to the 'anomaly' argument, the US Supreme Court considered that it would be equally anomalous

> 'to hold that a cargo owner, who has an unquestioned right under the law to recover full damages from a non-carrying vessel, can be compelled to give up a portion of that recovery to his carrier because of a stipulation exacted in a bill of lading. Moreover there is no indication that either the Harter Act or the Carriage of Goods by Sea Act was designed to alter the long-established rule that the full burden of the losses sustained by both ships in a both-to-blame collision is to be shared equally. Yet the very purpose of exacting this bill of lading stipulation is to enable one ship to escape its equal share of losses by shifting a part of its burden to its cargo owners . . . If that rule is to be changed, the Congress, not the shipowners, should change it'.[37]

Continuing adherence to this approach was demonstrated in the more recent case of *The Frances Hammer*[38] where, in a bill of lading, a choice of Danish law and jurisdiction clause was rejected on the ground that it was merely designed 'to avoid the law of the United States and to litigate in Denmark the validity of the both-to-blame clause'.[39]

Despite the attitude of US courts, both-to-blame clauses are still widely used in carriage contracts since their validity when incorporated in documents other than bills of lading has not yet been tested. Some support for a more optimistic view is to be found in *American Union Transport Inc* v *USA*[40] where a Californian court held valid a both-to-blame clause in a charterparty in a situation where the shipowner had contributed, under the 'divided damages' rule, towards a claim for cargo loss. The trial judge drew a distinction between bill of lading and charterparty contracts and indicated that in the latter the parties are free to make their 'own contract for carriage, including an exemption from liability for negligence – unless the provisions of the Harter Act are expressly incorporated in the charter agreement or bills of lading have been issued which fail to indicate that the ship is a private carrier'.[41] Particular stress was, however, laid on the fact that in this case no bills of lading were issued and that the charterers made use of the entire capacity of the vessel. Doubts must therefore exist as to the validity of a both-to-blame clause in a bill of lading issued under a charterparty once it is negotiated into the hands of a party other than the charterer.

10.2.3 RESTRAINT OF PRINCES

This exception is designed to cover any active and forcible intervention by a government or state authority in time of peace which prevents or interferes with performance of the

---

[36] Black J in *USA* v *Atlantic Mutual Ins Co* [1952] AMC 659 at p 661.
[37] *Ibid* at pp 663–4.
[38] [1975] 1 Lloyd's Rep 305.
[39] *Ibid* at p 307, *per* Wyatt DJ.
[40] [1976] AMC 1480.
[41] *Ibid* at p 1482.

carrier's obligations under a contract of affreightment. Examples of such intervention include restrictions on trade,[42] embargoes,[43] blockade[44] or the application of customs or quarantine regulations.

Actual forcible interference is not essential so long as there is an imminent threat of force being applied. Thus in *Rickards v Forrestal*[45] the owner of a German ship was entitled to rely on the exception when, on the outbreak of World War II, he complied with the orders of the German government by putting into a neutral port and depriving the plaintiff of his cargo. In the view of Lord Wright, the fact that the shipowner was in a neutral port and not subject to the direct control of the German government was irrelevant. 'There may be a restraint though the physical force of the state concerned is not immediately present. It is enough, I think, that there is an order of the state addressed to a subject of that state, acting with compelling force on him, decisively exacting his obedience and requiring him to do the act which effectively restrains the goods.'[46] Again, it is immaterial that the orders of the state authority cannot be enforced against a ship which habitually trades outside the jurisdiction if the owner is resident within the jurisdiction and can be subject to imprisonment on failure to comply.[47]

Shipowners faced with the imminent threat of state intervention may still rely on the exception to cover any loss resulting from such avoiding action as they may take. Some doubt, however, exists as to the degree of risk which must be established before such action is permissible. Thus in *Watts v Mitsui*,[48] where a vessel had been chartered to ship a cargo from a port in the Sea of Azov to Japan, the owner withdrew the vessel from the charter because of a fear that the Turkish government was on the point of closing the Dardanelles with the result that his ship would be trapped in the Black Sea. Although the House of Lords was of the opinion that the shipowner's apprehension was reasonable,[49] it held that the withdrawal was not covered by the exception 'restraint of princes'. In the opinion of Lord Loreburn, 'if the situation had been so menacing that a man of sound judgment would think it foolhardiness to proceed with the voyage, I should have regarded that as in fact a restraint of princes. It is true that mere apprehension will not suffice, but on the other hand it has never been held that a ship must continue her voyage till physical force is actually exercised.'[50] In contrast, the owner of a ship chartered to carry a cargo of phosphate rock from Florida to a Dutch port on the

---

[42] *Miller v Law Accident Ins Co* [1903] 1 KB 712.

[43] *Seabridge Shipping Ltd v Antco Shipping Ltd* [1977] 2 Lloyd's Rep 367.

[44] *Geipel v Smith* (1872) LR 7 QB 404.

[45] [1942] AC 50. See also Lord Reading CJ in *Sanday & Co v British & Foreign Marine Ins Co* [1915] 2 KB 781 at p 802: 'A political or executive act may . . . be an act of interference, and of forcible interference, notwithstanding that force is not actually exerted. The Executive has the power of compelling obedience to its orders by the exercise of force if necessary; the force need not be actually physically present when the master of a vessel submits to an order of the Executive. The master acts in obedience to such order without requiring the exertion of force to coerce him into submission, because it would be useless to refuse to submit.'

[46] [1942] AC 50 at p 81.

[47] *Furness Withy & Co v Banco* [1917] 2 KB 873.

[48] [1917] AC 227.

[49] In fact the Turkish government closed the Dardanelles some 25 days after the shipowner refused to nominate a vessel under the charter.

[50] [1917] AC 227 at p 236.

river Ems was held entitled to abort the charter and rely on the exception when the German army gained control of the river during World War I. In reply to the argument that the owners could have completed the contract by chartering a neutral ship, the trial judge commented: 'I cannot see my way to hold that the defendants were bound to pay large sums of money or to run big risks, or both, in order to deprive themselves of the protection of an exception inserted in the contract for their own benefit.'[51]

To what extent may the exception be relied on where the risk of state intervention is known to the parties at the time of contracting? In *Ciampa v British India Steam Nav Co*[52] a cargo of lemons loaded at Naples for London was severely damaged while being subjected to a process of deratisation in Marseilles as required by a decree of the French government. The shipowners were aware that such action was likely to be taken as the vessel had a foul bill of health having originally sailed from a plague-ridden port. In refusing to allow the shipowner to invoke the exception, Rowlatt J expressed the opinion that 'the facts which bring that law into operation must be facts which have supervened after the ship has started on the voyage in question. When facts exist which show conclusively that the ship was inevitably doomed before the commencement of the voyage to become subject to a restraint, I do not think that there is a "restraint of princes".'[53]

On the other hand, the value of exceptions would be severely curtailed if they were never applicable to risks which existed prior to the conclusion of the contract, particularly where such risks were unknown to the parties involved. In *The Loch Dee*[54] the charterer was permitted to rely on the laytime exception covering 'intervention of constituted authorities' when the time for loading was extended by local labour regulations which, unknown to the parties, prohibited stevedores from working between 9 p.m. and 6 a.m. In rebutting the argument that this had been local practice in the port for some time, Sellers J commented: 'In this contract there are exceptions dealing with delay by reason of ice, epidemics, labour or political disturbances. Any of these might in given circumstances be proved to have existed at the time the contract was made but, if the circumstances were unknown to the parties, it seems to me that they could be relied on if they existed and caused delay when the vessel arrived for loading and discharge.'[55]

Two final restrictions on the scope of the exception must be noted. First, it applies purely to acts of state authorities and not to non-governmental bodies such as mobs, rebels or guerrillas.[56] Secondly, while the exception covers acts of state it does not extend to provide protection against ordinary judicial process. So it was not available where goods were detained as the result of a civil action,[57] though it has been held that

---

[51] *Phosphate Mining Co v Rankin* (1915) 21 Com Cas 248 at p 251. See also *Nobel's Explosives v Jenkins* [1896] 2 QB 326.

[52] [1915] 2 KB 774.

[53] *Ibid* at p 779.

[54] (1948) 82 LlLR 430.

[55] *Ibid* at p 438. See also *Reardon Smith v Ministry of Agriculture* [1960] 1 QB 439 at pp 493–5; affd. [1962] 1 QB 42 at pp 83, 107, 128.

[56] *Nesbitt v Lushington* (1792) 4 TR 783. Cf. *The Silver Sky* [1981] 2 Lloyd's Rep 95 where requisitioning of a vessel by the leader of the FNLA, the party which ultimately lost the civil war in Angola, was held to fall within the exception 'restraint of princes'.

[57] *Finlay v Liverpool & Great Western SS Co* (1870) 23 LT 251.

the intervention of a special military court did not constitute ordinary judicial process for this purpose.[58]

The corresponding exception made applicable to bills of lading by Art IV rule 2(g) of the Hague/Visby Rules extends cover for the carrier to 'seizure under legal process'.

10.2.4 STRIKES OR LOCKOUTS

The protection afforded by this exception has expanded in line with developments in industrial relations over the past century. Originally envisaged as providing cover for shipowners in the event of withdrawal of labour resulting from a dispute as to wages or conditions of work, the term 'strike' was defined by Sankey J in 1915 as 'a general concerted refusal by workmen to work in consequence of an alleged grievance'.[59] Since that time the term has been more broadly interpreted to extend to a sympathetic strike where the workers involved had no personal grievance with their employers,[60] and to a case where the refusal to work a night shift involved no breach of contract on the part of the workforce.[61] In the latter case the trial judge commented that 'a strike does not cease to be a strike whether or not the appropriate epithet is "general", or "partial", "sympathetic" or "political"'.[62]

On the other hand, the withdrawal of labour must retain some connection, however tenuous, with an industrial dispute and consequently the exception has been held not to cover a stoppage of work by miners through fear of cholera,[63] or the refusal of a crew to sail because of the possibility of attack by enemy submarines.[64] Perhaps more questionable is the view expressed by the US Court of Appeals in *The Marilena P*[65] that the term 'strike' could cover the refusal of officers and crew, on political grounds, to sail with a cargo of military combat equipment to Vietnam.

An attempt to reconcile these cases and produce an all-embracing modern definition was made by Lord Denning MR in *The New Horizon*:[66] 'I think a strike is a concerted stoppage of work by men done with a view to improving their wages or conditions, or giving vent to a grievance, or making a protest about something or other, or supporting or sympathising with other workmen in such endeavour. It is distinct from a stoppage which is brought about by an external event such as a bombscare or by apprehension of danger.'

Authority suggests that the exception covers not only loss caused directly by the strike itself, but also consequential loss resulting from the after effects of the stoppage. So the charterers in *Leonis v Rank (No 2)*[67] could rely on the exception where loading

---

[58] *The Anita* [1970] 2 Lloyd's Rep 365; reversed on other grounds [1971] 1 Lloyd's Rep 487.
[59] *Williams Bros v Naamlooze* (1915) 21 Com Cas 253 at p 257.
[60] *The Laga* [1966] 1 Lloyd's Rep 582.
[61] *The New Horizon* [1975] 2 Lloyd's Rep 314.
[62] Ackner J in [1974] 2 Lloyd's Rep 210 at p 214.
[63] *Stephens v Harris* (1887) 57 LT 618 at p 619.
[64] *Williams Bros v Naamlooze* (1915) 21 Com Cas 253.
[65] [1969] 2 Lloyd's Rep 641.
[66] [1975] 2 Lloyd's Rep 314 at p 317.
[67] (1908) 13 Com Cas 295.

had been delayed owing to congestion following a strike which had been settled before the chartered vessel reached the loading port.[68]

The increasing impact of strikes on maritime trade in recent years has led to the traditional strike exception being supplemented by specific strike clauses in standard charter forms. These range from clauses which place the entire risk of time lost through strikes on the charterers,[69] to clauses which protect the charterer from liability for the resultant delay, but only during the continuance of the strike itself.[70] The Gencon general strike clause on the other hand, attempts to strike a balance between the interests of shipowner and charterer by relieving both parties from responsibility 'for the consequences of any strikes or lock-outs preventing or delaying the fulfilment of any obligations under this contract'.[71]

A completely different approach is adopted by the *Caspiana* clause which seeks to protect the shipowner from the expense of an idle ship being detained at a strikebound port. Should the port named in the charter prove to be affected by a strike, this clause permits him to discharge the cargo at 'any other safe or convenient port'. In such an event the consignee is not entitled to recover the cost of later transhipping the goods to their intended destination once the strike is over.[72] In view of the fact that it is almost impossible to assess in advance the likely cost to the cargo owner should this clause be invoked by the carrier, it is not surprising that such clauses are not popular with bankers where security for commercial credits is required.[73]

The corresponding strike exception incorporated in Art IV rule 2(j) of the Hague/Visby Rules is designed to give wide protection being made expressly applicable to 'strikes or lockouts or stoppage or restraint of labour from whatever cause, whether partial or general'.

10.2.5 DEFECTIVE PACKING

This exception is designed to cover the situation where goods have been packed in such a manner that they will not withstand the ordinary hazards likely to be encountered during transit. In essence it is a specific example of inherent vice and may even, in many cases, amount to neglect on the part of the shipper in failing to take reasonable care when shipping the goods. The use of packaging which is normal or customary in the trade will generally exonerate the shipper even though it cannot guarantee protection against every possible form of damage.[74]

Many cases of insufficiency of packing will be obvious on shipment, in which case it is advisable for the carrier to note the precise details on the bill of lading. But mere

---

[68] See also Willmer LJ in *Reardon Smith Line* v *Ministry of Agriculture* [1962] 1 QB 42 at p 102; *The Onisilos* [1971] 2 QB 501.
[69] The Baltic Conference special strike clause 1936.
[70] The Centrocon strike clause.
[71] 'Consequences' include the after effects of a strike: see *The Onisilos* [1971] 2 QB 501. See now Gencon 94 clause 16, which refers to 'strikes or lock-outs preventing or affecting *the actual loading or discharging of the cargo*'.
[72] See *Renton* v *Palmyra Trading Corp* [1957] AC 149.
[73] But see now UCP Art 26(iii)(a).
[74] See *Continex Inc* v *SS Flying Independent* [1952] AMC 1499 at p 1503.

knowledge of the state of packing will not prevent the carrier from later pleading the exception providing that the resultant damage or loss was in no way aggravated by any lack of care on his part.[75] Indeed, it has been agreed that such knowledge will not result in a higher degree of care being required of the carrier since 'the shipper cannot cast the burden of extra special stowage on the carrier by simply not packaging the shipment properly'.[76]

On the other hand, problems will arise where a clean bill of lading has been issued by a carrier who subsequently seeks to rely on the exception. So in *Silver v Ocean Steamship Corp*[77] clean bills were issued in respect of a consignment of frozen Chinese eggs which were shipped in 42 lb tins, loaded on trays of 84 tins each, without being protected by any form of packing. When many tins arrived at their destination severely damaged, the carrier was estopped from invoking the exception against a consignee who had relied in good faith on the clean bill. Greer LJ remarked that 'in this case, where the insufficiency [of packing] was obvious, the shipowners were nevertheless prepared to take the goods without complaint and give a clean bill that the goods were shipped in good order and condition. I think that the capacity of the goods safely to travel was part of their order and condition; and so, being apparent on the face of it, I cannot see how the shipowners can now say that the goods were insufficiently packed.'[78] In this respect defective packing differs from other forms of inherent vice which are not obvious to the carrier on shipment.[79]

10.3 THE HAGUE/VISBY EXCEPTIONS

The majority of exceptions incorporated into the Hague/Visby catalogue follow the traditional pattern outlined above and in this section it is intended to concentrate on the three exceptions which are unique to the Convention.

10.3.1 ACT, NEGLECT, OR DEFAULT OF THE MASTER, MARINER, PILOT, OR THE SERVANTS OF THE CARRIER IN THE NAVIGATION OR IN THE MANAGEMENT OF THE SHIP

Exceptions covering errors in navigation or in the management of a ship have a long history dating back to the nineteenth century and were frequently incorporated into bills of lading long before the advent of the Hague and Hague/Visby Rules. In its basic form, designed merely to provide protection for 'errors of navigation', the exception is inapplicable once negligence on the part of the carrier is established.[80] However, it is

---

[75] *Gould v SE & C Rly* [1920] 2 KB 186.
[76] *S M Wolff Co v SS Exiria* [1962] AMC 436 at p 441.
[77] [1930] 1 KB 416.
[78] *Ibid* at p 440. Scrutton LJ added (at p 427) 'I cannot think that a shipowner who receives, say, a wooden case broken open at one corner or side can describe it as "in apparent good order and condition" and afterwards prove the opposite.'
[79] See *supra*, at p 257.
[80] *The Satya Kailash* [1984] 1 Lloyd's Rep 588.

more commonly drafted to cover situations in which negligence is involved. The modern version first appeared in statutory form in s 3 of the US Harter Act 1893 which provided that, where the shipowner exercised due diligence to make his vessel seaworthy, he should not be liable 'for damage or loss resulting from faults or errors in navigation or in the management of said vessel'. A similar pattern was followed in the Hague and Hague/Visby Rules in Art IV rule 2(a), the text of which is quoted above.[81]

Despite its antiquity and the respectability of its lineage, the exception has been the target of considerable criticism from cargo interests and is regarded as somewhat of an anachronism in many parts of the world.[82] It affords a protection to the sea carrier which is not available in any other transport convention and it is noticeable that it has not been retained even for sea transport in the Hamburg Rules.[83]

The Hague/Visby exception covers fault in both the navigation and management of the ship. Little difficulty has been experienced in interpreting the phrase 'faults of navigation'. Thus it has been held to cover cargo damage where, due to the negligence of the master or crew, the vessel struck a reef,[84] ran aground[85] or collided with another vessel.[86] Again, where the Rules have been incorporated in a charterparty, the exception has extended beyond cargo damage to loss caused by negligent collision with the charterer's wharf,[87] or with the vessel to which the chartered ship was rendering lightering services.[88]

More problems have been encountered in seeking to distinguish fault in the management of the ship, which falls within the exception, from the carrier's duty under Art III rule 2 to take proper care of the cargo. Each case must be decided on its own facts but uncertainty has arisen because the same negligent act frequently affects both the safety of the vessel and the safety of the cargo. In such circumstances the courts tend to have regard to the property primarily affected by the conduct in question. In the words of Sir Francis Jeune in *The Glenochil*:[89] 'The distinction I intend to draw . . . is one between want of care of cargo and want of care of the vessel indirectly affecting the cargo.' This dictum was later amplified by Greer LJ[90] who expressed the distinction as follows:

> 'If the cause of the damage is solely, or even primarily, a neglect to take reasonable care of the cargo, the ship is liable, but if the cause of the damage is a neglect to take reasonable care of the

---

[81] For the purposes of construction of Art IV Rule 2(a), Lord Hailsham LC expressed the view in *Gosse Millerd Ltd* v *Canadian Government Merchant Marine Ltd* [1929] AC 223 at p 230, that he was 'unable to find any reason for supposing that the words, as used by the legislature in the Act of 1924, have any different meaning to that which has been judicially assigned to them when used in contracts for the carriage of goods by sea before that date'. The provision is retained unaltered in the Hague/Visby Rules which are attached as a Schedule to the Carriage of Goods by Sea Act 1971.

[82] See UNCTAD: *Report on Bills of Lading*, pp 39–40.

[83] See *supra*, at pp 217–18.

[84] *The Portland Trader* [1964] 2 Lloyd's Rep 443.

[85] *Complaint of Grace Line* [1974] AMC 1253.

[86] *The Xantho* (1887) 12 App Cas 503.

[87] *The Aliakmon Progress* [1978] 2 Lloyd's Rep 499.

[88] *The Satya Kailash* [1984] 1 Lloyd's Rep 588.

[89] [1896] P 10 at p 19.

[90] *Gosse Millerd* v *Canadian Government Merchant Marine* (1927) 29 LlLR 190 at p 200. Originally a dissenting judgment in the Court of Appeal, the view of Greer LJ was upheld on appeal by the House of Lords in [1929] AC 223.

ship, or some part of it, as distinct from the cargo, the ship is relieved from liability; for if the negligence is not negligence towards the ship, but only negligent failure to use the apparatus of the ship for the protection of the cargo, the ship is not so relieved.'

Thus negligent stowage,[91] or the failure properly to secure the cargo during discharge, is conduct primarily directed towards cargo care and any resultant damage is not covered by the exception. Similarly, in *Gosse Millerd* v *Canadian Government Merchant Marine*[92] a vessel had to go into dock for repairs and the hatches were left open to provide ease of access. Due to failure to replace the tarpaulins, rainwater penetrated the hold and damaged the cargo of tinplate. In the view of the House of Lords, as the tarpaulins were provided to protect the cargo, the conduct in question related to the care of cargo rather than management of the ship.

Conversely, where the primary objective is the safety of the vessel, it is immaterial for this purpose that the negligent conduct also affects cargo. So in the Canadian case of *Kalamazoo Paper Co* v *CPR Co*[93] a vessel was seriously damaged after hitting a rock and was beached in order to prevent her sinking. The cargo owners claimed for cargo damage alleging negligence on the part of master and crew in failing to use all available pumping facilities in order to keep the water level down after the vessel had grounded. The Supreme Court of Canada held that, in the circumstances, the use of the pumping machinery affected the general safety of the ship and consequently the actions of the crew fell within the 'management of the ship' exception.

'The further question is whether an act or omission in management is within the exception when at the same time and in the same mode it is an act or omission in relation to the care of cargo. It may be that duty to a ship as a whole takes precedence over duty to a portion of the cargo; but, without examining that question, the necessary effect of the language of Art III rule 2, "subject to the provisions of Art IV", seems to me to be that once it is shown that the omission is in the course of management, the exception applies, notwithstanding that it may be also an omission in relation to cargo. To construe it otherwise would be to add to the language of clause (a) the words "and not being a neglect in the care of the goods".'[94]

Nevertheless, the distinction is a fine one and, with every decision depending on its own particular facts, it is often difficult to forecast whether or not the exception will apply. Thus, after an earlier conflicting decision, it would appear that negligence in the maintenance or use of refrigeration equipment, or other of the ship's apparatus designed to protect cargo, would now fall outside the management exception.[95]

---

[91] *The Frances Salman* [1975] 2 Lloyd's Rep 355; *The Washington* [1976] 2 Lloyd's Rep 453.

[92] [1929] AC 223.

[93] [1950] 2 DLR 369.

[94] Rand J at *ibid* p 378. See also *Leval & Co* v *Colonial Steamship Co* [1961] 1 Lloyd's Rep 560. In both these cases the court took the view that the negligent conduct in question was directed primarily to ensure the safety of the vessel. Tetley, however, argues in *Marine Cargo Claims*, at p 399, that irrespective of the primary objective, 'where the single error is both in the management of the ship and in the care of the cargo, the carrier normally is not responsible because the error is, in effect, relative to the whole venture'.

[95] *Foreman & Ellams* v *Federal SN Co* (1928) 30 LlLR 52. Cf. *Rowson* v *Atlantic Transport Co* [1903] 2 KB 666 where the point was made that the refrigeration equipment in question was used to preserve both cargo and also the crew's food. This distinction was rejected by Wright J in *Foreman & Ellams* v *Federal SN Co*, at p 62.

10.3.2 FIRE, UNLESS CAUSED BY THE ACTUAL FAULT OF PRIVITY OF THE CARRIER

The Hague/Visby exception relating to fire excludes the carrier from responsibility for loss or damage arising or resulting from fire 'unless caused by the actual fault or privity of the carrier'.[96] Consequently, while a carrier is not liable for fire damage resulting from the negligent conduct of his servants or agents, for whose acts he would otherwise be vicariously liable, he will lose the protection of the exception where he is personally at fault. The presence or absence of such personal fault is primarily a question of fact to be decided by reference to all the circumstances of a particular case.[97]

While a decision on actual fault or privity is never an easy one, it is particularly difficult where the party involved is a public company. As such an organisation can only act through agents, it is often difficult to decide whether a particular negligent act is to be regarded as an act of the company itself or merely an act of its servants or agents. It follows, therefore, that the actual fault or privity which is required to exclude the exception is 'the fault or privity of somebody who is not merely a servant or agent for whom the company is liable upon the footing *respondeat superior*, but somebody for whom the company is liable because his action is the very action of the company itself'.[98] Such a person has been variously described as 'the directing mind',[99] 'the head or brain'[100] or the 'alter ego'[101] of the company.

In the case of a public company, its articles normally vest the right to exercise the company's powers in a board of directors and confer on the latter the power to delegate such exercise to a managing director. In these circumstances, the acts of such a managing director may properly be regarded as the acts of the company itself. So in *Lennard's Carrying Co v Asiatic Petroleum Co Ltd*[102] shipowners sought to limit their liability for fire damage to a cargo of benzine resulting from the vessel running aground in a storm due to lack of power caused by defective boilers. The shipowners had delegated management of their vessel to a firm, the managing director of which took an active part in the operation of the vessel. Although he was aware, or had reasonable means of knowing, of the defective condition of the boilers, he gave no special instructions to the ship's officers and took no steps to prevent the vessel going to sea in an unseaworthy

---

[96] Article IV Rule 2(b). The term 'actual fault or privity' also appeared in s 502(1) of the Merchant Shipping Act 1894, dealing with statutory exclusion of liability for fire damage, and in s 503 of the same Act, dealing with the overall limitation of shipowner liability. The definition of the term would appear to be identical in all three cases, and the examples cited in the following pages are drawn largely from cases interpreting these two sections of the Merchant Shipping Act.

[97] See Lord Brandon in *The Marion* [1984] 2 Lloyd's Rep 1 at p 4.

[98] Viscount Haldane LC in *Lennards Carrying Co v Asiatic Petroleum Co Ltd* [1915] AC 705 at p 713.

[99] Denning LJ in *Bolton (Engineering) Co Ltd v Graham & Sons Ltd* [1957] 1 QB 159 at p 172.

[100] Wright J in *Tempus Shipping Co v Louis Dreyfus* [1930] 1 KB 699 at p 710.

[101] Viscount Haldane LC in *Lennards Carrying Co v Asiatic Petroleum Co Ltd* [1915] AC 705 at p 715. The last phrase was criticised by Lord Reid in *Tesco Supermarkets Ltd v Nattras* [1971] 2 All ER 127 at p 132: 'In some cases the phrase *alter ego* has been used. When dealing with a company, the word *alter* is misleading. The person who speaks and acts as the company is not *alter*. He is identified with the company.' For a persuasive interpretation of Viscount Haldane's approach, see Lord Hoffman in *Meridian Global Funds v Securities Commission* [1995] 3 All ER 918 at pp 922–7.

[102] [1915] AC 705.

condition. His negligence in this regard was held to constitute 'actual fault or privity' on the part of the shipowners.[103]

Again, shipowners are entitled to delegate performance of many of their obligations to subordinates and, provided that they have exercised due care in their appointment, will normally be regarded as having discharged their obligations in this respect. The negligence of such agents will not normally amount to actual fault or privity so as to bar the shipowner from invoking the fire exception.[104] There would, however, appear not to be an unrestricted power of delegation even to an otherwise competent master. While a substantial number of reputable shipowners completely rely on the judgment of their masters in matters relating to the navigation and equipping of their vessels, recent cases suggest that the majority exercise varying degrees of supervision to ensure that their masters are performing their duties properly. In such circumstances, failure to exercise adequate supervision may amount to actual fault or privity on the part of shipowners, thus denying them the protection of the fire exception.[105]

This exception is rarely invoked since carriers in the past have preferred to rely on the somewhat similar protection afforded by s 502(1) of the Merchant Shipping Act 1894.[106] Indeed, even less reliance is likely to be placed on the exception in future following the replacement of s 502(1) by s 18 of the Merchant Shipping Act 1979, which came into force on 1 December 1986. Under the latter provision the burden of proof shifts to the cargo owner who, in order to recover for his loss, has to establish that the fire resulted from the carrier's 'personal act or omission, committed with intent to cause such loss, or recklessly, and with knowledge that such loss would probably result'.

The protection provided by the Hague/Visby Rules does, however, have two advantages over its statutory counterpart. First, the exception has general application to all 'carriers', as defined by the Rules, whereas the cover offered by the Merchant Shipping Acts extends only to owners of British ships. Secondly, the latter form of relief can only be relied on in respect of cargo damage resulting from fire on board the carrying vessel itself, whereas the Hague/Visby exception is designed to cover the entire carriage operation from tackle to tackle and so will provide relief for the carrier, for example, where cargo is damaged by a fire on board a lighter during the discharging operation.

Reliance cannot be placed on the exception where the operative cause of the loss is a failure on the part of the carrier to exercise due diligence, before and at the beginning of the voyage, to provide a seaworthy ship. Thus in *Maxine Footwear Co Ltd* v *Canadian Government Merchant Marine*[107] a deck officer, after loading had been completed, caused a fire by instructing the employee of an independent contractor to clear ice from the scupper pipes by the use of an oxyacetylene lamp, which resulted in the vessel having to be scuttled. While the cause of the fire did not involve the 'actual fault or privity' of the shipowners, they nevertheless could not rely on the exception since the negligence of the officer, which had necessitated the scuttling of the vessel, amounted to a failure to exercise due diligence to make the vessel seaworthy at the commencement of

---

[103] For a modern example, see *The Lady Gwendolen* [1965] 1 Lloyd's Rep 335.
[104] See *Tempus Shipping Co* v *Louis Dreyfus* [1930] 1 KB 699.
[105] See *The Marion* [1984] 2 Lloyd's Rep 1.
[106] See *infra* at pp 279–80.
[107] [1959] 2 Lloyd's Rep 105. Cf. *The Apostolis* [1997] 2 Lloyd's Rep 241.

the voyage. In the words of Lord Somervell,[108] 'Art III r 1 is an overriding obligation. If it is not fulfilled and the non-fulfilment causes the damage, the immunities of Art IV cannot be relied on.'

10.3.3 THE CATCH-ALL EXCEPTION

Having listed 16 specific instances in which the carrier's liability for damage or loss will be excluded, the Hague/Visby Rules conclude the catalogue in Art IV rule 2 with the following general exculpatory provision:

> 'any other cause arising without the actual fault or privity of the carrier, or without the fault or neglect of the agents or servants of the carrier, but the burden of proof shall be on the person claiming the benefit of this exception to show that neither the actual fault or privity of the carrier nor the fault or neglect of the agents or servants of the carrier contributed to the loss or damage.'[109]

In view of the disparity of the preceding 16 specified exceptions, there seems little possibility of applying the traditional *eiusdem generis* interpretation to the phrase 'any other cause' in this context, and the words must accordingly be taken on their face value. The carrier can therefore avoid liability for any damage or loss not falling within the named exceptions providing that he can establish that it occurred without his own fault or privity and[110] it did not result from any fault or neglect on the part of his servants or agents. Subsequent cases have established that the employees of an independent contractor engaged by the carrier must be regarded as the servants or agents of the carrier for this purpose.[111]

An example of a carrier successfully discharging this burden of proof is provided by the case of *Goodwin, Ferreira & Co v Lamport & Holt*[112] where a crate, being lowered into a lighter, broke open and its contents fell out damaging bales of cotton yarn already stowed in the lighter. The carrier avoided liability by establishing that the lid of the crate had been insecurely fastened on shipment and that the incident had involved no lack of care on the part of his servants or agents. There would appear to be a difference of opinion as to whether the carrier, in such circumstances, has the burden of proving the actual cause of the loss or damage in addition to proving the absence of negligence on his part.[113] In many cases the mere fact that the cause of loss is inexplicable means that the burden cannot be discharged. In other cases, however, the carrier may be able to establish a sound system of work even though he cannot pinpoint the precise cause of the damage. In the words of Atkinson J, 'It is not necessary for the defendants to establish exactly why and how the damage occurred, provided that they can disprove negligence; but, of course, it is not easy to do that unless they can establish some

---

[108] *Ibid* at p 113.
[109] Article IV rule 2(q).
[110] The Court of Appeal in *Hourani* v *Harrison* (1927) 32 Com Cas 305 held that the word 'or' in Art IV rule 2(q) must be read as 'and'.
[111] *Heyn* v *Ocean SS Co* (1927) 137 LT 158; *Leesh River Tea Co* v *British India SN Co* [1967] 2 QB 250.
[112] (1929) 34 LlLR 192.
[113] In favour of this view, see *Pendle & Rivet* v *Ellerman Lines Ltd* (1928) 29 LlLR 133 at p 136. Cf. *The Vermont* [1942] AMC 1407 at p 1410.

reasonably possible alternative explanation. If the damage is entirely unexplained, it is difficult to see how the onus can be discharged.'[114]

Problems have also arisen with regard to the applicability of the exceptions to cases of pilferage and theft. It was early held that such activities did not fall within the 'management of the ship' exception,[115] nor could the carrier invoke Art IV rule 2(q) where there had been theft of cargo by the carrier's servants or even by employees of a firm of stevedores engaged by the carrier to discharge the cargo.[116] Such actions were hardly committed 'without the fault or neglect of the agents or servants of the carrier'.

A questionable distinction was, however, drawn in *Leesh River Tea Co v British India SN Co*[117] where damage to cargo resulted from the theft of a storm valve cover by stevedores employed by the carrier to discharge a cargo of tea at Port Sudan. The carrier satisfied the court that the theft had involved no negligence on the part of the ship's officers and crew, but the question still remained as to whether he had to take responsibility for the acts of the stevedores who, admittedly, were independent contractors.

The Court of Appeal drew a distinction between thefts committed in the course of employment, i.e. thefts of cargo, and thefts which had no connection with the work the independent contractors were engaged to perform. As the theft of the storm valve cover formed no part of the discharging operation, the carrier was not required to take responsibility for it and could accordingly invoke the rule 2(q) exception to defeat the cargo owner's claim. Sellers LJ justified the decision in the following way:

> 'In the present case the act of the thief ought, I think, to be regarded as the act of a stranger. The thief in interfering with the ship and making her, as a consequence, unseaworthy, was performing no duty for the shipowner at all, neither negligently, nor deliberately, nor dishonestly. He was not in fact their servant . . . The appellants were only liable for his acts when he, as a servant of the stevedores, was acting on behalf of the appellants in the fulfilment of the work for which the stevedores had been engaged.'[118]

10.4 BARS TO THE EXCEPTIONS

As we have seen, once the cargo owner has established that the goods have been lost or damaged during transit, the burden of proof shifts to the carrier, if he is to avoid liability, to show that such loss or damage is covered by an exception. The same rule apparently applies whether the claim is made in respect of a charterparty or a bill of lading governed by the Hague/Visby Rules[119] and is based on the premise that the exception protects the shipowner from what would otherwise be 'the absolute liability of a common carrier'.[120] Unfortunately damage to cargo is not always attributable to a

---

[114] *Phillips & Co v Clan Line Steamers Ltd* (1943) 76 LlLR 58 at p 61.
[115] *Hourani v Harrison* (1927) 32 Com Cas 305 at p 310 *per* Bankes LJ; *Leesh River Tea Co v British India SN Co* [1966] 2 Lloyd's Rep 198 at p 199 *per* Sellers LJ.
[116] *Hourani v Harrison, supra.*
[117] [1966] 2 Lloyd's Rep 198.
[118] *Ibid* at p 200. The distinction is a trifle strained and has not gone unchallenged: see Tetley at pp 522–3.
[119] See Lloyd J in *The Hellenic Dolphin* [1978] 2 Lloyd's Rep 336 at p 339.
[120] See Willes J in *Notara v Henderson* (1872) LR 7 QB 225 at p 235.

single cause and, where a variety of factors are involved, it is important to draw a distinction between an immediate[121] or operative cause (*causa causans*, or *causa proxima*) and one which contributes to the loss, but is more remote (*causa sine qua non*). Only if the exception covers the former will the shipowner avoid liability.

So in *Hamilton v Pandorf* [122] a cargo of rice had been shipped under bills of lading which included an exception covering 'dangers and accidents at sea'. During the voyage rats gnawed a hole in a pipe which resulted in seawater escaping and damaging the cargo. The question at issue was whether the rats or the influx of water was the immediate and proximate cause of the loss. In holding that the shipowners were covered by the exception, Lord Fitzgerald expressed the view that 'The remote cause was in a certain sense the action of the rats on the lead pipe, but the immediate cause of the damage was the irruption of seawater from time to time through the injured pipe caused by the rolling of the ship as she proceeded on her voyage.'[123]

It therefore follows that if the evidence is inconclusive and the shipowner or carrier fails to establish the proximate cause of the loss, then he will be unable to rely on the exception.[124] Again, no protection will be afforded by the exception where the excepted peril could have been avoided by the exercise of reasonable care or where the operative cause of the loss was the unseaworthiness of the vessel or a fundamental breach of the contract of carriage. Brief reference must be made to each of these possibilities.

10.4.1 NEGLIGENCE

In the words of Willes J, 'The exception in the bill of lading only exempts the shipowner from the absolute liability of a common carrier, and not from the consequences of the want of reasonable skill, diligence and care.'[125] No peril is an 'act of God', 'restraint of princes', or 'danger of the sea' if its occurrence could have been avoided by the exercise of reasonable care.[126] However, once the carrier has established a prima facie case that the loss falls within the scope of an exception, the burden of proof shifts to the cargo owner to prove that in fact the operative cause of the loss was the carrier's negligence.[127] If he fails to discharge that burden, the carrier is entitled to rely on the exception.

10.4.2 UNSEAWORTHINESS

Similarly, a shipowner or carrier will not be allowed to invoke an exception where the cargo owner can establish that the immediate cause of the loss was not the excepted peril but the unseaworthiness of the vessel. Thus in *Standard Oil of New York v Clan Line Steamers*,[128] where a turret ship capsized in a storm, the shipowners were not

---

[121] *Per* Lord Watson in *Hamilton v Pandorf* (1887) 12 App Cas 518 at p 525.
[122] (1887) 12 App Cas 518.
[123] *Ibid* at p 528. NB The exception would not have been applicable if the immediate cause of the loss had been the action of the rats since such action would not be regarded as a danger peculiar to the sea.
[124] See Lord Brandon in *The Popi M* [1985] 2 Lloyd's Rep 1 at p 6.
[125] *Notara v Henderson* (1872) LR 7 QB 225 at p 235.
[126] See *Siordet v Hall* (1828) 4 Bing 607.
[127] *The Glendarroch* [1894] P 226. See also *Raymond & Reid v King Line Ltd* (1939) 64 LlLR 254.
[128] [1924] AC 100.

entitled to rely on the exception perils of the sea once the court was satisfied that the operative cause of the loss was their failure to instruct the master in the methods of handling a ship of this type. Such failure rendered the vessel unseaworthy.[129]

10.4.3 FUNDAMENTAL BREACH

According to the traditional view, in the event of a fundamental breach of contract, as for example the vessel deviating from the agreed course, the cargo owner could repudiate the contract with the result that the carrier could no longer rely on any of the contractual exceptions.[130] If, however, the cargo owner decided to waive the breach and continue with performance of the contract, the carrier was entitled once more to rely on the protection of the exemptions.[131] Following the decision of the House of Lords in *Photo Production Ltd* v *Securicor Transport*,[132] it would now appear to be a matter of construction whether a particular exception could be invoked by a shipowner in the aftermath of a fundamental breach of the contract of carriage.[133] An example of how such an approach might operate in practice is provided by the recent case of *The Kapitan Petko Voivoda*,[134] where cargo was stowed on deck in breach of an express undertaking for underdeck carriage. When the cargo suffered seawater damage as the result of the vessel running into heavy weather, the carrier sought to rely on the Hague Rules exceptions. Langley J took the view that 'An owner who contracts to carry goods under deck but in fact wrongfully carries them on deck cannot, I think, rely on the exemptions of "perils at sea" or "insufficiency of packing" to exclude liability if the cause of damage to the cargo is the deck carriage and it would not have occurred if the cargo had been carried under deck.'[135] On the other hand, if the loss would have been suffered in any event, irrespective of whether the cargo was stowed on or under deck, then the carrier might claim the protection of appropriate exemptions. Possible examples might be provided by loss resulting from fire, act of God or negligent navigation, but everything would depend on the facts of the particular case.

---

[129] See also *Maxine Footwear Ltd* v *Canadian Government Merchant Marine* [1959] AC 589; *The Farrandoc* [1967] 2 Lloyd's Rep 276.

[130] See *Morrison & Co* v *Shaw, Savill & Co* [1916] 2 KB 783 (charterparty); *Stag Line* v *Foscolo Mango* [1932] AC 328 (bill of lading).

[131] See *Hain SS Co* v *Tate & Lyle* (1936) 41 Com Cas 350; *Suisse Atlantique* v *NV Rotterdamsche Kolen Centrale* [1967] 1 AC 361.

[132] [1980] 1 Lloyd's Rep 545.

[133] For a full discussion of the effects of fundamental breach and deviation, see *supra* at pp 21 ff.

[134] [2003] 2 Lloyd's Rep 1.

[135] At p 7. This point was not contested when the case later went on appeal to the Court of Appeal.

11

LIMITATION OF LIABILITY

11.1 INTRODUCTION

One of the unique features of maritime law is the shipowner's right to limit his liability for loss or damage resulting from negligent navigation or management of his vessel. Originating in the nineteenth century, the limitation rule is one of the first examples of protectionism in the form of state support for the shipping industry. Its retention at the present day is justified not so much on its history as on its providing the shipowner with a calculable risk before embarking on a trading venture. According to Lord Denning MR, it 'is a rule of public policy which has its origin in history and its justification in convenience'.[1] The argument is that if the maximum liability of the shipowner can be assessed in advance then it should be easier and cheaper to obtain insurance cover – a factor also important to the injured party if he can thus be certain of recovery in the event of loss.

Historically two main systems of limitation of liability have developed over the years. In its earliest form, a shipowner's liability was limited to the value of his vessel together with the current freight.[2] This system still operates in many countries, including *inter alia* the United States, but has two serious disadvantages. On the one hand, the older and more decrepit the vessel, the more likely that claims will arise but the smaller will be the compensation fund. On the other hand where, as in the United States, the fund is limited to the value of the vessel after the casualty, plus the pending freight, only the minimum of compensation is likely to be recovered, particularly if the vessel is lost in the collision.[3]

The alternative formula based on the tonnage of the vessel was introduced in the United Kingdom in 1854,[4] and has subsequently been adopted in a series of international conventions drafted in the twentieth century. A fund is thus created, varying with the size of the vessel involved, out of which virtually all claims for personal injury and property damage have to be met.[5] Should the claims exceed the amount of the fund,

---

[1] *The Bramley Moore* [1964] P 200 at p 220. See also Griffiths LJ in *The Garden City (No 2)* [1984] 2 Lloyd's Rep 37 at p 44. 'It is a right given to promote the general health of trade and in truth is no more than a way of distributing the insurance risk.'

[2] A similar example of liability being limited to the value of the adventure is provided by the public company where liability is limited to the amount of capital invested in the business.

[3] A minimum of $400 per ton must, however, be made available in such an event to cover loss of life or personal injury: see 46 USCA para 183(b).

[4] Merchant Shipping Act 1854.

[5] Separate limits exist for oil pollution claims under the Merchant Shipping (Oil Pollution) Act 1971 and the Merchant Shipping Act 1974.

they are abated pro rata. While this formula often will produce a larger fund than under the old 'valuation' system, there is still the problem that such a method of calculation may unduly benefit the owners of smaller vessels, since the latter are often capable of inflicting an equal amount of damage to their larger counterparts.

Until recently limitation of liability in the United Kingdom was governed by s 503 of the Merchant Shipping Act 1894 as amended by the Merchant Shipping (Liability of Shipowners and Others) Act 1958,[6] which incorporated the provisions of the 1957 International Convention Relating to the Limitation of Liability of Sea Going Ships. As from 1 December 1986, however, this legislation was repealed by the Merchant Shipping Act 1979 which gave the 'force of law' to the provisions of the 1976 International Convention on Limitation of Liability for Maritime Claims. The latter Convention was drafted under the auspices of the International Maritime Organisation,[7] and its provisions are now to be found in Sch 7 of the Merchant Shipping Act 1995.

11.2 MERCHANT SHIPPING ACT 1995[8]

The need for a radical change in the limitation regime had been recognised following widespread criticism of the 1957 convention. In the space of some 20 years, inflation and fluctuations in the price of gold had so eroded the real value of the existing limits that it had been found necessary to establish a separate limit of liability for oil pollution claims[9] in order to ensure adequate levels of compensation, and the trend seemed likely to continue. Concern had also been expressed as to the impact of inflation on the level of liability of owners of smaller ships at a time when it was felt that the insurance market had the capacity to absorb the higher costs likely to result from a substantial rise in the limits.

The following are the main changes introduced by the 1979 Act.

11.2.1 PARTIES COVERED

Article 1.1 of the Convention, attached as Sch 7 to the 1995 Act, entitles shipowners and salvors to limit their liability in accordance with the provisions of the 1976 Convention. The term 'shipowner' is defined as including not only the owner of a vessel, but also a charterer, manager or an operator of a seagoing vessel.[10] The expression covers any type of charterer, whether time, voyage or by demise, although it was originally argued that the protection of limitation under the Convention was only

---

[6] For the reaction of the courts to forum shopping between the 1957 and 1976 Conventions, see *The Herceg Novi* [1998] 2 Lloyd's Rep 454; *Bouygues Offshore* v *Caspian Shipping Co* [1998] 2 Lloyd's Rep 461.

[7] As of 20 September 2003, the Convention was in force in 41 states including, *inter alia*, the United Kingdom and 10 other members of the EU, together with Australia, Japan, Liberia, Norway and Poland. For the law prior to 1 December 1986, see the first edition of this book, pp 260–5.

[8] For a general review, see Gaskell, N (ed) *Limitation of Liability – The New Law* (1986) and Griggs and Williams, *Limitation of Liability for Maritime Claims*, 3rd edn (1998).

[9] Merchant Shipping (Oil Pollution) Act 1971.

[10] Article 1.2. But a charterer might not be able to limit liability against claims brought by his shipowner: *The Aegean Sea* [1998] 2 Lloyd's Rep 39.

available to such charterers when acting in a manner equivalent to that of a shipowner e.g. in the management and operation of the vessel.[11] The Court of Appeal in *CMA CGM SA v Classica Shipping Ltd*[12] rejected this gloss on the word 'charterer', holding that in interpreting an international convention the words used must be given their natural meaning free from any English law preconceptions. Accordingly, a charterer was entitled to limit his liability, not only when acting *qua* shipowner, but also when acting in his normal capacity as a charterer, e.g. when defending an action by his shipowner for breach of charterparty. In the case in question fire and explosions aboard a vessel resulted in its abandonment. Ship and cargo were subsequently salvaged and the vessel required substantial repairs. The shipowners sought compensation claiming that the fire and explosions resulted from the shipment of dangerous cargo in breach of the charterparty, whereupon the charterers sought to limit their liability under the 1976 Convention. The Court of Appeal saw no objection to a charterer invoking the Convention limitation against a claim by his shipowner, provided that the particular claim fell within those listed in Art 2. In the words of Longmore LJ, 'a charterer's ability to limit will depend upon the type of claim that is brought against him rather than the capacity in which he was acting when his liability was incurred'.[13] In the event the court held that liability to indemnify for cargo claims discharged by the shipowners fell within Art 2, whereas claims in respect of loss of or damage to the ship did not. The latter were accordingly not subject to limitation.[14]

There may also be some doubt as to whether the term 'shipowner' can be construed to cover a ship repairer, shipbuilder or mortgagee. Such persons may, however, qualify in appropriate circumstances under Art 1.4, which extends the protection of the Convention to any person for whose act, neglect or default the shipowner is responsible, should such person be sued directly. Finally, although the shipowner may not be personally liable on a claim, Art 1.5 provides that, for limitation purposes, 'the liability of the shipowner shall include liability in an action brought against the vessel herself'.

One of the more important changes introduced by the 1976 Convention is the extension of the benefit of limitation to salvors. Prior to 1986 salvors were entitled, along with other shipowners, to limit their liability in respect of claims arising from the navigation or management of their vessels, but not for claims resulting from acts or omissions of persons either not on board the tug or not involved in its management. So the owner of a salvage tug in *The Tojo Maru*[15] was not able to plead limitation when one of his divers, operating in the sea, negligently damaged the vessel being salvaged.

---

[11] See David Steel J in *CMA CMG SA v Classica Shipping Ltd* [2003] 2 Lloyd's Rep 50 at p 54; see also *The Aegean Sea* [1998] 2 Lloyd's Rep 39 at p 49 *per* Thomas J: 'it was intended for claims by cargo interests and other third parties external to the operation of the ship against those responsible for the operation of the ship'.

[12] [2004] 1 Lloyd's Rep 460.

[13] [2004] 1 Lloyd's Rep, at p 469.

[14] 'We have decided that it is only in respect of damage to cargo and not in respect of damage to the ship (or consequential loss resulting from such damage) that the charterers in this case can limit their liability.' [2004] 1 Lloyd's Rep, at p 470 *per* Longmore LJ.

[15] [1972] AC 242.

Under the 1976 Convention, however, the right of limitation is extended to salvors, who constitute 'any person rendering services in direct connection with salvage operations'.[16] Servants or agents of the salvor, for whose acts or omissions the salvor would otherwise be liable, may similarly claim the benefit of limitation if they are sued personally.[17]

A further innovation in the 1976 Convention is the extension of cover to insurers of the party liable, who are entitled to limit their liability to the same extent as their assured.[18]

So far as the vessel involved in the incident is concerned, the provisions of the 1995 Act are applicable not only to a normal ship but also to 'any structure (whether completed or in course of completion) launched and intended for use in navigation as a ship or part of a ship'.[19] The right to limit extends to any ship, whether seagoing or not.[20]

11.2.2 TYPES OF CLAIM COVERED

An attempt has been made in the 1976 Convention to bring an increased range of claims within the ambit of the limitation fund. As with previous conventions, the primary thrust of the limitation provisions is directed at 'claims in respect of loss of life or personal injury or loss of or damage to property (including damage to harbour walls, basins and waterways and aids to navigation), occurring on board or in direct connection with the operation of the ship or with salvage operations and consequential loss resulting therefrom'.[21] Also covered are claims resulting from delay in the carriage of cargo or passengers by sea; claims in respect of the infringement of rights other than contractual rights; claims in respect of the raising, removal or destruction of wreck; claims in respect of the removal and destruction of cargo, and third-party claims in respect of measures taken to minimise the loss caused by the defendant.[22] Limitation will apply to all such claims whatever the basis of liability may be, and 'even if brought by way of recourse or for indemnity under a contract or otherwise'.[23]

Conversely, certain claims are specifically excluded from limitation under the Convention.[24] These include claims for salvage[25] or contribution in general average, claims for pollution and nuclear damage which are covered by separate liability regimes,[26] and claims for loss of life, personal injury or property damage caused by crew members where their contracts of service are governed by United Kingdom law.[27]

---

[16] Article 1.3.
[17] Article 1.4.
[18] Article 1.6.
[19] Merchant Shipping Act 1995, Sch 7 Part II para 12.
[20] *Ibid* para 2.
[21] Article 2.1(a).
[22] Article 2.1(b)–(f).
[23] Article 2.2.
[24] Article 3.
[25] But these do not include claims by a cargo owner against the owner of a salvaged ship for loss arising from breach of contract in failing to provide a seaworthy ship: *The Breydon Merchant* [1992] 1 Lloyd's Rep 373.
[26] That is, Merchant Shipping (Oil Pollution) Act 1971 and the Nuclear Installations Act 1965.
[27] Merchant Shipping Act 1995 s 185.

11.2.3 LIMITATION AMOUNT

The 1976 Convention introduced a substantial increase in the liability limits which have been further raised by the 1996 Protocol to the Convention which became operative from 13 May 2004.[28] The object of the Protocol is to compensate for inflation since 1976 and also to raise the limits for smaller ships to bring them into line with the cost of claims in respect of such vessels. Limitation is still to be based on tonnage, although in future it will be calculated in relation to gross tonnage as measured under the 1979 Tonnage Convention. This should result in a significant rise in the limits for certain types of vessel such as vehicle carriers and container ships. The Convention and Protocol also retain the format adopted by the 1957 Convention by providing separate and distinct limits for claims arising from loss of life and personal injury, as opposed to claims resulting from cargo damage and other losses. As with other modern conventions, the unit of account adopted for limitation purposes is the Special Drawing Right (SDR) on the International Monetary Fund.[29]

The following are the new limits operative from 13 May 2004:[30]

(i) *In respect of claims for loss of life or personal injury*

Vessel with tonnage not exceeding	2,000 tons	2 million SDRs
plus for each ton	2,001–30,000 tons	800 SDRs
plus for each ton	30,001–70,000 tons	600 SDRs
plus for each ton in excess of	70,000 tons	400 SDRs

---

[28] An Order in Council based on the powers contained in the new s 185(2A) of the Merchant Shipping Act 1995 (inserted by the Merchant Shipping and Maritime Security Act 1997 s 15) was made by Parliament on 19 May 1998 in order to give effect to the 1996 Protocol to the 1976 Convention when it received sufficient accessions to become effective. As of 5 March 2004 ten states have ratified or acceded to the Protocol which will enter into force on 13 May 2004.

[29] For definition, see *supra* at p 201.

[30] Thus in the case of claims for personal injury and property loss against a 50,000-ton vessel, the limitation fund would be calculated as follows:

'Personal' claims

Tonnage bands	Tons SDR rate	SDR total
0–2,000	–	2,000,000
2,001–30,000	28,000 × 800	22,400,000
30,001–50,000	20,000 × 600	12,000,000
		36,400,000

'Property' claims

Tonnage bands	Tons SDR rate	SDR total
0–2,000	–	1,000,000
2,001–30,000	28,000 × 400	11,200,000
30,001–50,000	20,000 × 300	6,000,000
		18,200,000
Total fund available		54,600,000

At a conversion rate on 6 March 2004 of SDR = £0.805 this would value the fund at £43,953,000 as compared with £18,649,837 under the previous 1976 Convention formula.

(ii) *In respect of claims for property damage or other loss*

Vessel with tonnage not exceeding	2,000 tons	1 million SDRs
plus for each ton	2,001–30,000 tons	400 SDRs
plus for each ton	30,001–70,000 tons	300 SDRs
plus for each ton in excess of	70,000 tons	200 SDRs[31]

States acceding to the 1996 Protocol were given a discretion as to the size of the general limits applicable to vessels with a tonnage of less than 300. In the case of the United Kingdom, by an Order in Council in 1998, the Department of Environment, Transport and the Regions opted for limits of one million SDRs for 'personal' claims and 500,000 SDRs for 'property' claims, i.e. half the minima laid down in the Protocol.[32]

Both the Convention and the Protocol retain the spill-over arrangement under which, once the fund set aside for personal injury claims has been exhausted, any outstanding personal injury claims will rank *pari passu* with claims for property damage or other losses against the fund nominally set aside for the latter claims. This means that where an incident gives rise solely to loss of life and personal injury claims, the potential fund available is the combined total of the respective limits set for personal injury and other claims. On the other hand, where only cargo claims are involved, the maximum sum available is the fund set aside after the limits for property and other claims have been applied.

11.2.4 BREAKING THE LIMITS

A radical change in the test to be applied for breaking the limits was introduced by Art 4 of the 1976 Convention which abolished the former concept of 'actual fault or privity' enshrined in the 1894 Merchant Shipping Act.[33] In future, in order to override the

---

[31] The following were the limits under the 1976 Convention prior to the coming into effect of the 1996 Protocol:

(i) *In respect of claims for loss of life or personal injury*

Vessel with tonnage not exceeding	500 tons	333,000 SDRs
plus for each ton	501–3,000 tons	500 SDRs
plus for each ton	3,001–30,000 tons	333 SDRs
plus for each ton	30,001–70,000 tons	250 SDRs
plus for each ton in excess of	70,000 tons	167 SDRs

(ii) *In respect of claims for property damage or other loss*

Vessel with tonnage not exceeding	500 tons	167,000 SDRs
plus for each ton	501–30,000 tons	167 SDRs
plus for each ton	30,001–70,000 tons	125 SDRs
plus for each ton in excess of	70,000 tons	83 SDRs

[32] The substantial increase in the limits for a 290 ton vessel is evident from the following figures:

Total fund	under 1976 Convention	500,000 SDRs	=	£402,500
	under 1996 Protocol	3,000,000 SDRs	=	£2,415,000
	under UK option	1,500,000 SDRs	=	£1,207,500

Calculated on basis of SDR value on 6 March 2004.

[33] For a full discussion of this concept, see *supra* at pp 268 ff.

limitation provisions, the claimant must prove that the loss or damage resulted from a personal act or omission of the party liable, 'committed with the intent to cause such loss or recklessly and with knowledge that such loss would probably result'. This new formulation of the test reveals a number of substantial alterations to the previous law on the subject. First, the burden of proof is shifted to the claimant so that, in cases of doubt, the party liable will be able to maintain the limit.[34] Secondly, the test is more strict, with the result that it will be much more difficult to break the limits. Not only must the loss result from a *personal* act or omission of the party liable, but it must be established that he either intended such loss or was reckless as to the consequences of his act or omission in the sense that he realised that such a loss would probably result.[35]

Problems still exist in identifying 'the party liable', particularly where the act or omission in question relates to the conduct of a public company. As such an organisation can only act through agents, it is often difficult to decide whether a particular act is to be regarded as the act of the company itself, or merely as a personal act of its servant or agents. Under the so-called '*alter ego*' test, the status of the individual concerned within the company hierarchy must be such that their acts may be properly regarded as the acts of the company itself. Membership of the board of directors or an equivalent post would seem to be a minimum requirement.[36] The acts of mere employees of the company,[37] or even of junior management, would not satisfy this test.

So far as the requisite mental element is concerned, this involves either a positive intent to cause the loss, or at least a realisation of the probable consequences of the conduct in question. It is doubtful whether such a state of mind could be attributed to the marine superintendent in *The Lady Gwendolen*[38] or to the parties liable in most of the other 'actual fault or privity' cases. Again, it would appear that in future, where duties have been delegated, 'the only personal act which is relevant must be the act of delegation. The fault of the delegate cannot be significant.'[39] The conclusion must be that the higher limits of liability introduced by the Convention have been balanced by a test which makes those limits virtually unbreakable.

---

[34] In such cases the claimant will have to bear the costs of failing to discharge the burden of proof.

[35] For further consideration of this point, see *supra* at p 204. For an authoritative discussion of the test to apply in such circumstances, see the judgment of Lord Hoffman in *Meridian Global Funds v Securities Commission* [1995] 3 All ER 918.

[36] *The Ert Stephanie* [1989] 1 Lloyd's Rep 349; *The Marion* [1984] 2 Lloyd's Rep 1; *The Lady Gwendolen* [1965] 1 Lloyd's Rep 335; *Lennard's Carrying Co v Asiatic Petroleum Co* [1915] AC 705; *The European Enterprise* [1989] 2 Lloyd's Rep 185.

[37] *The European Enterprise* [1989] 2 Lloyd's Rep 185.

[38] [1965] 1 Lloyd's Rep 335.

[39] Grime, RP, in Gaskell, N (ed) *Limitations of Liability – The New Law*, 1986, at p 108. For a full discussion of the implications of the new test, see pp 102–12 *ibid*.

12

FREIGHT

12.1 THE BASIC OBLIGATION

Freight is the consideration payable to the carrier for the carriage of goods from the port of shipment to the agreed destination. The obligation to pay freight can arise either under a voyage charter or a bill of lading contract, but must be clearly distinguished from the obligation to pay hire under a time charter. While the former payments are made in respect of the carriage of goods from one place to another, hire is payable for the right to use a vessel for a specific period of time irrespective of the extent to which it is employed by the charterer for the carriage of cargo.[1]

In the absence of agreement to the contrary, the common law presumes that freight is payable only on delivery of the goods to the consignee at the port of discharge. Payment of freight and delivery of goods are said to be concurrent conditions, in other words the carrier cannot demand payment of freight unless he is willing and able to deliver the goods at the place agreed. 'The true test of the right to freight is the question whether the service in respect of which the freight was contracted to be paid has been substantially performed, and, as a rule, freight is earned by the carriage and arrival of the goods ready to be delivered to the merchant . . .'[2] On the other hand, if goods are to be delivered by instalments, the consignee must, if required, pay for each delivery made and is not entitled to withhold payment until all the goods are delivered.

The contract of affreightment is said to be entire and indivisible, with the result that no freight is payable unless the cargo reaches the agreed destination. It is immaterial that the failure to do so is in no way attributable to the carrier as, for example, where ice in the Sea of Azov prevented the chartered ship from reaching the port of discharge.[3] Nor is it relevant that the occurrence which prevented performance is covered by an exception since an exception is intended to protect the carrier against an action for non-delivery of cargo and not to entitle him to freight which has not been earned.[4] From the cargo owner's standpoint, he has undertaken to pay freight as a *quid pro quo* for the safe delivery of his goods at the agreed destination. The only case where full freight becomes payable in such circumstances is where failure to reach the port of discharge is

---

[1] See Lord Denning MR in *The Nanfri* [1978] 2 Lloyd's Rep 132 at p 139. Hire under a time charter is frequently referred to as 'time freight' but Lord Denning drew attention to the confusion likely to arise from the use of this term since 'So different are the two concepts that I do not think the law as to "freight" can be applied indiscriminately to "hire".'
[2] Willes CJ in *Dakin v Oxley* (1864) 143 ER 938 at p 946.
[3] *Metcalfe v Britannia Ironworks Co* (1877) 2 QB 423.
[4] *Hunter v Prinsep* (1808) 10 East 378.

solely due to some act or default on the part of the cargo owner.[5] The carrier can, however, protect himself against such an eventuality in one of three ways. He can insure against such a loss of freight, he can stipulate for some proportion of the freight to be paid in advance, or he can tranship the goods and claim the full freight when they arrive at their destination.[6]

12.1.1 CALCULATION OF FREIGHT

Freight is normally assessed in relation to cargo quantity and, in such cases, the basis of the calculation will normally be specified in a freight clause in the contract of affreightment. The freight unit may take a variety of forms being quoted, for example, by weight, package or cubic measurement. Where the calculation is based on weight or measurement and, during transit, there is likely to be a variation in weight or volume of cargo, it is vital to ascertain the time at which such measurement is to be taken. The selection of the appropriate time is a matter of risk apportionment and most standard forms make provision for the assessment to take place either at the time of loading or at the time of discharge, leaving the final choice to the parties. Thus, where there is likely to be a reduction in the weight of cargo during transit due to the evaporation of liquid cargoes or loss in the normal handling of dry bulk cargoes, freight is usually assessed in relation to the amount of cargo delivered rather than the amount shipped.[7] Conversely, where cargo has a tendency to increase in weight due to absorption of moisture, then freight is likely to be assessed on the quantity shipped.[8]

12.1.2 DEDUCTIONS FROM FREIGHT

Where cargo arrives at its destination in a damaged state, or is short delivered, the agreed freight is nevertheless payable in full and the receiver is allowed no right of set-off even though the deterioration is so great that the cargo delivered is no longer worth the freight.[9] Lord Wilberforce in a recent case had no doubt 'that a claim in respect of cargo cannot be asserted by way of deduction from freight is a long established rule in English law'.[10] The consignee may, however, bring a cross-claim for compensation providing that the cause of action is not covered by an exception or is not time barred,[11] but he has no right to set-off entitling him to a deduction from freight unless such right is expressly incorporated into the contract of carriage.[12]

---

[5] *Cargo ex Galam* (1863) 15 ER 883.
[6] The right to tranship is a liberty and the shipowner is under no obligation to tranship. *The Fjord Wind* [1999] 1 Lloyd's Rep 307.
[7] See *Hansen* v *Harrold Bros* [1894] 1 QB 612.
[8] *The Metula* [1978] 1 Lloyd's Rep 5.
[9] *Dakin* v *Oxley* (1864) 143 ER 938. But damages for a subsequent repudiation of the contract of carriage can be set off against a claim for freight payable in advance. *The Dominique* [1988] 1 Lloyd's Rep 215.
[10] *Aries Tanker Corp* v *Total Transport* [1977] 1 Lloyd's Rep 334 at p 337. See also *The Brede* [1973] 2 Lloyd's Rep 333. The rule applies equally to land transport: *United Carriers Ltd* v *Heritage Food Group* [1995] 2 Lloyd's Rep 269.
[11] *Aries Tanker Corp* v *Total Transport, supra.*
[12] *The Olympic Brilliance* [1982] 2 Lloyd's Rep 206. Compare the position with regard to deductions from hire: *supra* at pp 100 ff.

The application of this rule has been described as arbitrary and there appears to be some doubt as to its rationale, but 'A rule is nevertheless capable of being a rule of law though no reason can be given for it.'[13] Lord Denning has, however, sought to justify the rule on policy grounds. In his opinion, 'The good conduct of business demands that freight should be paid according to the terms of the contract. Payment should not be held up because the goods are alleged to have been damaged in transit. If that were allowed, it would enable unscrupulous persons to make all sorts of unfounded allegations so as to avoid payment. In any case, even with the most scrupulous, it would lead to undesirable delay . . .'[14] Roskill LJ also suggests[15] that 'to alter the existing law would, or at least might, disturb the present distribution of risk between the shipowners' freight underwriters and their protection and indemnity association. At present, on the footing that there is no defence to a claim for freight, any liability of shipowners to cargo owners falls on the protection and indemnity association. If there were a defence to a claim for freight it is at least arguable that there would then be a loss of freight which would or might fall on the owners' freight underwriters and not on the protection and indemnity association.'

Freight is, however, not payable where the goods are so badly damaged on their arrival that they are unmerchantable in the sense that they no longer answer their commercial description. Thus no freight was payable on a cargo of solidified cement in *Duthie* v *Hilton*[16] which had been salvaged from a vessel that had been scuttled on the discovery of a fire in its hold. A similar result followed in *Asfar* v *Blundell*[17] where a cargo of dates, salved following a collision in the Thames, was found to be impregnated with oil and sewage and condemned as unfit for human consumption. The distinction between damaged cargo and goods which have lost their identity will always be a fine one but, in the words of Donaldson J, 'The question is whether an honest merchant would be forced to qualify the description applicable to the goods on shipment to such an extent as to destroy it. If the qualification destroys the description no freight has been earned because "the cargo" has not been delivered. If the description is merely qualified, "the cargo" has been delivered, albeit damaged or, as the case may be, contaminated.'[18]

12.1.3 THE EFFECT OF DEVIATION

If the traditional view of deviation still survives,[19] any unjustifiable deviation from the contractual voyage will amount to a fundamental breach of the contract of carriage, entitling the cargo owner to regard himself as discharged from all outstanding obligations under the contract. In such an event freight due under the contract on delivery of

---

[13] Lord Wilberforce in *Aries Tanker Corp* v *Total Transport* [1977] 1 Lloyd's Rep 334 at p 337. The reaction of Lord Simon (at p 340) can perhaps be gauged from his comment that 'Freight representing the original rule, stands uneroded, like an outcrop of pre-Cambrian amid the detritus of sedimentary deposits.' The US courts, however, appear to adopt the approach: see *Munson Steamship Line* v *Rosenthal* [1934] AMC 46.

[14] *The Brede* [1973] 2 Lloyd's Rep 333 at p 338.

[15] *Ibid* at p 347.

[16] (1868) LR 4 CP 138.

[17] [1896] 1 QB 123. See also *The Caspian Sea* [1980] 1 Lloyd's Rep 91.

[18] *The Caspian Sea* [1980] 1 Lloyd's Rep 91 at p 96.

[19] For a survey of the present position with regard to fundamental breach, see *supra* at p 21.

the goods would no longer be payable. Dicta suggest, however, that should the cargo nevertheless be carried safely to its destination, then the carrier would be able to claim a reasonable sum for freight based on a *quantum meruit* basis.[20]

12.2 ADVANCE FREIGHT

The parties to a contract of affreightment may expressly provide that the whole or part of the freight shall be payable in advance. Such a practice is frequently encountered in the liner trade and in many voyage charters and is a common requirement in transactions involving documentary credits.[21] There is, however, a strong presumption at common law that freight is only payable on delivery of the goods at destination and so any provision for advance payment must be clearly expressed. Thus in a case where goods were to be shipped from London to Lisbon, a term to the effect that 'freight for the said goods, being paid in London' was construed as indicating the place rather than the time of payment.[22]

The precise time at which freight is payable in advance may be expressed in a variety of ways such as 'on signing bills of lading', 'on sailing of vessel' or within a specified period following the occurrence of such an event.[23] Freight is then due at the time indicated and, if not paid, will remain due even though the goods are lost in transit and never reach their destination. On the other hand, should the cargo be lost or the contract be otherwise frustrated before the time fixed for payment, then the obligation to pay freight will be discharged. Accordingly, where freight was payable on 'final sailing' of the vessel, the obligation was discharged when the ship ran aground while being towed in a ship canal on its way from the docks to the open sea. In the opinion of Parke B, final sailing 'means her final departure from that port being out of the limits of that artificial cut and being at sea ready to proceed upon her voyage'.[24] Nevertheless, when freight under a voyage charter was payable 'on signing bills of lading' and the vessel sank shortly after sailing as the result of negligence of the crew, the charterer could not avoid liability for freight by failing to present the bills of lading for signature.[25]

Once freight has been paid in advance, it is not recoverable by the shipper even if the cargo is subsequently lost during the voyage, provided that such loss is covered by an exception in the relevant charterparty or bill of lading.[26] This appears to be the position at common law[27] but this is frequently reinforced by an express clause in the contract of

---

[20] *Hain Steamship Co* v *Tate & Lyle* (1936) 41 Com Cas 350 at pp 367–9 *per* Lord Wright.
[21] See UCP (1993 edn) Art 33.
[22] *Mashiter* v *Buller* (1807) 1 Camp 84.
[23] For example, 'within five days of master signing bills of lading': *The Lorna I* [1983] 1 Lloyd's Rep 373. Practical problems can arise in such cases where prepaid bills are required in support of documentary credits. The shipper may seek to delay payment until the end of the period permitted, while the shipowner will resist issuing prepaid bills, for obvious reasons, until he has actually received the freight.
[24] *Roelandts* v *Harrison* (1854) 156 ER 189 at p 195.
[25] *The Oriental Steamship Co Ltd* v *Tylor* [1893] 2 QB 518.
[26] If the loss or damage is not covered by an exception, the cargo owner can recover damages for non-delivery which will include any advance freight paid on the goods, together with the relevant insurance premium.
[27] See Sir John Donaldson MR in *The Lorna I* [1983] 1 Lloyd's Rep 373 at p 374.

carriage to the effect that freight is not refundable 'ship and/or cargo lost or not lost'. Advance freight is equally irrecoverable where the contract of carriage is frustrated before the cargo reaches its destination since, in such circumstances, there is no total failure of consideration within the rule established in the *Fibrosa* case,[28] and this situation was expressly excluded from the provisions of the Law Reform (Frustrated Contracts) Act 1943.

The principle that freight paid in advance is not refundable is unique to English law and finds no place in European legal systems, or even in the law of the United States,[29] where freight must be repaid to the charterer in the event of the cargo not reaching its destination.[30] An explanation of the special position accorded to advance freight was attempted by Hobhouse J in a recent case. 'Advance freight is not adjustable according to what subsequently occurs, it is not repayable in whole or in part even if the voyage is never completed. It is not treated as a contractual obligation to which the rules of failure of consideration, or partial failure, apply in the same way as in other branches of the law of contract. Once earned, advance freight is at the risk of the charterer and the subsequent incidents and misfortunes of the voyage do not entitle him to transfer any of that risk back to the shipowner.'[31]

The difference in approach between English and other legal systems appears to stem from the distinction drawn by Sir John Donaldson MR in *The Lorna I*[32] between the time when freight is payable and the time when freight is earned. Other legal systems appear to concentrate solely on the latter aspect and argue that if freight is not earned, it should be repayable. English law, on the other hand, regards both factors of equal importance. In the view of the Master of the Rolls, in the absence of special contractual provisions, freight is only earned when the goods are delivered at their destination. It is nevertheless possible to make freight payable in advance and, in such circumstances, 'a liability to pay advance freight does not *per se* affect the time when freight is earned. It is simply an obligation to make a payment on account of freight at a time when it has not yet been earned. However that obligation is subject to a customary incident capable of being varied or confirmed by express stipulation, that advance freight paid pursuant to the contract is not returnable or recoverable should the contract be frustrated before the freight can be earned.'[33]

In the case in question, the terms of the contract provided that advance freight was to be payable within five days of the master signing bills of lading, 'Freight non-returnable cargo and/or ship lost or not lost.' The vessel concerned was lost in heavy weather in the Black Sea before the expiry of the five-day period and the question at issue was whether

---

[28] *Fibrosa Spolka* v *Fairbairn Lawson* [1943] AC 32, see *supra* at pp 44–5.

[29] Poor W: *Charterparties and Ocean Bills of Lading* (5th edn, 1968) p 80 and cases there cited.

[30] The rule in England is, however, well established, Lord Selborne referring in 1875 to the 'peculiar rule of English mercantile law, that an advance on account of freight to be earned . . . is, in the absence of any stipulation to the contrary, an irrevocable payment at the risk of the shipper of the goods: *Allison* v *British Marine Ins Co* (1876) 1 AC 209 at p 253. See also Lord Wright in *Fibrosa Spolka* v *Fairbairn Lawson* [1943] AC 32 at p 67. Cf. the position in Scotland: *Watson* v *Shankland* (1871) Ct Sess 3rd series 142 at p 153.

[31] *The Dominique* [1987] 1 Lloyd's Rep 239 at p 246.

[32] [1983] 1 Lloyd's Rep 373.

[33] *Ibid* at p 374.

or not, in these circumstances, the charterer was liable to pay freight. The Court of Appeal took the view that no freight was either payable or earned before the expiry of the five-day period, by which time loss of vessel and cargo had frustrated the contract. The reference to freight being non-returnable in the event of the cargo being lost was construed as applying only to freight which had, or ought to have, been paid at the time the frustrating event occurred. At least one member of the court, however, was of the opinion that if the relevant freight had been paid during the five-day period, it would have been irrecoverable on the loss of the vessel.[34]

A good contrast is provided by the facts of *The Dominique*[35] where again freight was to be prepaid within five days of the signing of bills of lading but, in this case, 'full freight deemed to be earned on signing bills of lading, discountless and non-returnable, vessel and/or cargo lost or not lost . . .' The shipowners were in financial difficulties and when, during the performance of the charter, the vessel was arrested by a creditor, the charterer treated the failure of the shipowners to secure its release as a repudiatory breach of contract. The charterers were nevertheless held liable for freight since, although they had been given a five-day period in which to pay, freight was deemed to have been earned on the signing of bills of lading. In the view of Hobhouse J, 'There is thus a liability for freight as an existing debt owed by the charterer to the shipowner but the time at which that debt or liability must be discharged is postponed. The debt existed from the moment the bills of lading were signed.'[36]

The theory would appear to be that, once the liability for freight has accrued, either by the arrival of the date fixed for payment or as a result of freight being deemed to have been earned, it is treated as a liability in debt. Accordingly, the freight risk is transferred to the charterer and 'subsequent incidents and misfortunes of the voyage do not entitle him to transfer any of that risk back to the shipowner'.[37] From that point the freight risk is no longer insurable by the shipowner,[38] but is normally insured by the party making the advance payment as part of the value of the goods in respect of which the freight is paid. The practical economic burden of the risk is thus limited to the amount of the premium paid for the insurance cover.[39]

The incidence of risk is also used as a method of resolving a further problem with regard to the payment of advance freight. The question frequently arises, in relation to a payment made at the port of loading, whether such advance is on account of freight or merely a loan to the shipowner to cover ship's disbursements and current expenses. This is a question of interpretation of the terms of the contract and the intentions of the parties in each case. The burden of proof lies with the shipowner to establish that the payment was intended as advance freight since otherwise a loan would be recoverable. The usual solution to the problem is to ascertain which party is responsible for insuring

---

[34] O'Connor LJ at *ibid* p 376.

[35] [1987] 1 Lloyd's Rep 239.

[36] *Ibid* at p 245. On appeal ([1988] 1 Lloyd's Rep 215) the Court of Appeal confirmed that the entitlement to freight survived the repudiation, but held that the charterers were entitled to set off against such entitlement their claim for damages for loss resulting from the shipowners' repudiation of the charter.

[37] Hobhouse J in *The Dominique* [1987] 1 Lloyd's Rep 239 at p 246.

[38] *The Oriental Steamship Co Ltd* v *Tylor* [1893] 2 QB 518 at p 524.

[39] See UNCTAD: *Report on Charterparties*, pp 29–30.

the advance payment – if the shipper, then the payment must be intended as advance freight since a loan would not be at the shipper's risk.[40]

Where only part of the freight is payable in advance, such advance freight is regarded as part payment of the whole sum due on delivery with the result that, should any cargo be lost in transit, the merchant will only be liable for any balance if the overall freight due on the actual cargo delivered exceeds the amount paid in advance.[41] Alternatively, there will be no loss of freight paid in advance unless the freight due on the cargo eventually delivered is less than that paid in advance.

12.3 SPECIALISED TYPES OF FREIGHT

12.3.1 LUMP SUM FREIGHT

Freight may take the form of an agreed amount for the use of the whole, or part, of a ship to carry cargo on a given voyage instead of being calculated on the basis of the weight or measurement of cargo shipped.[42] Such a lump sum may still be recoverable in full even where the vessel fails to load the agreed amount of cargo provided that the failure is not due to any fault on the part of the shipowner as, for example, where it results from the shipper's failure to provide an adequate amount of cargo.[43] As with other forms of freight, lump sum freight is presumed to be payable on safe delivery of the cargo at the port of discharge, but the parties frequently provide for the whole, or a proportion, of the sum to be paid in advance.

When such freight is made payable on the 'right and true delivery' of the cargo at destination, it is not necessary for the whole of the cargo to be delivered before the carrier is entitled to payment of the lump sum freight. Thus, where part of a cargo shipped had been jettisoned on the vessel running aground, the court held the shipowner entitled to recover the full lump sum on safe delivery of the remaining goods at the port of discharge.[44] Lord Lindley pointed out that although freight was 'only payable on the right and true delivery of the cargo, those words are not taken literally but are understood to mean right and true delivery having regard to and excluding excepted perils'.[45] No judicial decision is available to indicate what precise proportion of the cargo must be delivered before freight is payable, but it is arguable that a reasonably substantial amount would be required.[46]

---

[40] *Hicks* v *Shield* (1857) 119 ER 1380 ('Cash for ship's disbursements to be advanced . . . free of interest, but subject to insurance.') NB Where any portion of the freight is payable in advance 'subject to insurance', the responsibility for insuring the advance falls on the shipper rather than the shipowner.

[41] See *Allison* v *Bristol Marine Ins Co* (1876) 1 App Cas 209.

[42] Query the difference between lump sum freight and the obligation to ship a 'full and complete' cargo at a fixed rate of freight per unit.

[43] *The Posidon* [2001] 1 Lloyd's Rep 697.

[44] *Williams & Co* v *Canton Ins Office Ltd* [1901] AC 462.

[45] *Ibid* at p 473. See also *The Norway* (1865) 13 LT 50; *The Tarva* [1973] 2 Lloyd's Rep 385.

[46] Colinvaux: *Carver's Carriage by Sea* (1982) (para 1675) argues that, as lump sum freight resembles a rent to be paid for the use of the vessel on the agreed voyages, 'it might well be contended that it is payable if she completes the voyage, whether with or without cargo'. On the other hand, it is difficult to see how the mere arrival of the vessel at the port of discharge can qualify as the 'right and true delivery of the cargo' necessary to trigger the obligation to pay freight. See Bramwell B in *Merchant Shipping Co* v *Armitage* (1873) LR 9 QB 99.

In the case cited, the loss of cargo was covered by an exception, but full freight would appear still to be payable even though the failure to deliver all the cargo shipped was attributable to fault on the part of the shipowner. In such an event the general rule against deductions from freight would operate and any resulting cargo claim would have to take the form of a separate action.[47]

Finally, it must be noted that the carrier is still entitled to claim the lump sum freight even though the cargo, or such proportion of it which reached the port of discharge, did not arrive in the original ship. The carrier is entitled to tranship the cargo if the vessel in which they were shipped becomes incapable of completing the voyage. He may even be able to recover where the cargo has been collected by the crew after being washed ashore from a stranded vessel.[48]

12.3.2 PRO RATA FREIGHT

The general rule at common law is that, in the absence of agreement to the contrary, no freight is payable unless the cargo is delivered at the agreed destination. Even though the carrier is excused from carrying the goods to the port of discharge by the intervention of an excepted peril, he is not entitled to claim freight proportional to the amount of the voyage completed. Thus in *Hunter* v *Prinsep*,[49] on a voyage from Honduras to London, the vessel was driven ashore on St Kitts and wrecked. Such of the cargo as was salvaged was put up for sale in St Kitts by the master without reference to the cargo owner. A subsequent claim for pro rata freight was denied on the ground that freight was only earned by delivery of the cargo at the agreed destination and that the master, by putting the goods up for sale in St Kitts, had clearly indicated that he had no intention of completing the journey.

On the other hand, the contract of affreightment may expressly provide for the payment of a proportion of the freight in specified circumstances, while the carrier will have a claim for pro rata freight where failure to deliver the cargo at destination results from the fault of the cargo owner. Thus the shipowner was entitled to pro rata freight on the failure of the charterer to respond to notice from the ship's master that the cargo was at risk in a salvage suit which resulted in the cargo being sold by order of the court.[50] An obligation to pay a proportion of the freight may also be implied where the cargo owner takes delivery of the goods short of destination in such circumstances as to raise the inference that he has dispensed with the need to carry them further.[51] Such an inference will not, however, be drawn from mere acceptance of the cargo short of destination unless the shipowner is able and willing to complete the carriage. 'To justify a claim for pro rata freight there must be a voluntary acceptance of the goods at an intermediate port in such a mode as to raise a fair inference that the further carriage of the goods was intentionally dispensed with.'[52] There was no scope for such an implication where the

---

[47] See *Williams & Co* v *Canton Ins Office Ltd* [1901] AC 462; *The Tarva* [1973] 2 Lloyd's Rep 385; *The Alfa Nord* [1977] 2 Lloyd's Rep 434.
[48] *Thomas* v *Harrowing Steamship Co* [1915] AC 58.
[49] (1808) 103 ER 818.
[50] *The Soblomsten* (1866) LR 1 A & E 293.
[51] *Christy* v *Row* (1808) 127 ER 849. Cf. *St Enoch Shipping Co* v *Phosphate Mining Co* [1916] 2 KB 624.
[52] Lord Coleridge CJ in *Metcalfe* v *Britannia Ironworks Co* (1877) 2 QBD 423 at p 427.

cargo owner accepted delivery of the goods under protest at a point some 300 miles short of the agreed port of discharge, when ice in the Sea of Azov prevented the vessel from completing her voyage.[53]

12.3.3 BACK FREIGHT

Where a carrier is prevented from delivering the cargo at the agreed destination for some reason beyond his control, such as the outbreak of war or the failure of the cargo owner to take delivery, then he must deal with the cargo in the owner's interest and at the owner's expense. If he is unable to obtain instructions from the cargo owner, he may land and warehouse the goods, tranship them, carry them on to another port or return them to the loading port – whichever action is the most appropriate in the circumstances. He is then entitled to recover the expenses involved as 'back freight'.[54]

The carrier is under no obligation to forward the cargo to the agreed destination, merely for the purpose of earning freight, when excepted perils have made it impossible to complete the voyage in the original ship. Nevertheless, if the freight is insured, where the cargo can be forwarded at an expense less than the freight at risk, it is the duty of the assured to forward and earn the freight or, by abandonment, give his freight underwriters the opportunity of so doing.

12.3.4 DEAD FREIGHT

Where the charterer has failed in his obligation to provide a 'full and complete cargo', the shipowner is entitled to damages for breach of contract – otherwise known as 'dead freight'. The shipowner, under such circumstances, is under a duty to mitigate his loss, being expected to take reasonable steps to procure alternative cargo. He is entitled to the cost of taking such action, together with the value of any freight still outstanding.[55]

The basis for the calculation of dead freight may be stipulated in the voyage charter in the form of a liquidated damages clause. Recent authority suggests, however, that such a clause does not necessarily limit the extent of damages recoverable for the breach, and that a shipowner may also be able to claim for the loss of demurrage consequent upon the failure to load the minimum agreed cargo.[56] In the absence of such provision, the amount due to the shipowner is calculated on the basis of the freight appropriate to the amount of unutilised cargo space less the expenses, if any, which the shipowner would normally have incurred in earning this freight.

No lien is available at common law for dead freight, but provision is normally made for one in the charterparty.[57]

---

[53] *Metcalfe* v *Britannia Ironworks Co* (1877) 2 QBD 423.

[54] See *Cargo ex Argos* (1873) LR 5 CP 134.

[55] *Wallems Rederi A/S* v *Muller & Co* [1927] 2 KB 99.

[56] *The Altus* [1985] 1 Lloyd's Rep 423. NB In this case different rates of demurrage were payable dependent on the amount of cargo loaded. The claim was based on the difference between the rate applicable to the amount actually loaded and that applicable to the amount agreed to be loaded. No claim was made for additional demurrage which would have been incurred for the extra time which would have been expended in loading the remainder of the cargo. The decision is therefore no authority on the latter point.

[57] See *Kish* v *Taylor* [1912] AC 604.

12.4 PAYMENT OF FREIGHT

12.4.1 PARTY FROM WHOM FREIGHT DUE

The party normally liable to pay freight is the party entering into the contract of affreightment with the carrier – namely, the charterer in the case of a voyage charterparty or the shipper in the case of a bill of lading contract. The contract of carriage may, however, provide for freight to be payable by other parties or the initial liability may be transferred by indorsement of the bill of lading.

(I) CHARTERPARTY FREIGHT

The charterer is the party primarily responsible for payment of freight due under a voyage charter and he remains liable even though he sub-charters the vessel or issues bills of lading to third parties reserving under them a similar amount of freight as that due under the charterparty. The shipowner is under no obligation to look first to the bill of lading holders for payment, nor does he lose his right of recourse against the charterer merely by waiving his lien and releasing the goods to the consignee without first securing payment of freight.

In many cases, however, the charterer may have no substantial interest in the contract of carriage once the cargo has been shipped as, for example, where he has shipped the goods as agent for a third party or where he has sold goods under a contract of sale which provides that he shall charter a vessel to ship them to the buyer. In such circumstances the charterparty will normally include a 'cesser clause' providing that the liability of the charterer for freight and other transport charges shall cease once the cargo has been loaded on the chartered vessel. Such a clause will be effective in discharging the charterer's liability for freight so long as the contract of carriage provides the shipowner with commensurate security in the form of a lien on the goods in question.[58] The cesser clause will not, however, relieve the charterer from liability as bill of lading holder.[59]

(II) BILL OF LADING FREIGHT

The shipper will normally be liable for the freight on goods shipped under a bill of lading unless the carrier is informed at the time of shipment that he is merely acting as agent on behalf of another party. He can be relieved of such liability either by an express term in the bill, or by the carrier giving credit to the consignee by, for example, accepting a bill of exchange drawn on the consignee for his own convenience.[60]

Once the shipper has transferred the bill to a consignee or indorsee, however, the liability for payment of bill of lading freight has been significantly modified following the repeal of the Bills of Lading Act 1855 by the Carriage of Goods by Sea Act 1992.[61] In view of the fact that the latter statute is applicable only to bills of lading issued on or after 16 September 1992, it will be necessary to consider the position under both regimes.

---

[58] For a full discussion of the effects of a cesser clause, see *infra* at pp 300–2.
[59] *Gullischen* v *Stewart* (1884) 11 QBD 186.
[60] *Strong* v *Hart* (1827) 6 B & C 160.
[61] For a full discussion of the provisions of the Carriage of Goods by Sea Act 1992, see *supra* at pp 137 ff.

(a) The law prior to 16 September 1992

Shipper.   The initial responsibility of the shipper for payment of freight survives the subsequent indorsement of the bill to a consignee or other indorsee. While such a consignee or indorsee then becomes personally liable for payment of freight as the result of the Bills of Lading Act 1855, s 2 expressly reserves the carrier's right of recourse against the shipper.

Consignees and indorsees.   The Bills of Lading Act 1855 provided the carrier with a statutory right to recover freight from any consignee or indorsee of a bill of lading to whom the property in the goods had passed as the result of its indorsement.[62] In the absence of such provision, the doctrine of privity of contract would normally prevent any action for freight being brought against a third party.

Two problems, however, still remained. The first concerned the situation where the Bills of Lading Act was not applicable as, for example, where the party indorsing the bill did not intend ownership in the goods to pass to the indorsee as a result of the indorsement.[63] Early authority suggested that in appropriate circumstances a party who presented a bill of lading and took delivery of the goods might be treated as impliedly promising to pay the freight. It was, however, repeatedly stressed that such an implication was one of fact in each case, and not one of law.[64] While such an inference may readily be drawn from a usage of trade or course of dealing between the parties,[65] it is perhaps more questionable when drawn in the abstract. Clearly such an implied contract would have to be supported by consideration, although this might arguably be provided by the carrier releasing the cargo without exercising his lien.[66]

The second problem related to the liability of the consignee or indorsee for advance freight which was still outstanding at the time he took delivery of the goods. Prima facie it would appear that they should be liable since s 1 of the Bills of Lading Act 1855 provided that, on indorsement of the bill, such a party should be treated 'as if the contract contained in the bill of lading had been made with himself'. It is, however, arguable that if such an indorsee was a transferee of the bill for value, who took it in ignorance of the fact that any freight was outstanding, it should not be difficult to construe an estoppel in his favour.

(b) The law after 16 September 1992

Shipper.   Here again, the initial responsibility of the shipper for payment of freight continues despite the indorsement of the bill of lading to a consignee or other indorsee. Section 3(3) of the Carriage of Goods by Sea Act 1992 provides that even where a subsequent consignee or indorsee becomes liable to pay freight, in accordance with the provisions of the Act, this is without prejudice to the continuing liability of the shipper, as original party to the contract of carriage.

---

[62] Bills of Lading Act 1855 s 1.

[63] See *Brandt* v *Liverpool* [1924] 1 KB 575 (where the bill of lading was indorsed in blank as security for a loan); *The Aliakmon* [1986] 1 Lloyd's Rep 1 (where the bill was indorsed to the consignees in order that they could obtain delivery of the goods from the carrier as agents on behalf of the shipper).

[64] See Parke B in *Moller* v *Young* (1855) 25 LJQB 94 at p 96.

[65] *Wilson* v *Kymer* (1813) 1 M & S 157.

[66] For a full discussion of *Brandt* v *Liverpool* and the implied contract theory, see *supra* at pp 140 ff.

Consignees and indorsees.   A consignee or indorsee, on obtaining title to sue under the 1992 Act,[67] does not become automatically subject to the obligations under the contract including the obligation to pay freight. Such obligations attach from the moment he seeks to enforce the contract, either by taking or demanding delivery of the goods from the carrier, making a claim under the contract of carriage or having taken or demanded delivery of the goods before acquiring title to sue.[68]

As to the question of liability for advance freight which is still outstanding at the time of taking delivery of the goods, the 1992 Act provides that a subsequent consignee or indorsee shall 'become subject to the same liabilities under that contract as if he had been a party to that contract'.[69] Here again, it is arguable whether estoppel might come to the rescue of a transferee for value who took the bill in ignorance of the outstanding freight.[70]

12.4.2 PARTY TO WHOM FREIGHT PAYABLE

Freight due under a voyage charter or bill of lading contract is normally payable to the party with whom the shipper entered into the contract of carriage, although the terms of that contract may provide otherwise. The carrier has complete freedom in designating the person to whom freight is payable. The initial obligation may, however, be changed before freight has accrued by the subsequent sale or mortgage of the vessel or the assignment of the freight to a third party. Where, in such circumstances, the party responsible for payment encounters conflicting claims, he would be well advised to interplead.

The following are the principal parties to whom freight may be payable:

(I) THE SHIPOWNER

The shipowner will normally be entitled to payment of voyage charter freight and, in the absence of any charterparty, to freight due under a bill of lading contract. The only exception arises in relation to a vessel chartered by demise where such freight is payable to the demise charterer.

In practice, freight will normally be collected by an authorised agent, which will usually be the loading broker, in the case where freight is payable at the loading port, or the master, where freight is payable on delivery. Payment to such an agent will discharge the consignee or assignee unless there is a custom of the trade to the contrary, or they have received notice that payment should be made to some other party.

Part owners of a vessel have a joint entitlement to freight in proportion to the number of shares they hold in the vessel. Their rights to participate in the vessel's earnings are governed by the law of partnership, and they usually appoint a managing owner or other joint agent to be responsible for collecting the freight.

---

[67] For a full discussion of obtaining title to sue, see *supra* pp 137 ff.
[68] Carriage of Goods by Sea Act 1992 s 3(1). But see *The Berge Sisar* [1998] 2 Lloyd's Rep 475.
[69] Section 3(1).
[70] Cf. the Hamburg Rules, Art 15.1(k), which requires the bill of lading to indicate the amount of freight, if any, payable by the consignee. Failure to do so amounts to conclusive evidence that no such freight is payable in favour of a consignee who, in good faith, has acted in reliance on the absence in the bill of lading of any such indication (Art 16.4).

(II) THE MASTER

The master is customarily authorised to collect the freight as agent of the shipowner, but cannot recover it by action except in the rare case where the contract of carriage has been made expressly with himself. In no circumstances can he sue where he has signed the bill of lading as agent on behalf of the shipowner.[71] As against the shipowner, the master has no right of set-off for wages or advances he has made on the ship's account.

(III) THE CHARTERER

Where a vessel has been chartered by demise, both sub-charter and bill of lading freights are payable to the demise charterer. In the case where vessels are time or voyage chartered however, the entitlement to bill of lading freights is a question of fact depending on the terms of the individual contract and the circumstances of the case.[72] In the majority of cases the bills are shipowner's bills since, although issued by the charterers, they are signed by the master or other agent on behalf of the shipowners. In such circumstances the shipowner is entitled to appoint agents to collect the freight on the bills at the port of discharge but, after deducting any outstanding charterfreight, is required to account for the balance to the charterer.[73] On the other hand, if the bills are signed by the master or other agent on behalf of the charterer, then they are treated as charterer's bills and the charterer is entitled to payment of any freight due under the contract of carriage.[74]

(IV) A PURCHASER OF THE SHIP

The sale of the vessel carries with it the entitlement to any freight which is in process of being earned at the time of sale and which is payable to the shipowner.[75]

(V) A MORTGAGEE OF THE SHIP

Unlike the position in sale, the mortgage of a ship does not *per se* include any entitlement to freight. Such entitlement does not arise until the mortgagee has taken either actual or constructive possession of the vessel. In the latter case notice to the charterer or consignee is sufficient for this purpose when the vessel is at sea provided that the mortgagee takes actual possession as soon as possible thereafter. On taking possession he is entitled to any freight in the course of being earned under the current contract of carriage but, in the case of advance freight, not if it has already been paid to the shipowner. The mortgagee is not, however, entitled to freight which has already accrued before he took possession, or in the case of charters, to any unpaid freight on previous voyages.[76]

Where there has been more than one mortgage of a vessel, priority as to entitlement to freight is governed by the date of registration of the mortgage rather than by the date of the mortgage itself.[77]

---

[71] *Repetto v Millar's Karri Forests* [1901] 2 KB 306.
[72] *Samuel v West Hartlepool SN Co* (1906) 11 Com Cas 115 at p 125 *per* Walton J.
[73] See *Molthes Rederi v Ellermans Wilson Line* (1926) 25 LlLR 259 at p 261 *per* Greer J.
[74] For a full discussion of the problem of identifying the carrier, see *supra* at pp 235 ff.
[75] *Lindsay v Gibbs* (1859) 22 Beav 522.
[76] *Shillito v Biggart* [1903] 1 KB 683.
[77] Merchant Shipping Act 1894 s 33.

(VI) ASSIGNEE OF FREIGHT

The right to freight can be assigned independently of the vessel and, provided that the requirements for the statutory form of assignment are complied with, the assignee can sue to recover freight in his own name. For this result to be achieved, the assignment must be in writing, it must be absolute and not conditional or by way of a charge, and written notice must be given to the debtor.[78] Such an assignment is subject to equities but, as between the parties, is immediately effective. In the event of successive assignments, the payor does not have to concern himself with the respective dates of these assignments but is entitled to pay the first assignee to give him notice.[79] Indeed, in the absence of any notice, he will obtain discharge by making payment to the party originally entitled.

An assignment of freight will take priority over any subsequent sale or mortgage of the vessel unless, at the time of the mortgage, the mortgagee had no notice of the assignment.[80] It will not, however, gain precedence over a prior sale of the vessel, since such a sale carries with it the right to any accruing freight. On the other hand, as a mortgagee gains no entitlement to freight until he takes possession of the vessel, a subsequent assignee will have priority as to freight which has already accrued at that time.

As any assignment is subject to equities, a charterer or consignee on paying freight will be able to set-off any debts due from the shipowner which have accrued before they received notice of the assignment.

(VII) AN UNDERWRITER

Where a vessel has been abandoned to an underwriter, he is entitled to any freight accruing thereafter. However, if the master has transhipped the cargo before abandonment, any freight resulting from the completion of the voyage is due to the owner of the abandoned vessel.

---

[78] Law of Property Act 1925 s 136(1). See *The Attika Hope* [1988] 1 Lloyd's Rep 439 (priority between assignees is governed by date of notice to the debtor).
[79] *Smith* v *Zigurds* [1934] AC 209.
[80] *Wilson* v *Wilson* (1872) LR 14 Eq 32.

13

SHIPOWNERS' LIENS

A lien is the right given to a shipowner to retain possession of the cargo at the port of discharge as security for the payment of freight or other charges. Such a right may, in certain circumstances, arise at common law or it may be provided for in an express term of the contract of carriage.

13.1 LIENS AT COMMON LAW

The shipowner's right to exercise a lien at common law arises independently of contract and is based exclusively on the ability of the shipowner to retain possession of the goods concerned. The right is restricted and is available at common law in three cases only:

(i)   *For the recovery of a general average contribution due from cargo.* In practice the shipowner will normally release the cargo to the consignee in return for the signing of an average bond or the provision of some other form of security.[1]

(ii) *For expenses incurred by the shipowner in protecting the cargo,* since the master has authority under an agency of necessity to take whatever steps are necessary to protect the cargo owner's interests during the voyage.[2]

(iii) *To recover the freight due on delivery of the cargo* under either the charter or bill of lading contract of carriage. No lien will, however, arise at common law for the recovery of other charges arising under the contract of carriage such as deadfreight, demurrage or damages for detention.

13.1.1 REQUIREMENTS FOR THE EXERCISE OF THE COMMON LAW LIEN FOR FREIGHT

Certain requirements must be met before the shipowner will be allowed to exercise the lien for freight. First, as the right is dependent on the shipowner retaining possession of the goods it will be lost as soon as the cargo is delivered to the consignee or his agent. For similar reasons a shipowner under a charter by demise has no lien for charter hire since under such a contract he does not retain possession of the vessel.

---

[1] *Hain SS Co v Tate & Lyle* (1936) 41 Com Cas 350.
[2] *Hingston v Wendt* (1876) 1 QBD 367 (shipowner had lien to cover cost of salvaging cargo when vessel driven ashore).

Secondly, exercise of the lien is dependent on payment of freight and delivery of cargo being treated as concurrent obligations. While this is normally the case,[3] there will be no entitlement to lien where the contract of carriage provides for the payment of freight at a date later than that fixed for delivery of cargo. Thus the shipowner in *Tamvaco v Simpson*[4] was unable to enforce a lien when the contract provided for half the freight to be paid by a bill of exchange which had not matured at the time the goods were to be delivered, despite the fact that by that time the shipper was already insolvent.

The right of lien is confined to the particular consignment of goods on which freight is due, although it may be exercised over the entire consignment even though only part of the freight is outstanding. Where a single contract is involved, the shipowner may exercise his lien over all the goods consigned to the same person on the same voyage, even where they have been consigned under different bills of lading. On the other hand, once the bills have been indorsed to different assignees, the shipowner's right of lien is restricted to those individual bills on which freight is outstanding. Where goods are delivered by instalments, there is normally a concurrent obligation to pay freight on the delivery of each instalment. Accordingly, exercise of any lien is confined to the particular instalment on which freight is due. Finally, where a chartered vessel is used as a general ship, the common law lien for the charter freight cannot be exercised against the goods of a third party which have been shipped under a bill of lading contract. Such a right must be conferred by an express term in the bill of lading.

Problems arise where the contract of carriage provides for freight to be payable in advance. The authorities would suggest that the common law lien cannot be exercised in respect of such freight, at least where the cargo is deliverable to a consignee other than the party responsible for payment of the advance freight.[5] Certainly, a shipowner would be estopped from enforcing the lien against a consignee or assignee who had taken up the bill in reliance on an express or implied representation that the freight had already been paid. Thus in *Gardner v Trechman*[6] the charterparty provided that bills of lading could be issued at any rate of freight but that, if the total amount due on bill freights fell short of the charter freight, the master was required to ensure that the balance was paid in advance by the charterer. In these circumstances the court held that the shipowner was not entitled to exercise a lien for the outstanding balance of the charter freight as against a third party holder of one of the bills.

In conclusion, it should be noted that the common law lien merely gives a right to retain possession of the goods, it confers no right of resale even where expenses are involved in their retention. In the case of a lien for charter freight, however, the shipowner may be able to recoup such losses by claiming demurrage for any resulting delay.

---

[3] *Tate v Meek* (1818) 8 Taunt 280.
[4] (1866) LR 1 CP 363.
[5] *Kitchener v Venus* (1859) 12 Moo PC 361. For the US position, see *Beverly Hills Nat Bank Co v Compania de Navegaciaon Almirante* [1971] AMC 890.
[6] (1884) 15 QBD 154.

13.2 EXPRESS CONTRACTUAL LIENS

Parties to a contract of carriage, whether under charter or bill of lading, invariably make express provision for appropriate liens rather than rely on the implied lien of the common law. In doing so they can provide not only security for the payment of freight, but also make provision for the refund of any other charges or losses incurred by the shipowner. Such clauses can be drafted in order to cover specific identified charges or in more general terms to encompass 'all charges whatsoever'. A typical example of the former type of clause is provided by clause 8 of the Gencon (1994) form:

> 'The owners shall have a lien on the cargo and on all sub-freights payable in respect of the cargo, for freight, deadfreight, demurrage, claims for damages and for all other amounts due under this Charter Party including costs of recovering same.'[7]

The more general alternative version is exemplified by clause 3 of Scancon:

> 'The owners shall have a lien on the cargo for any amount due under this contract and the necessary costs of recovering same.'[8]

13.2.1 CHARACTERISTICS OF CONTRACTUAL LIEN

As with the common law lien, exercise of a contractual lien depends on the shipowner retaining possession of the goods and consequently the right is lost as soon as the cargo comes into the hands of a consignee or assignee of the bill. Being a contractual lien, however, it is only enforceable against a party to the contract of carriage. Thus a lien incorporated in a time charter to provide security for unpaid hire is not enforceable against cargo of third parties shipped under a bill of lading even where such third parties have notice of the existence of the charterparty at the time their cargo was shipped. In refusing to enforce a lien clause in the head charter against cargo shipped by a sub-charterer, Lord Lindley held that such a clause did not

> 'entitle the shipowners to a lien on the goods of persons who have come under no contract with them . . . A right to seize one person's goods for another person's debt must be clearly and distinctly conferred before a court of justice can be expected to recognise it.'[9]

Such a lien would be enforceable if the charterparty clause was incorporated by an appropriate term in the bill of lading issued to the third-party shipper.[10]

More difficult problems of interpretation arise where the charterparty clause, instead of restricting exercise of the lien to charterer's cargo, expressly seeks to extend it to cover any cargo carried on the vessel. An example is provided by clause 18 of the NYPE form which confers on the shipowner 'a lien upon all cargoes and all sub-freights for any amounts due under this charter'.[11] Logically the doctrine of privity of contract should still be applicable, irrespective of the wording of the charterparty clause, and no lien

---

[7] See also Polcoalvoy 27.
[8] See also P & O Nedlloyd bill clause 14.
[9] *Turner* v *Haji Goolam* [1904] AC 826 at p 837.
[10] See *The Chrysovalandou Dyo* [1981] 1 Lloyd's Rep 159.
[11] See also Baltime 18.

should be enforceable against a third-party shipper unless it is expressly incorporated into the bill of lading contract. This was the view taken by Mocatta J in *The Agios Giorgis*[12] when he remarked that he was:

> 'unable to see how clause 18 can give the owners the right to detain cargo not belonging to the charterers and on which no freight was owing to the owners. There is no finding that the bills of lading contained any clause rendering the cargo shipped under them subject to this charterparty lien.'

A slightly different view, however, was expressed by Donaldson J in *The Aegnoussiotis*.[13] In that case the shipowner had sought to exercise the charterparty lien by temporarily suspending discharge of the consignee's cargo until outstanding hire had been paid. The point at issue here was not as to whether such action was justifiable *qua* consignees, but whether hire continued to be payable by the charterers during the period that discharge had been suspended. In the view of Donaldson J, clause 18 of the NYPE form, in so far as it sought to extend the lien to cover third-party cargo, was not entirely without effect. Under its provisions 'the time charterers accept an obligation to procure the creation of a contractual lien in favour of the owners',[14] presumably by ensuring that it is expressly incorporated as a term in the bill of lading contract. If they fail to do so, and the owners subsequently seek to assert a lien over third-party cargo, the normal doctrine of privity of contract will operate and such third parties will have a valid cause of action against the owners. But in such circumstances the charterers will not be allowed to take advantage of their own breach of contract with the result that, as against them, the purported exercise of the lien will be valid. The trial judge was accordingly of the opinion that, as against the charterers, hire continued to be payable during the suspension of the discharging operation. This decision is clearly one based on its own special facts and in no way undermines the basic proposition of law as stated in *The Agios Giorgis*.

One final point relates to the time at which the right of lien can be exercised:

> 'The essence of the exercise of a lien is the denial of possession of the cargo to someone who wants it.'[15]

On this basis Donaldson J in *The Mihalios Xilas*[16] held that the owners were not entitled to enforce the lien by halting the vessel at a bunkering port en route to the discharging port since no one wanted delivery of the cargo at that point. Such action would only be permissible if, due to special circumstances, the lien was not enforceable at the port of discharge as, for example, where the goods were consigned to a foreign government at their destination. On the other hand, the vessel having reached its destination, there appears to be no objection to the lien being exercised while lying off the port of discharge. To require otherwise

---

[12] [1976] 2 Lloyd's Rep 192 at p 204.
[13] [1977] 1 Lloyd's Rep 268.
[14] *Ibid*, at p 276.
[15] *Per* Donaldson J in *The Mihalios Xilas* [1978] 2 Lloyd's Rep 186 at p 191.
[16] [1978] 2 Lloyd's Rep 186.

'might involve unnecessary expense and in certain cases cause congestion in the port . . . [which] would seriously limit the commercial value of a lien. . . .'[17]

13.2.2 LIEN ON SUB-FREIGHTS

Many time charters provide that the lien for hire shall extend not only to cargo but also to sub-freights belonging to the charterers. This term presumably covers not only freight payable on bills of lading issued by the charterers, but also freight due on sub-charters.[18] The term 'lien' is a misnomer in this context since such sub-freights can never be regarded as being in the possession of the shipowner.[19] The clause merely gives the shipowner the right to intercept these sub-freights before they are paid to the charterer. Once they are in the hands of the charterer, the 'lien' is lost since

'such a lien does not confer the right to follow the money paid for freight into the pockets of the person receiving it simply because that money has been received in respect of a debt which was due for freight.'[20]

How then is such a lien on sub-freights exercised? Normally this will be achieved by notifying the bill of lading holder or sub-charterer that any freight due from him should be paid direct to the shipowner. In exercising such a lien, however, it is important to note that there are two alternative possibilities, depending on whether the contract of carriage was concluded by the third party with the owner or the charterer. Where bills of lading issued by charterers are signed by the master as agent on behalf of the owners, the contract of carriage is between shipper and shipowner. In the case of such an 'owner's contract',

'the legal right to the freight is in the owner and not in the charterer and the former can intervene at any time before the agent has received the freight and say to him: "I am no longer content that the charterer should collect the freight. If you collect it at all, you must collect it for me." If the agent then collects the freight it follows that the shipowner can sue for it as money had and received.'[21]

In the event of the charterer appointing an agent to collect the freight in these circumstances, such agent will be regarded at law as agent for both parties and can be required by the shipowner either to collect any outstanding freight on his behalf,[22] or to hand over any freight already collected.[23] There is, however, one proviso. Where such a lien is exercised by the shipowner, to recover charter hire, it can only be exercised in respect of hire which has already accrued due before the sub-freight came into the hands of the agent and not in respect of hire accruing after that date even though the

---

[17] *Per* Mocatta J in *The Chrysovalandou Dyo* [1978] 1 Lloyd's Rep 159 at p 165.
[18] But it does not cover hire due on a sub-time charter: *The Cebu (No 2)* [1990] 2 Lloyd's Rep 316.
[19] See Robert Goff J in *The Lancaster* [1980] 2 Lloyd's Rep 497 at p 501.
[20] *Per* Lord Alverstone CJ in *Tagart, Beaton & Co v Fisher* [1903] 1 KB 391 at p 395. See also *The Spiros C* [2000] 2 Lloyd's Rep 319 (sub-freight paid to charterer before contractually due).
[21] *Per* Greer J in *Molthes Rederi v Ellermans Wilson Line* (1926) 26 LlLR 259 at p 261.
[22] *Molthes Rederi v Ellermans Wilson Line* (1926) 26 LlLR 259.
[23] *Wehner v Dene Shipping Co* [1905] 2 KB 92.

relevant funds are still held by the agent.[24] An agent collecting freight in such circumstances is treated as acting solely as agent of the shipowner and so is not allowed to deduct disbursements incurred previously while acting as agent of the charterer.[25]

In the alternative situation where bills issued by charterers are signed on their own behalf, or by the master as agent for the charterers, the contract of carriage is between shipper and charterer and the legal right to freight is in the charterer. In the case of such 'charterer's contracts', the right of lien is required by the shipowner in order to intercept the freight before it is paid to the charterer or his agent since, once such sub-freights reach their hands, the lien is lost.[26] A recent High Court decision indicating that where the charterer is a company, such a shipowner's lien on sub-freights, in order to be enforceable, needed to be registered as a charge under the Companies Acts caused some disquiet in the market.[27] This was, however, quickly dispelled by s 93 of the Companies Act 1989 which removed any requirement for registration. Problems arise where bills are issued providing for freight to be payable in advance, since the charter lien on sub-freights will then effectively be lost. Nevertheless, the master may be obliged to sign such bills when tendered in cases where the charter authorises the charterer to present bills at any rate of freight without prejudice to the charter.[28] The only possible protection for the shipowner in these circumstances is to ensure that the bill incorporates the clause in the charterparty expressly giving a lien on the cargo for overdue charter hire. In practice such lien clauses are rarely acceptable in international c.i.f. contracts where commercial credits are involved. The terms of such credits invariably require freight to be pre-paid and also forbid the inclusion of a clause in the bill incorporating the terms of a charterparty.[29]

13.3 THE CESSER CLAUSE

Where goods are delivered under a bill of lading, the carrier normally looks to the receiver for any charges incidental to their transport, such as freight, and will usually be able to exercise a lien on the cargo in support of such claims. The same procedure will normally be followed where bills are issued under a charterparty, although in this case the charterer would normally remain liable for charges arising under the charter, including demurrage, damages for detention and dead freight. But the charterer may often not wish to retain responsibility for performance of the contract of carriage once the goods are loaded. He may, for example, have chartered the vessel to ship goods to an overseas

---

[24] *Ibid.*

[25] *Molthes Rederi v Ellermans Wilson Line (supra).*

[26] *Tagart, Beaton & Co v Fisher & Sons* [1903] 1 KB 391. For a similar approach by the US courts see *American Steel Barge Co v Chesapeake Coal Agency Co* 115 F 669.

[27] See *The Ugland Trailer* [1985] 2 Lloyd's Rep 372. The trial judge, Nourse J, admitted that the decision might come 'as something of a shock' to the market, since 'The evidence establishes that it has never been the practice to register a shipowner's lien on subfreights.' (At p 375.) See also *The Annangel Glory* [1988] 1 Lloyd's Rep 45.

[28] *The Shillito* (1897) 3 Com Cas 44.

[29] *The Nanfri* [1978] 2 Lloyd's Rep 132. See also UCP (1993) Art 23(a)(vi).

buyer, or he may have been acting as agent for an undisclosed principal. In order to relieve him of any such continuing liability, it became customary for the charterparty to include a 'cesser clause' providing that the charterer's liability for transport charges should cease once the cargo had been shipped. The wording of such clauses varied considerably, but the following is a typical example:

> 'Vessel to have a lien on the cargo for all freight, deadfreight, demurrage or average. . . . Charterer's liability under this charter to cease on cargo being shipped.'[30]

From the time the clause operated, the shipowner would be restricted to his remedies against the goods (i.e. lien) or under the bill of lading contract. Unless otherwise provided,[31] the clause is retrospective in effect and covers liabilities already incurred before loading is complete, as, for example, deadfreight or demurrage at the port of loading.[32] In approaching the construction of cesser clauses, the courts have been reluctant to take them at their face value. In the words of Donaldson J,

> 'cesser clauses are curious animals because it is now well established that they do not mean what they appear to say, namely, that the charterer's liability shall cease as soon as the cargo is on board. Instead, in the absence of special wording . . . , they mean that the charterer's liability shall cease if, and to the extent that, the owners have an alternative remedy by way of lien on the cargo.'[33]

Accordingly, the charterer will only be released from liability under the charter to the extent that the shipowner is given a co-extensive lien on the cargo. This construction is justified as being the only reasonable interpretation to be placed on the intention of the parties in the circumstances.[34] It is essential, therefore, that the charterparty liens are effectively incorporated into the bill of lading,[35] and that the wording of such clauses is adequate to cover the relevant charge.[36] Nor is the mere granting of a lien sufficient unless it can be effectively exercised by the shipowner. Such exercise may be prevented by the terms of the contract of carriage as, for example, where a charter provided that demurrage was not payable until one week after the date fixed for discharge of the cargo.[37] Again, a lien may not be legally capable of enforcement, as where a cargo is consigned to a foreign government which would not allow the lien to be exercised at the port of discharge.[38] As yet there is no authority as to whether the cesser clause would be effective in a case where exercise of the lien was not commercially practicable, or where the value of the cargo subject to the lien was not commensurate with the value of the

---

[30] Clauses 30 and 31 Baltimore Form C Berth Grain Charter. For other examples, see Norgrain 35, Polcoalvoy 27.

[31] See Gencon 8, Norgrain 34.

[32] *Kish* v *Cory* (1875) 10 QB 553. See also *Yone Susuki* v *Central Argentine Rly* [1928] AMC 1521.

[33] *Per* Donaldson J in *The Sinoe* [1971] 1 Lloyd's Rep 514 at p 516.

[34] See Pearson LJ in *Fidelitas Shipping* v *V/O Exportchleb* [1963] 2 Lloyd's Rep 113 at p 122.

[35] *Fidelitas Shipping* v *V/O Exportchleb* [1963] 2 Lloyd's Rep 113. For a discussion of the requirements for an effective incorporation of charterparty terms in a bill of lading, see *supra* at pp 239 ff.

[36] Thus a clause providing a lien for demurrage does not extend to a claim for damages for detention. *Clink* v *Radford* [1891] 1 QB 625.

[37] *The Athinoula* [1980] 2 Lloyd's Rep 481.

[38] *The Sinoe* [1971] 1 Lloyd's Rep 514. See also *The Aegis Britannic* [1987] 1 Lloyd's Rep 119.

claim, although provision for the latter contingency is often contained in the cesser clause itself.[39]

The strict *contra proferentem* approach adopted by the courts towards the construction of cesser clauses is perhaps not surprising in view of the criticism levelled at such clauses by the commercial world. On the one hand, they are not generally acceptable in transactions where commercial credits are involved.[40] From the shipowner's point of view, instead of a direct *in personam* action against the charterer, he is relegated to an uncertain, expensive and time consuming remedy against the cargo which it may not be commercially expedient to exercise. Viewed from the position of the bill of lading holder, he is required to accept liability for charges of the extent of which he is often unaware at the time of receiving the bill. Strong arguments have been advanced for outlawing the clause,[41] and it is noticeable that it has been omitted from many modern charter forms.[42]

---

[39] For example, Polcoalvoy 27. 'In respect of Owners' Claims protected by lien on the cargo the Charterer's liability under this charterparty shall cease on the cargo being loaded provided that the Owners have been able to obtain satisfaction of these claims by exercising the lien.'

[40] See Uniform Customs & Practice for Documentary Credits (1993 edn) Art 23(a)(vi).

[41] See UNCTAD: *Report on Charterparties* (1974) p 52.

[42] For example, Gencon 8; Shellvoy 5, clause 42.

Part Five

DISPUTE SETTLEMENT

14

DISPUTE SETTLEMENT

14.1 PROBLEMS OF CONFLICT OF LAWS

Contracts of carriage by sea frequently involve an international dimension, either because the parties involved are resident in different countries or because performance of the contract is required in a state other than that in which it was concluded. In the event of any dispute arising from such a contract, problems may ensue as to the court in which proceedings can be instituted and as to the appropriate law which is applicable to the transaction. Many of the standard bill of lading and charterparty forms make express provision for such an eventuality by including clauses specifying a particular forum and choice of law. In the absence of such clauses, both issues have to be decided by the courts after a review of the circumstances of each individual case.

14.1.1 CHOICE OF FORUM

Are parties to a contract of carriage allowed complete freedom of choice in selecting a forum, or is it required that the subject matter of the dispute has some connection with the chosen forum? The answer to this question may well depend on the particular court to which it is addressed and on the capacity in which that court is seised of the dispute. The question itself conceals two separate but interrelated subsidiary questions. To what extent will the nominated court accept jurisdiction and to what extent will other courts respect such a nomination by staying alternative actions commenced within their own jurisdictions? In general the selected forum is more likely to accept jurisdiction than is another forum to stay proceedings in deference to a choice of forum clause. The force of any application for a stay will depend upon whether the forum clause is exclusive or non-exclusive.[1]

Much may depend on the reasons for the selection of a particular forum. Litigants invariably prefer to sue in their own courts but where the parties originate from different jurisdictions some compromise is clearly necessary. Often the solution is to be found in selecting a respected neutral forum with expertise in the relevant subject matter.[2] Subject to statutory provisions largely stemming from international conventions to which the United Kingdom is a party,[3] English courts recognise the general principle of

---

[1] As to the distinction, see e.g. *Sinochem International Oil* v *Mobil Sales and Supply Corp* [2000] 1 Lloyd's Rep 670.

[2] See Burger CJ in *Zapata* v *The Bremen* [1972] 2 Lloyd's Rep 315 at p 318.

[3] See *infra* at pp 311 ff.

freedom of contract. They are normally prepared to accept jurisdiction even though the contract has no connection with the chosen forum. Thus in *The Chapparal*[4] where a Houston-based corporation had contracted with a German towage company to tow a drilling rig from Louisiana to Italy and the rig was damaged during transit, the English court was prepared to accept jurisdiction based on a London choice of forum clause, even though otherwise the transaction had no connection with the chosen forum.[5] In order to protect its proceedings an English court has power, subject to conventions, to grant an 'anti-suit' injunction to restrain a party subject to its jurisdiction from proceeding in a foreign court although, in the interests of comity, such jurisdiction will be exercised only if the proceedings are vexatious or oppressive in order to avoid the appearance of undue interference with the foreign court. In the absence of strong reasons to the contrary, such an injunction will ordinarily be granted where there is an exclusive English jurisdiction or arbitration agreement. Without such reasons such proceedings in a foreign court would be 'vexatious'.[6] Factors to be taken into account in deciding whether to issue such an injunction include any delay in seeking the injunction, the stage reached in the foreign proceedings, any risk of loss of security, whether any related proceedings would be outside the scope of the injunction, and whether it would result in a multiplicity of proceedings.[7] A grant would be inappropriate, for example, where the breach of the agreement was only arguable, or where any reliance on English law as the governing law of an arbitration agreement was not established to a high degree of probability.[8] It would also appear unlikely that an injunction would be granted where the litigation in the foreign courts is merely designed to provide security and does not involve the merits of the claim.[9]

In the converse situation English courts are prepared to recognise a foreign jurisdiction clause to the extent of granting a stay of any proceedings brought in an English court in contravention of such a clause.[10] Some of the principles applicable to granting a stay of English or foreign proceedings were formulated in the judgment of Brandon J in *The Eleftheria*.[11] While recognising that the court had an overriding discretion to control its own proceedings and prevent any attempt to oust its jurisdiction,[12] he took the view that in general the court should exercise this discretion by granting a stay

---

[4] [1968] 2 Lloyd's Rep 158.

[5] In deciding whether to uphold the agreement, the same factors are relevant as in relation to a foreign forum clause: *Akai Pty Ltd* v *People's Insurance Co Ltd* [1998] 1 Lloyd's Rep 90.

[6] See *Continental Bank* v *Aeakos Compania Naviera* [1994] 2 Lloyd's Rep 505; *The Angelic Grace* [1995] 1 Lloyd's Rep 87; *Turner* v *Grovit* [2002] 1 WLR 107; *Donohue* v *Armco Inc* [2002] 1 Lloyd's Rep 425. A pre-emptive strike contrary to the agreement would be vexatious. *Sabah Shipyard* v *Pakistan* [2003] 2 Lloyd's Rep 571.

[7] *Donohue* v *Armco Inc* [2002] 1 Lloyd's Rep 425; *The Epsilon Rosa* [2003] 2 Lloyd's Rep 509.

[8] *American International Specialty Lines Ass Co* v *Abbott Laboratories* [2002] EWHC 2714.

[9] See *The Lisboa* [1980] 2 Lloyd's Rep 546.

[10] *The Nile Rhapsody* [1994] 1 Lloyd's Rep 382. A similar attitude was adopted by the US Supreme Court in *Zapata* v *The Bremen* [1972] 2 Lloyd's Rep 315. As to the effect of the Brussels Convention, see *infra* pp 312–13.

[11] [1970] P 94 at pp 99–100. These principles were restated and elaborated on by Brandon J in *The El Amria* [1981] 2 Lloyd's Rep 119 but they were not, nor were they intended to be, comprehensive. See *Donohue* v *Armco Inc* [2002] 1 Lloyd's Rep 425.

[12] See also Denning LJ in *The Fehmarn* [1958] 1 WLR 159 at pp 161–2.

unless strong cause for not doing so was shown.[13] The burden of displacing this presumption would rest with the plaintiff, and the court, in reaching its decision, should take into account all the circumstances of the particular case. Among the relevant factors to be taken into consideration, Brandon J listed the following:

1 The country in which the evidence on the relevant issues of fact was situated or more readily available, together with the relative convenience and expense of trial as between English and foreign courts.[14]

2 The law applicable to the contract and whether it differed from English law. 'I recognise that an English court can and often does decide questions of foreign law on the basis of expert evidence from foreign lawyers . . . It seems to be clear, however, that in general, and other things being equal, it is more satisfactory for the law of a foreign country to be decided by the courts of that country.'[15]

3 The countries with which the parties are most closely connected.[16]

4 Whether the plaintiffs would be prejudiced by having to sue in a foreign court. For example, they might thereby be deprived of security for their claim,[17] faced with a time bar not applicable in England[18] or find themselves unable to enforce any judgment ultimately obtained. Similarly, it may be clear that, for political, racial or religious reasons, they would be unlikely to obtain a fair trial.[19]

In reaching its decision, however, the court should not be drawn into making a comparison between the merits of different legal systems. 'It is not only invidious in the extreme to attempt comparisons between two different systems of administering justice; it is in any case impossible on the hearing of an application of [this] kind . . . to examine the merits and demerits of the two systems in sufficient depth to reach a conclusion that either is to be preferred to the other.'[20] Nevertheless, in granting a stay it is permissible for the court to impose conditions seeking to ensure that the plaintiff is not disadvantaged by the proceedings being transferred to a foreign jurisdiction. Thus

---

[13] See *The Makefjell* [1976] 2 Lloyd's Rep 29; *The Biskra* [1983] 2 Lloyd's Rep 59; *The Frank Pais* [1986] 1 Lloyd's Rep 529; *Pirelli Cables Ltd* v *United Thai Shipping Corp* [2000] 1 Lloyd's Rep 663. Cf. *The Adolf Warski* [1976] 2 Lloyd's Rep 241.

[14] *The El Amria* [1981] 2 Lloyd's Rep 119. Cf. *The Star of Luxor* [1981] 1 Lloyd's Rep 139 (full and proper discovery available in Egypt).

[15] Brandon J in *The Eleftheria* [1970] P at p 105. Colinvaux in *Carver's Carriage by Sea* 13th edn, 1982 argues that in cases where English courts have refused a stay of proceedings, the decision has invariably been linked with a desire to secure the enforcement of the proper law of the contract: para 967.

[16] *The Kislovodsk* [1980] 1 Lloyd's Rep 183.

[17] Particularly in the case of a one-ship company whose vessel had been arrested in the United Kingdom.

[18] As to the effect of a claimant permitting time to run out in the country selected, see e.g. *The MC Pearl* [1997] 1 Lloyd's Rep 566; *Baghlaf Al Zafer Factory Co* v *Pakistan National Shipping Co* [1998] 2 Lloyd's Rep 229; *Pirelli Cables Ltd* v *United Thai Shipping Corp* [2000] 1 Lloyd's Rep 663.

[19] To these factors Brandon LJ later added the availability of a remedy in the English court, excessive delay in the foreign court and exceptionally serious defects in foreign procedures: see *The El Amria* [1981] 2 Lloyd's Rep 119. Where the issue relates to foreign procedures, further relevant factors for consideration are those outlined above in relation to the grant of an anti-suit injunction, see *supra* at p 306.

[20] Brandon LJ in *The El Amria* [1981] 2 Lloyd's Rep 119 at p 126. See also Lord Reid in *The Atlantic Star* [1973] 2 Lloyd's Rep 197 at p 200.

in *The Kislovodsk*[21] where Sheen J granted a stay of proceedings relating to a contract which contained a Russian jurisdiction clause, he made such stay conditional on the defendant providing satisfactory security to meet any judgment given by the Leningrad court and also on the plaintiff's witnesses being granted visas to attend the hearing.[22]

(I) WHERE NO CHOICE OF FORUM CLAUSE

Where the contract of carriage contains no choice of forum clause a claimant will normally seek to institute proceedings in the forum where the defendant resides or carries on business. Any judgment in his favour will accordingly be made easily enforceable against the defendant's assets. Occasionally, however, for procedural or other reasons it may be advantageous for the claimant to sue elsewhere in which case he will be faced with the problems as to whether the chosen court will accept or exercise jurisdiction and as to whether any judgment obtained will be effective if the defendant has no assets available within that jurisdiction.[23] Alternatively, the defendant may assert that the chosen forum is not appropriate on the grounds, *inter alia*, that there is a closer connection elsewhere or that lower costs or greater convenience would result from proceedings in an alternative forum (the principle of 'forum non conveniens'). Factors to be taken into consideration are identical to those relevant to service of a claim form on a defendant outside the country to establish English jurisdiction.[24] Where a foreign forum is not appropriate, an anti-suit injunction may be granted to protect English proceedings[25] but only where there has been unconscionable conduct in bringing them. The mere fact of instituting the proceedings is not sufficient in itself, but factors to be taken into consideration are those relevant to the appropriateness of the forum, including any non-exclusive jurisdiction agreement.[26]

So far as English courts are concerned, subject to Convention provisions, jurisdiction *in personam* is based on the ability to serve the claim form personally on the defendant, even though he is only temporarily resident in the country. The courts will also normally be prepared to act if the defendant voluntarily submits to the jurisdiction other than where the object of the appearance is merely to contest jurisdiction as, for example, in an attempt to protect property.[27] Jurisdiction *in rem* is also conferred in specified circumstances on the Admiralty Court following the serving of an *in rem* claim form within territorial waters on the vessel, or an earlier arrest of such a vessel, involved in the

---

[21] [1980] 1 Lloyd's Rep 183.

[22] *Baghlaf Al Zafer Factory Co v Pakistan National Shipping Co* (*supra* fn 16); *Baghlaf Al Zafer v Pakistan National Shipping Co (No 2)* [2000] 1 Lloyd's Rep 1 (reversing the stay when it became apparent that the undertaking might not be recognised by the foreign court). See also *Pirelli Cables Ltd v United Thai Shipping Corp* [2000] 1 Lloyd's Rep 663.

[23] A preliminary issue may involve the question of which court should decide jurisdiction (see *General Star v Stirling Cooke Brown* [2003] 1 Lloyd's Rep 19) and weight may be given to home or foreign proceedings properly started under the contract (*Ace Insurance v Zurich Insurance* [2000] 2 Lloyd's Rep 423).

[24] See *infra* at pp 309–10.

[25] But not elsewhere: *Airbus Industrie v Patel* [1999] 1 AC 119.

[26] See *Turner v Grovit* [2002] 1 WLR 107; *Sabah Shipyard v Pakistan* [2003] 2 Lloyd's Rep 571; *Royal Bank of Canada v Cooperative Centrale Raiffeisen* [2004] 1 Lloyd's Rep 471 (particularly the principles set out in paras 8–10).

[27] See *The Messianaki Tolmi* [1984] 1 Lloyd's Rep 266.

claim or any other ship beneficially owned by the defendant.[28] Such jurisdiction extends to 'any claim for loss of or damage to goods carried in a ship' and to 'any claim arising out of any agreement relating to the carriage of goods in a ship or to the use or hire of a ship'.[29]

In certain circumstances it is also possible to serve an *in personam* claim form on a person outside the jurisdiction. Apart from limitation actions, the relevant occasions on which such action is permissible are enumerated in Rule 6.20 of the Civil Procedure Rules[30] as follows:

(1) a claim is made for a remedy against a person domiciled within the jurisdiction;
   . . .

(5) a claim is made in respect of a contract where the contract –
   (a) was made within the jurisdiction;
   (b) was made by or through an agent trading or residing within the jurisdiction;
   (c) is governed by English law; or
   (d) contains a term to the effect that the court shall have jurisdiction to determine any claim in respect of the contract;

(6) a claim is made in respect of a breach of contract committed within the jurisdiction;
   . . .

(8) a claim is made in tort where –
   (a) damage was sustained within the jurisdiction; or
   (b) the damage sustained resulted from an act committed within the jurisdiction.[31]

Subject to legislative provisions (mainly based on Conventions), the procedure under Part 6 is not, however, available as of right and the claimant must first obtain the permission of the court to issue the claim form. 'Statutory authority has specified the particular circumstances in which the power *may* be exercised, but leaves it to the Court to decide whether [it is appropriate] to exercise its discretionary power in a particular case.'[32] The burden of proof rests on the claimant who must show: (i) a good arguable case that the matter falls within Part 6 (iii), (ii) that there is a serious issue to be tried, and (iii) that England is the appropriate forum.[33]

The principles on which to assess the appropriateness of England as the forum were enumerated by Lord Goff in *The Spiliada*.[34] The case involved an alleged breach of contract by shippers loading a cargo of wet sulphur which caused severe corrosion damage to the chartered vessel. Leave had been granted to the shipowners under RSC Order 11 to issue and serve a writ on the defendants in Vancouver on the basis that the contract

---

[28] See Supreme Court Act 1981 s 21(4); see also RSC Order 75. Service may in certain circumstances be on the defendant or his solicitor (*ibid*). Cf. *Amoco (UK) Exploration Co v British American Offshore Ltd* [1999] 2 Lloyd's Rep 772 (where not a party to contract).
[29] Supreme Court Act 1981 s 20(2)(g) and (h).
[30] Replacing Order 11 as from 25 March 2002.
[31] For an example, see the facts of *The Albaforth* [1984] 2 Lloyd's Rep 91. As to limitation and collision actions, see CPR Rules 61.4, 61.11.
[32] Lord Goff in *The Spiliada* [1987] 1 Lloyd's Rep 1 at p 13.
[33] *Seaconsar Far East Ltd v Bank Markazi* [1993] 4 All ER 456.
[34] [1987] 1 Lloyd's Rep 1.

in question incorporated a London arbitration clause and was accordingly governed by English law. In reviewing the authorities on service out of the jurisdiction, Lord Goff reached the conclusion that the principles involved bore 'a marked resemblance to the principles applicable in *forum non conveniens* cases'.[35]

In the latter cases, where proceedings have been commenced in England, the defendant is seeking a stay on the ground that England is not an appropriate forum since the relevant transaction is more closely connected with another forum where litigation could be conducted at substantially less inconvenience and expense. Following Lord Goff's approach, it is established that the same factors are relevant when considering a claimant's request that a case should be brought in England, although the defendant is outside the jurisdiction, as when considering a defendant's request that a case should not be heard in England even though he is within the jurisdiction. One situation is the 'obverse' of the other and the object in each case should be 'to identify the forum in which the case can be suitably tried for the interests of all parties and for the ends of justice'.[36] The difference lies in the burden of proof which rests with the party seeking the exercise of the court's discretion, i.e. with the claimant in 'service out' and with the defendant where a stay is requested.

In considering the question of the appropriate forum, the Lords confirmed that the court must take into consideration all the relevant circumstances including the convenience of all parties, the availability of evidence and witnesses, the law to be applied, the costs involved in litigating in a different forum, and whether substantial justice would be done in the foreign forum.[37] The overriding factor should be the suitability of the forum, and less emphasis is to be placed on the personal or juridical advantages of which the claimant would be deprived if the case was not heard by an English court. While such considerations should be taken into account, 'I do not think that the Court should be deterred from granting a stay of proceedings, or from exercising its discretion against granting leave under RSCO 11 simply because the plaintiff will be deprived of such an advantage, provided that the Court is satisfied that substantial justice will be done in the available appropriate forum.'[38] Thus, where a party resists a stay of proceedings on the ground that his claim would be time barred in the alternative jurisdiction, it would be appropriate to enquire whether he had acted unreasonably in allowing such time to elapse.[39]

---

[35] *Ibid* at p 13. There are numerous cases applying *The Spiliada*. See e.g. (carriage cases) *The Polessk* [1996] 2 Lloyd's Rep 40; *The Hamburg Star* [1994] 1 Lloyd's Rep 399; *The Varna No 2* [1994] 2 Lloyd's Rep 41; (limitation of liability) *Caltex* v *BP Shipping* [1996] 1 Lloyd's Rep 286.

[36] Lord Goff in *The Spiliada* [1987] 1 Lloyd's Rep at p 13.

[37] For an enumeration of similar factors to be taken into consideration in relation to the principle of *forum non conveniens*, see *The Atlantic Star* [1974] AC 436. As to substantial justice, see *Lubbe* v *Cape plc* [2002] 2 Lloyd's Rep 383. The customary guidance as to the dangers of procedural comparison applies in this context as in that of the jurisdiction clause. See e.g. *Lubbe* v *Cape plc* at p 393.

[38] Lord Goff: *The Spiliada* [1987] 1 Lloyd's Rep at p 14. See also *The Herceg Novi and Ming Galaxy* [1998] 2 Lloyd's Rep 454; *Lubbe* v *Cape plc* [2000] 2 Lloyd's Rep 383.

[39] For an example of not acting unreasonably in allowing time to elapse, see *Citi-March* v *Neptune Orient Lines* [1996] 2 All ER 545. Cf. *The MC Pearl* [1997] 1 Lloyd's Rep 566.

(II) CONVENTION JURISDICTIONAL FRAMEWORKS

(a) Conventions on particular matters

A number of Conventions incorporated by statute into English law contain jurisdictional provisions qualifying the general rules outlined above. Most of these conventions are concerned with particular matters having, by their nature, a transnational element.[40] In the case of carriage of goods by sea, neither the Hague nor the Hague/Visby Rules contain express jurisdiction provisions.[41] However, in *The Morviken*[42] the House of Lords held void a clause selecting a non-Hague/Visby jurisdiction in so far as the selection had the effect of derogating from the Rules, contrary to Art III rule 8. The decision therefore created a limitation on the freedom to select jurisdiction in respect of claims falling within the Rules.

(b) The European Conventions on Jurisdiction and Judgments[43]

In 1978 the United Kingdom became a party to the European Convention on Jurisdiction and the Enforcement of Judgments in Civil and Commercial Matters of 1968. The amended Convention became part of English law on 1 January 1987.[44] Within its scope it introduced an entirely novel jurisdictional structure and provided for recognition and enforcement of judgments.[45] It was also adapted to jurisdiction and judgments as between England, Scotland and Northern Ireland.[46] The Convention was replaced by Regulation 44/2001 as regards all EU member states with the exception of Denmark, in respect of legal proceedings instituted after 1 March 2002 and judgments in proceedings prior to that date under or akin to the Convention.[47] The Brussels Convention continues to apply as between Denmark and other member states.

The Lugano Convention follows the structure of the Brussels Convention – save that the European Court of Justice has no jurisdiction – and is operative between the EU member states, other EFTA states, Iceland, Norway, Switzerland and Poland. The EU Regulation 44/2001 has no effect on the Lugano Convention.

---

[40] For example, the Convention relating to the International Carriage of Goods by Road 1956.

[41] Cf. the Hamburg Rules, which contain detailed jurisdiction provisions in Art 21.

[42] [1983] 1 Lloyd's Rep 1. See *supra* at pp 184 ff.

[43] The conventions involved are the EC Convention on Jurisdiction and Judgments 1968 (the Brussels Convention) and the EFTA 'parallel' Convention (the Lugano Convention) as modified by Council Regulation (EC) No 44/2001.

[44] All members of the EU are parties to the Convention, and the Convention is amended on each accession. The current text is contained in SI 2000/1824.

[45] See Title III. These provisions apply to any judgment of a contracting state on subject matter falling within the Convention and require little formality. There are few grounds on which recognition or enforcement may be refused: see Arts 27, 28.

[46] Section 16, Schedule 4.

[47] The Civil Jurisdiction and Judgments Act 1982 is amended to take account of the Regulation SI 2001/3928, 3929.

(i) The Brussels Convention 1968

The Convention is incorporated directly into English law.[48] Subject to specified exceptions,[49] questions of *forum non conveniens*,[50] and anti-suit injunctions[51] it applies to any
claim involving a civil or commercial matter which comes before an English court.
The Convention recognises that other conventions may provide a different framework,
and provides that any such convention on a particular matter should have priority.[52]
So, for example, a case within both the EC Convention and the Hamburg Rules will be
governed by the latter, while the Conventions on Arrest of Sea Going Ships 1952 and
1999 provide for such arrest to be a basis of jurisdiction.

  The fundamental premise of the new regime is that jurisdiction should normally be
conferred on the courts of the contracting state in which the defendant is domiciled,
whether or not he be a national of that state.[53] In the case of certain claims, however, the
claimant may, at his option, bring a suit in the courts of another contracting state, provided that the dispute is linked with that state in one of a number of ways specified by
the Convention.[54] Thus in the case of a claim founded in tort, suit may be brought in the
courts of the state where the damage occurred, or in disputes relating to contract, in the
courts of the state in which performance was to take place.[55]

  To this general rule, however, the Convention provides a number of exceptions.
First, exclusive jurisdiction, regardless of domicile, is conferred on the courts of a contracting state with regard to certain specified types of proceedings.[56] These range from
testing the validity of the constitution or the decisions of a company with its seat in that
state, to disputing the validity of an entry in a public register maintained in that state.
Secondly, where one or more of the parties to a dispute are domiciled in a contracting

---

[48] Civil Jurisdiction and Judgments Act 1982 s 2(1).

[49] See Art 1(2). With the exception of arbitration, the excluded matters are not directly relevant to carriage of
goods by sea.

[50] As to courts of non-contracting states, see *Re Harrods* [1991] 4 All ER 334; *Ace Insurance* v *Zurich
Insurance* [2001] 1 Lloyd's Rep 618; and, despite Convention provisions for selection between competing
courts of contracting states (Arts 21–23, see *infra*), held to apply as between such states where the defendant
is not domiciled in a contracting state. *Sarrio* v *Kuwait Investment Authority* [1997] 1 Lloyd's Rep 113; *The
Xin Yang* [1996] 2 Lloyd's Rep 217. The issue of whether it remains open to an English court to apply
forum non conveniens in respect of a non-contracting state has been referred to the European Court:
Owusu v *Jackson* [2002] EWCA 877.

[51] See, for example, *The Kribi* [2001] 1 Lloyd's Rep 76. The power to grant such an injunction against other
courts within the scope of the Convention was referred to the European Court by the House of Lords
in *Turner* v *Grovit* [2002] 1 WLR 107 (the Court of Appeal having granted it [2002] QB 345). On
20 November 2003 Colomer AG gave his opinion that the power was inconsistent with the Convention
[2004] 1 Lloyd's Rep 216. The power may still be exercised: see *Through Transport Mutual Insurance* v
New India Assurance [2004] 1 Lloyd's Rep 206.

[52] Article 57. See *The Bergen* [1997] 1 Lloyd's Rep 380 (Arrest Convention).

[53] Article 2. An action *in rem* is within the Convention, the 'defendant' being the person having an interest in
the ship to protect: *The Deichland* [1989] 2 Lloyd's Rep 113. Should the defendant not be domiciled in a
contracting state, jurisdiction should be determined by the national law of the forum, subject to the
Convention giving contracting states 'exclusive jurisdiction' in certain matters (see Arts 4 and 16) and by
agreement of the parties (see Arts 17 and 18).

[54] Article 5.

[55] For example, see *Union Transport* v *Continental Lines* [1992] 1 Lloyd's Rep 229; *The Sea Maas* [1999] 2
Lloyd's Rep 281.

[56] Article 16.

state, effect will be given to any agreement by them to confer exclusive jurisdiction on a court of a particular contracting state.[57] Finally, a court of a contracting state before whom a defendant enters an appearance shall have jurisdiction provided that such appearance was not entered solely to contest the jurisdiction and that no other court has been granted exclusive jurisdiction by virtue of Article 16 of the Convention.[58]

There are further provisions to the effect that where suits involving the same parties and the same cause of action are brought in the courts of different contracting states, any court other than the court first seised of the matter must stay proceedings.[59] Similarly, where related actions are brought in the courts of different contracting states, any court other than the one first seised may stay its proceedings.[60]

It will be seen, therefore, that English courts are now required to apply two fundamentally different sets of jurisdictional rules depending on whether or not the particular case falls within the ambit of the Convention framework. The traditional approach of English law is that jurisdiction depends on service of a claim form on the defendant or the ship in England or, with permission of the court, on the defendant outside England. The formula adopted by the Convention, on the other hand, requires that, subject to certain specified exceptions, a defendant must be sued in his domicile. Service of a claim form remains necessary but it has a purely procedural role. The aim, in any event, is to make jurisdiction dependent on a substantive link between the dispute and the forum.

(ii) The Lugano Convention

This Convention, which matches the EC Convention discussed in the previous section, resulted from an agreement between EC member states and members of the European Free Trade Association (EFTA). It was enacted into English law by the Civil Jurisdiction and Judgments Act 1991.[61] The provisions of the Convention are parallel in almost all respects with those of the EC Convention, the respective rules relating to substantive jurisdiction differing only in respect of employment contracts. The Convention contains provisions setting out the mutual scope of the two Conventions.

The Lugano Convention will apply where the defendant is domiciled in an EFTA state or Poland and where the type of proceeding is such that, had the corresponding EC Convention been applicable, it would have created exclusive jurisdiction in a particular

---

[57] Article 17. This article sets out the formal requirements for such an agreement and also provides that, where no party to a jurisdiction clause is domiciled in a contracting state, no other contracting state may accept jurisdiction until the chosen court has declined it. The Arrest Convention is inconsistent with the mandatory application of a forum agreement under Art 17 and consequently upholding such an agreement remains discretionary: *The Bergen* [1997] 1 Lloyd's Rep 380. Incorporation of a jurisdiction clause by reference may satisfy the requirements. For an informative discussion, see *AIG Europe v QBE International Insurance* [2001] 2 Lloyd's Rep 268.

[58] Article 18.

[59] Article 21. An English court will not be seised of issue before relevant claim form has been both issued *and* served. *The Sargasso* [1994] 2 Lloyd's Rep 6.

[60] Article 22. The English view (held with considerable determination) that neither Art 21 nor Art 22 has any force where there is a jurisdiction agreement within Art 17 (*Continental Bank v Aeakos CN* [1994] 2 Lloyd's Rep 505) was not upheld by the European Court: *Gasser v MISAT* [2004] 1 Lloyd's Rep 222.

[61] Amended by SI 2000/1824 to reflect the accession of Poland to the Convention. The parties to the Convention are the EU member states, Iceland, Norway, Poland and Switzerland.

state. Similarly, the EFTA Convention will apply where suits, involving the same parties and the same cause of action (or related actions), are brought in two states, one of which is an EFTA state.

14.1.2 CHOICE OF LAW CLAUSE

Where the contract of carriage involves an international dimension, any resulting cargo claim will inevitably raise issues as to the applicable law. The common law rules on choice of law have been superseded by the Rome Convention on the Law Applicable to Contractual Obligations, which establishes a common framework for the states of the European Community. The Convention was incorporated into English law by the Contracts (Applicable Law) Act 1990 and is set out in Schedule 1 of that Act. It is applicable to all contracts, save those specifically excepted, entered into after it came into force on 1 April 1991. In large measure the approach of the Convention to the problem of choice of law is consistent with that taken by English courts prior to its enactment.

While the Convention applies to contracts of carriage, in order fully to appreciate its impact, a brief account of the common law prior to its enactment is appropriate.[62]

(1) THE LAW PRIOR TO THE CONVENTION AND IN SITUATIONS TO WHICH THE CONVENTION DOES NOT APPLY

Where international contracts of carriage are involved it may be invaluable to know in advance the national law which governs the agreement or any part of it,[63] since rights and remedies may differ radically in different legal systems. For this reason it has long been customary in contracts of affreightment to include an express choice of law clause in order to pre-empt any argument that may later arise. A variety of factors may influence the parties in selecting a particular legal system, ranging from the stronger bargaining power of one of the parties to the reputation of the system itself. There is some support for the view that it is preferable for the choice of law to follow the choice of forum since judges are presumably more competent in interpreting their own legal system.

(a) Express choice of law

English courts have in general been prepared to give effect to the expressed intention of the parties even though there is no connection between the particular subject matter of the dispute and the chosen law. Thus in *Vitafood Products* v *Unus Shipping Co*[64] the Privy Council gave effect to an English choice of law clause in a bill of lading covering a consignment of herring shipped in Newfoundland for New York. In rejecting the argument that the contract had no connection with England, Lord Wright categorically stated the view that 'where the English rule that intention is the test applies, and where there is an express statement by the parties of their intention to select the law of the contract, it is difficult to see what qualifications are possible, provided the intention

---

[62] There are also transactions which fall outside the Convention, e.g. arbitration or jurisdiction agreements.
[63] The 'proper law' as it was known.
[64] [1939] AC 277.

expressed is bona fide and legal and provided there is no reason for avoiding the choice on the ground of public policy'.[65]

Such wide freedom of choice is, however, subject to the provisos that the parties in exercising their choice are acting bona fide, that such choice is not contrary to the public policy of the state whose law would apply in the absence of any choice of law clause, and that there is no mandatory statutory provision prohibiting contracting out. So in *The Morviken*[66] a choice of law clause in a bill of lading issued in the United Kingdom was held void in so far as it infringed the minimum protection afforded to the cargo owner by the Carriage of Goods by Sea Act 1971.[67]

English courts have not, however, been prepared to recognise a 'floating' choice of law, i.e. a clause in the contract of carriage giving one of the parties the option of selecting the proper law of the contract. Thus in *The Iran Vojdan*[68] the trial judge refused to give effect to a clause in a bill of lading, covering a cargo shipped in Hamburg on an Iranian vessel, which gave the carrier the right of choice between German, Iranian and English law as the governing law of the contract. In the opinion of Bingham J, 'The proper law is something so fundamental to questions relating to the formulation, validity, interpretation and performance of a contract that it must, in my judgment, be built into the fabric of the contract from the start and cannot float in an indeterminate way until finally determined at the option of one party.'[69]

(b) Implied choice of law

In the absence of an express choice of law clause, the inclusion in the contract of a choice of forum clause, whether for litigation or arbitration, was at one time generally taken as an important indication of the proper law of the contract. In *Tzortzis* v *Monark Line*[70] a contract concluded in Stockholm for the sale of a vessel by Swedish owners to Greek buyers included a London arbitration clause. Although the Court of Appeal felt that otherwise the agreement had its closest and more real connection with Sweden, it nevertheless held that the inclusion of the arbitration clause 'raises an irresistible inference which overrides all other factors'.[71] One of the reasons given for such a conclusion was that the parties must have intended the arbitrators to apply the law with which they were most familiar.

Later cases suggested, however, that such a presumption was not conclusive and that the presence of an arbitration clause was only one of the factors to be taken into consideration when reaching a decision as to the proper law. In the view of Lord Diplock, 'strong as the implication may be, it can be rebutted as other implications of intention can be rebutted. It is not a positive rule of law which is independent of the intentions of

---

[65] *Ibid* at p 289.
[66] [1983] 1 Lloyd's Rep 1. See *supra* pp 186 ff.
[67] See also s 9 of the Sea-Carriage of Goods Act 1924 (Australia) which renders null and void any provision in a bill of lading covered by the Act which seeks to avoid the application of Australian law. *Ocean SS Co v Queensland State Wheat Board* [1941] 1 KB 402.
[68] [1984] 2 Lloyd's Rep 380. See also *The Armar* [1980] 2 Lloyd's Rep 450.
[69] The *Iran Vojdan* [1984] 2 Lloyd's Rep at p 385. But an arbitration clause giving a party an option of choice of forum does not necessarily imply a floating choice of law. *The Star Texas* [1993] 2 Lloyd's Rep 445.
[70] [1968] 1 Lloyd's Rep 337.
[71] *Per* Salmon LJ at *ibid* p 412.

the parties.'[72] Thus in the *Tunisienne* case,[73] a standard tanker voyage charterparty, negotiated in Paris between French shipowners and a Tunisian company for the carriage of a quantity of crude oil between Tunisian ports over a nine-month period, contained both a London arbitration clause and a clause providing that the contract should be 'governed by the laws of the flag of the vessel carrying the goods'. In these circumstances the House of Lords considered that the choice of London arbitration was not decisive and held that French law was the proper law of the contract. The majority of the court reached this conclusion by invoking the express choice of law clause while the minority relied on the general principle that the proper law was the law of the country with which the contract had its closest connection.[74] In upholding the original award of the arbitrator in this case, Lord Wilberforce observed that 'a question of the proper law of a commercial contract ought to be regarded as primarily a matter to be found by arbitrators: for after all the question is one of estimating competing factors in the light of commercial intention. . . .'[75]

(c) Where no choice indicated

Problems arose where the contract provided no express or implied indication of the law which the parties intended to govern their agreement. In such a case it was necessary to apply an objective test, taking into consideration the terms of the contract, the situation of the parties and all the surrounding circumstances. The general rule was that 'where the parties have not exercised their choice, the proper law of the contract is the system of law with which it has its closest and most real connection'.[76] In applying this test the court was entitled to take into consideration a variety of factors including the residence or nationality of the parties, the place where the contract was made, the place where the contract is to be performed, the location of the subject matter and, in charterparty cases, the law of the flag.[77] These indicators were originally treated as presumptions each of which raised a prima facie case in favour of a particular system of law, but with the advent of the 'connection' test, this view came to be regarded as outdated. No single factor was to be treated as providing a prima facie answer, but all must be taken into consideration.[78] An illustration of the application of the 'connection' test is provided by the Court of Appeal decision in *Coast Line Ltd* v *Hudig*.[79] English owners had chartered a vessel on a Gencon form to a Dutch firm for a voyage from Rotterdam to Drogheda in the Irish Republic and the question was whether the contract was governed by English or Dutch law. In finding in favour of English law as the proper law, Megaw LJ

---

[72] *Compagnie d'Armement Maritime* v *Compagnie Tunisienne de Navigation* [1971] AC 572 at p 609. Any such presumption is much less strong if there is a dual or alternative situs. *The Star Texas* [1993] 2 Lloyd's Rep 445.

[73] [1971] AC 572.

[74] See Lord Reid at *ibid* p 583.

[75] *Ibid* at p 596.

[76] Lord Diplock in *Compagnie d'Armement Maritime* v *Compagnie Tunisienne de Navigation* [1971] AC 572 at p 609.

[77] See *Lloyd* v *Guibert* (1865) 39 LJQB 241; *The Assunzione* [1954] P 150.

[78] See Megaw LJ in *Coast Lines Ltd* v *Hudig* [1972] 2 QB 34 at p 47. See also *The Stolt Marmaro* [1985] 2 Lloyd's Rep 428.

[79] [1972] 2 QB 34.

expressed the view that 'the fact that the subject matter of the charterparty was an English ship and that the whole of the transaction contemplated by the contract concerned the activities of that English ship in loading, carrying and discharging the cargo, produces the result that the transaction, viewed as a whole and weighing all the relevant factors has a closer and more real connection with English law than with the law of The Netherlands'.[80]

It was presumed that the same rules applied to a contract of carriage covered by a bill of lading, and the proper law depended on a construction of the terms of the bill in the light of the surrounding circumstances. Where the bill expressly incorporated the terms of a charterparty, however, the proper law of the charterparty generally also governed the bill.

(II) THE ROME CONVENTION[81]

(a) Scope of the Convention

The Convention, which came into force on 1 April 1991, applies to contractual obligations 'in any situation involving a choice of law between the laws of different countries',[82] irrespective of whether the contract or the parties have any connection with a contracting state. No definition of 'contractual obligation' is provided,[83] and presumably the interpretation of this term will be a matter for the national courts and, in the last resort, for the European Court. The Convention does, however, exclude certain contractual obligations from its scope.[84] Those of particular relevance to contracts of carriage by sea include, *inter alia*, arbitration agreements and choice of forum clauses; bills of exchange, cheques and promissory notes; and contracts of insurance covering risks situated within member states of the EU.[85] Such insurance contracts[86] are the subject of EU law, while in the other cases, questions of choice of law will be decided according to common law rules. The provisions of the Convention will also apply to cases of conflicts between the laws of different parts of the United Kingdom.[87]

(b) The applicable law

The Convention is broadly consistent with the common law in affording primacy to the intention of the parties: 'A contract shall be governed by the law chosen by the

---

[80] *Ibid* at p 47. Lord Denning MR, purporting to apply the same 'connection' test, held that, other factors being equally balanced, the law of the flag should prevail.

[81] All member states of the EU are parties to the Convention, but not all have become parties to the Treaties of Accession of Portugal and Spain (The Funchal Convention 1992) or of Austria, Finland and Sweden (The Accession Convention 1996). The UK is a party to both Conventions.

[82] Article 1.1.

[83] As to the need for taking a 'single international or autonomous view' in characterising an issue as 'contractual' for the purpose of the Convention, see *The Mount 1* [2001] 1 Lloyd's Rep 597. As to the need for restrictions on a claimant's ability to choose a governing law through formulating a claim, for example, in tort or contract, see Briggs [2003] LMCLQ 39.

[84] For a complete list, see Art 1.2.

[85] Article 1.3.

[86] See Baatz, Y, in Thomas, D (ed) *Modern Law of Marine Insurance*, 1996, Chapter 10.

[87] Section 2(3).

parties.'[88] Such choice may be express or may be inferred from the terms of the contract or the circumstances of the case, provided that it is established 'with reasonable certainty'.[89] Presumably, as at common law, the choice of a specific forum by the parties would be one of the factors to be taken into consideration.

A number of restrictions are, however, placed on the parties' freedom of choice. Thus courts are entitled to enforce the laws of the forum where they are mandatory irrespective of the law which would otherwise be applicable.[90] Again, parties will not be able to avoid a mandatory rule of a national state by the choice of a foreign law in circumstances where all the other relevant elements of the contract at the time of that choice are connected exclusively with that particular state.[91] For the purposes of both these provisions, 'mandatory rules' are defined as those 'which cannot be derogated from by contract'.[92] Similarly, a choice of law is not permissible if it either prejudices the application of international conventions to which a contracting state is a party,[93] or is 'manifestly incompatible with the public policy of the forum'.[94]

In the absence of any choice of law by the parties, 'the contract shall be governed by the law of the country with which it is most closely connected'.[95] While a decision as to the applicable law in these circumstances is largely a question of fact dependent on the facts of the particular case, the Convention departs from the common law approach in adopting a number of presumptions. The basic presumption is:

> 'that the contract is most closely connected with the country where the party who is to effect the performance which is characteristic of the contract has, at the time of conclusion of the contract, his habitual residence, or, in the case of a body corporate or incorporate, its central administration. However, if the contract is entered into in the course of that party's trade or profession, that country shall be the country in which the principal place of business is situated or, where under the terms of the contract the performance is to be effected through a place of business other than the principal place of business, the country in which that other place of business is situated.'[96]

This presumption is to be 'disregarded' if the characteristic performance cannot be determined, or 'it appears from the circumstances as a whole that the contract is most closely connected with another country'. The extent to which there is a substantive move away from the common law approach depends on the weight given to the presumption,[97] a matter not entirely settled in the English or Scottish courts.

---

[88] Article 3.1. Subject to the possibility of applying the law of a party's habitual residence the existence and validity of a contract is determined by the law which would govern if the contract was valid. (Art 8). The parties may also at any time agree to change the governing law (Art 3.2).

[89] *Ibid*. Applying also to any 'agreed' change. See *The Aeolian* [2001] 2 Lloyd's Rep 641.

[90] Article 7.2. This provision would presumably be in line with the decision in *The Morviken* [1983] 1 Lloyd's Rep 1. A provision permitting the application of foreign mandatory rules (Art 7.1) is not enacted into English law (s 2(2)).

[91] Article 3.3.

[92] *Ibid*.

[93] Article 21.

[94] Article 16.

[95] Article 4.1.

[96] Article 4.2. Some difficulty may be encountered in defining the term 'performance which is characteristic of the contract'. The presumption does not apply if this cannot be determined (Art 4.5).

[97] See *Definitely Maybe (Touring) Ltd* v *Marck Lieberberg* [2001] 1 WLR 1745.

In the case of contracts for the carriage of goods by sea,[98] this basic presumption is replaced by a presumption that the applicable law is that of the country in which, at the time the contract is concluded, the carrier has his principal place of business, provided that it is also the country in which the place of loading, or the place of discharge, or the principal place of business of the consignor is situated.[99] While this presumption will probably cover the majority of situations, in cases where its requirements are not met, the decision on the law most closely connected will have to be made on the facts of the case without the benefit of any presumption. Further, any presumption is to be disregarded where, from the circumstances as a whole, it appears that the contract is more closely connected with another country.[100]

Once a decision on the applicable law has been reached on the basis of the above rules, that law will be applied even though it is the law of a non-contracting state.[101]

(c) Interpretation of the Convention

The provisions of the Convention have so close an affinity with the pre-existing common law rules that it might be thought that, at least in the United Kingdom, the latter would play a dominant part in their interpretation. The 1990 Act, however, requires courts in the United Kingdom to take judicial notice 'of any decision of, or expression of opinion by, the European Court on any such question',[102] while the Convention itself requires that in interpreting its rules, 'regard shall be had to their international character and to the desirability of achieving uniformity in their interpretation and application'.[103] It seems likely, therefore, that the future development of choice of law rules will be influenced more by the European tradition than by their common law background.[104]

14.2 SECURITY FOR CLAIMS

Even though the claimant satisfies the jurisdictional requirements and obtains judgment from a competent court, there still remains the problem of obtaining satisfaction. 'An unsatisfied judgment against an assetless defendant is a pyrrhic victory.'[105] In the interval between judgment and execution, the defendant may have become insolvent or he may have made use of the opportunity to remove his assets out of the jurisdiction. Before embarking on arbitration or litigation, therefore, a claimant would be well

---

[98] These include single voyage charterparties and 'other contracts the main purpose of which is the carriage of goods' (Art 4.4).

[99] Article 4.4.

[100] Article 4.5. In such circumstances the basic presumption, where it would otherwise apply, is to be disregarded (*ibid*). For an application of Art 4.5, see *Bank of Baroda* v *Vysya Bank Ltd* [1994] 2 Lloyd's Rep 87.

[101] Article 2.

[102] Section 3(2). The Brussels Protocol, which is included in Sch 3 of the 1990 Act, and a second Protocol, confer jurisdiction on the European Court to give authoritative rulings on the interpretation of the Convention. However, the Protocols have not yet received sufficient ratifications to become effective.

[103] Article 18.

[104] See the approach of the Court of Appeal in *The Mount 1* [2001] 1 Lloyd's Rep 597.

[105] Thomas, DR *Maritime Liens*, 1980, p 73.

advised to seek some form of interim security in order to ensure that any possible judgment in his favour will be met. In English law there are two methods of obtaining such security. Their availability is not affected by either the Brussels or Lugano Conventions.

14.2.1 THE ACTION *IN REM*

Reference has already been made[106] to s 21(4) of the Supreme Court Act 1981 which, in respect of carriage claims, confers jurisdiction *in rem* on the Admiralty Court following the service of an *in rem* claim form within territorial waters on the ship in connection with which the claim arises.[107] Such jurisdiction is established where two requirements are met. First, the person who would be liable on the claim if sued *in personam* ('the relevant person') was, at the time the cause of the action arose, the owner or charterer of the ship or in possession or control of it. Secondly, at the time the action is brought, the ship is either beneficially owned ('as respects all the shares in it') or chartered by demise to that person. Alternatively, a similar action may be brought against any other ship which, at the time the action is brought, is beneficially owned by the 'relevant person'.[108]

Such a remedy is available for most claims arising under a contract of carriage by sea. The Act itself makes the procedure available in respect of 'any claim arising out of any agreement relating to the carriage of goods in a ship, or to the use or hire of a ship'.[109]

Jurisdiction *in rem is* exercisable over foreign as well as British ships, provided that they are located in British territorial waters at the time of service of the claim form. It has three main advantages. First, the party who would be liable *in personam*, and who is liable *in rem* because of his connection with the ship, need not be within the jurisdiction at the time proceedings are initiated against his ship. Secondly, the issue of the *in rem* claim form allows the claimant to secure the arrest of the ship.[110] The choice will then lie with the beneficial owner whether or not to acknowledge service of the claim form and defend the action. In the words of Sir George Jessel MR,

> 'You may in England and in most countries proceed against the ship. The writ [now claim form] may be issued against the owner of such a ship, and the owner may never appear, and you may get your judgment against the ship without a single person being named from beginning to end. That is an action *in rem*, and it is perfectly well understood that the judgment is against the ship.'[111]

Thirdly, on the issue of the claim form the claimant becomes a preferential creditor.

If the beneficial owner fails to acknowledge service of the claim form, authority would suggest that the value of the ship would represent the maximum limit of recovery

---

[106] See *supra* pp 308–9.

[107] Although not specifically provided for, it seems that an arrest prior to service acts as an alternative to service.

[108] Supreme Court Act 1981 s 21(4)(b).

[109] See s 20(2)(h).

[110] Property may be maintained under arrest if the action is stayed for arbitration or hearing in a foreign forum: Civil Jurisdiction and Judgments Act 1982 s 26; Arbitration Act 1996 s 11.

[111] *The City of Mecca* (1881) 5 PD 106 at p 112. But for the purposes of the Brussels and Lugano Conventions the reality that it is an action against a defendant is recognised (see fn 53 *supra*); such recognition now following (at least to an extent) in English law: *The Indian Grace No 2* [1988] AC 878.

for any claim.[112] In practice, however, the value of the ship normally far exceeds the value of the claim and consequently the action *in rem* may be viewed rather as a procedural device designed to induce the beneficial owner or demise charterer to enter an appearance in court and deposit bail or other security in order to obtain the release of the vessel.[113] Accordingly, the procedure serves a two-fold purpose in not only supplying a method of founding jurisdiction but also providing the claimant with the necessary security to ensure that any eventual judgment in his favour will be met.[114] Moreover the vessel, any bail deposited in substitution for it, or any bank or P & I guarantee, will provide a form of security immune from the consequences of any future events affecting the financial solvency of the defendant. In this regard the action *in rem* has a substantive consequence through the conferring of preferred creditor status or alternative security.

14.2.2 THE FREEZING INJUNCTION

This relatively recent form of security was invented by Lord Denning,[115] subsequently given statutory recognition by s 37(3) of the Supreme Court Act 1981, and now appears in the list of interim remedies in the Civil Procedure Rules.[116] It takes the form of an interlocutory injunction restraining a party to legal proceedings from removing moveable assets from the jurisdiction or otherwise disposing of them to the prejudice of the plaintiff pending judgment. It is a discretionary equitable remedy, failure to comply with which amounts to a contempt of court. The injunction has been found a particularly useful device where the defendant is out of the jurisdiction, to be used in conjunction with an application for permission to serve a claim form in respect of the substantive claim under the CPR Part 6(iii) replacing Order 11 of the Rules of the Supreme Court.[117] For the injunction to be granted, the defendant must be subject to the jurisdiction of the English Court,[118] and the claimant must have a good arguable cause of action. Where the defendant is out of the country, service of the claim form in respect of the injunction is itself governed by the CPR.[119] It is important to note, however, that the object of the injunction is merely to maintain the defendant's assets and so create a potential fund out of which any subsequent judgment can be satisfied. It is not designed in such an event to provide the claimant with any priority over other creditors. The

---

[112] See *The Longford* (1889) 14 PD 34; *The Burns* [1907] P 137. Cf. the comments of Brandon J in *The Conoco Britannia* [1972] 2 QB 543 at p 555. This would not, however, preclude a separate action *in personam* against the beneficial owner for any outstanding balance.

[113] But an inflated claim may lead to damages for wrongful detention: see *Gulf Azov v Idisi* [2001] 1 Lloyd's Rep 727.

[114] As to the provision of security in arbitration proceedings through an action *in rem*, see the Civil Jurisdiction and Judgments Act 1982 s 26; *The Tuyuti* [1984] 2 Lloyd's Rep 51.

[115] In *Nippon Yusen Kaisha v Karageorgis* [1975] 2 Lloyd's Rep 137 and *Mareva Compañia Naviera SA v International Bulk Carriers SA* [1975] 2 Lloyd's Rep 509 in which cases he invoked a discretionary power vested in the High Court under s 45 of the Supreme Court of Judicature Act 1925.

[116] CPR 25.1(1)(f). Until its incorporation into the CPR, it was known (after one of the initial cases) as the Mareva Injunction.

[117] See *supra* p 309. There will normally be a supporting order directing the defendant to disclose the location of assets. (See CPR 25.1(1)(g) and 25 PD.)

[118] An original restriction to foreigners outside the jurisdiction has long been abandoned.

[119] See Rule 6.20(4).

courts have repeatedly stressed that they are not seeking to rewrite the law of insolvency and that the injunction is not intended as a form of pre-trial attachment.[120]

It was early established that such an injunction would only issue where the claimant had a substantive cause of action within the jurisdiction.[121] However, legislative intervention has removed that restriction and the injunction is now available in support of both English and foreign proceedings.[122] A prerequisite for the exercise of the discretion in respect of foreign proceedings is whether, in the circumstances of the particular case, it is 'expedient' to grant interim relief, given that those proceedings are being conducted out of the jurisdiction.[123] Otherwise, there is no other fetter on the discretion.[124] Factors relevant to a finding of inexpediency include the effect on the management of the case in the foreign court, any policy of the foreign court to make orders which are not effective worldwide, the risk of inconsistency arising from an overlapping of orders made elsewhere and the risk of making an ineffective order.[125]

The popularity of the remedy quickly led to the formulation of a series of guidelines to prevent its abuse.[126] First, the party seeking the injunction should have a good arguable case against the defendant.[127] There should be a full and frank disclosure of all matters within his knowledge which are material to the case. Being an equitable remedy, any suspicion that he has failed to do so will result in the refusal of an injunction.[128] Secondly, the claimant should provide the court with full particulars of his claim together with a fair résumé of the points raised by the defendant in rebuttal. Thirdly, the claimant must provide grounds for believing that the defendant has assets against which the injunction can be directed. He will rarely be aware of the full extent of such assets, but proof of the existence of a bank account will be sufficient, even though it may be in overdraft.[129]

Fourthly, the claimant must provide grounds for believing that the assets are likely to be removed or dissipated before any judgment or award can be executed. In the words

---

[120] See *The Angel Bell* [1980] 1 Lloyd's Rep 632; *A/S Admiral Shipping* v *Portlink Ferries Ltd* [1984] 2 Lloyd's Rep 166; *Gangway Ltd* v *Caledonian Park Investments* [2001] 2 Lloyd's Rep 715.

[121] See *The Siskina* [1978] 1 Lloyd's Rep 1; *Mercedes Benz* v *Leiduck* [1995] 2 Lloyd's Rep 417.

[122] Civil Jurisdiction and Judgments Act 1982 s 25, as extended by SI 1997/302, 1997/278. As to arbitration, see Arbitration Act 1996 ss 2(3), 44(2)(e).

[123] Civil Jurisdiction and Judgments Act 1982 s 25(2). Under the Brussels Convention, the EU Council Regulation replacing it and, it would seem, the Lugano Convention, jurisdiction to grant interim relief as provided by national law follows from: (a) jurisdiction over the substantive claim or (b) the application of Art 24 permitting (*inter alia*) such relief in relation to assets having a 'real connecting link' with the forum: *Van Uden Maritime BV* v *Kommonditsgesellschaft Fiume* [1999] QB 1225.

[124] See *Crédit Suisse Fides Trust* v *Cuoghi* [1997] 3 All ER 724. However, the residence of the defendant and the location of the assets are clearly relevant factors. As to the relevance of the view of the foreign court, see *Refco Inc* v *Eastern Trading Co* [1999] 1 Lloyd's Rep 159. See also *Motorola Credit Corp* v *Uzan* [2003] EWCA 752 (reviewing the authorities).

[125] *Ibid* para 115.

[126] See Lord Denning MR in *The Genie* [1979] 2 Lloyd's Rep 184 at p 189. 'Much as I am in favour of the Mareva injunction, it must not be stretched too far lest it be endangered.'

[127] See *Yukong Line Ltd* v *Rendsburg Investments Corp* [2001] 2 Lloyd's Rep 113 and cases cited; *C Inc plc* v *L* [2001] 2 Lloyd's Rep 459.

[128] *The Assios* [1979] 1 Lloyd's Rep 331; or be a ground for discharge: *The Giovanna* [1999] 1 Lloyd's Rep 867.

[129] See *The Genie* [1979] 2 Lloyd's Rep 184; *Searose Ltd* v *Seatrain (UK) Ltd* [1981] 1 Lloyd's Rep 556.

of Lord Denning MR,[130] 'The mere fact that the defendant is abroad is not by itself sufficient. No one would wish any reputable foreign company to be plagued with a [freezing] injunction simply because it has agreed to London arbitration.' To decide otherwise would be a severe deterrent to any foreign party contemplating the inclusion of a London choice of forum clause in his contract. Accordingly, there must be some evidence drawn from the defendant's previous conduct or the circumstances of the case to raise the inference that there is a serious risk that he is likely to abscond or dispose of his assets prior to judgment being obtained.[131] Finally, the claimant must give an undertaking that he has sufficient funds to meet the costs should the eventual judgment go against him. In appropriate cases the court may require security to be given.[132]

Provided that these requirements are met, the freezing injunction can provide an effective form of security for a prospective litigant. Originally it was envisaged as a remedy available against foreigners outside the jurisdiction.[133] However, its scope has been progressively extended to cover defendants of any nationality, assets wherever found and, finally, proceedings in any state. That is not to say that the injunction will be as freely available against foreign assets as against assets located in England, or in respect of foreign as opposed to English proceedings, and the burden on the claimant will be particularly heavy where an injunction is sought against foreign assets in respect of proceedings conducted in a foreign state.[134]

The wide use being made of the injunction led to the fears of unnecessary inconvenience being caused to innocent third parties. So any order covering assets outside England will only apply to third parties if either they are subject to the jurisdiction of the English court and able to prevent breach of the order outside the jurisdiction, or the order is declared enforceable by the court in the relevant country.[135] In many instances the assets against which the injunction is directed are in the hands of banks or other third parties, who are expected to freeze the relevant account or other asset as soon as they are given notice of the injunction.[136] In such cases the claimant is required to give an undertaking to indemnify third parties against the expenses incurred in complying with the injunction,[137] while, in certain circumstances, the courts have refused to issue

---

[130] *The Genie, supra*, at p 189. See also *Refco Inc v Eastern Trading Co* [1999] 1 Lloyd's Rep 159; *The Giovanna* [1999] 1 Lloyd's Rep 867.

[131] See *Rathman v Othman* [1980] 2 Lloyd's Rep 565. Cf. *Esefka International v Central Bank of Nigeria* [1979] 1 Lloyd's Rep 445; *The Niedersachsen* [1983] 2 Lloyd's Rep 600.

[132] See *Esefka International v Central Bank of Nigeria, supra*.

[133] See *The Agrabele* [1979] 2 Lloyd's Rep 117 at p 120 *per* Lloyd J.

[134] See the comment of Lord Donaldson MR in the case of *Rosseel v Oriental Commercial & Shipping Ltd* [1990] 3 All ER 545 at p 546.

[135] See CPR 25 PD (sample form). See the standard form 23PD 13 and the *Admiralty and Commercial Courts Guide* Appendix 5. As to the evolvement of the conditions, see *Bank of China v NHM LLC* [2002] 2 Lloyd's Rep 506. The phrase 'able to prevent' means not only without committing a criminal offence or ignoring a court order but also not being in breach of contractual obligations.

[136] See *Z Ltd v A-Z and AA-LL* [1982] 1 Lloyd's Rep 240 at p 244. Any right of set-off in respect of any facility granted to the respondent before notification of the order will be excluded. See also guidance notes to standard form para 17. Where a bank has a prior charge, its duty is simply to act in good faith and in the ordinary course of business: *Gangway Ltd v Caledonian Park Investments* [2001] 2 Lloyd's Rep 715.

[137] See *Searose Ltd v Seatrain (UK) Ltd* [1981] 1 Lloyd's Rep 556 (expenses incurred in tracing branch of bank at which defendant's account held when no details given by plaintiff). See also *The Marie Leonhardt* [1981] 2 Lloyd's Rep 458. See CPR 25 PD (sample form).

an injunction where they considered it to constitute an unwarranted interference with the business of that third party.[138]

Restrictions have also been placed on the scope of the injunction even in respect of its application to the defendant himself. Thus the quantity of assets to be frozen will be limited to the amount of the claimant's claim, where that is quantifiable, while in appropriate circumstances the court will modify the injunction to allow a defendant to meet his ordinary trade debts in the normal course of business.[139] The reason for this latter indulgence in favour of the defendant is that, as discussed earlier, the object of the injunction is merely to prevent the dispersion of assets and not to provide the plaintiff with any priority over other creditors.

14.3 ARBITRATION

Most contracts of affreightment include a clause providing that any dispute arising thereunder shall be referred to arbitration. This is invariably the case in relation to charterparties, though arbitration clauses are less frequently found in bills of lading except where the bill incorporates an arbitration clause in the charterparty under which it is issued.[140] Arbitration differs from litigation in court in that the procedure is not available as of right in the event of any dispute, but is dependent on prior agreement between the parties. It also possesses many attractions to the prospective litigant. Its procedure is cheaper, speedier and less formal, many disputes being resolved by the arbitrator on a mere review of the documents. Again, arbitrators selected by the parties themselves are usually experts in the field who do not regard themselves as so strictly bound by precedent as the judiciary, being more prepared to make awards on the merits of the particular case before them. Finally, parties who are not anxious to have the details of their agreements publicised are attracted by the privacy associated with arbitral proceedings, since awards are not published in the United Kingdom.[141] The only major disadvantage associated with arbitration stems from the fact that a series of ad hoc awards generally unaccompanied by reasons, is not conducive to the establishment of the precedent necessary to make the law predictable.

14.3.1 THE ARBITRATION ACT 1996

As from 31 January 1997, the law of arbitration in England, Wales and Northern Ireland is governed by the provisions of the Arbitration Act 1996. Prior to this Act the relevant law was to be found in a series of three statutes, supplemented and interpreted by an extensive range of case law. The Arbitration Act 1950 consolidated most of the earlier basic arbitration legislation, the 1975 Act gave effect to the New York

---

[138] See *The Eletherios* [1982] 1 Lloyd's Rep 351; *Bank of China v NHM LLC* [2002] 2 Lloyd's Rep 506.
[139] See *A/S Admiral Shipping v Portlink Ferries Ltd* [1984] 2 Lloyd's Rep 166; *The Angel Bell* [1980] 1 Lloyd's Rep 632.
[140] For fuller discussion, see *supra* pp 235 ff.
[141] Cf. the position in the United States. It has recently been held that an arbitration agreement includes an implied duty of confidence: *Insurance Co v Lloyd's Syndicate* [1995] 1 Lloyd's Rep 272.

Convention on the enforcement of foreign arbitration awards, while the Arbitration Act 1979 sought to promote the greater finality of arbitration awards by limiting the supervisory powers of the English courts. The dispersion of the law between three statutes and the need to refer to a voluminous case law made the law difficult to access and resulted in unnecessary delay and expense. If English arbitration was to maintain its international reputation, rationalisation was urgently required.

A Departmental Advisory Committee established by the Department of Trade and Industry, and under the chairmanship of Saville LJ, drafted a new Bill specifically designed 'to restate and improve the law relating to arbitration pursuant to an arbitration agreement'. Not only was it designed to consolidate existing arbitration law, both statutory and common law, but also to introduce a number of significant changes with the object of providing a more flexible procedure. The underlying policy was to invest the parties with wide autonomy over the conduct of all aspects of arbitration proceedings, including the appointment of arbitrators, the procedure to be adopted, the powers of the arbitral tribunal and the scope of the arbitration award. Mandatory legislative provisions were to be restricted to a minimum and the interventionist powers of the court were limited to those essential to the maintenance of justice. The resulting statute received the Royal Assent in June 1996 and came into force on 31 January 1997, being applicable to all arbitrations commenced on or after that date.[142]

14.3.2 BASIC PRINCIPLES

(A) SEAT OF ARBITRATION

The 1996 Act introduced a new concept of the 'seat of the arbitration', which is identified as the juridical seat of the arbitration as distinct from the actual physical location of the arbitration proceedings.[143] While in the majority of cases the two will be interchangeable, in other cases the juridical seat may be located elsewhere, as for example where different parts of the proceedings are held in different countries. Such seat can be specified by the parties themselves in the arbitration agreement, or may be delegated to some other person or tribunal authorised by them for the purpose. In the absence of such specific designation, the seat must be determined objectively, having regard to the parties' agreement and all the relevant circumstances.[144] The provisions of the 1996 Act will apply where the seat of arbitration is in England, Wales or Northern Ireland.

(B) AUTONOMY OF THE PARTIES

Arbitration is founded on mutual agreement, a fact which the 1996 Act seeks to recognise by investing the parties with extensive powers over the conduct of arbitration proceedings. In general they are permitted to determine such matters as the size and composition of the arbitration tribunal,[145] the procedure to be adopted[146] and the

---

[142] For the law governing arbitration procedure prior to the 1996 Act, see the 2nd edition of this textbook, at pp 321–30.
[143] Arbitration Act 1996 s 2.
[144] Section 3.
[145] Sections 15–18.
[146] Sections 38–41.

availability or otherwise of a right of appeal to the High Court on a point of law.[147] Certain mandatory powers are, however, reserved to the court for reasons of public policy, such as the power to stay legal proceedings, to remove an arbitrator, or to enforce an arbitration award.[148] Otherwise the parties are granted a wide autonomy in regard to arbitration proceedings, many provisions of the Act being applicable 'unless the parties have agreed otherwise'.

(C) UNDERLYING PRINCIPLES

One of the unique features of the 1996 Act is an explicit statement of the guiding principles according to which the provisions of the statute are to be implemented. Thus section 1 states that 'the object of arbitration is to obtain the fair resolution of disputes by an impartial tribunal without unnecessary delay or expense', and in achieving this objective 'the parties should be free to agree how their disputes are resolved, subject only to such safeguards as are necessary in the public interest'. The parties are further enjoined to 'do all things necessary for the proper and expeditious conduct of the arbitration proceedings'.[149] The tribunal, on its part, is required 'to act fairly and impartially as between the parties, giving each party a reasonable opportunity of putting his case and dealing with that of his opponent, and . . . adopt procedures suitable to the circumstances of the particular case, avoiding unnecessary delay or expense, so as to provide a fair means for the resolution of the matters falling to be determined'.[150]

14.3.3 TYPES OF ARBITRATION

The parties are free to agree on the number of arbitrators to form the tribunal and on whether there is to be a chairman or umpire.[151] In the event of an arbitration clause not specifying the number of arbitrators to take part in adjudicating the dispute, s 15(3) of the 1996 Act provides that 'the tribunal shall consist of a sole arbitrator'.[152] The attraction of a single arbitrator lies in the reduced costs and the more speedy process resulting from the absence of any need to reach agreement with fellow arbitrators on procedural matters or the ultimate award. A serious problem can, however, arise where the two sides are not prepared to agree on the appointment. In such an event application can be made to the High Court to appoint an arbitrator[153] but experience has shown that such a process can be both time consuming and expensive. One accepted method of avoiding the problem is to include a provision in the arbitration clause for the arbitrator to be appointed by a named third party, for example the President of the Law Society or the Chairman of a Commodity Association.

Alternatively, the parties may provide for the reference of their dispute to 'three persons', in which case each party would appoint his own arbitrator and the two so

---

[147] Sections 69, 87(1).
[148] Listed in Sch 1 to the Act.
[149] Arbitration Act 1996 s 40(1).
[150] Section 33(1).
[151] Section 15(1).
[152] *The Villa* [1998] 1 Lloyd's Rep 195.
[153] Section 18(3)(d). See *The Villa* [1998] 1 Lloyd's Rep 195.

appointed would appoint a third as chairman of the tribunal.[154] In the event of any disagreement between the arbitrators as to the award, and in the absence of any agreement of the parties to the contrary, the decision of the majority will be binding.[155]

It is, however, more common in the United Kingdom for the arbitration agreement to provide for each party to appoint his own arbitrator and then for the two arbitrators themselves to appoint an umpire in the event of any disagreement between them. Such an umpire was not normally appointed until the disagreement had arisen, except where the arbitration procedure took the form of a formal hearing with the parties present. In the latter case the umpire was appointed in advance in order to obviate any possible need for a rehearing. The 1996 Act now gives statutory effect to this procedure by providing that the two arbitrators once appointed 'may appoint an umpire at any time after they themselves are appointed and shall do so before any substantive hearing or forthwith if they cannot agree on a matter relating to the arbitration'.[156] In the event of any disagreement between the arbitrators, the umpire is free to make an independent award as if he were a sole arbitrator.[157] Should either party refuse to co-operate by nominating his arbitrator then, after giving the appropriate notice, the other party may designate his nominee as the sole arbitrator and proceed with the hearing and award.[158]

Should the arbitration agreement provide for the appointment of two or other even number of arbitrators, without reference to the subsequent appointment of an umpire, the 1996 Act requires the appointment of an additional arbitrator as chairman of the tribunal.[159] The procedure would then follow that stipulated above for the appointment of 'three arbitrators', i.e. each party would appoint his own arbitrator and the two so appointed would appoint a third as chairman of the tribunal. In the event of any disagreement between the arbitrators as to the award, the decision of the majority will be binding.

Occasionally the contract may require the appointed arbitrator to be a 'commercial man', i.e. a person normally engaged in the relevant trade. It would appear that the category includes a full-time arbitrator, but not a lawyer practising in a particular commercial field.

14.3.4 COMMENCEMENT OF ARBITRATION

Section 14(1) of the 1996 Arbitration Act provides that the parties are free to agree when arbitration proceedings are to be regarded as commenced for the purposes of the Limitation Acts. In the absence of such agreement, 'where the arbitrator or arbitrators are to be appointed by the parties, arbitration proceedings are commenced in respect of a matter when one party serves on the other party or parties notice in writing requiring

---

[154] Section 16(5).
[155] Section 20(3).
[156] Section 16(6)(b). Provision is made in s 21(3) for the umpire to be supplied with the same documents and other materials as are supplied to the other arbitrators.
[157] Section 21(4).
[158] Section 17(2).
[159] Section 15(2).

him or them to appoint an arbitrator in respect of that matter'.[160] The parties are free to agree on the manner of service of such notice[161] but, in the absence of agreement, it may be served 'by any effective means'.[162]

14.3.5 APPEAL FROM ARBITRATION AWARD

Under the 1996 Act an appeal will lie to the High Court on a question of law arising out of an arbitration award, but only if the appeal is brought either with the consent of all the parties to the arbitration or with the leave of the court.[163] Any application for leave to appeal must be brought within 28 days of the date of the award and will only be granted if the court is satisfied –

'(a) that the determination of the question will substantially affect the rights of one or more of the parties,

(b) that the question is one which the tribunal was asked to determine,

(c) that, on the basis of the findings of fact in the award –
    (i)   the decision of the tribunal on the question is obviously wrong, or
    (ii) the question is one of general public importance and the decision of the tribunal is at least open to serious doubt, and

(d) that, despite the agreement of the parties to resolve the matter by arbitration, it is just and proper in all the circumstances for the court to determine the question.'[164]

In granting leave, the court is empowered to impose such conditions as it thinks fit, including the power to make an order in respect of security of costs.[165] On determining the appeal, the High Court may confirm, vary or set aside the arbitration award, or may remit it for reconsideration by the arbitration tribunal in the light of the court's opinion on the point of law involved.[166] No appeal will lie from the decision of a court of first instance except with the leave of that court, which shall not be given 'unless the court considers that the question is one of general importance or is one which for some other special reason should be considered by the Court of Appeal'.[167]

It is recognised, however, that no appeal is possible from an arbitration tribunal in the absence of a 'reasoned award' by the arbitrator and the new legislation requires an arbitrator to give reasons for his award 'unless it is an agreed award, or the parties have

---

[160] Section 14(4). Need not be a formal notice – copy of letter to arbitrator will suffice: *Seabridge Shipping* v *Orssleff's Eftf* [1999] 2 Lloyd's Rep 685.

[161] Section 76(1). See *The Pendrecht* [1980] 2 Lloyd's Rep 56 for the position prior to the 1996 Act. The same rule applies in relation to the 12-month time limit imposed by Art III rule 6 of the Hague/Visby Rules: *The Agios Lazarus* [1976] 2 Lloyd's Rep 47.

[162] Arbitration Act 1996 s 76(3).

[163] Section 69(1).

[164] Section 69(3).

[165] Section 70(8).

[166] Section 69(7).

[167] Section 69(8). The court has no power to grant leave to appeal unless the question of law involved relates to the law of England and Wales. See *Reliance Industries* v *Enron* [2002] 1 Lloyd's Rep 645 where the arbitrators were applying Indian law. See also *Athletic Union of Constantinople* v *National Basketball Assoc* [2002] 1 Lloyd's Rep 305.

agreed to dispense with reasons'.[168] It remains to be decided what degree of formality is required in the presentation of a reasoned award but it may be relevant to note that the courts took the view, in construing previous legislation on the subject, that 'All that is necessary is that the arbitrators should set out what, on their view of the evidence, did or did not happen and should explain succinctly why, in the light of what happened, they have reached their decision and what that decision is.'[169] Should the arbitrator give no reasons for his award, or reasons which the court considers insufficient, the court may require the arbitrator to state his reasons in sufficient detail to enable it to consider any question of law in the award which may arise on appeal.[170]

As the decision of the High Court to reject an application for leave to appeal is final, the question arises as to whether in these circumstances the court is still required to give reasons for its decision. The issue arose in *The Western Triumph*[171] where the claimant argued that the lack of adequate reasons for the rejection of his application amounted to a breach of his entitlement to a 'fair hearing' under s 6 of the Human Rights Act 1998. The Court of Appeal took the view that in the case of an appeal under s 69(3) of the 1996 Act it would generally only be necessary to identify the particular ground of appeal which the applicant had failed to establish without the need to say more. Only where the claimant contended that the tribunal's decision was obviously wrong in law, or open to serious doubt, may reasons be required. Such reasons, however, need only be brief, so as to show the losing party why it had lost and it may be sufficient merely to indicate that the court agreed with the reasons given by the arbitrators.

Finally, it must be noted that provision is made in the legislation for the parties to enter into an agreement excluding the right of appeal to the High Court from an arbitration award, and such agreement is presumed where the parties agree to dispense with reasons for the tribunal's award.[172] This right to exclude the court's jurisdiction in advance now extends to maritime contracts, thus reversing the position under the previous legislation.[173] On the other hand, in the case of a 'domestic arbitration agreement'[174] such an exclusion agreement, to be effective, must still be entered into after arbitration proceedings have commenced.[175]

RESTRICTIONS ON RIGHT OF APPEAL

Section 69 of the 1996 Act was clearly designed to promote a greater finality in arbitration awards by severely limiting the opportunities for appeal to the High Court. The

---

[168] Section 52(4). This reverses the previous position under s 1(6)(a) of the Arbitration Act 1979 which provided that the arbitrator was under no obligation to provide reasons for his award unless requested to do so in advance by one of the parties.

[169] Donaldson J in *Bremer* v *Westzucker* [1981] 2 Lloyd's Rep 130 at p 132. See also *Transcatalana* v *Incobrasa Brazileira* [1995] 1 Lloyd's Rep 215 at p 217 *per* Mance J.

[170] Arbitration Act 1996 s 70(4).

[171] [2002] 2 Lloyd's Rep 1.

[172] Section 69(1).

[173] Section 4(1)(a) of the Arbitration Act 1979 provided that any agreement seeking to exclude the right of appeal to the High Court in the case of any 'question or claim falling within the Admiralty jurisdiction of the High Court' was only effective if concluded after the commencement of arbitration proceedings.

[174] As defined in s 85(2) of the Arbitration Act 1996.

[175] Arbitration Act 1996 s 87(1).

criteria listed in the section for determining whether or not to grant leave to appeal constitute an expanded version of *The Nema*[176] guidelines which, in turn, represent the reaction of the House of Lords to previous legislation on the same subject.[177] Until judicial reaction to the new legislation is forthcoming, useful guidance may possibly be derived from brief reference to the views expressed in *The Nema* and associated case law.[178]

In approaching the question of leave to appeal, the House of Lords in *The Nema* took the view that, even though questions of law were involved, a distinction had to be drawn between awards concerning one-off contracts, in which the wording was unlikely to be repeated, and those involving standard terms, the construction of which was of general interest to the commercial community. In the latter case an authoritative ruling from the court served a useful function in establishing certainty and predictability. On the other hand, in the case of the one-off contract, Lord Diplock felt that it was far from self-evident that the decision of an experienced arbitrator, selected by the parties for his expertise in the trade, was not to be preferred to that of one of the House of Lords itself.[179]

Lord Diplock then proceeded to outline the factors which a court should take into consideration in deciding how to exercise its discretion.

> 'What the Judge should normally ask himself in this type of arbitration, particularly where the events relied on are one-off events, is not whether he agrees with the decision reached by the arbitrator, but: does it appear on a perusal of the award either that the arbitrator misdirected himself in law or that his decision was such that no reasonable arbitrator could reach.'[180]

Even so, a thorough review of the award was not necessary.

> 'Leave should not normally be given unless it is apparent to the Judge upon a mere perusal of the reasoned award itself without the benefit of adversarial argument, that the meaning ascribed to the clause by the arbitrator is obviously wrong: but if on such perusal it appears to the Judge that it is possible argument might persuade him, despite first impression to the contrary, that the arbitrator might be right, he should not grant leave; the parties should be left to accept, for better or worse, the decision of the tribunal that they had chosen to decide the matter in the first instance.'[181]

More flexibility was, however, permissible where the construction of standard terms was involved, particularly where such construction 'would add significantly to the clarity and certainty of English commercial law'.[182] But even here leave to appeal should not be granted unless the court was satisfied that a strong prima facie case had been made out that the arbitrator's construction was wrong.

---

[176] [1981] 2 Lloyd's Rep 239.
[177] Section 1(4) of the Arbitration Act 1979 provided that the High Court should not grant leave to appeal 'unless it considers that, having regard to all the circumstances, the determination of the question of law concerned could substantially affect the rights of one or more of the parties to the arbitration agreement'. Cf. 1996 Act s 69(3)(a).
[178] The 1996 Act does not exclude reference to existing case law which is compatible with the new legislation. See s 81.
[179] *The Nema* [1981] 2 Lloyd's Rep 239 at p 243.
[180] *Ibid* at p 248. See also *The Safeer* [1994] 1 Lloyd's Rep 637.
[181] At p 247.
[182] At p 248.

The criteria formulated by Lord Diplock have been applied in subsequent cases.[183] Thus leave to appeal has been refused in cases involving the interpretation of one-off clauses in bills of lading[184] and charterparties[185] and also in a case where the court considered that a decision on the point of law involved would add nothing whatever to the clarity or certainty of English law.[186] Conversely, leave was granted where the issue involved the construction of a technical war risk clause of wide application[187] and where a question of EEC law was relevant.[188]

14.3.6 OTHER CHALLENGES TO AN AWARD

In addition to the right of appeal on a point of law, the parties are permitted to challenge an arbitration award on grounds of lack of substantive jurisdiction[189] or serious irregularity affecting the tribunal, the proceedings or the award.[190] In the latter case the Act lists a series of specific irregularities, one or more of which might constitute a 'serious irregularity' provided that in the circumstances, and in the opinion of the court, they will cause substantial injustice to the applicant.

14.3.7 CONTROL BY THE COURT OF ARBITRATION PROCEEDINGS

As it is contrary to public policy at common law to seek to oust the jurisdiction of the courts, the High Court in England has inherited supervisory powers over arbitration proceedings. These powers have been substantially curtailed by the 1996 Act with the object of granting the parties greater autonomy over the conduct of arbitration proceedings and casting the courts in more of a supportive than interventionist role. Such remaining control is exercised in a variety of forms.

(I) POWER TO STAY PROCEEDINGS

Where a party to an arbitration agreement institutes an action in court in contravention of that agreement, the other party may request the court to stay such proceedings. In such circumstances the court is required to grant a stay 'unless satisfied that the arbitration agreement is null and void, inoperative or incapable of being performed'.[191]

---

[183] For further elucidation of the *Nema* rules, see Lord Diplock in *The Antaios (No 2)* [1984] 2 Lloyd's Rep 235. The majority of the Court of Appeal has expressed the view that these criteria are not applicable to applications for leave to appeal from a decision of the High Court to the Court of Appeal: *The Baleares* [1991] 2 Lloyd's Rep 318.

[184] *The Kerman* [1982] 1 Lloyd's Rep 62. See the judgment of Parker J for a reformulation of Lord Diplock's criteria.

[185] *National Rumour Co v Lloyd Libra* [1982] 1 Lloyd's Rep 472. Cf. *The Sanko Honour* [1985] 1 Lloyd's Rep 418.

[186] *The Vimeira* [1983] 2 Lloyd's Rep 424.

[187] *The Apex* [1982] 1 Lloyd's Rep 476. Cf. *The Safeer* [1994] 1 Lloyd's Rep 637.

[188] *Bulk Oil v Sun International* [1983] 1 Lloyd's Rep 655.

[189] Arbitration Act 1996 s 67.

[190] Section 68.

[191] Arbitration Act 1996 s 9(4). *The Halki* [1998] 1 Lloyd's Rep 49. Also applies to third-party proceedings for indemnity: *Wealands v CLC Contractors* [1999] 2 Lloyd's Rep 739. Section 1(1) of the Arbitration Act 1975 listed an additional ground for denying a stay in the context of a non-domestic arbitration: namely, that there was in fact no dispute between the parties. This option has been omitted from the 1996 Act.

In the case of a 'domestic arbitration',[192] however, the court may also deny a stay if satisfied 'that there are other sufficient grounds for not requiring the parties to abide by the arbitration agreement'.[193] Under legislation prior to the 1996 Act, the court was given an unfettered discretion in the case of a domestic arbitration whether or not to grant a stay.[194] In practice, however, the courts normally held the parties to an arbitration agreement freely entered into, and the burden of proof of showing cause why a stay should not be granted rested with the party opposing the application.[195] The courts may well adopt a similar approach to the 1996 legislation.

(II) REVOCATION OF AUTHORITY AND REMOVAL OF ARBITRATOR

Under the 1996 Act the parties are free to specify in their arbitration agreement the circumstances in which the authority of the arbitrator may be revoked, in whole or in part.[196] In the absence of such agreement, his authority can only be withdrawn by the parties acting jointly or by an arbitral or other institution or person vested by the parties with authority to take such action.[197] So far as intervention by the court is concerned, its powers are restricted to the removal of the arbitrator rather than the revocation of his authority. In this regard the previous more abstract concept of misconduct[198] has been abandoned in favour of a clear statement as to the specific grounds on which an arbitrator may be removed by the court. Section 24(1) provides that application to remove an arbitrator may be made to the court on any of the following grounds –

'(a) that circumstances exist that give rise to justifiable doubts as to his impartiality;

(b) that he does not possess the qualifications required by the arbitration agreement;

(c) that he is physically or mentally incapable of conducting the proceedings or that there are justifiable doubts as to his capacity to do so;

(d) that he has refused or failed –
  (i) properly to conduct the proceedings, or
  (ii) to use all reasonable dispatch in conducting the proceedings or making an award,

and that substantial injustice has been or will be caused to the applicant.'

(III) DELAY IN PROSECUTING THE CLAIM

One issue which exercised the courts over many years was the extent of their power to strike out a claim in arbitration on the ground of undue delay in its prosecution. While parties are normally required to nominate their arbitrators within a given time, no time restriction was imposed by the common law on the prosecution of arbitration proceedings even though the resultant delay might seriously prejudice a fair hearing. In the

---

[192] As defined in s 85(2) of the 1996 Act.
[193] Section 86(2)(b).
[194] Arbitration Act 1950 s 4(1).
[195] *Heyman* v *Darwins Ltd* [1942] AC 356 at p 388.
[196] Arbitration Act 1996 s 23(1).
[197] Section 23(3).
[198] See Arbitration Act 1950 s 23. See also Thomas, DR, 'Removal of Arbitrators by Court' [1982] LMCLJ 186.

opinion of Lord Diplock in *Bremer Vulcan v South India Shipping Corp*,[199] the High Court had no general supervisory powers over the conduct of arbitration proceedings more extensive that those conferred on it by the then current Arbitration Acts. In his view arbitration differed from litigation in that the submission of a dispute to arbitration was voluntary, being based on the agreement of the parties, with the result that any obligation to proceed with reasonable dispatch arising from such agreement was mutual. If a party was not satisfied with the speed of prosecution of a particular claim, his remedy was to apply to the arbitrator for directions. In such an event an arbitrator was entitled to fix a date for the hearing and then to proceed to make an award on the merits on the basis of whatever evidential material was then available to him. In the absence of such an application, however, the arbitrator was under no obligation to act on his own initiative, but was entitled to assume that both parties were satisfied with the way in which the proceedings were progressing.

The problem was finally resolved by legislation in the form of s 102 of the Courts and Legal Services Act 1990,[200] now re-enacted in s 41(3) of the 1996 Arbitration Act. This provision invests the arbitral tribunal with the power to dismiss any claim referred to it, provided that two requirements are satisfied. There must be inordinate and inexcusable delay by the claimant in pursuing the claim, and such delay must either create a substantial risk that it will not be possible to have a fair trial of the issues involved or result in serious prejudice to the respondent.[201] It will be noted that the power to dismiss a claim is vested in the arbitration tribunal rather than the High Court, and that the parties can exclude such power by an appropriate clause in the arbitration agreement.

14.3.8 ENFORCEMENT OF ARBITRATION AWARDS

Once a final award is made by an arbitration tribunal in England, Wales or Northern Ireland it may, by leave of the High Court, be enforced in the same way as a judgment or order of the court to the same effect.[202] Having obtained an award, however, the successful claimant may discover that the defendant has insufficient assets within the jurisdiction to meet his claim. The question then arises as to what extent arbitration awards are exportable and enforceable in other jurisdictions. Under the 1958 New York Convention provision is made for the mutual enforcement of awards in states adhering to the Convention, provided that certain basic requirements are met. In the United Kingdom the Convention, originally implemented by the Arbitration Act 1975, is now incorporated in Part III of the 1996 Act.

A party seeking to enforce a foreign award is required to produce documentary evidence in the form of the duly authenticated original award together with the original arbitration agreement. Alternatively, duly certified copies of either document will

---

[199] [1981] 1 Lloyd's Rep 253 at p 259.

[200] Effected by a new s 13A inserted in the Arbitration Act 1950. This section was held to be retrospective in *The Bouccra* [1994] 1 Lloyd's Rep 251.

[201] In *Lazenby v McNicholas Construction Co* [1995] 2 Lloyd's Rep 30, Rix J refused an application to dismiss a claim for inordinate delay under s 13A of the Arbitration Act 1950 made within the six-year limitation period for a contractual claim.

[202] Arbitration Act 1996 s 66(1).

suffice.[203] Any enforcement of the award is subject to certain safeguards designed to protect the party against whom it is invoked. Accordingly, enforcement may be refused if the latter can establish any impropriety in the original arbitration proceedings, such as a procedural defect or a failure to grant him a fair hearing, or he can prove that enforcement of the award would be contrary to the public policy of the enforcing state.[204] Subject to these safeguards a foreign award may be enforced, by leave of the High Court, in the same manner as a judgment or order of the court to the same effect, or may be relied on by the successful party by way of defence or set-off.[205] In view of the number of states which have ratified or adhered to the New York Convention, it would appear that an arbitration award may be more marketable than a court judgment.

---

[203] Section 102. Where either document is in a foreign language an officially certified translation of it is required to be deposited: s 102(2).
[204] For a full list of the grounds for refusal of enforcement, see Arbitration Act 1996 s 103.
[205] Section 101.

15

BREACH OF CONTRACT

15.1 FORMS OF BREACH

A breach of contract occurs when one party refuses or fails to perform one or more of the obligations he has undertaken in pursuance of that contract. Such a breach may take one of three forms. The party in default may either expressly repudiate liability under the contract, do some act which renders further performance of the contract impossible, or simply fail to perform when performance is due. Thus, in the context of a time charterparty, the shipowner may alternatively repudiate his obligation to provide the chartered vessel,[1] may render further performance of the charterparty impossible by selling the vessel to a third party,[2] or may withdraw the vessel during the currency of the charter.[3] In the first two cases the breach may occur not only during the course of performance of the contract but also before either party is entitled to demand performance from the other. The effect of any breach is to give rise to an automatic right of action for damages and, in certain cases, may entitle the innocent party to treat himself as discharged from all further obligations under the contract.

15.1.1 ANTICIPATORY BREACH

Where a party repudiates his obligations in advance of the date fixed for performance of the contract, this is categorised as an anticipatory breach and entitles the party not in default to bring an action for breach immediately without the necessity of waiting until performance is due. In the words of Lord Campbell, 'where there is a contract to do an act on a future day, there is a relation constituted between the parties in the meantime by the contract, and they impliedly promise in the meantime that neither will do anything to the prejudice of the other inconsistent with that relation'.[4] But such an anticipatory breach does not automatically terminate the contractual obligation for, to be effective, the repudiation must be accepted by the other party. 'Repudiation by one party standing alone does not terminate the contract. It takes two to end it, by repudiation on the one side and acceptance of the repudiation on the other.'[5]

---

[1] *The Super Servant Two* [1990] 1 Lloyd's Rep 1.
[2] *Lord Strathcona Steamship Co Ltd v Dominion Coal Co* [1926] AC 108.
[3] *The Nanfri* [1979] AC 757.
[4] *Hochster v De la Tour* (1853) 2 E&B 678 at p 689. An alternative explanation was provided by Cockburn CJ in *Frost v Knight* (1872) LR 7 Ex 111 at p 114. 'The promisee has an inchoate right to the performance of the bargain, which becomes complete when the time for performance has arrived. In the meantime he has a right to have the contract kept open as a subsisting and effective contract.'
[5] Viscount Simon in *Heymans v Darwins Ltd* [1942] AC 356 at p 361.

So in *The Simona*[6] a vessel was chartered for the carriage of a cargo of steel from Durban to Bilbao with a laycan of 3–9 July and an option to cancel on 9 July. Subsequently the owners nominated the vessel for 13–16 July and then telexed the charterers requesting an appropriate extension of the cancelling date. The charterers refused and immediately gave notice of cancellation of the charter. This notice, having been given in advance of the contractual cancelling date of 9 July, constituted an anticipatory breach of the charter. The owners, however, chose to ignore the breach and gave a revised notice of readiness to load on 8 July. In holding that the contract still subsisted despite the anticipatory breach, Lord Ackner remarked that 'when one party wrongfully refuses to perform obligations, this will not automatically bring the contract to an end. The innocent party has an option. He may either accept the wrongful repudiation as determining the contract and sue for damages or he may ignore or reject the attempt to determine the contract and affirm its continued existence.'[7]

If he elects to waive the anticipatory breach, the obligations under the contract continue as before unaffected by the attempted repudiation. 'In that case he keeps the contract alive for the benefit of the other party, as well as his own; he remains subject to all its obligations and liabilities and enables the other party not only to complete the contract, if so advised, notwithstanding his previous repudiation of it, but also to take advantage of any supervening circumstance which would justify him in declining to complete it.'[8] If, therefore, in the interval between the anticipatory breach and the date fixed for performance, the fulfilment of the contract is rendered impossible or otherwise frustrated, both parties are discharged from all further obligations under the agreement.[9] Similarly, the party originally in default may take advantage of any other occurrence which would discharge the contract in normal circumstances, while the party having waived the breach will then be unable to recover damages for the earlier repudiation. Accordingly the charterer in *The Simona*[10] was entitled to invoke the cancellation clause when the chartered vessel was not available for loading by the cancellation date notwithstanding his earlier anticipatory breach.

Should the innocent party, however, decide to accept the anticipatory breach, he may bring an action for damages immediately. In such an event, damages for breach are assessed as at the date fixed for performance and not as at the date of actual breach. The option, therefore, goes only to the question of breach and not to the question of damages.[11]

15.2 THE EFFECTS OF BREACH

The terms of a contract are obviously not all of equal importance. While the performance of certain obligations is essential to the continued existence of the contract, the performance of others may be so incidental that the objects of the contract can be

---

[6] [1988] 2 Lloyd's Rep 199.
[7] *Ibid* at p 203.
[8] Cockburn CJ in *Frost* v *Knight* (1872) LR 7 Ex 111 at p 112.
[9] See e.g. *Avery* v *Bowden* (1855) 5 E&B 714.
[10] [1988] 2 Lloyd's Rep 199.
[11] *Roper* v *Johnson* (1873) LR 8 CP 167.

substantially achieved even though these obligations are not met in their entirety. There also exists a third category of terms, the effects of the breach of which will vary depending on the nature of the breach and the circumstances of the case.

15.2.1 CONDITIONS AND WARRANTIES

The terms of a contract have been traditionally classified as either conditions or warranties. A condition is a basic term, non-performance of which would render performance of the remaining terms something substantially different from what was originally intended. Consequently, the breach of such a term would entitle the party not in default to treat the contract as repudiated and himself as discharged from performance of all outstanding obligations under the contract. Conversely, a warranty is a minor term, breach of which can be adequately compensated for by the award of damages. The breach of such a term will not therefore release the innocent party from performance of his contractual obligations.

The distinction is well drawn by Diplock LJ in the case of *Hong Kong Fir Shipping* Co v *Kawasaki*.[12] In his view,

> [there are some obligations] 'of which it can be predicated that every breach of such an undertaking must give rise to an event which will deprive the party not in default of substantially the whole benefit which it was intended that he should obtain from the contract. And such a stipulation . . . is a "condition". So, too, there may be other simple contractual undertakings of which it can be predicated that no breach can give rise to an event which will deprive the party not in default of substantially the whole benefit which it was intended that he should obtain from the contract; and such a stipulation . . . is a "warranty".'

While it may be easy to recognise such a distinction in principle, it may be more difficult to apply it in practice to the facts of a particular case. To assist in this process, certain guidelines have been established to determine whether a particular term should be classified as a condition. First, an obligation may be designated as a condition by statute. A typical example is provided by sections 12–15 of the Sale of Goods Act 1979 which seek to classify the obligations of the parties to a contract for the sale of goods. Statutory intervention is, however, rare in the context of carriage of goods by sea. Secondly, judicial precedent may categorise a particular undertaking as a condition. Thus the obligation not to deviate from the contractual voyage[13] and the requirement not to deliver goods in the absence of production of the relevant bill of lading have both been held to have this status.[14] Similarly, in *The Mihalis Angelos*,[15] the Court of Appeal held that where a shipowner gave notice of readiness to load, there was an implied condition that he honestly, and on reasonable grounds, believed the forecast to be accurate.

Thirdly, the parties themselves may expressly designate a particular obligation as a condition, although the mere use of the word 'condition' is not conclusive, since the circumstances surrounding their agreement may indicate that the parties had no intention

---

[12] [1962] 2 QB 26 at p 69.
[13] See *supra* at pp 16 ff.
[14] See *supra* at pp 157–8.
[15] [1971] 1 QB 164.

of using the word in its technical sense.[16] Again, there is some doubt as to the status of express terms providing that one party may terminate a contract on the occurrence of a specific event. Examples are provided by the provision in a time charter permitting the shipowner to withdraw the vessel on default in payment of hire by the charterer,[17] and by the cancellation clause in a voyage charter which allows the charterer to terminate the contract if the vessel is not delivered by a specific date.[18] In both cases the effect of the operation of the clause is similar to the effect of a breach of condition in that the innocent party is entitled to treat himself as discharged from all outstanding obligations under the contract. This fact has led some judges to categorise such terms as conditions.[19] But the effects are not identical in all respects. Thus the voyage charterer who exercises the right to cancel is not entitled to damages for any delay involved in the vessel failing to meet the cancellation date unless such delay is the result of the shipowner's failure to exercise reasonable dispatch.[20] Again, the better view is that the shipowner who withdraws his vessel on default in payment of hire is not able to claim damages for the unexpired period of the time charter unless such default in payment amounts to a repudiatory breach by the charterer, which will rarely be the case.[21] It would, therefore, seem preferable not to classify such terms as 'conditions' in the technical sense, but simply to regard them as clauses conferring on the innocent party no more than a contractual option to terminate the contract on the occurrence of the specified event.[22]

Finally, in the absence of other indicators, the intention of the parties to treat a particular term as a condition may be implied from the nature of the contract and the surrounding circumstances. Thus time clauses in mercantile contracts have generally been treated as conditions by the courts on the grounds that 'parties to commercial transactions should be entitled to know their rights at once and should not, when possible, be required to wait upon events before those rights can be determined'.[23] In *Bunge* v *Tradax Export*[24] there was an agreement to buy a quantity of soya bean meal 'f.o.b. one US Gulf port at seller's option'. The buyers, on their part, were required to give 15 days' notice of nomination of a vessel to load the cargo. In the event, the sellers sought to treat the buyers' failure to give the required notice as a repudiatory breach. The House of Lords had no hesitation in categorising the notice requirement as a condition and felt such a decision was justified 'in the case of time clauses in mercantile contracts'.[25] Lord Roskill expressed the view that 'in a mercantile contract when a term has to be performed by one party as a condition precedent to the ability of the other party

---

[16] *Wickman* v *Schuler* [1974] AC 235.

[17] See *supra* at pp 102 ff.

[18] See *supra* at pp 66–7.

[19] For example, Lord Diplock in *The Afovos* [1983] 1 Lloyd's Rep 335 at p 341. See also Lord Roskill in *Bunge* v *Tradax Export* [1981] 2 Lloyd's Rep 1 at p 12.

[20] See *supra* at p 66.

[21] See *supra* at p 108.

[22] Brandon J in *The Brimnes* [1972] 2 Lloyd's Rep 465 at p 482, when discussing the effect of the withdrawal clause in the NYPE charter, 'reached the conclusion that there is nothing in [that clause] which clearly shows that the parties intended the obligation to pay hire punctually to be an essential term of the contract, as distinct from being a term for breach of which an express right to withdraw was given'.

[23] Lord Roskill in *Bunge* v *Tradax Export* [1981] 2 Lloyd's Rep 1 at p 12.

[24] [1981] 2 Lloyd's Rep 1.

[25] *Ibid* p 6 *per* Lord Wilberforce.

to perform another term, especially an essential term such as the nomination of a single loading port, the term as to time for the performance of the former obligation will in general fall to be treated as a condition'.[26] On this basis time has been held to be of the essence in f.o.b. sales contracts where a seller undertook to nominate a loading port by a specified date 'at latest',[27] and where a buyer was under an obligation to open a documentary credit by the date agreed for shipment of the goods.[28]

More difficulty arises in cases where performance extends over a considerable period of time. During this period one party may be required to carry out a series of acts as, for example, the time charterer who is under an obligation to pay hire semi-monthly in advance throughout the charterparty. In the absence of an express contractual provision to the contrary,[29] failure to pay one instalment on time will rarely, if ever, be treated as a repudiatory breach. 'The reason is, that such delay in payment of one half-monthly instalment would not have the effect of depriving the owners of substantially the whole benefit which it was the intention of the parties that the owners should obtain from the . . . charter.'[30]

Only where the circumstances surrounding the non-payment indicate a clear intention on the part of the defaulting party to be no longer bound by the contractual obligation will the breach be regarded as repudiatory. Two factors are important in ascertaining such an intention. First, the ratio of the breach to the contract as a whole – is the proportion unperformed trivial or vital to the main purpose of the contract? Secondly, is there any great likelihood that the breach will be repeated? So the late payment of one out of forty-eight instalments of hire could hardly be treated as a serious breach of contract, whereas an express refusal to pay any further instalments would evince a clear intention no longer to be bound by the contractual obligations.

15.2.2 INTERMEDIATE TERMS

Not all contractual obligations fall conveniently into the traditional division between conditions and warranties. There are some terms, the consequences of the breach of which may range from the trivial to the very serious. Thus the failure to provide a seaworthy ship may result from 'the presence of trivial defects easily and rapidly remediable as well as by defects which must inevitably result in a total loss of the vessel'.[31] It would therefore be inequitable to provide a uniform remedy across the board. Such terms have been described as 'intermediate' or 'innominate' terms. Only in cases where 'the event . . . has the effect of depriving the other party of substantially the whole benefit which it was the intention of the parties that he should obtain from the

---

[26] [1981] 2 Lloyd's Rep 1 at p 15.

[27] *Gill & Duffus* v *Société pour L'Exportation des Sucres* [1986] 1 Lloyd's Rep 322. See also *The Mavro Vetranic* [1985] 1 Lloyd's Rep 580.

[28] *Stach Ltd* v *Baker Bosley Ltd* [1958] 2 QB 130.

[29] Most charterparties contain a standard withdrawal clause to cover this eventuality. See *supra* at pp 102–3.

[30] Diplock LJ in *The Afovos* [1983] 1 Lloyd's Rep 335 at p 341. In this case the shipowners had withdrawn their vessel without complying with the notice requirement in the charter withdrawal clause and so had to justify their action on the basis of common law principles.

[31] Diplock LJ in *Hong Kong Fir Shipping Co* v *Kawasaki* [1962] 2 QB 26 at p 71. For a full treatment of the effects of unseaworthiness, see *supra* at pp 9 ff.

contract'[32] can the party not in default treat it as a repudiatory breach. So in *Hong Kong Fir Shipping Co* v *Kawasaki*,[33] where a vessel time chartered for a period of 24 months was off-hire for 20 weeks during the first six months of the charter as the result of initial unseaworthiness, the Court of Appeal held that the breach was not sufficiently serious to entitle the charterer to treat the contract as discharged.

The recognition of a category of intermediate terms provides a more flexible and equitable remedy and courts have been encouraged not to be 'overready to construe terms as conditions unless the contract clearly requires the Court so to do'.[34] Conversely, however, there are practical problems since the concept introduces a greater degree of uncertainty into the law. A victim of the breach who decides to treat it as repudiatory can never be sure that he has made the correct decision until the conclusion of any subsequent litigation or arbitration proceedings. The charterer in *Hong Kong Fir Shipping Co* v *Kawasaki*[35] who, after losing 20 weeks of the charter, treated the breach of the seaworthiness obligation as repudiatory and chartered another vessel, subsequently discovered that he had made the wrong decision, as the result of which he found himself in repudiatory breach. The reaction of certain judges has been to stress the need for certainty in commercial transactions. 'One of the important elements of the law is predictability. At any rate in commercial law there are obvious and substantial advantages in having, where possible, a firm and definite rule for a particular class of legal relationship, e.g., the legal categorisation of a particular definable type of contractual clause in common use.'[36]

There will inevitably be a conflict between the desire for predictability in commercial matters and the need to deal equitably in individual cases. The object of the courts should be to seek to strike a reasonable balance between the two. In the opinion of Lord Roskill, 'the basic principles of construction for determining whether or not a particular term is a condition remains as before, always bearing in mind on the one hand the need for certainty and, on the other, the desirability of not, where legitimate, allowing rescission where the breach complained of is highly technical and where damages would clearly be an adequate remedy'.[37]

15.2.3 THE EFFECTS OF A REPUDIATORY BREACH

Once a defaulting party commits a breach of condition or otherwise demonstrates a clear intention not to perform his obligations under the contract, the innocent party has the option of treating the contract as discharged. The breach itself does not automatically discharge all outstanding obligations. For the party not in default

'may, notwithstanding the so-called repudiation, insist on holding his co-contractor to the bargain and continue to render due performance on his part. In that event the co-contractor has

---

[32] Lord Diplock in *Photo Production* v *Securicor* [1980] 1 Lloyd's Rep 545 at p 553. See also *The Seaflower* [2000] 2 Lloyd's Rep 37.
[33] [1962] 2 QB 26.
[34] Lord Roskill in *Bunge* v *Tradax Export* [1981] 2 Lloyd's Rep 1 at p 14.
[35] [1962] 2 QB 26.
[36] Megaw LJ in *The Mihalis Angelos* [1970] 2 All ER 125 at p 138.
[37] *Bunge Corp* v *Tradax Export* [1981] 2 Lloyd's Rep 1 at p 14.

the opportunity of withdrawing from his false position and, even if he does not, may escape ultimate liability because of some supervening event not due to his own fault which excuses or puts an end to further performance . . . Alternatively the other party may rescind the contract, or (as it is sometimes expressed) "accept the repudiation", by so acting as to make it plain that, in view of the wrongful action of the other party who has repudiated, he claims to treat the contract as at an end, in which case he can sue at once for damages.'[38]

(I) AFFIRMATION OF THE CONTRACT

Despite the repudiatory nature of the breach, the party not in default may decide to waive it and continue with performance of the contract. On the one hand, further performance of the contract may be profitable despite the breach, or the breach may only be technical as, for example, a minor deviation causing no material loss. Such a waiver has the following effects:

1 Once the option has been exercised it cannot be retracted, although the conduct of the parties will not be treated as a waiver if, at the time of the alleged waiver, they were unaware of the breach. Thus parties to a contract of carriage will not be regarded as having waived the breach if they take delivery of cargo at the port of discharge in ignorance of the fact that the vessel has deviated en route.[39]

2 The contractual obligations will continue with full force and the party originally in default will be able to rely on all exceptions and limitation of liability provisions throughout performance of the remaining obligations under the contract.[40] He will also be able to take advantage of any subsequent event which frustrates the contract.[41]

3 The injured party may still recover damages for any loss suffered as a result of the breach.

(II) ACCEPTANCE OF REPUDIATORY BREACH

Where the innocent party elects to accept the repudiatory breach, he is at once discharged from performance of all outstanding obligations under the contract and entitled to sue for damages. In the absence of an express declaration of intent, problems may arise in establishing as a question of fact whether such an election can be inferred from the conduct of the party not in default. There is authority for the view that 'an act of acceptance of a repudiation requires no particular form: a communication does not have to be couched in the language of acceptance. It is sufficient that the communication or conduct clearly and unequivocally conveys to the repudiating party that the aggrieved party is treating the contract as at an end.'[42] Thus in *The Santa Clara*,[43] where a cargo of propane sold on c.i.f. terms had not been loaded by the agreed date, the buyer sent a telex repudiating the contract. On the facts, the buyer's action was held to constitute an anticipatory breach of the sale contract. The loading was nevertheless completed and the

---

[38] Viscount Simon in *Heyman* v *Darwins Ltd* [1942] AC 356 at p 361.
[39] *Hain SS Co* v *Tate & Lyle* [1936] 41 Com Cas 350.
[40] *Suisse Atlantique* [1967] 1 AC 361.
[41] *Avery* v *Bowden* (1856) 6 E & B 953.
[42] Lord Steyn in *The Santa Clara* [1996] 2 Lloyd's Rep 225 at p 229.
[43] [1996] 2 Lloyd's Rep 225.

vessel sailed, but neither party took any further steps to perform the contract. In a subsequent action for damages brought by the seller, the question arose as to whether his failure to act amounted to an acceptance of the buyer's repudiatory breach. In the opinion of Lord Steyn, 'sometimes in the practical world of businessmen an omission to act may be as pregnant with meaning as a positive declaration'.[44] In the event, the seller's failure to tender a bill of lading to the buyer – a pre-condition to payment of the price under a c.i.f. contract – was held to justify the arbitrator in inferring an election to accept the buyer's anticipatory breach. Moreover, the court went so far as to suggest that it was not even necessary for the aggrieved party personally to notify the party in breach of his election. 'It is sufficient that the fact of the election comes to the repudiating party's attention, e.g. notification by an unauthorised broker or other intermediary may be sufficient.'[45]

While acceptance of a repudiatory breach relieves the innocent party from all outstanding obligations, it does not discharge the entire contract and its other provisions remain in full force. Any other result would remove the juridical basis for any claim for damages. Consequently, 'such actions for breach will be subject to the exceptions, limitation clauses and other provisions of the contract'.[46]

15.3 THE ACTION FOR DAMAGES

The object of any litigation or arbitration is normally to obtain compensation for losses resulting from breach of the contract of affreightment. The party injured by the breach is entitled to claim damages whether or not the breach is sufficiently serious to allow him to regard the contract as having been discharged.[47] In approaching the problem of assessing such compensation, the courts have to deal with two distinct issues: first, the question of remoteness of damage and, secondly, the question of measure of damages. Monetary compensation cannot be recovered for every loss resulting from the breach of a contract of carriage since, on practical grounds, the party in default cannot be made liable for consequences which are unreasonably remote or unexpected. The problem of remoteness of damage, therefore, concerns the identification of the types of loss resulting from a breach which are sufficiently relevant and 'proximate' to be made the subject of compensation. Liability having been established for a particular type of loss, the next step is to quantify the amount of compensation which can be recovered in respect of that loss. The general rule here is that the injured party must be placed, so far as money can do it, in the same situation as if the contract had been performed.

---

[44] *Ibid* at p 230.
[45] [1996] 2 Lloyd's Rep 225 at p 230.
[46] Including arbitration clauses: see *Heyman* v *Darwins Ltd* [1942] AC 356. The traditional view was that the unique feature of breach of a fundamental term (as opposed to breach of a condition) was that once the repudiatory breach was accepted the party in default could no longer rely for protection on the terms of the contract. Following the cases of *Suisse Atlantique* [1967] 1 AC 361 and *Photo Production* v *Securicor* [1980] AC 827, it would now appear that it is a matter of construction as to whether such terms are applicable to a particular breach. See *supra* at pp 21–2.
[47] For a full account of the remedies available for breach of contract, see Cheshire and Fifoot: Chapter 21; Treitel: Chapter 21.

The two issues of remoteness of damage and measure of damages will now be considered separately in more detail, after which a number of other factors related to the assessment of damages will be briefly discussed.

15.3.1 REMOTENESS OF DAMAGE

The traditional test for liability was authoritatively stated by the Court of Exchequer Chamber in the nineteenth-century case of *Hadley* v *Baxendale*.[48] In the words of Alderson B, the only loss which is sufficiently proximate is 'such as may fairly and reasonably be considered either arising naturally, i.e. according to the usual course of things, from such breach of contract itself, or such as may reasonably be supposed to have been in the contemplation of both parties, at the time they made the contract, as the probable result of the breach of it'.

Two distinct types of damage emerge from this test. First, the natural and normal loss which any reasonable man would expect and, secondly, abnormal loss arising from special circumstances for which the defaulter will only be liable if they are expressly drawn to his attention before or at the time he enters into the contract.[49] Liability for normal loss may, however, be extended where the defaulter is experienced in a particular trade or has special knowledge of the surrounding circumstances. In such an event he will be able to make a far more accurate assessment of the actual loss likely to result from his breach of contract, with the result that his liability will be correspondingly increased.[50] So the shipowner in *The Heron II*[51] who delivered late was liable for the fall in the market price of sugar since, with his knowledge of the market in Basrah, 'if he had thought about the matter he must have realised that at least it was not unlikely that the sugar would be sold in the market at market price on arrival'.[52] In practice, however, such knowledge will rarely be imputed to a mere carrier, for he 'commonly knows less than a seller about the purposes for which the buyer or consignee needs the goods, or about other "special circumstances" which may cause exceptional loss if due delivery is withheld'.[53]

While all the factors enumerated above are still relevant, the modern tendency is no longer to state the concept of remoteness enshrined in *Hadley* v *Baxendale* in terms of

---

[48] (1854) 9 Ex 341 at p 354.

[49] The earlier view was that mere knowledge of special circumstances was not sufficient to increase the defaulter's liability, particularly in the case of a carrier. Asquith LJ, in *Victoria Laundry (Windsor) Ltd* v *Newman Industries* [1949] 2 KB 528 at p 539, expressed the opinion that 'where knowledge of special circumstances is relied on as enhancing the damages recoverable, that knowledge must have been brought home to the defendant at the time of the contract in such circumstances that the defendant impliedly undertook to bear any special loss referable to a breach in those special circumstances'. The requirement for such an implied undertaking was questioned by the Lords in *The Heron II* [1969] 1 AC 350 at p 421, and no longer seems to be the law. See Robert Goff J in *The Pegase* [1981] 1 Lloyd's Rep 175 at pp 181–2.

[50] See *Victoria Laundry (Windsor) Ltd* v *Newman Industries* [1949] 2 KB 528; *Fletcher* v *Tayleur* (1855) 17 CB 21.

[51] [1969] 1 AC 350.

[52] Lord Reid, *ibid* at p 382.

[53] Asquith LJ in *Victoria Laundry (Windsor) Ltd* v *Newman Industries* [1949] 2 KB 528 at p 537. See also *Wilson* v *Lancs & Yorks Rly* (1861) 9 CB (NS) 632. Cf. *Schulze* v *GE Rly* (1887) 19 QBD 30.

two separate rules, but rather in the terms of a single proposition. The injured party is only entitled to recover such part of the loss actually resulting from the breach of contract as was reasonably within his contemplation at the time of concluding the contract. In the view of Robert Goff J, 'This approach accords very much to what actually happens in practice; the Courts have not been over-ready to pigeon-hole the cases under one or other of the so-called rules in *Hadley* v *Baxendale*, but rather to decide each case on the basis of the relevant knowledge of the defendant.'[54]

In applying this test of reasonable contemplation, one final factor has to be taken into consideration by the courts. What is the required degree of probability that the contemplated events will occur? Liability would appear to depend on the parties envisaging the possibility of such loss rather than its inevitability, although the precise degree of possibility or probability was lost in a welter of semantic argument in the case of *The Heron II*.[55] Members of the House of Lords disapproved of earlier suggestions that a particular consequence of a breach was sufficiently proximate if the likelihood of its occurrence was a 'serious possibility' or was 'on the cards',[56] but signally failed to come up with a viable alternative test. The expressions favoured to describe the required degree of probability ranged from suggesting that the loss must be a 'real danger' or one 'liable' or 'not unlikely' to occur. On one point, however, their Lordships were unanimous. A higher degree of probability is required to satisfy the test of remoteness in contract than in tort, where liability is based on reasonable foresight. Their Lordships justified the distinction on the ground that a party injured by a breach of contract, unlike the victim of a tort, has ample opportunity to inform the other party in advance, at the time of contracting, of the likely consequences of any breach.[57]

The operation of the remoteness rules in practice can best be illustrated by a selection of examples drawn from various types of carriage contract.

(I) BREACH OF CHARTERPARTY OBLIGATIONS

The owner who fails to make his vessel available at the agreed time under a voyage charterparty will realise that, as the result of his breach, the charterer will be unable to ship his cargo as originally intended. The appropriate damages recoverable under the remoteness test will accordingly be the extra cost of making alternative arrangements for the shipment of that cargo.[58] Any loss of profits on resale of the cargo resulting from the breach will be too remote unless the likelihood of such loss had been brought to the attention of the carrier at the time of contracting.[59] Conversely, the normal loss to the shipowner following the failure of the charterer to provide either any cargo, or a full cargo, will be restricted to the loss of the freight involved.

---

[54] *The Pegase* [1981] 1 Lloyd's Rep 175 at p 183.

[55] [1969] 1 AC 350.

[56] See Asquith LJ in *Victoria Laundry (Windsor) Ltd* v *Newman Industries* [1949] 2 KB at p 540.

[57] See Lord Reid in *The Heron II* [1969] 1 AC 350 at pp 385–6. He suggested that a party to a contract 'who wishes to protect himself against a risk which to the other party would appear to be unusual . . . can direct the other party's attention to it before the contract is made. In tort, however, there is no opportunity for the injured party to protect himself in that way . . .'.

[58] *The Almare Seconda* [1981] 2 Lloyd's Rep 433.

[59] *Panalpina* v *Densil Underwear Ltd* [1981] 1 Lloyd's Rep 187.

In the case of a time charter, where the owner either fails to deliver the vessel or repudiates his obligations during the currency of the charter, the natural consequence is that the charterer is deprived of the use of the vessel. If there is an available market for chartering in a substitute, 'the damages will generally be assessed on the basis of the difference between the contract rate for the . . . charterparty period and the market rate for the chartering in of a substitute vessel for that period'.[60] Loss of expected profit on the use of the vessel will normally be too remote unless on the facts it can be brought within the ambit of the reasonable contemplation criteria.[61]

(II) FAILURE OF THE CARRIER TO DELIVER GOODS

Where goods have been lost in transit, the normal loss to the consignee is the value of the goods at the time and place of delivery less the cost of freight and insurance.[62] Any special significance which the goods had for the consignee is irrelevant unless it was in the reasonable contemplation of the carrier at the time of the conclusion of the contract. So in *British Columbia Sawmill Co v Nettleship*[63] the defendant had contracted to carry a large quantity of machinery to Canada for the erection of a sawmill. The machinery had been packed into crates, but the carrier had not been informed of the contents of each particular crate. In fact, all the master parts required for the erection of the sawmill had been packed into a single crate which was subsequently lost in transit. While the plaintiffs were entitled to recover the market value of the lost parts, a claim for loss of profits, caused by a twelve-month delay in the erection of the sawmill while the lost parts were replaced, was held to be too remote. The carrier 'is not to be made liable for damages beyond what may fairly be presumed to have been contemplated by the parties at the time of entering into the contract. It must have been something which could have been foreseen and reasonably expected . . .'[64] As the carrier was unaware of the vital importance of the contents of this particular crate, it was not within his contemplation that its loss would result in such a prolonged delay in the construction of the sawmill.

(III) GOODS DAMAGED IN TRANSIT

Where goods are damaged in transit, the loss resulting in the normal course of events is the reduction in value of the goods at the time and place of delivery. Compensation is then based on the difference between the respective market values of the goods at destination in a sound condition as compared with the actual condition in which they were delivered.[65] Any loss of profits on resale is irrecoverable unless it was within the contemplation of the parties at the time of contracting.

---

[60] Robert Goff J in *The Elena D'Amico* [1980] 1 Lloyd's Rep 75 at p 87.

[61] Loss of normal profits may, however, be a factor to be taken into consideration in assessing damages when a time chartered vessel is delivered late. See Viscount Simonds in *Adamastos Shipping Co Ltd v Anglo-Saxon Petroleum Co* [1959] AC 133.

[62] There will be no such deduction where the freight is payable in advance. *Rodocanachi v Milburn* (1886) 18 QBD 67.

[63] (1868) LR 3 CP 499.

[64] Bovill CJ at *ibid* pp 505-6.

[65] *The Welsh Endeavour* [1984] 1 Lloyd's Rep 400.

(IV) GOODS DELIVERED SHORT OF DESTINATION

The normal loss recoverable in such a situation is the expense of transporting the goods to the contractual destination.[66]

(V) DELAY IN DELIVERY OF THE GOODS

Delay in delivery of goods may result in a variety of different types of loss for the consignee. Not only will he be deprived of the use of the goods in the meantime, but a possible forward sale may be frustrated by the delay. In addition, the physical quality of the goods may deteriorate or there might be a substantial fall in their market value. Most of these types of loss are covered by the principles outlined above. Damages are not recoverable for the loss of forward sales or the inability of the consignee to use the goods for some special purpose unless the relevant circumstances have been drawn to the attention of the defaulter at the time of contracting.[67] On the contrary, compensation for the normal deterioration in quality of perishable goods resulting from the delay would not be too remote.

More difficulty arises where the loss relates solely to a fall in the market value of the goods during the period of delay. Where late delivery occurs under a contract for the sale of goods, the position is straightforward and the appropriate measure of damages is the difference between the market price of equivalent goods at the respective dates of due and actual delivery.[68] Where delay in delivery occurs in a contract of carriage, however, the issue appears to have been treated historically as a question of remoteness,[69] rather than merely one of measure of damages. Accordingly, the question addressed by the courts has been whether such a fall in the market could reasonably have been expected to have been in the contemplation of the parties when they concluded the contract. Distinctions have been drawn between fluctuations of a regular seasonal kind and those which might be considered unusual and unexpected. Thus in *The Ardennes*[70] where a cargo of oranges was delivered late as the result of deviation by the carrier, the plaintiff shipper recovered for a substantial fall in the market which had occurred in the meantime. Such fluctuations were seasonal and dependent on the quantity of oranges available. In the circumstances, 'all parties must have been aware that the earlier the goods arrived the better would be the price'.[71] The position was clarified to some extent by the House of Lords in *The Heron II*[72] where a ship had been chartered to carry a cargo of sugar from Constanza to Basrah. As a result of the vessel deviating to pick up additional cargo, the sugar arrived in Basrah 10 days later than scheduled by which time there had been a substantial fall in the market price. While the shipowner was aware that there was a market for sugar in Basrah and that the consignees were sugar merchants, he was not aware that they intended to sell the sugar on the market immediately

---

[66] *Monarch Steamship Co Ltd* v *Karlshamns Oljefabriker* [1949] AC 196.

[67] See *The Pegase* [1981] 1 Lloyd's Rep 175.

[68] *Heskell* v *Continental Express Ltd* [1950] 1 All ER 1033; *Wertheim* v *Chicoutimi Pulp Co* [1911] AC 301 at p 308.

[69] See *The Parana* (1877) 2 PD 118 at p 123. Cf. *The Heron II* [1969] 1 AC 350.

[70] [1951] 1 KB 55.

[71] Lord Goddard CJ at *ibid* p 61.

[72] [1969] 1 AC 350.

on its arrival. Nevertheless, their Lordships held that 'on the facts of this case the parties must be assumed to have contemplated that there would be a punctual delivery to the port of discharge, and that port having a market in sugar, there was a real danger that as a result of a delay in breach of contract the charterer would miss the market and would suffer loss accordingly'.[73]

15.3.2 MEASURE OF DAMAGES

Having decided that a defaulter is liable for a particular consequence of a breach, the next question is to ascertain how much he has to pay. The general underlying principle is that the party in breach is liable to pay such monetary compensation as will place the injured party in the position he would have enjoyed had the contract been performed.[74] The rule as to measure of damages in contract is, therefore, slightly different from the principle of *restitutio in integrum* in tort, under which a tortfeasor is required to restore the party injured to the position he enjoyed before the tort was committed.

(I) THE RULE IN OPERATION

In the event of non-delivery of goods by a carrier, the loss to the consignee is the money required to purchase equivalent goods on the open market at the time and place fixed for delivery, less a deduction to cover the cost of freight and insurance. He is thereby enabled to purchase equivalent goods on the open market without loss to himself and so is placed in the same position as if the contract had been performed.[75] If the consignee, in the meantime, has entered into a forward sale, the price at which he has agreed to resell the goods cannot be taken into consideration in assessing damages, whether it is lower[76] or higher[77] than the market price.

The contrast between the contract and market price will also provide the prima facie rule for quantifying damages for other breaches of contracts of affreightment, such as the repudiation by a shipowner of a time or voyage charter. The principle is appropriate 'because the existence of an available market will generally mean that the innocent party can, at the date of breach, acquire a substitute from the market'.[78] By adopting such a procedure the object of the contract is achieved.

(II) ABSENCE OF AVAILABLE MARKET

With such importance being attached to market value in quantifying damages for breach of contract, an obvious difficulty arises where there is no available market for the goods in question at the place fixed for delivery. This is a problem which is frequently encountered in relation to contracts of carriage. This situation arose in *O'Hanlan v GW Ry*[79]

---

[73] Lord Upjohn at *ibid* p 428. Lord Pearce (at p 415) saw such a result as a 'serious possibility', while Lord Reid (at p 388) considered it as 'not unlikely' to occur.

[74] See Parke B in *Robinson v Harman* (1848) 1 Ex 850 at p 855; Lord Wright in *Monarch Steamship Co Ltd v Karlshamns Oljefabriker* [1949] AC 196 at p 220.

[75] Cf. Sale of Goods Act 1979 s 51(3) for the equivalent position in sale.

[76] *Williams Bros v Agius* [1914] AC 510.

[77] *The Arpad* [1934] P 189.

[78] Robert Goff J in *The Pegase* [1981] 1 Lloyd's Rep 175 at p 183.

[79] (1865) 6 B & S 484. See also *The Pegase* [1981] 1 Lloyd's Rep 175 at p 185.

where the defendant carriers had failed to deliver a consignment of cloth which they had undertaken to transport from Leeds to Neath. At the material time there was no whole-sale market in Neath. In these circumstances Blackburn J laid down the general principle that where there is no market 'either from the smallness of the place or the scarcity of the particular goods, the value at the time and place of delivery would have to be ascertained as a fact by the jury, taking into consideration various matters, including, in addition to the cost price and expenses of transit, the reasonable profits of the importer.'[80] When the court is making such an estimate, it may take into consideration the price at which the particular goods have been resold by the consignee as valuable evidence of their actual value at the time and place of delivery.[81] But a resale price is only one of the factors to be taken into consideration and it will be readily rejected if proved to be an unreliable guide.[82]

15.3.3 OTHER RELEVANT CONSIDERATIONS IN ASSESSING DAMAGES

(I) DUTY TO MITIGATE

Damages will not be awarded for losses which might reasonably have been avoided by the claimant, since he is expected to take whatever action is reasonably open to him in order to mitigate his loss. While it has been stressed in recent cases that a claimant is under no duty to mitigate in the strict sense, but can take whatever action he considers best in his own business interests, nevertheless the consequences of such action cannot necessarily be charged to the wrongdoer. 'A defendant is only liable for such part of the plaintiff's loss as is properly to be regarded as caused by the defendant's breach of duty.'[83] By failing to take available steps to mitigate, the claimant may run the risk of the court holding that the resultant loss is not attributable to the original breach. Thus, on the failure of the owner to deliver a chartered ship, it would be advisable for the char-terer, on a rising market, to hire a substitute vessel. Any expenses incurred in mitigating the ultimate loss will be recoverable as part of the damages while, if the claimant avoids loss by chartering a substitute vessel at a more advantageous rate, only nominal dam-ages will be recoverable. A claimant is not expected to risk further loss in an attempt to mitigate[84] or to take action which would ruin his commercial reputation.[85] Whether or not reasonable steps have been taken to mitigate is a question of fact in each case.[86]

Problems can arise where an injured party refuses to accept a repudiatory breach and holds the party in default to his contract. Even though such conduct is unreasonable, the contract nevertheless remains alive and no requirement for mitigating action arises.

---

[80] (1865) 6 B & S at p 491.
[81] This was done in *Patrick* v *Russo-British Grain Export Co* [1927] 2 KB 535. Salter J pointed out (at p 538): 'If there is no market the value must be otherwise ascertained, and a resale price may be some evidence of such value.'
[82] *The Arpad* [1934] P 189 at p 230.
[83] Sir John Donaldson MR in *The Solholt* [1983] 1 Lloyd's Rep 605 at p 608; see also Robert Goff J in *The Elena D'Amico* [1980] 1 Lloyd's Rep 75 at p 89.
[84] *Pilkington* v *Wood* [1953] Ch 770.
[85] *Finlay* v *Kwik Hoo Tong* [1929] 1 KB 400.
[86] *Payzu* v *Saunders* [1919] 2 KB 581. See also *Kaines (UK) Ltd* v *Osterreichische* [1993] 2 Lloyd's Rep 1.

Such an option is, of course, only available in a situation where further performance of the contract requires no co-operation on the part of the party in default. So in *White & Carter (Councils) Ltd v McGregor*[87] the respondents had hired advertising space on litter bins which the appellants supplied to local councils throughout Great Britain. Although the respondents cancelled the order almost immediately, the appellants refused to accept the repudiation and proceeded to prepare the advertisement plates which they attached to the bins before delivering them for use by the local councils. By a majority of three to two the House of Lords held that the respondents were liable for the full contract price as the appellants were under no duty to accept the repudiation and mitigate the resultant loss.

The decision has been subject to much criticism,[88] but is subject to the proviso that the rule is not applicable where the claimant 'has no legitimate interest, financial or otherwise, in performing the contract rather than claiming damages'.[89] This situation arose in *The Alaskan Trader*[90] where a chartered ship suffered a serious engine breakdown following which the charterers indicated that they had no further use for the vessel. The owners refused to treat the charterers' conduct as repudiation of the charter and proceeded to repair the vessel at a cost of $800,000. They then placed it at the disposal of the charterers for the remainder of the charter period. In the view of the High Court they were not entitled to the hire as they had no legitimate interest in keeping the contract alive.

(II) ASSESSMENT BY THE PARTIES

The parties may themselves assess the damages payable in the event of breach and incorporate such assessment as a term of the contract of carriage. Such a provision will be enforced by the courts if it forms a genuine pre-estimate of the loss which is likely to flow from the breach, and the claimant will not be allowed to recover more than that amount from the defaulting party.[91] Such a sum is termed 'liquidated damages'. On the other hand, damages may be fixed at a figure higher than any loss which can reasonably be expected, as a threat to secure performance of the contract. This sum is termed a 'penalty' and will not be enforced by the courts since it would undermine the compensatory nature of damages. The law considers that the promisee is adequately compensated by recovering his actual loss. A typical example of a liquidated damages clause in a contract of carriage is provided by the demurrage clause in a voyage charterparty which fixes the compensation to be paid in the event of the charterer detaining the vessel in port beyond the agreed lay days.[92]

In construing such a clause, the courts look to the intentions of the parties rather than to the actual words used. A clause will be presumed to be a penalty if the stipulated

---

[87] [1962] AC 413.

[88] See Goodhart 78 LQR 263; Cheshire and Fifoot pp 685–7; Treitel pp 1016–19.

[89] Lord Reid in *White & Carter (Councils) Ltd v McGregor* [1962] AC 413 at p 431.

[90] [1983] 2 Lloyd's Rep 645. See also *The Puerto Buitrago* [1976] 1 Lloyd's Rep 250; *Stocznia v Latvian Shipping* [1996] 2 Lloyd's Rep 132; *The Dynamic* [2003] 2 Lloyd's Rep 693 cf. *The Odenfeld* [1978] 2 Lloyd's Rep 357.

[91] *Cellulose Acetate Silk Co v Widnes Foundry Ltd* [1933] AC 20.

[92] For a full discussion of the characteristics of a demurrage clause, see *supra* at pp 76 ff.

figure is 'extravagant and unconscionable'[93] in comparison with the greatest loss that could possibly flow from the breach. Thus a demurrage clause will not be enforceable if it provides for a level of compensation for overrunning the lay days which is far in excess of any possible market rates.[94]

15.4 REMEDIES OTHER THAN DAMAGES

The common law remedy of damages for breach of contract may, in appropriate circumstances, be supplemented by the equitable remedies of specific performance and injunction. While the common law action is available as of right, the equitable remedies are discretionary and this fact limits their usefulness in the context of charterparties and bill of lading contracts. A combination of three principles renders recourse to these remedies inappropriate in the majority of cases. First, they can only be invoked where damages provide an inadequate remedy for the consequences of the breach in question. Secondly, the courts will rarely grant specific performance of a contract for the provision of services and, finally, they are reluctant to require specific performance of a contract which would require constant supervision by the court. While none of these factors might individually be decisive, the combination of all three has the result that few, if any, contracts of carriage are required to be specifically performed at the present day.

15.4.1 SPECIFIC PERFORMANCE

There are few, if any, examples of a decree of specific performance being granted in respect of a charterparty. In the context of breach of a voyage charter, Lord Chelmsford LC as early as 1858 in the case of *De Mattos* v *Gibson*[95] refused such a remedy on the ground that it would be impossible for the court to supervise the due performance of such a contract. Lord Diplock was equally emphatic in denying its relevance in the context of breach of a time charter, which he categorised as a contract for services, and, 'Being a contract for services it is thus the very prototype of a contract which before the fusion of law and equity a Court would never grant specific performance . . . In the event of failure to render the promised services, the party to whom they were to be rendered would be left to pursue such remedies in damages for breach of contract as he might have at common law.'[96]

It is true that in a different context ways have been found to surmount these two obstacles. Thus it has been held that specific performance might be granted of a building contract if the obligations under the contract are sufficiently clearly defined and their enforcement would not involve superintendence by the court to an unacceptable

---

[93] Lord Dunedin in *Dunlop Tyre Co* v *New Garage Ltd* [1915] AC 79 at p 86.
[94] It will not be treated as a penalty, however, if it names a figure substantially lower than the market rate. See
   Suisse Atlantique v *N Rotterdamsche Kolen Centrale* [1967] 1 AC 361.
[95] (1858) 4 De G & J 276.
[96] *The Scaptrade* [1983] 2 Lloyd's Rep 253 at p 257.

degree.[97] Again, the ban on enforcing contracts for the provision of services may only strictly be relevant where personal services are involved.[98] Nevertheless, decrees of specific performance are rarely granted to enforce obligations arising under charterparties or bill of lading contracts. Perhaps the decisive factor is that in the overwhelming majority of cases alternative vessels or services are readily available with the result that damages provide an adequate remedy. Only in a case where the vessel or the services required possess some unique characteristic fundamental to the particular contract might a decree of specific performance be justified.

15.4.2 INJUNCTION

A similar approach has been adopted by the courts towards an application for an injunction in the event of breach of a contract of carriage. This is particularly true where the grant of an injunction would be in substance equivalent to a decree of specific performance in that the party in default would be left with no option but to perform the contract. For this reason Lord Diplock in *The Scaptrade*[99] refused to grant an injunction to prevent a shipowner under a time charter from withdrawing his vessel for late payment of hire. In his view, 'To grant an injunction restraining the shipowner from exercising his right of withdrawal of the vessel from the service of the charterer, though negative in form, is pregnant with an affirmative order to the shipowner to perform the contract; juristically it is indistinguishable from a decree of specific performance of a contract to render services; and in respect of that category of contracts, even in the event of breach, this is a remedy that English courts have always disclaimed any jurisdiction to grant.'

Temporary injunctions have, however, been granted from time to time, on breach of charterparty obligations, in order to preserve the *status quo* pending trial of the issue involved.[100] These cases mostly involve time charters and, in particular, the right of the shipowner to withdraw his vessel failing punctual payment of the hire. Following the dicta of Lord Diplock in *The Scaptrade*,[101] it would seem more appropriate to grant the injunction in terms restraining the shipowner from employing his ship otherwise than in accordance with the charter, rather than the more positive form used in earlier cases restraining him from withdrawing the vessel from the service of the charterer. In the case of *Lord Strathcona* v *Dominion Coal Co*,[102] the Privy Council was even prepared to

---

[97] *Wolverhampton Corp* v *Emmons* [1901] 1 QB 515. See also *Posner* v *Scott-Lewis* [1987] Ch 25; Megarry J in *Tito* v *Waddell (No 2)* [1977] Ch 106 at p 321, 'The real question is whether there is a sufficient definition to what has to be done in order to comply with the order of the Court.'

[98] 'The reasons why the court is reluctant to decree specific performance of a contract for personal services (and I would regard it as a strong reluctance rather than a rule) are, I think, more complex and more firmly bottomed on human nature . . . In general, no doubt, the inconvenience and mischief of decreeing specific performance of most such contracts will greatly outweigh the advantages, and specific performance will be refused. But I do not think that it should be assumed that as soon as any element of personal service or continuous services can be discerned in a contract the court will, without more, refuse specific performance.' *Giles* v *Morris* [1972] 1 All ER 960 at pp 969–70.

[99] [1983] 2 Lloyd's Rep 253 at p 257.

[100] See *The Chrysovalandou Dyo* [1981] 1 Lloyd's Rep 159; *The Balder London* [1983] 1 Lloyd's Rep 492.

[101] See *supra* at pp 106–7.

[102] [1926] AC 108. See also *De Mattos* v *Gibson* (1858) 4 De G & J 276, where a similar restraint was imposed on a mortgagee.

issue an injunction restraining the purchaser of a vessel from using it otherwise than in accordance with a pre-existing long-term charter. This is an isolated decision, strongly criticised in later cases,[103] and its effect appears to be restricted to its own special facts, the most significant of which was that the purchaser had actual notice of the charter-party at the time of completion of the conveyance.

---

[103] See *Port Line* v *Ben Line* [1958] 2 QB 146.

APPENDICES

BILLS OF LADING ACT 1855
(18 & 19 Vict c 111)

WHEREAS, by the custom of merchants, a bill of lading of goods being transferable by endorsement, the property in goods may thereby pass to the endorsee, but nevertheless all rights in respect of the contract contained in the bill of lading continue in the original shipper or owner; and it is expedient that such rights should pass with the property: And whereas it frequently happens that the goods in respect of which bills of lading purport to be signed have not been laden on board, and it is proper that such bills of lading in the hands of a bona fide holder for value should not be questioned by the master or other person signing the same on the ground of the goods not having been laden as aforesaid:

1. Consignees, and endorsees of bills of lading empowered to sue. – Every consignee of goods named in a bill of lading, and every endorsee of a bill of lading, to whom the property in the goods therein mentioned shall pass upon or by reason of such consignment or endorsement, shall have transferred to and vested in him all rights of suit, and be subject to the same liabilities in respect of such goods as if the contract contained in the bill of lading had been made with himself

2. Saving as to stoppage in transitu, and claims for freight, etc. – Nothing herein contained shall prejudice or affect any right of stoppage *in transitu*, or any right to claim freight against the original shipper or owner, or any liability of the consignee or endorsee by reason or in consequence of his being such consignee or endorsee, or of his receipt of the goods by reason or in consequence of such consignment or endorsement.

3. Bill of lading in hands of consignee, etc., conclusive evidence of shipment as against master, etc. – Every bill of lading in the hands of a consignee or endorsee for valuable consideration, representing goods to have been shipped on board a vessel, shall be conclusive evidence of such shipment as against the master or other person signing the same, notwithstanding that such goods or some part thereof may not have been so shipped, unless such holder of the bill of lading shall have had actual notice at the time of receiving the same that the goods had not been in fact laden on board: Provided, that the master or other person so signing may exonerate himself in respect of such misrepresentation by showing that it was caused without any default on his part, and wholly by the fraud of the shipper, or of the holder, or some person under whom the holder claims.

INTERNATIONAL CONVENTION FOR THE UNIFICATION OF CERTAIN RULES OF LAW RELATING TO BILLS OF LADING, BRUSSELS, AUGUST 25, 1924

(The Hague Rules)

Article I

In this convention the following words are employed with the meanings set out below:

- *(a)* "Carrier" includes the owner or the charterer who enters into a contract of carriage with a shipper.
- *(b)* "Contract of carriage" applies only to contracts of carriage covered by a bill of lading or any similar document of title, in so far as such document relates to the carriage of goods by sea, including any bill of lading or any similar document as aforesaid issued under or pursuant to a charter party from the moment at which such bill of lading or similar document of title regulates the relations between a carrier and a holder of the same.
- *(c)* "Goods" includes goods, wares, merchandise, and articles of every kind whatsoever except live animals and cargo which by the contract of carriage is stated as being carried on deck and is so carried.
- *(d)* "Ship" means any vessel used for the carriage of goods by sea.
- *(e)* "Carriage of goods" covers the period from the time when the goods are loaded on to the time they are discharged from the ship.

Article II

Subject to the provisions of Article VI, under every contract of carriage of goods by sea the carrier, in relation to the loading, handling, stowage, carriage, custody, care and discharge of such goods, shall be subject to the responsibilities and liabilities and entitled to the rights and immunities hereafter set forth.

Article III

1. The carrier shall be bound before and at the beginning of the voyage to exercise due diligence to –

- *(a)* Make the ship seaworthy.
- *(b)* Properly man, equip and supply the ship.
- *(c)* Make the holds, refrigerating and cool chambers, and all other parts of the ship in which goods are carried, fit and safe for their reception, carriage and preservation.

2. Subject to the provisions of Article IV, the carrier shall properly and carefully load, handle, stow, carry, keep, care for, and discharge the goods carried.

3. After receiving the goods into his charge the carrier or the master or agent of the carrier shall, on demand of the shipper, issue to the shipper a bill of lading showing among other things –

(a)   The leading marks necessary for identification of the goods as the same are furnished in writing by the shipper before the loading of such goods starts, provided such marks are stamped or otherwise shown clearly upon the goods if uncovered, or on the cases or coverings in which such goods are contained, in such a manner as should ordinarily remain legible until the end of the voyage.

(b)   Either the number of packages or pieces, or the quantity, or weight, as the case may be, as furnished in writing by the shipper.

(c)   The apparent order and condition of the goods.

Provided that no carrier, master or agent of the carrier shall be bound to state or show in the bill of lading any marks, number, quantity, or weight which he has reasonable ground for suspecting not accurately to represent the goods actually received, or which he has had no reasonable means of checking.

4. Such a bill of lading shall be *prima facie* evidence of the receipt by the carrier of the goods as therein described in accordance with paragraph 3(a), (b) and (c).

5. The shipper shall be deemed to have guaranteed to the carrier the accuracy at the time of shipment of the marks, number, quantity and weight, as furnished by him, and the shipper shall indemnify the carrier against all loss, damages and expenses arising or resulting from inaccuracies in such particulars. The right of the carrier to such indemnity shall in no way limit his responsibility and liability under the contract of carriage to any person other than the shipper.

6. Unless notice of loss or damage and the general nature of such loss or damage be given in writing to the carrier or his agent at the port of discharge before or at the time of the removal of the goods into the custody of the person entitled to delivery thereof under the contract of carriage, or, if the loss or damage be not apparent, within three days, such removal shall be *prima facie* evidence of the delivery by the carrier of the goods as described in the bill of lading.

If the loss or damage is not apparent, the notice must be given within three days of the delivery of the goods.

The notice in writing need not be given if the state of the goods has, at the time of their receipt, been the subject of joint survey or inspection.

In any event the carrier and the ship shall be discharged from all liability in respect of loss or damage unless suit is brought within one year after delivery of the goods or the date when the goods should have been delivered.

In the case of an actual or apprehended loss or damage the carrier and the receiver shall give all reasonable facilities to each other for inspecting and tallying the goods.

7. After the goods are loaded the bill of lading to be issued by the carrier, master, or agent of the carrier, to the shipper shall, if the shipper so demands, be a "shipped" bill of lading, provided that if the shipper shall have previously taken up any document of title to such goods, he shall surrender the same as against the issue of the "shipped" bill of lading, but at the option of the carrier such document of title may be noted at the port of shipment by the carrier, master, or agent with the name or names of the ship or ships upon which the goods have been shipped and the date or dates of shipment, and when so noted, if it shows the particulars mentioned in paragraph 3 of Article III, shall for the purpose of this article be deemed to constitute a "shipped" bill of lading.

8. Any clause, covenant, or agreement in a contract of carriage relieving the carrier or the ship from liability for loss or damage to, or in connexion with, goods arising from negligence, fault, or failure in the duties and obligations provided in this article or lessening such liability otherwise than as provided in this convention, shall be null and void and of no effect. A benefit of insurance in favour of the carrier or similar clause shall be deemed to be a clause relieving the carrier from liability.

Article IV

1. Neither the carrier nor the ship shall be liable for loss or damage arising or resulting from unseaworthiness unless caused by want of due diligence on the part of the carrier to make the ship seaworthy, and to secure that the ship is properly manned, equipped and supplied, and to make the holds, refrigerating and cool chambers and all other parts of the ship in which goods are carried fit and safe for their reception, carriage and preservation in accordance with the provisions of paragraph 1 of Article III. Whenever loss or damage has resulted from unseaworthiness the burden of proving the exercise of due diligence shall be on the carrier or other person claiming exemption under this article.

2. Neither the carrier nor the ship shall be responsible for loss or damage arising or resulting from –

   (a)   Act, neglect, or default of the master, mariner, pilot, or the servants of the carrier in the navigation or in the management of the ship.
   (b)   Fire, unless caused by the actual fault or privity of the carrier.
   (c)   Perils, dangers and accidents of the sea or other navigable waters.
   (d)   Act of God.
   (e)   Act of war.
   (f)   Act of public enemies.
   (g)   Arrest or restraint of princes, rulers or people, or seizure under legal process.
   (h)   Quarantine restrictions.
   (i)   Act of omission of the shipper or owner of the goods, his agent or representative.
   (j)   Strikes or lockouts or stoppage or restraint of labour from whatever cause, whether partial or general.
   (k)   Riots and civil commotions.
   (l)   Saving or attempting to save life or property at sea.
   (m)   Wastage in bulk or weight or any other loss or damage arising from inherent defect, quality or vice of the goods.
   (n)   Insufficiency of packing.
   (o)   Insufficiency or inadequacy of marks.
   (p)   Latent defects not discoverable by due diligence.
   (q)   Any other cause arising without the actual fault or privity of the carrier, or without the fault or neglect of the agents or servants of the carrier, but the burden of proof shall be on the person claiming the benefit of this exception to show that neither the actual fault or privity of the carrier nor the fault or neglect of the agents or servants of the carrier contributed to the loss or damage.

3. The shipper shall not be responsible for loss or damage sustained by the carrier or the ship arising or resulting from any cause without the act, fault or neglect of the shipper, his agents or his servants.

4. Any deviation in saving or attempting to save life or property at sea or any reasonable deviation shall not be deemed to be an infringement or breach of this convention or of the

contract of carriage, and the carrier shall not be liable for any loss or damage resulting therefrom.

5. Neither the carrier nor the ship shall in any event be or become liable for any loss or damage to or in connexion with goods in an amount exceeding £100 per package or unit, or the equivalent of that sum in other currency unless the nature and value of such goods have been declared by the shipper before shipment and inserted in the bill of lading.

This declaration if embodied in the bill of lading shall be *prima facie* evidence, but shall not be binding or conclusive on the carrier.

By agreement between the carrier, master or agent of the carrier and the shipper another maximum amount than that mentioned in this paragraph may be fixed, provided that such maximum shall not be less than the figure above named.

Neither the carrier nor the ship shall be responsible in any event for loss or damage to, or in connexion with, goods if the nature or value thereof has been knowingly misstated by the shipper in the bill of lading.

6. Goods of an inflammable, explosive or dangerous nature to the shipment whereof the carrier, master or agent of the carrier has not consented with knowledge of their nature and character, may at any time before discharge be landed at any place, or destroyed or rendered innocuous by the carrier without compensation and the shipper of such goods shall be liable for all damages and expenses directly or indirectly arising out of or resulting from such shipment. If any such goods shipped with such knowledge and consent shall become a danger to the ship or cargo, they may in like manner be landed at any place, or destroyed or rendered innocuous by the carrier without liability on the part of the carrier except to general average, if any.

Article V

A carrier shall be at liberty to surrender in whole or in part all or any of his rights and immunities or to increase any of his responsibilities and obligations under this convention, provided such surrender or increase shall be embodied in the bill of lading issued to the shipper. The provisions of this convention shall not be applicable to charter parties, but if bills of lading are issued in the case of a ship under a charter party they shall comply with the terms of this convention. Nothing in these rules shall be held to prevent the insertion in a bill of lading of any lawful provision regarding general average.

Article VI

Notwithstanding the provisions of the preceding articles, a carrier, master or agent of the carrier and a shipper shall in regard to any particular goods be at liberty to enter into any agreement in any terms as to the responsibility and liability of the carrier for such goods, and as to the rights and immunities of the carrier in respect of such goods, or his obligation as to seaworthiness, so far as this stipulation is not contrary to public policy, or the care or diligence of his servants or agents in regard to the loading, handling, stowage, carriage, custody, care and discharge of the goods carried by sea, provided that in this case no bill of lading has been or shall be issued and that the terms agreed shall be embodied in a receipt which shall be a non-negotiable document and shall be marked as such.

Any agreement so entered into shall have full legal effect.

Provided that this article shall not apply to ordinary commercial shipments made in the ordinary course of trade, but only to other shipments where the character or condition of the property to be carried or the circumstances, terms and conditions under which the carriage is to be performed are such as reasonably to justify a special agreement.

Article VII

Nothing herein contained shall prevent a carrier or a shipper from entering into any agreement, stipulation, condition, reservation or exemption as to the responsibility and liability of the carrier or the ship for the loss or damage to, or in connexion with, the custody and care and handling of goods prior to the loading on, and subsequent to, the discharge from the ship on which the goods are carried by sea.

Article VIII

The provisions of this convention shall not affect the rights and obligations of the carrier under any statute for the time being in force relating to the limitation of the liability of owners of seagoing vessels.

Article IX

The monetary units mentioned in this convention are to be taken to be gold value.

Those contracting States in which the pound sterling is not a monetary unit reserve to themselves the right of translating the sums indicated in this convention in terms of pound sterling into terms of their own monetary system in round figures.

The national laws may reserve to the debtor the right of discharging his debt in national currency according to the rate of exchange prevailing on the day of the arrival of the ship at the port of discharge of the goods concerned.

Article X

The provisions of this convention shall apply to all bills of lading issued in any of the contracting States.

Article XI

After an interval of not more than two years from the day on which the convention is signed the Belgian Government shall place itself in communication with the Governments of the high contracting parties which have declared themselves prepared to ratify the convention, with a view to deciding whether it shall be put into force. The ratifications shall be deposited at Brussels at a date to be fixed by agreement among the said Governments. The first deposit of ratifications shall be recorded in a procès-verbal signed by the representatives of the Powers which take part therein and by the Belgian Minister for Foreign Affairs.

The subsequent deposit of ratifications shall be made by means of a written notification, addressed to the Belgian Government and accompanied by the instrument of ratification.

A duly certified copy of the procès-verbal relating to the first deposit of ratifications, of the notifications referred to in the previous paragraph, and also of the instruments of ratification accompanying them, shall be immediately sent by the Belgian Government through the diplomatic channel to the Powers who have signed this convention or who have acceded to it. In the cases contemplated in the preceding paragraph, the said Government shall inform them at the same time of the date on which it received the notification.

Article XII

Non-signatory States may accede to the present convention whether or not they have been represented at the International Conference at Brussels.

A State which desires to accede shall notify its intention in writing to the Belgian Government, forwarding to it the document of accession, which shall be deposited in the archives of the said Government.

The Belgian Government shall immediately forward to all the States which have signed or acceded to the convention a duly certified copy of the notification and of the act of accession, mentioning the date on which it received the notification

Article XIII

The high contracting parties may at the time of signature, ratification or accession declare that their acceptance of the present convention does not include any or all of the self-governing dominions, or of the colonies, overseas possessions, protectorates or territories under their sovereignty or authority, and they may subsequently accede separately on behalf of any self-governing dominion, colony, overseas possession, protectorate or territory excluded in their declaration. They may also denounce the convention separately in accordance with its provisions in respect of any self-governing dominion, or any colony, overseas possession, protectorate or territory under their sovereignty or authority.

Article XIV

The present convention shall take effect, in the case of the States which have taken part in the first deposit of ratifications, one year after the date of the protocol recording such deposit. As respects the States which ratify subsequently or which accede, and also in cases in which the convention is subsequently put into effect in accordance with Article XIII, it shall take effect six months after the notifications specified in paragraph 2 of Article XI and paragraph 2 of Article XII have been received by the Belgian Government.

Article XV

In the event of one of the contracting States wishing to denounce the present convention, the denunciation shall be notified in writing to the Belgian Government, which shall immediately communicate a duly certified copy of the notification to all the other States, informing them of the date on which it was received.

The denunciation shall only operate in respect of the State which made the notification, and on the expiry of one year after the notification has reached the Belgian Government.

Article XVI

Any one of the contracting States shall have the right to call for a fresh conference with a view to considering possible amendments.

A State which would exercise this right should notify its intention to the other States through the Belgian Government, which would make arrangements for convening the Conference.

Done at Brussels, in a single copy, August 25, 1924.

PROTOCOL OF SIGNATURE

At the time of signing the International Convention for the Unification of certain Rules of Law relating to Bills of Lading the Plenipotentiaries whose signatures appear below have adopted this Protocol, which will have the same force and the same value as if its provisions were inserted in the text of the convention to which it relates.

The High Contracting Parties may give effect to this convention either by giving it the force of law or by including in their national legislation in a form appropriate to that legislation the rules adopted under this convention.

They may reserve the right –

1. To prescribe that in the cases referred to in paragraph 2(c) to (p) of Article IV the holder of a bill of lading shall be entitled to establish responsibility for loss or damage arising from the personal fault of the carrier or the fault of his servants which are not covered by paragraph (a).
2. To apply Article VI in so far as the national coasting trade is concerned to all classes of goods without taking account of the restriction set out in the last paragraph of that article.

Done at Brussels, in a single copy, August 25, 1924.

CARRIAGE OF GOODS BY SEA ACT 1971

(1971 c 190)

An Act to amend the law with respect to the carriage of goods by sea. [8th April 1971]

BE IT ENACTED by the Queen's most Excellent Majesty, by and with the advice and consent of the Lords Spiritual and Temporal, and Commons, in this present Parliament assembled, and by the authority of the same, as follows:

1. – (1) In this Act, 'the Rules' means the International Convention for the unification of certain rules of law relating to bills of lading signed at Brussels on 25 August 1924, as amended by the Protocol signed at Brussels on 23 February 1968 and by the protocol signed at Brussels on 21 December 1979.

(2) The provisions of the Rules, as set out in the Schedule to this Act, shall have the force of law.

(3) Without prejudice to subsection (2) above, the said provisions shall have effect (and have the force of law) in relation to and in connection with the carriage of goods by sea in ships where the port of shipment is a port in the United Kingdom, whether or not the carriage is between ports in two different States within the meaning of Article X of the Rules.

(4) Subject to subsection (6) below, nothing in this section shall be taken as applying anything in the Rules to any contract for the carriage of goods by sea, unless the contract expressly or by implication provides for the issue of a bill of lading or any similar document of title.

[(5) – Repealed by the Merchant Shipping Act 1981, Sch.]

(6) Without prejudice to Article X*(c)* of the Rules, the Rules shall have the force of law in relation to –
   (a)   any bill of lading if the contract contained in or evidenced by it expressly provides that the Rules shall govern the contract, and
   (b)   any receipt which is a non-negotiable document marked as such if the contract contained in or evidenced by it is a contract for the carriage of goods by sea which expressly provides that the Rules are to govern the contract as if the receipt were a bill of lading,
but subject, where paragraph *(b)* applies, to any necessary modifications and in particular with the omission in Article III of the Rules of the second sentence of paragraph 4 and of paragraph 7.

(7) If and so far as the contract contained in or evidenced by a bill of lading or receipt within para-graph *(a)* or *(b)* of subsection (6) above applies to deck cargo or live animals, the Rules as given the force of law by that subsection shall have effect as if Article I*(c)* did not exclude deck cargo and live animals.
   In this subsection "deck cargo" means cargo which by the contract of carriage is stated as being carried on deck and is so carried.

Conversion of special drawing rights into sterling
1A. – (1) For the purposes of Article IV of the Rules the value on a particular day of one special drawing right shall be treated as equal to such a sum in sterling as the International Monetary Fund have fixed as being the equivalent of one special drawing right –

(a)   for that day; or

(b)   if no sum has been so fixed for that day, for the last day before that day for which a sum has been so fixed.

(2) A certificate given by or on behalf of the Treasury stating –

(a)   that a particular sum in sterling has been fixed as aforesaid for a particular day; or

(b)   that no sum has been so fixed for a particular day and that a particular sum in sterling has been so fixed for a day which is the last day for which a sum has been so fixed before the particular day,

shall be conclusive evidence of those matters for the purposes of subsection (1) above; and a document purporting to be such a certificate shall in any proceedings be received in evidence and, unless the contrary is proved, be deemed to be such a certificate.

(3) The Treasury may charge a reasonable fee for any certificate given in pursuance of subsection (2) above, and any fee received by the Treasury by virtue of this subsection shall be paid into the Consolidated Fund.

2. – (1) If Her Majesty by Order in Council certifies to the following effect, that is to say, that for the purposes of the Rules

(a)   a State specified in the Order is a contracting State, or is a contracting State in respect of any place or territory so specified,
or

(b)   any place or territory specified in the Order forms part of a State so specified (whether a contracting State or not),

the Order shall, except so far as it has been superseded by a subsequent Order, be conclusive evidence of the matters so certified.

(2) An Order in Council under this section may be varied or revoked by a subsequent Order in Council.

3. – There shall not be implied in any contract for the carriage of goods by sea to which the Rules apply by virtue of this Act any absolute undertaking by the carrier of the goods to provide a seaworthy ship.

4. – (1) Her Majesty may by Order in Council direct that this Act shall extend, subject to such exceptions, adaptations and modifications as may be specified in the Order, to all or any of the following territories, that is:

(a)   any colony (not being a colony for whose external relations a country other than the United Kingdom is responsible),

(b)   any country outside Her Majesty's dominions in which Her Majesty has jurisdiction in right of Her Majesty's Government of the United Kingdom.

(2) An Order in Council under this section may contain such transitional and other consequential and incidental provisions as appear to Her Majesty to be expedient, including provisions amending or repealing any legislation about the carriage of goods by sea forming part of the law of any of the territories mentioned in paragraphs *(a)* and *(b)* above.

(3) An Order in Council under this section may be varied or revoked by a subsequent Order in Council.

5. – (1) Her Majesty may by Order in Council provide that section 1(3) of this Act shall have effect as if the reference therein to the United Kingdom included a reference to all or any of the following territories, that is –

(a) the Isle of Man;

(b) any of the Channel Islands specified in the Order;

(c) any colony specified in the Order (not being a colony for whose external relations a country other than the United Kingdom is responsible);

(d) any associated state (as defined by section 1(3) of the West Indies Act 1967) specified in the Order;

(e) any country specified in the Order, being a country outside Her Majesty's dominions in which Her Majesty has jurisdiction in right of Her Majesty's Government of the United Kingdom.

(2) An Order in Council under this section may be varied or revoked by a subsequent Order in Council.

6. – (1) This Act may be cited as the Carriage of Goods by Sea Act 1971.

(2) It is hereby declared that this Act extends to Northern Ireland.

(3) The following enactments shall be repealed, that is –

(a) the Carriage of Goods by Sea Act 1924,

(b) section 12(4)(a) of the Nuclear Installations Act 1965,

and without prejudice to section 38(1) of the Interpretation Act 1889, the reference to the said Act of 1924 in section 1(1)(i)(ii) of the Hovercraft Act 1968 shall include a reference to this Act.

(4) It is hereby declared that for the purposes of Article VIII of the Rules section 186 of the Merchant Shipping Act 1995 (which entirely exempts shipowners and others in certain circumstances from liability for loss of, or damage to, goods) is a provision relating to limitation of liability.

(5) This Act shall come into force on such day as Her Majesty may by Order in Council appoint, and, for the purposes of the transition from the law in force immediately before the day appointed under this subsection to the provisions of this Act, the Order appointing the day may provide that those provisions shall have effect subject to such transitional provisions as may be contained in the Order.

SCHEDULE

The Hague Rules as amended by the Brussels Protocol 1968.

Article I

In these Rules the following words are employed, with the meaning set out below:

(a) "Carrier" includes the owner or the charterer who enters into a contract of carriage with a shipper.

(b) "Contract of carriage" applies only to contracts of carriage covered by a bill of lading or any similar document of title, in so far as such document relates to the carriage of goods by sea, including any bill of lading or any similar document as aforesaid issued under or pursuant to a charter party from the moment at which such bill of lading or similar document of title regulates the relations between a carrier and a holder of the same.

(c) "Goods" includes goods, wares, merchandise, and articles of every kind whatsoever except live animals and cargo which by the contract of carriage is stated as being carried on deck and is so carried.

(d) "Ship" means any vessel used for the carriage of goods by sea.

(e) "Carriage of goods" covers the period from the time when the goods are loaded on to the time they are discharged from the ship.

Article II

Subject to the provisions of Article VI, under every contract of carriage of goods by sea the carrier, in relation to the loading, handling, stowage, carriage, custody, care and discharge of such goods, shall be subject to the responsibilities and liabilities, and entitled to the rights and immunities hereinafter set forth.

Article III

1. The carrier shall be bound before and at the beginning of the voyage to exercise due diligence to –

(a) Make the ship seaworthy.

(b) Properly man, equip and supply the ship.

(c) Make the holds, refrigerating and cool chambers, and all other parts of the ship in which goods are carried, fit and safe for their reception, carriage and preservation.

2. Subject to the provisions of Article IV, the carrier shall properly and carefully load, handle, stow, carry, keep, care for, and discharge the goods carried.

3. After receiving the goods into his charge the carrier or the master or agent of the carrier shall, on demand of the shipper, issue to the shipper a bill of lading showing among other things –

(a) The leading marks necessary for identification of the goods as the same are furnished in writing by the shipper before the loading of such goods starts, provided such marks are stamped or otherwise shown clearly upon the goods if uncovered, or on the cases or coverings in which such goods are contained, in such a manner as should ordinarily remain legible until the end of the voyage.

(b) Either the number of packages or pieces, or the quantity, or weight, as the case may be, as furnished in writing by the shipper.

(c) The apparent order and condition of the goods.

Provided that no carrier, master or agent of the carrier shall be bound to state or show in the bill of lading any marks, number, quantity, or weight which he has reasonable ground for suspecting not accurately to represent the goods actually received, or which he has had no reasonable means of checking.

4. Such a bill of lading shall be prima facie evidence of the receipt by the carrier of the goods as therein described in accordance with paragraph 3*(a)*, *(b)* and *(c)*. However, proof to the contrary shall not be admissible when the bill of lading has been transferred to a third party acting in good faith.

5. The shipper shall be deemed to have guaranteed to the carrier the accuracy at the time of shipment of the marks, number, quantity and weight, as furnished by him, and the shipper shall indemnify the carrier against all loss, damages and expenses arising or resulting from inaccuracies in such particulars. The right of the carrier to such indemnity shall in no way limit his responsibility and liability under the contract of carriage to any person other than the shipper.

6. Unless notice of loss or damage and the general nature of such loss or damage be given in writing to the carrier or his agent at the port of discharge before or at the time of the removal of the goods into the custody of the person entitled to delivery thereof under the contract of carriage, or, if the loss or damage be not apparent, within three days, such removal shall be prima facie evidence of the delivery by the carrier of the goods as described in the bill of lading.

The notice in writing need not be given if the state of the goods has, at the time of their receipt, been the subject of joint survey or inspection.

Subject to paragraph 6*bis* the carrier and the ship shall in any event be discharged from all liability whatsoever in respect of the goods, unless suit is brought within one year of their delivery or of the date when they should have been delivered. This period may, however, be extended if the parties so agree after the cause of action has arisen.

In the case of any actual or apprehended loss or damage the carrier and the receiver shall give all reasonable facilities to each other for inspecting and tallying the goods.

6*bis*. An action for indemnity against a third person may be brought even after the expiration of the year provided for in the preceding paragraph if brought within the time allowed by the law of the Court seised of the case. However, the time allowed shall be not less than three months, commencing from the day when the person bringing such action for indemnity has settled the claim or has been served with process in the action against himself.

7. After the goods are loaded the bill of lading to be issued by the carrier, master, or agent of the carrier, to the shipper shall, if the shipper so demands, be a "shipped" bill of lading, provided that if the shipper shall have previously taken up any document of title to such goods, he shall surrender the same as against the issue of the "shipped" bill of lading, but at the option of the carrier such document of title may be noted at the port of shipment by the carrier, master, or agent with the name or names of the ship or ships upon which the goods have been shipped and the date or dates of shipment, and when so noted, if it shows the particulars mentioned in paragraph 3 of Article III, shall for the purpose of this article be deemed to constitute a "shipped" bill of lading.

8. Any clause, covenant, or agreement in a contract of carriage relieving the carrier or the ship from liability for loss or damage to, or in connection with, goods arising from negligence, fault or failure in the duties and obligations provided in this article or lessening such liability otherwise than as provided in these Rules, shall be null and void and of no effect. A benefit of insurance in favour of the carrier or similar clause shall be deemed to be a clause relieving the carrier from liability.

Article IV

1. Neither the carrier nor the ship shall be liable for loss or damage arising or resulting from unseaworthiness unless caused by want of due diligence on the part of the carrier to make the ship seaworthy, and to secure that the ship is properly manned, equipped and supplied, and to make the holds, refrigerating and cool chambers and all other parts of the ship in which goods are carried fit and safe for their reception, carriage and preservation in accordance with the provisions of paragraph 1 of Article III. Whenever loss or damage has resulted from unseaworthiness the burden of proving the exercise of due diligence shall be on the carrier or other person claiming exemption under this article.

2. Neither the carrier nor the ship shall be responsible for loss or damage arising or resulting from –

   (a) Act, neglect, or default of the master, mariner, pilot, or the servants of the carrier in the navigation or in the management of the ship.
   (b) Fire, unless caused by the actual fault or privity of the carrier.
   (c) Perils, dangers and accidents of the sea or other navigable waters.
   (d) Act of God.
   (e) Act of war.
   (f) Act of public enemies.
   (g) Arrest or restraint of princes, rulers or people, or seizure under legal process.
   (h) Quarantine restrictions.
   (i) Act or omission of the shipper or owner of the goods, his agent or representative.
   (j) Strikes or lockouts or stoppage or restraint of labour from whatever cause, whether partial or general.
   (k) Riots and civil commotions.
   (l) Saving or attempting to save life or property at sea.
   (m) Wastage in bulk or weight or any other loss or damage arising from inherent defect, quality or vice of the goods.
   (n) Insufficiency of packing.
   (o) Insufficiency or inadequacy of marks.
   (p) Latent defects not discoverable by due diligence.
   (q) Any other cause arising without the actual fault or privity of the carrier, or without the fault or neglect of the agents or servants of the carrier, but the burden of proof shall be on the person claiming the benefit of this exception to show that neither the actual fault or privity of the carrier nor the fault or neglect of the agents or servants of the carrier contributed to the loss or damage.

3. The shipper shall not be responsible for loss or damage sustained by the carrier or the ship arising or resulting from any cause without the act, fault or neglect of the shipper, his agents or his servants.

4. Any deviation in saving or attempting to save life or property at sea or any reasonable deviation shall not be deemed to be an infringement or breach of these Rules or of the contract of carriage, and the carrier shall not be liable for any loss or damage resulting therefrom.

5.(a) Unless the nature and value of such goods have been declared by the shipper before shipment and inserted in the bill of lading, neither the carrier nor the ship shall in any event be or become liable for any loss or damage to or in connection with the goods in an amount exceeding 666.67 units of account per package or unit or 2 units of account per kilogramme weight of the goods lost or damaged, whichever is the higher.

(b) The total amount recoverable shall be calculated by reference to the value of such goods at the place and time at which the goods are discharged from the ship in accordance with the contract or should have been so discharged.

The value of the goods shall be fixed according to the commodity exchange price, or, if there be no such price, according to the current market price, or, if there be no commodity exchange price or current market price, by reference to the normal value of goods of the same kind and quality.

(c) Where a container, pallet or similar article of transport is used to consolidate goods, the number of packages or units enumerated in the bill of lading as packed in such article of transport shall be deemed the number of packages or units for the purpose of this paragraph as far as these packages or units are concerned. Except as aforesaid such article of transport shall be considered the package or unit.

(d) The unit of account mentioned in this Article is the special drawing right as defined by the International Monetary Fund. The amounts mentioned in sub-paragraph *(a)* of this paragraph shall be converted into national currency on the basis of the value of that currency on a date to be determined by the law of the Court seised of the case.

(e) Neither the carrier nor the ship shall be entitled to the benefit of the limitation of liability provided for in this paragraph if it is proved that the damage resulted from an act or omission of the carrier done with intent to cause damage, or recklessly and with knowledge that damage would probably result.

(f) The declaration mentioned in sub-paragraph *(a)* of this paragraph, if embodied in the bill of lading, shall be prima facie evidence, but shall not be binding or conclusive on the carrier.

(g) By agreement between the carrier, master or agent of the carrier and the shipper other maximum amounts than those mentioned in sub-paragraph *(a)* of this paragraph may be fixed, provided that no maximum amount so fixed shall be less than the appropriate maximum mentioned in that sub-paragraph.

(h) Neither the carrier nor the ship shall be responsible in any event for loss or damage to, or in connection with, goods if the nature or value thereof has been knowingly misstated by the shipper in the bill of lading.

6. Goods of an inflammable, explosive or dangerous nature to the shipment whereof the carrier, master or agent of the carrier has not consented with knowledge of their nature and character, may at any time before discharge be landed at any place, or destroyed or rendered innocuous by the carrier without compensation and the shipper of such goods shall be liable for all damages and expenses directly or indirectly arising out of or resulting from such shipment. If any such goods shipped with such knowledge and consent shall become a danger to the ship or cargo, they may in like manner be landed at any place, or destroyed or rendered innocuous by the carrier without liability on the part of the carrier except to general average, if any.

Article IV *bis*

1. The defences and limits of liability provided for in these Rules shall apply in any action against the carrier in respect of loss or damage to goods covered by a contract of carriage whether the action be founded in contract or in tort.

2. If such an action is brought against a servant or agent of the carrier (such servant or agent not being an independent contractor), such servant or agent shall be entitled to avail himself of the defences and limits of liability which the carrier is entitled to invoke under these Rules.

3. The aggregate of the amounts recoverable from the carrier, and such servants and agents, shall in no case exceed the limit provided for in these Rules.

4. Nevertheless, a servant or agent of the carrier shall not be entitled to avail himself of the provisions of this article, if it is proved that the damage resulted from an act or omission of the servant or agent done with intent to cause damage or recklessly and with knowledge that damage would probably result.

Article V

A carrier shall be at liberty to surrender in whole or in part all or any of his rights and immunities or to increase any of his responsibilities and obligations under these Rules, provided such surrender or increase shall be embodied in the bill of lading issued to the shipper. The provisions of these Rules shall not be applicable to charter parties, but if bills of lading are issued in the case of a ship under a charter party they shall comply with the terms of these Rules. Nothing in these Rules shall be held to prevent the insertion in a bill of lading of any lawful provision regarding general average.

Article VI

Notwithstanding the provisions of the preceding articles, a carrier, master or agent of the carrier and a shipper shall in regard to any particular goods be at liberty to enter into any agreement in any terms as to the responsibility and liability of the carrier for such goods, and as to the rights and immunities of the carrier in respect of such goods, or his obligation as to seaworthiness, so far as this stipulation is not contrary to public policy, or the care or diligence of his servants or agents in regard to the loading, handling, stowage, carriage, custody, care and discharge of the goods carried by sea, provided that in this case no bill of lading has been or shall be issued and that the terms agreed shall be embodied in a receipt which shall be a non-negotiable document and shall be marked as such.

Any agreement so entered into shall have full legal effect.

Provided that this article shall not apply to ordinary commercial shipments made in the ordinary course of trade, but only to other shipments where the character or condition of the property to be carried or the circumstances, terms and conditions under which the carriage is to be performed are such as reasonably to justify a special agreement.

Article VII

Nothing herein contained shall prevent a carrier or a shipper from entering into any agreement, stipulation, condition, reservation or exemption as to the responsibility and liability of the carrier or the ship for the loss or damage to, or in connection with, the custody and care and handling of goods prior to the loading on, and subsequent to the discharge from, the ship on which the goods are carried by sea.

Article VIII

The provisions of these Rules shall not affect the rights and obligations of the carrier under any statute for the time being in force relating to the limitation of the liability of owners of sea-going vessels.

Article IX

These Rules shall not affect the provisions of any International Convention or national law governing liability for nuclear damage.

Article X

The provisions of these Rules shall apply to every bill of lading relating to the carriage of goods between ports in two different States if:

(a) the bill of lading is issued in a contracting State,

or

(b) the carriage is from a port in a contracting State,

or

(c) the contract contained in or evidenced by the bill of lading provides that these Rules or legislation of any State giving effect to them are to govern the contract,

whatever may be the nationality of the ship, the carrier, the shipper, the consignee, or any other interested person.

[The last two paragraphs of this article are not reproduced. They require contracting States to apply the Rules to bills of lading mentioned in the article and authorise them to apply the Rules to other bills of lading.]

[Articles 11 to 16 of the International Convention for the unification of certain rules of law relating to bills of lading signed at Brussels on 25 August 1924 are not reproduced. They deal with the coming into force of the Convention, procedure for ratification, accession and denunciation, and the right to call for a fresh conference to consider amendments to the Rules contained in the Convention.]

CARRIAGE OF GOODS BY SEA ACT 1992

(1992 c 50)

An Act to replace the Bills of Lading Act 1855 with new provision with respect to bills of lading and certain other shipping documents. [16th July 1992]

Be it enacted by the Queen's most Excellent Majesty, by and with the advice and consent of the Lords Spiritual and Temporal, and Commons, in this present Parliament assembled, and by the authority of the same, as follows:

1.(1) This Act applies to the following documents, that is to say:
   (a) any bill of lading;
   (b) any sea waybill; and
   (c) any ship's delivery order.

(2) References in this Act to a bill of lading:
   (a) do not include references to a document which is incapable of transfer either by indorsement or, as a bearer bill, by delivery without indorsement; but
   (b) subject to that, do include references to a received for shipment bill of lading.

(3) References in this Act to a sea waybill are references to any document which is not a bill of lading but:
   (a) is such a receipt for goods as contains or evidences a contract for the carriage of goods by sea; and
   (b) identifies the person to whom delivery of the goods is to be made by the carrier in accordance with that contract.

(4) References in this Act to a ship's delivery order are references to any document which is neither a bill of lading nor a sea waybill but contains an undertaking which:
   (a) is given under or for the purposes of a contract for the carriage by sea of the goods to which the document relates, or of goods which include those goods; and
   (b) is an undertaking by the carrier to a person identified in the document to deliver the goods to which the document relates to that person.

(5) The Secretary of State may by regulations make provision for the application of this Act to cases where a telecommunication system or any other information technology is used for effecting transactions corresponding to:
   (a) the issue of a document to which this Act applies;
   (b) the indorsement, delivery or other transfer of such a document; or
   (c) the doing of anything else in relation to such a document.

(6) Regulations under subsection (5) above may:
   (a) make such modifications of the following provisions of this Act as the Secretary of State considers appropriate in connection with the application of this Act to any case mentioned in that subsection; and
   (b) contain supplemental, incidental, consequential and transitional provision;
and the power to make regulations under that subsection shall be exercisable by statutory instrument subject to annulment in pursuance of a resolution of either House of Parliament.

2.(1) Subject to the following provisions of this section, a person who becomes:
   (a) the lawful holder of a bill of lading;

(b) the person who (without being an original party to the contract of carriage) is the person to whom delivery of the goods to which a sea waybill relates is to be made by the carrier in accordance with that contract; or

(c) the person to whom delivery of the goods to which a ship's delivery order relates is to be made in accordance with the undertaking contained in the order,

shall (by virtue of becoming the holder of the bill or, as the case may be, the person to whom delivery is to be made) have transferred to and vested in him all rights of suit under the contract of carriage as if he had been a party to that contract.

(2) Where, when a person becomes the lawful holder of a bill of lading, possession of the bill no longer gives a right (as against the carrier) to possession of the goods to which the bill relates, that person shall not have any rights transferred to him by virtue of subsection (1) above unless he becomes the holder of the bill:

(a) by virtue of a transaction effected in pursuance of any contractual or other arrangements made before the time when such a right to possession ceased to attach to possession of the bill; or

(b) as a result of the rejection to that person by another person of goods or documents delivered to the other person in pursuance of any such arrangements.

(3) The rights vested in any person by virtue of the operation of subsection (1) above in relation to a ship's delivery order:

(a) shall be so vested subject to the terms of the order; and

(b) where the goods to which the order relates form a part only of the goods to which the contract of carriage relates, shall be confined to rights in respect of the goods to which the order relates.

(4) Where, in the case of any document to which this Act applies:

(a) a person with any interest or right in or in relation to goods to which the document relates sustains loss or damage in consequence of a breach of the contract of carriage; but

(b) subsection (1) above operates in relation to that document so that rights of suit in respect of that breach are vested in another person,

the other person shall be entitled to exercise those rights for the benefit of the person who sustained the loss or damage to the same extent as they could have been exercised if they had been vested in the person for whose benefit they are exercised.

(5) Where rights are transferred by virtue of the operation of subsection (1) above in relation to any document, the transfer for which that subsection provides shall extinguish any entitlement to those rights which derives:

(a) where that document is a bill of lading, from a person's having been an original party to the contract of carriage; or

(b) in the case of any document to which this Act applies, from the previous operation of that subsection in relation to that document;

but the operation of that subsection shall be without prejudice to any rights which derive from a person's having been an original party to the contract contained in, or evidenced by, a sea waybill and, in relation to a ship's delivery order, shall be without prejudice to any rights deriving otherwise than from the previous operation of that subsection in relation to that order.

3.(1) Where subsection (1) of section 2 of this Act operates in relation to any document to which this Act applies and the person in whom rights are vested by virtue of that subsection:

(a) takes or demands delivery from the carrier of any of the goods to which the document relates;

(b) makes a claim under the contract of carriage against the carrier in respect of any of those goods; or

(c) is a person who, at a time before those rights were vested in him, took or demanded delivery from the carrier of any of those goods,

that person shall (by virtue of taking or demanding delivery or making the claim or, in a case falling within paragraph (c) above, of having the rights vested in him) become subject to the same liabilities under that contract as if he had been a party to that contract.

(2) Where the goods to which a ship's delivery order relates form a part only of the goods to which the contract of carriage relates, the liabilities to which any person is subject by virtue of the operation of this section in relation to that order shall exclude liabilities in respect of any goods to which the order does not relate.

(3) This section, so far as it imposes liabilities under any contract on any person, shall be without prejudice to the liabilities under the contract of any person as an original party to the contract.

4. A bill of lading which:
   (a) represents goods to have been shipped on board a vessel or to have been received for shipment on board a vessel; and
   (b) has been signed by the master of the vessel or by a person who was not the master but had the express, implied or apparent authority of the carrier to sign bills of lading,
shall, in favour of a person who has become the lawful holder of the bill, be conclusive evidence against the carrier of the shipment of the goods or, as the case may be, of their receipt for shipment.

5.(1) In this Act:

'bill of lading', 'sea waybill' and 'ship's delivery order' shall be construed in accordance with section 1 above;
'the contract of carriage':
   (a) in relation to a bill of lading or sea waybill, means the contract contained in or evidenced by that bill or waybill; and
   (b) in relation to a ship's delivery order, means the contract under or for the purposes of which the undertaking contained in the order is given;
'holder', in relation to a bill of lading, shall be construed in accordance with subsection (2) below;
'information technology' includes any computer or other technology by means of which information or other matter may be recorded or communicated without being reduced to documentary form; and
'telecommunication system' has the same meaning as in the Telecommunications Act 1984.

(2) References in this Act to the holder of a bill of lading are references to any of the following persons, that is to say:
   (a) a person with possession of the bill who, by virtue of being the person identified in the bill, is the consignee of the goods to which the bill relates;
   (b) a person with possession of the bill as a result of the completion, by delivery of the bill, of any indorsement of the bill or, in the case of a bearer bill, of any other transfer of the bill;
   (c) a person with possession of the bill as a result of any transaction by virtue of which he would have become a holder falling within paragraph (a) or (b) above had not the transaction been effected at a time when possession of the bill no longer gave a right (as against the carrier) to possession of the goods to which the bill relates;
and a person shall be regarded for the purposes of this Act as having become the lawful holder of a bill of lading wherever he has become the holder of the bill in good faith.

(3) References in this Act to a person's being identified in a document include references to his being identified by a description which allows for the identity of the person in question to be

varied, in accordance with the terms of the document, after its issue; and the reference in section 1(3)(b) of this Act to a document's identifying a person shall be construed accordingly.

(4) Without prejudice to sections 2(2) and 4 above, nothing in this Act shall preclude its operation in relation to a case where the goods to which a document relates:

(a) cease to exist after the issue of the document; or

(b) cannot be identified (whether because they are mixed with other goods or for any other reason);

and references in this Act to the goods to which a document relates shall be construed accordingly.

(5) The preceding provisions of this Act shall have effect without prejudice to the application, in relation to any case, of the rules (the Hague-Visby Rules) which for the time being have the force of law by virtue of section 1 of the Carriage of Goods by Sea Act 1971.

6.(1) This Act may be cited as the Carriage of Goods by Sea Act 1992.

(2) The Bills of Lading Act 1855 is hereby repealed.

(3) This Act shall come into force at the end of the period of two months beginning with the day on which it is passed; but nothing in this Act shall have effect in relation to any document issued before the coming into force of this Act.

(4) This Act extends to Northern Ireland.

UNITED NATIONS CONVENTION ON THE CARRIAGE OF GOODS BY SEA, 1978

(The Hamburg Rules)

Preamble

THE STATES PARTIES TO THIS CONVENTION,

HAVING RECOGNIZED the desirability of determining by agreement certain rules relating to the carriage of goods by sea,

HAVE DECIDED to conclude a Convention for this purpose and have thereto agreed as follows:

PART I. GENERAL PROVISIONS

Article 1. Definitions

In this Convention:

1. "Carrier" means any person by whom or in whose name a contract of carriage of goods by sea has been concluded with a shipper.

2. "Actual carrier" means any person to whom the performance of the carriage of the goods, or of part of the carriage, has been entrusted by the carrier, and includes any other person to whom such performance has been entrusted.

3. "Shipper" means any person by whom or in whose name or on whose behalf a contract of carriage of goods by sea has been concluded with a carrier, or any person by whom or in whose name or on whose behalf the goods are actually delivered to the carrier in relation to the contract of carriage by sea.

4. "Consignee" means the person entitled to take delivery of the goods.

5. "Goods" includes live animals; where the goods are consolidated in a container, pallet or similar article of transport or where they are packed, "goods" includes such article of transport or packaging if supplied by the shipper.

6. "Contract of carriage by sea" means any contract whereby the carrier undertakes against payment of freight to carry goods by sea from one port to another; however, a contract which involves carriage by sea and also carriage by some other means is deemed to be a contract of carriage by sea for the purposes of this Convention only in so far as it relates to the carriage by sea.

7. "Bill of lading" means a document which evidences a contract of carriage by sea and the taking over or loading of the goods by the carrier, and by which the carrier undertakes to deliver the goods against surrender of the document. A provision in the document that the goods are to be delivered to the order of a named person, or to order, or to bearer, constitutes such an undertaking.

8. "Writing" includes, inter alia, telegram and telex.

Article 2. Scope of application

1. The provisions of this Convention are applicable to all contracts of carriage by sea between two different States, if:

(a) the port of loading as provided for in the contract of carriage by sea is located in a Contracting State, or

(b) the port of discharge as provided for in the contract of carriage by sea is located in a Contracting State, or

(c) one of the optional ports of discharge provided for in the contract of carriage by sea is the actual port of discharge and such port is located in a Contracting State, or

(d) the bill of lading or other document evidencing the contract of carriage by sea is issued in a Contracting State, or

(e) the bill of lading or other document evidencing the contract of carriage by sea provides that the provisions of this Convention or the legislation of any State giving effect to them are to govern the contract.

2. The provisions of this Convention are applicable without regard to the nationality of the ship, the carrier, the actual carrier, the shipper, the consignee or any other interested person.

3. The provisions of this Convention are not applicable to charter-parties. However, where a bill of lading is issued pursuant to a charter-party, the provisions of the Convention apply to such a bill of lading if it governs the relation between the carrier and the holder of the bill of lading, not being the charterer.

4. If a contract provides for future carriage of goods in a series of shipments during an agreed period, the provisions of this Convention apply to each shipment. However, where a shipment is made under a charter-party, the provisions of paragraph 3 of this article apply.

Article 3. Interpretation of the Convention

In the interpretation and application of the provisions of this Convention regard shall be had to its international character and to the need to promote uniformity.

PART II. LIABILITY OF THE CARRIER

Article 4. Period of responsibility

1. The responsibility of the carrier for the goods under this Convention covers the period during which the carrier is in charge of the goods at the port of loading, during the carriage and at the port of discharge.

2. For the purpose of paragraph 1 of this article, the carrier is deemed to be in charge of the goods

(a) from the time he has taken over the goods from:

    (i) the shipper, or a person acting on his behalf; or

    (ii) an authority or other third party to whom, pursuant to law or regulations applicable at the port of loading, the goods must be handed over for shipment;

(b) until the time he has delivered the goods:

    (i) by handing over the goods to the consignee; or

    (ii) in cases where the consignee does not receive the goods from the carrier, by placing them at the disposal of the consignee in accordance with the contract or with the law or with the usage of the particular trade, applicable at the port of discharge; or

    (iii) by handing over the goods to an authority or other third party to whom, pursuant to law or regulations applicable at the port of discharge, the goods must be handed over.

3. In paragraphs 1 and 2 of this article, reference to the carrier or to the consignee means, in addition to the carrier or the consignee, the servants or agents, respectively of the carrier or the consignee.

Article 5. Basis of liability

1. The carrier is liable for loss resulting from loss of or damage to the goods, as well as from delay in delivery, if the occurrence which caused the loss, damage or delay took place while the goods were in his charge as defined in article 4, unless the carrier proves that he, his servants or agents took all measures that could reasonably be required to avoid the occurrence and its consequences.

2. Delay in delivery occurs when the goods have not been delivered at the port of discharge provided for in the contract of carriage by sea within the time expressly agreed upon or, in the absence of such agreement, within the time which it would be reasonable to require of a diligent carrier, having regard to the circumstances of the case.

3. The person entitled to make a claim for the loss of goods may treat the goods as lost if they have not been delivered as required by article 4 within 60 consecutive days following the expiry of the time for delivery according to paragraph 2 of this article.

4. (a) The carrier is liable

    (i) for loss of or damage to the goods or delay in delivery caused by fire, if the claimant proves that the fire arose from fault or neglect on the part of the carrier, his servants or agents;

    (ii) for such loss, damage or delay in delivery which is proved by the claimant to have resulted from the fault or neglect of the carrier, his servants or agents, in taking all measures that could reasonably be required to put out the fire and avoid or mitigate its consequences.

(b) In case of fire on board the ship affecting the goods, if the claimant or the carrier so desires, a survey in accordance with shipping practices must be held into the cause and circumstances of the fire, and a copy of the surveyor's report shall be made available on demand to the carrier and the claimant.

5. With respect to live animals, the carrier is not liable for loss, damage or delay in delivery resulting from any special risks inherent in that kind of carriage. If the carrier proves that he has complied with any special instructions given to him by the shipper respecting the animals and that, in the circumstances of the case, the loss, damage or delay in delivery could be attributed to such risks, it is presumed that the loss, damage or delay in delivery was so caused, unless there is proof that all or a part of the loss, damage or delay in delivery resulted from fault or neglect on the part of the carrier, his servants or agents.

6. The carrier is not liable, except in general average, where loss, damage or delay in delivery resulted from measures to save life or from reasonable measures to save property at sea.

7. Where fault or neglect on the part of the carrier, his servants or agents combines with another cause to produce loss, damage or delay in delivery the carrier is liable only to the extent that the loss, damage or delay in delivery is attributable to such fault or neglect, provided that the carrier proves the amount of the loss, damage or delay in delivery not attributable thereto.

Article 6. Limits of liability

1. (a) The liability of the carrier for loss resulting from loss of or damage to goods according to the provisions of article 5 is limited to an amount equivalent to 835 units of account per package or other

shipping unit or 2.5 units of account per kilogramme of gross weight of the goods lost or damaged, whichever is the higher.

(b) The liability of the carrier for delay in delivery according to the provisions of article 5 is limited to an amount equivalent to two and a half times the freight payable for the goods delayed, but not exceeding the total freight payable under the contract of carriage of goods by sea.

(c) In no case shall the aggregate liability of the carrier, under both subparagraphs (a) and (b) of this paragraph, exceed the limitation which would be established under subparagraph (a) of this paragraph for total loss of the goods with respect to which such liability was incurred.

2. For the purpose of calculating which amount is the higher in accordance with paragraph 1(a) of this article, the following rules apply:

(a) Where a container, pallet or similar article of transport is used to consolidate goods, the package or other shipping units enumerated in the bill of lading, if issued, or otherwise in any other document evidencing the contract of carriage by sea, as packed in such article of transport are deemed packages or shipping units. Except as aforesaid the goods in such article of transport are deemed one shipping unit.

(b) In cases where the article of transport itself has been lost or damaged, that article of transport, if not owned or otherwise supplied by the carrier, is considered one separate shipping unit.

3. Unit of account means the unit of account mentioned in article 26.

4. By agreement between the carrier and the shipper, limits of liability exceeding those provided for in paragraph 1 may be fixed.

Article 7. *Application to non-contractual claims*

1. The defences and limits of liability provided for in this Convention apply in any action against the carrier in respect of loss or damage to the goods covered by the contract of carriage by sea, as well as of delay in delivery whether the action is founded in contract, in tort or otherwise.

2. If such an action is brought against a servant or agent of the carrier, such servant or agent, if he proves that he acted within the scope of his employment, is entitled to avail himself of the defences and limits of liability which the carrier is entitled to invoke under this Convention.

3. Except as provided in article 8, the aggregate of the amounts recoverable from the carrier and from any persons referred to in paragraph 2 of this article shall not exceed the limits of liability provided for in this Convention.

Article 8. *Loss of right to limit responsibility*

1. The carrier is not entitled to the benefit of the limitation of liability provided for in article 6 if it is proved that the loss, damage or delay in delivery resulted from an act or omission of the carrier done with the intent to cause such loss, damage or delay, or recklessly and with knowledge that such loss, damage or delay would probably result.

2. Notwithstanding the provisions of paragraph 2 of article 7, a servant or agent of the carrier is not entitled to the benefit of the limitation of liability provided for in article 6 if it is proved that the loss, damage or delay in delivery resulted from an act or omission of such servant or agent, done with the intent to cause such loss, damage or delay, or recklessly and with knowledge that such loss, damage or delay would probably result.

Article 9. *Deck cargo*

1. The carrier is entitled to carry the goods on deck only if such carriage is in accordance with an agreement with the shipper or with the usage of the particular trade or is required by statutory rules or regulations.

2. If the carrier and the shipper have agreed that the goods shall or may be carried on deck, the carrier must insert in the bill of lading or other document evidencing the contract of carriage by sea a statement to that effect. In the absence of such a statement the carrier has the burden of proving that an agreement for carriage on deck has been entered into; however, the carrier is not entitled to invoke such an agreement against a third party, including a consignee, who has acquired the bill of lading in good faith.

3. Where the goods have been carried on deck contrary to the provisions of paragraph 1 of this article or where the carrier may not under paragraph 2 of this article invoke an agreement for carriage on deck, the carrier, notwithstanding the provisions of paragraph 1 of article 5, is liable for loss of or damage to the goods, as well as for delay in delivery, resulting solely from the carriage on deck, and the extent of his liability is to be determined in accordance with the provisions of article 6 or article 8 of this Convention, as the case may be.

4. Carriage of goods on deck contrary to express agreement for carriage under deck is deemed to be an act or omission of the carrier within the meaning of article 8.

Article 10. *Liability of the carrier and actual carrier*

1. Where the performance of the carriage or part thereof has been entrusted to an actual carrier,

whether or not in pursuance of a liberty under the contract of carriage by sea to do so, the carrier nevertheless remains responsible for the entire carriage according to the provisions of this Convention. The carrier is responsible, in relation to the carriage performed by the actual carrier, for the acts and omissions of the actual carrier and of his servants and agents acting within the scope of their employment.

2. All the provisions of this Convention governing the responsibility of the carrier also apply to the responsibility of the actual carrier for the carriage performed by him. The provisions of paragraphs 2 and 3 of article 7 and of paragraph 2 of article 8 apply if an action is brought against a servant or agent of the actual carrier.

3. Any special agreement under which the carrier assumes obligations not imposed by this Convention or waives rights conferred by this Convention affects the actual carrier only if agreed to by him expressly and in writing. Whether or not the actual carrier has so agreed, the carrier nevertheless remains bound by the obligations or waivers resulting from such special agreement.

4. Where and to the extent that both the carrier and the actual carrier are liable, their liability is joint and several.

5. The aggregate of the amounts recoverable from the carrier, the actual carrier and their servants and agents shall not exceed the limits of liability provided for in this Convention.

6. Nothing in this article shall prejudice any right of recourse as between the carrier and the actual carrier.

Article 11. Through carriage

1. Notwithstanding the provisions of paragraph 1 of article 10, where a contract of carriage by sea provides explicitly that a specified part of the carriage covered by the said contract is to be performed by a named person other than the carrier, the contract may also provide that the carrier is not liable for loss, damage or delay in delivery caused by an occurrence which takes place while the goods are in the charge of the actual carrier during such part of the carriage. Nevertheless, any stipulation limiting or excluding such liability is without effect if no judicial proceedings can be instituted against the actual carrier in a court competent under paragraph 1 or 2 of article 21. The burden of proving that any loss, damage or delay in delivery has been caused by such an occurrence rests upon the carrier.

2. The actual carrier is responsible in accordance with the provisions of paragraph 2 of article 10 for loss, damage or delay in delivery caused by an occurrence which takes place while the goods are in his charge.

PART III. LIABILITY OF THE SHIPPER

Article 12. General rule

The shipper is not liable for loss sustained by the carrier or the actual carrier, or for damage sustained by the ship, unless such loss or damage was caused by the fault or neglect of the shipper, his servants or agents. Nor is any servant or agent of the shipper liable for such loss or damage unless the loss or damage was caused by fault or neglect on his part.

Article 13. Special rules on dangerous goods

1. The shipper must mark or label in a suitable manner dangerous goods as dangerous.

2. Where the shipper hands over dangerous goods to the carrier or an actual carrier, as the case may be, the shipper must inform him of the dangerous character of the goods and, if necessary, of the precautions to be taken. If the shipper fails to do so and such carrier or actual carrier does not otherwise have knowledge of their dangerous character:

(a) the shipper is liable to the carrier and any actual carrier for the loss resulting from the shipment of such goods, and

(b) the goods may at any time be unloaded, destroyed or rendered innocuous, as the circumstances may require, without payment of compensation.

3. The provisions of paragraph 2 of this article may not be invoked by any person if during the carriage he has taken the goods in his charge with knowledge of their dangerous character.

4. If, in cases where the provisions of paragraph 2, subparagraph (b), of this article do not apply or may not be invoked, dangerous goods become an actual danger to life or property, they may be unloaded, destroyed or rendered innocuous, as the circumstances may require, without payment of compensation except where there is an obligation to contribute in general average or where the carrier is liable in accordance with the provisions of article 5.

PART IV. TRANSPORT DOCUMENTS

Article 14. Issue of bill of lading

1. When the carrier or the actual carrier takes the goods in his charge, the carrier must, on demand of the shipper, issue to the shipper a bill of lading.

2. The bill of lading may be signed by a person having authority from the carrier. A bill of lading signed by the master of the ship carrying the goods is deemed to have been signed on behalf of the carrier.

3. The signature on the bill of lading may be in handwriting, printed in facsimile, perforated,

stamped, in symbols, or made by any other mechanical or electronic means, if not inconsistent with the law of the country where the bill of lading is issued.

Article 15. Contents of bill of lading

1. The bill of lading must include, *inter alia*, the following particulars:

(a) the general nature of the goods, the leading marks necessary for identification of the goods, an express statement, if applicable, as to the dangerous character of the goods, the number of packages or pieces, and the weight of the goods or their quantity otherwise expressed, all such particulars as furnished by the shipper;

(b) the apparent condition of the goods;

(c) the name and principal place of business of the carrier;

(d) the name of the shipper;

(e) the consignee if named by the shipper;

(f) the port of loading under the contract of carriage by sea and the date on which the goods were taken over by the carrier at the port of loading;

(g) the port of discharge under the contract of carriage by sea;

(h) the number of originals of the bill of lading, if more than one;

(i) the place of issuance of the bill of lading;

(j) the signature of the carrier or a person acting on his behalf;

(k) the freight to the extent payable by the consignee or other indication that freight is payable by him;

(l) the statement referred to in paragraph 3 of article 23;

(m) the statement, if applicable, that the goods shall or may be carried on deck;

(n) the date or the period of delivery of the goods at the port of discharge if expressly agreed upon between the parties; and

(o) any increased limit or limits of liability where agreed in accordance with paragraph 4 of article 6.

2. After the goods have been loaded on board, if the shipper so demands, the carrier must issue to the shipper a "shipped" bill of lading which, in addition to the particulars required under paragraph 1 of this article, must state that the goods are on board a named ship or ships, and the date or dates of loading. If the carrier has previously issued to the shipper a bill of lading or other document of title with respect to any of such goods, on request of the carrier, the shipper must surrender such document in exchange for a "shipped" bill of lading. The carrier may amend any previously issued document in order to meet the shipper's demand for a "shipped" bill of lading if, as amended, such document includes all the information required to be contained in a "shipped" bill of lading.

3. The absence in the bill of lading of one or more particulars referred to in this article does not affect the legal character of the document as a bill of lading provided that it nevertheless meets the requirements set out in paragraph 7 of article 1.

Article 16. Bills of lading: reservations and evidentiary effect

1. If the bill of lading contains particulars concerning the general nature, leading marks, number of packages or pieces, weight or quantity of the goods which the carrier or other person issuing the bill of lading on his behalf knows or has reasonable grounds to suspect do not accurately represent the goods actually taken over or, where a "shipped" bill of lading is issued, loaded, or if he had no reasonable means of checking such particulars, the carrier or such other person must insert in the bill of lading a reservation specifying these inaccuracies, grounds of suspicion or the absence of reasonable means of checking.

2. If the carrier or other person issuing the bill of lading on his behalf fails to note on the bill of lading the apparent condition of the goods, he is deemed to have noted on the bill of lading that the goods were in apparent good condition.

3. Except for particulars in respect of which and to the extent to which a reservation permitted under paragraph 1 of this article has been entered:

(a) the bill of lading is *prima facie* evidence of the taking over or, where a "shipped" bill of lading is issued, loading, by the carrier of the goods as described in the bill of lading; and

(b) proof to the contrary by the carrier is not admissible if the bill of lading has been transferred to a third party, including a consignee, who in good faith has acted in reliance on the description of the goods therein.

4. A bill of lading which does not, as provided in paragraph 1, subparagraph (k) of article 15, set forth the freight or otherwise indicate that freight is payable by the consignee or does not set forth demurrage incurred at the port of loading payable by the consignee, is *prima facie* evidence that no freight or such demurrage is payable by him. However, proof to the contrary by the carrier is not admissible when the bill of lading has been transferred to a third party, including a consignee, who in good faith has acted in reliance on the absence in the bill of lading of any such indication.

Article 17. *Guarantees by the shipper*

1. The shipper is deemed to have guaranteed to the carrier the accuracy of particulars relating to the general nature of the goods, their marks, number, weight and quantity as furnished by him for insertion in the bill of lading. The shipper must indemnify the carrier against the loss resulting from inaccuracies in such particulars. The shipper remains liable even if the bill of lading has been transferred by him. The right of the carrier to such indemnity in no way limits his liability under the contract of carriage by sea to any person other than the shipper.

2. Any letter of guarantee or agreement by which the shipper undertakes to indemnify the carrier against loss resulting from the issuance of the bill of lading by the carrier, or by a person acting on his behalf, without entering a reservation relating to particulars furnished by the shipper for insertion in the bill of lading, or to the apparent condition of the goods, is void and of no effect as against any third party, including a consignee, to whom the bill of lading has been transferred.

3. Such letter of guarantee or agreement is valid as against the shipper unless the carrier or the person acting on his behalf, by omitting the reservation referred to in paragraph 2 of this article, intends to defraud a third party, including a consignee, who acts in reliance on the description of the goods in the bill of lading. In the latter case, if the reservation omitted relates to particulars furnished by the shipper for insertion in the bill of lading, the carrier has no right of indemnity from the shipper pursuant to paragraph 1 of this article.

4. In the case of intended fraud referred to in paragraph 3 of this article the carrier is liable, without the benefit of the limitation of liability provided for in this Convention, for the loss incurred by a third party, including a consignee, because he has acted in reliance on the description of the goods in the bill of lading.

Article 18. *Documents other than bills of lading*

Where a carrier issues a document other than a bill of lading to evidence the receipt of the goods to be carried, such a document is *prima facie* evidence of the conclusion of the contract of carriage by sea and the taking over by the carrier of the goods as therein described.

PART V. CLAIMS AND ACTIONS

Article 19. *Notice of loss, damage or delay*

1. Unless notice of loss or damage, specifying the general nature of such loss or damage, is given in writing by the consignee to the carrier not later than the working day after the day when the goods were handed over to the consignee, such handing over is *prima facie* evidence of the delivery by the carrier of the goods as described in the document of transport or if no such document has been issued, in good condition.

2. Where the loss or damage is not apparent, the provisions of paragraph 1 of this article apply correspondingly if notice in writing is not given within 15 consecutive days after the day when the goods were handed over to the consignee.

3. If the state of the goods at the time they were handed over to the consignee has been the subject of a joint survey or inspection by the parties, notice in writing need not be given of loss or damage ascertained during such survey or inspection.

4. In the case of any actual or apprehended loss or damage the carrier and the consignee must give all reasonable facilities to each other for inspecting and tallying the goods.

5. No compensation shall be payable for loss resulting from delay in delivery unless a notice has been given in writing to the carrier within 60 consecutive days after the day when the goods were handed over to the consignee.

6. If the goods have been delivered by an actual carrier, any notice given under this article to him shall have the same effect as if it had been given to the carrier, and any notice given to the carrier shall have effect as if given to such actual carrier.

7. Unless notice of loss or damage, specifying the general nature of the loss or damage, is given in writing by the carrier or actual carrier to the shipper not later than 90 consecutive days after the occurrence of such loss or damage or after the delivery of the goods in accordance with paragraph 2 of article 4, whichever is later, the failure to give such notice is *prima facie* evidence that the carrier or the actual carrier has sustained no loss or damage due to the fault or neglect of the shipper, his servants or agents.

8. For the purpose of this article, notice given to a person acting on the carrier's or the actual carrier's behalf, including the master or the officer in charge of the ship, or to a person acting on the shipper's behalf is deemed to have been given to the carrier, to the actual carrier or to the shipper, respectively.

Article 20. *Limitation of actions*

1. Any action relating to carriage of goods under this Convention is time-barred if judicial or arbitral proceedings have not been instituted within a period of two years.

2. The limitation period commences on the day on which the carrier has delivered the goods or part

thereof or, in cases where no goods have been delivered, on the last day on which the goods should have been delivered.

3. The day on which the limitation period commences is not included in the period.

4. The person against whom a claim is made may at any time during the running of the limitation period extend that period by a declaration in writing to the claimant. This period may be further extended by another declaration or declarations.

5. An action for indemnity by a person held liable may be instituted even after the expiration of the limitation period provided for in the preceding paragraphs if instituted within the time allowed by the law of the State where proceedings are instituted. However, the time allowed shall not be less than 90 days commencing from the day when the person instituting such action for indemnity has settled the claim or has been served with process in the action against himself.

Article 21. Jurisdiction

1. In judicial proceedings relating to carriage of goods under this Convention the plaintiff, at his option, may institute an action in a court which, according to the law of the State where the court is situated, is competent and within the jurisdiction of which is situated one of the following places:

(a) the principal place of business or, in the absence thereof, the habitual residence of the defendant; or

(b) the place where the contract was made provided that the defendant has there a place of business, branch or agency through which the contract was made; or

(c) the port of loading or the port of discharge; or

(d) any additional place designated for that purpose in the contract of carriage by sea.

2. (a) Notwithstanding the preceding provisions of this article, an action may be instituted in the courts of any port or place in a Contracting State at which the carrying vessel or any other vessel of the same ownership may have been arrested in accordance with applicable rules of the law of that State and of international law. However, in such a case, at the petition of the defendant, the claimant must remove the action, at his choice, to one of the jurisdictions referred to in paragraph 1 of this article for the determination of the claim, but before such removal the defendant must furnish security sufficient to ensure payment of any judgment that may subsequently be awarded to the claimant in the action.

(b) All questions relating to the sufficiency or otherwise of the security shall be determined by the court of the port or place of the arrest.

3. No judicial proceedings relating to carriage of goods under this Convention may be instituted in a place not specified in paragraph 1 or 2 of this article. The provisions of this paragraph do not constitute an obstacle to the jurisdiction of the Contracting States for provisional or protective measures.

4. (a) Where an action has been instituted in a court competent under paragraph 1 or 2 of this article or where judgment has been delivered by such a court, no new action may be started between the same parties on the same grounds unless the judgment of the court before which the first action was instituted is not enforceable in the country in which the new proceedings are instituted;

(b) for the purpose of this article the institution of measures with a view to obtaining enforcement of a judgment is not to be considered as the starting of a new action;

(c) for the purpose of this article, the removal of an action to a different court within the same country, or to a court in another country, in accordance with paragraph 2 (a) of this article, is not to be considered as the starting of a new action.

5. Notwithstanding the provisions of the preceding paragraphs, an agreement made by the parties, after a claim under the contract of carriage by sea has arisen, which designates the place where the claimant may institute an action, is effective.

Article 22. Arbitration

1. Subject to the provisions of this article, parties may provide by agreement evidenced in writing that any dispute that may arise relating to carriage of goods under this Convention shall be referred to arbitration.

2. Where a charter-party contains a provision that disputes arising thereunder shall be referred to arbitration and a bill of lading issued pursuant to the charter-party does not contain a special annotation providing that such provision shall be binding upon the holder of the bill of lading, the carrier may not invoke such provision as against a holder having acquired the bill of lading in good faith.

3. The arbitration proceedings shall, at the option of the claimant, be instituted at one of the following places:

(a) a place in a State within whose territory is situated:

(i) the principal place of business of the defendant or, in the absence thereof, the habitual residence of the defendant; or

(ii) the place where the contract was made, provided that the defendant has there a place of business, branch or agency through which the contract was made; or

(iii) the port of loading or the port of discharge; or

(b) any place designated for that purpose in the arbitration clause or agreement.

4. The arbitrator or arbitration tribunal shall apply the rules of this Convention.

5. The provisions of paragraphs 3 and 4 of this article are deemed to be part of every arbitration clause or agreement, and any term of such clause or agreement which is inconsistent therewith is null and void.

6. Nothing in this article affects the validity of an agreement relating to arbitration made by the parties after the claim under the contract of carriage by sea has arisen.

PART VI. SUPPLEMENTARY PROVISIONS

Article 23. *Contractual stipulations*

1. Any stipulation in a contract of carriage by sea, in a bill of lading, or in any other document evidencing the contract of carriage by sea is null and void to the extent that it derogates, directly or indirectly, from the provisions of this Convention. The nullity of such a stipulation does not affect the validity of the other provisions of the contract or document of which it forms a part. A clause assigning benefit of insurance of the goods in favour of the carrier, or any similar clause, is null and void.

2. Notwithstanding the provisions of paragraph 1 of this article, a carrier may increase his responsibilities and obligations under this Convention.

3. Where a bill of lading or any other document evidencing the contract of carriage by sea is issued it must contain a statement that the carriage is subject to the provisions of this Convention which nullify any stipulation derogating therefrom to the detriment of the shipper or the consignee.

4. Where the claimant in respect of the goods has incurred loss as a result of a stipulation which is null and void by virtue of the present article, or as a result of the omission of the statement referred to in paragraph 3 of this article, the carrier must pay compensation to the extent required in order to give the claimant compensation in accordance with the provisions of this Convention for any loss of or damage to the goods as well as for delay in delivery. The carrier must, in addition, pay compensation for costs incurred by the claimant for the purpose of exercising his right, provided that costs incurred in the action where the foregoing provision is invoked are to be determined in accordance with the law of the State where proceedings are instituted.

Article 24. *General average*

1. Nothing in this Convention shall prevent the application of provisions in the contract of carriage by sea or national law regarding the adjustment of general average.

2. With the exception of article 20, the provisions of this Convention relating to the liability of the carrier for loss of or damage to the goods also determine whether the consignee may refuse contribution in general average and the liability of the carrier to indemnify the consignee in respect of any such contribution made or any salvage paid.

Article 25. *Other conventions*

1. This Convention does not modify the rights or duties of the carrier, the actual carrier and their servants and agents, provided for in international conventions or national law relating to the limitation of liability of owners of seagoing ships.

2. The provisions of articles 21 and 22 of this Convention do not prevent the application of the mandatory provisions of any other multilateral convention already in force at the date of this Convention relating to matters dealt with in the said articles, provided that the dispute arises exclusively between parties having their principal place of business in States members of such other convention. However, this paragraph does not affect the application of paragraph 4 of article 22 of this Convention.

3. No liability shall arise under the provisions of this Convention for damage caused by a nuclear incident if the operator of a nuclear installation is liable for such damage:

(a) under either the Paris Convention of 29 July 1960 on Third Party Liability in the Field of Nuclear Energy as amended by the Additional Protocol of 28 January 1964 or the Vienna Convention of 21 May 1963 on Civil Liability for Nuclear Damage, or

(b) by virtue of national law governing the liability for such damage, provided that such law is in all respects as favourable to persons who may suffer damage as either the Paris or Vienna Conventions.

4. No liability shall arise under the provisions of this Convention for any loss of or damage to or delay in delivery of luggage for which the carrier is responsible under any international convention or national law relating to the carriage of passengers and their luggage by sea.

5. Nothing contained in this Convention prevents a Contracting State from applying any other international convention which is already in force at the date of this Convention and which applies mandatorily to contracts of carriage of goods primarily by a mode of transport other than transport by sea. This

provision also applies to any subsequent revision or amendment of such international convention.

Article 26. Unit of account

1. The unit of account referred to in article 6 of this Convention is the Special Drawing Right as defined by the International Monetary Fund. The amounts mentioned in article 6 are to be converted into the national currency of a State according to the value of such currency at the date of judgment or the date agreed upon by the parties. The value of a national currency, in terms of the Special Drawing Right, of a Contracting State which is a member of the International Monetary Fund is to be calculated in accordance with the method of valuation applied by the International Monetary Fund in effect at the date in question for its operations and transactions. The value of a national currency in terms of the Special Drawing Right of a Contracting State which is not a member of the International Monetary Fund is to be calculated in a manner determined by that State.

2. Nevertheless, those States which are not members of the International Monetary Fund and whose law does not permit the application of the provisions of paragraph 1 of this article may, at the time of signature, or at the time of ratification, acceptance, approval or accession or at any time thereafter, declare that the limits of liability provided for in this Convention to be applied in their territories shall be fixed as:

12,500 monetary units per package or other shipping unit or 37.5 monetary units per kilogramme of gross weight of the goods.

3. The monetary unit referred to in paragraph 2 of this article corresponds to sixty-five and a half milligrammes of gold of millesimal fineness nine hundred. The conversion of the amounts referred to in paragraph 2 into the national currency is to be made according to the law of the State concerned.

4. The calculation mentioned in the last sentence of paragraph 1 and the conversion mentioned in paragraph 3 of this article is to be made in such a manner as to express in the national currency of the Contracting State as far as possible the same real value for the amounts in article 6 as is expressed there in units of account. Contracting States must communicate to the depositary the manner of calculation pursuant to paragraph 1 of this article, or the result of the conversion mentioned in paragraph 3 of this article, as the case may be, at the time of signature or when depositing their instruments of ratification, acceptance, approval or accession, or when availing themselves of the option provided for in paragraph 2 of this article and whenever there is a

change in the manner of such calculation or in the result of such conversion.

PART VII. FINAL CLAUSES

Article 27. Depositary

The Secretary-General of the United Nations is hereby designated as the depositary of this Convention.

Article 28. Signature, ratification, acceptance, approval, accession

1. This Convention is open for signature by all States until 30 April 1979 at the Headquarters of the United Nations, New York.

2. This Convention is subject to ratification, acceptance or approval by the signatory States.

3. After 30 April 1979, this Convention will be open for accession by all States which are not signatory States.

4. Instruments of ratification, acceptance, approval and accession are to be deposited with the Secretary-General of the United Nations.

Article 29. Reservations

No reservations may be made to this Convention.

Article 30. Entry into force

1. This Convention enters into force on the first day of the month following the expiration of one year from the date of deposit of the 20th instrument of ratification, acceptance, approval or accession.

2. For each State which becomes a Contracting State to this Convention after the date of the deposit of the 20th instrument of ratification, acceptance, approval or accession, this Convention enters into force on the first day of the month following the expiration of one year after the deposit of the appropriate instrument on behalf of that State.

3. Each Contracting State shall apply the provisions of this Convention to contracts of carriage by sea concluded on or after the date of the entry into force of this Convention in respect of that State.

Article 31. Denunciation of other conventions

1. Upon becoming a Contracting State to this Convention, any State party to the International Convention for the Unification of Certain Rules relating to Bills of Lading signed at Brussels on 25 August 1924 (1924 Convention) must notify the

Government of Belgium as the depositary of the 1924 Convention of its denunciation of the said Convention with a declaration that the denunciation is to take effect as from the date when this Convention enters into force in respect of that State.

2. Upon the entry into force of this Convention under paragraph 1 of article 30, the depositary of this Convention must notify the Government of Belgium as the depositary of the 1924 Convention of the date of such entry into force, and of the names of the Contracting States in respect of which the Convention has entered into force.

3. The provisions of paragraphs 1 and 2 of this article apply correspondingly in respect of States parties to the Protocol signed on 23 February 1968 to amend the International Convention for the Unification of Certain Rules relating to Bills of Lading signed at Brussels on 25 August 1924.

4. Notwithstanding article 2 of this Convention, for the purposes of paragraph 1 of this article, a Contracting State may, if it deems it desirable, defer the denunciation of the 1924 Convention and of the 1924 Convention as modified by the 1968 Protocol for a maximum period of five years from the entry into force of this Convention. It will then notify the Government of Belgium of its intention. During this transitory period, it must apply to the Contracting States this Convention to the exclusion of any other one.

Article 32. Revision and amendment

1. At the request of not less than one-third of the Contracting States to this Convention, the depositary shall convene a conference of the Contracting States for revising or amending it.

2. Any instrument of ratification, acceptance, approval or accession deposited after the entry into force of an amendment to this Convention, is deemed to apply to the Convention as amended.

Article 33. Revision of the limitation amounts and unit of account on monetary unit

1. Notwithstanding the provisions of article 32, a conference only for the purpose of altering the amount specified in article 6 and paragraph 2 of article 26, or of substituting either or both of the units defined in paragraphs 1 and 3 of article 26 by other units is to be convened by the depositary in accordance with paragraph 2 of this article. An alteration of the amounts shall be made only because of a significant change in their real value.

2. A revision conference is to be convened by the depositary when not less than one-fourth of the Contracting States so request.

3. Any decision by the conference must be taken by a two-thirds majority of the participating States. The amendment is communicated by the depositary to all the Contracting States for acceptance and to all the States signatories of the Convention for information.

4. Any amendment adopted enters into force on the first day of the month following one year after its acceptance by two-thirds of the Contracting States. Acceptance is to be effected by the deposit of a formal instrument to that effect, with the depositary.

5. After entry into force of an amendment a Contracting State which has accepted the amendment is entitled to apply the Convention as amended in its relations with Contracting States which have not within six months after the adoption of the amendment notified the depositary that they are not bound by the amendment.

6. Any instrument of ratification, acceptance, approval or accession deposited after the entry into force of an amendment to this Convention, is deemed to apply to the Convention as amended.

Article 34. Denunciation

1. A Contracting State may denounce this Convention at any time by means of a notification in writing addressed to the depositary.

2. The denunciation takes effect on the first day of the month following the expiration of one year after the notification is received by the depositary. Where a longer period is specified in the notification, the denunciation takes effect upon the expiration of such longer period after the notification is received by the depositary.

DONE at Hamburg, this thirty-first day of March one thousand nine hundred and seventy-eight, in a single original, of which the Arabic, Chinese, English, French, Russian and Spanish texts are equally authentic.

IN WITNESS WHEREOF the undersigned plenipotentiaries, being duly authorized by their respective Governments, have signed the present Convention.

ANNEX II

COMMON UNDERSTANDING ADOPTED BY THE UNITED NATIONS CONFERENCE ON THE CARRIAGE OF GOODS BY SEA

It is the common understanding that the liability of the carrier under this Convention is based on the principle of presumed fault or neglect. This means that, as a rule, the burden of proof rests on the carrier but, with respect to certain cases, the provisions of the Convention modify this rule.

CMI UNIFORM RULES FOR SEA WAYBILLS

1. Scope of Application

(i)   These Rules shall be called the 'CMI Uniform Rules for Sea Waybills'.

(ii) They shall apply when adopted by a contract of carriage which is not covered by a bill of lading or similar document of title, whether the contract be in writing or not.

2. Definitions

In these Rules:

'Contract of carriage' shall mean any contract of carriage subject to these Rules which is to be performed wholly or partly by sea.

'Goods' shall mean any goods carried or received for carriage under a contract of carriage.

'Carrier' and 'Shipper' shall mean the parties named in or identifiable as such from the contract of carriage.

'Consignee' shall mean the party named in or identifiable as such from the contract of carriage, or any person substituted as consignee in accordance with rule 6(i).

'Right of Control' shall mean the rights and obligations referred to in rule 6.

3. Agency

(i)   The shipper on entering into the contract of carriage does so not only on his own behalf but also as agent for and on behalf of the consignee, and warrants to the carrier that he has authority so to do.

(ii) This rule shall apply if, and only if, it be necessary by the law applicable to the contract of carriage so as to enable the consignee to sue and be sued thereon. The consignee shall be under no greater liability than he would have been had the contract of carriage been covered by a bill of lading or similar document of title.

4. Rights and Responsibilities

(i)   The contract of carriage shall be subject to any International Convention or National Law which is, or if the contract of carriage had been covered by a bill of lading or similar document of title would have been, compulsorily applicable thereto. Such convention or law shall apply notwithstanding anything inconsistent therewith in the contract of carriage.

(ii) Subject always to subrule (i), the contract of carriage is governed by:
    (a)   these Rules;
    (b)   unless otherwise agreed by the parties, the carrier's standard terms and conditions for the trade, if any, including any terms and conditions relating to the non-sea part of the carriage;
    (c)   any other terms and conditions agreed by the parties.

(iii) In the event of any inconsistency between the terms and conditions mentioned under subrule (ii)(b) or (c) and these Rules, these Rules shall prevail.

5. Description of the Goods

(i)   The shipper warrants the accuracy of the particulars furnished by him relating to the goods, and shall indemnify the carrier against any loss, damage or expense resulting from any inaccuracy.

(ii) In the absence of reservation by the carrier, any statement in a sea waybill or similar document as to the quantity or condition of the goods shall

    (a) as between the carrier and the shipper be prima facie evidence of receipt of the goods as so stated,

    (b) as between the carrier and the consignee be conclusive evidence of receipt of the goods as so stated, and proof to the contrary shall not be permitted, provided always that the consignee has acted in good faith.

6. Right of Control

(i) Unless the shipper has exercised his option under subrule (ii) below, he shall be the only party entitled to give the carrier instructions in relation to the contract of carriage. Unless prohibited by the applicable law, he shall be entitled to change the name of the consignee at any time up to the consignee claiming delivery of the goods after their arrival at destination, provided he gives the carrier reasonable notice in writing, or by some other means acceptable to the carrier, thereby undertaking to indemnify the carrier against any additional expense caused thereby.

(ii) The shipper shall have the option, to be exercised not later than the receipt of the goods by the carrier, to transfer the right of control to the consignee. The exercise of this option must be noted on the sea waybill or similar document, if any. Where the option has been exercised the consignee shall have such rights as are referred to in subrule (i) above and the shipper shall cease to have such rights.

7. Delivery

(i) The carrier shall deliver the goods to the consignee upon production of proper identification.

(ii) The carrier shall be under no liability for wrong delivery if he can prove that he has exercised reasonable care to ascertain that the party claiming to be the consignee is in fact that party.

8. Validity

In the event of anything contained in these Rules or any such provisions as are incorporated into the contract of carriage by virtue of rule 4, being inconsistent with the provisions of any International Convention or National Law compulsorily applicable to the contract of carriage, such Rules and provisions shall to that extent but no further be null and void.

CMI RULES FOR ELECTRONIC BILLS OF LADING

1. Scope of Application

These Rules shall apply whenever the parties so agree.

2. Definitions

a. 'Contract of Carriage' means any agreement to carry goods wholly or partly by sea.

b. 'EDI' means Electronic Data Interchange, i.e. the interchange of trade data effected by teletransmission.

c. 'UN/EDIFACT' means the United Nations Rules for Electronic Data Interchange for Administration, Commerce and Transport.

d. 'Transmission' means one or more messages electronically sent together as one unit of dispatch which includes heading and terminating data.

e. 'Confirmation' means a Transmission which advises that the content of a Transmission appears to be complete and correct, without prejudice to any subsequent consideration or action that the content may warrant.

f. 'Private Key' means any technically appropriate form, such as a combination of numbers and/or letters, which the parties may agree for securing the authenticity and integrity of a Transmission.

g. 'Holder' means the party who is entitled to the rights described in Article 7(a) by virtue of its possession of a valid Private Key.

h. 'Electronic Monitoring System' means the device by which a computer system can be examined for the transactions that it recorded, such as a Trade Data Log or an Audit Trail.

i. 'Electronic Storage' means any temporary, intermediate or permanent storage of electronic data including the primary and the back-up storage of such data.

3. Rules of procedure

a. When not in conflict with these Rules, the Uniform Rules of Conduct for Interchange of Trade Data by Teletransmission, 1987 (UNCID) shall govern the conduct between the parties.

b. The EDI under these Rules should conform with the relevant UN/EDIFACT standards. However, the parties may use any other method of trade data interchange acceptable to all of the users.

c. Unless otherwise agreed, the document format for the Contract of Carriage shall conform to the UN Layout Key or compatible national standard for bills of lading.

d. Unless otherwise agreed, a recipient of a Transmission is not authorised to act on a Transmission unless he has sent a Confirmation.

e. In the event of a dispute arising between the parties as to the data actually transmitted, an Electronic Monitoring System may be used to verify the data received. Data concerning other transactions not related to the data in dispute are to be considered as trade secrets and thus not available for examination. If such data are unavoidably revealed as part of the examination of the Electronic Monitoring System, they must be treated as confidential and not released to any outside party or used for any other purpose.

f.   Any transfer of rights to the goods shall be considered to be private information, and shall not be released to any outside party not connected to the transport or clearance of the goods.

4. Form and content of the receipt message

a.   The carrier, upon receiving the goods from the shipper, shall give notice of the receipt of the goods to the shipper by a message at the electronic address specified by the shipper.

b.   This receipt message shall include:
   (i)   the name of the shipper;
   (ii) the description of the goods, with any representations and reservations, in the same tenor as would be required if a paper bill of lading were issued;
   (iii) the date and place of the receipt of the goods;
   (iv) a reference to the carrier's terms and conditions of carriage; and
   (v)   the Private Key to be used in subsequent Transmissions.
   The shipper must confirm this receipt message to the carrier, upon which Confirmation the shipper shall be the Holder.

c.   Upon demand of the Holder, the receipt message shall be updated with the date and place of shipment as soon as the goods have been loaded on board.

d.   The information contained in (ii), (iii) and (iv) of paragraph (b) above including the date and place of shipment if updated in accordance with paragraph (c) of this Rule, shall have the same force and effect as if the receipt message were contained in a paper bill of lading.

5. Terms and conditions of the Contract of Carriage

a   It is agreed and understood that whenever the carrier makes a reference to its terms and conditions of carriage, these terms and conditions shall form part of the Contract of Carriage.

b.   Such terms and conditions must be readily available to the parties to the Contract of Carriage.

c.   In the event of any conflict or inconsistency between such terms and conditions and these Rules, these Rules shall prevail.

6. Applicable law

The Contract of Carriage shall be subject to any international convention or national law which would have been compulsorily applicable if a paper bill of lading had been issued.

7. Right of Control and Transfer

a.   The Holder is the only party who may, as against the carrier:

   (1)   claim delivery of the goods;

   (2)   nominate the consignee or substitute a nominated consignee for any other party, including itself;

   (3)   transfer the Right of Control and Transfer to another party;

   (4)   instruct the carrier on any other subject concerning the goods, in accordance with the terms and conditions of the Contract of Carriage, as if he were the holder of a paper bill of lading.

b.   A transfer of the Right of Control and Transfer shall be effected: (i) by notification of the current Holder to the carrier of its intention to transfer its Right of Control and Transfer to a proposed new Holder, and (ii) confirmation by the carrier of such notification message, whereupon (iii) the carrier shall transmit the information as referred to in article 4 (except for the Private Key) to the proposed new Holder, whereafter (iv) the proposed new Holder shall advise the carrier of its acceptance of the Right of Control and Transfer, whereupon (v) the carrier shall cancel the current Private Key and issue a new Private Key to the new Holder.

c.   If the proposed new Holder advises the carrier that it does not accept the Right of Control and Transfer or fails to advise the carrier of such acceptance within a reasonable time, the proposed transfer of the Right of Control and Transfer shall not take place. The carrier shall notify the current Holder accordingly and the current Private Key shall retain its validity.

d.   The transfer of the Right of Control and Transfer in the manner described above shall have the same effects as the transfer of such rights under a paper bill of lading.

8. The Private Key

a.   The Private Key is unique to each successive Holder. It is not transferable by the Holder. The carrier and the Holder shall each maintain the security of the Private Key.

b.   The carrier shall only be obliged to send a Confirmation of an electronic message to the last Holder to whom it issued a Private Key, when such Holder secures the Transmission containing such electronic message by the use of the Private Key.

c.   The Private Key must be separate and distinct from any means used to identify the Contract of Carriage, and any security password or identification used to access the computer network.

9. Delivery

a.   The carrier shall notify the Holder of the place and date of intended delivery of the goods. Upon such notification the Holder has a duty to nominate a consignee and to give adequate delivery instructions to the carrier with verification by the Private Key. In the absence of such nomination, the Holder will be deemed to be the consignee.

b.   The carrier shall deliver the goods to the consignee upon production of proper identification in accordance with the delivery instructions specified in paragraph (a) above; such delivery shall automatically cancel the Private Key.

c.   The carrier shall be under no liability for misdelivery if it can prove that it exercised reasonable care to ascertain that the party who claimed to be the consignee was in fact that party.

10. Option to receive a paper document

a.   The Holder has the option at any time prior to delivery of the goods to demand from the carrier a paper bill of lading. Such document shall be made available at a location to be determined by the Holder, provided that no carrier shall be obliged to make such document available at a place where it has no facilities and in such instance the carrier shall only be obliged to make the document available at the facility nearest to the location determined by the Holder. The carrier shall not be responsible for delays in delivering the goods resulting from the Holder exercising the above option.

b.   The carrier has the option at any time prior to delivery of the goods to issue to the Holder a paper bill of lading unless the exercise of such option could result in undue delay or disrupts the delivery of the goods.

c.   A bill of lading issued under Rules 10(a) or (b) shall include: (i) the information set out in the receipt message referred to in Rule 4 (except for the Private Key); and (ii) a statement to the effect that the bill of lading has been issued upon termination of the procedures for EDI under the CMI Rules for Electronic Bills of Lading. The aforementioned bill of lading shall be issued at the option of the Holder either to the order of the Holder whose name for this purpose shall then be inserted in the bill of lading or 'to bearer'.

d.   The issuance of a paper bill of lading under Rule 10(a) or (b) shall cancel the Private Key and terminate the procedures for EDI under these Rules. Termination of these procedures by the Holder or the carrier will not relieve any of the parties to the Contract of Carriage of their rights, obligations or liabilities while performing under the present Rules nor of their rights, obligations or liabilities under the Contract of Carriage.

e.   The Holder may demand at any time the issuance of a print-out of the receipt message referred to in Rule 4 (except for the Private Key) marked as 'non-negotiable copy'. The issuance of such a print-out shall not cancel the Private Key nor terminate the procedures for EDI.

11. Electronic data is equivalent to writing

The carrier and the shipper and all subsequent parties utilizing these procedures agree that any national or local law, custom or practice requiring the Contract of Carriage to be evidenced in writing and signed, is satisfied by the transmitted and confirmed electronic data residing on computer data storage media displayable in human language on a video screen or as printed out by a computer. In agreeing to adopt these Rules, the parties shall be taken to have agreed not to raise the defence that this contract is not in writing.

53-0

PART I

THE BALTIC AND INTERNATIONAL MARITIME COUNCIL (BIMCO)
STANDARD BAREBOAT CHARTER
CODE NAME: "BARECON 89"

1. Shipbroker

2. Place and date

3. Owners/Place of business

4. Bareboat charterers (Charterers)/Place of business

5. Vessel's name, Call Sign and Flag (Cl. 9(c))

6. Type of Vessel

7. GRT/NRT

8. When/Where built

9. Total DWT (abt.) in metric tons on summer freeboard

10. Class (Cl. 9)

11. Date of last special survey by the Vessel's classification society

12. Further particulars of Vessel (also indicate minimum number of months' validity of class certificates agreed acc. to Cl. 14)

First issued by
The Baltic and International Maritime Council (BIMCO), Copenhagen
in 1974 as "Barecon 'A'" and "Barecon 'B'"
Revised and amalgamated 1989

13. Port or Place of delivery (Cl. 2)	14. Time for delivery (Cl. 3)	15. Cancelling date (Cl. 4)
	16. Port or Place of redelivery (Cl. 14)	
17. Running days' notice if other than stated in Cl. 3	18. Frequency of dry-docking if other than stated in Cl. 5(f)	
19. Trading Limits (Cl. 5)		
20. Charter period	21. Charter hire (Cl. 10)	
22. Rate of interest payable acc. to Cl. 10(f) and, if applicable, acc. to PART IV	23. Currency and method of payment (Cl. 10)	

(continued)

PART I

"BARECON 89" Standard Bareboat Charter

(continued)

24. Place of payment; also state beneficiary and bank account (Cl. 10)

25. Bank guarantee/bond (sum and place) (Cl. 22) (optional)

26. Mortgage(s), if any, (state whether Cl. 11(a) or (b) applies; if 11(b) applies state date of Deed(s) of Covenant and name of Mortgagee(s)/Place of business) (Cl. 11)

27. Insurance (marine and war risks) (state value acc. to Cl. 12(f) or, if applicable, acc. to Cl. 13(k)) (also state if Cl. 13 applies)

28. Additional insurance cover, if any, for Owners' account limited to (Cl. 12(b)) or, if applicable, (Cl. 13(g))

29. Additional insurance cover, if any, for Charterers' account limited to (Cl. 12(b)) or, if applicable, (Cl. 13(g))

30. Latent defects (only to be filled in if period other than stated in Cl. 2)

31. War cancellation (indicate countries agreed) (Cl. 24)

32. Brokerage commission and to whom payable (Cl. 25)

33. Law and arbitration (state 26.1., 26.2., or 26.3. of Cl. 26 as agreed; if 26.3. agreed, also state place of arbitration) (Cl. 26)

34. Number of additional clauses covering special provisions, if agreed

35. Newbuilding Vessel (indicate with "yes" or "no" whether Part III applies) (optional)	36. Name and place of Builders (only to be filled in if Part III applies)
37. Vessel's Yard Building No. (only to be filled in if Part III applies)	38. Date of Building Contract (only to be filled in if Part III applies)
39. Hire/Purchase agreement (indicate with "yes" or "no" whether Part IV applies) (optional)	40. Bareboat Charter Registry (indicate with "yes" or "no" whether Part V applies) (optional)
41. Flag and Country of the Bareboat Charter Registry (only to be filled in if Part V applies)	42. Country of the Underlying Registry (only to be filled in if Part V applies)

PREAMBLE. – It is mutually agreed that this Contract shall be performed subject to the conditions contained in this Charter which shall include PART I and PART II. In the event of a conflict of conditions, the provisions of PART I shall prevail over those of PART II to the extent of such conflict but no further. It is further mutually agreed that PART III and/or PART IV and/or PART V shall only apply and shall only form part of this Charter if expressly agreed and stated in the Boxes 35, 39 and 40. If PART III and/or PART IV and/or PART V apply, it is further mutually agreed that in the event of a conflict of conditions, the provisions of PART I and PART II shall prevail over those of PART III and/or PART IV and/or PART V to the extent of such conflict but no further.

Signature (Owners)

Signature (Charterers)

Printed and sold by Fr. G. Knudtzons Bogtrykkeri A/S, 55 Toldbodgade, DK-1253 Copenhagen K, Telefax +45 33 93 11 84 by authority of The Baltic and International Maritime Council (BIMCO), Copenhagen

PART II
"BARECON 89" Standard Bareboat Charter

1. Definitions

In this Charter, the following terms shall have the meanings hereby assigned to them:

"The Owners" shall mean the person or company registered as Owners of the Vessel.

"The Charterers" shall mean the Bareboat charterers and shall not be construed to mean a time charterer or a voyage charterer.

2. Delivery *(not applicable to newbuilding vessels)*

The Vessel shall be delivered and taken over by the Charterers at the port or place indicated in Box 13, in such ready berth as the Charterers may direct.

The Owners shall before and at the time of delivery exercise due diligence to make the Vessel seaworthy and in every respect ready in hull, machinery and equipment for service under this Charter. The Vessel shall be properly documented at time of delivery.

The delivery to the Charterers of the Vessel and the taking over of the Vessel by the Charterers shall constitute a full performance by the Owners of all the Owners' obligations under Clause 2, and thereafter the Charterers shall not be entitled to make or assert any claim against the Owners on account of any conditions, representations or warranties expressed or implied with respect to the Vessel but the Owners shall be responsible for repairs or renewals occasioned by latent defects in the Vessel, her machinery or appurtenances, existing at the time of delivery under the Charter, provided such defects have manifested themselves within 18 months after delivery unless otherwise provided in Box 30.

3. Time for Delivery *(not applicable to newbuilding vessels)*

The Vessel to be delivered not before the date indicated in Box 14 unless with the Charterers' consent.

Unless otherwise agreed in Box 17, the Owners to give the Charterers not less than 30 running days' preliminary and not less than 14 days' definite notice of the date on which the Vessel is expected to be ready for delivery.

The Owners to keep the Charterers closely advised of possible changes in the Vessel's position.

4. Cancelling *(not applicable to newbuilding vessels)*

Should the Vessel not be delivered latest by the cancelling date indicated in Box 15, the Charterers to have the option of cancelling this Charter without prejudice to any claim the Charterers may otherwise have on the Owners under the Charter.

If it appears that the Vessel will be delayed beyond the cancelling date, the Owners shall, as soon as they are in a position to state with reasonable certainty the day on which the Vessel should be ready, give notice thereof to the Charterers asking whether they will exercise their option of cancelling, and the option must then be declared within one hundred and sixty-eight (168) hours of the receipt by the Charterers of such notice. If the Charterers do not then exercise their option of cancelling, the seventh day after the readiness date stated in the Owners' notice shall be regarded as a new cancelling date stated for the purpose of this Clause.

8. Inventories and Consumable Oil and Stores

A complete inventory of the Vessel's entire equipment, outfit, appliances and of all consumable stores on board the Vessel shall be made by the Charterers in conjunction with the Owners on delivery and again on redelivery of the Vessel. The Charterers and the Owners, respectively, shall at the time of delivery and redelivery take over and pay for all bunkers, lubricating oil, water and unbroached provisions, paints, oils, ropes and other consumable stores in the said Vessel at the then current market prices at the ports of delivery and redelivery, respectively.

9. Maintenance and Operation

(a) The Vessel shall during the Charter period be in the full possession and at the absolute disposal for all purposes of the Charterers and under their complete control in every respect. The Charterers shall maintain the Vessel, her machinery, boilers, appurtenances and spare parts in a good state of repair, in efficient operating condition and in accordance with good commercial maintenance practice and, except as provided for in Clause 13 (l), they shall keep the Vessel with unexpired classification of the class indicated in Box 10 and with other required certificates in force at all times.

The Charterers to take immediate steps to have the necessary repairs done within a reasonable time failing which the Owners shall have the right of withdrawing the Vessel from the service of the Charterers without noting any protest and without prejudice to any claim the Owners may otherwise have against the Charterers under the Charter.

Unless otherwise agreed, in the event of any improvement, structural changes or expensive new equipment becoming necessary for the continued operation of the Vessel by reason of new class requirements or by compulsory legislation costing more than 5 per cent. of the Vessel's marine insurance value as stated in Box 27, then the extent, if any, to which the rate of hire shall be varied and the ratio in which the cost of compliance shall be shared between the parties concerned in order to achieve a reasonable distribution thereof as between the Owners and the Charterers having regard, inter alia, to the length of the period remaining under the Charter, shall in the absence of agreement, be referred to arbitration according to Clause 26.

The Charterers are required to establish and maintain financial security or responsibility in respect of oil or other pollution damage as required by any government, including Federal, state or municipal or other division or authority thereof, to enable the Vessel, without penalty or charge, lawfully to enter, remain at, or leave any port, place, territorial or contiguous waters of any country, state or municipality in performance of this Charter without any delay. This obligation shall apply whether or not such requirements have been lawfully imposed by such government or division or authority thereof. The Charterers shall make and maintain all arrangements by bond or otherwise as may be necessary to satisfy such requirements at the Charterers' sole expense and the Charterers shall indemnify the Owners against all consequences whatsoever (including loss of time) for any failure or inability to do so.

TOVALOP SCHEME. *(Applicable to oil tank vessels only).* – The Charterers are required to enter the Vessel under the **TOVALOP SCHEME** or under any similar compulsory scheme upon delivery under this Charter and to maintain her so during the currency of this Charter.

(b) The Charterers shall at their own expense and by their own procurement man, victual, navigate, operate, supply, fuel and repair the Vessel whenever

5. Trading Limits

The Vessel shall be employed in lawful trades for the carriage of suitable lawful merchandise within the trading limits indicated in Box 19.

The Charterers undertake not to employ the Vessel or suffer the Vessel to be employed otherwise than in conformity with the terms of the instruments of insurance (including any warranties expressed or implied therein) without first obtaining the consent to such employment of the Insurers and complying with such requirements as to extra premium or otherwise as the Insurers may prescribe. If required, the Charterers shall keep the Owners and the Mortgagees advised of the intended employment of the Vessel.

The Charterers also undertake not to employ the Vessel or suffer her employment in any trade or business which is forbidden by the law of any country to which the Vessel may sail or is otherwise illicit or in carrying illicit or prohibited goods or in any manner whatsoever which may render her liable to condemnation, destruction, seizure or confiscation.

Notwithstanding any other provisions contained in this Charter it is agreed that nuclear fuels or radioactive products or waste are specifically excluded from the cargo permitted to be loaded or carried under this Charter. This exclusion does not apply to radio-isotopes used or intended to be used for any industrial, commercial, agricultural, medical or scientific purposes provided the Owners' prior approval has been obtained to loading thereof.

6. Surveys *(not applicable to newbuilding vessel(s))*

Survey on Delivery and Redelivery. – The Owners and Charterers shall each appoint surveyors for the purpose of determining and agreeing in writing the condition of the Vessel at the time of delivery and redelivery hereunder. The Owners shall bear all expenses of the On-Survey including loss of time, if any, and the Charterers shall bear all expenses of the Off-Survey including loss of time, if any, at the rate of hire per day or pro rata, also including in each case the cost of any docking and undocking, if required, in connection herewith.

7. Inspection

Inspection. – The Owners shall have the right at any time to inspect or survey the Vessel or instruct a duly authorised surveyor to carry out such survey on their behalf to ascertain the condition of the Vessel and satisfy themselves that the Vessel is being properly repaired and maintained. Inspection or survey in dry-dock shall be made only when the Vessel shall be in dry-dock for the Charterers' purpose. However, the Owners shall have the right to require the Vessel to be dry-docked for inspection if the Charterers are not docking her at normal classification intervals. The fees for such inspection or survey shall in the event of the Vessel being found to be in the condition provided in Clause 9 of this Charter be payable by the Owners and shall be paid by the Charterers only in the event of the Vessel being found to require repairs or maintenance in order to achieve the condition so provided. All time taken in respect of inspection, survey or repairs shall count as time on hire and shall form part of the Charter period.

The Charterers shall also permit the Owners to inspect the Vessel's log books wherever requested and shall whenever required by the Owners furnish them with full information regarding any casualties or other accidents or damage to the Vessel. For the purpose of this Clause, the Charterers shall keep the Owners advised of the intended employment of the Vessel.

required during the Charter period and they shall pay all charges and expenses of every kind and nature whatsoever incidental to their use and operation of the Vessel under this Charter, including any foreign general municipality and/or state taxes. The Master, officers and crew of the Vessel shall be the servants of the Charterers for all purposes whatsoever, even if for any reason appointed by the Owners.

Charterers shall comply with the regulations regarding officers and crew in force in the country of the Vessel's flag or any other applicable law.

(c) During the currency of this Charter, the Vessel shall retain her present name as indicated in Box 5 and shall remain under and fly the flag as indicated in Box 5. Provided, however, that the Charterers shall have the liberty to paint the Vessel in their own colours, install and display their funnel insignia and fly their own house flag. Painting and re-painting, instalment and re-instalment to be for the Charterers' account and time used thereby to count as time on hire.

(d) The Charterers shall make no structural changes in the Vessel or changes in the machinery, boilers, appurtenances or spare parts thereof without in each instance first securing the Owners' approval thereof. If the Owners so agree, the Charterers shall, if the Owners so require, restore the Vessel to its former condition before the termination of the Charter.

(e) The Charterers shall have the use of all outfit, equipment, and appliances on board the Vessel at the time of delivery, provided the same or their substantial equivalent shall be returned to the Owners on redelivery in the same good order and condition as when received, ordinary wear and tear excepted. The Charterers shall from time to time during the Charter period replace such items of equipment as shall be so damaged or worn as to be unfit for use. The Charterers are to procure that all repairs to or replacement of any damaged, worn or lost parts or equipment be effected in such manner (both as regards workmanship and quality of materials) as not to diminish the value of the Vessel. The Charterers have the right to fit additional equipment at their expense and risk but the Charterers shall remove such equipment at the end of the period if requested by the Owners.

Any equipment including radio equipment on hire on the Vessel at time of delivery shall be kept and maintained by the Charterers and the Charterers shall assume the obligations and liabilities of the Owners under any lease contracts in connection therewith and shall reimburse the Owners for all expenses incurred in connection therewith, also for any new equipment required in order to comply with radio regulations.

(f) The Charterers shall dry-dock the Vessel and clean and paint her underwater parts whenever the same may be necessary, but not less than once in every eighteen calendar months after delivery unless otherwise agreed in Box 18.

10. Hire

(a) The Charterers shall pay to the Owners for the hire of the Vessel at the lump sum per calendar month as indicated in Box 21 commencing on and from the date and hour of her delivery to the Charterers and at and after the agreed lump sum for any part of a month. Hire to continue until the date and hour when the Vessel is redelivered by the Charterers to her Owners.

(b) Payment of Hire, except for the first and last month's Hire, if sub-clause (c) of this Clause is applicable, shall be made in cash without discount every month in advance on the first day of each month in the currency and in the manner indicated in Box 23 and at the place mentioned in Box 24.

PART II
"BARECON 89" Standard Bareboat Charter

(c) Payment of Hire for the first and last month's Hire if less than a full month 200
shall be calculated proportionally according to the number of days in the 201
particular calendar month and advance payment to be effected accordingly. 202
(d) Should the Vessel be lost or missing, Hire to cease from the date and time 203
when she was lost or last heard of. Any Hire paid in advance to be adjusted 204
accordingly. 205
(e) Time shall be of the essence in relation to payment of Hire hereunder. In 206
default of payment beyond a period of seven running days, the Owners shall 207
have the right to withdraw the Vessel from the service of the Charterers 208
without noting any protest and without interference by any court or any other 209
formality whatsoever, and shall, without prejudice to any other claim the 210
Owners may otherwise have against the Charterers under the Charter, be 211
entitled to damages in respect of all costs and losses incurred as a result of 212
the Charterers' default and the ensuing withdrawal of the Vessel. 213
(f) Any delay in payment of Hire shall entitle the Owners to an interest at the 214
rate per annum as agreed in Box 22. If Box 22 has not been filled in the current 215
market rate in the country where the Owners have their Principal Place of 216
Business shall apply. 217

11. Mortgage 218
°) (a) Owners warrant that they have not effected any mortgage of the Vessel. 219
°) (b) The Vessel chartered under this Charter is financed by a mortgage 220
according to the Deed(s) of Covenant annexed to this Charter and as stated in 221
Box 26. By their counter-signature on the Deed(s) of Covenant, the 222
Charterers undertake to have acquainted themselves with all terms, 223
conditions and provisions of the said Deed(s) of Covenant. The Charterers 224
undertake that they will comply with all instructions or directions in 225
regard to the employment, insurances, repairs and maintenance of the 226
Vessel, etc., as laid down in the Deed(s) of Covenant or as may be directed 227
from time to time during the currency of the Charter by the Mortgagee(s) in 228
conformity with the Deed(s) of Covenant. 229
°) (c) The Owners warrant that they have not effected any mortgage(s) other 230
than stated in Box 26 and that they will not effect any other mortgage(s) 231
without the prior consent of the Charterers. 232
°) *(Optional, Clauses 11 (a) and 11 (b) are alternatives; indicate alternative agreed* 233
in Box 26). 234

12. Insurance and Repairs 235
(a) During the Charter period the Vessel shall be kept insured by the 236
Charterers at their expense against marine, war and Protection and Indemnity 237
risks in such form as the Owners shall in writing approve, which approval 238
shall not be unreasonably withheld. Such marine, war and P. and I. 239
insurances shall be arranged by the Charterers to protect the interests of both 240
the Owners and the Charterers and mortgagees (if any), and the Charterers 241
shall be at liberty to protect under such insurances the interests of any 242
managers they may appoint. All insurance policies shall be in the joint names 243
of the Owners and the Charterers as their interests may appear. 244
If the Charterers fail to arrange and keep any of the insurances provided 245
for under the provisions of sub-clause (a) above in the manner described 246
therein, the Owners shall notify the Charterers whereupon the Charterers 247
shall rectify the position within seven running days, failing which Owners 248
shall have the right to withdraw the Vessel from the service of the Charterers 249
without prejudice to any claim the Owners may otherwise have against the 250
Charterers. 251

Charterers at their expense against Protection and Indemnity risks in such 303
form as the Owners shall in writing approve which approval shall not be 304
unreasonably withheld. If the Charterers fail to arrange and keep any of the 305
insurances provided for under the provisions of sub-clause (b) in the manner 306
described therein, the Owners shall notify the Charterers whereupon the 307
Charterers shall rectify the position within seven running days, failing which 308
the Owners shall have the right to withdraw the Vessel from the service of the 309
Charterers without prejudice to any claim the Owners may otherwise have 310
against the Charterers. 311
(c) In the event that any act or negligence of the Charterers shall vitiate any of 312
the insurance herein provided, the Charterers shall pay to the Owners all 313
losses and indemnify the Owners against all claims and demands which 314
would otherwise have been covered by such insurance. 315
(d) The Charterers shall, subject to the approval of the Owners or Owners' 316
Underwriters, effect all insured repairs, and the Charterers shall undertake 317
settlement of all miscellaneous expenses and liabilities, to the extent of coverage 318
under the insurances provided for under the provisions of sub-clause (a) of 319
this Clause. The Charterers to be secured reimbursement through the 320
Owners' Underwriters for such expenditures upon presentation of accounts. 321
(e) The Charterers to remain responsible for and to effect repairs and 322
settlement of costs and expenses incurred thereby in respect of all other 323
repairs not covered by the insurances and/or not exceeding any possible 324
franchise(s) or deductibles provided for in the insurances. 325
(f) All time used for repairs under the provisions of sub-clause (d) and (e) of 326
this Clause and for repairs of latent defects according to Clause 2 above, 327
including any deviation, shall count as time on hire and shall form part of the 328
Charter period. 329
The Owners shall not be responsible for any expenses as are incident to the 330
use and operation of the Vessel for such time as may be required to make 331
such repairs. 332
(g) If the conditions of the above insurances permit additional insurance to be 333
placed by the parties such cover shall be limited to the amount for each party 334
set out in Box 28 and Box 29, respectively. The Owners or the Charterers as 335
the case may be shall immediately furnish the other party with particulars of 336
any additional insurance effected, including copies of any cover notes or 337
policies and the written consent of the Insurers of any such required 338
insurance in any case where the consent of such Insurers is necessary. 339
(h) Should the Vessel become an actual, constructive, compromised or 340
agreed total loss under the insurances required under sub-clause (a) of this 341
Clause, all insurance payments for such loss shall be paid to the Owners, who 342
shall distribute the moneys between themselves and the Charterers 343
according to their respective interests. 344
(i) If the Vessel becomes an actual, constructive, compromised or agreed 345
total loss under the insurances arranged by the Owners in accordance with 346
sub-clause (a) of this Clause, this Charter shall terminate as of the date of 347
such loss. 348
(j) The Charterers shall upon the request of the Owners, promptly execute 349
such documents as may be required to enable the Owners to abandon the 350
Vessel to Insurers and claim a constructive total loss. 351
(k) For the purpose of insurance coverage against marine and war risks under 352
the provisions of sub-clause (a) of this Clause, the value of the Vessel is the 353
sum indicated in Box 27. 354
(l) Notwithstanding anything contained in Clause 9 (a), it is agreed that under 355

The Charterers shall, subject to the approval of the Owners and the 252
Underwriters, effect all insured repairs and shall undertake settlement of all 253
costs in connection with such repairs as well as insured charges, expenses 254
and liabilities (reimbursement to be secured by the Charterers from the 255
Underwriters) to the extent of coverage under the insurances herein provided 256
for. 257

The Charterers also to remain responsible for and to effect repairs and 258
settlement of costs and expenses incurred thereby in respect of all other 259
repairs not covered by the insurances and/or not exceeding any possible 260
franchise(s) or deductibles provided for in the insurances. 261

All time used for repairs under the provisions of sub-clause (a) of this Clause 262
and for repairs of latent defects according to Clause 2 above including any 263
deviation shall count as time on hire and shall form part of the Charter period. 264

(b) If the conditions of the above insurances permit additional insurance to be 265
placed by the parties, such cover shall be limited to the amount for each party 266
set out in Box 28 and Box 29, respectively. The Owners or the Charterers as 267
the case may be shall immediately furnish the other party with particulars of 268
any additional insurance effected, including copies of any cover notes or 269
policies and the written consent of the insurers of any such required 270
insurance in any case where the consent of such insurers is necessary. 271

(c) Should the Vessel become an actual, constructive, compromised or 272
agreed total loss under the insurances required under sub-clause (a) of 273
Clause 12, all insurance payments for such loss shall be paid to the Mort- 274
gagee, if any, in the manner described in the Deed(s) of Covenant, who shall 275
distribute the moneys between themselves, the Owners and the Charterers 276
according to their respective interests. The Charterers undertake to notify the 277
Owners and the Mortgagee, if any, of any occurrences in consequence of 278
which the Vessel is likely to become a Total Loss as defined in this Clause. 279

(d) If the Vessel becomes an actual, constructive, compromised or agreed 280
total loss under the insurances arranged by the Charterers in accordance 281
with sub-clause (a) of this Clause, this Charter shall terminate as of the date of 282
such loss. 283

(e) The Owners shall upon the request of the Charterers, promptly execute 284
such documents as may be required to enable the Charterers to abandon the 285
Vessel to insurers and claim a constructive total loss. 286

(f) For the purpose of insurance coverage against marine and war risks under 287
the provisions of sub-clause (a) of this Clause, the value of the Vessel is the 288
sum indicated in Box 27. 289

13. Insurance, Repairs and Classification 290

(Optional, only to apply if expressly agreed and stated in Box 27, in which event 291
Clause 12 shall be considered deleted) 292

(a) During the Charter period the Vessel shall be kept insured by the Owners 293
at their expense against marine and war risks under the form of policy or 294
policies attached hereto. The Owners and/or insurers shall not have any right 295
of recovery or subrogation against the Charterers on account of loss of or any 296
damage to the Vessel or her machinery or appurtenances covered by such 297
insurance, or on account of payments made to discharge claims against or 298
liabilities of the Vessel or the Owners covered by such insurance. All 299
insurance policies shall be in the joint names of the Owners and the 300
Charterers as their interests may appear. 301

(b) During the Charter period the Vessel shall be kept insured by the 302

the provisions of Clause 13, if applicable, the Owners shall keep the Vessel 357
with unexpired classification in force at all times during the Charter period. 358

14. Redelivery 359

The Charterers shall at the expiration of the Charter period redeliver the 360
Vessel at a safe and ice-free port or place as indicated in Box 16. The 361
Charterers shall give the Owners not less than 30 running days' preliminary 362
and not less than 14 days' definite notice of expected date, range of ports of 363
redelivery or port or place of redelivery. Any changes thereafter in Vessel's 364
position shall be notified immediately to the Owners. 365

Should the Vessel be ordered on a voyage by which the Charter period may 366
be exceeded the Charterers to have the use of the Vessel to enable them to 367
complete the voyage, provided it could be reasonably calculated that the 368
voyage would allow redelivery about the time fixed for the termination of the 369
Charter. 370

The Vessel shall be redelivered to the Owners in the same or as good 371
structure, state, condition and class as that in which she was delivered, fair 372
wear and tear not affecting class excepted. 373

The Vessel upon redelivery shall have her survey cycles up to date and class 374
certificates valid for at least the number of months agreed in Box 12. 375

15. Non-Lien and Indemnity 376

The Charterers will not suffer, nor permit to be continued, any lien or 377
encumbrance incurred by them or their agents, which might have priority over 378
the title and interest of the Owners in the Vessel. 379

The Charterers further agree to fasten to the Vessel in a conspicuous place 380
and to keep so fastened during the Charter period a notice reading as 381
follows:— 382

"This Vessel is the property of (name of Owners). It is under charter to (name 383
of Charterers) and by the terms of the Charter Party neither the Charterers nor 384
the Master have any right, power or authority to create, incur or permit to be 385
imposed on the Vessel any lien whatsoever." 386

The Charterers shall indemnify and hold the Owners harmless against any 387
lien of whatsoever nature arising upon the Vessel during the Charter period 388
while she is under the control of the Charterers, and against any claims 389
against the Owners arising out of or in relation to the operation of the Vessel 390
by the Charterers. Should the Vessel be arrested by reason of claims or liens 391
arising out of her operation hereunder by the Charterers, the Charterers shall 392
at their own expense take all reasonable steps to secure that within a 393
reasonable time the Vessel is released and at their own expense put up bail to 394
secure release of the Vessel. 395

16. Lien 396

The Owners to have a lien upon all cargoes and sub-freights belonging to the 397
Charterers and any Bill of Lading freight for all claims under this Charter, and 398
the Charterers to have a lien on the Vessel for all moneys paid in advance and 399
not earned. 400

17. Salvage 401

All salvage and towage performed by the Vessel shall be for the Charterers' 402
benefit and the cost of repairing damage occasioned thereby shall be borne 403
by the Charterers. 404

PART II
"BARECON 89" Standard Bareboat Charter

405

18. Wreck Removal

In the event of the Vessel becoming a wreck or obstruction to navigation the 406
Charterers shall indemnify the Owners against any sums whatsoever which 407
the Owners shall become liable to pay and shall pay in consequence of the 408
Vessel becoming a wreck or obstruction to navigation. 409

410

19. General Average

General Average, if any, shall be adjusted according to the York-Antwerp 411
Rules 1974 or any subsequent modification thereof current at the time of the 412
casualty. 413

The Charter Hire not to contribute to General Average. 414

415

20. Assignment and Sub-Demise

The Charterers shall not assign this Charter nor sub-demise the Vessel 416
except with the prior consent in writing of the Owners which shall not be 417
unreasonably withheld and subject to such terms and conditions as the 418
Owners shall approve. 419

420

21. Bills of Lading

The Charterers are to procure that all Bills of Lading issued for carriage of 421
goods under this Charter shall contain a Paramount Clause incorporating any 422
legislation relating to Carrier's liability for cargo compulsorily applicable in 423
the trade; if no such legislation exists, the Bills of Lading shall incorporate the 424
British Carriage of Goods by Sea Act. The Bills of Lading shall also contain the 425
amended New Jason Clause and the Both-to-Blame Collision Clause. 426

The Charterers agree to indemnify the Owners against all consequences or 427
liabilities arising from the Master, officers or agents signing Bills of Lading or 428
other documents. 429

430

22. Bank Guarantee

The Charterers undertake to furnish, before delivery of the Vessel, a first class 431
bank guarantee or bond in the sum and at the place as indicated in Box 25 as 432
guarantee for full performance of their obligations under this Charter. 433
(Optional, only to apply if Box 25 filled in). 434

460

24. War

(a) The Vessel unless the consent of the Owners be first obtained not to be 461
ordered nor continue to any place or on any voyage nor be used on any 462
service which will bring her within a zone which is dangerous as the result of 463
any actual or threatened act of war, hostilities, warlike operations, acts of 464
piracy or of hostility or malicious damage against this or any other vessel or 465
its cargo by any person, body or State whatsoever, revolution, civil war, civil 466
commotion or the operation of international law, nor be exposed in any way to 467
any risks or penalties whatsoever consequent upon the imposition of 468
Sanctions, nor carry any goods that may in any way expose her to any risks of 469
seizure, capture, penalties or any other interference of any kind whatsoever 470
by the belligerent or fighting powers or parties or by any Government or Ruler. 471

(b) The Vessel to have liberty to comply with any orders or directions as to 472
departure, arrival, routes, ports of call, stoppages, destination, delivery or in 473
any other wise whatsoever given by the Government of the nation under 474
whose flag the Vessel sails or any other Government or any person (or body) 475
acting or purporting to act with the authority of such Government or by any 476
committee or person having under the terms of the war risks insurance on the 477
Vessel the right to give any such orders or directions. 478

(c) In the event of outbreak of war (whether there be a declaration of war or 479
not) between any two or more of the countries as stated in Box 31, both the 480
Owners and the Charterers shall have the right to cancel this Charter, 481
whereupon the Charterers shall redeliver the Vessel to the Owners in 482
accordance with Clause 14, if she has cargo on board after discharge thereof 483
at destination, or if debarred under this Clause from reaching or entering it at 484
a near open and safe port as directed by the Owners, or if she has no cargo on 485
board, at the port at which she then is or if at sea at a near open and safe port 486
as directed by the Owners. In all cases hire shall continue to be paid in 487
accordance with Clause 10 and except as aforesaid all other provisions of this 488
Charter shall apply until redelivery. 489

490

25. Commission

The Owners to pay a commission at the rate indicated in Box 32 to the Brokers 491
named in Box 32 on any Hire paid under the Charter but in no case less than is 492
necessary to cover the actual expenses of the Brokers and a reasonable fee 493
for their work. If the full Hire is not paid owing to breach of Charter by either of 494
the parties the party liable therefor to indemnify the Brokers against their loss 495
of commission. 496

Should the parties agree to cancel the Charter, the Owners to indemnify the 497
Brokers against any loss of commission but in such case the commission not 498
to exceed the brokerage on one year's Hire. 499

23. Requisition/Acquisition 435

(a) In the event of the Requisition for Hire of the Vessel by any governmental or 436
other competent authority (hereinafter referred to as "Requisition for Hire") 437
irrespective of the date during the Charter period when "Requisition for Hire" 438
may occur and irrespective of the length thereof and whether or not it be for 439
an indefinite or a limited period of time, and irrespective of whether it may or 440
will remain in force for the remainder of the Charter period, this Charter shall 441
not be deemed thereby or thereupon to be frustrated or otherwise terminated 442
and the Charterers shall continue to pay the stipulated hire in the manner 443
provided by this Charter until the time when the Charter would have 444
terminated pursuant to any of the provisions hereof always provided however 445
that in the event of "Requisition for Hire" any Requisition Hire or 446
compensation received or receivable by the Owners shall be payable to the 447
Charterers during the remainder of the Charter period or the period of the 448
"Requisition for Hire" whichever be the shorter. 449

The Hire under this Charter shall be payable to the Owners from the same time 450
as the Requisition Hire is payable to the Charterers. 451

(b) In the event of the Owners being deprived of their ownership in the Vessel 452
by any Compulsory Acquisition of the Vessel or requisition for title by any 453
governmental or other competent authority (hereinafter referred to as 454
"Compulsory Acquisition"), then, irrespective of the date during the Charter 455
period when "Compulsory Acquisition" may occur, this Charter shall be 456
deemed terminated as of the date of such "Compulsory Acquisition". In such 457
event Charter Hire to be considered as earned and to be paid up to the date 458
and time of such "Compulsory Acquisition". 459

26. Law and Arbitration 500

°) 26.1. This Charter shall be governed by English law and any dispute arising 501
out of this Charter shall be referred to arbitration in London, one arbitrator 502
being appointed by each party, in accordance with the Arbitration Acts 1950 503
and 1979 or any statutory modification or re-enactment thereof for the time 504
being in force. On the receipt by one party of the nomination in writing of the 505
other party's arbitrator, that party shall appoint their arbitrator within fourteen 506
days, failing which the decision of the single Arbitrator appointed shall apply. 507
If two Arbitrators properly appointed shall not agree they shall appoint an 508
umpire whose decision shall be final. 509

°) 26.2. Should any dispute arise out of this Charter, the matter in dispute shall 510
be referred to three persons at New York, one to be appointed by each of the 511
parties hereto, and the third by the two so chosen; their decision or that of any 512
two of them shall be final, and for purpose of enforcing any award, this 513
agreement may be made a rule of the Court. 514
The arbitrators shall be members of the Society of Maritime Arbitrators, Inc. of 515
New York and the proceedings shall be conducted in accordance with the 516
rules of the Society. 517

°) 26.3. Any dispute arising out of this Charter shall be referred to arbitration at 518
the place indicated in Box 33, subject to the law and procedures applicable 519
there. 520

26.4. If Box 33 in Part I is not filled in, sub-clause 26.1. of this Clause shall 521
apply. 522
°) 26.1., 26.2. and 26.3. are alternatives; indicate alternative agreed in Box 33. 523

OPTIONAL PART

"BARECON 89" Standard Bareboat Charter

PART III

PROVISIONS TO APPLY FOR NEWBUILDING VESSELS ONLY

(Optional, only to apply if expressly agreed and stated in Box 35)

Specifications and Building Contract

(a) The Vessel shall be constructed in accordance with the Building Contract (hereafter called "the Building Contract") as annexed to this Charter, made between the Builders and the Owners and in accordance with the specifications and plans annexed thereto, such Building Contract, specifications and plans having been counter-signed as approved by the Charterers. 1–6

(b) No change shall be made in the Building Contract or in the specifications or plans of the Vessel as approved by the Charterers as aforesaid, without the Charterers' consent. 7–9

(c) The Charterers shall have the right to send their representative to the Builders' Yard to inspect the Vessel during the course of her construction to satisfy themselves that construction is in accordance with such approved specifications and plans as referred to under sub-clause (a) of this Clause. 10–13

(d) The Vessel shall be built in accordance with the Building Contract and shall be of the description set out therein provided nevertheless that the Charterers shall be bound to accept the Vessel from the Owners on the date of delivery by the Builders as having been completed and constructed in accordance with the Building Contract and the Charterers undertake that after having so accepted the Vessel they will not thereafter raise any claims against the Owners in respect of the Vessel's performance or specification or defects if any except that in respect of any repair or replacement of any defects which appear within the first 12 months from delivery the Owners shall use their best endeavours to recover any expenditure incurred in remedying such defects from the Builders, but shall only be liable to the Charterers to the extent the Owners have a valid claim against the Builders under the guarantee clause of the Building Contract (a copy whereof has been supplied to the Charterers) provided that the Charterers shall be bound to accept such sums as the Owners are able to recover under this clause and shall make no claim upon the Owners for any difference between the amounts so recovered and the actual expenditure incurred on repairs or replacements or for any loss of time incurred thereby. 14–30

Time and Place of Delivery

(a) Subject to the Vessel having completed her acceptance trials including trials of cargo equipment in accordance with the Building Contract and specifications to the satisfaction of the Charterers, the Owners shall give and the Charterers shall take delivery of the Vessel afloat when ready for delivery at the Builders' Yard or some other safe and readily accessible dock, wharf or place as may be agreed between the parties hereto and the Builders. Under the Building Contract the Builders have estimated that the Vessel will be ready for delivery to the Owners as therein provided but the delivery date for the purpose of this Charter shall be the date when the Vessel is in fact ready for delivery by the Builders after completion of trials whether that be before or after as indicated in the Building Contract. Notwithstanding the foregoing, the Charterers shall not be obliged to take delivery of the Vessel until she has been classed and documented as provided in this Charter and free for transfer to the flag she has to fly. Subject as aforesaid the Charterers shall not be entitled to refuse acceptance of delivery of the Vessel and upon and after such acceptance the Charterers shall not be entitled to make any claim against the Owners in respect of any conditions, representations or 32–47

warranties, whether express or implied, as to the seaworthiness of the Vessel or in respect of delay in delivery or otherwise howsoever. 48–49

(b) If for any reason other than a default by the Owners under the Building Contract, the Builders become entitled under that Contract not to deliver the Vessel to the Owners, the Owners shall upon giving to the Charterers written notice of Builders becoming so entitled, be excused from giving delivery of the Vessel to the Charterers and upon receipt of such notice by the Charterers this Charter shall cease to have effect. 50–55

(c) If for any reason the Owners become entitled under the Building Contract to reject the Vessel the Owners shall, before exercising such right of rejection, consult the Charterers and thereupon 56–58

i) if the Charterers do not wish to take delivery of the Vessel they shall inform the Owners within seven (7) days by notice in writing and upon receipt by the Owners of such notice this Charter shall cease to have effect; or 59–61

ii) if the Charterers wish to take delivery of the Vessel they may by notice in writing within seven (7) days require the Owners to negotiate with the Builders as to the terms on which delivery should be taken and/or refrain from exercising their right to rejection and upon receipt of such notice the Owners shall commence such negotiations and/or take delivery of the Vessel from the Builders and deliver her to the Charterers; 62–67

iii) in no circumstances shall the Charterers be entitled to reject the Vessel unless the Owners are able to reject the Vessel from the Builders; 68–69

iv) if this Charter terminates under sub-clause (b) or (c) of this Clause, the Owners shall thereafter not be liable to the Charterers for any claim under or arising out of this Charter or its termination. 70–72

Guarantee Works

If not otherwise agreed, the Owners authorize the Charterers to arrange for the guarantee works to be performed in accordance with the building contract terms, and hire to continue during the period of guarantee works. The Charterers have to advise the Owners about the performance to the extent the Owners may request. 73–77

Name of Vessel

The name of the Vessel shall be mutually agreed between the Owners and the Charterers and the Vessel shall be painted in the colours, display the funnel insignia and fly the house flag as required by the Charterers. 78–81

Survey on Redelivery

The Owners and the Charterers shall appoint surveyors for the purpose of determining and agreeing in writing the condition of the Vessel at the time of re-delivery. 82–85

Without prejudice to Clause 14 (Part II), the Charterers shall bear all survey expenses and all other costs, if any, including the cost of docking and undocking, if required, as well as all repair costs incurred. 86–88

The Charterers shall also bear all loss of time spent in connection with any docking and undocking as well as repairs, which shall be paid at the rate of Hire per day or pro rata. 89–91

PART IV
HIRE/PURCHASE AGREEMENT

(Optional, only to apply if expressly agreed and stated in Box 39)

On expiration of this Charter and provided the Charterers have fulfilled their obligations according to Part I and II as well as Part III, if applicable, it is agreed, that on payment of the last month's hire instalment as per Clause 10 the Charterers have purchased the Vessel with everything belonging to her and the Vessel is fully paid for.

If the payment of the instalment due is delayed for less than 7 running days or for reason beyond the Charterers' control, the right of withdrawal under the terms of Clause 10(e) of Part II shall not be exercised. However, any delay in payment of the instalment due shall entitle the Owners to an interest at the rate per annum as agreed in Box 22. If Box 22 has not been filled in the current market rate in the country where the Owners have their Principal Place of Business shall apply.

In the following paragraphs the Owners are referred to as 'the Sellers and the Charterers as the Buyers.

The Vessel shall be delivered by the Sellers and taken over by the Buyers on expiration of the Charter.

The Sellers guarantee that the Vessel, at the time of delivery, is free from all encumbrances and maritime liens or any debts whatsoever other than those arising from anything done or not done by the Buyers or any existing mortgage agreed not to be paid off by the time of delivery. Should any claims, which have been incurred prior to the time of delivery be made against the Vessel, the Sellers hereby undertake to indemnify the Buyers against all consequences of such claims to the extent it can be proved that the Sellers are responsible for such claims. Any taxes, notarial, consular and other charges and expenses connected

with the purchase and registration under Buyers' flag, shall be for Buyers' account. Any taxes, consular and other charges and expenses connected with closing of the Sellers' register, shall be for Sellers' account.

In exchange for payment of the last month's hire instalment the Sellers shall furnish the Buyers with a Bill of Sale duly attested and legalized, together with a certificate setting out the registered encumbrances, if any. On delivery of the Vessel the Sellers shall provide for deletion of the Vessel from the Ship's Register and deliver a certificate of deletion to the Buyers.

The Sellers shall, at the time of delivery, hand to the Buyers all classification certificates (for hull, engines, anchors, chains, etc.), as well as all plans which may be in Sellers' possession.

The Wireless Installation and Nautical Instruments, unless on hire, shall be included in the sale without any extra payment.

The Vessel with everything belonging to her shall be at Sellers' risk and expense until she is delivered to the Buyers, subject to the conditions of this Contract and the Vessel with everything belonging to her shall be delivered and taken over as she is at the time of delivery, after which the Sellers shall have no responsibility for possible faults or deficiencies of any description.

The Buyers undertake to pay for the repatriation of the Captain, officers and other personnel if appointed by the Sellers to the port where the Vessel entered the Bareboat Charter as per Clause 2 (Part II) or to pay the equivalent cost for their journey to any other place.

	1
	2
	3
	4
	5
	6
	7
	8
	9
	10
	11
	12
	13
	14
	15
	16
	17
	18
	19
	20
	21
	22
	23
	24
	25
	26
	27
	28
	29
	30
	31
	32
	33
	34
	35
	36
	37
	38
	39
	40
	41
	42
	43
	44
	45

PART V
PROVISIONS TO APPLY FOR VESSELS REGISTERED IN A BAREBOAT CHARTER REGISTRY

(Optional, only to apply if expressly agreed and stated in Box 40)

Definitions

For the purpose of this PART V, the following terms shall have the meanings hereby assigned to them:

"The Bareboat Charter Registry" shall mean the registry of the State whose flag the Vessel will fly and in which the Charterers are registered as the bareboat charterers during the period of the Bareboat Charter.

"The Underlying Registry" shall mean the registry of the State in which the Owners of the Vessel are registered as Owners and to which jurisdiction and control of the Vessel will revert upon termination of the Bareboat Charter Registration.

Mortgage

The Vessel chartered under this Charter is financed by a mortgage and the provisions of Clause 11 (b) (Part II) shall apply.

1 Termination of Charter by Default

If the Vessel chartered under this Charter is registered in a Bareboat Charter Registry as stated in Box 41, and if the Owners shall default in the payment of any amounts due under the mortgage(s) specified in Box 26, the Charterers shall, if so required by the mortgagee, direct the Owners to re-register the Vessel in the Underlying Registry as shown in Box 42.

In the event of the Vessel being deleted from the Bareboat Charter Registry as stated in Box 41, due to a default by the Owners in the payment of any amounts due under the mortgage(s), the Charterers shall have the right to terminate this Charter forthwith and without prejudice to any other claim they may have against the Owners under this Charter.

	1
	2
	3
	4
	5
	6
	7
	8
	9
	10
	11
	12
	13
	14
	15
	16
	17
	18
	19
	20
	21
	22
	23

1. Shipbroker

RECOMMENDED
THE BALTIC AND INTERNATIONAL MARITIME COUNCIL
UNIFORM GENERAL CHARTER (AS REVISED 1922, 1976 and 1994)
(To be used for trades for which no specially approved form is in force)
CODE NAME: "GENCON"

Part I

2. Place and date

3. Owners/Place of business (Cl. 1)

4. Charterers/Place of business (Cl. 1)

5. Vessel's name (Cl. 1)

6. GT/NT (Cl. 1)

7. DWT all told on summer load line in metric tons (abt.) (Cl. 1)

8. Present position (Cl. 1)

9. Expected ready to load (abt.) (Cl. 1)

10. Loading port or place (Cl. 1)

11. Discharging port or place (Cl. 1)

12. Cargo (also state quantity and margin in Owners' option, if agreed; if full and complete cargo not agreed state "part cargo" (Cl. 1)

13. Freight rate (also state whether freight prepaid or payable on delivery) (Cl. 4)

14. Freight payment (state currency and method of payment; also beneficiary and bank account) (Cl. 4)

15. State if vessel's cargo handling gear shall not be used (Cl. 5)

16. Laytime (if separate laytime for load. and disch. is agreed, fill in a) and b). If total laytime for load. and disch., fill in c) only) (Cl. 6)

(a) Laytime for loading

17. Shippers/Place of business (Cl. 6)

(b) Laytime for discharging

18. Agents (loading) (Cl. 6)

(c) Total laytime for loading and discharging

19. Agents (discharging) (Cl. 6)

20. Demurrage rate and manner payable (loading and discharging) (Cl. 7)

21. Cancelling date (Cl. 9)

22. General Average to be adjusted at (Cl. 12)

23. Freight Tax (state if for the Owners' account (Cl. 13 (c))

24. Brokerage commission and to whom payable (Cl. 15)

25. Law and Arbitration (state 19 (a), 19 (b) or 19 (c) of Cl. 19; if 19 (c) agreed also state Place of Arbitration) (if not filled in 19 (a) shall apply) (Cl. 19)

(a) State maximum amount for small claims/shortened arbitration (Cl. 19)

26. Additional clauses covering special provisions, if agreed

It is mutually agreed that this Contract shall be performed subject to the conditions contained in this Charter Party which shall include Part I as well as Part II. In the event of a conflict of conditions, the provisions of Part I shall prevail over those of Part II to the extent of such conflict.

Signature (Owners)

Signature (Charterers)

Printed and sold by Fr. G. Knudtzon Ltd., 55 Toldbodgade, DK-1253 Copenhagen K. Telefax +45 33 93 11 84 by authority of The Baltic and International Maritime Council (BIMCO), Copenhagen

PART II

"Gencon" Charter (As Revised 1922, 1976 and 1994)

1. It is agreed between the party mentioned in Box 3 as the Owners of the Vessel named in Box 5, of the GT/NT indicated in Box 6 and carrying about the number of metric tons of deadweight capacity all told on summer loadline stated in Box 7, now in position as stated in Box 8 and expected ready to load under this Charter Party about the date indicated in Box 9, and the party mentioned as the Charterers in Box 4 that:

The said Vessel shall, as soon as her prior commitments have been completed, proceed to the loading port(s) or place(s) stated in Box 10 or so near thereto as she may safely get and lie always afloat, and there load a full and complete cargo (if shipment of deck cargo agreed same to be at the Charterers' risk and responsibility) as stated in Box 12, which the Charterers bind themselves to ship, and being so loaded the Vessel shall proceed to the discharging port(s) or place(s) stated in Box 11 as ordered on signing Bills of Lading, or so near thereto as she may safely get and lie always afloat, and there deliver the cargo.

2. Owners' Responsibility Clause

The Owners are to be responsible for loss of or damage to the goods or for delay in delivery of the goods only in case the loss, damage or delay has been caused by personal want of due diligence on the part of the Owners or their Manager to make the Vessel in all respects seaworthy and to secure that she is properly manned, equipped and supplied, or by the personal act or default of the Owners or their Manager.

And the Owners are not responsible for loss, damage or delay arising from any other cause whatsoever, even from the neglect or default of the Master or crew or some other person employed by the Owners on board or ashore for whose acts they would, but for this Clause, be responsible, or from unseaworthiness of the Vessel on loading or commencement of the voyage or at any time whatsoever.

3. Deviation Clause

The Vessel has liberty to call at any port or ports in any order, for any purpose, to sail without pilots, to tow and/or assist Vessels in all situations, and also to deviate for the purpose of saving life and/or property.

4. Payment of Freight

(a) The freight at the rate stated in Box 13 shall be paid in cash calculated on the intaken quantity of cargo.

(b) *Prepaid.* If according to Box 13 freight is to be paid on shipment, it shall be deemed earned and non-returnable, Vessel and/or cargo lost or not lost.

Neither the Owners nor their agents shall be required to sign or endorse bills of lading showing freight prepaid unless the freight due to the Owners has actually been paid.

(c) *On delivery.* If according to Box 13 freight, or part thereof, is payable at destination it shall not be deemed earned until the cargo is thus delivered. Notwithstanding the provisions under (a), if freight or part thereof is payable on delivery of the cargo the Charterers shall have the option of paying the freight on delivered weight/quantity provided such option is declared before breaking bulk and the weight/quantity can be ascertained by official weighing machine, joint draft survey or tally.

Cash for Vessel's ordinary disbursements at the port of loading to be advanced by the Charterers, if required, at highest current rate of exchange, subject to two (2) per cent to cover insurance and other expenses.

readiness at loading port to be given to the Shippers named in Box 17 or if not named, to the Charterers or their agents named in Box 18. Notice of readiness at the discharging port to be given to the Receivers or, if not known, to the Charterers or their agents named in Box 19.

If the loading/discharging berth is not available on the Vessel's arrival at or off the port of loading/discharging, the Vessel shall be entitled to give notice of readiness within ordinary office hours on arrival there, whether in free pratique or not, whether customs cleared or not. Laytime or time on demurrage shall then count as if she were in berth and in all respects ready for loading/ discharging provided that the Master warrants that she is in fact ready in all respects. Time used in moving from the place of waiting to the loading/ discharging berth shall not count as laytime.

If, after inspection, the Vessel is found not to be ready in all respects to load/ discharge time lost after the discovery thereof until the Vessel is again ready to load/discharge shall not count as laytime.

Time used before commencement of laytime shall count.

* *Indicate alternative (a) or (b) as agreed, in Box 16.*

7. Demurrage

Demurrage at the loading and discharging port is payable by the Charterers at the rate stated in Box 20 in the manner stated in Box 20 per day or pro rata for any part of a day. Demurrage shall fall due day by day and shall be payable upon receipt of the Owners' invoice.

In the event the demurrage is not paid in accordance with the above, the Owners shall give the Charterers 96 running hours written notice to rectify the failure. If the demurrage is not paid at the expiration of this time limit and if the vessel is in or at the loading port, the Owners are entitled at any time to terminate the Charter Party and claim damages for any losses caused thereby.

8. Lien Clause

The Owners shall have a lien on the cargo and on all sub-freights payable in respect of the cargo, for freight, deadfreight, demurrage, claims for damages and for all other amounts due under this Charter Party including costs of recovering same.

9. Cancelling Clause

(a) Should the Vessel not be ready to load (whether in berth or not) on the cancelling date indicated in Box 21, the Charterers shall have the option of cancelling this Charter Party.

(b) Should the Owners anticipate that, despite the exercise of due diligence, the Vessel will not be ready to load by the cancelling date, they shall notify the Charterers thereof without delay stating the expected date of the Vessel's readiness to load and asking whether the Charterers will exercise their option of cancelling the Charter Party, or agree to a new cancelling date.

Such option must be declared by the Charterers within 48 running hours after the receipt of the Owners' notice. If the Charterers do not exercise their option of cancelling, then this Charter Party shall be deemed to be amended such that the seventh day after the new readiness date stated in the Owners' notification to the Charterers shall be the new cancelling date.

The provisions of sub-clause (b) of this Clause shall operate only once, and in case of the Vessel's further delay, the Charterers shall have the option of cancelling the Charter Party as per sub-clause (a) of this Clause.

5. Loading/Discharging

(a) Costs/Risks

The cargo shall be brought into the holds, loaded, stowed and/or trimmed, tallied, lashed and/or secured and taken from the holds and discharged by the Charterers, free of any risk, liability and expense whatsoever to the Owners. The Charterers shall provide and lay all dunnage material as required for the proper stowage and protection of the cargo on board, the Owners allowing the use of all dunnage available on board. The Charterers shall be responsible for and pay the cost of removing their dunnage after discharge of the cargo under this Charter Party and time to count until dunnage has been removed.

(b) Cargo Handling Gear

Unless the Vessel is gearless or unless it has been agreed between the parties that the Vessel's gear shall not be used and stated as such in Box 15, the Owners shall throughout the duration of loading/discharging give free use of the Vessel's cargo handling gear and of sufficient motive power to operate all such cargo handling gear. All such equipment to be in good working order. Unless caused by negligence of the stevedores, time lost by breakdown of the Vessel's cargo handling gear or motive power – pro rata the total number of cranes/winches required at that time for the loading/discharging of cargo under this Charter Party – shall not count as laytime or time on demurrage.

On request the Owners shall provide free of charge cranemen/winchmen from the crew to operate the Vessel's cargo handling gear, unless local regulations prohibit this, in which latter event shore labourers shall be for the account of the Charterers. Cranemen/winchmen shall be under the Charterers' risk and responsibility and as stevedores be deemed as their servants but shall always work under the supervision of the Master.

(c) Stevedore Damage

The Charterers shall be responsible for damage (beyond ordinary wear and tear) to any part of the Vessel caused by Stevedores. Such damage shall be notified as soon as reasonably possible by the Master to the Charterers or their agents and to their Stevedores, failing which the Charterers shall not be held responsible. The Master shall endeavour to obtain the Stevedores' written acknowledgement of liability.

The Charterers are obliged to repair any stevedore damage prior to completion of the voyage, but must repair stevedore damage affecting the Vessel's seaworthiness or class before the Vessel sails from the port where such damage was caused or found. All additional expenses incurred shall be for the account of the Charterers and any time lost shall be for the account of and shall be paid to the Owners by the Charterers at the demurrage rate.

6. Laytime

* (a) Separate laytime for loading and discharging

The cargo shall be loaded within the number of running days/hours as indicated in Box 16, weather permitting, Sundays and holidays excepted, unless used, in which event time used shall count.

The cargo shall be discharged within the number of running days/hours as indicated in Box 16, weather permitting, Sundays and holidays excepted, unless used, in which event time used shall count.

* (b) Total laytime for loading and discharging

The cargo shall be loaded and discharged within the number of total running days/hours as indicated in Box 16, weather permitting, Sundays and holidays excepted, unless used, in which event time used shall count.

(c) Commencement of laytime (loading and discharging)

Laytime for loading and discharging shall commence at 13.00 hours, if notice of readiness is given up to and including 12.00 hours, and at 06.00 hours next working day if notice given during office hours after 12.00 hours. Notice of

10. Bills of Lading

Bills of Lading shall be presented and signed by the Master as per the "Congenbill" Bill of Lading form, Edition 1994, without prejudice to this Charter Party, or by the Owners' agents provided written authority has been given by Owners to the agents, a copy of which is to be furnished to the Charterers. The Charterers shall indemnify the Owners against all consequences or liabilities that may arise from the signing of bills of lading as presented to the extent that the terms or contents of such bills of lading impose or result in the imposition of more onerous liabilities upon the Owners than those assumed by the Owners under this Charter Party.

11. Both-to-Blame Collision Clause

If the Vessel comes into collision with another vessel as a result of the negligence of the other vessel and any act, neglect or default of the Master, Mariner, Pilot or the servants of the Owners in the navigation or in the management of the Vessel, the owners of the cargo carried hereunder will indemnify the Owners against all loss or liability to the other or non-carrying vessel or her owners in so far as such loss or liability represents loss of, or damage to, or any claim whatsoever of the owners of said cargo, paid or payable by the other or non-carrying vessel or her owners to the owners of said cargo and set-off, recouped or recovered by the other or non-carrying vessel or her owners as part of their claim against the carrying Vessel or the Owners.

The foregoing provisions shall also apply where the owners, operators or those in charge of any vessel or vessels or objects other than, or in addition to, the colliding vessels or objects are at fault in respect of a collision or contact.

12. General Average and New Jason Clause

General Average shall be adjusted in London unless otherwise agreed in Box 22 according to York-Antwerp Rules 1994 and any subsequent modification thereof. Proprietors of cargo to pay the cargo's share in the general expenses even if same have been necessitated through neglect or default of the Owners' servants (see Clause 2).

If General Average is to be adjusted in accordance with the law and practice of the United States of America, the following Clause shall apply: "In the event of accident, danger, damage or disaster before or after the commencement of the voyage, resulting from any cause whatsoever, whether due to negligence or not, for which, or for the consequence of which, the Owners are not responsible, by statute, contract or otherwise, the cargo shippers, consignees or the owners of the cargo shall contribute with the Owners in General Average to the payment of any sacrifices, losses or expenses of a General Average nature that may be made or incurred and shall pay salvage and special charges incurred in respect of the cargo. If a salving vessel is owned or operated by the Owners, salvage shall be paid for as fully as if the said salving vessel or vessels belonged to strangers. Such deposit as the Owners, or their agents, may deem sufficient to cover the estimated contribution of the goods and any salvage and special charges thereon shall, if required, be made by the cargo, shippers, consignees or owners of the goods to the Owners before delivery.".

13. Taxes and Dues Clause

(a) On Vessel -The Owners shall pay all dues, charges and taxes customarily levied on the Vessel, howsoever the amount thereof may be assessed.

(b) On cargo -The Charterers shall pay all dues, charges, duties and taxes customarily levied on the cargo, howsoever the amount thereof may be assessed.

(c) On freight -Unless otherwise agreed in Box 23, taxes levied on the freight shall be for the Charterers' account.

PART II
"Gencon" Charter (As Revised 1922, 1976 and 1994)

14. Agency
In every case the Owners shall appoint their own Agent both at the port of loading and the port of discharge. 207 208 209

15. Brokerage 210
A brokerage commission at the rate stated in Box 24 on the freight, dead-freight and demurrage earned is due to the party mentioned in Box 24. 211 212
In case of non-execution 1/3 of the brokerage on the estimated amount of freight to be paid by the party responsible for such non-execution to the Brokers as indemnity for the latter's expenses and work. In case of more voyages the amount of indemnity to be agreed. 213 214 215 216

16. General Strike Clause 217
(a) If there is a strike or lock-out affecting or preventing the actual loading of the cargo, or any part of it, when the Vessel is ready to proceed from her last port or at any time during the voyage to the port or ports of loading or after her arrival there, the Master or the Owners may ask the Charterers to declare, that they agree to reckon the laydays as if there were no strike or lock-out. Unless the Charterers have given such declaration in writing (by telegram, if necessary) within 24 hours, the Owners shall have the option of cancelling this Charter Party. If part cargo has already been loaded, the Owners must proceed with same, (freight payable on loaded quantity only) having liberty to complete with other cargo on the way for their own account. 218 219 220 221 222 223 224 225 226 227
(b) If there is a strike or lock-out affecting or preventing the actual discharging of the cargo on or after the Vessel's arrival at or off port of discharge and same has not been settled within 48 hours, the Charterers shall have the option of keeping the Vessel waiting until such strike or lock-out is at an end against paying half demurrage after expiration of the time provided for discharging until the strike or lock-out terminates and thereafter full demurrage shall be payable until the completion of discharging, or of ordering the Vessel to a safe port where she can safely discharge without risk of being detained by strike or lock-out. Such orders to be given within 48 hours after the Master or the Owners have given notice to the Charterers of the strike or lock-out affecting the discharge. On delivery of the cargo at such port, all conditions of this Charter Party and of the Bill of Lading shall apply and the Vessel shall receive the same freight as if she had discharged at the original port of destination, except that if the distance to the substituted port exceeds 100 nautical miles, the freight on the cargo delivered at the substituted port to be increased in proportion. 228 229 230 231 232 233 234 235 236 237 238 239 240 241 242 243
(c) Except for the obligations described above, neither the Charterers nor the Owners shall be responsible for the consequences of any strikes or lock-outs preventing or affecting the actual loading or discharging of the cargo. 244 245 246

17. War Risks ("Voywar 1993") 247
(1) For the purpose of this Clause, the words: 248
(a) The "Owners" shall include the shipowners, bareboat charterers, disponent owners, managers or other operators who are charged with the management of the Vessel, and the Master; and 249 250 251
(b) "War Risks" shall include any war (whether actual or threatened), act of war, civil war, hostilities, revolution, rebellion, civil commotion, warlike operations, the laying of mines (whether actual or reported), acts of piracy, acts of terrorists, acts of hostility or malicious damage, blockades (whether imposed against all Vessels or imposed selectively against 252 253 254 255 256

(5) The Vessel shall have liberty:- 314
(a) to comply with all orders, directions, recommendations or advice as to departure, arrival, routes, sailing in convoy, ports of call, stoppages, destinations, discharge of cargo, delivery or in any way whatsoever which are given by the Government of the Nation under whose flag the Vessel sails, or other Government to whose laws the Owners are subject, or any other Government which so requires, or any body or group acting with the power to compel compliance with their orders or directions; 315 316 317 318 319 320 321
(b) to comply with the orders, directions or recommendations of any war risks underwriters who have the authority to give the same under the terms of the war risks insurance; 322 323 324
(c) to comply with the terms of any resolution of the Security Council of the United Nations, any directives of the European Community, the effective orders of any other Supranational body which has the right to issue and give the same, and with national laws aimed at enforcing the same to which the Owners are subject, and to obey the orders and directions of those who are charged with their enforcement; 325 326 327 328 329 330
(d) to discharge at any other port any cargo or part thereof which may render the Vessel liable to confiscation as a contraband carrier; 331 332
(e) to call at any other port to change the crew or any part thereof or other persons on board the Vessel when there is reason to believe that they may be subject to internment, imprisonment or other sanctions; 333 334 335
(f) where cargo has not been loaded or has been discharged by the Owners under any provisions of this Clause, to load other cargo for the Owners' own benefit and carry it to any other port or ports whatsoever, whether backwards or forwards or in a contrary direction to the ordinary or customary route. 336 337 338 339 340
(6) If in compliance with any of the provisions of sub-clauses (2) to (5) of this Clause anything is done or not done, such shall not be deemed to be a deviation, but shall be considered as due fulfilment of the Contract of Carriage. 341 342 343 344

18. General Ice Clause 345
Port of loading 346
(a) In the event of the loading port being inaccessible by reason of ice when the Vessel is ready to proceed from her last port or at any time during the voyage or on the Vessel's arrival or in case frost sets in after the Vessel's arrival, the Master for fear of being frozen in is at liberty to leave without cargo, and this Charter Party shall be null and void. 347 348 349 350 351
(b) If during loading the Master, for fear of the Vessel being frozen in, deems it advisable to leave, he has liberty to do so with what cargo he has on board and to proceed to any other port or ports with option of completing cargo for the Owners' benefit for any port or ports including port of discharge. Any part cargo thus loaded under this Charter Party to be forwarded to destination at the Vessel's expense but against payment of freight, provided that no extra expenses be thereby caused to the Charterers, freight being paid on quantity delivered (in proportion if lumpsum), all other conditions as per this Charter Party. 352 353 354 355 356 357 358 359 360
(c) In case of more than one loading port, and if one or more of the ports are closed by ice, the Master or the Owners to be at liberty either to load the part cargo at the open port and fill up elsewhere for their own account as under section (b) or to declare the Charter Party null and void unless the Charterers agree to load full cargo at the open port. 361 362 363 364 365

Vessels of certain flags or ownership, or against certain cargoes or crews 257
or otherwise howsoever), by any person, body, terrorist or political group, 258
or the Government of any state whatsoever, which, in the reasonable 259
judgement of the Master and/or the Owners, may be dangerous or are 260
likely to be or to become dangerous to the Vessel, her cargo, crew or other 261
persons on board the Vessel. 262

(2) If at any time before the Vessel commences loading, it appears that, in the 263
reasonable judgement of the Master and/or the Owners, performance of 264
the Contract of Carriage, or any part of it, may expose, or is likely to expose, 265
the Vessel, her cargo, crew or other persons on board the Vessel to War 266
Risks, the Owners may give notice to the Charterers cancelling this 267
Contract of Carriage, or may refuse to perform such part of it as may 268
expose, or may be likely to expose, the Vessel, her cargo, crew or other 269
persons on board the Vessel to War Risks; provided always that if this 270
Contract of Carriage provides that loading or discharging is to take place 271
within a range of ports, and at the port or ports nominated by the Charterers 272
the Vessel, her cargo, crew, or other persons onboard the Vessel may be 273
exposed, or may be likely to be exposed, to War Risks, the Owners shall 274
first require the Charterers to nominate any other safe port which lies 275
within the range for loading or discharging, and may only cancel this 276
Contract of Carriage if the Charterers shall not have nominated such safe 277
port or ports within 48 hours of receipt of notice of such requirement. 278

(3) The Owners shall not be required to continue to load cargo for any voyage, 279
or to sign Bills of Lading for any port or place, or to proceed or continue on 280
any voyage, or on any part thereof, or to proceed through any canal or 281
waterway, or to proceed to or remain at any port or place whatsoever, 282
where it appears, either after the loading of the cargo commences, or at 283
any stage of the voyage thereafter before the discharge of the cargo is 284
completed, that, in the reasonable judgement of the Master and/or the 285
Owners, the Vessel, her cargo (or any part thereof), crew or other persons 286
on board the Vessel (or any one or more of them) may be, or are likely to be, 287
exposed to War Risks. If it should so appear, the Owners may by notice 288
request the Charterers to nominate a safe port for the discharge of such 289
cargo or any part thereof, and if within 48 hours of the receipt of such 290
notice, the Charterers shall not have nominated such a port, the Owners 291
may discharge the cargo at any safe port of their choice (including the port 292
of loading) in complete fulfilment of the Contract of Carriage. The Owners 293
shall be entitled to recover from the Charterers the extra expenses of such 294
discharge and, if the discharge takes place at any port other than the 295
loading port, to receive the full freight as though the cargo had been 296
carried to the discharging port and if the extra distance exceeds 100 miles, 297
to additional freight which shall be the same percentage of the freight 298
contracted for as the percentage which the extra distance represents to 299
the distance of the normal and customary route, the Owners having a lien 300
on the cargo for such expenses and freight. 301

(4) If at any stage of the voyage after the loading of the cargo commences, it 302
appears that, in the reasonable judgement of the Master and/or the 303
Owners, the Vessel, her cargo, crew or other persons on board the Vessel 304
may be, or are likely to be, exposed to War Risks on any part of the route 305
(including any canal or waterway) which is normally and customarily used 306
in a voyage of the nature contracted for, and there is another longer route 307
to the discharging port, the Owners shall give notice to the Charterers that 308
this route will be taken. In this event the Owners shall be entitled, if the total 309
extra distance exceeds 100 miles, to additional freight which shall be the 310
same percentage of the freight contracted for as the percentage which the 311
extra distance represents to the distance of the normal and customary 312
route. 313

Port of discharge 366

(a) Should ice prevent the Vessel from reaching port of discharge the 367
Charterers shall have the option of keeping the Vessel waiting until the re- 368
opening of navigation and paying demurrage or of ordering the Vessel to a safe 369
and immediately accessible port where she can safely discharge without risk of 370
detention by ice. Such orders to be given within 48 hours after the Master or the 371
Owners have given notice to the Charterers of the impossibility of reaching port 372
of destination. 373

(b) If during discharging the Master for fear of the Vessel being frozen in deems 374
it advisable to leave, he has liberty to do so with what cargo he has on board and 375
to proceed to the nearest accessible port where she can safely discharge. 376

(c) On delivery of the cargo at such port, all conditions of the Bill of Lading shall 377
apply and the Vessel shall receive the same freight as if she had discharged at 378
the original port of destination, except that if the distance of the substituted port 379
exceeds 100 nautical miles, the freight on the cargo delivered at the substituted 380
port to be increased in proportion. 381

19. Law and Arbitration 382

* (a) This Charter Party shall be governed by and construed in accordance with 383
English law and any dispute arising out of this Charter Party shall be referred to 384
arbitration in London in accordance with the Arbitration Acts 1950 and 1979 or 385
any statutory modification or re-enactment thereof for the time being in force. 386
Unless the parties agree upon a sole arbitrator, one arbitrator shall be 387
appointed by each party and the arbitrators so appointed shall appoint a third 388
arbitrator, the decision of the three-man tribunal thus constituted or any two of 389
them, shall be final. On the receipt by one party of the nomination in writing of 390
the other party's arbitrator, that party shall appoint their arbitrator within 391
fourteen days, failing which the decision of the single arbitrator appointed shall 392
be final. 393

For disputes where the total amount claimed by either party does not exceed 394
the amount stated in Box 25** the arbitration shall be conducted in accordance 395
with the Small Claims Procedure of the London Maritime Arbitrators 396
Association. 397

* (b) This Charter Party shall be governed by and construed in accordance with 398
Title 9 of the United States Code and the Maritime Law of the United States and 399
should any dispute arise out of this Charter Party, the matter in dispute shall be 400
referred to three persons at New York, one to be appointed by each of the 401
parties hereto, and the third by the two so chosen; their decision or that of any 402
two of them shall be final, and for purpose of enforcing any award, this 403
agreement may be made a rule of the Court. The proceedings shall be 404
conducted in accordance with the rules of the Society of Maritime Arbitrators, 405
Inc. 406

For disputes where the total amount claimed by either party does not exceed 407
the amount stated in Box 25** the arbitration shall be conducted in accordance 408
with the Shortened Arbitration Procedure of the Society of Maritime Arbitrators, 409
Inc. 410

* (c) Any dispute arising out of this Charter Party shall be referred to arbitration at 411
the place indicated in Box 25, subject to the procedures applicable there. The 412
laws of the place indicated in Box 25 shall govern this Charter Party. 413

(d) If Box 25 in Part I is not filled in, sub-clause (a) of this Clause shall apply. 414

* (a), (b) and (c) are alternatives; indicate alternative agreed in Box 25. 415

** Where no figure is supplied in Box 25 in Part I, this provision only shall be void but 416
the other provisions of this Clause shall have full force and remain in effect. 417

Issued July 1987

Code word for this Charter Party

"SHELLVOY 5"

Voyage Charter Party

LONDON,   19

PREAMBLE

IT IS THIS DAY AGREED between   1

of   2

(hereinafter referred to as "Owners") being owners/disponent owners of the   3

motor/steam tank vessel called   4

(hereinafter referred to as "the vessel")   5

and   of   6

(hereinafter referred to as "Charterers")   7

that the service for which provision is herein made shall be subject to the terms and conditions of this charter   8
which includes Part I and Part II. In the event of any conflict between the provisions of Part I and Part II hereof,   9
the provisions of Part I shall prevail.   10

PART I   11

(A) Description of vessel   Owners guarantee that at the date hereof the vessel:-   12
    13

    (i)   Is classed   14

    (ii)   Has a deadweight of   tonnes (1000 kg.) on a salt-water draft on assigned summer freeboard   15
        of   m.   16

    (iii)   Has a capacity available for the cargo of   tonnes (1000 kg.) 5% more or less in Owners'   17
        option.   18

(iv)	Is fully fitted with heating systems for all cargo tanks capable of maintaining cargo at a temperature of up to _____ degrees Celsius.	19 20
(v)	Has tanks coated as follows:-	21
(vi)	Is equipped with cranes/derricks capable of lifting to and supporting at the vessel's port and starboard manifolds submarine hoses of up to _____ tonnes (1000 kg.) in weight.	22 23
(vii)	Has cargo pumps capable of discharging a full cargo within _____ hours or maintaining a back pressure of _____ at the vessel's manifold (provided shore facilities permit and the cargo does not have a kinematic viscosity exceeding 600 centistokes at the discharge temperature required by Charterers).	24 25 26 27
(viii)	Has or will have carried the following three cargoes immediately prior to loading under this charter:-	28
	Last	29
	2.	30
	3.	31
(ix)	Has a crude oil washing system complying with the requirements of the International Convention for the Prevention of Pollution from Ships 1973 as modified by the Protocol of 1978 ("MARPOL 73/78").	32 33
(x)	Has an operational inert gas system.	34
(xi)	Has on board all papers and certificates required by any applicable law, in force as at the date of this charter, to enable the vessel to perform the charter service without any delay.	35 36
(xii)	Is entered in _____ P&I Club.	37
(B) Position/ Readiness	Now _____ Expected ready to load	38 39
(C) Laydays	Commencing Noon Local Time on _____ (Commencement Date)	40
	Terminating Noon Local Time on _____ (Termination Date)	41

Issued July 1987

PART I

                                                      "SHELLVOY 5"

                                                          PAGE 2

(D) Loading Port(s)/ Range   one or more ports at Charterers' option   42 43 44

(E) Discharging Port(s)/ Range   one or more ports at Charterers' option   45 46 47

(F) Cargo description   Charterers' option   48 49

Maximum temperature on loading   degrees Celsius   50

(G) Freight rate   At   % of the rate for the voyage as provided for in the Worldwide Tanker Nominal Freight Scale current at the date of commencement of loading (hereinafter referred to as "Worldscale") per ton (2240lbs)/tonne (1000Kg).   51 52 53

(H) Freight payable to   54 55

(I) Laytime   running hours   56

(J) Demurrage per day (or pro rata)   57 58 59

(K) ETAs	All radio messages sent by the master to Charterers shall be addressed to	60
(L) Special provisions		61 62
Signatures	**IN WITNESS WHEREOF**, the parties have caused this charter consisting of the Preamble, Parts I and II to be executed as of the day and year first above written.	63 64
	By	65
	By	66

Issued July 1987

"SHELLVOY 5"

PART II

Condition of vessel

1.   Owners shall exercise due diligence to ensure that from the time when the obligation to proceed to the loading port(s) attaches and throughout the charter service –

(a)   the vessel and her hull, machinery, boilers, tanks, equipment and facilities are in good order and condition and in every way equipped and fit for the service required; and

(b)   the vessel has a full and efficient complement of master, officers and crew;

and to ensure that before and at the commencement of any laden voyage the vessel is in all respects fit to carry the cargo specified in Part I(F).

Cleanliness of tanks

2.   Whilst loading, carrying and discharging cargo the master shall at all times use due diligence to keep the tanks, lines and pumps of the vessel clean for the cargo specified in Part I(F). It shall be for the master alone to decide whether the vessel's tanks, lines and pumps are suitably clean. However, the decision of the master shall be without prejudice to the right of Charterers, should any contamination or damage subsequently be found, to contend that the same was caused by inadequate cleaning and/or some breach of this or any other Clause of this charter.

Voyage

3.   Subject to the provisions of this charter the vessel shall perform her service with utmost despatch and shall proceed to such berths as Charterers may specify, in any port or ports within Part I(D) nominated by Charterers, or so near thereunto as she may safely get and there, always safely afloat, load a full cargo, but not in excess of the maximum quantity consistent with the International Load Line Convention for the time being in force and, being so loaded, proceed as ordered on signing bills of lading to such berths as Charterers may specify, in any port or ports within Part I(E) nominated by Charterers, or so near thereunto as she may safely get and there, always safely afloat, discharge the cargo.

Charterers shall nominate loading and discharging ports, and shall specify loading and discharging berths, in sufficient time to avoid delay or deviation to the vessel. Subject to the foregoing, and provided it does not cause delay or deviation to the vessel, Charterers shall have the option of ordering the vessel to safe areas at sea for wireless orders.

In this charter, "berth" means any berth, wharf, dock, anchorage, submarine line, a position alongside any vessel or lighter or any other loading or discharging point whatsoever to which Charterers are entitled to order the vessel hereunder, and "port" means any port or location at sea to which the vessel may proceed in accordance with the terms of this charter.

Safe berth

4.   Charterers shall exercise due diligence to order the vessel only to ports and berths which are safe for the vessel and to ensure that transhipment operations conform to standards not less than those set out in the latest edition of ICS/OCIMF Ship-to-Ship Transfer Guide (Petroleum). Notwithstanding anything contained in this charter, Charterers do not warrant the safety of any port, berth or transhipment operation and Charterers shall

not be liable for loss or damage arising from any unsafety if they can prove that due diligence was exercised in the giving of the order. — 100, 101

Freight

5. Freight shall be earned concurrently with delivery of cargo at the nominated discharging port or ports and shall be paid by Charterers to Owners without any deductions in United States Dollars at the rate(s) specified in Part I(G) on the gross Bill of Lading quantity as furnished by the shipper (subject to Clauses 8 and 40), upon receipt by Charterers of notice of completion of final discharge of cargo, provided that no freight shall be payable on any quantity in excess of the maximum quantity consistent with the International Load Line Convention for the time being in force. — 102, 103, 104, 105, 106, 107

If the vessel is ordered to proceed on a voyage for which a fixed differential is provided in Worldscale, such fixed differential shall be payable without applying the percentage referred to in Part I(G). — 108, 109

If cargo is carried between ports and/or by a route for which no freight rate is expressly quoted in Worldscale, then the parties shall, in the absence of agreement as to the appropriate freight rate, apply to Worldscale Association (London) Ltd., or Worldscale Association (NYC) Inc, for the determination of an appropriate Worldscale freight rate. — 110, 111, 112, 113

Save in respect of the time when freight is earned, the location of any transhipment at sea pursuant to Clause 26(2) shall not be an additional nominated port for the purposes of this charter (including this Clause 5) and the freight rate for the voyage shall be the same as if such transhipment had not taken place. — 114, 115, 116

Dues and other charges

6. Dues and other charges upon the vessel, including those assessed by reference to the quantity of cargo loaded or discharged, and any taxes on freight whatsoever shall be paid by Owners, and dues and other charges upon the cargo shall be paid by Charterers. However, notwithstanding the foregoing, where under a provision of Worldscale a due or charge is expressly for the account of Owners or Charterers then such due or charge shall be payable in accordance with such provision. — 117, 118, 119, 120, 121

Loading and discharging cargo

7. The cargo shall be loaded into the vessel at the expense of Charterers and, up to the vessel's permanent hose connections, at Charterers' risk. The cargo shall be discharged from the vessel at the expense of Owners and, up to the vessel's permanent hose connections, at Owners' risk. Owners shall, unless otherwise notified by Charterers or their agents, supply at Owners' expense all hands, equipment and facilities required on board for mooring and unmooring and connecting and disconnecting hoses for loading and discharging. — 122, 123, 124, 125, 126

Deadfreight

8. Charterers need not supply a full cargo, but if they do not freight shall nevertheless be paid as if the vessel had been loaded with a full cargo. — 127, 128

The term "full cargo" as used throughout this charter means a cargo which, together with any collected washings (as defined in Clause 40) retained on board pursuant to the requirements of MARPOL 73/78, fills the vessel to either her applicable deadweight or her capacity stated in Part I(A)(iii), whichever is less, while leaving sufficient space in the tanks for the expansion of cargo. — 129, 130, 131, 132

Shifting

9.   Charterers shall have the right to require the vessel to shift at ports of loading and/or discharging from a loading or discharging berth within port limits and back to the same or to another such berth once or more often on payment of all additional expenses incurred. For the purposes of freight payment and shifting the places grouped in Port and Terminal Combinations in Worldscale are to be considered as berths within a single port. If at any time before cargo operations are completed it becomes dangerous for the vessel to remain at the specified berth as a result of wind or water conditions, Charterers shall pay all additional expenses of shifting from any such berth and back to that or any other specified berth within port limits (except to the extent that any fault of the vessel contributed to such danger).   133 134 135 136 137 138 139 140

Subject to Clause 14(a) and (c) time spent shifting shall count against laytime or if the vessel is on demurrage for demurrage.   141 142

Charterers' failure to give orders

10.   If the vessel is delayed due to Charterers' breach of Clause 3 Charterers shall, subject to the terms hereof, compensate Owners in accordance with Clause 15(1) and (2) as if such delay were time exceeding the laytime.   143 144 145

The period of such delay shall be calculated   146

(i)   from 6 hours after Owners notify Charterers that the vessel is delayed awaiting nomination of loading port until such nomination has been received by Owners, or   147 148

(ii) from 6 hours after the vessel gives notice of readiness at the loading port until commencement of loading   149 150

as the case may be, subject always to the same exceptions as those set out in Clause 14. Any period of delay in respect of which Charterers pay compensation pursuant to this Clause 10 shall be excluded from any calculation of time for laytime or demurrage made under any other Clause of this charter.   151 152 153

Periods of delay hereunder shall be cumulative for each port, and Owners may demand compensation after the vessel has been delayed for a total of 20 running days, and thereafter after each succeeding 5 running days of delay and at the end of any delay. Each such demand shall show the period in respect of which compensation is claimed and the amount due. Charterers shall pay the full amount due within 14 days after receipt of Owners' demand. Should Charterers fail to make any such payments Owners shall have the right to terminate this charter by giving written notice to Charterers or their agents, without prejudice to any claims which Charterers or Owners may have against each other under this charter or otherwise.   154 155 156 157 158 159 160

Laydays/ Termination

11.   Should the vessel not be ready to load by noon local time on the termination date set out in Part I(C) Charterers shall have the option of terminating this charter unless the vessel has been delayed due to Charterers' change of orders pursuant to Clause 26, in which case the laydays shall be extended by the period of such delay.   161 162 163 164

However, if Owners reasonably conclude that, despite the exercise of due diligence, the vessel will not be ready to load by noon on the termination date, Owners may, as soon as they are able to state with reasonable certainty a new date when the vessel will be ready, give notice to Charterers declaring the new readiness date and asking Charterers to elect whether or not to terminate this charter. Unless Charterers within 4 days after such   165 166 167 168 notice or within 2 days after the termination date (whichever is earlier) declare this charter terminated, Part I(C) shall be deemed to be amended such that the new readiness date stated shall be the commencement date and the second day thereafter shall be the termination date. [169] [170] [171]

The provisions of this Clause and the exercise or non-exercise by Charterers of their option to terminate shall not prejudice any claims which Charterers or Owners may have against each other. [172] [173]

Laytime

12. The laytime for loading, discharging and all other Charterers' purposes whatsoever shall be the number of running hours specified in Part I(I). Charterers shall have the right to load and discharge at all times, including night, provided that they shall pay for all extra expenses incurred ashore. [174] [175] [176]

Notice of readiness/ Running time

13. (1) Subject to the provisions of Clauses 13(3) and 14, if the vessel loads or discharges cargo other than by transhipment at sea [177] [178] [179]

(a) Time at each loading or discharging port shall commence to run 6 hours after the vessel is in all respects ready to load or discharge and written notice thereof has been tendered by the master or Owners' agents to Charterers or their agents and the vessel is securely moored at the specified loading or discharging berth. However, if the vessel does not proceed immediately to such berth time shall commence to run 6 hours after (i) the vessel is lying in the area where she was ordered to wait or, in the absence of any such specific order, in a usual waiting area and (ii) written notice of readiness has been tendered and (iii) the specified berth is accessible. A loading or discharging berth shall be deemed inaccessible only for so long as the vessel is or would be prevented from proceeding to it by bad weather, tidal conditions, ice, awaiting daylight pilot or tugs, or port traffic control requirements (except those requirements resulting from the unavailability of such berth or of the cargo). [180] [181] [182] [183] [184] [185] [186] [187] [188] [189] [190]

If Charterers fail to specify a berth at any port, the first berth at which the vessel loads or discharges the cargo or any part thereof shall be deemed to be the specified berth at such port for the purposes of this Clause. [191] [192] [193]

Notice shall not be tendered before commencement of laydays and notice tendered by radio shall qualify as written notice provided it is confirmed in writing as soon as reasonably possible. [194] [195] [196]

(b) Time shall continue to run [197] [198]

(i) until cargo hoses have been disconnected, or

(ii) if the vessel is delayed for Charterers' purposes for more than one hour after disconnection of cargo hoses, until the termination of such delay provided that if the vessel waits at any place other than the berth, time on passage to such other place, from disconnecting of hoses to remooring/anchorage at such other place, shall not count. [199] [200] [201] [202]

(2) If the vessel loads or discharges cargo by transhipment at sea time shall count from the arrival of the vessel at the transhipment area or from commencement of the laydays, whichever is later, and, subject to Clause 14(c), shall run until transhipment has been completed and the vessels have separated.

(3) Notwithstanding anything else in this Clause 13, if Charterers start loading or discharging the vessel before time would otherwise start to run under this charter, time shall run from commencement of such loading or discharging.

(4) For the purposes of this Clause 13 and of Clause 14 "time" shall mean laytime or time counting for demurrage, as the case may be.

Suspension of time

14. Time shall not count when

(a) spent on inward passage from the vessel's waiting area to the loading or discharging berth specified by Charterers, even if lightening occurred at such waiting area; or

(b) spent in handling ballast except to the extent that cargo operations are carried on concurrently and are not delayed thereby; or

(c) lost as a result of
  (i) breach of this Charter by Owners; or
  (ii) any cause attributable to the vessel, including breakdown or inefficiency of the vessel; or
  (iii) strike, lock-out, stoppage or restraint of labour of master, officers or crew of the vessel or tug boats or pilot.

Demurrage

15. (1) Charterers shall pay demurrage at the rate specified in Part I(J).

If the demurrage rate specified in Part I(J) is expressed as a percentage of Worldscale such percentage shall be applied to the demurrage rate applicable to vessels of a similar size to the vessel as provided in Worldscale or, for the purpose of clause 10 and/or if this charter is terminated prior to the commencement of loading, in the Worldwide Tanker Nominal Freight Scale current at the termination date specified in Part I(C).

Demurrage shall be paid per running day or pro rata for part thereof for all time which, under the provisions of this charter, counts against laytime or for demurrage and which exceeds the laytime specified in Part I(I). Charterers' liability for exceeding the laytime shall be absolute and shall not in any case be subject to the provisions of Clause 32.

(2) If, however, all or part of such demurrage arises out of or results from fire or explosion at ports of loading and/or discharging in or about the plant of Charterers, shippers or consignees of the cargo (not being a fire or explosion caused by the negligence or wilful act or omission of Charterers, shippers or consignees of the cargo or their respective servants or agents), act of God, act of war, riot, civil commotion, or arrest or restraint of princes rulers or peoples, the rate of demurrage shall be reduced by half for such demurrage or such part thereof.

(3)   Owners shall notify Charterers within 60 days after completion of discharge if demurrage has been incurred and any demurrage claim together with supporting documentation shall be submitted within 90 days after completion of discharge. If Owners fail to give notice of or to submit any such claim within the time limits aforesaid, Charterers' liability for such demurrage shall be extinguished.

Vessel inspection

16.   Charterers shall have the right, but no duty, to have a representative attend on board the vessel at any loading and/or discharging ports (except locations at sea) and the master and Owners shall co-operate to facilitate his inspection of the vessel and observation of cargo operations. However, such right, and the exercise or non-exercise thereof, shall in no way reduce the master's or Owners' authority over, or responsibility to Charterers and third parties for, the vessel and every aspect of her operation, nor increase Charterers' responsibilities to Owners or third parties for the same.

Cargo inspection

17.   Without prejudice to Clause 2 hereof, Charterers shall have the right to require inspection of the vessel's tanks at loading and/or discharging ports (except locations at sea) to ascertain the quantity and quality of the cargo, water and residues on board. Depressurisation of the tanks to permit inspection and/or ullaging shall be carried out in accordance with the recommendations in the latest edition of the International Safety Guide for Oil Tankers and Terminals. Charterers shall also have the right to inspect and take samples from the bunker tanks and other non-cargo spaces. Any delay to the vessel caused by such inspection and measurement or associated depressurising/repressurising of tanks shall count against laytime, or if the vessel is on demurrage, for demurrage.

Cargo measurement

18.   The master shall ascertain the contents of all tanks before and after loading and before and after discharging, and shall prepare tank-by-tank ullage reports of the cargo, water and residues on board which shall be promptly made available to Charterers or their representative if requested. Each such ullage report shall show actual ullage/dips, and densities at observed and standard temperature (15°Celsius). All quantities shall be expressed in cubic metres at both observed and standard temperature.

Inert gas

19.   The vessel's inert gas system (if any) shall comply with Regulation 62, Chapter II-2 of the 1974 Safety of Life at Sea Convention as modified by the Protocol of 1978 and Owners warrant that such system shall be operated in accordance with the guidance given in the IMO publication "Inert Gas Systems (1983)". Should the inert gas system fail, Section 8 (Emergency Procedures) of the said IMO publication shall be strictly adhered to and time lost as a consequence of such failure shall not count against laytime or, if the vessel is on demurrage, for demurrage.

Crude oil washing

20.   If the vessel is equipped for crude oil washing Charterers shall have the right to require the vessel to crude oil wash those tanks in which the cargo is carried. If crude oil washing is required by Charterers or any competent authority, any additional discharging time thereby incurred shall count against laytime or, if the vessel is on demurrage, for demurrage, and the number of hours specified in Part I(A)(vii) shall be increased by 0.75 hours per cargo tank washed.

237
238
239
240
241
242
243
244
245
246
247
248
249
250
251
252
253
254
255
256
257
258
259
260
261
262
263
264
265
266
267
268
269

Over age insurance	21. Any additional insurance on the cargo required because of the age of the vessel shall be for Owners' account.
Ice	22. The vessel shall not be required to force ice or to follow icebreakers. If the master finds that a nominated port is inaccessible due to ice, the master shall immediately notify Charterers requesting revised orders and shall remain outside the ice-bound area; and if after arrival at a nominated port there is danger of the vessel being frozen in, the vessel shall proceed to the nearest safe and ice free position and at the same time request Charterers to give revised orders.

In either case if the affected port is

(i) the first or only loading port and no cargo has been loaded, Charterers shall either nominate another port, or give notice cancelling this charter in which case they shall pay at the demurrage rate in Part I(J) for the time from the master's notification aforesaid or from notice of readiness on arrival, as the case may be, until the time such cancellation notice is given;

(ii) a loading port and part of the cargo has been loaded, Charterers shall either nominate another port, or order the vessel to proceed on the voyage without completing loading in which case Charterers shall pay for any deadfreight arising therefrom;

(iii) a discharging port, Charterers shall either nominate another port or order the vessel to proceed to or return to and discharge at the nominated port. If the vessel is ordered to proceed to or return to a nominated port, Charterers shall bear the risk of the vessel being damaged whilst proceeding to or returning to or at such port, and the whole period from the time when the master's request for revised orders is received by Charterers until the vessel can safely depart after completion of discharge shall count against laytime or, if the vessel is on demurrage, for demurrage.

If, as a consequence of Charterers revising orders pursuant to this clause, the nominated port(s) or the number or rotation of ports is changed freight, shall nevertheless be paid for the voyage which the vessel would otherwise have performed had the orders not been so revised, such freight to be increased or reduced by the amount by which, as a result of such revision of orders,

(a) the time used including any time awaiting revised orders (which shall be valued at the demurrage rate in Part I(J)),

(b) the bunkers consumed (which shall be valued at the bunker costs at the port at which bunkers were last taken) and

(c) the port charges

for the voyage actually performed are greater or less than those that would have been incurred on the voyage which, but for the revised orders under this Clause, the vessel would have performed.

Quarantine	23. Time lost due to quarantine shall not count against laytime or for demurrage unless such quarantine was in force at the time when the affected port was nominated by Charterers.

270
271

272
273
274
275
276

277
278
279
280
281
282
283
284
285
286
287
288
289
290

291
292
293
294
295
296
297
298
299
300
301

302
303

Agency

24. The vessel's agents shall be nominated by Charterers at nominated ports of loading and discharging. 304

Such agents, although nominated by Charterers, shall be employed and paid by Owners. 305

Charterers' obligation at shallow draft port/ Lightening in port

25. (1) (a) If the vessel, with the quantity of cargo then on board, is unable due to inadequate depth of water in the port safely to reach any specified discharging berth and discharge the cargo there always safely afloat, Charterers shall specify a location within port limits where the vessel can discharge sufficient cargo into vessels or lighters to enable the vessel safely to reach and discharge cargo at such discharging berth, and the vessel shall lighten at such location. 306 307 308 309 310

(b) If the vessel is lightened pursuant to Clause 25(1)(a) then, for the purposes of the calculation of laytime and demurrage, the lightening place shall be treated as the first discharging berth within the port where such lightening occurs. 311 312 313

Charterers' orders/ Change of orders/ Part cargo transhipment

26. (1) If, after loading and/or discharging ports have been nominated, Charterers wish to vary such nominations or their rotation, Charterers may give revised orders subject to Part I(D) and/or (E), as the case may be. Charterers shall reimburse Owners at the demurrage rate provided in Part I(J) for any deviation or delay which may result therefrom and shall pay at replacement price for any extra bunkers consumed. 314 315 316 317

Charterers shall not be liable for any other loss or expense which is caused by such variation unless promptly on receipt of the revised orders Owners notify Charterers of the expectation of such loss or expense in which case, unless Charterers promptly revoke such orders, Charterers shall be liable to reimburse Owners for any such loss or expense proven. 318 319 320 321

(2) Subject to Clause 33(6), Charterers may order the vessel to load and/or discharge any part of the cargo by transhipment at sea in the vicinity of any nominated port or en route between two nominated ports, in which case Charterers shall reimburse Owners at the demurrage rate specified in Part I(J) for any additional steaming time and/or delay which may be incurred as a consequence of proceeding to and from the location at sea of such transhipment and, in addition, Charterers shall pay at replacement price for any extra bunkers consumed. 322 323 324 325 326

Heating of cargo

27. If Charterers require cargo heating the vessel shall, on passage to and whilst at discharging port(s), maintain the cargo at the loaded temperature or at the temperature stated in Part I(A)(iv), whichever is the lower. Charterers may request that the temperature of the cargo be raised above or lowered below that at which it was loaded, in which event Owners shall use their best endeavours to comply with such request and Charterers shall pay at replacement price for any additional bunkers consumed and any consequential delay to the vessel shall count against laytime or, if the vessel is on demurrage, for demurrage. 327 328 329 330 331 332

ETA

28. Owners undertake that, unless Charterers require otherwise, the master shall:

(a) advise Charterers by radio immediately on leaving the final port of call on the previous voyage or within 48 hours after the time and date of this charter, whichever is the later, of the time and date of the vessel's expected arrival at the first loading port or, if the loading range is in the Arabian Gulf, the time of her expected arrival off Quoin Island;

(b) confirm or amend such advice not later than 72 hours and again not later than 24 hours before the vessel is due at the first loading port or, in the case of a loading range in the Arabian Gulf, off Quoin Island;

(c) advise Charterers by radio immediately after departure from the final loading port, of the vessel's expected time of arrival at the first discharging port or the area at sea to which the vessel has been instructed to proceed for wireless orders, and confirm or amend such advice not later than 72 hours and again not later than 24 hours before the vessel is due at such port or area;

(d) immediately radio any variation of more than six hours from expected times of arrival at loading or discharging ports, Quoin Island or such area at sea to Charterers;

(e) address all radio messages in accordance with Part I(K).

Owners shall be responsible for any consequences or additional expenses arising as a result of non-compliance with this Clause.

Packed cargo

29. Charterers have the option of shipping products and/or general cargo in available dry cargo space, the quantity being subject to the master's discretion. Freight shall be payable at the bulk rate in accordance with Clause 5 and Charterers shall pay in addition all expenses incurred solely as a result of the packed cargo being carried. Delay occasioned to the vessel by the exercise of such option shall count against laytime or, if the vessel is on demurrage, for demurrage.

Subletting/ Assignment

30. Charterers shall have the option of sub-chartering the vessel and/or of assigning this charter to any person or persons, but Charterers shall always remain responsible for the due fulfilment of all the terms and conditions of this charter.

Liberty

31. The vessel shall be at liberty to tow or be towed, to assist vessels in all positions of distress, to call at any port or ports for bunkers, to sail without pilots, and to deviate for the purpose of saving life or property or for the purpose of embarking or disembarking persons spares or supplies by helicopter or for any other reasonable purpose.

Exceptions

32. (a) The vessel, her master and Owners shall not, unless otherwise in this charter expressly provided, be liable for any loss or damage or delay or failure arising or resulting from any act, neglect or default of the master, pilots, mariners or other servants of Owners in the navigation or management of the vessel; fire unless caused by the actual fault or privity of Owners; collision or stranding; dangers and accidents of the sea; explosion, bursting of boilers, breakage of shafts or any latent defect in hull, equipment or machinery; provided, however, that Part I(A) and Clauses 1 and 2 hereof shall be unaffected by the foregoing. Further, neither the vessel, her master or Owners, nor Charterers shall, unless otherwise in this charter expressly provided, be liable for any loss

or damage or delay or failure in performance hereunder arising or resulting from act of God, act of war, act of public enemies, seizure under legal process, quarantine restrictions, strikes, lock-outs, restraints of labour, riots, civil commotions or arrest or restraint of princes rulers or people.

(b) Nothing in this charter shall be construed as in any way restricting, excluding or waiving the right of Owners or of any other relevant persons to limit their liability under any available legislation or law.

(c) Clause 32(a) shall not apply to or affect any liability of Owners or the vessel or any other relevant person in respect of

(i) loss of or damage caused to any berth, jetty, dock, dolphin, buoy, mooring line, pipe or crane or other works or equipment whatsoever at or near any port to which the vessel may proceed under this charter, whether or not such works or equipment belong to Charterers, or

(ii) any claim (whether brought by Charterers or any other person) arising out of any loss of or damage to or in connection with the cargo. Any such claim shall be subject to the Hague-Visby Rules or the Hague Rules, as the case may be, which ought pursuant to Clause 37 hereof to have been incorporated in the relevant bill of lading (whether or not such Rules were so incorporated), or, if no such bill of lading is issued, to the Hague-Visby Rules.

Bills of lading

33. (1) Subject to the provisions of this Clause Charterers may require the master to sign lawful bills of lading for any cargo in such form as Charterers direct.

(2) The signing of bills of lading shall be without prejudice to this charter and Charterers hereby indemnify Owners against all liabilities that may arise from signing bills of lading to the extent that the same impose liabilities upon Owners in excess of or beyond those imposed by this charter.

(3) All bills of lading presented to the master for signature, in addition to complying with the requirements of Clauses 35, 36 and 37, shall include or effectively incorporate clauses substantially similar to the terms of Clauses 22, 33(7) and 34.

(4) All bills of lading presented for signature hereunder shall show a named port of discharge. If when bills of lading are presented for signature discharging port(s) have been nominated hereunder, the discharging port(s) shown on such bills of lading shall be in conformity with the nominated port(s). If at the time of such presentation no such nomination has been made hereunder, the discharging port(s) shown on such bills of lading must be within Part I(E) and shall be deemed to have been nominated hereunder by virtue of such presentation.

(5) Article III Rules 3 and 5 of the Hague-Visby Rules shall apply to the particulars included in the bills of lading as if Charterers were the shippers, and the guarantee and indemnity therein contained shall apply to the description of the cargo furnished by or on behalf of Charterers.

  (6) Notwithstanding any other provisions of this charter, Owners shall not be obliged to comply with 402
any orders from Charterers to discharge all or part of the cargo 403
   (i) at any port other than that shown on the bills of lading (except as provided in Clauses 22 or 404
    34) and/or 405
   (ii) without presentation of an original bill of lading 406
unless they have received from Charterers both written confirmation of such orders and an indemnity acceptable 407
to Owners. 408

  (7) The master shall not be required or bound to sign bills of lading for any blockaded port or for any 409
port which the master or Owners in his or their discretion consider dangerous or impossible to enter or reach. 410

  (8) Charterers hereby warrant that on each and every occasion that they issue orders under Clauses 411
22, 26, 34 or 38 they will have the authority of the holders of the bills of lading to give such orders, and that such 412
bills of lading will not be transferred to any person who does not concur therein. 413

War risks 34. (1) If 414
   (a) any loading or discharging port to which the vessel may properly be ordered under the 415
    provisions of this charter or bills of lading issued pursuant to this charter be blockaded, or 416
   (b) owing to any war, hostilities, warlike operation, civil commotions, revolutions, or the 417
    operation of international law (i) entry to any such loading or discharging port or the loading 418
    or discharging of cargo at any such port be considered by the master or Owners in his or their 419
    discretion dangerous or prohibited or (ii) it be considered by the master or Owners in his or 420
    their discretion dangerous or impossible or prohibited for the vessel to reach any such 421
    loading or discharging port. 422
Charterers shall have the right to order the cargo or such part of it as may be affected to be loaded or discharged at 423
any other loading or discharging port within the ranges specified in Part I(D) or (E) respectively (provided such 424
other port is not blockaded and that entry thereto or loading or discharging of cargo thereat or reaching the same 425
is not in the master's or Owners' opinion dangerous or impossible or prohibited). 426

  (2) If no orders be received from Charterers within 48 hours after they or their agents have received 427
from Owners a request for the nomination of a substitute port, then 428
   (a) if the affected port is the first or only loading port and no cargo has been loaded, this charter 429
    shall terminate forthwith; 430
   (b) if the affected port is a loading port and part of the cargo has already been loaded, 431
    the vessel may proceed on passage and Charterers shall pay for any deadfreight so 432
    incurred; 433

(c) if the affected port is a discharging port, Owners shall be at liberty to discharge the cargo at any port which they or the master may in their or his discretion decide on (whether within the range specified in Part I(E) or not) and such discharging shall be deemed to be due fulfilment of the contract or contracts of affreightment so far as cargo so discharged is concerned.

(3) If in accordance with Clause 34(1) or (2) cargo is loaded or discharged at any such other port, freight shall be paid as for the voyage originally nominated. such freight to be increased or reduced by the amount by which, as a result of loading or discharging at such other port,

(a) the time on voyage including any time awaiting revised orders (which shall be valued at the demurrage rate in Part I(J)).

(b) the bunkers consumed (which shall be valued at the bunker costs at the port at which bunkers were last taken), and

(c) the port charges

for the voyage actually performed are greater or less than those which would have been incurred on the voyage originally nominated Save as aforesaid, the voyage actually performed shall be treated for the purpose of this Charter as if it were the voyage originally nominated.

(4) The vessel shall have liberty to comply with any directions or recommendations as to departure, arrival, routes, ports of call, stoppages, destinations, zones, waters, delivery or in any otherwise whatsoever given by the government of the nation under whose flag the vessel sails or any other government or local authority including any de facto government or local authority or by any person or body acting or purporting to act as or with the authority of any such government or authority or by any committee or person having under the terms of the war risks insurance on the vessel the right to give any such directions or recommendations. If by reason of or in compliance with any such directions or recommendations anything is done or is not done. such shall not be deemed a deviation.

If by reason of or in compliance with any such directions or recommendations the vessel does not proceed to the discharging port or ports originally nominated or to which she may have been properly ordered under the provisions of this charter or bills of lading issued pursuant to this charter. the vessel may proceed to any discharging port on which the master or Owners in his or their discretion may decide and there discharge the cargo. Such discharging shall be deemed to be due fulfilment of the contract or contracts of affreightment and Owners shall be entitled to freight as if discharging had been effected at the port or ports originally nominated or to which the vessel may have been properly ordered under the provisions of this charter or bills of lading issued pursuant to this charter. All extra expenses involved in reaching and discharging the cargo at any such other discharging port shall be paid by Charterers and Owners shall have a lien on the cargo for all such extra expenses.

Both to blame clause

35.   If the liability for any collision in which the vessel is involved while performing this charter falls to be determined in accordance with the laws of the United States of America, the following clause, which shall be included in all bills of lading issued pursuant to this charter shall apply:–   467 468 469

"If the vessel comes into collision with another vessel as a result of the negligence of the other vessel and any act, neglect or default of the master, mariner, pilot or the servants of the Carrier in the navigation or in the management of the vessel, the owners of the cargo carried hereunder will indemnify the Carrier against all losses or liability to the other or non-carrying vessel or her owners in so far as such loss or liability represents loss of, or damage to, or any claim whatsoever of the owners of the said cargo, paid or payable by the other or non-carrying vessel or her owners to the owners of the said cargo and set off, recouped or recovered by the other or non-carrying vessel or her owners as part of their claim against the carrying vessel or the Carrier.   470 471 472 473 474 475 476

The foregoing provisions shall also apply where the owners, operators or those in charge of any vessel or vessels or objects other than, or in addition to, the colliding vessels or objects are at fault in respect of a collision or contact."   477 478 479

General average/ New Jason Clause

36.   General average shall be payable according to the York/Antwerp Rules, 1974, and shall be adjusted in London, but should the adjustment be made in accordance with the law and practice of the United States of America, the following clause, which shall be included in all bills of lading issued pursuant to this charter, shall apply:–   480 481 482 483

"In the event of accident, danger, damage or disaster before or after the commencement of the voyage, resulting from any cause whatsoever, whether due to negligence or not, for which, or for the consequence of which, the Carrier is not responsible, by statute, contract or otherwise, the cargo, shippers, consignees or owners of the cargo shall contribute with the Carrier in general average to the payment of any sacrifices, losses or expenses of a general average nature that may be made or incurred and shall pay salvage and special charges incurred in respect of the cargo.   484 485 486 487 488 489

If a salving vessel is owned or operated by the Carrier, salvage shall be paid for as fully as if the said salving vessel or vessels belonged to strangers. Such deposit as the Carrier or its agents may deem sufficient to cover the estimated contribution of the cargo and any salvage and special charges thereon shall, if required, be made by the cargo, shippers, consignees or owners of the cargo to the Carrier before delivery."   490 491 492 493

Clause paramount

37.   The following clause shall be included in all bills of lading issued pursuant to this charter:–   494 495 496

"CLAUSE PARAMOUNT

(1)   Subject to sub-clause (2) hereof, this bill of lading shall be governed by, and have effect subject to, the rules contained in the International Convention for the Unification of Certain Rules relating to Bills of Lading signed at Brussels on 25th August 1924 (hereafter the "Hague Rules") as amended by the Protocol signed   497 498 499

at Brussels on 23rd February 1968 (hereafter the "Hague-Visby Rules"). Nothing herein contained shall be deemed to be either a surrender by the Carrier of any of his rights or immunities or an increase of any of his responsibilities or liabilities under the Hague-Visby Rules. — 500 / 501 / 502

(2) If there is governing legislation which applies the Hague Rules compulsorily to this bill of lading, to the exclusion of the Hague-Visby Rules, then this bill of lading shall have effect subject to the Hague Rules. Nothing herein contained shall be deemed to be either a surrender by the Carrier of any of his rights or immunities or an increase of any of his responsibilities or liabilities under the Hague Rules. — 503 / 504 / 505 / 506

(3) If any term of this bill of lading is repugnant to the Hague-Visby Rules, or the Hague Rules if applicable, such term shall be void but no further. — 507 / 508

(4) Nothing in this bill of lading shall be construed as in any way restricting, excluding or waiving the right of any relevant party or person to limit his liability under any available legislation and/or law." — 509 / 510

Back loading

38. Charterers may order the vessel to load a part cargo at any nominated discharging port, and to discharge such part cargo at a port(s) to be nominated by Charterers within the range specified in Part I(E) and within the rotation of the discharging ports previously nominated, provided that such part cargo is of the description specified in Part I(F) and that the master in his absolute discretion determines that this cargo can be loaded, segregated and discharged without risk of contamination by, or of, any other cargo remaining on board. — 511 / 512 / 513 / 514 / 515

Charterers shall pay a lump sum freight in respect of such part cargo calculated at the demurrage rate specified in Part I(J) on any additional time used by the vessel as a result of loading, carrying or discharging such part cargo. — 516 / 517 / 518

Any additional expenses, including port charges, incurred as a result of loading or discharging such part cargo shall be for Charterers' account. — 519 / 520

Bunkers

39. Owners shall give Charterers or any other company in the Royal Dutch/Shell Group of Companies first option to quote for the supply of bunker requirements for the performance of this charter. — 521 / 522

Oil pollution prevention

40. (1) Owners shall ensure that the master shall:- — 523

(a) comply with MARPOL 73/78 including in particular and without limitation Regulation 9, Chapter II of the International Convention for the Prevention of Pollution from Ships 1973; — 524 / 525

(b) collect the drainings and any tank washings into a suitable tank or tanks and, after maximum separation of free water, discharge the bulk of such water overboard, consistent with the above regulations; and — 526 / 527 / 528

(c) thereafter notify Charterers promptly of the amounts of oil and free water so retained on board and details of any other washings retained on board from earlier voyages (together called the "collected washings"). — 529 / 530 / 531

(2) On being so notified, Charterers, in accordance with their rights under this Clause (which shall include without limitation the right to determine the disposal of the collected washings), shall before the vessel's arrival at the loading berth (or if already arrived as soon as possible thereafter) give instructions as to how the collected washings shall be dealt with. Owners shall ensure that the master on the vessel's arrival at the loading berth (or if already arrived as soon as possible thereafter) shall arrange in conjunction with the cargo suppliers for the measurement of the quantity of the collected washings and shall record the same in the vessel's ullage record.	532 533 534 535 536 537 538
(3) Charterers may require the collected washings to be discharged ashore at the loading port, in which case no freight shall be payable on them.	539 540
(4) Alternatively Charterers may require either that the cargo be loaded on top of the collected washings and the collected washings be discharged with the cargo, or that they be kept separate from the cargo in which case Charterers shall pay for any deadfreight incurred thereby in accordance with Clause 8 and shall, if practicable, accept discharge of the collected washings at the discharging port or ports.	541 542 543 544
In either case, provided that the master has reduced the free water in the collected washings to a minimum consistent with the retention on board of the oil residues in them and consistent with sub-Clause (1)(a) above, freight in accordance with Clause 5 shall be payable on the quantity of the collected washings as if such quantity were included in a bill of lading and the figure therefor furnished by the shipper provided, however, that	545 546 547 548
(i) if there is provision in this charter for a lower freight rate to apply to cargo in excess of an agreed quantity, freight on the collected washings shall be paid at such lower rate (provided such agreed quantity of cargo has been loaded) and	549 550 551
(ii) if there is provision in this charter for a minimum cargo quantity which is less than a full cargo, then whether or not such minimum cargo quantity is furnished, freight on the collected washings shall be paid as if such minimum cargo quantity had been furnished, provided that no freight shall be payable in respect of any collected washings which are kept separate from the cargo and not discharged at the discharge port.	552 553 554 555 556
(5) Whenever Charterers require the collected washings to be discharged ashore pursuant to this Clause, Charterers shall provide and pay for the reception facilities, and the cost of any shifting therefor shall be for Charterers' account. Any time lost discharging the collected washings and/or shifting therefor shall count against laytime or, if the vessel is on demurrage, for demurrage.	557 558 559 560

TOVALOP

41. Owners warrant that the vessel:	561
(i) is a tanker owned by a Participating Owner in TOVALOP	562
and	563
(ii) is entered in the P&I Club stated in Part I(A)(xii)	564
and will so remain during the currency of this charter.	565

When an escape or discharge of Oil occurs from the vessel and causes or threatens to cause Pollution Damage, or when there is the Threat of an escape or discharge of Oil (i.e. a grave and imminent danger of the escape or discharge of Oil which, if it occurred, would create a serious danger of Pollution Damage, whether or not an escape or discharge in fact subsequently occurs), then Charterers may, at their option upon notice to Owners or master, undertake such measures as are reasonably necessary to prevent or minimise such Pollution Damage or to remove the Threat, unless Owners promptly undertake the same. Charterers shall keep Owners advised of the nature and result of any such measures taken by them and, if time permits, the nature of the measures intended to be taken by them. Any of the aforementioned measures taken by Charterers shall be deemed taken on Owners' authority and as Owners' agents, and shall be at Owners' expense except to the extent that:

(1) any such escape or discharge or Threat was caused or contributed to by Charterers, or
(2) by reason of the exceptions set out in Article III, paragraph 2, of the 1969 International Convention on Civil Liability for Oil Pollution Damage or any protocol thereto, Owners are or, had the said Convention applied to such escape or discharge or to the Threat, would have been, exempt from liability for the same, or
(3) the cost of such measures together with all other liabilities, costs and expenses of Owners arising out of or in connection with such escape or discharge or Threat exceeds the maximum liability applicable to the vessel under TOVALOP as at the time of such escape or discharge or threat, save and insofar as Owners shall be entitled to recover such excess under either the 1971 International Convention on the Establishment of an International Fund for Compensation for Oil Pollution Damage or under CRISTAL

PROVIDED ALWAYS that if Owners in their absolute discretion consider said measures should be discontinued, Owners shall so notify Charterers and thereafter Charterers shall have no right to continue said measures under the provisions of this Clause and all further liability to Charterers under this Clause shall thereupon cease.

The above provisions are not in derogation of such other rights as Charterers or Owners may have under this charter or may otherwise have or acquire by law or any international convention or TOVALOP.

The term ''TOVALOP'' means the Tanker Owners' Voluntary Agreement Concerning Liability for Oil Pollution dated 7th January 1969, as amended from time to time, and the term ''CRISTAL'' means the Contract Regarding an Interim Supplement to Tanker Liability for Oil Pollution dated 14th January 1971, as amended from time to time. The terms ''Participating Owner'', ''Oil'' and, ''Pollution Damage'' shall for the purposes of this clause have the meanings ascribed to them in TOVALOP.

Lien

42. Owners shall have an absolute lien upon the cargo and all subfreights for all amounts due under this charter and the cost of recovery thereof including any expenses whatsoever arising from the exercise of such lien.

566
567
568
569
570
571
572
573
574
575
576
577
578
579
580
581
582
583
584
585
586

587
588
589
590

591
592

593
594
595
596
597

598
599

Law and litigation

43. (a)   This charter shall be construed and the relations between the parties determined in accordance with the laws of England.

(b)   any dispute arising under this charter shall be decided by the English Courts to whose jurisdiction the parties hereby agree.

(c)   Notwithstanding the foregoing, but without prejudice to any party's right to arrest or maintain the arrest of any maritime property, either party may, by giving written notice of election to the other party, elect to have any such dispute referred to the arbitration of a single arbitrator in London in accordance with the provisions of the Arbitration Act 1950, or any statutory modification or re-enactment thereof for the time being in force.

(i)   A party shall lose its right to make such an election only if:
   (a)   it receives from the other party a written notice of dispute which –
     (1) states expressly that a dispute has arisen out of this charter;
     (2) specifies the nature of the dispute; and
     (3) refers expressly to this clause 43(c) and;
   (b)   it fails to give notice of election to have the dispute referred to arbitration not later than 30 days from the date of receipt of such notice of dispute.

(ii)   the parties hereby agree that either party may –
   (a)   appeal to the High Court on any question of law arising out of an award;
   (b)   apply to the High Court for an order that the arbitrator state the reasons for his award;
   (c)   give notice to the arbitrator that a reasoned award is required; and
   (d)   apply to the High Court to determine any question of law arising in the course of the reference.

(d)   It shall be a condition precedent to the right of any party to a stay of any legal proceedings in which maritime property has been, or may be, arrested in connection with a dispute under this charter, that that party furnishes to the other party security to which that other party would have been entitled in such legal proceedings in the absence of a stay.

Construction

44.   The side headings have been included in this charter for convenience of reference only and shall in no way affect the construction hereof.

600
601
602
603
604
605
606
607
608
609
610
611
612
613
614
615
616
617
618
619
620
621
622
623
624
625
626
627

SHELL February 1999 amendments/additions/deletions to SHELLVOY 5 Charter Party Issued July 1987

Part I

Delete (A) Description of vessel line 12 and insert:

"(A) 1 – Description of vessel – Owners guarantee that at the date hereof, and from the time when the obligation to proceed to the loadport(s) attaches, the vessel"

(iii) delete and insert: "Has capacity for cargo of _____ m3"

(vii) delete and insert: "Discharges a full cargo (whether homogenous or multi grade) within 24 hours or can maintain a back pressure of 100 PSI at the vessel's manifold and Owners guarantee such minimum performance provided shore facilities permit. The discharge guarantee shall only be applicable provided the kinematic viscosity does not exceed 600 centistokes at the discharge temperature required by Charterers. If the kinematic viscosity only exceeds 600 centistokes on part of the cargo or particular grade(s) then the discharge guarantee shall continue to apply to all other cargo/grades."

(xii) delete and insert: "Is entered in the .... P&I Club, being a member of the International Group of P&I Clubs."

Insert (A) 11: "Maintenance/Restoration – throughout the Charter service, Owners shall ensure that the vessel shall be maintained, or that they shall take all steps necessary to promptly restore vessel to be, within the description in Part I(A)1 and any questionnaires requested by Charterers or within information provided by Owners."

(G) Insert in line 51: "New" before "Worldwide Tanker Nominal Freight Scale".

(K) ETAs –

Each Charterer to insert own instruction here.

.... for STASCO (as Charterers) use:

"STASCO LONDON OTS/141 TELEX G919651 SHEL A G or G94016255 OTS G, copied to other parties as advised in Charterers' voyage instructions."

All telexes must begin with the vessel name at the start of the subject line (no inverted commas, or use of MT/SS preceding the vessel name).

Part II

Clause 1 – Condition of vessel – delete and insert:

"Owners shall exercise due diligence to ensure that from the time when the obligation to proceed to the loading port(s) attaches and throughout the charter service –

(a) the vessel and her hull, machinery, boilers, tanks, equipment and facilities are in good order and condition and in every way equipped and fit for the service required; and

(b) the vessel has a full and efficient complement of master, officers and crew;

and to ensure that before and at the commencement of any laden voyage the vessel is in all respects fit to carry the cargo specified in Part I(F). For the avoidance of doubt, references to equipment in this Charter shall include but not be limited to computers and computer systems, and such equipment shall (inter alia) be required (i) to continue to function, and not suffer a loss of functionality and accuracy (whether logical or mathematical) as a result of the run date or dates being processed, irrespective of the century in which the dates fall, and (ii) to recognise the year 2000 as a leap year and accept 29 February 2000 as a valid date."

Clause 2 – Cleanliness of tanks – delete and insert:

"Whilst loading, carrying and discharging the cargo the Master shall at all times keep the tanks, lines and pumps of the vessel always clean for the cargo. Unless otherwise agreed between Owners and Charterers the vessel shall present for loading with cargo tanks ready and subject to following paragraphs, if vessel fitted with Inert Gas System (IGS), fully inerted.

Charterers shall have the right to inspect vessel's tanks prior to loading and the vessel shall abide by Charterers' instructions with regard to tank or tanks which the vessel is required to present ready for entry and inspection. If Charterers' inspector is not satisfied with the cleanliness of the vessel's tanks, Owners shall clean them in their time and at their expense to the satisfaction of Charterers' inspector, provided that nothing herein shall affect the responsibilities and obligations of the Master and Owners in respect of the loading, carriage and care of cargo under this Charter nor prejudice the rights of Charterers, should any contamination or damage subsequently be found, to contend that the same was caused by inadequate cleaning and/or some breach of this or any other clause of this Charter.

Notwithstanding that the vessel, if equipped with IGS, shall present for loading with all cargo tanks fully inerted, any time used for de-inerting (provided that such de-inerting takes place after laytime or demurrage time has commenced or would, but for this clause, have commenced) and/or re-inerting those tanks that at Charterers' specific request were gas freed for inspection, shall count as laytime or if on demurrage for demurrage, provided the tank or tanks inspected found to be suitable.

If the vessel's tanks are inspected and rejected, time used for de-inerting shall not count towards laytime or demurrage, and laytime or demurrage time shall not commence or recommence, as the case may be, until the tanks have been re-inspected, approved by Charterers' inspector, and re-inerted."

Clause 3 Voyage – delete 2nd paragraph lines 88–91 and insert:

"Charterers shall nominate loading and discharging ports, and shall specify loading and discharging berths. In addition Charterers shall have the option at any time of ordering the vessel to safe areas at sea for wireless orders. Any delay or deviation arising as a result of the exercise of such option shall be compensated by Charterers in accordance with the terms of Clause 26(1)."

Clause 4 Safe berth – add to end of line 101:

"or if such loss or damage was caused by an act of war or civil commotion within the trading areas defined in Part 1 (D/E)."

Clause 8 Deadfreight – add at end of line 132:

"If under Part I(F) vessel is chartered for a minimum quantity and the vessel is unable to load such quantity due to having reached her capacity as stated in Part I(A)1(iii), always leaving sufficient space for expansion of cargo, then without prejudice to any claims which Charterers may have against Owners, no deadfreight between the quantity loaded and the quantity shown in Part I(F) shall be due."

Clause 13 – Notice of readiness/Running time

Delete in line 177/178 words "if the vessel loads or discharges cargo other than by transhipment at sea".

Insert in line 189 a "comma" between "daylight" and "pilot".

Clause (b) – delete and insert:

"Time shall:

(i) Continue to run until the cargo hoses have been disconnected.

(ii) Recommence two hours after disconnection of hoses if the vessel is delayed for Charterers' purposes and shall continue until the termination of such delay provided that if the vessel waits at any place other than the berth, any time or part of the time on passage to such other place that occurs after two hours from disconnection of hoses shall not count."

(2) Delete and insert:

"If the vessel loads or discharges cargo by transhipment at sea time shall commence in accordance with Clause 13(1)(a) as amended, and run until transhipment has been completed and the vessels have separated, always subject to Clause 14."

Clause 15 Demurrage

(1) Insert in line 226 "New" before "Worldwide Tanker Nominal Freight Scale".

(2) Insert in line 231 after explosion "or strike or failure/breakdown of plant and/or machinery".

(3) Delete and insert:

"Owners shall notify Charterers within 60 days after completion of discharge if demurrage has been incurred and any demurrage claim shall be fully and correctly documented, and received by Charterers, within 90 days after completion of discharge. If Owners fail to give notice of or to submit any such claim with documentation, as required herein, within the limits aforesaid, Charterers' liability for such demurrage shall be extinguished."

Clause 20 Crude oil washing – delete and insert:

"If the vessel is equipped for crude oil washing Charterers shall have the right to require the vessel to crude oil wash, concurrently with discharge, those tanks in which Charterers' cargo is carried. If crude oil washing is required by Charterers or any competent authority, any additional discharge time thereby incurred, always subject to the next succeeding sentences, shall count against laytime or, if the vessel is on demurrage, for demurrage. The number of hours specified in Part I(A)1(vii) as amended shall be increased by 0.6 hours per cargo tank washed, always subject to a maximum increase of 8 hours. If vessel fails to maintain 100 PSI throughout the discharge then any time over 24 hours, plus the additional discharge performance allowance under this clause, shall not count as laytime or demurrage, if on demurrage. This does not reduce Owners' liability for vessel to perform her service with utmost despatch."

Clause 32 Exceptions – delete (ii) and insert:

"any claim (whether brought by Charterers or any other person) arising out of any loss of or damage to or in connection with the cargo. Any such claim shall be subject to The Hague-Visby Rules or The Hague Rules or the Hamburg Rules as the case may be, which ought pursuant to Clause 37 hereof to have been incorporated in the relevant bill of lading (whether or not such Rules were so incorporated), or if no such bill of lading is issued to The Hague-Visby Rules unless the Hamburg Rules compulsorily apply in which case to the Hamburg Rules."

Clauses 36 General average/New Jason Clause – delete first paragraph and insert:

"General average shall be payable according to the York/Antwerp Rules as amended 1994 and shall be adjusted in London. All disputes relating to General Average shall be resolved in London in accordance with English Law. Without prejudice to the foregoing, should the adjustment be made in accordance with the Law and practice of the United States of America the following clause, which shall be included in all Bills of Lading issued pursuant to this Charter, shall apply."

Clause 37 Clause paramount – delete and insert:

"The following clause shall be included in all bills of lading issued pursuant to this charter:

(1) Subject to sub-clauses (2) or (3) hereof, this bill of lading shall be governed by, and have effect subject to, the rules contained in the International Convention for the Unification of Certain Rules relating to Bills of Lading signed at Brussels on 25th August 1924 (hereafter the "Hague Rules") as amended by the Protocol signed at Brussels on 23rd February 1968 (hereafter The "Hague-Visby Rules"). Nothing contained herein shall be deemed to be either a surrender by the carrier of any of his rights or immunities or any increase of any of his responsibilities or liabilities under the Hague-Visby Rules.

(2) If there is governing legislation which applies the Hague Rules compulsorily to this bill of lading, to the exclusion of the Hague-Visby Rules, then this bill of lading shall have effect subject to the Hague Rules. Nothing herein contained shall be deemed to be either a surrender by the carrier of any of his rights or immunities or an increase of any of his responsibilities or liabilities under the Hague Rules.

(3) If there is governing legislation which applies the Hamburg Rules compulsorily to this Bill of Lading to the exclusion of the Hague-Visby Rules, then this Bill of Lading shall have effect subject to the Hamburg Rules. Nothing herein contained shall be deemed to be either a surrender by the carrier of any of his rights or immunities or an increase of any of his responsibilities or liabilities under the Hamburg Rules.

(4) If any term of this bill of lading is repugnant to the Hague-Visby Rules, or Hague Rules or Hamburg Rules, if applicable, such term shall be void to that extent but no further.

(5) Nothing in this bill of lading shall be construed as in any way restricting, excluding or waiving the right of any relevant party or person to limit his liability under any available legislation and/or law."

Clause 38 Backloading – delete and insert:

"Charterers may order the vessel to discharge and/or backload a part or full cargo at any nominated port within the loading/discharging ranges specified within Part I(D/E) and within the rotation of the ports previously nominated, provided that any cargo loaded is of the description specified in Part I(F) and that the Master in his reasonable discretion determines that the cargo can be loaded, segregated and discharged without risk of contamination by, or of any other cargo.

Charterers shall pay in respect of loading, carrying and discharging such cargo as follows:

(1) A lumpsum freight calculated at the demurrage rate specified in Part I(J) on any additional port time used by the vessel; and

(2) any additional expenses, including port charges incurred, and

(3) if the vessel is fixed on a Worldscale rate in Part I(G) then freight shall always be paid for the whole voyage at the rate(s) specified in Part I(G) on the largest cargo quantity carried on any ocean leg."

Clause 40 (1) Oil pollution prevention

Insert new sub paragraph (d) "Not to load on top of such 'collected washing' without specific instructions from Charterers"

Clause 41 TOVALOP – delete and insert:

"ITOPF Clause

Owners warrant that throughout the duration of this Charter the vessel will be:

(i) owned or demise chartered by a member of the 'International Tanker Owners Pollution Federation Limited', and

(ii) entered in the Protection and Indemnity (P&I) Club stated in Part I(A)1(xii) as amended."

Clause 43 Law and litigation – delete in line 607 "Arbitration Act 1950" and insert "Arbitration Act 1996".

PART I

THE BALTIC AND INTERNATIONAL MARITIME CONFERENCE
UNIFORM TIME-CHARTER (Box Layout 1974)
CODE NAME: "BALTIME 1939"

1. Shipbroker

2. Place and date

3. Owners/Place of business

4. Charterers/Place of business

5. Vessel's name

6. GRT/NRT

7. Class

8. Indicated horse power

9. Total tons d.w. (abt.) on Board of Trade summer freeboard

10. Cubic feet grain/bale capacity

11. Permanent bunkers (abt.)

12. Speed capability in knots (abt.) on a consumption in tons (abt.) of

13. Present position

14. Period of hire (Cl. 1)

15. Port of delivery (Cl. 1)

16. Time of delivery (Cl. 1)

17. (a) Trade limits (Cl. 2)

Adopted by
the Documentary Committee of the Chamber
of Shipping of the United Kingdom
and the Documentary Committee of The Japan
Shipping Exchange, Inc.

Issued ²/₃/1909
Amended ¹³/₃/1911
Amended ⁴/₃/1912
Amended ¹³/₃/1920
Amended ¹/₃/1939
Amended ¹/₁/1950
Amended ¹/₁/1974

(b) Cargo exclusions specially agreed

18. Bunkers on re-delivery (state min. and max. quantity) (Cl. 5)

19. Charter hire (Cl. 6)

20. Hire payment (state currency, method and place of payment; also beneficiary and bank account) (Cl. 6)

21. Place or range of re-delivery (Cl. 7)

22. War (only to be filled in if Section (C) agreed) (Cl. 21)

23. Cancelling date (Cl. 22)

24. Place of arbitration (only to be filled in if place other than London agreed) (Cl. 23)

25. Brokerage commission and to whom payable (Cl. 25)

26. Numbers of additional clauses covering special provisions, if agreed

It is mutually agreed that this Contract shall be performed subject to the conditions contained in this Charter which shall include Part I as well as Part II. In the event of a conflict of conditions, the provisions of Part I shall prevail over those of Part II to the extent of such conflict.

Signature (Owners)

Signature (Charterers)

Printed and sold by Fr. G. Knudtzon Ltd., 55, Toldbodgade, Copenhagen, by authority of The Baltic and International Maritime Conference, Copenhagen.

40-0

Copyright, published by The Baltic and International Maritime Conference, Copenhagen

PART II
"BALTIME 1939" Uniform Time-Charter (Box Layout 1974)

It is agreed between the party mentioned in Box 3 as Owners of the Vessel named in Box 5 of the gross/net Register tonnage indicated in Box 6, classed as stated in Box 7 and of indicated horse power as stated in Box 8, carrying about the number of tons deadweight indicated in Box 9 on Board of Trade summer freeboard inclusive of bunkers, stores, provisions and boiler water, having as per builder's plan a cubic-feet grain/bale capacity as stated in Box 10, exclusive of permanent bunkers, which contain about the number of tons stated in Box 11, and fully loaded capable of steaming about the number of knots indicated in Box 12 in good weather and smooth water on a consumption of about the number of tons best Welsh coal or oil-fuel stated in Box 12, now in position as stated in Box 13 and the party mentioned as Charterers in Box 4, as follows: (1–16)

1. Period/Port of Delivery/Time of Delivery
The Owners let, and the Charterers hire the Vessel for a period of the number of calendar months indicated in Box 14 from the time (not a Sunday or a legal Holiday unless taken over) the Vessel is delivered and placed at the disposal of the Charterers between 9 a.m. and 6 p.m., or between 9 a.m. and 2 p.m. if on Saturday, at the port stated in Box 15 in such available berth where she can safely lie always afloat, as the Charterers may direct, she being in every way fitted for ordinary cargo service. The Vessel to be delivered at the time indicated in Box 16. (17–27)

2. Trade
The Vessel to be employed in lawful trades for the carriage of lawful merchandise only between good and safe ports or places where she can safely lie always afloat within the limits stated in Box 17.
No live stock nor injurious, inflammable or dangerous goods (such as acids, explosives, calcium carbide, ferro silicon, naphtha, motor spirit, tar, or any of their products) to be shipped. (28–36)

3. Owners to Provide
The Owners to provide and pay for all provisions and wages, for insurance of the Vessel, for all deck and engine-room stores and maintain her in a thoroughly efficient state in hull and machinery during service. The Owners to provide one winchman per hatch. If further winchmen are required, or if the stevedores refuse or are not permitted to work with the Crew, the Charterers to provide and pay qualified shore-winchmen. (37–45)

4. Charterers to Provide
The Charterers to provide and pay for all coals including galley coal, oil-fuel, water for boilers, port charges, pilotages (whether compulsory or not), canal steersmen, boatage, lights, tug-assistance, consular charges (except those pertaining to the Master, Officers and Crew), canal, dock and other dues and charges, including any foreign general municipality or state taxes, also all dock, harbour and tonnage dues at the ports of delivery and re-delivery (unless incurred through cargo carried before delivery or (46–55)

8. Cargo Space
The whole reach and burthen of the Vessel, including lawful deck-capacity to be at the Charterers' disposal, reserving proper and sufficient space for the Vessel's Master, Officers, Crew, tackle, apparel, furniture, provisions and stores. (113–118)

9. Master
The Master to prosecute all voyages with the utmost despatch and to render customary assistance with the Vessel's Crew. The Master to be under the orders of the Charterers as regards employment, agency, or other arrangements. The Charterers to indemnify the Owners against all consequences or liabilities arising from the Master, Officers or Agents signing Bills of Lading or other documents or otherwise complying with such orders, as well as from any irregularity in the Vessel's papers or for overcarrying goods. The Owners not to be responsible for shortage, mixture, marks, nor for number of pieces or packages, nor for damage to or claims on cargo caused by bad stowage or otherwise. If the Charterers have reason to be dissatisfied with the conduct of the Master, Officers, or Engineers, the Owners, on receiving particulars of the complaint, promptly to investigate the matter, and, if necessary and practicable, to make a change in the appointments. (119–137)

10. Directions and Logs
The Charterers to furnish the Master with all instructions and sailing directions and the Master and Engineer to keep full and correct logs accessible to the Charterers or their Agents. (138–142)

11. Suspension of Hire etc.
(A) In the event of drydocking or other necessary measures to maintain the efficiency of the Vessel, deficiency of men or Owners' stores, break-down of machinery, damage to hull or other accident, either hindering or preventing the working of the Vessel and continuing for more than twenty-four consecutive hours, no hire to be paid in respect of any time lost thereby during the period in which the Vessel is unable to perform the service immediately required. Any hire paid in advance to be adjusted accordingly.
(B) In the event of the Vessel being driven into port or to anchorage through stress of weather, trading to shallow harbours or to rivers or ports with bars or suffering an accident to her cargo, any detention of the Vessel and/or expenses resulting from such detention to be for the Charterers' account even if such detention and/or expenses, or the cause by reason of which either is incurred, be due to, or be contributed to by, the negligence of the Owners' servants. (143–162)

12. Cleaning Boilers
Cleaning of boilers whenever possible to be done during service, but if impossible the Charterers to give the Owners necessary time for cleaning. Should the Vessel (163–166)

overtime paic to Officers and Crew according to the hours and rates stated in the Vessel's articles. (224–225)

18. Lien
The Owners to have a lien upon all cargoes and sub-freights belonging to the Time-Charterers and any Bill of Lading freight for all claims under this Charter, and the Charterers to have a lien on the Vessel for all moneys paid in advance and not earned. (226–231)

19. Salvage
All salvage and assistance to other vessels to be for the Owners' and the Charterers' equal benefit after deducting the Master's and Crew's proportion and all legal and other expenses including hire paid under the charter for time lost in the salvage, also repairs of damage and coal or oil-fuel consumed. The Charterers to be bound by all measures taken by the Owners in order to secure payment of salvage and to fix its amount. (232–240)

20. Sublet
The Charterers to have the option of subletting the Vessel, giving due notice to the Owners, but the original Charterers always remain responsible to the Owners for due performance of the Charter. (241–245)

21. War
(A) The Vessel unless the consent of the Owners be first obtained not to be ordered nor continue to any place or on any voyage nor be used on any service which will bring her within a zone which is dangerous as the result of any actual or threatened act of war, war hostilities, warlike operations, acts of piracy or of hostility or malicious damage against this or any other vessel or its cargo by any person, body or State whatsoever, revolution, civil war, civil commotion or the operation of international law, nor be exposed in any way to any risks or penalties whatsoever consequent upon the imposition of Sanctions, nor carry any goods that may in any way expose her to any risks of seizure, capture, penalties or any other interference of any kind whatsoever by the belligerent or fighting powers or parties or by any Government or Ruler.
(B) Should the Vessel approach or be brought or ordered within such zone, or be exposed in any way to the said risks, (1) the Owners to be entitled from time to time to insure their interests in the Vessel and/or hire against any of the risks like y to be involved therein on such terms as they shall think fit, the Charterers to make a refund to the Owners of the premium on demand; and (2) notwithstanding the terms of Clause 11 hire to be paid for all time lost including any lost owing to loss of or injury to the Master, Officers, or Crew or to the action of the Crew in refusing to proceed to such zone or to be exposed to such risks.
(C) In the event of the wages of the Master, Officers and/or Crew or the cost of provisions and/or stores for deck and/or engine room and/or insurance premiums being increased by reason of or during the existence of any of the matters mentioned in section (A) the amount of any (246–277)

after re-delivery), agencies, commissions, also to arrange and pay for loading, trimming, stowing (including dunnage and shifting boards, excepting any already on board), unloading, weighing, tallying and delivery of cargoes, surveys on hatches, meals supplied to officials and men in their service and all other charges and expenses whatsoever including detention and expenses through quarantine (including cost of fumigation and disinfection).

All ropes, slings and special runners actually used for loading and discharging and any special gear, including special ropes, hawsers and chains required by the custom of the port for mooring to be for the Charterers' account. The Vessel to be fitted with winches, derricks, wheels and ordinary runners capable of handling lifts up to 2 tons.

5. Bunkers
The Charterers at port of delivery and the Owners at port of re-delivery to take over and pay for all coal or oil-fuel remaining in the Vessel's bunkers at current price at the respective ports.
The Vessel to be re-delivered with not less than the number of tons and not exceeding the number of tons of coal or oil-fuel in the Vessel's bunkers stated in Box 18.

6. Hire
The Charterers to pay as hire the rate stated in Box 19 per 30 days, commencing in accordance with Clause 1 until her re-delivery to the Owners.
Payment
Payment of hire to be made in cash, in the currency stated in Box 20, without discount, every 30 days, in advance, and in the manner prescribed in Box 20.
In default of payment the Owners to have the right of withdrawing the Vessel from the service of the Charterers, without noting any protest and without interference by any court or any other formality whatsoever and without prejudice to any claim the Owners may otherwise have on the Charterers under the Charter.

7. Re-delivery
The Vessel to be re-delivered on the expiration of the Charter in the same good order as when delivered to the Charterers (fair wear and tear excepted) at an ice-free port in the Charterers' option at the place or within the range stated in Box 21, between 9 a.m. and 6 p.m., and 9 a.m. and 2 p.m. on Saturday, but the day of re-delivery shall not be a Sunday or legal holiday.
Notice
The Charterers to give the Owners not less than ten days' notice at which port and on about which day the Vessel will be re-delivered.
Should the Vessel be ordered on a voyage by which the Charter period will be exceeded the Charterers to have the use of the Vessel to enable them to complete the voyage, provided it could be reasonably calculated that the voyage would allow re-delivery about the time fixed for the termination date the Charterers to pay the market rate if higher than the rate stipulated herein.

be detained beyond 48 hours hire to cease until again ready.

13. Responsibility and Exemption
The Owners only to be responsible for delay in delivery of the Vessel or for delay during the currency of the Charter and for loss or damage to goods onboard, if such delay or loss has been caused by want of due diligence on the part of the Owners or their Manager in making the Vessel seaworthy and fitted for the voyage or any other personal act or omission or default of the Owners or their Manager. The Owners not to be responsible in any other case nor for damage or delay whatsoever and howsoever caused even if caused by the neglect or default of their servants.
The Owners not to be liable for loss or damage arising or resulting from strikes, lock-outs or stoppage or restraint of labour (including the Master, Officers or Crew) whether partial or general.
The Charterers to be responsible for loss or damage caused to the Vessel or to the Owners by goods being loaded contrary to the terms of the Charter or by improper or careless bunkering or loading, stowing or discharging or any other improper or negligent act on their part or that of their servants.

14. Advances
The Charterers or their Agents to advance to the Master, if required, necessary funds for ordinary disbursements for the Vessel's account at any port charging only interest at 6 per cent p.a., such advances to be deducted from hire.

15. Excluded Ports
The Vessel not to be ordered to nor bound to enter: a) any place where fever or epidemics are prevalent or to which the Master, Officers and Crew by law are not bound to follow the Vessel.
Ice
b) any ice-bound place or any place where lights, lightships, marks and buoys are or are likely to be withdrawn by reason of ice on the Vessel's arrival or where there is risk that ordinarily the Vessel will not be able on account of ice to reach the place or to get out after having completed loading or discharging. The Vessel not to be obliged to force ice. If on account of ice the Master considers it dangerous to remain at the loading or discharging place for fear of the Vessel being frozen in and/or damaged, he has liberty to sail to a convenient open place and await the Charterers' fresh instructions.
Unforeseen detention through any of above causes to be for the Charterers' account.

16. Loss of Vessel
Should the Vessel be lost or missing, hire to cease from the date when she was lost. If the date of loss cannot be ascertained half hire to be paid from the date the Vessel was last reported until the calculated date of arrival at the destination. Any hire paid in advance to be adjusted accordingly.

17. Overtime
The Vessel to work day and night if required. The Charterers to refund the Owners their outlays for all

increase to be added to the hire and paid by the Charterers on production of the Owners' account therefor, such account being rendered monthly.
(D) The Vessel to have liberty to comply with any orders or directions as to departure, arrival, routes, ports of call, stoppages, destination, delivery or in any other wise whatsoever given by the Government of the nation under whose flag the Vessel sails or any other Government or any person (or body) acting or purporting to act with the authority of such Government or by any committee or person having under the terms of the war risks insurance on the Vessel the right to give any such orders or directions.
(E) In the event of the nation under whose flag the Vessel sails becoming involved in war, hostilities, warlike operations, revolution, or civil commotion, both the Owners and the Charterers may cancel the Charter and, unless otherwise agreed, the Vessel to be re-delivered to the Owners at the port of destination or, if prevented through the provisions of section (A) from reaching or entering it, then at a near open and safe port at the Owners' option, after discharge of any cargo on board.
(F) If in compliance with the provisions of this clause anything is done or is not done, such not to be deemed a deviation.
Section (C) is optional and should be considered deleted unless agreed according to Box 22.

22. Cancelling
Should the Vessel not be delivered by the date indicated in Box 23, the Charterers to have the option of cancelling.
If the Vessel cannot be delivered by the cancelling date, the Charterers, if required, to declare within 48 hours after receiving notice thereof whether they cancel or will take delivery of the Vessel.

23. Arbitration
Any dispute arising under the Charter to be referred to arbitration in London (or such other place as may be agreed according to Box 24) one Arbitrator to be nominated by the Owners and the other by the Charterers, and in case the Arbitrators shall not agree then to the decision of an Umpire to be appointed by them, the award of the Arbitrators or the Umpire to be final and binding upon both parties.

24. General Average
General Average to be settled according to York/Antwerp Rules, 1974. Hire not to contribute to General Average.

25. Commission
The Owners to pay a commission at the rate stated in Box 25 to the party mentioned in Box 25 on any hire paid under the Charter, but in no case less than is necessary to cover the actual expenses of the Brokers and a reasonable fee for their work. If the full hire is not paid owing to breach of Charter by either of the parties the party liable therefor to indemnify the Brokers against their loss of commission.
Should the parties agree to cancel the Charter, the Owners to indemnify the Brokers against any loss of commission but in such case the commission not to exceed the brokerage on one year's hire.

The New York Produce Exchange Form
"NYPE"

Time Charter

GOVERNMENT FORM

Approved by the New York Produce Exchange

November 6th, 1913—Amended October 20th, 1921; August 6th, 1931; October 3rd, 1946

1 **This Charter Party,** made and concluded in .... day of ....19......

2 Between .... of ....

3 Owners of the good $\left\{\begin{array}{l}\text{Steamship}\\\text{Motorship}\end{array}\right\}$ ....

4 of .... tons gross register, and .... tons net register, having engines of .... indicated horse power

5 and with hull, machinery and equipment in a thoroughly efficient state, and classed ....

6 at .... of about .... cubic feet bale capacity, and about .... tons of 2240 lbs.

7 deadweight capacity (cargo and bunkers, including fresh water and stores not exceeding one and one-half percent of ship's deadweight capacity,

8 allowing a minimum of fifty tons) on a draft of .... feet .... inches on .... Summer freeboard, inclusive of permanent bunkers,

9 which are of the capacity of about .... tons of fuel, and capable of steaming, fully laden, under good weather

10 conditions about .... knots on a consumption of about .... tons of best Welsh coal—best grade fuel oil—best grade Diesel oil,

11 now ....

12 and .... Charterers of the City of ....

13 **Witnesseth,** That the said Owners agree to let, and the said Charterers agree to hire the said vessel, from the time of delivery, for

14 about .... within below mentioned trading limits.

15 Charterers to have liberty to sublet the vessel for all or any part of the time covered by this Charter, but Charterers remaining responsible for

16 the fulfillment of this Charter Party.

17 Vessel to be placed at the disposal of the Charterers, at ....

18

19

20 in such dock or at such wharf or place (where she may safely lie, always afloat, at all times of tide, except as otherwise provided in clause No. 6), as

21 the Charterers may direct. If such dock, wharf or place be not available time to count as provided for in clause No. 5. Vessel on her delivery to be

22 ready to receive cargo with clean-swept holds and tight, staunch, strong and in every way fitted for the service, having water ballast, winches and

23 donkey boiler with sufficient steam power, or if not equipped with donkey boiler, then other power sufficient to run all the winches at one and the same

24 time (and with full complement of officers, seamen, engineers and firemen for a vessel of her tonnage), to be employed, in carrying lawful merchan-

25 dise, including petroleum or its products, in proper containers, excluding ....

26 (vessel is not to be employed in the carriage of Live Stock, but Charterers are to have the privilege of shipping a small number on deck at their risk,

27 all necessary fittings and other requirements to be for account of Charterers), in such lawful trades, between safe port and/or ports in British North

28 America, and/or United States of America, and/or West Indies, and/or Central America, and/or Caribbean Sea, and/or Gulf of Mexico, and/or

29 Mexico, and/or South America .... and/or Europe

30 and/or Africa, and/or Asia, and/or Australia, and/or Tasmania, and/or New Zealand, but excluding Magdalena River, River St. Lawrence between

31 October 31st and May 15th, Hudson Bay and all unsafe ports; also excluding, when out of season, White Sea, Black Sea and the Baltic,

32 ....

33 ....

34 ....

NEW YORK PRODUCE EXCHANGE FORM

35 as the Charterers or their Agents shall direct, on the following conditions:

36 1. That the Owners shall provide and pay for all provisions, wages and consular shipping and discharging fees of the Crew; shall pay for the
37 insurance of the vessel, also for all the cabin, deck, engine-room and other necessary stores, including boiler water and maintain her class and keep
38 the vessel in a thoroughly efficient state in hull, machinery and equipment for and during the service.

39 2. That the Charterers shall provide and pay for all the fuel except as otherwise agreed, Port Charges, Pilotages, Agencies, Commissions,
40 Consular Charges (except those pertaining to the Crew) and all other usual expenses except those before stated, but when the vessel puts into
41 a port for causes for which vessel is responsible, then all such charges incurred shall be paid by the Owners. Fumigations ordered because of
42 illness of the crew to be for Owners account. Fumigations ordered because of cargoes carried or ports visited while vessel is employed under this
43 charter to be for Charterers account. All other fumigations to be for Charterers account after vessel has been on charter for a continuous period
44 of six months or more.

45 Charterers are to provide necessary dunnage and shifting boards, also any extra fittings requisite for a special trade or unusual cargo, but
46 Owners to allow them the use of any dunnage and shifting boards already aboard vessel. Charterers to have the privilege of using shifting boards
47 for dunnage, they making good any damage thereto.

48 3. That the Charterers, at the port of delivery, and the Owners, at the port of re-delivery, shall take over and pay for all fuel remaining on
49 board the vessel at the current prices in the respective ports, the vessel to be delivered with not less than ....tons and not more than
50 ....tons and to be re-delivered with not less than....................tons and not more than....................tons.

51 4. That the Charterers shall pay for the use and hire of the said Vessel at the rate of ....days

52 ....United States Currency per ton on vessel's total deadweight carrying capacity, including bunkers and
53 stores, on..summer freeboard, per Calendar Month, commencing on and from the day of her delivery, as aforesaid, and at
54 and after the same rate for any part of a month; hire to continue until the hour of the day of her re-delivery in like good order and condition, ordinary
55 wear and tear excepted, to the Owners (unless lost) at ....unless otherwise mutually agreed. Charterers are to give Owners not less than..................days

56 notice of vessel's expected date of re-delivery, and probable port.

57 5. Payment of said hire to be made in New York in cash in United States Currency, semi-monthly in advance, and for the last half month or
58 part of same the approximate amount of hire, and should same not cover the actual time, hire is to be paid for the balance day by day, as it becomes
59 due, if so required by Owners, unless bank guarantee or deposit is made by the Charterers, otherwise failing the punctual and regular payment of the
60 hire, or bank guarantee, or on any breach of this Charter Party, the Owners shall be at liberty to withdraw the vessel from the service of the Char-
61 terers, without prejudice to any claim they (the Owners) may otherwise have on the Charterers. Time to count from 7 a.m. on the working day
62 following that on which written notice of readiness has been given to Charterers or their Agents before 4 p.m., but if required by Charterers, they
63 to have the privilege of using vessel at once, such time used to count as hire.

64 Cash for vessel's ordinary disbursements at any port may be advanced as required by the Captain, by the Charterers or their Agents, subject
65 to 2½% commission and such advances shall be deducted from the hire. The Charterers, however, shall in no way be responsible for the application
66 of such advances.

67 6. That the cargo or cargoes be laden and/or discharged in any dock or at any wharf or place that Charterers or their Agents may
68 direct, provided the vessel can safely lie always afloat at any time of tide, except at such places where it is customary for similar size vessels to safely
69 lie aground.

70 7. That the whole reach of the Vessel's Hold, Decks, and usual places of loading (not more than she can reasonably stow and carry), also
71 accommodations for Supercargo, if carried, shall be at the Charterers' disposal, reserving only proper and sufficient space for Ship's officers, crew,
72 tackle, apparel, furniture, provisions, stores and fuel. Charterers have the privilege of passengers as far as accommodations allow, Charterers
73 paying Owners...per day per passenger for accommodations and meals. However, it is agreed that in case any fines or extra expenses are
74 incurred in the consequence of the carriage of passengers, Charterers are to bear such risk and expense.

75 8. That the Captain shall prosecute his voyages with the utmost despatch, and shall render all customary assistance with ship's crew and
76 boats. The Captain (although appointed by the Owners), shall be under the orders and directions of the Charterers as regards employment and
77 agency; and Charterers are to load, stow, and trim the cargo at their own expense under the supervision of the Captain, who is to sign Bills of Lading for
78 cargo as presented, in conformity with Mate's or Tally Clerk's receipts.

79 9. That if the Charterers shall have reason to be dissatisfied with the conduct of the Captain, Officers, or Engineers, the Owners shall on
80 receiving particulars of the complaint, investigate the same, and, if necessary, make a change in the appointments.

81 10. That the Charterers shall have permission to appoint a Supercargo, who shall accompany the vessel and see that voyages are prosecuted

NEW YORK PRODUCE EXCHANGE FORM

83 with the utmost despatch. He is to be furnished with free accommodation, and same fare as provided for Captain's table, Charterers paying at the
84 rate of $1.00 per day. Owners to victual Pilots and Customs Officers, and also, when authorized by Charterers or their Agents, to victual Tally
85 Clerks, Stevedore's Foreman, etc., Charterers paying at the current rate per meal, for all such victualling.
86   11. That the Charterers shall furnish the Captain from time to time with all requisite instructions and sailing directions, in writing, and the
87 Captain shall keep a full and correct Log of the voyage or voyages, which are to be patent to the Charterers or their Agents, and furnish the Char-
88 terers, their Agents or Supercargo, when required, with a true copy of daily Logs, showing the course of the vessel and distance run and the con-
89 sumption of fuel.
90   12. That the Captain shall use diligence in caring for the ventilation of the cargo.
91   13. That the Charterers shall have the option of continuing this charter for a further period of ....
92 ....
93 on giving written notice thereof to the Owners or their Agents ....days previous to the expiration of the first-named term, or any declared option.
94   14. That if required by Charterers, time not to commence before ....and should vessel
95 not have given written notice of readiness on or before .... but not later than 4 p.m. Charterers or
96 their Agents to have the option of cancelling this Charter at any time not later than the day of vessel's readiness.
97   15. That in the event of the loss of time from deficiency of men or stores, fire, breakdown or damages to hull, machinery or equipment,
98 grounding, detention by average accidents to ship or cargo, drydocking for the purpose of examination or painting bottom, or by any other cause
99 preventing the full working of the vessel, the payment of hire shall cease for the time thereby lost; and if upon the voyage the speed be reduced by
100 defect in or breakdown of any part of her hull, machinery or equipment, the time so lost, and the cost of any extra fuel consumed in consequence
101 thereof, and all extra expenses shall be deducted from the hire.
102   16. That should the Vessel be lost, money paid in advance and not earned (reckoning from the date of loss or being last heard of) shall be
103 returned to the Charterers at once. The act of God, enemies, fire, restraint of Princes, Rulers and People, and all dangers and accidents of the Seas,
104 Rivers, Machinery, Boilers and Steam Navigation, and errors of Navigation throughout this Charter Party, always mutually excepted.
105   The vessel shall have the liberty to sail with or without pilots, to tow and to be towed, to assist vessels in distress, and to deviate for the
106 purpose of saving life and property.
107   17. That should any dispute arise between Owners and the Charterers, the matter in dispute shall be referred to three persons at New York,
108 one to be appointed by each of the parties hereto, and the third by the two so chosen; their decision or that of any two of them, shall be final, and for
109 the purpose of enforcing any award, this agreement may be made a rule of the Court. The Arbitrators shall be commercial men.
110   18. That the Owners shall have a lien upon all cargoes, and all sub-freights for any amounts due under this Charter, including General Aver-
111 age contributions, and the Charterers to have a lien on the Ship for all monies paid in advance and not earned, and any overpaid hire or excess
112 deposit to be returned at once. Charterers will not suffer, nor permit to be continued, any lien or encumbrance incurred by them or their agents, which
113 might have priority over the title and interest of the owners in the vessel.
114   19. That all derelicts and salvage shall be for Owners' and Charterers' equal benefit after deducting Owners' and Charterers' expenses and
115 Crew's proportion. General Average shall be adjusted, stated and settled, according to Rules 1 to 15, inclusive, 17 to 22, inclusive, and Rule F of
116 York-Antwerp Rules 1924, at such port or place in the United States as may be selected by the carrier, and as to matters not provided for by these
117 Rules, according to the laws and usages at the port of New York. In such adjustment disbursements in foreign currencies shall be exchanged into
118 United States money at the rate prevailing on the last day of discharge at the port or place of final discharge of such damaged cargo from the ship. Average agreement or
119 the rate prevailing on the last day of discharge at the port or place of final discharge of such damaged cargo from the ship. Average agreement or
120 bond and such additional security, as may be required by the carrier, must be furnished before delivery of the goods. Such cash deposit as the carrier
121 or his agents may deem sufficient as additional security for the contribution of the goods and for any salvage and special charges thereon, shall, if
122 required, be made by the goods, shippers, consignees or owners of the goods to the carrier before delivery. Such deposit shall, at the option of the
123 carrier, be payable in United States money and be remitted to the adjuster. When so remitted the deposit shall be held in a special account at the
124 place of adjustment in the name of the adjuster pending settlement of the General Average and refunds or credit balances, if any, shall be paid in
125 United States money.
126   In the event of accident, danger, damage, or disaster, before or after commencement of the voyage resulting from any cause whatsoever,
127 whether due to negligence or not, for which, or for the consequence of which, the carrier is not responsible, by statute, contract, or otherwise, the
128 goods, the shipper and the consignee, jointly and severally, shall contribute with the carrier in general average to the payment of any sacrifices,
129 losses, or expenses of a general average nature that may be made or incurred, and shall pay salvage and special charges incurred in respect of the
130 goods. If a salving ship is owned or operated by the carrier, salvage shall be paid for as fully and in the same manner as if such salving ship or
131 ships belonged to strangers.

NEW YORK PRODUCE EXCHANGE FORM

Provisions as to General Average in accordance with the above are to be included in all bills of lading issued hereunder.

20. Fuel used by the vessel while off hire, also for cooking, condensing water, or for grates and stoves to be agreed to as to quantity, and the cost of replacing same, to be allowed by Owners.

21. That as the vessel may be from time to time employed in tropical waters during the term of this Charter, Vessel is to be docked at a convenient place, bottom cleaned and painted whenever Charterers and Captain think necessary, at least once in every six months, reckoning from time of last painting, and payment of the hire to be suspended until she is again in proper state for the service.

22. Owners shall maintain the gear of the ship as fitted, providing gear (for all derricks) capable of handling lifts up to three tons, also providing ropes, falls, slings and blocks. If vessel is fitted with derricks capable of handling heavier lifts, Owners are to provide necessary gear for same, otherwise equipment and gear for heavier lifts shall be for Charterers' account. Owners also to provide on the vessel lanterns and oil for night work, and vessel to give use of electric light when so fitted, but any additional lights over those on board to be at Charterers' expense. The Charterers to have the use of any gear on board the vessel.

23. Vessel to work night and day, if required by Charterers, and all winches to be at Charterers' disposal during loading and discharging; steamer to provide one winchman per hatch to work winches day and night, as required, Charterers agreeing to pay officers, engineers, winchmen, deck hands and donkeymen for overtime work done in accordance with the working hours and rates stated in the ship's articles. If the rules of the port, or labor unions, prevent crew from driving winches, shore Winchmen to be paid by Charterers. In the event of a disabled winch or winches, or insufficient power to operate winches, Owners to pay for shore engine, or engines, in lieu thereof, if required, and pay any loss of time occasioned thereby.

24. It is also mutually agreed that this Charter is subject to all the terms and provisions of and all the exemptions from liability contained in the Act of Congress of the United States approved on the 13th day of February, 1893, and entitled "An Act relating to Navigation of Vessels, etc.," in respect of all cargo shipped under this charter to or from the United States of America. It is further subject to the following clauses, both of which are to be included in all bills of lading issued hereunder:

U.S.A. Clause Paramount

This bill of lading shall have effect subject to the provisions of the Carriage of Goods by Sea Act of the United States, approved April 16, 1936, which shall be deemed to be incorporated herein, and nothing herein contained shall be deemed a surrender by the carrier of any of its rights or immunities or an increase of any of its responsibilities or liabilities under said Act. If any term of this bill of lading be repugnant to said Act to any extent, such term shall be void to that extent, but no further.

Both-to-Blame Collision Clause

If the ship comes into collision with another ship as a result of the negligence of the other ship and any act, neglect or default of the Master, mariner, pilot or the servants of the Carrier in the navigation or in the management of the ship, the owners of the goods carried hereunder will indemnify the Carrier against all loss or liability to the other or non-carrying ship or her owners in so far as such loss or liability represents loss of, or damage to, or any claim whatsoever of the owners of said goods, paid or payable by the other or non-carrying ship or her owners to the owners of said goods and set off, recouped or recovered by the other or non-carrying ship or her owners as part of their claim against the carrying ship or carrier.

25. The vessel shall not be required to enter any ice-bound port, or any port where lights or light-ships have been or are about to be withdrawn by reason of ice, or where there is risk that in the ordinary course of things the vessel will not be able on account of ice to safely enter the port or to get out after having completed loading or discharging.

26. Nothing herein stated is to be construed as a demise of the vessel to the Time Charterers. The owners to remain responsible for the navigation of the vessel, insurance, crew, and all other matters, same as when trading for their own account.

27. A commission of 2¼ per cent is payable by the Vessel and Owners to

....

on hire earned and paid under this Charter, and also upon any continuation or extension of this Charter.

28. An address commission of 2¼ per cent payable to .... on the hire earned and paid under this Charter.

.... By cable authority from .... As .... For Owners

BROKERS.

The original Charter Party in our possession.

52-1

Code Name: "NYPE 93"
Recommended by:
The Baltic and International Maritime Council (BIMCO)
The Federation of National Associations of
Ship Brokers and Agents (FONASBA)

TIME CHARTER©

New York Produce Exchange Form
Issued by the Association of Ship Brokers and Agents (U.S.A.), Inc.

November 6th, 1913 - Amended October 20th, 1921; August 6th, 1931; October 3rd, 1946;
Revised June 12th, 1981; September 14th 1993.

THIS CHARTER PARTY, made and concluded in	1
this ....day of..19...	2
Between...	3
....	4
<u>Owners</u> of the Vessel described below, and..	5
....	6
....	7
<u>Charterers</u>.	8

<u>Description of Vessel</u>   9

Name .... Flag .... Built ....(year).	10
Port and number of Registry	11
Classed...in..	12
Deadweight...long*/metric* tons (cargo and bunkers, including freshwater and	13
stores not exceeding .... long*/metric* tons) on a salt water draft of	14
on summer freeboard.	15
Capacity .... cubic feet grain...................................cubic feet bale space.	16
Tonnage.. GT/GRT.	17
Speed about .... knots, fully laden, in good weather conditions up to and including maximum	18
Force .... on the Beaufort wind scale, on a consumption of about .... long*/metric*	19
tons of......................................	20

* Delete as appropriate.	21
For further description see Appendix "A" (if applicable)	22

1. <u>Duration</u>	23
The Owners agree to let and the Charterers agree to hire the Vessel from the time of delivery for a period	24
of..	25
....	26
....	27
....within below mentioned trading limits.	28

2.   <u>Delivery</u>   29

The Vessel shall be placed at the disposal of the Charterers at   30
....   31
....   32
.... The Vessel on her delivery   33
shall be ready to receive cargo with clean-swept holds and tight, staunch, strong and in every way fitted   34
for ordinary cargo service, having water ballast and with sufficient power to operate all cargo-handling gear   35
simultaneously.   36

The Owners shall give the Charterers not less than ....days notice of expected date of   37
delivery.   38

3.   <u>On-Off Hire Survey</u>   39

Prior to delivery and redelivery the parties shall, unless otherwise agreed, each appoint surveyors, for their   40
respective accounts, who shall not later than at first loading port/last discharging port respectively, conduct   41
joint on-hire/off-hire surveys, for the purpose of ascertaining quantity of bunkers on board and the condition   42
of the Vessel. A single report shall be prepared on each occasion and signed by each surveyor, without   43
prejudice to his right to file a separate report setting forth items upon which the surveyors cannot agree.   44
If either party fails to have a representative attend the survey and sign the joint survey report, such party   45
shall nevertheless be bound for all purposes by the findings in any report prepared by the other party.   46
On-hire survey shall be on Charterers' time and off-hire survey on Owners' time.   47

4.   <u>Dangerous Cargo/Cargo Exclusions</u>   48

(a) The Vessel shall be employed in carrying lawful merchandise excluding any goods of a dangerous,   49
injurious, flammable or corrosive nature unless carried in accordance with the requirements or   50
recommendations of the competent authorities of the country of the Vessel's registry and of ports of   51
shipment and discharge and of any intermediate countries or ports through whose waters the Vessel must   52
pass. Without prejudice to the generality of the foregoing, in addition the following are specifically   53
excluded: livestock of any description, arms, ammunition, explosives, nuclear and radioactive materials,   54
....   55
....   56
....   57
....   58
....   59
....   60
....   61
....   62
....   63
....   64

(b)   If IMO-classified cargo is agreed to be carried, the amount of such cargo shall be limited to   65
.... tons and the Charterers shall provide the Master with any evidence he may   66
reasonably require to show that the cargo is packaged, labelled, loaded and stowed in accordance with IMO   67
regulations, failing which the Master is entitled to refuse such cargo or, if already loaded, to unload it at   68
the Charterers' risk and expense.   69

5.   <u>Trading Limits</u>   70

The Vessel shall be employed in such lawful trades between safe ports and safe places   71
within..   72

....excluding   73

....   74

....   75

....as the Charterers shall direct.   76

6.   Owners to Provide   77

The Owners shall provide and pay for the insurance of the Vessel, except as otherwise provided, and for   78
all provisions, cabin, deck, engine-room and other necessary stores, including boiler water; shall pay for   79
wages, consular shipping and discharging fees of the crew and charges for port services pertaining to the   80
crew; shall maintain the Vessel's class and keep her in a thoroughly efficient state in hull, machinery and   81
equipment for and during the service, and have a full complement of officers and crew.   82

7.   Charterers to Provide   83

The Charterers, while the Vessel is on hire, shall provide and pay for all the bunkers except as otherwise   84
agreed; shall pay for port charges (including compulsory watchmen and cargo watchmen and compulsory   85
garbage disposal), all communication expenses pertaining to the Charterers' business at cost, pilotages,   86
towages, agencies, commissions, consular charges (except those pertaining to individual crew members   87
or flag of the Vessel), and all other usual expenses except those stated in Clause 6, but when the Vessel   88
puts into a port for causes for which the Vessel is responsible (other than by stress of weather), then all   89
such charges incurred shall be paid by the Owners. Fumigations ordered because of illness of the crew   90
shall be for the Owners' account. Fumigations ordered because of cargoes carried or ports visited while   91
the Vessel is employed under this Charter Party shall be for the Charterers' account. All other fumigations   92
shall be for the Charterers'account after the Vessel has been on charter for a continuous period of six   93
months or more.   94

The Charterers shall provide and pay for necessary dunnage and also any extra fittings requisite for a   95
special trade or unusual cargo, but the Owners shall allow them the use of any dunnage already aboard   96
the Vessel. Prior to redelivery the Charterers shall remove their dunnage and fittings at their cost and in   97
their time.   98

8.   Performance of Voyages   99

(a) The Master shall perform the voyages with due despatch, and shall render all customary assistance   100
with the Vessel's crew. The Master shall be conversant with the English language and (although   101
appointed by the Owners) shall be under the orders and directions of the Charterers as regards   102
employment and agency; and the Charterers shall perform all cargo handling, including but not limited to   103
loading, stowing, trimming, lashing, securing, dunnaging, unlashing, discharging, and tallying, at their risk   104
and expense, under the supervision of the Master.   105

(b) If the Charterers shall have reasonable cause to be dissatisfied with the conduct of the Master or   106
officers, the Owners shall, on receiving particulars of the complaint, investigate the same, and, if   107
necessary, make a change in the appointments.   108

9.   Bunkers   109

(a) The Charterers on delivery, and the Owners on redelivery, shall take over and pay for all fuel and   110
diesel oil remaining on board the Vessel as hereunder. The Vessel shall be delivered with: 111
.... long*/metric* tons of fuel oil at the price of .... per ton;   112
.....................................tons of diesel oil at the price of .... per ton. The vessel shall   113
be redelivered with: .... tons of fuel oil at the price of................................... per ton;   114
.... tons of diesel oil at the price of .... per ton.   115

Same tons apply throughout this clause.   116

(b) The Charterers shall supply bunkers of a quality suitable for burning in the Vessel's engines and   117
auxiliaries and which conform to the specification(s) as set out in Appendix A.   118

The Owners reserve their right to make a claim against the Charterers for any damage to the main engines   119
or the auxiliaries caused by the use of unsuitable fuels or fuels not complying with the agreed   120
specification(s). Additionally, if bunker fuels supplied do not conform with the mutually agreed   121
specification(s) or otherwise prove unsuitable for burning in the Vessel's engines or auxiliaries, the Owners   122
shall not be held responsible for any reduction in the Vessel's speed performance and/or increased bunker   123
consumption, nor for any time lost and any other consequences.   124

10.   Rate of Hire/Redelivery Areas and Notices   125

The Charterers shall pay for the use and hire of the said Vessel at the rate of $.................................   126
U.S. currency, daily, **or** $................................. U.S. currency per ton on the Vessel's total deadweight   127
carrying capacity, including bunkers and stores, on .... summer freeboard, per 30 days,   128
commencing on and from the day of her delivery, as aforesaid, and at and after the same rate for any part   129
of a month; hire shall continue until the hour of the day of her redelivery in like good order and condition,   130
ordinary wear and tear excepted, to the Owners (unless Vessel lost) at.................................   131
....   132
....   133
.... unless otherwise mutually agreed.   134

The Charterers shall give the Owners not less than .... days notice of the Vessel's   135
expected date and probable port of redelivery.   136

For the purpose of hire calculations, the times of delivery, redelivery or termination of charter shall be   137
adjusted to GMT.   138

11.   Hire Payment   139

(a)   *Payment*   140

Payment of Hire shall be made so as to be received by the Owners or their designated payee in   141
...., viz...   142
....   143
....   144
....in   145
.... currency, or in United States Currency, in funds available to the   146
Owners on the due date, 15 days in advance, and for the last month or part of same the approximate   147
amount of hire, and should same not cover the actual time, hire shall be paid for the balance day by day   148
as it becomes due, if so required by the Owners. Failing the punctual and regular payment of the hire,   149
or on any fundamental breach whatsoever of this Charter Party, the Owners shall be at liberty to   150
withdraw the Vessel from the service of the Charterers without prejudice to any claims they (the Owners)   151
may otherwise have on the Charterers.   152

At any time after the expiry of the grace period provided in Sub-clause 11 (b) hereunder and while the   153
hire is outstanding, the Owners shall, without prejudice to the liberty to withdraw, be entitled to withhold   154
the performance of any and all of their obligations hereunder and shall have no responsibility whatsoever   155
for any consequences thereof, in respect of which the Charterers hereby indemnify the Owners, and hire   156
shall continue to accrue and any extra expenses resulting from such withholding shall be for the   157
Charterers' account.   158

(b)   *Grace Period*   159

Where there is failure to make punctual and regular payment of hire due to oversight, negligence, errors   160
or omissions on the part of the Charterers or their bankers, the Charterers shall be given by the Owners   161
.... clear banking days (as recognized at the agreed place of payment) written notice to rectify the   162
failure, and when so rectified within those .... days following the Owners' notice, the payment shall 163
stand as regular and punctual.   164

Failure by the Charterers to pay the hire within .... days of their receiving the Owners' notice as   165
provided herein, shall entitle the Owners to withdraw as set forth in Sub-clause 11 (a) above.   166

(c)   *Last Hire Payment*   167

Should the Vessel be on her voyage towards port of redelivery at the time the last and/or the penultimate   168
payment of hire is/are due, said payment(s) is/are to be made for such length of time as the Owners and   169
the Charterers may agree upon as being the estimated time necessary to complete the voyage, and taking   170
into account bunkers actually on board, to be taken over by the Owners and estimated disbursements for   171
the Owners' account before redelivery. Should same not cover the actual time, hire is to be paid for the   172
balance, day by day, as it becomes due. When the Vessel has been redelivered, any difference is to be   173
refunded by the Owners or paid by the Charterers, as the case may be.   174

(d)   *Cash Advances*   175

Cash for the Vessel's ordinary disbursements at any port may be advanced by the Charterers, as required   176
by the Owners, subject to 2½ percent commission and such advances shall be deducted from the hire.   177
The Charterers, however, shall in no way be responsible for the application of such advances.   178

12.   **Berths**   179

The Vessel shall be loaded and discharged in any safe dock or at any safe berth or safe place that   180
Charterers or their agents may direct, provided the Vessel can safely enter, lie and depart always afloat   181
at any time of tide.   182

13.   **Spaces Available**   183

(a) The whole reach of the Vessel's holds, decks, and other cargo spaces (not more than she can   184
reasonably and safely stow and carry), also accommodations for supercargo, if carried, shall be at the   185
Charterers' disposal, reserving only proper and sufficient space for the Vessel's officers, crew, tackle,   186
apparel, furniture, provisions, stores and fuel.   187

(b) In the event of deck cargo being carried, the Owners are to be and are hereby indemnified by the   188
Charterers for any loss and/or damage and/or liability of whatsoever nature caused to the Vessel as a   189
result of the carriage of deck cargo and which would not have arisen had deck cargo not been loaded.   190

14.   **Supercargo and Meals**   191

The Charterers are entitled to appoint a supercargo, who shall accompany the Vessel at the Charterers'   192
risk and see that voyages are performed with due despatch. He is to be furnished with free   193
accommodation and same fare as provided for the Master's table, the Charterers paying at the rate of   194
.... per day. The Owners shall victual pilots and customs officers, and also, when   195
authorized by the Charterers or their agents, shall victual tally clerks, stevedore's foreman, etc.,   196
Charterers paying at the rate of .... per meal for all such victualling.   197

15.   <u>Sailing Orders and Logs</u>   198

The Charterers shall furnish the Master from time to time with all requisite instructions and sailing   199
directions, in writing, in the English language, and the Master shall keep full and correct deck and engine   200
logs of the voyage or voyages, which are to be patent to the Charterers or their agents, and furnish the   201
Charterers, their agents or supercargo, when required, with a true copy of such deck and engine logs,   202
showing the course of the Vessel, distance run and the consumption of bunkers. Any log extracts   203
required by the Charterers shall be in the English language.   204

16.   <u>Delivery/Cancelling</u>   205

If required by the Charterers, time shall not commence before .... and should the   206
Vessel not be ready for delivery on or before..but not later than..........hours,   207
the Charterers shall have the option of cancelling this Charter Party.   208

      Extension of Cancelling   209

If the Owners warrant that, despite the exercise of due diligence by them, the Vessel will not be ready   210
for delivery by the cancelling date, and provided the Owners are able to state with reasonable certainty   211
the date on which the Vessel will be ready, they may, at the earliest seven days before the Vessel is   212
expected to sail for the port or place of delivery, require the Charterers to declare whether or not they will   213
cancel the Charter Party. Should the Charterers elect not to cancel, or should they fail to reply within two   214
days or by the cancelling date, whichever shall first occur, then the seventh day after the expected date   215
of readiness for delivery as notified by the Owners shall replace the original cancelling date. Should the   216
Vessel be further delayed, the Owners shall be entitled to require further declarations of the Charterers   217
in accordance with this Clause.   218

17.   <u>Off Hire</u>   219

In the event of loss of time from deficiency and/or default and/or strike of officers or crew, or deficiency   220
of stores, fire, breakdown of, or damages to hull, machinery or equipment, grounding, detention by the   221
arrest of the Vessel, (unless such arrest is caused by events for which the Charterers, their servants,   222
agents or subcontractors are responsible), or detention by average accidents to the Vessel or cargo unless   223
resulting from inherent vice, quality or defect of the cargo, drydocking for the purpose of examination or   224
painting bottom, or by any other similar cause preventing the full working of the Vessel, the payment of   225
hire and overtime, if any, shall cease for the time thereby lost. Should the Vessel deviate or put back   226
during a voyage, contrary to the orders or directions of the Charterers, for any reason other than accident   227
to the cargo or where permitted in lines 257 to 258 hereunder, the hire is to be suspended from the time   228
of her deviating or putting back until she is again in the same or equidistant position from the destination   229
and the voyage resumed therefrom. All bunkers used by the Vessel while off hire shall be for the Owners'   230
account. In the event of the Vessel being driven into port or to anchorage through stress of weather,   231
trading to shallow harbors or to rivers or ports with bars, any detention of the Vessel and/or expenses   232
resulting from such detention shall be for the Charterers' account. If upon the voyage the speed be   233
reduced by defect in, or breakdown of, any part of her hull, machinery or equipment, the time so lost, and   234
the cost of any extra bunkers consumed in consequence thereof, and all extra proven expenses may be   235
deducted from the hire.   236

18.   <u>Sublet</u>   237

Unless otherwise agreed, the Charterers shall have the liberty to sublet the Vessel for all or any part of   238
the time covered by this Charter Party, but the Charterers remain responsible for the fulfillment of this   239
Charter Party.   240

19.   <u>Drydocking</u>   241

The Vessel was last drydocked 242

*(a) The Owners shall have the option to place the Vessel in drydock during the currency of this Charter   243
at a convenient time and place, to be mutually agreed upon between the Owners and the Charterers, for   244
bottom cleaning and painting and/or repair as required by class or dictated by circumstances.   245

*(b) Except in case of emergency no drydocking shall take place during the currency of this Charter   246
Party.   247

* *Delete as appropriate*   248

20.   <u>Total Loss</u>   249

Should the Vessel be lost, money paid in advance and not earned (reckoning from the date of loss or   250
being last heard of) shall be returned to the Charterers at once.   251

21.   <u>Exceptions</u>   252

The act of God, enemies, fire, restraint of princes, rulers and people, and all dangers and accidents of the   253
seas, rivers, machinery, boilers, and navigation, and errors of navigation throughout this Charter, always   254
mutually excepted.   255

22.   <u>Liberties</u>   256

The Vessel shall have the liberty to sail with or without pilots, to tow and to be towed, to assist vessels   257
in distress, and to deviate for the purpose of saving life and property.   258

23.   <u>Liens</u>   259

The Owners shall have a lien upon all cargoes and all sub-freights and/or sub-hire for any amounts due   260
under this Charter Party, including general average contributions, and the Charterers shall have a lien on   261
the Vessel for all monies paid in advance and not earned, and any overpaid hire or excess deposit to be   262
returned at once.   263

The Charterers will not directly or indirectly suffer, nor permit to be continued, any lien or encumbrance,   264
which might have priority over the title and interest of the Owners in the Vessel. The Charterers   265
undertake that during the period of this Charter Party, they will not procure any supplies or necessaries   266
or services, including any port expenses and bunkers, on the credit of the Owners or in the Owners' time.   267

24.   <u>Salvage</u>   268

All derelicts and salvage shall be for the Owners' and the Charterers' equal benefit after deducting   269
Owners' and Charterers' expenses and crew's proportion.   270

25.   <u>General Average</u>   271

General average shall be adjusted according to York-Antwerp Rules 1974, as amended 1990, or any   272
subsequent modification thereof, in .... and settled in   273
currency.   274

The Charterers shall procure that all bills of lading issued during the currency of the Charter Party will 275
contain a provision to the effect that general average shall be adjusted according to York-Antwerp Rules 276
1974, as amended 1990, or any subsequent modification thereof and will include the "New Jason 277
Clause" as per Clause 31. 278

Time charter hire shall not contribute to general average. 279

26. **Navigation** 280

Nothing herein stated is to be construed as a demise of the Vessel to the Time Charterers. The Owners 281
shall remain responsible for the navigation of the Vessel, acts of pilots and tug boats, insurance, crew, 282
and all other matters, same as when trading for their own account. 283

27. **Cargo Claims** 284

Cargo claims as between the Owners and the Charterers shall be settled in accordance with the Inter-Club 285
New York Produce Exchange Agreement of February 1970, as amended May, 1984, or any subsequent 286
modification or replacement thereof. 287

28. **Cargo Gear and Lights** 288

The Owners shall maintain the cargo handling gear of the Vessel which is as follows:........................... 289
.... 290
.... 291
.... 292
providing gear (for all derricks or cranes) capable of lifting capacity as described. The Owners shall also 293
provide on the Vessel for night work lights as on board, but all additional lights over those on board shall 294
be at the Charterers' expense. The Charterers shall have the use of any gear on board the Vessel. If 295
required by the Charterers, the Vessel shall work night and day and all cargo handling gear shall be at the 296
Charterers' disposal during loading and discharging. In the event of disabled cargo handling gear, or 297
insufficient power to operate the same, the Vessel is to be considered to be off hire to the extent that 298
time is actually lost to the Charterers and the Owners to pay stevedore stand-by charges occasioned 299
thereby, unless such disablement or insufficiency of power is caused by the Charterers' stevedores. If 300
required by the Charterers, the Owners shall bear the cost of hiring shore gear in lieu thereof, in which 301
case the Vessel shall remain on hire. 302

29. **Crew Overtime** 303

In lieu of any overtime payments to officers and crew for work ordered by the Charterers or their agents, 304
the Charterers shall pay the Owners, concurrently with the hire ....per month 305
or pro rata. 306

30. **Bills of Lading** 307

(a) The Master shall sign the bills of lading or waybills for cargo as presented in conformity with mates 308
or tally clerk's receipts. However, the Charterers may sign bills of lading or waybills on behalf of the 309
Master, with the Owner's prior written authority, always in conformity with mates or tally clerk's receipts. 310

(b) All bills of lading or waybills shall be without prejudice to this Charter Party and the Charterers shall indemnify the Owners against all consequences or liabilities which may arise from any inconsistency between this Charter Party and any bills of lading or waybills signed by the Charterers or by the Master at their request.

(c) Bills of lading covering deck cargo shall be claused: "Shipped on deck at Charterers', Shippers' and Receivers' risk, expense and responsibility, without liability on the part of the Vessel, or her Owners for any loss, damage, expense or delay howsoever caused."

31.   **Protective Clauses**

This Charter Party is subject to the following clauses all of which are also to be included in all bills of lading or waybills issued hereunder:

(a)   CLAUSE PARAMOUNT

"This bill of lading shall have effect subject to the provisions of the Carriage of Goods by Sea Act of the United States, the Hague Rules, or the Hague-Visby Rules, as applicable, or such other similar national legislation as may mandatorily apply by virtue of origin or destination of the bills of lading, which shall be deemed to be incorporated herein and nothing herein contained shall be deemed a surrender by the carrier of any of its rights or immunities or an increase of any of its responsibilities or liabilities under said applicable Act. If any term of this bill of lading be repugnant to said applicable Act to any extent, such term shall be void to that extent, but no further."

and

(b)   BOTH-TO-BLAME COLLISION CLAUSE

"If the ship comes into collision with another ship as a result of the negligence of the other ship and any act, neglect or default of the master, mariner, pilot or the servants of the carrier in the navigation or in the management of the ship, the owners of the goods carried hereunder will indemnify the carrier against all loss or liability to the other or non-carrying ship or her owners insofar as such loss or liability represents loss of, or damage to, or any claim whatsoever of the owners of said goods, paid or payable by the other or non-carrying ship or her owners to the owners of said goods and set off, recouped or recovered by the other or non-carrying ship or her owners as part of their claim against the carrying ship or carrier.

The foregoing provisions shall also apply where the owners, operators or those in charge of any ships or objects other than, or in addition to, the colliding ships or objects are at fault in respect to a collision or contact."

and

(c)   NEW JASON CLAUSE

"In the event of accident, danger, damage or disaster before or after the commencement of the voyage resulting from any cause whatsoever, whether due to negligence or not, for which, or for the consequences of which, the carrier is not responsible, by statute, contract, or otherwise, the goods, shippers, consignees, or owners of the goods shall contribute with the carrier in general average to the payment of any sacrifices, losses, or expenses of a general average nature that may be made or incurred, and shall pay salvage and special charges incurred in respect of the goods.

If a salving ship is owned or operated by the carrier, salvage shall be paid for as fully as if salving ship or ships belonged to strangers. Such deposit as the carrier or his agents may deem sufficient to cover the estimated contribution of the goods and any salvage and special charges thereon shall, if required, be made by the goods, shippers, consignees or owners of the goods to the carrier before delivery."

and   353

(d)   U.S. TRADE - DRUG CLAUSE   354
"In pursuance of the provisions of the U.S. Anti Drug Abuse Act 1986 or any re-enactment thereof, the   355
Charterers warrant to exercise the highest degree of care and diligence in preventing unmanifested   356
narcotic drugs and marijuana to be loaded or concealed on board the Vessel.   357

Non-compliance with the provisions of this clause shall amount to breach of warranty for consequences   358
of which the Charterers shall be liable and shall hold the Owners, the Master and the crew of the Vessel   359
harmless and shall keep them indemnified against all claims whatsoever which may arise and be made   360
against them individually or jointly. Furthermore, all time lost and all expenses incurred, including fines,   361
as a result of the Charterers' breach of the provisions of this clause shall be for the Charterer's account   362
and the Vessel shall remain on hire.   363

Should the Vessel be arrested as a result of the Charterers' non-compliance with the provisions of this   364
clause, the Charterers shall at their expense take all reasonable steps to secure that within a reasonable   365
time the Vessel is released and at their expense put up the bails to secure release of the Vessel.   366

The Owners shall remain responsible for all time lost and all expenses incurred, including fines, in the   367
event that unmanifested narcotic drugs and marijuana are found in the possession or effects of the   368
Vessel's personnel."   369

and   370

(e)   WAR CLAUSES   371
"(i) No contraband of war shall be shipped. The Vessel shall not be required, without the consent of the   372
Owners, which shall not be unreasonably withheld, to enter any port or zone which is involved in a state   373
of war, warlike operations, or hostilities, civil strife, insurrection or piracy whether there be a declaration 374
of war or not, where the Vessel, cargo or crew might reasonably be expected to be subject to capture,   375
seizure or arrest, or to a hostile act by a belligerent power (the term "power" meaning any de jure or de   376
facto authority or any purported governmental organization maintaining naval, military or air forces).   377

(ii) If such consent is given by the Owners, the Charterers will pay the provable additional cost of insuring   378
the Vessel against hull war risks in an amount equal to the value under her ordinary hull policy but not   379
exceeding a valuation of... In addition, the Owners may purchase and the   380
Charterers will pay for war risk insurance on ancillary risks such as loss of hire, freight disbursements,   381
total loss, blocking and trapping, etc. If such insurance is not obtainable commercially or through a   382
government program, the Vessel shall not be required to enter or remain at any such port or zone.   383

(iii) In the event of the existence of the conditions described in (i) subsequent to the date of this Charter,   384
or while the Vessel is on hire under this Charter, the Charterers shall, in respect of voyages to any such   385
port or zone assume the provable additional cost of wages and insurance properly incurred in connection   386
with master, officers and crew as a consequence of such war, warlike operations or hostilities.   387

(iv) Any war bonus to officers and crew due to the Vessel's trading or cargo carried shall be for the   388
Charterers' account."   389

32.   <u>War Cancellation</u>   390

In the event of the outbreak of war (whether there be a declaration of war or not) between any two or   391
more of the following countries:...   392
....   393
....   394
....   395
either the Owners or the Charterers may cancel this Charter Party. Whereupon, the Charterers shall   396
redeliver the Vessel to the Owners in accordance with Clause 10; if she has cargo on board, after   397
discharge thereof at destination, or, if debarred under this Clause from reaching or entering it, at a near   398
open and safe port as directed by the Owners; or, if she has no cargo on board, at the port at which she   399
then is; or, if at sea, at a near open and safe port as directed by the Owners. In all cases hire shall   400
continue to be paid in accordance with Clause 11 and except as aforesaid all other provisions of this   401
Charter Party shall apply until redelivery.   402

33.   <u>Ice</u>   403

The Vessel shall not be required to enter or remain in any icebound port or area, nor any port or area   404
where lights or lightships have been or are about to be withdrawn by reason of ice, nor where there is   405
risk that in the ordinary course of things the Vessel will not be able on account of ice to safely enter and   406
remain in the port or area or to get out after having completed loading or discharging. Subject to the   407
Owners' prior approval the Vessel is to follow ice-breakers when reasonably required with regard to her   408
size, construction and ice class.   409

34.   <u>Requisition</u>   410

Should the Vessel be requisitioned by the government of the Vessel's flag during the period of this Charter   411
Party, the Vessel shall be deemed to be off hire during the period of such requisition, and any hire paid   412
by the said government in respect of such requisition period shall be retained by the Owners. The period   413
during which the Vessel is on requisition to the said government shall count as part of the period provided   414
for in this Charter Party.   415

If the period of requisition exceeds .... months, either party shall have the option   416
of cancelling this Charter Party and no consequential claim may be made by either party.   417

35.   <u>Stevedore Damage</u>   418

Notwithstanding anything contained herein to the contrary, the Charterers shall pay for any and all   419
damage to the Vessel caused by stevedores provided the Master has notified the Charterers and/or their   420
agents in writing as soon as practical but not later than 48 hours after any damage is discovered. Such   421
notice to specify the damage in detail and to invite Charterers to appoint a surveyor to assess the extent   422
of such damage.   423

(a) In case of any and all damage(s) affecting the Vessel's seaworthiness and/or the safety of the crew   424
and/or affecting the trading capabilities of the Vessel, the Charterers shall immediately arrange for repairs   425
of such damage(s) at their expense and the Vessel is to remain on hire until such repairs are completed   426
and if required passed by the Vessel's classification society.   427

(b) Any and all damage(s) not described under point (a) above shall be repaired at the Charterers' option,   428
before or after redelivery concurrently with the Owners' work. In such case no hire and/or expenses will   429
be paid to the Owners except and insofar as the time and/or the expenses required for the repairs for   430
which the Charterers are responsible, exceed the time and/or expenses necessary to carry out the   431
Owners' work.   432

36.   **Cleaning of Holds**   433

The Charterers shall provide and pay extra for sweeping and/or washing and/or cleaning of holds between   434
voyages and/or between cargoes provided such work can be undertaken by the crew and is permitted by   435
local regulations, at the rate of................................. per hold.   436

In connection with any such operation, the Owners shall not be responsible if the Vessel's holds are not   437
accepted or passed by the port or any other authority. The Charterers shall have the option to re-deliver   438
the Vessel with unclean/unswept holds against a lumpsum payment of.......................in lieu of cleaning.   439

37.   **Taxes**   440

Charterers to pay all local, State, National taxes and/or dues assessed on the Vessel or the Owners   441
resulting from the Charterers' orders herein, whether assessed during or after the currency of this Charter   442
Party including any taxes and/or dues on cargo and/or freights and/or sub-freights and/or hire (excluding   443
taxes levied by the country of the flag of the Vessel or the Owners).   444

38.   **Charterers' Colors**   445

The Charterers shall have the privilege of flying their own house flag and painting the Vessel with their   446
own markings. The Vessel shall be repainted in the Owners' colors before termination of the Charter   447
Party. Cost and time of painting, maintaining and repainting those changes effected by the Charterers   448
shall be for the Charterers' account.   449

39.   **Laid Up Returns**   450

The Charterers shall have the benefit of any return insurance premium receivable by the Owners from their   451
underwriters as and when received from underwriters by reason of the Vessel being in port for a minimum   452
period of 30 days if on full hire for this period or pro rata for the time actually on hire.   453

40.   **Documentation**   454

The Owners shall provide any documentation relating to the Vessel that may be required to permit the   455
Vessel to trade within the agreed trade limits, including, but not limited to certificates of financial   456
responsibility for oil pollution, provided such oil pollution certificates are obtainable from the Owners'   457
P & I club, valid international tonnage certificate, Suez and Panama tonnage certificates, valid certificate   458
of registry and certificates relating to the strength and/or serviceability of the Vessel's gear.   459

41.   **Stowaways**   460

(a)   (i) The Charterers warrant to exercise due care and diligence in preventing stowaways in gaining   461
         access to the Vessel by means of secreting away in the goods and/or containers shipped by the   462
         Charterers.   463

         (ii) If, despite the exercise of due care and diligence by the Charterers, stowaways have gained   464
         access to the Vessel by means of secreting away in the goods and/or containers shipped by the   465
         Charterers, this shall amount to breach of charter for the consequences of which the Charterers   466
         shall be liable and shall hold the Owners harmless and shall keep them indemnified against all   467
         claims whatsoever which may arise and be made against them. Furthermore, all time lost and all   468
         expenses whatsoever and howsoever incurred, including fines, shall be for the Charterers' account   469
         and the Vessel shall remain on hire.   470

(iii) Should the Vessel be arrested as a result of the Charterers' breach of charter according to   471
sub-clause (a)(ii) above, the Charterers shall take all reasonable steps to secure that, within a   472
reasonable time, the Vessel is released and at their expense put up bail to secure release of the   473
Vessel.   474

(b)   (i) If, despite the exercise of due care and diligence by the Owners, stowaways have gained   475
access to the Vessel by means other than secreting away in the goods and/or containers shipped   476
by the Charterers, all time lost and all expenses whatsoever and howsoever incurred, including   477
fines, shall be for the Owners' account and the Vessel shall be off hire.   478

(ii) Should the Vessel be arrested as a result of stowaways having gained access to the Vessel   479
by means other than secreting away in the goods and/or containers shipped by the Charterers,   480
the Owners shall take all reasonable steps to secure that, within a reasonable time, the Vessel   481
is released and at their expense put up bail to secure release of the Vessel.   482

42.   Smuggling   483

In the event of smuggling by the Master, Officers and/or crew, the Owners shall bear the cost of any   484
fines, taxes, or imposts levied and the Vessel shall be off hire for any time lost as a result thereof.   485

43.   Commissions   486

A commission of...................... percent is payable by the Vessel and the Owners to..........................   487
....   488
....   489
....   490
on hire earned and paid under this Charter, and also upon any continuation or extension of this Charter.   491

44.   Address Commission   492

An address commission of .... percent is payable to...   493
....   494
....   495
....on hire earned and paid under this Charter.   496

45.   Arbitration   497

(a)   NEW YORK   498
All disputes arising out of this contract shall be arbitrated at New York in the following manner, and   499
subject to U.S. Law: 500

One Arbitrator is to be appointed by each of the parties hereto and a third by the two so chosen. Their   501
decision or that of any two of them shall be final, and for the purpose of enforcing any award, this   502
agreement may be made a rule of the court. The Arbitrators shall be commercial men, conversant with   503
shipping matters. Such Arbitration is to be conducted in accordance with the rules of the Society of   504
Maritime Arbitrators Inc.   505

For disputes where the total amount claimed by either party does not exceed US $ ....**   506
the arbitration shall be conducted in accordance with the Shortened Arbitration Procedure of the Society   507
of Maritime Arbitrators Inc.   508

(b)   LONDON   509
All disputes arising out of this contract shall be arbitrated at London and, unless the parties agree   510
forthwith on a single Arbitrator, be referred to the final arbitrament of two Arbitrators carrying on business   511
in London who shall be members of the Baltic Mercantile & Shipping Exchange and engaged in Shipping,   512
one to be appointed by each of the parties, with power to such Arbitrators to appoint an Umpire. No   513
award shall be questioned or invalidated on the ground that any of the Arbitrators is not qualified as   514
above, unless objection to his action be taken before the award is made. Any dispute arising hereunder   515
shall be governed by English Law.   516

For disputes where the total amount claimed by either party does not exceed US $ ....** 517
the arbitration shall be conducted in accordance with the Small Claims Procedure of the London Maritime   518
Arbitrators Association.   519

* *Delete para (a) or (b) as appropriate*   520

** *Where no figure is supplied in the blank space this provision only shall be void but the other provisions*   521
of this clause shall have full force and remain in effect.   522

If mutually agreed, clauses .... to ...., both inclusive, as attached hereto are fully   523
incorporated in this Charter Party.   524

Code word for this Charter Party
"SHELLTIME 4"

Issued December 1984

Time Charter Party

LONDON,   19

IT IS THIS DAY AGREED between

of   (hereinafter referred to as "Owners"), being owners of the

good   vessel called   1
                                                                                                                                                2
                                                                                                                                                3

(hereinafter referred to as "the vessel") described as per Clause 1 hereof and   4

of   (hereinafter referred to as "Charterers"):   5

Description and   1.   At the date of delivery of the vessel under this charter   6
Condition of   (a)   she shall be classed: 7
Vessel   (b)   she shall be in every way fit to carry crude petroleum and/or its products;   8

                            (c)   she shall be tight, staunch, strong, in good order and condition, and in every way fit for the   9
service, with her machinery, boilers, hull and other equipment (including but not limited to hull stress calculator   10
and radar) in a good and efficient state;   11
                            (d)   her tanks, valves and pipelines shall be oil-tight;   12
                            (e)   she shall be in every way fitted for burning   13
                                  at sea – fueloil with a maximum viscosity of   Centistokes at 50 degrees Centigrade/any   14
                                  commercial grade of fueloil ("ACGFO") for main propulsion, marine diesel oil/ACGFO   15
                                  for auxiliaries   16
                                  in port – marine diesel oil/ACGFO for auxiliaries: 17

                            (f)   she shall comply with the regulations in force so as to enable her to pass through the Suez and   18
Panama Canals by day and night without delay;   19
                            (g)   she shall have on board all certificates, documents and equipment required from time to time by   20
any applicable law to enable her to perform the charter service without delay;   21
                            (h)   she shall comply with the description in Form B appended hereto, provided however that if there   22
is any conflict between the provisions of Form B and any other provision, including this Clause 1, of this charter   23
such other provision shall govern.   24

Shipboard Personnel and their Duties

2. (a)   At the date of delivery of the vessel under this charter
(i)   she shall have a full and efficient complement of master, officers and crew for a vessel of her tonnage, who shall in any event be not less than the number required by the laws of the flag state and who shall be trained to operate the vessel and her equipment competently and safely;
(ii)   all shipboard personnel shall hold valid certificates of competence in accordance with the requirements of the law of the flag state;
(iii)   all shipboard personnel shall be trained in accordance with the relevant provisions of the International Convention on Standards of Training, Certification and Watchkeeping for Seafarers, 1978;
(iv)   there shall be on board sufficient personnel with a good working knowledge of the English language to enable cargo operations at loading and discharging places to be carried out efficiently and safely and to enable communications between the vessel and those loading the vessel or accepting discharge therefrom to be carried out quickly and efficiently.
(b)   Owners guarantee that throughout the charter service the master shall with the vessel's officers and crew, unless otherwise ordered by Charterers,
(i)   prosecute all voyages with the utmost despatch;
(ii)   render all customary assistance; and
(iii)   load and discharge cargo as rapidly as possible when required by Charterers or their agents to do so, by night or by day, but always in accordance with the laws of the place of loading or discharging (as the case may be) and in each case in accordance with any applicable laws of the flag state.

Duty to Maintain

3. (i)   Throughout the charter service Owners shall, whenever the passage of time, wear and tear or any event (whether or not coming within Clause 27 hereof) requires steps to be taken to maintain or restore the conditions stipulated in Clauses 1 and 2(a), exercise due diligence so to maintain or restore the vessel.
(ii)   If at any time whilst the vessel is on hire under this charter the vessel fails to comply with the requirements of Clauses 1, 2(a) or 10 then hire shall be reduced to the extent necessary to indemnify Charterers for such failure. If and to the extent that such failure affects the time taken by the vessel to perform any services under this charter, hire shall be reduced by an amount equal to the value, calculated at the rate of hire, of the time so lost.
   Any reduction of hire under this sub-Clause (ii) shall be without prejudice to any other remedy available to Charterers, but where such reduction of hire is in respect of time lost, such time shall be excluded from any calculation under Clause 24.
(iii)   If Owners are in breach of their obligation under Clause 3(i) Charterers may so notify Owners in writing; and if, after the expiry of 30 days following the receipt by Owners of any such notice, Owners have failed to demonstrate to Charterers' reasonable satisfaction the exercise of due diligence as required in Clause 3(i), the vessel shall be off-hire, and no further hire payments shall be due, until Owners have so demonstrated that they are exercising such due diligence.
   Furthermore, at any time while the vessel is off-hire under this Clause 3 Charterers have the option to terminate this charter by giving notice in writing with effect from the date on which such notice of termination is received by Owners or from any later date stated in such notice. This sub-Clause (iii) is without prejudice to any rights of Charterers or obligations of Owners under this charter or otherwise (including without limitation Charterers' rights under Clause 21 hereof).

Period Trading Limits

4.   Owners agree to let and Charterers agree to hire the vessel for a period of commencing from the time and date of delivery of the vessel, for the purpose of carrying all lawful merchandise (subject always to Clause 28) including in particular | 65 66 67

in any part of the world, as Charterers shall direct, subject to the limits of the current British Institute Warranties and any subsequent amendments thereof. Notwithstanding the foregoing, but subject to Clause 35, Charterers may order the vessel to ice-bound waters or to any part of the world outside such limits provided that Owners consent thereto (such consent not to be unreasonably withheld) and that Charterers pay for any insurance premium required by the vessel's underwriters as a consequence of such order. | 68 69 70 71 72

Charterers shall use due diligence to ensure that the vessel is only employed between and at safe places (which expression when used in this charter shall include ports, berths, wharves, docks, anchorages, submarine lines, alongside vessels or lighters, and other locations including locations at sea) where she can safely lie always afloat. Notwithstanding anything contained in this or any other clause of this charter, Charterers do not warrant the safety of any place to which they order the vessel and shall be under no liability in respect thereof except for loss or damage caused by their failure to exercise due diligence as aforesaid. Subject as above, the vessel shall be loaded and discharged at any places as Charterers may direct, provided that Charterers shall exercise due diligence to ensure that any ship-to-ship transfer operations shall conform to standards not less than those set out in the latest published edition of the ICS/OCIMF Ship-to-Ship Transfer Guide. | 73 74 75 76 77 78 79 80 81

The vessel shall be delivered by Owners at a port in | 82

at Owners' option and redelivered to Owners at a port in | 83

at Charterers' option. | 84

Laydays/ Cancelling

5.   The vessel shall not be delivered to Charterers before   and Charterers shall have the option of cancelling this charter if the vessel is not ready and at their disposal on or before | 85 86

Owners to Provide

6.   Owners undertake to provide and to pay for all provisions, wages, and shipping and discharging fees and all other expenses of the master, officers and crew; also, except as provided in Clauses 4 and 34 hereof, for all insurance on the vessel, for all deck, cabin and engine-room stores, and for water; for all drydocking, overhaul, maintenance and repairs to the vessel; and for all fumigation expenses and de-rat certificates. Owners' obligations under this Clause 6 extend to all liabilities for customs or import duties arising at any time during the performance of this charter in relation to the personal effects of the master, officers and crew, and in relation to the stores, provisions and other matters aforesaid which Owners are to provide and pay for and Owners shall refund to Charterers any sums Charterers or their agents may have paid or been compelled to pay in respect of any such liability. Any amounts allowable in general average for wages and provisions and stores shall be credited to Charterers insofar as such amounts are in respect of a period when the vessel is on-hire. | 87 88 89 90 91 92 93 94 95 96

Charterers to Provide	7. Charterers shall provide and pay for all fuel (except fuel used for domestic services), towage and pilotage and shall pay agency fees, port charges, commissions, expenses of loading and unloading cargoes, canal dues and all charges other than those payable by Owners in accordance with Clause 6 hereof, provided that all charges for the said items shall be for Owners' account when such items are consumed, employed or incurred for Owners' purposes or while the vessel is off-hire (unless such items reasonably relate to any service given or distance made good and taken into account under Clause 21 or 22); and provided further that any fuel used in connection with a general average sacrifice or expenditure shall be paid for by Owners.
Rate of Hire	8. Subject as herein provided, Charterers shall pay for the use and hire of the vessel at the rate of per day, and pro rata for any part of a day, from the time and date of her delivery (local time) until the time and date of her redelivery (local time) to Owners.
Payment of Hire	9. Subject to Clause 3 (iii), payment of hire shall be made in immediately available funds to:

Account
in per calendar month in advance, less:
(i) any hire paid which Charterers reasonably estimate to relate to off-hire periods, and
(ii) any amounts disbursed on Owners' behalf, any advances and commission thereon, and charges which are for Owners' account pursuant to any provision hereof, and
(iii) any amounts due or reasonably estimated to become due to Charterers under Clause 3 (ii) or 24 hereof,

any such adjustments to be made at the due date for the next monthly payment after the facts have been ascertained. Charterers shall not be responsible for any delay or error by Owners' bank in crediting Owners account provided that Charterers have made proper and timely payment.
In default of such proper and timely payment,
(a) Owners shall notify Charterers of such default and Charterers shall within seven days of receipt of such notice pay to Owners the amount due including interest, failing which Owners may withdraw the vessel from the service of Charterers without prejudice to any other rights Owners may have under this charter or otherwise; and

(b) Interest on any amount due but not paid on the due date shall accrue from the day after that date up to and including the day when payment is made, at a rate per annum which shall be 1% above the U.S. Prime Interest Rate as published by the Chase Manhattan Bank in New York at 12.00 New York time on the due date, or, if no such interest rate is published on that day, the interest rate published on the next preceding day on which such a rate was so published, computed on the basis of a 360 day year of twelve 30-day months, compounded semi-annually.

97
98
99
100
101
102
103
104
105
106
107
108
109
110
111
112
113
114
115
116
117
118
119
120
121
122
123
124
125
126
127
128

Space Available to Charterers

10. The whole reach, burthen and decks of the vessel and any passenger accommodation (including Owners' suite) shall be at Charterers' disposal, reserving only proper and sufficient space for the vessel's master, officers, crew, tackle, apparel, furniture, provisions and stores, provided that the weight of stores on board shall not, unless specially agreed, exceed   tonnes at any time during the charter period. `129` `130` `131` `132`

Overtime

11. Overtime pay of the master, officers and crew in accordance with ship's articles shall be for Charterers' account when incurred, as a result of complying with the request of Charterers or their agents, for loading, discharging, heating of cargo, bunkering or tank cleaning. `133` `134` `135`

Instructions and Logs

12. Charterers shall from time to time give the master all requisite instructions and sailing directions, and he shall keep a full and correct log of the voyage or voyages, which Charterers or their agents may inspect as required. The master shall when required furnish Charterers or their agents with a true copy of such log and with properly completed loading and discharging port sheets and voyage reports for each voyage and other returns as Charterers may require. Charterers shall be entitled to take copies at Owners' expense of any such documents which are not provided by the master. `136` `137` `138` `139` `140` `141`

Bills of Lading

13. (a) The master (although appointed by Owners) shall be under the orders and direction of Charterers as regards employment of the vessel, agency and other arrangements, and shall sign bills of lading as Charterers or their agents may direct (subject always to Clauses 35(a) and 40) without prejudice to this charter. Charterers hereby indemnify Owners against all consequences or liabilities that may arise
(i) from signing bills of lading in accordance with the directions of Charterers or their agents, to the extent that the terms of such bills of lading fail to conform to the requirements of this charter, or (except as provided in Clause 13(b)) from the master otherwise complying with Charterers or their agents' orders;
(ii) from any irregularities in papers supplied by Charterers or their agents.
(b) Notwithstanding the foregoing. Owners shall not be obliged to comply with any orders from Charterers to discharge all or part of the cargo
(i) at any place other than that shown on the bill of lading and/or
(ii) without presentation of an original bill of lading
unless they have received from Charterers both written confirmation of such orders and an indemnity in a form acceptable to Owners. `142` `143` `144` `145` `146` `147` `148` `149` `150` `151` `152` `153` `154` `155`

Conduct of Vessel's Personnel

14. If Charterers complain of the conduct of the master or any of the officers or crew, Owners shall immediately investigate the complaint. If the complaint proves to be well founded, Owners shall, without delay, make a change in the appointments and Owners shall in any event communicate the result of their investigations to Charterers as soon as possible. `156` `157` `158` `159`

Bunkers at Delivery and Redelivery

15. Charterers shall accept and pay for all bunkers on board at the time of delivery, and Owners shall on redelivery (whether it occurs at the end of the charter period or on the earlier termination of this charter) accept and pay for all bunkers remaining on board, at the then-current market prices at the port of delivery or redelivery, as the case may be, or if such prices are not available payment shall be at the then-current market prices at the `160` `161` `162` `163`

nearest port at which such prices are available; provided that if delivery or redelivery does not take place in a port payment shall be at the price paid at the vessel's last port of bunkering before delivery or redelivery, as the case may be. Owners shall give Charterers the use and benefit of any fuel contracts they may have in force from time to time, if so required by Charterers, provided suppliers agree.

Stevedores. Pilots. Tugs

16.   Stevedores when required shall be employed and paid by Charterers, but this shall not relieve Owners from responsibility at all times for proper stowage, which must be controlled by the master who shall keep a strict account of all cargo loaded and discharged. Owners hereby indemnify Charterers, their servants and agents against all losses, claims, responsibilities and liabilities arising in any way whatsoever from the employment of pilots, tugboats or stevedores, who although employed by Charterers shall be deemed to be the servants of and in the service of Owners and under their instructions (even if such pilots, tugboat personnel or stevedores are in fact the servants of Charte...'s their agents or any affiliated company); provided, however, that

(i)   the foregoing indemnity shall not exceed the amount to which Owners would have been entitled to limit their liability if they had themselves employed such pilots, tugboats or stevedores, and

(ii)   Charterers shall be liable for any damage to the vessel caused by or arising out of the use of stevedores, fair wear and tear excepted, to the extent that Owners are unable by the exercise of due diligence to obtain redress therefor from stevedores.

Supernumeraries

17.   Charterers may send representatives in the vessel's available accommodation upon any voyage made under this charter. Owners finding provisions and all requisites as supplied to officers, except liquors, Charterers paying at the rate of   per day for each representative while on board the vessel.

Sub-letting

18.   Charterers may sub-let the vessel, but shall always remain responsible to Owners for due fulfilment of this charter.

Final Voyage

19.   If when a payment of hire is due hereunder Charterers reasonably expect to redeliver the vessel before the next payment of hire would fall due, the hire to be paid shall be assessed on Charterers' reasonable estimate of the time necessary to complete Charterers' programme up to redelivery, and from which estimate Charterers may deduct amounts due or reasonably expected to become due for

(i)   disbursements on Owners' behalf or charges for Owners' account pursuant to any provision hereof, and

(ii)   bunkers on board at redelivery pursuant to Clause 15.

Promptly after redelivery any overpayment shall be refunded by Owners or any underpayment made good by Charterers.

If at the time this charter would otherwise terminate in accordance with Clause 4 the vessel is on a ballast voyage to a port of redelivery or is upon a laden voyage. Charterers shall continue to have the use of the vessel at the same rate and conditions as stand herein for as long as necessary to complete such ballast voyage, or to complete such laden voyage and return to a port of redelivery as provided by this charter, as the case may be.

Loss of Vessel

20. Should the vessel be lost, this charter shall terminate and hire shall cease at noon on the day of her loss: should the vessel be a constructive total loss, this charter shall terminate and hire shall cease at noon on the day on which the vessel's underwriters agree that the vessel is a constructive total loss; should the vessel be missing, this charter shall terminate and hire shall cease at noon on the day on which she was last heard of. Any hire paid in advance and not earned shall be returned to Charterers and Owners shall reimburse Charterers for the value of the estimated quantity of bunkers on board at the time of termination, at the price paid by Charterers at the last bunkering port.

Off-hire

21. (a) On each and every occasion that there is loss of time (whether by way of interruption in the vessel's service or, from reduction in the vessel's performance, or in any other manner)

(i) due to deficiency of personnel or stores; repairs; gas-freeing for repairs; time in and waiting to enter dry dock for repairs; breakdown (whether partial or total) of machinery, boilers or other parts of the vessel or her equipment (including without limitation tank coatings); overhaul, maintenance or survey; collision, stranding, accident or damage to the vessel; or any other similar cause preventing the efficient working of the vessel; and such loss continues for more than three consecutive hours (if resulting from interruption in the vessel's service) or cumulates to more than three hours (if resulting from partial loss of service); or

(ii) due to industrial action, refusal to sail, breach of orders or neglect of duty on the part of the master, officers or crew; or

(iii) for the purpose of obtaining medical advice or treatment for or landing any sick or injured person (other than a Charterers' representative carried under Clause 17 hereof) or for the purpose of landing the body of any person (other than a Charterers' representative), and such loss continues for more than three consecutive hours; or

(iv) due to any delay in quarantine arising from the master, officers or crew having had communication with the shore at any infected area without the written consent or instructions of Charterers or their agents, or to any detention by customs or other authorities caused by smuggling or other infraction of local law on the part of the master, officers, or crew; or

(v) due to detention of the vessel by authorities at home or abroad attributable to legal action against or breach of regulations by the vessel, the vessel's owners, or Owners (unless brought about by the act or neglect of Charterers); then

without prejudice to Charterers' rights under Clause 3 or to any other rights of Charterers hereunder or otherwise the vessel shall be off-hire from the commencement of such loss of time until she is again ready and in an efficient state to resume her service from a position not less favourable to Charterers than that at which such loss of time commenced; provided, however, that any service given or distance made good by the vessel whilst off-hire shall be taken into account in assessing the amount to be deducted from hire.

(b) If the vessel fails to proceed at any guaranteed speed pursuant to Clause 24, and such failure arises wholly or partly from any of the causes set out in Clause 21(a) above, then the period for which the vessel shall be off-hire under this Clause 21 shall be the difference between

(i) the time the vessel would have required to perform the relevant service at such guaranteed speed, and

198
199
200
201
202
203
204

205
206
207
208
209
210
211
212
213
214
215
216
217
218
219
220
221
222
223
224
225
226
227
228
229
230
231
232
233
234
235

(ii) the time actually taken to perform such service (including any loss of time arising from interruption in the performance of such service).

For the avoidance of doubt, all time included under (ii) above shall be excluded from any computation under Clause 24.

(c) Further and without prejudice to the foregoing, in the event of the vessel deviating (which expression includes without limitation putting back, or putting into any port other than that to which she is bound under the instructions of Charterers) for any cause or purpose mentioned in Clause 21(a), the vessel shall be off-hire from the commencement of such deviation until the time when she is again ready and in an efficient state to resume her service from a position not less favourable to Charterers than that at which the deviation commenced, provided, however, that any service given or distance made good by the vessel whilst so off-hire shall be taken into account in assessing the amount to be deducted from hire. If the vessel, for any cause or purpose mentioned in Clause 21 (a), puts into any port other than the port to which she is bound on the instructions of Charterers, the port charges, pilotage and other expenses at such port shall be borne by Owners. Should the vessel be driven into any port or anchorage by stress of weather hire shall continue to be due and payable during any time lost thereby.

(d) If the vessel's flag state becomes engaged in hostilities, and Charterers in consequence of such hostilities find it commercially impracticable to employ the vessel and have given Owners written notice thereof then from the date of receipt by Owners of such notice until the termination of such commercial impracticability the vessel shall be off-hire and Owners shall have the right to employ the vessel on their own account.

(e) Time during which the vessel is off-hire under this charter shall count as part of the charter period.

Periodical Drydocking

22. (a) Owners have the right and obligation to drydock the vessel at regular intervals of

On each occasion Owners shall propose to Charterers a date on which they wish to drydock the vessel, not less than _____ before such date, and Charterers shall offer a port for such periodical drydocking and shall take all reasonable steps to make the vessel available as near to such date as practicable.

Owners shall put the vessel in drydock at their expense as soon as practicable after Charterers place the vessel at Owners' disposal clear of cargo other than tank washings and residues. Owners shall be responsible for and pay for the disposal into reception facilities of such tank washings and residues and shall have the right to retain any monies received therefor, without prejudice to any claim for loss of cargo under any bill of lading or this charter.

(b) If a periodical drydocking is carried out in the port offered by Charterers (which must have suitable accommodation for the purpose and reception facilities for tank washings and residues), the vessel shall be off-hire from the time she arrives at such port until drydocking is completed and she is in every way ready to resume Charterers' service and is at the position at which she went off-hire or a position no less favourable to Charterers, whichever she first attains. However,

(i) provided that Owners exercise due diligence in gas-freeing, any time lost in gas-freeing to the standard required for entry into drydock for cleaning and painting the hull shall not count as off-hire, whether lost on passage to the drydocking port or after arrival there (notwithstanding Clause 21), and

(ii) any additional time lost in further gas-freeing to meet the standard required for hot work or entry to cargo tanks shall count as off-hire, whether lost on passage to the drydocking port or after arrival there.

Any time which, but for sub-Clause (i) above, would be off-hire, shall not be included in any calculation under Clause 24.

The expenses of gas-freeing, including without limitation the cost of bunkers, shall be for Owners account.

(c) If Owners require the vessel, instead of proceeding to the offered port to carry out periodical drydocking at a special port selected by them, the vessel shall be off-hire from the time when she is released to proceed to the special port until she next presents for loading in accordance with Charterers instructions, provided, however, that Charterers shall credit Owners with the time which would have been taken on passage at the service speed had the vessel not proceeded to drydock. All fuel consumed shall be paid for by Owners but Charterers shall credit Owners with the value of the fuel which would have been used on such notional passage calculated at the guaranteed daily consumption for the service speed, and shall further credit Owners with any benefit they may gain in purchasing bunkers at the special port.

(d) Charterers shall, insofar as cleaning for periodical drydocking may have reduced the amount of tank-cleaning necessary to meet Charterers requirements, credit Owners with the value of any bunkers which Charterers calculate to have been saved thereby, whether the vessel drydocks at an offered or a special port.

Ship Inspection

23. Charterers shall have the right at any time during the charter period to make such inspection of the vessel as they may consider necessary. This right may be exercised as often and at such intervals as Charterers in their absolute discretion may determine and whether the vessel is in port or on passage. Owners affording all necessary co-operation and accommodation on board provided, however,

(i) that neither the exercise nor the non-exercise nor anything done or not done in the exercise or non-exercise, by Charterers of such right shall in any way reduce the master's or Owners authority over, or responsibility to Charterers or third parties for, the vessel and every aspect of her operation, nor increase Charterers' responsibilities to Owners or third parties for the same; and

(ii) that Charterers shall not be liable for any act, neglect or default by themselves, their servants or agents in the exercise or non-exercise of the aforesaid right.

Detailed Description and Performance

24. (a) Owners guarantee that the speed and consumption of the vessel shall be as follows:-

Average speed in knots

Laden

Maximum average bunker consumption
main propulsion – auxiliaries
fuel oil/diesel oil   fuel oil/diesel oil
tonnes   tonnes

Ballast

    The foregoing bunker consumptions are for all purposes except cargo heating and tank cleaning

and shall be pro-rated between the speeds shown.

    The service speed of the vessel is _____ knots laden and _____ knots in ballast and in the absence

of Charterers' orders to the contrary the vessel shall proceed at the service speed. However if more than one

laden and one ballast speed are shown in the table above Charterers shall have the right to order the vessel to

steam at any speed within the range set out in the table (the "ordered speed").

    If the vessel is ordered to proceed at any speed other than the highest speed shown in the table.

and the average speed actually attained by the vessel during the currency of such order exceeds such ordered

speed plus 0.5 knots (the "maximum recognised speed"), then for the purpose of calculating any increase or

decrease of hire under this Clause 24 the maximum recognised speed shall be used in place of the average speed

actually attained.

    For the purposes of this charter the "guaranteed speed" at any time shall be the then-current

ordered speed or the service speed, as the case may be

    The average speeds and bunker consumptions shall for the purposes of this Clause 24 be

calculated by reference to the observed distance from pilot station to pilot station on all sea passages during each

period stipulated in Clause 24 (c), but excluding any time during which the vessel is (or but for Clause 22 (b) (i)

would be) off-hire and also excluding "Adverse Weather Periods", being (i) any periods during which reduction

of speed is necessary for safety in congested waters or in poor visibility (ii) any days, noon to noon, when winds

exceed force 8 on the Beaufort Scale for more than 12 hours.

307
308
309
310
311
312
313
314
315
316
317
318
319
320
321
322
323
324
325
326

(b)   If during any year from the date on which the vessel enters service (anniversary to anniversary) the vessel falls below or exceeds the performance guaranteed in Clause 24(a) then if such shortfall or excess results 327
328
329

(i)   from a reduction or an increase in the average speed of the vessel, compared to the speed guaranteed in Clause 24(a), then an amount equal to the value at the hire rate of the time so lost or gained, as the case may be, shall be deducted from or added to the hire paid; 330
331
332

(ii)   from an increase or a decrease in the total bunkers consumed, compared to the total bunkers which would have been consumed had the vessel performed as guaranteed in Clause 24(a), an amount equivalent to the value of the additional bunkers consumed or the bunkers saved, as the case may be, based on the average price paid by Charterers for the vessel's bunkers in such period, shall be deducted from or added to the hire paid. 333
334
335
336
337

The addition to or deduction from hire so calculated for laden and ballast mileage respectively shall be adjusted to take into account the mileage steamed in each such condition during Adverse Weather Periods, by dividing such addition or deduction by the number of miles over which the performance has been calculated and multiplying by the same number of miles plus the miles steamed during the Adverse Weather Periods, in order to establish the total addition to or deduction from hire to be made for such period. 338
339
340
341
342

Reduction of hire under the foregoing sub-Clause (b) shall be without prejudice to any other remedy available to Charterers. 343

(c)   Calculations under this Clause 24 shall be made for the yearly periods terminating on each successive anniversary of the date on which the vessel enters service, and for the period between the last such anniversary and the date of termination of this charter if less than a year. Claims in respect of reduction of hire arising under this Clause during the final year or part year of the charter period shall in the first instance be settled in accordance with Charterers' estimate made two months before the end of the charter period. Any necessary adjustment after this charter terminates shall be made by payment by Owners to Charterers or by Charterers to Owners as the case may require. 344
345
346
347
348
349
350

Payments in respect of increase of hire arising under this Clause shall be made promptly after receipt by Charterers of all the information necessary to calculate such increase. 351
352

Salvage   25.   Subject to the provisions of Clause 21 hereof, all loss of time and all expenses (excluding any damage to or loss of the vessel or tortious liabilities to third parties) incurred in saving or attempting to save life or in successful or unsuccessful attempts at salvage shall be borne equally by Owners and Charterers provided that Charterers shall not be liable to contribute towards any salvage payable by Owners arising in any way out of services rendered under this Clause 25. 353
354
355
356
357

All salvage and all proceeds from derelicts shall be divided equally between Owners and Charterers after deducting the master's, officers' and crew's share. 358
359

Lien   26.   Owners shall have a lien upon all cargoes and all freights, sub-freights and demurrage for any amounts due under this charter; and Charterers shall have a lien on the vessel for all monies paid in advance and not earned, and for all claims for damages arising from any breach by Owners of this charter. 360
361
362

363
364
365
366
367
368
369
370
371
372
373
374
375
376
377
378
379
380
381
382
383
384
385
386

387
388
389
390

391
392
393
394
395
396

397
398
399

Exceptions

27. (a) The vessel, her master and Owners shall not, unless otherwise in this charter expressly provided, be liable for any loss or damage or delay or failure arising or resulting from any act, neglect or default of the master, pilots, mariners or other servants of Owners in the navigation or management of the vessel: fire, unless caused by the actual fault or privity of Owners; collision or stranding; dangers and accidents of the sea: explosion, bursting of boilers, breakage of shafts or any latent defect in hull, equipment or machinery; provided, however, that Clauses 1, 2, 3 and 24 hereof shall be unaffected by the foregoing. Further, neither the vessel, her master or Owners, nor Charterers shall, unless otherwise in this charter expressly provided, be liable for any loss or damage or delay or failure in performance hereunder arising or resulting from act of God, act of war, seizure under legal process, quarantine restrictions, strikes, lock-outs, riots, restraints of labour, civil commotions or arrest or restraint of princes, rulers or people.

(b) The vessel shall have liberty to sail with or without pilots, to tow or go to the assistance of vessels in distress and to deviate for the purpose of saving life or property.

(c) Clause 27(a) shall not apply to or affect any liability of Owners or the vessel or any other relevant person in respect of

(i) loss or damage caused to any berth, jetty, dock, dolphin, buoy, mooring line, pipe or crane or other works or equipment whatsoever at or near any place to which the vessel may proceed under this charter, whether or not such works or equipment belong to Charterers, or

(ii) any claim (whether brought by Charterers or any other person) arising out of any loss of or damage to or in connection with cargo. All such claims shall be subject to the Hague-Visby Rules or the Hague Rules, as the case may be, which ought pursuant to Clause 38 hereof to have been incorporated in the relevant bill of lading (whether or not such Rules were so incorporated) or, if no such bill of lading is issued, to the Hague-Visby Rules.

(d) In particular and without limitation, the foregoing subsections (a) and (b) of this Clause shall not apply to or in any way affect any provision in this charter relating to off-hire or to reduction of hire.

Injurious Cargoes

28. No acids, explosives or cargoes injurious to the vessel shall be shipped and without prejudice to the foregoing any damage to the vessel caused by the shipment of any such cargo, and the time taken to repair such damage, shall be for Charterers' account. No voyage shall be undertaken, nor any goods or cargoes loaded, that would expose the vessel to capture or seizure by rulers or governments.

Grade of Bunkers

29. Charterers shall supply marine diesel oil/fuel oil with a maximum viscosity of   Centistokes at 50 degrees Centigrade/ACGFO for main propulsion and diesel oil/ACGFO for the auxiliaries. If Owners require the vessel to be supplied with more expensive bunkers they shall be liable for the extra cost thereof.

Charterers warrant that all bunkers provided by them in accordance herewith shall be of a quality complying with the International Marine Bunker Supply Terms and Conditions of Shell International Trading Company and with its specification for marine fuels as amended from time to time.

Disbursements

30. Should the master require advances for ordinary disbursements at any port, Charterers or their agents shall make such advances to him, in consideration of which Owners shall pay a commission of two and a half per cent, and all such advances and commission shall be deducted from hire.

Laying-up   31.   Charterers shall have the option. after consultation with Owners. of requiring Owners to lay up the vessel at a safe place nominated by Charterers. in which case the hire provided for under this charter shall be adjusted to reflect any net increases in expenditure reasonably incurred or any net saving which should reasonably be made by Owners as a result of such lay-up. Charterers may exercise the said option any number of times during the charter period.   400 / 401 / 402 / 403 / 404

Requisition   32.   Should the vessel be requisitioned by any government. de facto or de jure. during the period of this charter. the vessel shall be off-hire during the period of such requisition. and any hire paid by such government in respect of such requisition period shall be for Owners' account. Any such requisition period shall count as part of the charter period.   405 / 406 / 407 / 408

Outbreak of War   33.   If war or hostilities break out between any two or more of the following countries: U.S.A.. U.S.S.R.. P.R.C.. U.K.. Netherlands–both Owners and Charterers shall have the right to cancel this charter.   409 / 410

Additional War Expenses   34.   If the vessel is ordered to trade in areas where there is war (de facto or de jure) or threat of war. Charterers shall reimburse Owners for any additional insurance premia. crew bonuses and other expenses which are reasonably incurred by Owners as a consequence of such orders. provided that Charterers are given notice of such expenses as soon as practicable and in any event before such expenses are incurred. and provided further that Owners obtain from their insurers a waiver of any subrogated rights against Charterers in respect of any claims by Owners under their war risk insurance arising out of compliance with such orders.   411 / 412 / 413 / 414 / 415 / 416

War Risks   35.   (a)   The master shall not be required or bound to sign bills of lading for any place which in his or Owners' reasonable opinion is dangerous or impossible for the vessel to enter or reach owing to any blockade. war. hostilities. warlike operations. civil war. civil commotions or revolutions.   417 / 418 / 419

     (b)   If in the reasonable opinion of the master or Owners it becomes. for any of the reasons set out in Clause 35(a) or by the operation of international law. dangerous. impossible or prohibited for the vessel to reach or enter. or to load or discharge cargo at. any place to which the vessel has been ordered pursuant to this charter (a "place of peril"). then Charterers or their agents shall be immediately notified by telex or radio messages. and Charterers shall thereupon have the right to order the cargo. or such part of it as may be affected. to be loaded or discharged. as the case may be. at any other place within the trading limits of this charter (provided such other place is not itself a place of peril). If any place of discharge is or becomes a place of peril. and no orders have been received from Charterers or their agents within 48 hours after dispatch of such messages. then Owners shall be at liberty to discharge the cargo or such part of it as may be affected at any place which they or the master may in their or his discretion select within the trading limits of this charter and such discharge shall be deemed to be due fulfilment of Owners' obligations under this charter so far as cargo so discharged is concerned.   420 / 421 / 422 / 423 / 424 / 425 / 426 / 427 / 428 / 429 / 430

     (c)   The vessel shall have liberty to comply with any directions or recommendations as to departure. arrival. routes. ports of call. stoppages. destinations. zones. waters. delivery or in any other wise whatsoever given by the government of the state under whose flag the vessel sails or any other government or local authority or by any person or body acting or purporting to act as or with the authority of any such government or local   431 / 432 / 433 / 434 authority including any de facto government or local authority or by any person or body acting or purporting to act as or with the authority of any such government or local authority or by any committee or person having under the terms of the war risks insurance on the vessel the right to give any such directions or recommendations. If by reason of or in compliance with any such directions or recommendations anything is done or is not done, such shall not be deemed a deviation.

If by reason of or in compliance with any such direction or recommendation the vessel does not proceed to any place of discharge to which she has been ordered pursuant to this charter, the vessel may proceed to any place which the master or Owners in his or their discretion select and there discharge the cargo or such part of it as may be affected. Such discharge shall be deemed to be due fulfilment of Owners' obligations under this charter so far as cargo so discharged is concerned.

Charterers shall procure that all bills of lading issued under this charter shall contain the Chamber of Shipping War Risks Clause 1952.

Both to Blame Collision Clause

36. If the liability for any collision in which the vessel is involved while performing this charter falls to be determined in accordance with the laws of the United States of America. the following provision shall apply:

"If the ship comes into collision with another ship as a result of the negligence of the other ship and any act. neglect or default of the master mariner. pilot or the servants of the carrier in the navigation or in the management of the ship. the owners of the cargo carried hereunder will indemnify the carrier against all loss. or liability to the other or non-carrying ship or her owners in so far as such loss or liability represents loss of. or damage to. or any claim whatsoever of the owners of the said cargo. paid or payable by the other or non-carrying ship or her owners to the owners of the said cargo and set off. recouped or recovered by the other or non-carrying ship or her owners as part of their claim against the carrying ship or carrier."

"The foregoing provisions shall also apply where the owners. operators or those in charge of any ship or ships or objects other than. or in addition to. the colliding ships or objects are at fault in respect of a collision or contact."

Charterers shall procure that all bills of lading issued under this charter shall contain a provision in the foregoing terms to be applicable where the liability for any collision in which the vessel is involved falls to be determined in accordance with the laws of the United States of America.

New Jason Clause

37. General average contributions shall be payable according to the York/Antwerp Rules. 1974. and shall be adjusted in London in accordance with English law and practice but should adjustment be made in accordance with the law and practice of the United States of America. the following provision shall apply:

"In the event of accident. danger. damage or disaster before or after the commencement of the voyage. resulting from any cause whatsoever. whether due to negligence or not. for which. or for the consequence of which. the carrier is not responsible by statute. contract or otherwise. the cargo. shippers. consignees or owners of the cargo shall contribute with the carrier in general average to the payment of any sacrifices. losses or expenses of a general average nature that may be made or incurred and shall pay salvage and special charges incurred in respect of the cargo."

"If a salving ship is owned or operated by the carrier. salvage shall be paid for as fully as if the said salving ship or ships belonged to strangers. Such deposit as the carrier or his agents may deem sufficient to cover

435
436
437
438
439
440
441
442
443
444
445
446
447
448
449
450
451
452
453
454
455
456
457
458
459
460
461
462
463
464
465
466
467
468
469
470
471
472

the estimated contribution of the cargo and any salvage and special charges thereon shall, if required, be made by the cargo shippers, consignees or owners of the cargo to the carrier before delivery."

Charterers shall procure that all bills of lading issued under this charter shall contain a provision in the foregoing terms, to be applicable where adjustment of general average is made in accordance with the laws and practice of the United States of America.

Clause Paramount

38. Charterers shall procure that all bills of lading issued pursuant to this charter shall contain the following clause:

"(1) Subject to sub-clause (2) hereof, this bill of lading shall be governed by, and have effect subject to, the rules contained in the International Convention for the Unification of Certain Rules relating to Bills of Lading signed at Brussels on 25th August 1924 (hereafter the "Hague Rules") as amended by the Protocol signed at Brussels on 23rd February 1968 (hereafter the "Hague-Visby Rules"). Nothing contained herein shall be deemed to be either a surrender by the carrier of any of his rights or immunities or any increase of any of his responsibilities or liabilities under the Hague-Visby Rules."

"(2) If there is governing legislation which applies the Hague Rules compulsorily to this bill of lading, to the exclusion of the Hague-Visby Rules, then this bill of lading shall have effect subject to the Hague Rules. Nothing herein contained shall be deemed to be either a surrender by the carrier of any of his rights or immunities or an increase of any of his responsibilities or liabilities under the Hague Rules."

"(3) If any term of this bill of lading is repugnant to the Hague-Visby Rules, or Hague Rules if applicable, such term shall be void to that extent but no further."

"(4) Nothing in this bill of lading shall be construed as in any way restricting, excluding or waiving the right of any relevant party or person to limit his liability under any available legislation and/or law."

TOVALOP

39. Owners warrant that the vessel is:
    (i)   a tanker in TOVALOP and
    (ii) properly entered in   P & I Club

and will so remain during the currency of this charter.

When an escape or discharge of Oil occurs from the vessel and causes or threatens to cause Pollution Damage, or when there is the threat of an escape or discharge of Oil (i.e. a grave and imminent danger of the escape or discharge of Oil which, if it occurred, would create a serious danger of Pollution Damage, whether or not an escape or discharge in fact subsequently occurs), then Charterers may, at their option, upon notice to Owners or master, undertake such measures as are reasonably necessary to prevent or minimise such Pollution Damage or to remove the Threat, unless Owners promptly undertake the same. Charterers shall keep Owners advised of the nature and result of any such measures taken by them and, if time permits, the nature of the measures intended to be taken by them. Any of the aforementioned measures taken by Charterers shall be deemed taken on Owners' authority as Owners' agent, and shall be at Owners' expense except to the extent that:

    (1)   any such escape or discharge or Threat was caused or contributed to by Charterers, or

    (2)   by reason of the exceptions set out in Article III, paragraph 2, of the 1969 International

473
474
475
476
477

478
479
480
481
482
483
484
485
486
487
488
489
490
491
492
493

494
495
496

497
498
499
500
501
502
503
504
505
506
507
508

Convention on Civil Liability for Oil Pollution Damage, Owners are or, had the said Convention applied to such escape or discharge or to the Threat, would have been exempt from liability for the same, or

(3)   the cost of such measures together with all other liabilities, costs and expenses of Owners arising out of or in connection with such escape or discharge or Threat exceeds one hundred and sixty United States Dollars (US $160) per ton of the vessel's Tonnage or sixteen million eight hundred thousand United States Dollars (US $16,800,000), whichever is the lesser, save and insofar as Owners shall be entitled to recover such excess under either the 1971 International Convention on the Establishment of an International Fund for Compensation for Oil Pollution Damage or under CRISTAL;

PROVIDED ALWAYS that if Owners in their absolute discretion consider said measures should be discontinued, Owners shall so notify Charterers and thereafter Charterers shall have no right to continue said measures under the provisions of this Clause 39 and all further liability to Charterers under this Clause 39 shall thereupon cease.

The above provisions are not in derogation of such other rights as Charterers or Owners may have under this charter or may otherwise have or acquire by law or any International Convention or TOVALOP.

The term "TOVALOP" means the Tanker Owners' Voluntary Agreement Concerning Liability for Oil Pollution dated 7th January 1969, as amended from time to time, and the term "CRISTAL" means the Contract Regarding an Interim Supplement to Tanker Liability for Oil Pollution dated 14th January 1971, as amended from time to time. The terms "Oil", "Pollution Damage", and "Tonnage" shall for the purposes of this Clause 39 have the meanings ascribed to them in TOVALOP.

Export
Restrictions

40.   The master shall not be required or bound to sign bills of lading for the carriage of cargo to any place to which export of such cargo is prohibited under the laws, rules or regulations of the country in which the cargo was produced and/or shipped.

Charterers shall procure that all bills of lading issued under this charter shall contain the following clause:

"If any laws rules or regulations applied by the government of the country in which the cargo was produced and/or shipped, or any relevant agency thereof, impose a prohibition on export of the cargo to the place of discharge designated in or ordered under this bill of lading, carriers shall be entitled to require cargo owners forthwith to nominate an alternative discharge place for the discharge of the cargo, or such part of it as may be affected, which alternative place shall not be subject to the prohibition, and carriers shall be entitled to accept orders from cargo owners to proceed to and discharge at such alternative place. If cargo owners fail to nominate an alternative place within 72 hours after they or their agents have received from carriers notice of such prohibition, carriers shall be at liberty to discharge the cargo or such part of it as may be affected by the prohibition at any safe place on which they or the master may in their or his absolute discretion decide and which is not subject to the prohibition, and such discharge shall constitute due performance of the contract contained in this bill of lading so far as the cargo so discharged is concerned".

The foregoing provision shall apply mutatis mutandis to this charter, the references to a bill of lading being deemed to be references to this charter.

509
510
511
512
513
514
515
516
517
518
519
520
521
522
523
524
525
526
527

528
529
530
531
532
533
534
535
536
537
538
539
540
541
542
543
544
545
546

Law and Litigation

41. (a) This charter shall be construed and the relations between the parties determined in accordance with the laws of England.

(b) Any dispute arising under this charter shall be decided by the English Courts to whose jurisdiction the parties hereby agree.

(c) Notwithstanding the foregoing, but without prejudice to any party's right to arrest or maintain the arrest of any maritime property, either party may, by giving written notice of election to the other party, elect to have any such dispute referred to the arbitration of a single arbitrator in London in accordance with the provisions of the Arbitration Act 1950, or any statutory modification or re-enactment thereof for the time being in force.

  (i) A party shall lose its right to make such an election only if:

    (a) it receives from the other party a written notice of dispute which –

      (1) states expressly that a dispute has arisen out of this charter;

      (2) specifies the nature of the dispute; and

      (3) refers expressly to this clause 41(c)

    and

    (b) it fails to give notice of election to have the dispute referred to arbitration not later than 30 days from the date of receipt of such notice of dispute.

  (ii) The parties hereby agree that either party may –

    (a) appeal to the High Court on any question of law arising out of an award;

    (b) apply to the High Court for an order that the arbitrator state the reasons for his award;

    (c) give notice to the arbitrator that a reasoned award is required; and

    (d) apply to the High Court to determine any question of law arising in the course of the reference.

(d) It shall be a condition precedent to the right of any party to a stay of any legal proceedings in which maritime property has been, or may be, arrested in connection with a dispute under this charter, that that party furnishes to the other party security to which that other party would have been entitled in such legal proceedings in the absence of a stay.

Construction

42. The side headings have been included in this charter for convenience of reference and shall in no way affect the construction hereof.

SHELLTIME 4 STANDARD CHARTERPARTY AMENDMENTS AND ADDITIONS

BASIS SHELLTIME 4 issued December 1984

1. AMENDMENTS TO STANDARD TEXT

Lines 6 and 25 After "charter" add "and throughout the charter period".

Clause 3 After line 59 add:

"Owners shall advise charterers immediately, in writing, should the vessel fail an inspection by, but not limited to, a governmental and/or port state authority, and/or terminal and/or major charterer of similar tonnage. Owners shall simultaneously advise charterers of their proposed course of action to remedy the defects which have caused the failure of such inspection.

If, in charterers' reasonably held view, failure of such inspection prevents normal commercial operations, charterers have the option to place the vessel offhire from the date and time that she fails such inspection until the date and time that the vessel passes a reinspection by the same organisation, which shall be in a position no less favourable to charterers than that at which she went offhire."

Clause 8

Insert to line 106 after "Owners":

"These rates are inclusive of overtime."

Clause 11 Delete.

Clause 15 Delete and insert the following:

"Charterers shall accept and pay for all bunkers at the time of delivery and owners shall on redelivery (whether it occurs at the end of the charter period or on the earlier termination of this charter) accept and pay for all bunkers remaining on board at the price actually paid, on a first in first out basis. Such prices are to be supported by paid invoices.

Vessel to be delivered to and redelivered from the charter period with a minimum quantity of bunkers on board sufficient to reach the nearest main bunkering port.

Notwithstanding anything contained in this charter party all bunkers on board the vessel shall, throughout the duration of this charter, remain the property of the charterer and can only be purchased on the terms specified in the charter party at the end of the charter period or on the earlier termination of the charter, whichever occurs first."

Clause 17 line 182 Insert "USD 15.00".

Clause 21 line 256 Add "Any periods of offhire earned under clause 21 and 22 may be added to the charter period in charterers' option".

Clause 22 Delete and insert "vessel shall be dry-docked in an emergency only".

Clause 24 Add just before line 308:

"Vessel performance to be guaranteed up to and including Beaufort 5 on a penalty only basis." Clause to be suitably amended.

Clause 27 Delete lines 380–4 inclusive and insert:

"(ii) any claim (whether brought by charterers or any other person) arising out of any loss of or damage to or in connection with the cargo. Any such claim shall be subject to the Hague-Visby Rules or the Hague Rules or the Hamburg Rules as the case may be, which ought pursuant to Clause 38 hereof to have been incorporated in the relevant Bill of Lading (whether or not such Rules were so incorporated), or if no such Bill of Lading is issued to the Hague-Visby Rules unless the Hamburg Rules compulsorily apply in which case to the Hamburg Rules."

Clause 29 Insert in line 396 after fuels "in accordance with ISO Standards RMG35".

Add:

"Owners to provide charterers with a copy of results of the test programme with DNV."

Clause 33 Delete "USSR" and insert the following:

"the countries or republics having been part of the former USSR (except that declaration of war solely between any two or more of the countries or republics having been part of the former USSR shall be exempted)."

Clause 37 Delete first paragraph and insert:

"General average shall be payable according to the York/Antwerp Rules as amended 1994 and shall be adjusted in London. All disputes relating to General Average shall be resolved in London in accordance with English Law. Without prejudice to the foregoing, should the adjustment be made in accordance with the Law and practice of the United States of America the following clause, which shall be included in all Bills of Lading issued pursuant to this time charter, shall apply:"

Clause 38 Delete and insert:

"Charterers shall procure that all Bills of Lading issued pursuant to this charter shall contain the following clause:

(1) Subject to sub-clause (2) or (3) hereof, this Bill of Lading shall be governed by and have the effect subject to the rules contained in the International Convention for the Unification of Certain Rules relating to Bills of Lading signed at Brussels on 25th August 1924 (hereafter the "Hague Rules") as amended by the Protocol signed at Brussels on 23rd February 1968 (hereafter the "Hague-Visby Rules"). Nothing contained herein shall be deemed to be either a surrender by the carrier of any of his rights or immunities or any increase of any of his responsibilities or liabilities under the Hague-Visby Rules."

"(2) If there is governing legislation which applies the Hague Rules compulsorily to this Bill of Lading, to the exclusion of the Hague-Visby Rules, then this Bill of Lading shall have effect subject to the Hague Rules. Nothing herein contained shall be deemed to be either a surrender by the carrier of any of his rights or immunities or an increase of any of his responsibilities or liabilities under the Hague Rules."

"(3) If there is governing legislation which applies the United Nations Convention on the Carriage of Goods by Sea 1978 (hereafter the "Hamburg Rules") compulsorily to this Bill of Lading to the exclusion of the Hague-Visby Rules, then this Bill of Lading shall have effect subject to the Hamburg Rules. Nothing herein contained shall be deemed to be either a surrender by the carrier of any of his rights or immunities or an increase of any of his responsibilities or liabilities under the Hamburg Rules."

"(4) If any term of this Bill of Lading is repugnant to the Hague-Visby Rules, or Hague Rules or Hamburg Rules, if applicable, such term shall be void to that extent but no further."

"(5) Nothing in this Bill of Lading shall be construed as in any way restricting, excluding or waiving the right of any relevant party or person to limit his liability under any available legislation and/or law."

Clause 39 Delete and insert new additional ITOPF clause 15.

LINER BILL OF LADING

(Liner terms approved by The Baltic and International Maritime Conference)

Code Name: "CONLINEBILL"

Amended January 1st, 1950, August 1st, 1952, January 1st, 1973, July 1st, 1974, August 1st, 1976, January 1st, 1978.

1. Definition.
Wherever the term "Merchant" is used in this Bill of Lading, it shall be deemed to include the Shipper, the Receiver, the Consignee, the Holder of the Bill of Lading and the Owner of the cargo.

2. General Paramount Clause.
The Hague Rules contained in the International Convention for the Unification of certain rules relating to Bills of Lading, dated Brussels the 25th August 1924 as enacted in the country of shipment shall apply to this contract. When no such enactment is in force in the country of shipment, the corresponding legislation of the country of destination shall apply, but in respect of shipments to which no such enactments are compulsorily applicable, the terms of the said Convention shall apply.
Trades where Hague-Visby Rules apply.
In trades where the International Brussels Convention 1924 as amended by the Protocol signed at Brussels on February 23rd 1968 – The Hague-Visby Rules – apply compulsorily, the provisions of the respective legislation shall be considered incorporated in this Bill of Lading. The Carrier takes all reservations possible under such applicable legislation, relating to the period before loading and after discharging and while the goods are in the charge of another Carrier, and to deck cargo and live animals.

3. Jurisdiction.
Any dispute arising under this Bill of Lading shall be decided in the country where the carrier has his principal place of business, and the law of such country shall apply except as provided elsewhere herein.

4. Period of Responsibility.
The Carrier or his Agent shall not be liable for loss of or damage to the goods during the period before loading and after discharge from the vessel, howsoever such loss or damage arises.

5. The Scope of Voyage.
As the vessel is engaged in liner service the intended voyage shall not be limited to the direct route but shall be deemed to include any proceeding or returning to or stopping or slowing down at or off any ports or places for any reasonable purpose connected with the service including maintenance of vessel and crew.

6. Substitution of Vessel, Transhipment and Forwarding.
Whether expressly arranged beforehand or otherwise, the Carrier shall be at liberty to carry the goods to their port of destination by the said or other vessel or vessels either belonging to the Carrier or others, or

hours before the vessel's arrival there. In the absence of such declaration the Carrier may elect to discharge at the first or any other optional port and the contract of carriage shall then be considered as having been fulfilled. Any option can be exercised for the total quantity under this Bill of Lading only.

11. Freight and Charges.
(a) Prepayable freight, whether actually paid or not, shall be considered as fully earned upon loading and non-returnable in any event. The Carrier's claim for any charges under this contract shall be considered definitely payable in like manner as soon as the charges have been incurred.
Interest at 5 per cent., shall run from the date when freight and charges are due.
(b) The Merchant shall be liable for expenses of fumigation and of gathering and sorting loose cargo and of weighing onboard and expenses incurred in repairing damage to and replacing of packing due to excepted causes and for all expenses caused by extra handling of the cargo for any of the aforementioned reasons.
(c) Any dues, duties, taxes and charges which under any denomination may be levied on any basis such as amount of freight, weight of cargo or tonnage of the vessel shall be paid by the Merchant.
(d) The Merchant shall be liable for all fines and/or losses which the Carrier, vessel or cargo may incur through non-observance of Custom House and/or import or export regulations.
(e) The Carrier is entitled in case of incorrect declaration of contents, weights, measurements or value of the goods to claim double the amount of freight which would have been due if such declaration had been correctly given. For the purpose of ascertaining the actual facts, the Carrier reserves the right to obtain from the Merchant the original invoice and to have the contents inspected and the weight, measurement or value verified.

12. Lien.
The Carrier shall have a lien for any amount due under this contract and costs of recovering same and shall be entitled to sell the goods privately or by auction to cover any claims.

13. Delay.
The Carrier shall not be responsible for any loss sustained by the Merchant through delay of the goods unless caused by the Carrier's personal gross negligence.

14. General Average and Salvage.
General Average to be adjusted at any port or place at Carrier's

discharge the cargo at port of loading or any other safe and convenient port.
(d) The discharge under the provisions of this clause of any cargo for which a Bill of Lading has been issued shall be deemed due fulfilment of the contract. If in connection with the exercise of any liberty under this clause any extra expenses are incurred, they shall be paid by the Merchant in addition to the freight, together with return freight if any and a reasonable compensation for any extra services rendered to the goods.
(e) If any situation referred to in this clause may be anticipated, or if for any such reason the vessel cannot safely and without delay reach or enter the loading port or must undergo repairs, the Carrier may cancel the contract before the Bill of Lading is issued.
(f) The Merchant shall be informed if possible.

17. Identity of Carrier.
The Contract evidenced by this Bill of Lading is between the Merchant and the Owner of the vessel named herein (or substitute) and it is therefore agreed that said Shipowner only shall be liable for any damage or loss due to any breach or non-performance of any obligation arising out of the contract of carriage, whether or not relating to the vessel's seaworthiness. If, despite the foregoing, it is adjudged that any other is the Carrier and/or bailee of the goods shipped hereunder, all limitations of, and exonerations from, liability provided for by law or by this Bill of Lading shall be available to such other.
It is further understood and agreed that as the Line, Company or Agents who has executed this Bill of Lading for and on behalf of the Master is not a principal in the transaction, said Line, Company or Agents shall not be under any liability arising out of the contract of carriage, nor as Carrier nor bailee of the goods.

18. Exemptions and Immunities of all servants and agents of the Carrier.
It is hereby expressly agreed that no servant or agent of the Carrier (including every independent contractor from time to time employed by the Carrier) shall in any circumstances whatsoever be under any liability whatsoever to the Merchant for any loss, damage or delay arising or resulting directly or indirectly from any act, neglect or default on his part while acting in the course of or in connection with his employment and, but without prejudice to the generality of the foregoing provisions in this clause, every exemption, limitation, condition and liberty herein contained and every right, exemption from liability, defence and immunity of whatsoever nature applicable to the Carrier or to which the Carrier is entitled hereunder shall also be

by other means of transport, proceeding either directly or indirectly to such port and to carry the goods or part of them beyond their port of destination, and to tranship, land and store the goods either on shore or afloat and reship and forward the same at Carrier's expense but at Merchant's risk. When the ultimate destination at which the Carrier may have engaged to deliver the goods is other than the vessel's port of discharge, the Carrier acts as Forwarding Agent only.

The responsibility of the Carrier shall be limited to the part of the transport performed by him on vessels under his management and no claim will be acknowledged by the Carrier for damage or loss arising during any other part of the transport even though the freight for the whole transport has been collected by him.

7. Lighterage.

Any lightering in or off ports of loading or ports of discharge to be for the account of the Merchant.

8. Loading, Discharging and Delivery

of the cargo shall be arranged by the Carrier's Agent unless otherwise agreed.

Loading, storing and delivery shall be for the Merchant's account.

Loading and discharging may commence without previous notice.

The Merchant or his Assign shall tender the goods when the vessel is ready to load and as fast as the vessel can receive and – but only if required by the Carrier – also outside ordinary working hours notwithstanding any custom of the port. Otherwise the Carrier shall be relieved of any obligation to load such cargo and the vessel may leave the port without further notice and deadfreight is to be paid.

The Merchant or his Assign shall take delivery of the goods and continue to receive the goods as fast as the vessel can deliver and – but only if required by the Carrier – also outside ordinary working hours notwithstanding any custom of the port. Otherwise the Carrier shall be at liberty to discharge the goods and any discharge to be deemed a true fulfilment of the contract, or alternatively to act under Clause 16.

The Merchant shall bear all overtime charges in connection with tendering and taking delivery of the goods as above.

If the goods are not applied for within a reasonable time, the Carrier may sell the same privately or by auction.

The Merchant shall accept his reasonable proportion of unidentified loose cargo.

9. Live Animals and Deck Cargo

shall be carried subject to the Hague Rules as referred to in Clause 2 hereof with the exception that notwithstanding anything contained in Clause 19 the Carrier shall not be liable for any loss or damage resulting from any act, neglect or default of his servants in the management of such animals and deck cargo.

10. Options.

The port of discharge for optional cargo must be declared to the vessel's Agents at the first of the optional ports not later than 48

option and to be settled according to the York–Antwerp Rules 1974.

In the event of accident, danger, damage or disaster before or after commencement of the voyage resulting from any cause whatsoever, whether due to negligence or not, for which or for the consequence of which the Carrier is not responsible by statute, contract or otherwise, the Merchant shall contribute with the Carrier in General Average to the payment of any sacrifice, losses or expenses of a General Average nature that may be made or incurred, and shall pay salvage and special charges incurred in respect of the goods. If a salving vessel is owned or operated by the Carrier, salvage shall be paid for as fully as if the salving vessel or vessels belonged to strangers.

15. Both-to-Blame Collision Clause. (This clause to remain in effect even if unenforcible in the Courts of the United States of America.)

If the vessel comes into collision with another vessel as a result of the negligence of the other vessel and any act, negligence or default of the Master, Mariner Pilot or the servants of the Carrier in the navigation or in the management of the vessel, the Merchant will indemnify the Carrier against all loss or liability to the other or non-carrying vessel or her Owner in so far as such loss or liability represents loss of or damage to or any claim whatsoever of the owner of the said goods paid or payable by the other or non-carrying vessel or her Owner to the owner of said cargo and set-off, or recouped or recovered by the other or non-carrying vessel or her Owner as part of his claim against the carrying vessel or Carrier. The foregoing provisions shall also apply where the Owner, operator or those in charge of any vessel or vessels or objects other than, or in addition to, the colliding vessels or objects are at fault in respect of a collision or contact.

16. Government directions, War, Epidemics, Ice, Strikes, etc.

(a) The Master and the Carrier shall have liberty to comply with any order or directions or recommendations in connection with the transport under this contract given by any Government or Authority, or anybody acting or purporting to act on behalf of such Government or Authority, or having under the terms of the insurance on the vessel the right to give such orders or directions or recommendations.

(b) Should it appear that the performance of the transport would expose the vessel or any goods onboard to risk of seizure or damage or delay, resulting from war, warlike operations, blockade, riots, civil commotions or piracy, or any person onboard to the risk of loss of life or freedom, or that any such risk has increased, the Master may discharge the cargo at port of loading or any other safe and convenient port.

(c) Should it appear that epidemics, quarantine, ice – labour troubles, labour obstructions, strikes, lock-outs, any of which onboard or on shore – difficulties in loading or discharging would prevent the vessel from leaving the port of loading or reaching or entering the port of discharge or there discharging in the usual manner and leaving again, all of which safely and without delay, the Master may

available and shall extend to protect every such servant or agent of the Carrier acting as aforesaid and for the purpose of all the foregoing provisions of this clause the Carrier is or shall be deemed to be acting as agent or trustee on behalf of and for the benefit of all persons who are or might be his servants or agents from time to time (including independent contractors as aforesaid) and all such persons shall to this extent be or be deemed to be parties to the contract evidenced by this Bill of Lading.

The Carrier shall be entitled to be paid by the Merchant on demand any sum recovered or recoverable by the Merchant or any other from such servant or agent of the Carrier for any such loss, damage or delay or otherwise.

19. Optional Stowage. Unitization.

(a) Goods may be stowed by the Carrier as received, or, at Carrier's option, by means of containers, or similar articles of transport used to consolidate goods.

(b) Containers, trailers and transportable tanks, whether stowed by the Carrier or received by him in a stowed condition from the Merchant, may be carried on or under deck without notice to the Merchant.

(c) The Carrier's liability for cargo stowed as aforesaid shall be governed by the Hague Rules as defined above notwithstanding the fact that the goods are being carried on deck and the goods shall contribute to general average and shall receive compensation in general average.

ADDITIONAL CLAUSES
(To be added if required in the contemplated trade).

A. Demurrage.

The Carrier shall be paid demurrage at the daily rate per ton of the vessel's gross register tonnage as indicated on Page 2 if the vessel is not loaded or discharged with the dispatch set out in Clause 8, any delay in waiting for berth at or off port to count. Provided that if the delay is due to causes beyond the control of the Merchant, 24 hours shall be deducted from the time on demurrage.

Each Merchant shall be liable towards the Carrier for a proportionate part of the total demurrage due, based upon the total freight on the goods to be loaded or discharged at the port in question.

No Merchant shall be liable in demurrage for any delay arisen only in connection with goods belonging to other Merchants.

The demurrage in respect of each parcel shall not exceed its freight. (This Clause shall only apply if the Demurrage Box on Page 2 is filled in).

B. U.S. Trade. Period of Responsibility.

In case the Contract evidenced by this Bill of Lading is subject to the U.S. Carriage of Goods by Sea Act, then the provisions stated in said Act shall govern before loading and after discharge and throughout the entire time the goods are in the Carrier's custody.

LINER BILL OF LADING

Page 2

B/L No.

Reference No.

Shipper

Consignee

Notify address

Pre-carriage by*

Place of receipt by pre-carrier*

Vessel

Port of loading

Port of discharge

Place of delivery by on-carrier*

Marks and Nos.	Number and kind of packages; description of goods	Gross weight	Measurement

Particulars furnished by the Merchant

Freight details, charges etc.

Daily demurrage rate (additional Clause A)

* Applicable only when document used as a Through Bill of Lading

Printed and sold
by Fr. G. Knudtzon. Ltd.. 55. Toldbodgade. Copenhagen,
by authority of The Baltic and International Maritime Conference.
(BIMCO). Copenhagen.

SHIPPED on board in apparent good order and condition, weight, measure, marks, numbers, quality, contents and value unknown, for carriage to the Port of Discharge or so near thereunto as the Vessel may safely get and lie always afloat, to be delivered in the like good order and condition at the aforesaid Port unto Consignees or their Assigns, they paying freight as indicated to the left plus other charges incurred in accordance with the provisions contained in this Bill of Lading. In accepting this Bill of Lading the Merchant expressly accepts and agrees to all its stipulations on both pages, whether written, printed, stamped or otherwise incorporated, as fully as if they were all signed by the Merchant.
One original Bill of Lading must be surrendered duly endorsed in exchange for the goods or delivery order.
I N   W I T N E S S whereof the Master of the said Vessel has signed the number of original Bills of Lading stated below, all of this tenor and date, one of which being accomplished, the others to stand void.

Freight payable at

Place and date of issue

Number of original Bs/L

Signature

BILL OF LADING

TO BE USED WITH CHARTER-PARTIES
CODE NAME: "CONGENBILL"
EDITION 1994
ADOPTED BY
THE BALTIC AND INTERNATIONAL MARITIME COUNCIL (BIMCO)

Conditions of Carriage

(1) All terms and conditions, liberties and exceptions of the Charter Party, dated as overleaf, including the Law and Arbitration Clause, are herewith incorporated.

(2) **General Paramount Clause.**

    (a) The Hague Rules contained in the International Convention for the Unification of certain rules relating to Bills of Lading, dated Brussels the 25th August 1924 as enacted in the country of shipment, shall apply to this Bill of Lading. When no such enactment is in force in the country of shipment, the corresponding legislation of the country of destination shall apply, but in respect of shipments to which no such enactments are compulsorily applicable, the terms of the said Convention shall apply.

    (b) *Trades where Hague-Visby Rules apply.*

    In trades where the International Brussels Convention 1924 as amended by the Protocol signed at Brussels on February 23rd 1968 – the Hague-Visby Rules – apply compulsorily, the provisions of the respective legislation shall apply to this Bill of Lading.

    (c) The Carrier shall in no case be responsible for loss of or damage to the cargo, howsoever arising prior to loading into and after discharge from the Vessel or while the cargo is in the charge of another Carrier, nor in respect of deck cargo or live animals.

(3) **General Average.**

General Average shall be adjusted, stated and settled according to York-Antwerp Rules 1994, or any subsequent modification thereof, in London unless another place is agreed in the Charter Party.

Cargo's contribution to General Average shall be paid to the Carrier even when such average is the result of a fault, neglect or error of the Master, Pilot or Crew. The Charterers, Shippers and Consignees expressly renounce the Belgian Commercial Code, Part II, Art. 148.

(4) **New Jason Clause.**

In the event of accident, danger, damage or disaster before or after the commencement of the voyage, resulting from any cause whatsoever, whether due to negligence or not, for which, or for the consequence of which, the Carrier is not responsible, by statute, contract or otherwise, the cargo, shippers, consignees or the owners of the cargo shall contribute with the Carrier in General Average to the payment of any sacrifices, losses or expenses of a General Average nature that may be made or incurred and shall pay salvage and special charges incurred in respect of the cargo. If a salving vessel is owned or operated by the Carrier, salvage shall be paid for as fully as if the said salving vessel or vessels belonged to strangers. Such deposit as the Carrier, or his agents, may deem sufficient to cover the estimated contribution of the goods and any salvage and special charges thereon shall, if required, be made by the cargo, shippers, consignees or owners of the goods to the Carrier before delivery.

(5) **Both-to-Blame Collision Clause.**

If the Vessel comes into collision with another vessel as a result of the negligence of the other vessel and any act, neglect or default of the Master, Mariner, Pilot or the servants of the Carrier in the navigation or in the management of the Vessel, the owners of the cargo carried hereunder will indemnify the Carrier against all loss or liability to the other or non-carrying vessel or her owners in so far as such loss or liability represents loss of, or damage to, or any claim whatsoever of the owners of said cargo, paid or payable by the other or non-carrying vessel or her owners to the owners of said cargo and set-off, recouped or recovered by the other or non-carrying vessel or her owners as part of their claim against the carrying Vessel or the Carrier.

The foregoing provisions shall also apply where the owners, operators or those in charge of any vessel or vessels or objects other than, or in addition to, the colliding vessels or objects are at fault in respect of a collision or contact.

For particulars of cargo, freight,
destination, etc., see overleaf.

CODE NAME: "CONGENBILL". EDITION 1994

Shipper

BILL OF LADING

TO BE USED WITH CHARTER-PARTIES

B/L No.

Reference No.

Consignee

Notify address

Vessel	Port of loading

Port of discharge

Shipper's description of goods   Gross weight

(of which   on deck at Shipper's risk; the Carrier not
being responsible for loss or damage howsoever arising)

Freight payable as per
CHARTER-PARTY dated ....

FREIGHT ADVANCE.
Received on account of freight:

....

Time used for loading .... days .... hours.

SHIPPED at the Port of Loading in apparent good order and condition on board the Vessel for carriage to the Port of Discharge or so near thereto as she may safely get the goods specified above.

Weight, measure, quality, quantity, condition, contents and value unknown.

IN WITNESS whereof the Master or Agent of the said Vessel has signed the number of Bills of Lading indicated below all of this tenor and date, any one of which being accomplished the others shall be void.

FOR CONDITIONS OF CARRIAGE SEE OVERLEAF

Freight payable at	Place and date of issue
Number of original Bs/L	Signature

Printed and sold by
Fr. G. Knudtzons Bogtrykkeri A/S, 55 Toldbodgade, DK-1253 Copenhagen K,
Telefax +45 33 93 11 84
by authority of The Baltic and International Maritime Council
(BIMCO), Copenhagen.

Bill of Lading for Combined Transport shipment or Port to Port shipment

Shipper

B/L No.:
Booking Ref.:
Shipper's Ref.:

P&O Nedlloyd

Consignee or Order

Notify Party/Address (It is agreed that no responsibility shall attach to the Carrier or his Agents for failure to notify (see clause 20 on reverse))

Place of Receipt (Applicable only when this document is used as a Combined Transport Bill of Lading)

Place of Delivery (Applicable only when this document is used as a Combined Transport Bill of Lading)

Vessel and Voy. No.

Port of Loading

Port of Discharge

Marks and Nos; Container Nos; | Number and kind of Packages; description of Goods | Gross Weight (kg) | Measurement (cbm)

Above particulars as declared by Shipper, but not acknowledged by the Carrier (see clause 11)

* Total No. of Containers/Packages received by the Carrier

Received by the Carrier from the Shipper in apparent good order and condition (unless otherwise noted herein) the total number or quantity of Containers or other packages or units indicated in the box opposite entitled "*Total No. of Containers/Packages received by the Carrier for Carriage subject to all the terms and conditions hereof (INCLUDING THE TERMS AND CONDITIONS ON THE REVERSE HEREOF AND THE TERMS AND CONDITIONS OF THE CARRIER'S APPLICABLE TARIFF) from the Place of Receipt or the Port of Loading, whichever is applicable, to the Port of Discharge or the Place of Delivery, whichever is applicable. If the acknowledged tally is of Containers, this indicates that the Container has been packed and sealed by the Merchant at his premises without the Carrier being represented and able to check or verify either the tally of Goods or the stowage, which are consequently unknown to him (See Clause 8). The Merchant accepts that, except by special arrangement or pursuant to Clause 9 hereof, Containers are not weighed by the Carrier at any time. If the Carrier so requires, before he arranges delivery of the Goods one original Bill of Lading, duly endorsed, must be surrendered by the Merchant to the Carrier at the Port of Discharge or at some other location acceptable to the Carrier. In accepting this Bill of Lading the Merchant expressly accepts and agrees to all its terms and conditions whether printed, stamped or written, or otherwise incorporated, notwithstanding the non-signing of this Bill of Lading by the Merchant. Without prejudice to the generality of this reference, attention is drawn, inter-alia, to Clause 12 (Shipper's/Merchant's Responsibility), 19 (Dangerous Goods) and 24 (Law & Jurisdiction).

Movement

Freight and Charges (indicate whether prepaid or collect):

Origin Inland Haulage Charge ....

Origin Terminal Handling/LCL Service Charge ... ...

Ocean Freight   ... ...

Destination Terminal Handling/LCL Service Charge ...

Destination Inland Haulage Charge   ... ...

Freight Payable at

Number of Original Bills of Lading

Place and Date of Issue

IN WITNESS of the contract herein contained the number of originals stated opposite has been issued, one of which being accomplished the other(s) to be void
FOR P&O NEDLLOYD LTD, AS CARRIER*

ORIGINAL

P&O Nedlloyd

*OPERATING IN PARTNERSHIP WITH P&O NEDLLOYD BV

8/PONL B/L5 8/00

ICS

C/T B/L

April 78

444049

TERMS AND CONDITIONS
(Enlarged print available from the Carrier or his agents.)

1. DEFINITIONS
In this Bill of Lading the word: –

"Carrier" means the party named in the Signature box on the face hereof.

"Merchant" includes any Person who at any time has been or becomes the Shipper, Holder, Consignee, Receiver of the Goods, any Person who owns or is entitled to the possession of the Goods or of this Bill of Lading and any Person acting on behalf of any such Person.

"Holder" means any Person for the time being in possession of (or entitled to the possession of) this Bill of Lading.

"Person" includes an individual, group, company or other entity.

"Sub-Contractor" includes (but is not limited to) owners and operators of vessels (other than the Carrier), stevedores, terminal and groupage operators, road, rail and air transport operators and any independent contractor employed by the Carrier in performance of the Carriage and any sub-sub-contractors thereof.

"indemnify" includes defend, indemnify and hold harmless whether or not the obligation to indemnify arises out of negligent or non-negligent acts or omissions of the Carrier, his servants, agents or Sub-Contractors.

"Goods" means the whole or any part of the cargo received from the Shipper and includes the packing and any equipment or Container not supplied by or on behalf of the Carrier.

"Container" includes any container, trailer, transportable tank, flat or pallet, or any similar article used to consolidate goods and any ancillary equipment.

"Carriage" means the whole or any part of the operations and services undertaken by the Carrier in respect of the Goods covered by this Bill of Lading.

"Port of Loading" means any port at which the Goods are loaded on board any vessel (which may not necessarily be the vessel named overleaf) for Carriage under this Bill of Lading.

"Port of Discharge" means any port at which the Goods are discharged from any vessel (which may not necessarily be the vessel named overleaf) after Carriage under this Bill of Lading.

"Vessel" means any waterborne craft used in the Carriage under this Bill of Lading which may be a feeder vessel or an ocean vessel.

"Combined Transport" arises if the Place of Receipt and/or the Place of Delivery are indicated on the face hereof in the relevant spaces.

"Port to Port" arises if the Carriage is not Combined Transport.

"Shipped on Board" relates only to the Container into which the Goods are manifested.

"Freight" includes all charges payable to the Carrier in accordance with the applicable Tariff and this Bill of Lading.

"Hague Rules" means the provisions of the International Convention for the Unification of Certain Rules relating to Bills of Lading signed at Brussels on 25th August, 1924 and includes the amendments by the Protocol signed at Brussels on 23rd February, 1968, but only if such amendments are compulsorily applicable to this Bill of Lading. (It is expressly provided that nothing in this Bill of Lading shall be construed as contractually applying said Rules as amended by said Protocol).

2. CARRIER'S TARIFF
The terms and conditions of the Carrier's applicable Tariff are incorporated herein. Particular attention is drawn to the terms and conditions therein relating to container and vehicle demurrage. Copies of the relevant provisions of the applicable Tariff are obtainable from the Carrier or his agents upon request. In the case of inconsistency between this Bill of Lading and the applicable Tariff, this Bill of Lading shall prevail.

3. WARRANTY
The Merchant warrants that in agreeing to the terms and conditions hereof he is, or has the authority of the Person owning or entitled to the possession of the Goods and this Bill of Lading.

4. SUB-CONTRACTING AND INDEMNITY
(1) The Carrier shall be entitled to sub-contract the Carriage on any terms whatsoever.

(2) The Merchant undertakes that no claim or allegation shall be made against any Person whomsoever by whom the Carriage is performed or undertaken (including all Sub-Contractors of the Carrier), other than the Carrier, which imposes or attempts to impose upon any such Person, or any vessel owned by any such Person, any liability whatsoever in connection with the Goods or the Carriage of the Goods, whether or not arising out of negligence on the part of such Person and, if any such claim or allegation should nevertheless be made, the Merchant will indemnify the Carrier against all consequences thereof. Without prejudice to the foregoing every such Person or vessel shall have the benefit of every right, defence, limitation and liberty of whatsoever nature herein contained or otherwise available to the Carrier (including, but not limited to Clause 24 hereof) as if such provisions were expressly for his benefit, and in entering into this contract, the Carrier, to the extent of these provisions, does so not only on his own behalf but also as agent and trustee for such Persons or vessel.

(3) The provisions of Clause 4 (2), including but not limited to the undertakings of the Merchant contained therein, shall extend to claims or allegations of whatsoever nature against other Persons chartering space on the carrying vessel.

(4) The Merchant further undertakes that no claim or allegation in respect of the Goods shall be made against the Carrier by any Person other than in accordance with the terms and conditions of this Bill of Lading which imposes or attempts to impose upon the Carrier any liability whatsoever in connection with the Goods or the Carriage of the Goods, whether or not arising out of negligence on the part of the Carrier and, if any such claim or allegation should nevertheless be made, to indemnify the Carrier against all consequences thereof.

5. CARRIER'S RESPONSIBILITY PORT-TO-PORT SHIPMENT
If Carriage is Port-to-Port, the liability (if any) of the Carrier for loss, damage or delay to the Goods occurring from and during loading onto any vessel up to and during discharge from that vessel or from another vessel into which the Goods have been transhipped shall be determined in accordance with any national law making the Hague Rules compulsorily applicable to this Bill of Lading, or in any other case in accordance with the Hague Rules, Articles 1–8 inclusive only.

Unless Clause 25 applies, the Carrier shall be under no liability whatsoever for loss, damage or delay to the Goods, howsoever occurring, if such loss or damage arises prior to loading onto or subsequent to discharge from a vessel. Notwithstanding the above, in case and to the extent that any applicable law provides for any additional period of responsibility, the Carrier shall have the benefit of every right, defence, limitation and liberty in the Hague Rules as applied by this clause during that period, notwithstanding that the loss, damage or delay did not occur at sea.

In the event of the Goods being discharged at a port other than the Port of Discharge nominated in this Bill of Lading and forwarded to the nominated Port of Discharge by whatever means, the Hague Rules as referred to in paragraph 1 of this clause shall continue to apply until delivery at the nominated Port of Discharge, notwithstanding that Carriage may not be by sea.

6. CARRIER'S RESPONSIBILITY/ COMBINED TRANSPORT
If Carriage is Combined Transport, the Carrier undertakes to perform and/or in his own name to procure performance of the Carriage from the Place of Receipt or the Port of Loading whichever is applicable, to the Port of Discharge or the Place of Delivery, whichever is applicable, and, save as is otherwise provided for in this Bill of Lading, the Carrier shall be liable for loss, damage or delay occurring during the Carriage only to the extent set out below.

(1) *If the stage of the Carriage during which loss or damage occurred is not known*

(a) *Exclusions*

If the stage of the Carriage during which the loss, damage or delay occurred is not known, the Carrier shall be relieved of liability for any loss, damage or delay if such loss, damage or delay was caused by:

(i) an act or omission of the Merchant,

(ii) insufficiency of or defective condition of packing or marking,

(iii) handling, loading, stowage or unloading of the Goods by or on behalf of the Merchant (see Clause 8),

(iv) inherent vice of the Goods,

(v) strike, lock-out, stoppage or restraint of labour, from whatever cause, whether partial or general,

(vi) a nuclear incident,

(vii) any cause or event which the Carrier could not avoid and the consequences whereof he could not prevent by the exercise of reasonable diligence,

(viii) any act or omission of the Carrier the consequences of which he could not reasonably have foreseen,

(ix) compliance with instructions of any Person entitled to give them.

(b) *Burden of Proof*

The burden of proof that the loss, damage or delay was due to one or more of the causes or events specified in this Clause 6 (1) shall rest upon the Carrier. Save that if the Carrier establishes that, in the circumstances of the case, the loss or damage could be attributed to one or more of the causes or events specified in Clause 6 (1) (a) (ii), (iii) or (iv), it shall be presumed that it was so caused. The Merchant shall, however, be entitled to prove that the loss or damage was not, in fact, caused either wholly or partly by one or more of these causes or events.

(c) *Limitation of Liability*

Except as provided in Clauses 7 (2), 7 (3), and 27, if Clause 6 (1) operates total compensation shall in no circumstances whatsoever and howsoever arising exceed 2 SDRs per kilo of the gross weight of the Goods lost or damaged. (SDR means Special Drawing Right as defined by the International Monetary Fund). Limitation of liability for delay shall be as provided in the applicable international convention or national law, in the absence of which the Carrier accepts no liability whatsoever for delay, howsoever caused (see Clause 7 (4)).

(2) *If the state of the Carriage during which the loss or damage occurred is known*

Notwithstanding anything provided for in Clause 6 (1) and subject to Clauses 15 and 16, if it is known during which stage of the Carriage the loss, damage or delay occurred, the liability of the Carrier in respect of such loss, damage or delay shall be determined:

(a) by the provisions contained in any international convention or national law which provisions:–

(i) cannot be departed from by private contract to the detriment of the Merchant, and

(ii) would have applied if the Merchant had made a separate and direct contract with the Carrier in respect of the particular stage of the carriage during which the loss, damage or delay occurred and received as evidence thereof any particular document which must be issued in order to make such international convention or national law applicable, or

(b) if no international convention or national law would apply by virtue of Clause 6 (2) (a), by the Hague Rules, Articles 1–8 inclusive only if the loss, damage or delay is known to have occurred during waterborne Carriage, or

(c) by the provisions of Clause 6 (1) if the provisions of Clause 6 (2) (a) and (b) above do not apply.

For the purposes of Clause 6 (2), references in the Hague Rules to carriage by sea shall be deemed to include references to all waterborne Carriage and the Hague Rules shall be construed accordingly.

(3) *If the Place of Receipt or Place of Delivery is not named on the face hereof*

Subject to Clauses 5 and 25,

(a) if the Place of Receipt is not named on the face hereof, the Carrier shall be under no liability whatsoever for loss, damage or delay to the Goods, howsoever occurring, if such loss, damage or delay arises prior to loading onto the vessel.

(b) if the Place of Delivery is not named on the face hereof, the Carrier shall be under no liability whatsoever for loss, damage or delay to the Goods, howsoever occurring, if such loss or damage arises subsequent to discharge from the vessel.

(4) *Notice of Claim*

Unless Clause 25 applies, the Carrier shall be deemed prima facie to have effected timely delivery of the Goods as described in this Bill of Lading unless notice of loss, damage or delay to the Goods, indicating the general nature of such loss, damage or delay, shall have been given in writing to the Carrier or to his representative at the Place of Delivery (or the Port of Discharge if no Place of Delivery is named on the face hereof) before or at the time of removal of the Goods into the custody of the Person entitled to delivery thereof under this Bill of Lading, or, if the loss or damage is not apparent, within three working days thereafter.

(5) *Time-bar*

Unless Clause 25 applies, the Carrier shall be discharged of all liability whatsoever in respect of the Goods, unless suit is brought and notice

thereof given to the Carrier within nine months after delivery of the Goods or, if the Goods are not delivered, ten months after the date of issue of this Bill of lading.

7. SUNDRY LIABILITY PROVISIONS

(1) *Basis of Compensation*

Unless Clause 25 applies, compensation shall be calculated by reference to the value of the Goods at the place and time they are delivered to the Merchant, or at the place and time they should have been delivered. For the purpose of determining the extent of the Carrier's liability for loss, damage or delay to the Goods, the sound value of the Goods is agreed to be the FOB/FCA invoice value plus freight and insurance if paid.

(2) *Hague Rules Limitation*

If the Hague Rules are applicable by national law, the liability of the Carrier shall in no event exceed the limit provided in the applicable national law. If the Hague Rules are applicable otherwise than by national law, in determining the liability of the Carrier the liability shall in no event exceed £100 sterling per package or unit.

(3) *Ad Valorem*

The Merchant agrees and acknowledges that the Carrier has no knowledge of the value of the Goods, and that higher compensation than that provided for in this Bill of Lading may not be claimed unless, with the consent of the Carrier, the value of the Goods declared by the Shipper prior to the commencement of the Carriage is stated in this Bill of Lading and extra Freight paid, if required. In that case, the amount of the declared value shall be substituted for the limits laid down in this Bill of Lading. Any partial loss or damage shall be adjusted pro rata on the basis of such declared value.

(4) *Delay*

(a) Unless Clause 25 applies, the Carrier does not undertake that the Goods shall arrive at the Port of Discharge or Place of Delivery at any particular time or to meet any particular market or use, and the Carrier shall in no circumstances whatsoever and howsoever arising be liable for direct, indirect or consequential loss or damage caused by delay.

(b) However, if Clause 25 applies, unless a latest date of delivery is shown on the face hereof and any required premium paid, timely delivery shall be considered to have been made if the Goods are made available to the Merchant at the Port of Discharge or Place of Delivery, as the case may be, within 60 days after the date published in the P&O Nedlloyd Inbound Schedule against the Port of Discharge nominated therein for the relevant ocean Vessel. The Carrier shall be entitled to all the defences, exceptions and limitations provided in the applicable international convention or national law and this Bill of Lading.

(5) *Scope of Application*

(a) The terms and conditions of this Bill of Lading shall at all times govern all responsibilities of the Carrier in connection with or arising out of the supply of a Container to the Merchant, not only during the Carriage, but also during the periods prior to and/or subsequent to the Carriage.

(b) The rights, defences, limitations and liberties of whatsoever nature provided for in this Bill of Lading shall apply in any action against the Carrier for loss, damage or delay, howsoever occurring and whether the action be founded in contract or in tort and even if the loss, damage or delay arose as a result of unseaworthiness, negligence or breach of a fundamental term of this contract.

(c) Save as is otherwise provided for in this Bill of Lading, the Carrier shall in no circumstances whatsoever and howsoever arising be liable for direct or indirect or consequential loss or damage or loss of profits.

(6) *Inspection by Authorities*

If by order of the authorities at any place, a Container has to be opened for the Goods to be inspected, the Carrier will not be liable for any loss, damage or delay incurred as a result of any opening, unpacking inspection or repacking. The Carrier shall be entitled to recover the cost of such opening, unpacking, inspection and repacking from the Merchant.

8. SHIPPER-PACKED CONTAINERS

If a Container has not been packed by or on behalf of the Carrier:

(1) The Carrier shall not be liable for loss, damage or delay to the Goods caused by matters beyond his control, including, inter alia, without prejudice to the generality of this exclusion:

(a) the manner in which the Container has been packed, or

(b) the unsuitability of the Goods for carriage in the Container supplied, or

(c) the unsuitability or defective condition of the Container or the incorrect setting of any temperature controls thereof, provided that, if the Container has been supplied by or on behalf of the Carrier, this unsuitability, defective condition or incorrect setting could have been apparent upon inspection by the Merchant at or prior to the time when the Container was packed, or

(d) packing temperature controlled Goods that are not at the correct temperature for Carriage.

(2) The Shipper is responsible for the packing and sealing of all Shipper-Packed Containers and, if a Shipper-Packed Container is delivered by the Carrier with its original seal as affixed by the Shipper intact, the Carrier shall not be liable for any shortages of Goods ascertained at delivery. If, nevertheless, a claim for shortage is made against the Carrier by any Person whomsoever, the Merchant agrees to indemnify the Carrier against the cost of any such claim, plus any costs incurred in respect thereof.

(3) The Merchant shall indemnify the Carrier against any loss, damage, liability or expense whatsoever and howsoever arising caused by one or more of the matters referred to in Clause 8 (1), save that, if the loss, damage, liability or expense was caused by a matter referred to in Clause 8 (1) (c), the Merchant shall not be liable to indemnify the Carrier in respect thereof unless the proviso referred to in that Clause applies.

9. INSPECTION OF GOODS

The Carrier or any Person to whom the Carrier has sub-contracted the Carriage or any Person authorised by the Carrier shall be entitled, but under no obligation, to open any Container or package at any time and to inspect, weigh and/or measure the Goods and/or weigh the Container.

10. CARRIAGE AFFECTED BY CONDITION OF GOODS

If it appears at any time that, due to their condition, the Goods cannot safely or properly be carried or carried further, either at all or without incurring any additional expense or taking any measure(s) in relation to the Container or the Goods, the Carrier may, without notice to the Merchant (but as his agent only), take any measure(s) and/or incur any additional expense to carry or to continue the Carriage thereof, and/or sell or dispose of the Goods, and/or abandon the Carriage and/or store them ashore or afloat, under cover or in the open, at any place, whichever the Carrier, in his absolute discretion, considers most appropriate, which abandonment, storage, sale or disposal shall be deemed to constitute due delivery under this Bill of Lading. The Merchant shall indemnify the Carrier against any additional expense so incurred.

11. DESCRIPTION OF GOODS

(1) This Bill of Lading shall be prima facie evidence of the receipt by the Carrier from the Shipper in apparent good order and condition, except as otherwise noted, of the total number of containers or other packages or units indicated in the box on the face hereof entitled "*Total No. of Containers/Packages received by the Carrier".

(2) Except as provided in Clause 11 (1), no representation is made by the Carrier as to the weight, contents, measure, quantity, quality, description, condition, marks, numbers or value of the Goods, and the Carrier shall be under no responsibility whatsoever in respect of such description or particulars, which are unknown to him.

It is agreed that, whilst he retains the right so to do at his sole discretion, the Carrier is not at any time under any obligation to weigh any Container or open any Container to make any check on the Goods therein or their stowage (see Clause 9).

(3) If any particulars of any Letter of Credit and/or Import Licence and/or Sale Contract and/or Invoice or Order number and/or details of any contract to which the Carrier is not a party are shown on the face of this Bill of Lading, such particulars are included solely at the request of the Merchant for his convenience. The Merchant agrees that the inclusion of such particulars shall not be regarded as a declaration of value and in no way increases the Carrier's liability under this Bill of Lading. The Merchant further agrees to indemnify the Carrier against all consequences of including such particulars in this Bill of Lading. The Merchant acknowledges that, except when the provisions of Clause 7 (3) apply, the value of the Goods is unknown to the Carrier.

12. SHIPPER'S/MERCHANTS RESPONSIBILITY

(1) All of the Persons coming within the definition of Merchant in Clause 1 shall be jointly and severally liable to the Carrier for the due fulfilment of all obligations undertaken by the Merchant in this Bill of Lading and remain so liable throughout Carriage, notwithstanding their having transferred this Bill of Lading and/or title to the Goods to another party.

(2) The Shipper warrants to the Carrier that the particulars relating to the Goods as set out overleaf have been checked by the Shipper on

receipt of this Bill of Lading and that such particulars, and any other particulars furnished by or on behalf of the Shipper, are adequate and correct. The Shipper also warrants that the Goods are lawful goods and contain no contraband. If the Container is not supplied by or on behalf of the Carrier, the Shipper further warrants that the Container meets all ISO and/or other international safety standards and is fit in all respects for Carriage by the Carrier.

(3) The Merchant shall indemnify the Carrier against all claims, losses, damages, fines and expenses arising or resulting from any breach of any of the warranties in Clause 12(2) hereof or from any other cause in connection with the Goods for which the Carrier is not responsible.

(4) The Merchant shall comply with all regulations or requirements of Customs, port and other authorities, and shall bear and pay all duties, taxes, fines, imposts, expenses or losses (including, without prejudice to the generality of the foregoing, Freight for any additional Carriage undertaken) incurred or suffered in respect of the Goods, and shall indemnify the Carrier in respect thereof.

(5) If Containers supplied by or on behalf of the Carrier are unpacked at the Merchant's premises, the Merchant is responsible for returning the empty Containers free from labels etc, with interiors brushed clean, odour free and in every respect fit for immediate reuse, to the point or place designated by the Carrier, his servants or agents, within the time prescribed. Should a Container not be returned as required above within the time prescribed, the Carrier is entitled to take such steps as he considers appropriate for the account of the Merchant and the Merchant shall be liable for any detention, loss or expense incurred as a result thereof.

(6) Containers released into the care of the Merchant for packing, unpacking of any other purpose whatsoever are at the sole risk of the Merchant until redelivered to the Carrier. The Merchant shall indemnify the Carrier for all loss and/or damage to such Containers occurring during such period. The Merchant shall also indemnify the Carrier for any loss, damage, injury, fines or expenses caused or incurred by such Containers whilst in his control.

13. FREIGHT

(1) Freight shall be deemed fully earned on receipt of the Goods by the Carrier and shall be paid and non-returnable in any event.

(2) The Merchant's attention is drawn to the stipulations concerning currency in which the Freight is to be paid, rate of exchange, devaluation and other contingencies relative to Freight in the applicable Tariff.

(3) Freight has been calculated on the basis of particulars furnished by or on behalf of the Shipper. If the particulars furnished by or on behalf of the Shipper are incorrect, it is agreed that a sum equal to double the correct Freight less the Freight charged shall be payable as liquidated damages to the Carrier.

(4) All Freight shall be paid without any set-off, counter-claim, deduction or stay of execution before delivery of the Goods.

14. LIEN

The Carrier shall have a lien on the Goods and any documents relating thereto for all sums payable to the Carrier under this contract. The Carrier shall also have a lien against the Merchant on the Goods and any documents relating thereto for all sums due from him to the Carrier under any other contract. The Carrier may exercise his lien at any time and at any place at his sole discretion, whether the contractual Carriage is completed or not. In any event any lien shall extend to cover the cost of recovering the sums due and for that purpose the Carrier shall have the right to sell the Goods by public auction or private treaty, without notice to the Merchant at any time and at any place at the sole discretion of the Carrier.

15. OPTIONAL STOWAGE AND DECK CARGO

(1) The Goods may be packed by the Carrier in Containers and consolidated with other goods in Containers.

(2) Goods, whether or not packed in Containers, may be carried on deck or under deck, at the sole discretion of the Carrier, without notice to the merchant. All such Goods whether carried on deck or under deck, shall participate in general average and shall be deemed to be within the definition of goods for the purposes of the Hague Rules and shall be carried subject to those Rules.

(3) Notwithstanding Clause 15 (2), in the case of Goods which are stated on the face hereof as being carried on deck and which are so carried the Hague Rules shall not apply and the Carrier shall be under no liability whatsoever for loss, damage or delay, howsoever arising, whether or not caused by negligence on the part of the Carrier, his servants, Agents, or Sub-Contractors.

16. LIVE ANIMALS

The Hague Rules shall not apply to the Carriage of live animals, which are carried at the sole risk of the Merchant. The Carrier shall be under no liability whatsoever for any injury, illness, death, delay or destruction to such live animals howsoever arising. Should the Master in his sole discretion consider that any live animal is likely to be injurious to any other live animal or any person or property on board, or to cause the vessel to be delayed or impeded in the prosecution of its voyage, such live animal may be destroyed and thrown overboard without any liability attaching to the Carrier. The Merchant shall indemnify the Carrier against all or any extra costs incurred for any reason whatsoever in connection with the Carriage of any live animal.

17. METHODS AND ROUTES OF CARRIAGE

(1) The Carrier may at any time and without notice to the Merchant:
(a) use any means of carriage whatsoever,
(b) transfer the Goods from one conveyance to another, including but not limited to transhipping or carrying them on another vessel than that named on the face hereof,
(c) unpack and remove the Goods which have been packed into a Container and forward them in a Container or otherwise,
(d) proceed by any route in his discretion (whether or not the nearest or most direct or customary or advertised route), at any speed, and proceed to or stay at any place or port whatsoever, once or more often and in any order,
(e) load or unload the Goods at any place or port (whether or not such port is named overleaf as the Port of Loading or Port of Discharge) and store the Goods at any such place or port,
(f) comply with any orders or recommendations given by any government or authority, or any Person acting or purporting to act as or on behalf of such government or authority, or having under the terms of any insurance on any conveyance employed by the Carrier the right to give orders or directions,
(g) permit the vessel to proceed with or without pilots, to tow or be towed, or to be dry-docked, with or without Goods and/or Containers on board.
(2) The liberties set out in Clause 17 (1) may be invoked by the Carrier for any purpose whatsoever, whether or not connected with the Carriage of the Goods, including but not limited to loading or unloading other goods, bunkering, undergoing repairs, adjusting instruments, picking up or landing any persons, including but not limited to persons involved with the operation or maintenance of the vessel and assisting vessels in all situations. Anything done in accordance with Clause 17 (1) or any delay arising therefrom shall be deemed to be within the contractual Carriage and shall not be a deviation.
(3) By tendering Goods for Carriage without any written request for Carriage in a specialised Container, or for Carriage otherwise than in a Container, the Merchant accepts that Carriage may properly be undertaken in a general purpose container, carried on or under deck at the Carrier's sole discretion.

18. MATTERS AFFECTING PERFORMANCE

If at any time the Carriage, the vessel or other goods on board the vessel are or are likely to be affected by any hindrance, risk, delay, difficulty or disadvantage of any kind (other than the inability of the Goods, due to their condition, safely or properly to be carried or carried further) and howsoever arising (even though the circumstances giving rise to such hindrance, risk, delay, difficulty or disadvantage existed at the time this contract was entered into or the Goods were received for Carriage), the Carrier (whether or not the Carriage is commenced) may, without prior notice to the Merchant and at the sole discretion of the Carrier, either:–
(a) Carry the Goods to the contracted Port of Discharge or Place of Delivery, whichever is applicable, by an alternative route to that indicated in this Bill of Lading or that which is usual for Goods consigned to that Port of Discharge or Place of Delivery. If the Carrier elects to invoke the terms of this Clause 18 (a) then, notwithstanding the provisions of Clause 17 hereof, he shall be entitled to charge such additional Freight as the Carrier may determine.
or
(b) Suspend the Carriage of the Goods and store them ashore or afloat upon the terms of this Bill of Lading and endeavour to forward them as soon as possible, but the Carrier makes no representations as to the maximum period of such suspension of Carriage. If the Carrier elects to invoke the terms of this Clause 18 (b) then notwithstanding the provisions of Clause 17 hereof, he shall be entitled to charge such additional Freight as the Carrier may determine.
or

(c) Abandon the Carriage of the Goods and place them at the Merchant's disposal at any place or port which the Carrier may deem safe and convenient, whereupon the responsibility of the Carrier in respect of such Goods shall cease. The Carrier shall nevertheless be entitled to full Freight on the Goods received for Carriage, and the Merchant shall pay any additional costs of the Carriage to, and delivery and storage at, such place or port. If the Carrier elects to use an alternative route under Clause 18 (a) or to suspend the Carriage under Clause 18 (b) this shall not prejudice his right subsequently to abandon the Carriage.

19. DANGEROUS GOODS

(1) No Goods which are or may become dangerous, inflammable, damaging or injurious (including radio-active materials), or which are or may become liable to damage any property whatsoever or injure any person whomsoever, shall be tendered to the Carrier for Carriage without his express consent in writing, and without the Container as well as the Goods themselves being distinctly marked on the outside so as to indicate the nature and character of any such Goods and so as to comply with any applicable laws, regulations or requirements. If any such Goods are delivered to the Carrier without such written consent and/or marking, or if in the opinion of the Carrier the Goods are or are liable to become of a dangerous, inflammable, damaging or injurious nature, they may at any time be destroyed, disposed of, abandoned, or rendered harmless without compensation to the Merchant and without prejudice to the Carrier's right to Freight.
(2) The Merchant undertakes that such Goods are packed in a manner adequate to withstand the risks of Carriage having regard to their nature and in compliance with all laws or regulations which may be applicable during the Carriage. In particular but without prejudice to the generality of this Clause 19 (2), if the Goods are not packed into the Container by or on behalf of the Carrier, the Merchant undertakes that incompatible Goods are not packed in the same Container.
(3) Whether or not the Merchant was aware of the nature of the Goods, the Merchant shall indemnify the Carrier against all claims, losses, damages or expenses arising in consequence of the Carriage of such Goods.
(4) Nothing contained in this Clause shall deprive the Carrier of any of his rights provided for elsewhere.

20. NOTIfiCATION AND DELIVERY

(1) Any mention herein of parties to be notified of the arrival of the Goods is solely for information of the Carrier, and failure to give such notification shall not involve the Carrier in any liability nor relieve the Merchant of any obligation hereunder.
(2) The Merchant shall take delivery of the Goods within the time provided in the Carrier's applicable Tariff (see Clause 2). If the Merchant fails to do so the Carrier shall be entitled, without notice, to unpack the Goods if packed in Containers and/or to store the Goods ashore, afloat, in the open or under cover, at the sole risk of the Merchant. Such storage shall constitute due delivery hereunder, and thereupon the liability of the Carrier in respect of the Goods stored as aforesaid shall wholly cease, and the costs of such storage (if paid or payable by the Carrier or any agent or Sub-Contractor of the Carrier) shall forthwith upon demand be paid by the Merchant to the Carrier.
(3) If the Merchant fails to take delivery of the Goods within thirty days of delivery becoming due under Clause 20 (2), or if in the opinion of the Carrier they are likely to deteriorate, decay, become worthless or incur charges whether for storage or otherwise in excess of their value, the Carrier may, without prejudice to any other rights which he may have against the Merchant, without notice and without any responsibility whatsoever attaching to him, sell, destroy or dispose of the Goods and apply any proceeds of sale in reduction of the sums due to the Carrier from the Merchant.
(4) Refusal by the Merchant to take delivery of the Goods in accordance with the terms of this Clause and/or to mitigate any loss or damage thereto shall constitute a waiver by the Merchant to the Carrier of any claim whatsoever relating to the Goods or the Carriage thereof.
(5) In the event of the Carrier agreeing to a request of the Merchant to amend the Place of Delivery stated herein without stipulating any particular terms and conditions to apply during said amended Carriage, to the extent provided by the applicable Tariff the terms and conditions of this Bill of Lading shall continue to apply, but only until the Goods are delivered by the Carrier to the Merchant at the amended Place of Delivery. Once the applicable Tariff ceases to provide for the continued application of the terms and conditions of the Bill of Lading

or, if the Carrier declines to extend the Bill of Lading terms to the amended Place of Delivery, then the Carrier shall act as agent only of the Merchant in arranging for delivery of the Goods to amended Place of Delivery but shall then be under no liability whatsoever for loss, damage or delay to the Goods, howsoever arising, for the period of amended Carriage.

If the Carrier agrees to make multiple point deliveries of an FCL Container, this contract terminates upon presentation of the sealed Container at the first place of delivery. Thereafter the Carrier acts as agent only to arrange any further deliveries.

(6) If, at the place where the Carrier is entitled to call upon the Merchant to take delivery of the Goods under Clause 20 (2) the Carrier is obliged to hand over the Goods into the custody of any Customs, port or other authority, such hand-over shall constitute due delivery to the Merchant under this Bill of Lading.

(7) This Bill of Lading shall not be a negotiable document of title unless consigned "to order", "to the order of . . .", or "to bearer". If not so consigned but instead consigned directly to a nominated party, this shall be a "Straight" Bill and, at the sole discretion of the Carrier, delivery may be made to the nominated party only upon proof of identity, as if this Bill of Lading were a Waybill. Such delivery shall constitute due delivery hereunder.

21. FCL MULTIPLE BILLS OF LADING

(1) Goods will only be delivered in a Container to the Merchant if all Bills of Lading in respect of the contents of the Container have been surrendered authorising delivery to a single Merchant at a single Place of Delivery. In the event that this requirement is not fulfilled the Carrier may unpack the Container and, in respect of Goods for which Bills of Lading have been surrendered, deliver them to the Merchant on an LCL basis. Such delivery shall constitute due delivery hereunder, but will only be effected against payment by the Merchant of LCL Service Charges and any charges appropriate to LCL Goods (as laid down in the Tariff) together with the actual costs incurred for any additional services rendered.

(2) If this is an FCL multiple Bill of Lading (as evidenced by the qualification of the tally acknowledged overleaf to the effect that it is "One of . . . part cargoes in the Container"), then the Goods detailed overleaf are said to comprise part of the contents of the Container indicated. If the Carrier is required to deliver the Goods to more than one Merchant and if all or part of the total Goods within the Container consists of bulk Goods or unappropriated Goods, or is or becomes mixed or unmarked or unidentifiable, the Holders of Bills of Lading relating to Goods within the Container shall take delivery thereof (including any damaged portion) and bear any shortage in such proportions as the Carrier shall in his absolute discretion determine, and such delivery shall constitute due delivery hereunder.

22. GENERAL AVERAGE & SALVAGE

(1) In the event of accident, danger, damage or disaster before or after the commencement of the voyage, resulting from any cause whatsoever, due to negligence or not, for which, or for the consequences of which, the Carrier is not responsible, by statute, contract or otherwise, the Merchant shall contribute with the Carrier in general average to the payment of any sacrifices, losses or expenses of a general average nature that may be made or incurred, and shall pay salvage and special charges incurred in respect of the Goods.

(2) Any general average on a vessel operated by the Carrier shall be adjusted according to the York/Antwerp Rules of 1994 or any subsequent amendment thereto authorised by the CMI at any port or place and in any currency at the option of and by an adjuster appointed by the Carrier with the test of reasonableness in the Rule Paramount being made on the basis of what was known at the time of the general average act and not subsequently with the benefit of hindsight. Any general average on a vessel not operated by the Carrier (whether a seagoing or inland waterways vessel) shall be adjusted according to the requirements of the operator of that vessel. In either case the Merchant shall give such cash deposit or other security as the Carrier may deem sufficient to cover the estimated general average contribution of the Goods. Any security, other than cash deposits, must be given by a party acceptable to and with assets in a jurisdiction nominated by the Carrier. Such security must be provided before delivery if the Carrier so requires, or, if the Carrier does not so require, within three months of the delivery of the Goods, whether or not at the time of delivery the Merchant had notice of the Carrier's lien. The Carrier shall be under no obligation to exercise any lien for general average contribution due to the Merchant.

(3) Conversion into the currency of the adjustment shall be calculated at the rate prevailing on the date of payment for disbursements and on the date of completion of discharge of the vessel for allowances, contributory values, etc.

(4) If a salving vessel is owned or operated by the Carrier, salvage shall be paid for as fully as if the salving vessel or vessels belonged to strangers.

(5) In the event of the Master in his sole discretion or in consultation with owners considering that salvage services are needed, the Merchant agrees that the Master may act as his agent to procure such services to Goods and that the Carrier may act as his agent to settle salvage remuneration, without any prior consultation with the Merchant in both cases.

(6) If the Merchant contests payment of contribution to general average, salvage, salvage charges and/or special charges to Goods on any grounds whatsoever or fails to make payment of contribution within three months of the issue of the adjustment thereof, whether or not prior security has been provided, the Merchant shall pay interest for the period in excess of three months on the contribution due at two percent per annum above the base lending rate of the central bank of the country in whose currency the adjustment is issued, in addition to the contribution due.

(7) In the event of any general average credit balances due to Merchants still being unclaimed 5 years after the date of issue of the adjustment, these shall be paid to the Carrier, who will hold such credit balances pending application by the Merchants entitled thereto.

23. VARIATION OF THE CONTRACT

No servant or agent of the Carrier shall have the power to waive or vary any of the terms of this Bill of Lading, unless such waiver or variation is in writing and is specifically authorised or ratified in writing by the Carrier.

24. LAW AND JURISDICTION

(1) Unless Clause 25 or 27 applies, any claim against the Carrier under this Bill of Lading shall be determined according to English law and exclusively in the High Court of Justice in London. The merchant irrevocably submits to this jurisdiction.

(2) The Carrier shall be entitled to pursue any claim against the Merchant in London according to English Law or in any jurisdiction in which the Merchant has assets but then in accordance with the local law of that jurisdiction.

(3) Nothing herein shall prevent the parties to any claim or dispute under this Bill of Lading from agreeing to submit the claim or dispute to arbitration by mutually acceptable arbitrator(s) on mutually acceptable terms at a mutually acceptable venue.

25. VALIDITY

In the event that anything herein contained is inconsistent with any applicable international convention or national law which cannot be departed from by private contract, the provisions hereof shall to the extent of such inconsistency but no further be null and void.

26. LIMITATION OF LIABILITY

For the avoidance of doubt it is hereby agreed by the Merchant that the Carrier qualifies and shall be regarded as a person entitled to limit liability under the relevant Convention on the Limitation of Liability for Maritime Claims, notwithstanding that the Carrier may have procured space on board the Vessel concerned by means of a Slot Charterparty, Bill of Lading or some other contract of carriage.

Except to the extent that mandatory law to the contrary applies in the appropriate jurisdiction (in which case said law shall apply), the size of the fund to which the Carrier may limit liability shall be identical to that proportion of the limitation fund by which the actual carrier is entitled to limit which is (or would be) available for the Carrier's claims against the actual carrier.

27. USA CLAUSE PARAMOUNT (if applicable)

(1) If Carriage includes carriage to, from or through a port in the United States of America, this Bill of Lading shall be subject to the United States Carriage of Goods by Sea Act 1936 (US COGSA), the terms of which are incorporated herein and shall be paramount throughout Carriage by sea and the entire time that the Goods are in the actual custody of the Carrier on his Sub-Contractor at the sea terminal in the United States of America before loading onto the vessel and after discharge therefrom, as the case may be.

(2) The Carrier shall not be liable in any capacity whatsoever for loss, damage or delay to the Goods while the Goods are in the United States of America away from the sea terminal and are not in the actual

custody of the Carrier. At these times the Carrier acts as agent only to procure Carriage by Persons (one or more) under the usual terms and conditions of those Persons. If, for any reason, the Carrier is denied the right to act as agent only at these times, his liability for loss, damage or delay to the goods shall be determined in accordance with Clause 6 hereof.

(3) If US COGSA applies the liability of the Carrier and/or the vessel shall not exceed US$ 500 per package or customary freight unit (in accordance with Section 1304(5) thereof), unless the value of the Goods has been declared on the face hereof, in which case Clause 7(3) shall apply.

(4) Notwithstanding the provisions of Clause 24, if Carriage includes Carriage to, from or through a port in the United States of America, the Merchant may refer any claim or dispute to the United States District Court for the Southern District of New York in accordance with the laws of the United States of America.

P & O NEDLLOYD LIMITED, BEAGLE HOUSE, BRAHAM STREET, LONDON E1 8EP

COMMON SHORT FORM BILL OF LADING

UK Customs Assigned No.

B/L No.

Shipper's Reference

F/Agent's Reference

Shipper

Consignee (if "Order" state Notify Party and Address)

Name of Carrier

The contract evidenced by this Short Form Bill of Lading is subject to the exceptions, limitations, conditions and liberties (including those relating to pre-carriage and on-carriage) set out in the Carrier's Standard Conditions applicable to the voyage covered by this Short Form Bill of Lading and operative on its date of issue.

If the carriage is one where the provisions of the Hague Rules contained in the International Convention for unification of certain rules relating to Bills of Lading dated Brussels on 25th August, 1924, as amended by the Protocol signed at Brussels on 23rd February, 1968 (the Hague Visby Rules) are compulsorily applicable under Article X, the said Standard Conditions contain or shall be deemed to contain a Clause giving effect to the Hague Visby Rules. Otherwise, except as provided below, the said Standard Conditions contain or shall be deemed to contain a Clause giving effect to the provisions of the Hague Rules.

The Carrier hereby agrees that to the extent of any inconsistency the said Clause shall prevail over the exceptions, limitations, conditions and liberties set out in the Standard Conditions in respect of any period to which the Hague Rules or the Hague Visby Rules by their terms apply. Unless the Standard Conditions expressly provide otherwise, neither the Hague Rules nor the Hague Visby Rules shall apply to this contract where the goods carried hereunder consist of live animals or cargo which by this contract is stated as being carried on deck and is so carried.

Notwithstanding anything contained in the said Standard Conditions, the term Carrier in this Short Form Bill of Lading shall mean the Carrier named on the front thereof.

A copy of the Carrier's said Standard Conditions applicable hereto may be inspected or will be supplied on request at the office of the Carrier or the Carrier's Principal Agents.

Notify Party and Address (leave blank if stated above)

Pre-Carriage by*

|Place of Receipt by Pre-Carrier*

Vessel

|Port of Loading

Port of Discharge

|Place of Delivery by On-Carrier*

Marks and Nos: Container No.   Number and kind of packages; Description of Goods

|Gross Weight |Measurement

*Applicable only when document used as a Through Bill of Lading

© GCBS 1979

AVAILABLE FROM

THE CARLTON BERRY CO. LTD.

PRINTERS TO LLOYD'S OF LONDON

PHONE: 01-623 7100 Extn. 3166

Particulars declared by Shipper

Freight Details: Charges etc.

RECEIVED FOR CARRIAGE as above in apparent good order and condition, unless otherwise stated hereon, the goods described in the above particulars.

IN WITNESS whereof the number of original Bills of Lading stated below have been signed, all of this tenor and date, one of which being accomplished the others to stand void.

Ocean Freight Payable at

Number of Original Bs/L

Place and Date of Issue

Signature for Carrier; Carrier's Principal Place of Business

GCBS
CSF
BL
1979

710

Printed by The Carlton Berry Co. Ltd.
Authorised and licensed by the
General Council of British Shipping.

55-0

B/L No.

Reference No.

N e g o t i a b l e
COMBINED TRANSPORT BILL OF LADING

Revised 1995

Code Name: "COMBICONBILL"
Shipper

Consigned to order of

Notify party/address

Place of receipt

Ocean Vessel

Port of loading

Port of discharge

Place of delivery

Freight payable at

Number of original Bills of Lading

Marks and Nos.

Quantity and description of goods

Gross weight, kg. Measurement, m³

Particulars above declared by Shipper

Freight and charges

RECEIVED the goods in apparent good order and condition and, as far as ascertained by reasonable means of checking, as specified above unless otherwise stated.

The Carrier, in accordance with and to the extent of the provisions contained in this Bill of Lading, and with liberty to sub-contract, undertakes to perform and/or in his own name to procure performance of the combined transport and the delivery of the goods, including all services related thereto, from the place and time of taking the goods in charge to the place and time of delivery and accepts responsibility for such transport and such services.

One of the Bills of Lading must be surrendered duly endorsed in exchange for the goods or delivery order.

IN WITNESS whereof TWO (2) original Bills of Lading have been signed, if not otherwise stated above, one of which being accomplished the other(s) to be void.

Place and date of issue

Shipper's declared value of ....

subject to payment of above extra charge.

Signed for

.... as Carrier

by ....

As agent(s) only to the Carrier

p.t.o.

Note:

The Merchant's attention is called to the fact that according to Clauses 10 to 12 and Clause 24 of this Bill of Lading, the liability of the Carrier is, in most cases, limited in respect of loss of or damage to the goods and delay.

COMBINED TRANSPORT BILL OF LADING

Adopted by The Baltic and International Maritime Council in January, 1971 (as revised 1995)

Code Name: "COMBICONBILL"

I. GENERAL PROVISIONS

1. Applicability.
Notwithstanding the heading "Combined Transport", the provisions set out and referred to in this Bill of Lading shall also apply, if the transport as described in this Bill of Lading is performed by one mode of transport only.

2. Definitions.
"Carrier" means the party on whose behalf this Bill of Lading has been signed.
"Merchant" includes the Shipper, the Receiver, the Consignor, the Consignee, the holder of this Bill of Lading and the owner of the goods.

3. Carrier's Tariff.
The terms of the Carrier's applicable Tariff at the date of shipment are incorporated herein. Copies of the relevant provisions of the applicable Tariff are available from the Carrier upon request. In the case of inconsistency between this Bill of Lading and the applicable Tariff, this Bill of Lading shall prevail.

4. Time Bar.
All liability whatsoever of the Carrier shall cease unless suit is brought within 9 months after delivery of the goods or the date when the goods should have been delivered.

5. Law and Jurisdiction.
Disputes arising under this Bill of Lading shall be determined by the courts and in accordance with the law at the place where the Carrier has his principal place of business.

II. PERFORMANCE OF THE CONTRACT

6. Methods and Routes of Transportation.
(1) The Carrier is entitled to perform the transport and all services related thereto in any reasonable manner and by any reasonable means, methods and routes.
(2) In accordance herewith, for instance, in the event of carriage by sea, vessels may sail with or without pilots, undergo repairs, adjust equipment, drydock and tow vessels in all situations.

7. Optional Stowage.
(1) Goods may be stowed by the Carrier by means of containers, trailers, transportable tanks, flats, pallets, or similar articles of transport used to consolidate goods.
(2) Containers, trailers, transportable tanks and covered flats, whether stowed by the Carrier or received by him in a stowed condition from the Merchant, may be carried on or under deck without notice to the Merchant.

8. Hindrances etc. Affecting Performance.
(1) The Carrier shall use reasonable endeavours to complete the transport and to deliver the goods at the place designated for delivery.
(2) If at any time the performance of the contract as evidenced by this Bill of Lading is or will be affected by any hindrance, risk, delay, difficulty or disadvantage of whatsoever kind, and if by virtue of sub-clause 8 (1) the Carrier has no duty to complete the performance of the contract, the Carrier (whether or not the transport is commenced) may elect to:
(a) treat the performance of this Contract as terminated and place the goods at the Merchant's disposal at any place which the Carrier shall deem safe and convenient; or

be calculated by reference to the value of such goods at the place and time they are delivered to the Merchant in accordance with the contract or should have been so delivered.
(2) The value of the goods shall be fixed according to the commodity exchange price or, if there be no such price, according to the current market price or, if there be no commodity exchange price or current market price, by reference to the normal value of goods of the same kind and quality.
(3) Compensation shall not, however, exceed two Special Drawing Rights per kilogramme of gross weight of the goods lost or damaged.
(4) Higher compensation may be claimed only when, with the consent of the Carrier, the value for the goods declared by the Shipper which exceeds the limits laid down in this Clause has been stated on the face of this Bill of Lading at the place indicated. In that case the amount of the declared value shall be substituted for that limit.

11. Special Provisions for Liability and Compensation
(1) Notwithstanding anything provided for in Clauses 9 and 10 of this Bill of Lading, if it can be proved where the loss or damage occurred, the Carrier and the Merchant shall, as to the liability of the Carrier, be entitled to require any such liability to be determined by the provisions contained in any international convention or national law, which provisions:
(a) cannot be departed from by private contract, to the detriment of the claimant, and
(b) would have applied if the Merchant had made a separate and direct contract with the Carrier in respect of the particular stage of transport where the loss or damage occurred and received as evidence thereof any particular document which must be issued if such international convention or national law shall apply.
(2) Insofar as there is no mandatory law applying to carriage by sea by virtue of the provisions of sub-clause 11 (1), the liability of the Carrier in respect of any carriage by sea shall be determined by the International Brussels Convention 1924 as amended by the Protocol signed at Brussels on February 23rd 1968 – The Hague/Visby Rules. The Hague/Visby Rules shall also determine the liability of the Carrier in respect of carriage by inland waterways as if such carriage were carriage by sea. Furthermore, they shall apply to all goods, whether carried on deck or under deck.

12. Delay, Consequential Loss, etc.
If the Carrier is held liable in respect of delay, consequential loss or damage other than loss of or damage to the goods, the liability of the Carrier shall be limited to the freight for the transport covered by this Bill of Lading, or to the value of the goods as determined in Clause 10, whichever is the lesser.

13. Notice of Loss of or Damage to the Goods
(1) Unless notice of loss of or damage to the goods, specifying the general nature of such loss or damage, is given in writing by the Merchant to the Carrier when the goods are handed over to the Merchant, such handing over is *prima facie* evidence of the Delivery by the Carrier of the goods as described in this Bill of Lading.
(2) Where the loss or damage is not apparent, the same *prima facie* effect shall apply if notice in writing is not given within three (3) consecutive days after the day when the goods were handed over to the Merchant.

loss or expense incurred by the Carrier, if such loss, damage or expense has been caused by:
(a) negligent filling, packing or stowing of the container;
(b) the contents being unsuitable for carriage in container; or
(c) the unsuitability or defective condition of the container unless the container has been supplied by the Carrier and the unsuitability or defective condition would not have been apparent upon reasonable inspection at or prior to the time when the container was filled, packed or stowed.
(2) The provisions of sub-clause (1) of this Clause also apply with respect to trailers, transportable tanks, flats and pallets which have not been filled, packed or stowed by the Carrier.
(3) The Carrier does not accept liability for damage due to the unsuitability or defective condition of reefer equipment or trailers supplied by the Merchant.

18. Dangerous Goods.
(1) The Merchant shall comply with all internationally recognised requirements and all rules which apply according to national law or by reason of international Convention, relating to the carriage of goods of a dangerous nature, and shall in any event inform the Carrier in writing of the exact nature of the danger before goods of a dangerous nature are taken into charge by the Carrier and indicate to him, if need be, the precautions to be taken.
(2) Goods of a dangerous nature which the Carrier did not know were dangerous, may, at any time or place, be unloaded, destroyed, or rendered harmless, without compensation; further, the Merchant shall be liable for all expenses, loss or damage arising out of their handing over for carriage or of their carriage.
(3) If any goods shipped with the knowledge of the Carrier as to their dangerous nature shall become a danger to any person or property, they may in like manner be landed at any place or destroyed or rendered innocuous by the Carrier without liability on the part of the Carrier except to General Average, if any.

19. Return of Containers
(1) For the purpose of this Clause the Consignor shall mean the person who concludes this Contract with the Carrier and the Consignee shall mean the person entitled to receive the goods from the Carrier.
(2) Containers, pallets or similar articles of transport supplied by or on behalf of the Carrier shall be returned to the Carrier in the same order and condition as handed over to the Merchant, normal wear and tear excepted, with interiors clean and within the time prescribed in the Carrier's tariff or elsewhere.
(3) (a) The Consignor shall be liable for any loss of, damage to, or delay, including demurrage, of such articles, incurred during the period between handing over to the Consignor and return to the Carrier for carriage.
(b) The Consignor and the Consignee shall be jointly and severally liable for any loss of, damage to, or delay, including demurrage, of such articles, incurred during the period between handing over to the Consignee and return to the Carrier.

(b) deliver the goods at the place designated for delivery.

(3) If the goods are not taken delivery of by the Merchant within a reasonable time after the Carrier has called upon him to take delivery, the Carrier shall be at liberty to put the goods in safe custody on behalf of the Merchant at the latter's risk and expense.

(4) In any event the Carrier shall be entitled to full freight for goods received for transportation and additional compensation for extra costs resulting from the circumstances referred to above.

III. CARRIER'S LIABILITY

9. Basic Liability.

(1) The Carrier shall be liable for loss of or damage to the goods occurring between the time when he receives the goods into his charge and the time of delivery.

(2) The Carrier shall be responsible for the acts and omissions of any person of whose services he makes use for the performance of the contract of carriage evidenced by this Bill of Lading.

(3) The Carrier shall, however, be relieved of liability for any loss of or damage if such loss or damage arose or resulted from:

(a) The wrongful act or neglect of the Merchant.

(b) Compliance with the instructions of the person entitled to give them.

(c) The lack of, or defective conditions of packing in the case of goods which, by their nature, are liable to wastage or to be damaged when not packed or when not properly packed.

(d) Handling, loading, stowage or unloading of the goods by or on behalf of the Merchant.

(e) Inherent vice of the goods.

(f) Insufficiency or inadequacy of marks or numbers on the goods, covering, or unit loads.

(g) Strikes or lock-outs or stoppages or restraints of labour from whatever cause whether partial or general.

(h) Any cause or event which the Carrier could not avoid and the consequence whereof he could not prevent by the exercise of reasonable diligence.

(4) Where under sub-clause 9 (3) the Carrier is not under any liability in respect of some of the factors causing the loss or damage, he shall only be liable to the extent that those factors for which he is liable under this Clause have contributed to the loss or damage.

(5) The burden of proving that the loss or damage was due to one or more of the causes or events, specified in (a), and (b) and (f) of sub-clause 9 (3) shall rest upon the Carrier.

(6) When the Carrier establishes that in the circumstances of the case, the loss or damage could be attributed to one or more of the causes or events, specified in (c) to (g) of sub-clause 9 (3), it shall be presumed that it was so caused. The Merchant shall, however, be entitled to prove that the loss or damage was not, in fact, caused either wholly or partly by one or more of the causes or events.

10. Amount of Compensation

(1) When the Carrier is liable for compensation in respect of loss of or damage to the goods, such compensation shall

14. Defences and Limits for the Carrier, Servants, etc.

(1) The defences and limits of liability provided for in this Bill of Lading shall apply in any action against the Carrier for loss of damage to or in connection with the goods whether the action can be founded in contract or in tort.

(2) The Carrier shall not be entitled to the benefit of the limitation of liability provided for in sub-clause 10 (3), if it is proved that the loss or damage resulted from a personal act or omission of the Carrier done with intent to cause such loss or damage or recklessly and with knowledge that damage would probably result.

(3) The Merchant undertakes that no claim shall be made against any servant, agent or other persons whose services the Carrier has used in order to perform this Contract and if any claim should nevertheless be made, to indemnify the Carrier against all consequences thereof.

(4) However, the provisions of this Bill of Lading apply whenever claims relating to the performance of this Contract are made against any servant, agent or other person whose services the Carrier has used in order to perform this Contract, whether such claims are founded in contract or in tort. In entering into this Contract, the Carrier, to the extent of such provisions, does so not only on his own behalf but also as agent or trustee for such persons. The aggregate liability of the Carrier and such persons shall not exceed the limits in Clauses 10, 11 and 24, respectively.

IV. DESCRIPTION OF GOODS

15. Carrier's Responsibility.

The information in this Bill of Lading shall be *prima facie* evidence of the taking in charge by the Carrier of the goods as described by such information, unless a contrary indication, such as "shipper's weight, load and count", "shipper-packed container" or similar expressions, have been made in the printed text or superimposed on the Bill of Lading. Proof to the contrary shall not be admissible when the Bill of Lading has been transferred, or the equivalent electronic data interchange message has been transmitted to and acknowledged by the Consignee who in good faith has relied and acted thereon.

16. Shipper's Responsibility.

The Shipper shall be deemed to have guaranteed to the Carrier the accuracy, at the time the goods were taken in charge by the Carrier, of the description of the goods, marks, number, quantity and weight, as furnished by him, and the Shipper shall defend, indemnify and hold harmless the Carrier against all loss, damage and expenses arising or resulting from inaccuracies in or inadequacy of such particulars. The right of the Carrier to such indemnity shall in no way limit his responsibility and liability under this Bill of Lading to any person other than the Shipper. The Shipper shall remain liable even if the Bill of Lading has been transferred by him.

17. Shipper-packed Containers, etc.

(1) If a container has not been filled, packed or stowed by the Carrier, the Carrier shall not be liable for any loss of or damage to its contents and the Merchant shall cover any

V. FREIGHT AND LIEN

20. Freight.

(1) Freight shall be deemed earned when the goods have been taken in charge by the Carrier and shall be paid in any event.

(2) The Merchant's attention is drawn to the stipulations concerning currency in which the freight and charges are to be paid, rate of exchange, devaluation and other contingencies relative to freight and charges in the relevant tariff conditions. If no such stipulation as to devaluation exists or is applicable the following shall apply:

If the currency in which freight and charges are quoted is devalued between the date of the freight agreement and the date when the freight and charges are paid, then all freight and charges shall be automatically and immediately increased in proportion to the extent of the devaluation of the said currency.

(3) For the purpose of verifying the freight basis, the Carrier reserves the right to have the contents of containers, trailers or similar articles of tranport inspected in order to ascertain the weight, measurement, value, or nature of the goods.

21. Lien.

The Carrier shall have a lien on the goods for any amount due under this Contract and for the costs of recovering the same, and may enforce such lien in any reasonable manner, including sale or disposal of the goods.

VI. MISCELLANEOUS PROVISIONS

22. General Average.

(1) General Average shall be adjusted at any port or place at the Carrier's option, and to be settled according to the York-Antwerp Rules 1994, or any modification thereof, this covering all goods, whether carried on or under deck. The New Jason Clause as approved by BIMCO to be considered as incorporated herein.

(2) Such security including a cash deposit as the Carrier may deem sufficient to cover the estimated contribution of the goods and any salvage and special charges thereon, shall, if required, be submitted to the Carrier prior to delivery of the goods.

23. Both-to-Blame Collision Clause.

The Both-to-Blame Collision Clause as adopted by BIMCO shall be considered incorporated herein.

24. U.S. Trade.

(1) In case the contract evidenced by this Bill of Lading is subject to the Carriage of Goods by Sea Act of the United States of America, 1936 (U.S. COGSA), then the provisions stated in the said Act shall govern before loading and after discharge and throughout the entire time the goods are in the Carrier's custody.

(2) If the U.S. COGSA applies, and unless the nature and value of the goods have been declared by the shipper before the goods have been handed over to the Carrier and inserted in this Bill of Lading, the Carrier shall in no event be or become liable for any loss or damage to the goods in an amount exceeding USD 500 per package or customary freight unit.

NON-NEGOTIABLE SEA WAYBILL

Shipper

UK Customs Assigned No.

SWB No.

Shipper's Reference

F/Agent's Reference

Consignee

Name of Carrier

Notify Party and Address (leave blank if stated above)

The contract evidenced by this Waybill is subject to the exceptions, limitations, conditions and liberties (including those relating to pre-carriage and on-carriage) set out in the Carrier's Standard Conditions of Carriage applicable to the voyage covered by this Waybill and operative on its date of issue. If the carriage is one where had a Bill of Lading been issued the provisions of the Hague Rules contained in the International Convention for unification of certain rules relating to Bills of Lading dated Brussels 25th August 1924, as amended by the Protocol signed at Brussels on the 23rd February, 1968 (the Hague Visby Rules) would have been compulsorily applicable under Article X, the said Standard Conditions contain or shall be deemed to contain a Clause giving effect to the Hague Visby Rules. Otherwise the said Standard Conditions contain or shall be deemed to contain a Clause giving effect to the provisions of the Hague Rules. In neither case shall the proviso to the first sentence of Article V of the Hague Rules or the Hague Visby Rules apply. The Carrier hereby agrees: (i) that to the extent of any inconsistency the said clause shall prevail over the said Standard Conditions in respect of any period to which the Hague Rules or the Hague Visby Rules by their terms apply and (ii) that for the purpose of the terms of this Contract of Carriage this Waybill falls within the definition of Article 1(b) of the Hague Rules and the Hague Visby Rules.
The Shipper accepts the said Standard Conditions on his own behalf and on behalf of the Consignee and the owner of the goods and warrants that he has authority to do so. The Consignee by presenting this Waybill and/or requesting delivery of the goods further undertakes all liabilities of the Shipper hereunder such undertaking being additional and without prejudice to the Shipper's own liability. The benefits of the contract evidenced by this Waybill shall thereby be transferred to the Consignee or other persons presenting this Waybill.
Notwithstanding anything contained on the front thereof the term Carrier in this Waybill shall mean the Carrier named on the front thereof.
A copy of the Carrier's said Standard Conditions applicable hereto may be inspected or will be supplied on request at the office of the Carrier or the Carrier's Principal Agents.

Pre-Carriage by* | Place of Receipt by Pre-Carrier*

Vessel | Port of Loading

Port of Discharge | Place of Delivery by On-Carrier*

Marks and Nos:	Container No.	Number and kind of packages: Description of Goods	Gross Weight	Measurement

AVAILABLE FROM

*Applicable only when document used as a Through Bill of Lading

THE CARLTON BERRY CO. LTD.

PRINTERS TO LLOYD'S OF LONDON

PHONE: 01-623 7100 Extn. 3166

Particulars declared by Shipper

Freight Details. Charges etc.

RECEIVED FOR CARRIAGE as above in apparent good order and condition, unless otherwise stated hereon, the goods described in the above particulars.

Ocean Freight Payable at

Place and Date of Issue

Signature for Carrier; Carrier's Principal Place of Business

GCBS
SWB
1979

711

Printed by The Carlton Berry Co. Ltd
Authorised and licensed by the
General Council of British Shipping.

Non-Negotiable Waybill for Combined Transport shipment or Port to Port shipment

Shipper

Waybill No.:

Booking Ref.:

Shipper's Ref.:

P&O Nedlloyd

Consignee   (If the name shown in this space is a Bank, the Bank named is specifically excluded from the list of parties coming within the definition of Merchant in the Carrier's contract of carriage and incurs no liability to the Carrier under said contract unless applying for delivery in its own name.)

Notify Party/Address   (It is agreed that no responsibility shall attach to the Carrier or his Agents for failure to notify)

Place of Receipt   (Applicable only when this document is used as a Combined Transport Waybill)

Place of Delivery   (Applicable only when this document is used as a Combined Transport Waybill)

Vessel and Voy. No.

Port of Loading

Port of Discharge

Marks and Nos; Container Nos;   Number and kind of Packages; description of Goods   Gross Weight (kg)   Measurement (cbm)

WAYBILL

Above particulars as declared by Shipper, but not acknowledged by the Carrier

* Total No. of Containers/Packages received by the Carrier

Received by the Carrier from the Shipper in apparent good order and condition (unless otherwise noted herein) the total number or quantity of Containers or other packages or units indicated in the box opposite entitled "Total No. of Containers/Packages received by the Carrier" for Carriage from the Place of Receipt or the Port of Loading, whichever applicable, to the Port of Discharge or the Place of Delivery, whichever applicable, SUBJECT TO THE TERMS OF THE CARRIER'S STANDARD BILL OF LADING TERMS AND CONDITIONS AND TARIFF FOR THE RELEVANT TRADE, WHICH ARE MUTATIS MUTANDIS APPLICABLE TO THIS WAYBILL (copies of which may be obtained from the Carrier or his agents). Except for live animals and Goods which are stated herein to be carried on deck and are so carried, these terms and conditions are warranted by the Carrier in respect of the sea portion of the Carriage to apply the Hague Rules or Hague Visby Rules, whichever would have been applicable if this Waybill were a Bill of Lading. In either case the provisions of Article III Rule 4 of the Hague Visby Rules are deemed to be incorporated herein.

The contract evidenced by this Waybill is deemed to be a contract of carriage as defined in Article 1 (b) of the Hague Rules and Hague Visby Rules. However this Waybill is not a document of title to the Goods.

Delivery will be made to the Consignee named, or his authorised agents, on production of proof of identity at the Port of Discharge or the Place of Delivery, whichever applicable. Should the Consignee require delivery to a party and/or premises other than as shown above in the "Consignee" box, then written instructions must be given by the Consignee to the Carrier or his agent. Unless the Shipper expressly waives his right to control the Goods until delivery by means of a clause on the face hereof, such instructions from the Consignee will be subject to any instruction to the contrary by the Shipper.

Movement

Unless instructed to the contrary by the Shipper prior to the commencement of Carriage and noted accordingly on the face hereof, the Carrier will, subject to the aforesaid terms and conditions, process cargo claims with the Consignee. Claims settlement, if any, shall be a complete discharge of the Carrier's liability to the Shipper. The Shipper accepts the said standard terms and conditions on his own behalf, on behalf of the Consignee and the Owner of the Goods, and authorises the Consignee to bring suit against the Carrier in his own name but as agent of the Shipper, and warrants that he has authority so to accept and authorise. The Shipper further undertakes that no claim or allegation in respect of the Goods shall be made against the Carrier by any person other than in accordance with the terms and conditions of this Waybill.

Freight and Charges (indicate whether prepaid or collect):

Origin Inland Haulage Charge ... ...

Origin Terminal Handling/LCL Service Charge ... ...

Ocean Freight ... ...

Destination Terminal Handling/LCL Service Charge ...

Destination Inland Haulage Charge ... ...

ICS
C/T B/L
April 78

This Waybill is issued subject to the CMI Uniform Rules For Sea Waybills

Place and Date of Issue

IN WITNESS whereof this Waybill is signed.

FOR P&O NEDLLOYD LTD, AS CARRIER.*

P&O Nedlloyd

168047

P&O Nedlloyd Ltd, Beagle House, Braham Street, London E1 8EP

11/PONL W/B3 8/00

*OPERATING IN PARTNERSHIP WITH P&O NEDLLOYD B.V.

INDEX